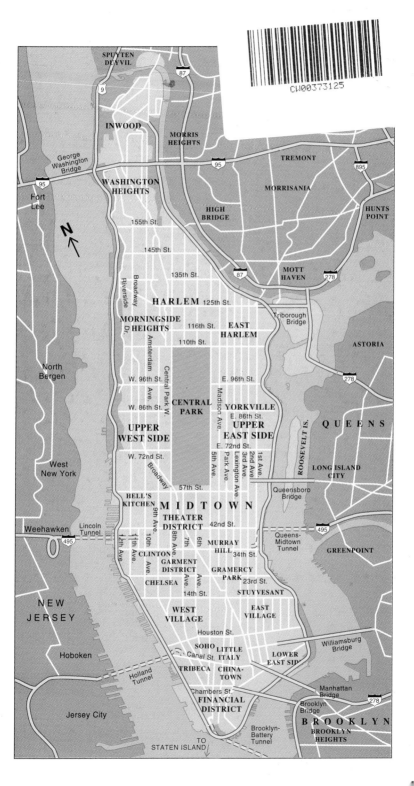

SPUYTEN
DUYVIL

87
9

INWOOD

MORRIS
HEIGHTS

TREMONT

95

895

George
Washington
Bridge

95

Fort
Lee

WASHINGTON
HEIGHTS

MORRISANIA

HIGH
BRIDGE

HUNTS
POINT

155th St.

145th St.

135th St.

87

MOTT
HAVEN

278

N

Broadway
Riverside
Dr.

HARLEM 125th St.

Triborough
Bridge

MORNINGSIDE
HEIGHTS

116th St.

EAST
HARLEM

110th St.

ASTORIA

North
Bergen

Amsterdam

Central Park W.

W. 96th St.

E. 96th St.

278

W. 86th St.

Madison Ave.

CENTRAL
PARK

YORKVILLE
UPPER
EAST SIDE

E. 86th St.

QUEENS

UPPER
WEST SIDE

W. 72nd St.

E. 72nd St.

5th Ave.
Park Ave.
Lexington Ave.
3rd Ave.
2nd Ave.
1st Ave.

ROOSEVELT IS.

West
New York

Broadway

57th St.

LONG ISLAND
CITY

Queensboro
Bridge

Weehawken

HELL'S
KITCHEN

Lincoln
Tunnel

495

MIDTOWN

9th Ave.
8th Ave.
10th Ave.
11th Ave.
12th Ave.

THEATER
DISTRICT

42nd St.

7th
6th

Queens-
Midtown
Tunnel

495

GREENPOINT

CLINTON

MURRAY
HILL

34th St.

GARMENT
DISTRICT

GRAMERCY
PARK

Ave.
Ave.

CHELSEA

23rd St.

NEW

14th St.

STUYVESANT

JERSEY

WEST
VILLAGE

EAST
VILLAGE

Hoboken

Houston St.

Williamsburg
Bridge

SOHO LITTLE
ITALY

Canal St.

LOWER
EAST SIDE

Holland
Tunnel

TRIBECA

CHINA-
TOWN

Manhattan
Bridge

278

Chambers St.

Jersey City

FINANCIAL
DISTRICT

Brooklyn
Bridge

BROOKLYN

BROOKLYN
HEIGHTS

TO
STATEN ISLAND

Brooklyn-
Battery
Tunnel

New York City Subways

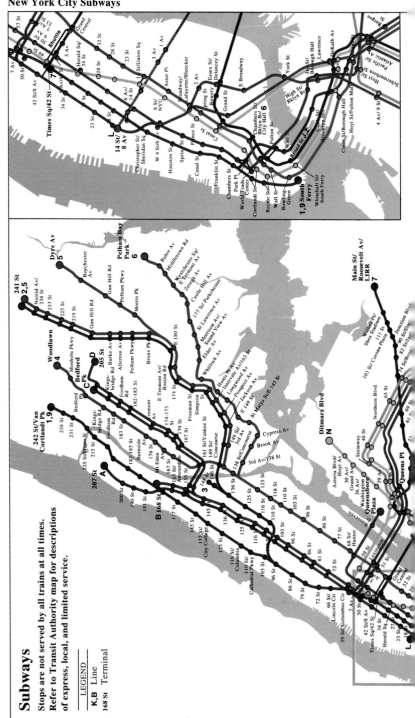

Subways

Stops are not served by all trains at all times.
Refer to Transit Authority map for descriptions
of express, local, and limited service.

LEGEND

K,B Line

168 St Terminal

Downtown Manhattan

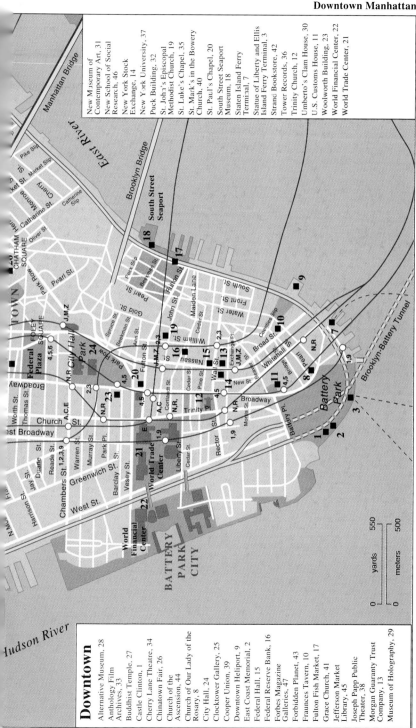

Midtown Manhattan

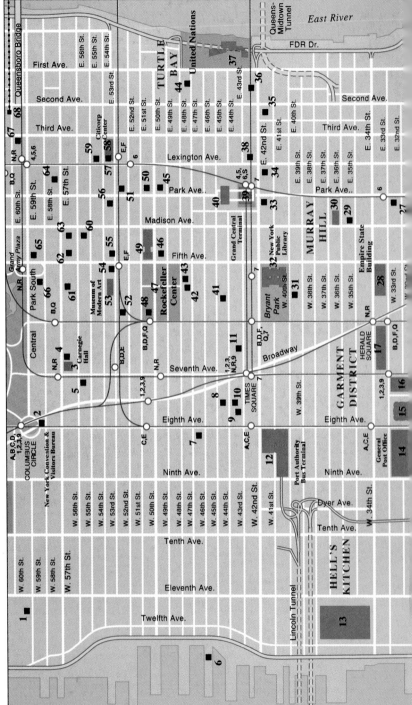

Midtown Manhattan

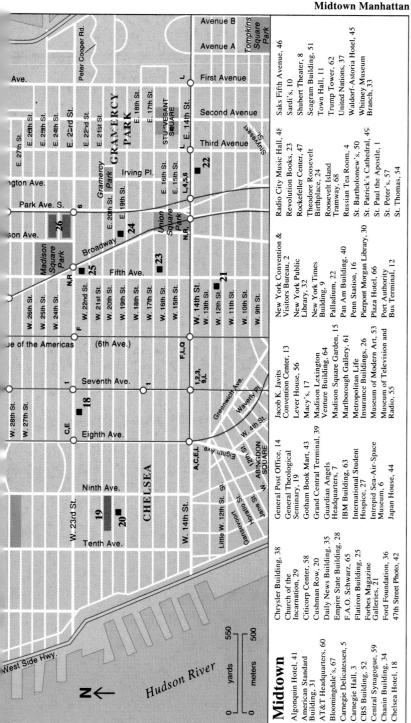

Midtown

Algonquin Hotel, 41
American Standard Building, 31
AT&T Headquarters, 60
Bloomingdale's, 67
Carnegie Delicatessen, 5
Carnegie Hall, 3
CBS Building, 52
Central Synagogue, 59
Chanin Building, 34
Chelsea Hotel, 18

Chrysler Building, 38
Church of the Incarnation, 29
Citicorp Center, 58
Cushman Row, 20
Daily News Building, 35
Empire State Building, 28
F.A.O. Schwarz, 65
Flatiron Building, 25
Forbes Magazine Galleries, 21
Ford Foundation, 36
47th Street Photo, 42

General Post Office, 14
General Theological Seminary, 19
Gotham Book Mart, 43
Grand Central Terminal, 39
Guardian Angels Headquarters, 7
IBM Building, 63
International Student Hospice, 27
Intrepid Sea-Air-Space Museum, 6
Japan House, 44

Jacob K. Javits Convention Center, 13
Lever House, 56
Macy's, 17
Madison Lexington Venture Building, 64
Madison Square Garden, 15
Marlborough Gallery, 61
Metropolitan Life Insurance Buildings, 26
Museum of Modern Art, 53
Museum of Television and Radio, 55

New York Convention & Visitors Bureau, 2
New York Public Library, 32
New York Times Building, 9
Palladium, 22
Pan Am Building, 40
Penn Station, 16
Pierpont Morgan Library, 30
Plaza Hotel, 66
Port Authority Bus Terminal, 12

Radio City Music Hall, 4
Revolution Books, 23
Rockefeller Center, 47
Theodore Roosevelt Birthplace, 24
Roosevelt Island Tramway, 68
Russian Tea Room, 4
St. Bartholomew's, 50
St. Patrick's Cathedral, 49
St. Paul the Apostle, 1
St. Peter's, 57
St. Thomas, 54

Saks Fifth Avenue, 46
Sardi's, 10
Shubert Theater, 8
Seagram Building, 51
Town Hall, 7
Trump Tower, 62
United Nations, 37
Waldorf-Astoria Hotel, 45
Whitney Museum Branch, 33

Uptown

American Museum of Natural History, 53

The Ansonia, 55

The Arsenal, 25

Asia Society, 14

Belvedere Castle, 36

Bethesda Fountain, 33

Blockhouse No. 1, 42

Bloomingdale's, 22

Bridle Path, 30

Cathedral of St. John the Divine, 47

Central Park Zoo, 24

Chess and Checkers House, 28

Children's Museum of Manhattan, 51

Children's Zoo, 26

China House, 19

Cleopatra's Needle, 38

Columbia University, 46

Conservatory Garden, 2

Cooper-Hewitt Museum, 7

The Dairy, 27

Dakota Apartments, 56

Delacorte Theater, 37

El Museo del Barrio, 1

Fordham University, 60

Frick Museum, 13

Gracie Mansion, 10

Grant's Tomb, 45

Great Lawn, 39

Guggenheim Museum, 9

Hayden Planetarium (at the American Museum of Natural History), 53

Hector Memorial, 50

Hotel des Artistes, 57

Hunter College, 16

International Center of Photography, 5

Jewish Museum, 6

The Juilliard School (at Lincoln Center), 59

Lincoln Center, 59

Loeb Boathouse, 34

Masjid Malcolm Shabazz , 43

Metropolitan Museum of Art, 11

Mt. Sinai Hospital, 4

Museum of American Folk Art, 58

Museum of American Illustration, 21

Museum of the City of New York, 3

National Academy of Design, 8

New York Convention & Visitors Bureau, 61

New York Historical Society, 54

New York Hospital, 15

Plaza Hotel, 23

Police Station (Central Park), 40

Rockefeller University, 20

7th Regiment Armory, 17

Shakespeare Garden, 35

Soldiers and Sailors Monument, 49

Strawberry Fields, 32

Studio Museum in Harlem, 44

Symphony Space, 48

Tavern on the Green, 31

Temple Emanu-El, 18

Tennis Courts, 41

Whitney Museum of American Art, 12

Wollman Rink, 29

Zabar's, 52

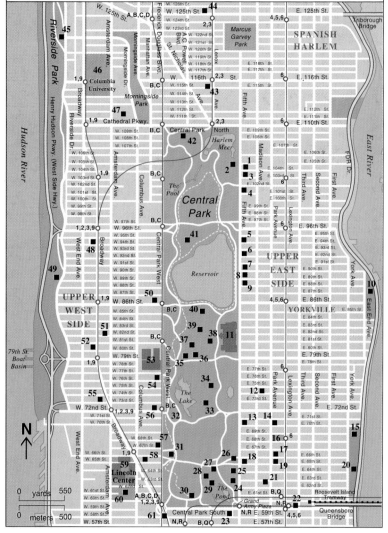

Let's Go

NEW YORK CITY

is the best book for anyone traveling on a budget. Here's why:

No other guidebook has as many budget listings.

In New York City we list over 2,500 budget travel bargains. We tell you the cheapest way to get around, and where to get an inexpensive and satisfying meal once you've arrived. We give hundreds of money-saving tips that anyone can use, plus invaluable advice on discounts and deals for students, children, families, and senior travelers.

Let's Go researchers have to make it on their own.

Our Harvard-Radcliffe researcher-writers travel on budgets as tight as your own—no expense accounts, no free hotel rooms.

Let's Go is completely revised each year.

We don't just update the prices, we go back to the place. If a charming café has become an overpriced tourist trap, we'll replace the listing with a new and better one.

No other guidebook includes all this:

Honest, engaging coverage of the city and beyond; up-to-the-minute prices, directions, addresses, phone numbers, and opening hours; in-depth essays on local culture, history, and politics; comprehensive listings on transportation; straight advice on work and study, budget accommodations, sights, nightlife, and food; detailed maps; and much more.

Let's Go is for anyone who wants to see New York City on a budget.

Books by Let's Go, Inc.

EUROPE

Let's Go: Europe

Let's Go: Austria & Switzerland

Let's Go: Britain & Ireland

Let's Go: Eastern Europe

Let's Go: France

Let's Go: Germany

Let's Go: Greece & Turkey

Let's Go: Ireland

Let's Go: Italy

Let's Go: London

Let's Go: Paris

Let's Go: Spain & Portugal

NORTH & CENTRAL AMERICA

Let's Go: USA & Canada

Let's Go: Alaska & The Pacific Northwest

Let's Go: California

Let's Go: New York City

Let's Go: Washington, D.C.

Let's Go: Mexico

MIDDLE EAST & ASIA

Let's Go: Israel & Egypt

Let's Go: Thailand

Let's Go

The Budget Guide to

NEW YORK CITY

1995

James Dylan Ebenhoh
Editor

Written by
Let's Go, Inc.
A subsidiary of
Harvard Student Agencies, Inc.

MACMILLAN

HELPING LET'S GO

If you have suggestions or corrections, or just want to share your discoveries, drop us a line. We read every piece of correspondence, whether a 10-page e-mail letter, a velveteen Elvis postcard, or, as in one case, a collage. All suggestions are passed along to our researcher-writers. Please note that mail received after May 5, 1995 will probably be too late for the 1996 book, but will be retained for the following edition.

Address mail to:

Let's Go: New York City
Let's Go, Inc.
1 Story Street
Cambridge, MA 02138
USA

Or send e-mail to:
.letsgo@delphi.com

In addition to the invaluable travel advice our readers share with us, many are kind enough to offer their services as researchers or editors. Unfortunately, the charter of Let's Go, Inc. and Harvard Student Agencies, Inc. enables us to employ only currently enrolled Harvard-Radcliffe students.

About Let's Go

Back in 1960, a few students at Harvard University got together to produce a 20-page pamphlet offering a collection of tips on budget travel in Europe. For three years, Harvard Student Agencies, a student-run nonprofit corporation, had been doing a brisk business booking charter flights to Europe; this modest, mimeographed packet was offered to passengers as an extra. The following year, students traveling to Europe researched the first full-fledged edition of *Let's Go: Europe*, a pocket-sized book featuring advice on shoestring travel, irreverent write-ups of sights, and a decidedly youthful slant.

Throughout the 60s, the guides reflected the times: one section of the 1968 *Let's Go: Europe* talked about "Street Singing in Europe on No Dollars a Day." During the 70s, *Let's Go* gradually became a large-scale operation, adding regional European guides and expanding coverage into North Africa and Asia. The 80s saw the arrival of *Let's Go: USA & Canada* and *Let's Go: Mexico*, as well as regional North American guides; in the 90s we introduced five in-depth city guides to Paris, London, Rome, New York City, and Washington, DC. And as the budget travel world expands, so do we; the first edition of *Let's Go: Thailand* hit the shelves last year, and this year's edition adds coverage of Malaysia, Singapore, Tokyo, and Hong Kong.

This year we're proud to announce the birth of *Let's Go: Eastern Europe*—the most comprehensive guide to this renascent region, with more practical information and insider tips than any other. *Let's Go: Eastern Europe* brings our total number of titles, with their spirit of adventure and reputation for honesty, accuracy, and editorial integrity, to 21.

We've seen a lot in 35 years. *Let's Go: Europe* is now the world's #1 best selling international guide, translated into seven languages. And our guides are still researched, written, and produced entirely by students who know first-hand how to see the world on the cheap.

Every spring, we recruit over 100 researchers and 50 editors to write our books anew. Come summertime, after several months of training, researchers hit the road for seven weeks of exploration, from Bangkok to Budapest, Anchorage to Ankara. With pen and notebook in hand, a few changes of underwear stuffed in our backpacks, and a budget as tight as yours, we visit every *pensione*, *palapa*, pizzeria, café, club, campground, or castle we can find to make sure you'll get the most out of *your* trip.

We've put the best of our discoveries into the book you're now holding. A brand-new edition of each guide hits the shelves every year, only months after it is researched, so you know you're getting the most reliable, up-to-date, and comprehensive information available. The budget travel world is constantly changing, and where other guides quickly become obsolete, our annual research keeps you abreast of the very latest travel insights. And even as you read this, work on next year's editions is well underway.

At *Let's Go*, we think of budget travel not only as a means of cutting down on costs, but as a way of breaking down a few walls as well. Living cheap and simple on the road brings you closer to the real people and places you've been saving up to visit. This book will ease your anxieties and answer your questions about the basics—to help *you* get off the beaten track and explore. We encourage you to put *Let's Go* away now and then and strike out on your own. As any seasoned traveler will tell you, the best discoveries are often those you make yourself. If you find something worth sharing, drop us a line. We're at Let's Go, Inc., 1 Story Street, Cambridge, MA, 02138, USA (e-mail: letsgo@delphi.com).

Happy travels!

Contents

Maps

Acknowledgments

Whoa nellie. I definitely couldn't have done this alone. Tim Perlstein was a last-minute savior (actually, well before the last minute), and his sense of humor, as well as his uncanny ability to be hungry at the same time as I, made the summer a blast. Marc Zelanko prodded me gently all summer and was rewarded with a number of thankless tasks in the wee hours. Pete Keith came through in the crunch with his fruitful negotiations with the bigwigs, and Alexis Averbuck and Liz Stein fielded stupid questions about everything from computers to rotting meat. Amelia Kaplan offered a number of wonderful suggestions (Tarrytown notwithstanding), and Dave Overcamp, John Donahue, Steve Burt, Maia Gemmill, and Ben Peskoe were proofing fiends. Scott Croft at the NYC Visitors Bureau also helped out in a big way with his prompt fax in the hour of crisis. The whole office kept up my spirits: Mike Farbiarz validated my love for GBV, Sean Desmond threw a mean slider, Matt Heid had a helluva lawn Nova, Dan Glover and Emily Hobson organized some wicked footie, and Natalie Boutin, Amy Cooper, and Tanya Bezreh always showered me with kindness. Back at the ranch, Julie Cooper and Jen Cox were fellow late-night TV addicts; their friendship meant everything to me after hellish days at the office. Kardyhm Kelly, as always, filled my days (and my belly) with joy and love, and Daryna McKeand taught me the joys of Spanish pop. Jake Kuttothara, Mark Hren, and Vic Ortiz-de-Montellano made lengthy treks from the West and shared some great summer times with me. Thanks also to Gaunt and the Turks for rockin' the (Middle) East. Peace Corps Pat Machniak is to be thanked for years of fun; he will be missed. Finally, my parents and sister deserve my utmost love; this book is for them. —JDE

STAFF

Editor	James Dylan Ebenhoh
Managing Editor	Marc David Zelanko
Publishing Director	Pete Keith
Production Manager	Alexis G. Averbuck
Production Assistant	Elizabeth J. Stein
Financial Manager	Matt Heid
Assistant General Manager	Anne E. Chisholm
Sales Group Manager	Sherice R. Guillory
Sales Department Coordinator	Andrea N. Taylor
Sales Group Representatives	Eli K. Aheto
	Timur Okay Harry Hiçyılmaz
	Arzhang Kamerei
	Hollister Jane Leopold
	David L. Yuan
President	Lucienne D. Lester
General Manager	Richard M. Olken

Researcher-Writers

Rita A. Hao   *Manhattan, New Haven, Hoboken, Jersey City, and Princeton*
This riot grrrl extraordinaire wasted no time in fleeing the cruel North for her new haven, overcoming hesitation about life in a bigger burg than Knoxville to tear up this town. Rita told it like it was, forgoing the incorporation of any wedge-shaped "nails" in favor of making the rarefied culture of the city palpable. (In other words, she told it like it was.) Rita always had an eye for the bizarre and funky, deciphering pop culture prophecies in bus billboards and Barbra boutiques. She battled public urination and rowdy, ramen-hurling slackers to whip Hoboken up from scratch, and she caused many an expressway pile-up on her sassy tour of Jersey malldom. Densely packed midtown blocks and seemingly barren outer zones were both enlivened by Rita's wit and thorough researching. Along the way, she made many friends, including a home-made, punk rock Barbie—hand-crafted to fill the void caused from missing Bikini Kill one too many times.

Benjamin Peskoe   *Manhattan, Queens, Staten Island, Long Island*
The legend of Superstar Ben Peskoe accosted me from day one, with glowing adjectives and exclamation points whizzing around like gerbils on speed. Peer pressure became less of a factor after our party line connection, and when he slid off the slopes to Cambridge I started to believe the hype. As a writer, Ben was amazingly meticulous, organized, and eloquent. As a researcher, he went head-to-head with rush hour Long Island traffic in a clunker of a rental car, searched for quaint farmhouses in the middle of unwelcoming slums, and skidded down slippery, meat-laden streets on the prowl for wholesomeness. Ben somehow managed to find everything he was looking for, and SoHo, TriBeCa, and west Midtown especially benefited from his insane slaving. A glutton for punishment, BenPoe spent countless hours back at One Story St. picking up the slack for slow-poke editors, and his fame ensured that I was always surrounded by a throng of admirers (not my own). Ben is everything that is great about *Let's Go*—plain and simple.

Michael Sonnenschein   *Manhattan, Brooklyn, Bronx, Atlantic City*
After his memorable gig as a toddler-sitter, Mike also fled Boston, but he clearly found his niche in the surreal world of parading mermaids, indie hipsters, naked mini-ravers, and bemused old folks. Brooklyn, the East Village, and the Lower East Side were the sites of much exploration and expansion, as Mike somehow managed to avoid all contact with sharp skyscrapers in favor of exposing the oft-overshadowed down-to-earth, as well as trolling the grotty underground. Atlantic City, for all its glitz and glamor, somehow ended up leaving Mike spellbound by the outright *weirdness* of it all (although we're sure he had a few trysts with Lady Luck). Look for more of his insights into surreal mundanity on a horror flick screen near you.

Matt Ware   *Princeton*

How To Use This Book

New York City has been the subject of thousands of books covering every aspect of life in the big city, from Broadway to busing and street gangs to game shows. *This* book is neither an academic exegesis nor a crack investigative report. *Let's Go* opens up New York City to those who want to experience its leading-edge nightlife, get the most out of world-class museums, or simply enjoy a good hot dog and a good view. We give you the scoop on the city's history and where to see it for yourself; we tell you what the local newspapers are and what to use them for. We help you budget your time and your money, telling you where to go what to expect when you get there.

New York City: An Introduction fills you in on New York's history, politics, people, architecture, music, and literature. **Essentials** offers practical advice. **Planning Your Trip** will help you get to New York and tells you what to expect when you arrive. We get you into town from the airport, and we offer special tips and resources for students, seniors, women, gays and lesbians, travelers with disabilities, families, and travelers with special diets.

Once you're in the Big Apple, **Getting Around** will help you navigate the city by subway, bus, taxi, bicycle, on foot, and even by Rollerblade. **Getting Acquainted** tells you where to bank, obtain medical care, and use the bathroom and fills you in about mail, telephones, and how to stay safe.

In the **Accommodations** section, hostels and hotels are listed in order of value, based on price, location, safety, and comfort, as determined by our gimlet-eyed researcher-writers. **Eating & Drinking** includes reviews of more than 250 places to eat and drink, along with a full list of restaurants cross-referenced by type of food, price ("Splurge"), hours ("Open Late"), and atmosphere ("Outdoor Dining"), plus our own top picks. We also list some of our favorite watering holes. Organized by neighborhood, the **Sights** chapters allow you to guide yourself around the city, telling you when to look up, when to pay an entrance fee, and when to just say no. **Museums** and **Galleries,** New York's pride and joy, are covered in sections of their own. **Sports** gives you the complete roundup on both spectator sports and a surprisingly wide array of participatory sports in the city. **Shopping** tells you where to buy rhino teeth or a good book, and **Entertainment & Nightlife** helps you find live jazz or delve into New York's nighttime underworld. Ironically, we also help you get out of New York, with daytrips to **Long Island, Atlantic City, Princeton,** and **New Haven.**

Check out the **Appendices** for a quick-reference list of free things to do and see, and nearly 100 annual events that take place in or around New York City.

A NOTE TO OUR READERS

The information for this book is gathered by *Let's Go*'s researchers during the late spring and summer months. Each listing is derived from the assigned researcher's opinion based upon his or her visit at a particular time. The opinions are expressed in a candid and forthright manner. Other travelers might disagree. Those traveling at a different time may have different experiences since prices, dates, hours, and conditions are always subject to change. You are urged to check beforehand to avoid inconvenience and surprises. Travel always involves a certain degree of risk, especially in low-cost areas. When traveling, especially on a budget, you should always take particular care to ensure your safety.

New York City:
An Introduction

This rural America thing. It's a joke.
——*Edward Koch, former mayor of New York City*

■■■ HISTORY

Since New York's early days, outsiders have regarded it with wonder and alarm. The city has a history of dramatic and often ungainly growth; services and infrastructure have rarely kept up with the rapid pace of expansion. In the 1600s, root pigs ran wild in the streets. In the 1700s, the city's water supply was so fouled that even the horses refused to drink it. And in the 19th and 20th centuries, New York's mean streets and corrupt bosses became emblems of troubled urbanity, of the malignant, treacherous maelstrom of life in the big city. But for the city's long-term residents, and for the continuously arriving seekers of a better life, the magic produced by that stunning growth compensates for the drawbacks. New York scoffs at the timid compromises of other cities. It boasts the most immigrants, the tallest skyscrapers, the trickiest con artists. Even the vast gray blocks of concrete have an indomitable charm. "There is more poetry in a block of New York than in 20 daisied lanes," said O. Henry, returning from a prosaic and dull vacation in rural Westchester. In the country, he said, "there was too much fresh scenery and fresh air. What I need is a steam heated flat and no vacation or exercise."

New York's vaunted self-sufficiency began early. The colony was founded in 1624 by the Dutch West Indies Company as a trading post, but England soon asserted rival claims to the land. While the home countries squabbled, the colonists went about their business: trading beaver skins, colorful wampum, and silver with the neighboring Native Americans. In 1626, New York's tradition of great bargains began when Peter Minuit bought the island for 60 guilders, or just under $24.

The land was rich and abundant, making European guidance hardly necessary. "Wild pigeons are as thick as the sparrows in Holland...Children and pigs multiply here rapidly," gloated one colonist. When the Dutch West Indies Company did try to interfere, the settlers resented it. Calvinist Peter Stuyvesant, the governor appointed by Holland in the middle of the 17th century, instituted rigid reforms on the happy-go-lucky settlement. He shot hogs, closed taverns, and whipped Quakers, sparking protest and complaint among the citizens. Inexplicably, the physically challenged Stuyvesant has since become a local folk hero. Schools and businesses in New York are named for him and people refer to him fondly as "Peg-Leg" Peter.

Because the early colonists were less than enthralled by Dutch rule, they put up only token resistance when the British finally invaded the settlement in 1664. The new British governors were less noxious if only because they were less effective; an astounding number never even made it to the colony: some got lost en route from England, a handful went down at sea, and others decided that New England was a more attractive spot and went there. Between 1664 and 1776, there were 22 hiatuses in governance.

Left to its own devices, the city continued to grow. In 1754, higher education came to New York in the form of King's College (renamed Columbia University). By the late 1770s the city had become a major port with a population of 20,000. The preoccupation with prosperity engendered by this early success meant that New Yorkers would be rather dull to the first whiffs of revolution. British rule was good for business—and, then as now, the dollar (or at least the gold coin) ruled in the soon-to-be capital of capitalism.

HISTORY

The new American army, understandably, made no great efforts to protect the ungrateful city, and New York was held by the British throughout the war. The American Revolution was a rough time for poor New York. It had "a most melancholy appearance, being deserted and pillaged," wrote one observer. Fire destroyed a quarter of the city in 1776, ships spontaneously exploded, and the general atmosphere of chaos was interrupted only by sporadic games of cricket. When the defeated British army finally left in 1783, most people were relieved—except for 6000 Tory loyalists, who followed the British out of New York and went on to Nova Scotia.

With its buildings in heaps of rubble and a third of its population off roaming Canada, New York made a valiant effort to rebuild. Somewhat unexpectedly, it succeeded. "The progress of the city is, as usual, beyond all calculations," wrote one rapturous citizen. New York served a brief stint as the nation's capital; about the same time it acquired a bank and the first stock exchange, which met under a buttonwood tree on Wall Street. The Randel Plan simplified the organization of the city streets in 1811, establishing Manhattan's grid scheme. Merchants built mansions on the new streets, along with tenements for the increasing numbers of immigrants from Eastern and Northern Europe.

Administration and services continued to lag behind growth. New York became the largest U.S. city early in the 19th century, but pigs, dogs, and chickens continued to run freely. Fires and riots lent precariousness to the streetlife, while the foul water supply precipitated a cholera epidemic. The notorious corruption of Tammany Hall, a political machine set in motion in the 1850s and operative for nearly a century, aggravated the already desperate situation. "The New Yorker belongs to a community worse governed by lower and baser scum than any city in Western Christendom," complained George Strong.

Still, New Yorkers remained loyal to the city, often neglecting national concerns in favor of local interests. New York initially opposed the Civil War, its desire to protect trade with the South outweighing Abolitionist principles. Abraham Lincoln, the *New York Times* wrote dismissively in 1860, was "a lawyer who has some local reputation in Illinois." The attack on Fort Sumter made New York rally to the Northern side, but a conscription act in 1863 led to the infamous Draft Riots, which cost a thousand lives.

After the war, New York entered a half-century of peace and prosperity; during this time the elements of urban modernity began to coalesce. The Metropolitan Museum of Art was founded in 1870, and Bloomingdale's opened its venerable doors in 1872. Frederick Law Olmsted created Central Park on 82 rolling acres at the tail end of the century; the Flatiron building, the first skyscraper, was erected in 1902. The city had thus spread out, both horizontally and vertically. "It'll be a great place if they ever finish it," O. Henry quipped.

Booming construction and burgeoning culture industries helped generate a sort of urban bliss. Mayor Fiorello LaGuardia brought the city safely out of the Great Depression, and post-World War II prosperity brought still more immigrants and businesses to the city. But even as the country—and the rest of the world—celebrated New York as the capital of the 20th century, the cracks in the city's foundations became apparent. By the 1960s, crises in public transportation, education, and housing exacerbated racial tensions and fostered the consolidation of a criminal underclass.

City officials raised taxes to provide more services, but higher taxes drove middle-class residents as well as corporations out of the city. As a series of recessions and budget crises swamped the government, critics charged that Mayor Robert Wagner's only response was "dedicated inactivity." By 1975, the city was pleading with the federal government to rescue it from impending bankruptcy—and was rebuffed. The *Daily News* headline the next day read "Ford to New York: Drop Dead."

But New York, as has been its wont, bounced back. Budget wizard Felix Rohatyn trimmed the city's budget. The city's massive (if goofy) "I Love New York" campaign spread cheery hearts on bumper stickers. Large manufacturing, which had gone south and west of New York, was supplanted by fresh money from high finance and infotech, the big Reaganaut growth industries. In the '80s Wall Street was hip again, or at least grotesquely profitable, and the city seemed to recover some of its lost vitality.

As the rosy blush of the '80s faded to gray '90s recession, the city's problems seemed to reappear in full force. Bizarre outbreaks of violence, particularly violence against women, received national attention; racial bigotry, and threats of violent direct action, littered the newspapers and street-corners; and budget problems necessitated cuts in education and the police force. Nowadays, there are signs of life and renewed commitment in the urban blightscape: a recent resurgence of community activism and do-it-yourself politics is a glimmer of hope. Community policing, for example, has recently produced considerable drops in crime, and formerly seamy areas like Times Square—not to mention the entire subway system—are now on the mend. New York's history of heroic comebacks is not yet over, at least in the hearts of its citizens. Former mayor Ed Koch's inaugural speech echoes the sentiments of generations. "New York is not a problem," Koch educated. "New York is a stroke of genius."

■■■ ETHNIC NEW YORK

> *To Europe she was America, to America she was the gateway of the earth. But to tell the story of New York would be to write a social history of the world.*
>
> —H.G. Wells

In 1643, Jesuit missionary Isaac Jogues wrote a description of a lively New Amsterdam fort. Among the 500 people living in this 17th-century melting-pot community were artisans, soldiers, trappers, sailors, and slaves—and no fewer than 18 languages were spoken in this motley assemblage.

New Yorkers have always claimed a wide range of national origins. The first black settlement began in today's SoHo in 1644. Germans and Irish came over between 1840 and 1860; in 1855, European-born immigrants constituted nearly half of New York's population.

After the Civil War, a massive wave of immigration began, cresting around the turn of the century. Europeans left famine, religious persecution, and political unrest in their native lands for the perils of seasickness and the promise of America. German and Irish immigrants were eventually joined, beginning in 1890, by Italians, Lithuanians, Russians, Poles, and Greeks.

Immigrants worked long hours in disgusting and unsafe conditions for meager wages; only the Triangle Shirtwaist Fire of 1911, which killed 146 female factory workers, brought about enough public protest to force stricter regulations on working conditions. Meanwhile, Tammany Hall-based "ward bosses" stepped in to take care of the confused new arrivals, helping them find jobs and housing and even providing them with emergency funds in case of illness or accident. All the immigrants needed to produce in return were their votes for the incumbent city government. But later, in the 1920s, the U.S. Congress restricted immigration from Europe, and the Great Depression of the '30s brought it to a virtual halt.

Today the melting pot simmers with more than seven million people speaking 80 languages. New York has more Italians than Rome, more Irish than Dublin, and more Jews than Jerusalem. Immigrants from Asia and the Caribbean now make up most of the incoming population. The cultural diversity resulting from past and present immigration has recently made non-Hispanic whites a minority in the City for the first time ever. New York continues easily to absorb those who navigate to its shores; while it takes years or lifetimes to blend into other cities, newcomers become New Yorkers almost instantly.

■■■ POLITICS

New York's political history is a murky one. Corruption, typified by "Boss" William Tweed and Tammany Hall, was long its hallmark, and honest politicians have had difficulty being effective.

In the 1850s, Tweed took charge of Tammany and began promising money and jobs to people—often new immigrants—who agreed to vote for his candidates. With Tweed's men ruling city government, embezzling and kickbacks were routine. Tweed managed to rob the city of somewhere between 20 and 300 million dollars. When citizens complained in 1871, Tweed said defiantly, "Well, what are you going to do about it?" Although a *New York Times* exposé led to Tweed's downfall in 1875, Tammany continued to try to influence elections without him.

Occasional reform movements bucked Tammany's power. In 1894, for example, Teddy Roosevelt was appointed to the police department. Dressed in a cape, he sallied forth at night like a judicial Masked Avenger, searching for policemen who were sleeping on the job or consorting with prostitutes. Even more successful as a reformer was Fiorello LaGuardia, New York's immensely popular mayor from 1933-1945. "Nobody wants me but the people," he said as he reorganized the government and revitalized the city.

Since the 1960s, politicians have grappled with social and economic problems. John B. Lindsay ran in 1965 with the slogan "He is fresh and everyone else is tired," but even his freshness wilted under the barrage of crime, drought, race problems, and labor unrest. After its bankruptcy crisis, the city slowly began to rebound. Ed Koch became America's most visible mayor, appearing on *Saturday Night Live* and providing an endless stream of quotables. And the economic boom of the late '80s made Wall Street—and, by extension, New York—glamorous and fashionable. In 1988, David Dinkins was elected on a platform of harmonious growth and continued prosperity, leading even habitual cynics to retain hope for the future of the city.

During Dinkins's tenure the city government was reformed when the Supreme Court abolished the Board of Estimate system, under which each borough president had one vote. (This system was blatantly unfair, since borough populations range from Brooklyn's 2.8 million to Staten Island's 350,000.) The old system was replaced with a 35-member City Council, and now each borough can initiate zoning, propose legislation, and deal with contractors on its own.

Dinkins ultimately failed to achieve his vision of racial harmony, though, and the continuing fiscal crises and persistent crime rate led to his defeat to Rudy Giuliani in the 1993 mayoral election. The campaign and the eventual election-night tallies were strongly divided along racial lines; many moderate whites who had supported Dinkins in 1988 defected to the side of Giuliani, who addressed a number of intertwining fears with a campaign that could be summed up in two words: Safety First. Since his election, Giuliani has made an effort to increase police presence in the city, though a widely publicized commission report in July 1994 on persistent, widespread police corruption in the past decade has not increased the populace's confidence in the "beat cop." Giuliani has also attempted to trim the city's annual budget, but ongoing fiscal miscalculations and vehement opposition to his cuts promise to make the path to austerity a contentious one.

■■■ ARCHITECTURE

A hundred times have I thought New York is a catastrophe and fifty times: It is a beautiful catastrophe.

—Le Corbusier

THE EARLY YEARS AND EUROPEAN INFLUENCE

New York has always warmed to the latest trends in architecture, hastily demolishing old buildings to make way for their stylistic successors. In the 19th century the surging rhythm of endless destruction and renewal seemed to attest to the city's vigor and enthusiasm. Walt Whitman praised New York's "pull-down-and-build-over-again spirit," and *The Daily Mirror* was an isolated voice when, in 1831, it criticized the city's "irreverence for antiquity."

By the 20th century, many found that irreverence troubling. New York's history was quickly disappearing under the steamroller of modernization. Mounting public concern climaxed when developers destroyed gracious Penn Station in 1965, and the Landmarks Preservation Commission was created in response. Since then, the LPC has been vigorously designating buildings to protect. Developers, meanwhile, seek loopholes and air-rights to explode city buildings into the sky.

Despite the rear-guard efforts of the LPC, traces of pre-Revolutionary New York are hard to find. The original Dutch settlement consisted mostly of traditional homes with gables and stoops. One example from 1699, the restored Vechte-Corte-lyou House, stands near Fifth Ave. and 3rd St. in Brooklyn. The British, however, built over most of these with Federal-style buildings like St. Paul's Church on Madison Ave.

Even after the British had been forced out, their architectural tastes lingered, influencing the townhouses built by their prosperous colonists. Through the early 19th century, American architects continued to incorporate such Federal details as dormer windows, stoops, and doors with columns and fan lights. Federal houses still line Charlton St. and northern Vandam St., while the old City Hall, built by D.C. mastermind Pierre L'Enfant in 1802, applies Federal detailing to a public building.

The Greek Revival of the 1820s and 30s added porticoes and iron laurel wreaths to New York's streets. If you see a house with uneven bricks, it probably predates the 1830s, when machines started making bricks. Greek Revival prevails on Washington Square North. It also pops up on Lafayette St. and on W. 20th St. Grey granite St. Peter's, built in 1838, was the first Greek Revival Catholic Church in New York.

While cadging from the old country and the classical tradition, Americans did manage to introduce some architectural innovations. Beginning in the 1850s, thousands of brownstones (made from cheap stone quarried in New Jersey) sprang up all over New York. Next to skyscrapers, the brownstone townhouse may be New York's most characteristic structure. Although beyond most people's means today, the houses were middle-class residences back then—the rich lived in block-long mansions on Fifth Avenue, and apartments were for the poor.

The social hierarchy of buildings was scandalized in 1883, when the luxurious Dakota apartment house (later John Lennon's home) went up. The building's name derives from its location on the far side of Central Park; it was so far removed from the social center of town, local wits joked, that it might as well be in Dakota Territory. But the relatively cheap, sumptuously appointed apartments offered an attractive alternative to the soaring real estate prices of Midtown. Soon, similar apartment buildings, like the Ansonia, were built in Harlem and on the Upper West Side.

In the 1890s American architects studying abroad brought the Beaux Arts style back from France and captivated the nation. Beaux Arts, which blended Classical detail with lavish decoration, stamped itself on structures built through the 1930s. Especially fine examples are the New York Customs House, built by Cass Gilbert, and the New York Public Library, originally built to house James Lenox's overflowing book collection. Lenox, a wealthy recluse, accumulated so many books that keeping track of them in his apartment was nearly impossible; when he wanted to read one he already possessed, he often had to go out and buy another copy. He donated his collection to the city in 1895.

Architects lavished gracious Beaux Arts detailing on the first specimens of New York's quintessential structure—the skyscraper. Made possible by the invention of the elevator in 1857, skyscrapers soon became the city's architectural trademark.

THE SKYSCRAPER: AN AMERICAN AESTHETIC

Permissive new building codes at the turn of the 20th century allowed the first skyscrapers to sprout. Initial response was mixed. The Flatiron building, erected in 1902, was triangular in shape and only 6 ft. wide at its point; its wind currents blew women's skirts up, and people feared it would topple. But tall buildings proved a useful invention in a city forever short on space, and others soon joined the Flatiron.

In 1913, Cass Gilbert gilded the 55-story Woolworth Building with Gothic flourishes, piling terracotta salamanders onto antique "W"s. The Empire State Building and the Chrysler Building, fashioned from stone and steel and built like rockets, stand testimony to America's romance with science and space. Over the years, more dizzying buildings have joined the throng.

But not all New York monoliths look the same, and the urban landscape does have quirks and personality. Learn to read between the skylines and you'll be able to distinguish and date just about every tower. New York's succession of zoning laws can be a better architectural guide than I.M. Pei.

Does the building have a ziggurat on top? Look like a wedding cake? Zoning restrictions of the late 1940s stipulated that tall buildings had to be set back at the summit. New York's first curtain of pure glass was the 1950 United Nations Secretariat Building, an air-conditioning nightmare. The building quickly inspired Lever House, a 24-story glass box. Then, in 1958, Ludwig Mies Van der Rohe and Philip Johnson created the Seagram Building, a glass tower set behind a plaza on Park Avenue. Crowds soon gathered to mingle, sunbathe, and picnic, much to the surprise of planners and builders. A delighted planning commission began offering financial incentives to every builder who offset a highrise with public open space. Over the next decade, many architects stuck empty plazas next to their towering office complexes. Some of them looked a little too empty to the picky planning commission, which changed the rules in 1975 to stipulate that every plaza should provide public seating. By the late '70s, plazas were moved indoors: high-tech atriums with gurgling fountains, bevis fronds, and pricey cafés began to flourish.

The leanest skyscrapers you will see date from the early '80s, when shrewd developers realized they could get office space, bypass zoning regulations, *and* receive a bonus from the commission if they hoisted up "sliver" buildings. Composed largely of elevators and stairs, the disturbingly anorexic newcomers were generally disliked. Those tired of living in the shadow of shafts altered zoning policy in 1983 so that structural planning would encourage more room for air and sun.

Builders have finally recognized the overcrowding problem in East Midtown and expanded their horizons somewhat. New residential complexes have risen on the Upper East Side above 95th St.; in the near future you can expect high-flying office complexes to stomp out the West Midtown culture of the 40s and 50s. Some developers have even ventured into the sagebrush splendor of Queens. And with the restructuring of the city government in 1989, citizens now have a greater say in development projects in their community.

The planning commission that oversees the beautiful catastrophe now takes overcrowding and environmental issues into account when it makes its decisions. As an added safeguard, the Landmarks Preservation Commission lurks ever-vigilant, ensuring that New York does not destroy its past as it steamrolls into the future.

■■■ MUSIC

Music in New York City rocks hard in every genre and style. Classical music-related performances flourish uptown, especially at the series of halls composing Lincoln Center (Avery Fisher Hall is home to the **New York Philharmonic**). The 92nd Street Y is another showcase for serious music. Each summer the **Next Wave Festival** takes over the Brooklyn Academy of Music, offering spectacular, offbeat happenings, crackpot fusions of classical music, theater, and performance art.

In 1976 ambitious avant-garde poets and sometime musicians took over the campy glam-rock scene in downtown barroom clubs like **CBGB's** and **Max's Kansas City:** bands and performers like the Ramones, Patti Smith, Richard Hell, Television, and Blondie combined venom, wit, and a calculated stupidity to invent **punk**. Ever since, New York has convulsed with musical shocks; the New Wave became the **No Wave** when speed-freaking bizarro intellectuals (in bands like DNA, the

Contortions, and Red Transistor) pared rock down to a minimum and added honking saxophone squalor. In the '80s angry kids imported **hardcore** from Washington, D.C.: a bevy of fast-rocking, non-drinking, non-smoking bands packed Sunday all-ages shows at CBGB's. In the '80s and early '90s the **"post-punk"** scene crystallized around bands like Sonic Youth, Yo La Tengo, and Pussy Galore, producing short, finely crafted bursts of musical energy. You can find obscure or out-of-print vinyl in one of the city's many used record stores; prices are absurd, but the selection far surpasses that of any other North American city (see Shopping: Record Stores).

Rap and **hip-hop** began here, on the streets of New York's neighborhoods, and the list of New York artists reads like the text of *Who's Who in Urban Music:* KRS-1, Chuck D, MC Lyte, LL Cool J, Run-DMC, EPMD, and Queen Latifah (who leaped across the river from Jersey). Grandmaster Flash and Bronx DJ Afrika Bambaataa laid the foundations in the late '70s and early '80s with records rooted deeply in electronic processing, scratching, and sampling. In 1979, the Sugarhill Gang (see Sights: Harlem for more on Sugar Hill) released "Rapper's Delight," widely considered the first true rap record. For a clearer glimpse of the hip-hop scene in New York (and across the country) pick up a copy of New York-based *The Source,* the genre's premier fanzine (thicker and glossier than before).

Jazz has been associated with the sound of the big city since the music's inception. Duke Ellington played here in the '20s and '30s. **Minton's Playhouse** in Harlem was home to Thelonious Monk and one of the birthplaces of **bebop,** a highly-sophisticated jazz variant with a hard-edged sensibility. Miles Davis, Charlie Parker, Dizzy Gillespie, Max Roach, Tommy Potter, Bud Powell, and many others contributed to the New York sound of the late '40s and '50s, when beatniks, hepcats, and poor old souls filled 52nd St. clubs. **Free-jazz** pioneer Cecil Taylor and spaceman Sun Ra set up shop here during the '60s and '70s. Today, wonko experimentalists like John Zorn and James Blood Ulmer plot to destroy music at clubs like the **Knitting Factory;** meanwhile, in Brooklyn, a loose grouping of like-minded musicians called M-Base mixes hot funk with cool jazz, to good effect.

New York is the place to catch new music. Nearly every performer who comes to the States plays here, and thousands of local bands compete to make a statement and win an audience. Venues range from stadiums to concert halls to back-alley sound-systems. Whatever your inclination, New York's expansive musical scene should be able to satisfy it. (See Entertainment & Nightlife: Music.)

■■■ LITERARY NEW YORK

New York's reputation as the literary capital of the Americas—and arguably the English-speaking world—has deep historical roots. English-born **William Bradford,** perhaps the city's first literary man of note, was appointed public printer—America's first—here in 1698. He went on to found the country's first newspaper, the *New York Gazette,* in 1725.

Even before it had become the publishing center of the country (supplanting Boston around the mid-19th century), New York was home to many of the pioneers of the national literature. Some of these writers—**Herman Melville** for example—knew neither of their own nor of New York's impending literary fame. Melville, born in 1819 at 6 Pearl St. in lower Manhattan, was so disheartened by the critics' response to *Moby Dick* that he took a job at a New York customs house for four dollars a day and died unrecognized and unappreciated; to top it off, the *Times* called him Henry in his obituary. **Washington Irving** knew better how to work a room. Born at 131 William St., the author of *Knickerbocker's History of New York* made a name for himself penning satirical essays on New York society "from the beginning of the world to the end of the Dutch dynasty." In a moment of classic coinage, Irving gave New York its enduring pen-name, Gotham City. Other lower Manhattan writers of the times included **William Cullen Bryant, James Fenimore Cooper,** and **Walt Whitman,** who hung around for a while to work on the magazine *Aurora* and to rhapsodize in free verse on the Brooklyn Bridge and "Manahatta."

American writers have traditionally lived on the fringes of the culture. Appropriately, most New York writers have lived on the *geographic* fringes of their city— either well above (in Harlem) or below (in the Village and on the Lower East Side) New York's social and commercial centers. Maybe these writers have sought the critical perspective that comes with living at a distance. Maybe, as in **Edgar Allen Poe's** pitiful case, they were so brutally poor they had no choice in the matter. Poe, who rented a house all the way out in the rural Bronx, earned so little he used to send his aging mother-in-law to scour nearby fields for edible roots.

Literary deadbeats, hacks, and bohunks followed the wave of mostly Italian immigrants and Bohemians streaming into the Greenwich Village area in the early 20th century. Among the young-and-poor crowd were **Willa Cather, John Reed,** and **Theodore Dreiser,** pioneers of the mature American novel. For over fifty years the Village would be one of America's most important neighborhoods, hosting a full spectrum of poets, essayists, and novelists, including **Marianne Moore, Hart Crane, e.e. cummings, Edna St. Vincent Millay, John Dos Passos,** and **Thomas Wolfe.**

Although too expensive for most Village writers, spiffy Washington Square— immortalized by **Henry James's** book of that name and by **Edith Wharton's** *Age of Innocence*—was nevertheless the center of the literary scene. Radiating off the square to the north were the legendary **Salamagundi Club** (47 Fifth Ave. at 11th St.); the Cedar Tavern, one time gathering place for Beats **Allen Ginsberg** and **Jack Kerouac;** and the cobblestoned Washington Mews, home to **Sherwood Anderson** (No. 54), **"Jaundice" John Dos Passos** (in the studio between No. 14 and 15), and innumerable others. To the south of the Square once stood the boarding houses where **O. Henry** and **Eugene O'Neill** kicked it, and 133 MacDougal is the spot where O'Neill revved up his **Provincetown Players.** Down Bleecker and MacDougal you'll find some of the coffee houses the Beats made famous, along with former residences of James Fenimore Cooper (145 Bleecker), Theodore Dreiser, and **James Agee** (172 Bleecker). West of the square are the former pads of **Richard Wright, Edward Albee** (238 W. 4th St.), **Sinclair Lewis** (69 Charles St.), **Hart Crane** (79 Charles St.), and **Thomas Wolfe** (263 West 11th St.). **Dylan Thomas** was one of many writers who gassed up at the White Horse Tavern (567 Hudson St.). Few, however, were as unfortunate as Thomas, who, after pumping a purported 18 shots of scotch through his shredded gut, lapsed into a fatal coma.

The West Village, of course, did not have exclusive rights on New York's writerly set. On the other side of Broadway, the now-thriving, once-affordable East Village was headquarters to Kerouac and Ginsberg, **Amiri Baraka (Le Roi Jones),** and **W.H. Auden** (who spent a couple of decades at 77 St. Mark's Place, basement entrance). Many a writer has whiled away his or her dying days in relative obscurity at the **Chelsea Hotel** (on 23rd St. between Seventh and Eighth Ave.). Among the luckier of tenants have been **Arthur Miller** and **Vladimir Nabokov.** In midtown lurks the legendary **Algonquin Hotel** (59 W. 44th St.). In 1919 the wits of the Round Table—writers like **Robert Benchley, Dorothy Parker, Alexander Woollcott,** and **Franklin P. Adams**—made this hotel the site of their famous weekly lunch meetings. The Algonquin is the birthplace of the *New Yorker* magazine.

The **Gotham Book Mart** (41 W. 47th St.), established in 1920, has long been one of New York's most important literary hangouts. The store is famous for its second-story readings, which hosted some of the biggest writers of the century and attracted all of literary New York. During the years when *Ulysses* was banned in the U.S., those in the know came to the Gotham to buy imported copies under the counter. Check out the memorabilia and old photographs that document the bookstore's history. **Columbia University** has long been the intellectual magnet of the Upper West Side. The roving Beat crowd contaminated the area in the late '40s while Ginsberg was studying at the college. His friends were known to join him at the old West End Café (2911 Broadway). Unlike the White Horse, this delicatessen/bar doesn't play up its highfalutin' past.

The Renaissance that exploded in the Harlem of the '20s is one of the most important moments in American literary history. Novels like **George Schuyler's** *Black No*

More and **Claude McKay's** *Home to Harlem* are energized accounts of the throbbing, grizzled underworld of speakeasies and nightclubs. **Zora Neale Hurston,** an anthropology student at Columbia, helped plug the college intellectual scene into the hypercreative buzz up in Harlem, while **Langston Hughes** and his circle were busy founding radical journals. A downtown crowd of lefties, artists, and alternative lifestylists bypassed Midtown altogether in their relentless (often ignorantly condescending) explorations into black culture. For the next generation's impressions of this amazing neighborhood, look to the writings of **James Baldwin, Anne Petry,** and **Ralph Ellison,** whose *Invisible Man* captures a tense and disappointed post-Renaissance Harlem. Also see **Nathan Huggins's** *Harlem Renaissance*.

■■■ JOURNALISM AND PUBLICATIONS

New York, the premiere society of information abundance, is a sounding board for the rest of the global village. ABC, CBS, NBC, two wire services, umpteen leading magazines, and more newspapers than anywhere else in the world have taken up residence here. Publicists, preachers, advertisers, sociologists, and community activists jockey for position, hoping to make enough noise to be heard above the information din. The stakes are immense, the opportunities unparalleled; the high concentration of media here amplifies every sound. Broadsheets, graffiti, posters, and billboards provide additional media outlets, public spaces for high-profile intervention. Meanwhile, a strange underground world opens up on public-access television, if you can find a friend with cable.

New York's romance with the media began almost three centuries ago. The city's first newspaper, the *Gazette,* appeared in 1725. Ten years later, John Peter Zenger, editor of the *New-York Weekly Journal,* was charged with libel for satirizing public officials. His description of the city recorder as "a large spaniel...that has lately strayed from his kennel with his mouth full of fulsome panegyrics" was seen as especially offensive. The governor threw Zenger into jail and burned copies of his paper in public. When the court acquitted him, it set a precedent for what would become a great U.S. tradition—the freedom of the press.

The city soon became the center of the nation's rapidly developing print network. Horace Greeley's *Tribune,* based in New York, became America's first nationally distributed paper; Greeley told young men all around the country to "Go West." In the mid-19th century, Nassau Street was dubbed "Newspaper Row."

Today New York supports well over 100 different newspapers, reflecting the diversity of its urban landscape. Weekly ethnic papers cater to the black, Hispanic, Irish, Japanese, Chinese, Indian, Korean, and Greek communities, among others. Candidates for local office frequently court voters in these communities by seeking endorsements from their papers. Other papers cater to the patrician, the pensive, and the prurient.

The *New York Post* and the *Daily News,* the city's two major tabloid dailies, are famous for their less-than-demure sensibilities. The *News,* recently "rescued" by now-dead Robert Maxwell, has slightly better taste—it doesn't use red ink, and it reports fewer gruesome murders. *Post* headlines, often printed in unwieldy lettering three inches high, can have a nasty, toothsome ring. One of the *Post's* more brilliant offerings read "Headless Body Found in Topless Bar." Both papers have editorial policies more conservative than their headlines, as well as comics, advice pages, gossip columns, and horoscopes. The *Post* has a great sports section and both have good metropolitan coverage. *New York Newsday* also offers thorough local coverage. After more than 40 years as a successful Long Island paper—with a youngish staff, some entertaining columnists and a special Sunday section just for the kids—*Newsday* recently decided to make the jump to city tabloid and is trying hard to compete with the worst of its peers.

If you do want to read about headless bodies, the *New York Times* will not satisfy you. The distinguished elder statesman of the city papers, the *Times* deals soberly and thoroughly with the news. Its editorial page provides a nationally respected forum for policy debates, and its political endorsements are prized by candidates across the country. Praise from its Book Review section can revitalize living authors and immortalize dead ones, and its Sunday crossword puzzles enliven brunches from Fresno to Tallahassee. Recently, the *Times* began "National Editions" geared toward audiences outside the city. But it remains centered on New York. Theater directors, nervous politicians, and other fervent readers even make late-night news-stand runs to buy the hefty Sunday *Times* around midnight on Saturday.

The largest weekly leftist newspaper in the country, the *Village Voice* captures a lot of the spirit of the city (each Wednesday) you won't find in the dailies. Printed on the same kind of paper as the conservative *Post* and *Daily News,* it has nothing else in common with them. Don't search here for syndicated advice columnists, baseball statistics, or the bikini-clad woman *du jour.* The *Voice* prefers to stage lively political debates and print quirky reflections on New York life. It also sponsors some good investigative city reporting—and the city's most intriguing set of per-sonal ads. Twice-yearly special editions examine new music and literary trends. Aging rock-modernist Robert Christgau's music columns grace the *Voice* every week, while the movie reviews are some of the most substantial (and sometimes most considered) in the nation. The *New York Press,* a free weekly, also has good club and nightlife listings in addition to entertaining articles on politics and culture.

The *Wall Street Journal* and the Upper East Side's *New York Observer* fill out the news spectrum. The *Observer* prints articles and commentary on city politics on its dapper pink pages. The *Journal* gives a quick world-news summary on page one for breakfasting brokers more interested in the market pages. With its pen-and-ink drawings, market strategies, and continual obsession with the price of gold, the *Journal* offers an alternate view of the world.

Magazines rise and fall constantly in New York, but a few have managed to endure. The rarefied *New Yorker* publishes fiction and poetry by well-known authors and the occasional fledgling discovery. Even its ads contain measured prose. Its world-famous cover by Saul Steinberg, showing the rest of the world dwarfed by New York, reflects the perspective of the typical New Yorker and of the city's liter-ary scene. *The New Yorker* also carries the most thorough listings and reviews of films and events—and the finest cartoons—in the tri-state area. *New York* magazine also prints extensive listings but focuses on the city's (wealthy) lifestyle. Its final pages can prove very entertaining: they hold impossible British crossword puzzles, monthly word-game contests, and a slew of desperate personal ads.

■■■ ETIQUETTE

Like the French and the Visigoths, New Yorkers have a widespread reputation for rudeness. For most of them, lack of politeness is not a matter of principle; it's a strat-egy for survival. Nowhere is the anonymous rhythm of urban life more pounding than in New York City. Cramped into tiny spaces, millions of people find them-selves confronting one another every day, rudderless in a vast sea of humanity. If the comfort of strangers seems overshadowed by the confusion, keep in mind that it's partly a question of scale. The city, by the most fundamental human standards, is just too big and heterogeneous and jumbled. And people react by keeping to them-selves, especially in public. But if you feel that the city is intolerably unfriendly, try to note the small humanitarian gestures that appear in unlikely places.

▦ Essentials

PLANNING YOUR TRIP

Millions of penniless immigrants disembarked at Ellis Island with visions of streets paved with gold, but they quickly learned to survive in New York. You can too.

Use your address book as a supplementary travel guide; staying with friends, enemies, and remote acquaintances greatly reduces the cost of living in New York. The off-season helps too: in May and September the weather improves, the crowds of tourists thin, and prices plummet. Facilities and sights don't close in the off-season—the city that never sleeps doesn't care much for hibernation either.

Travel offices, tourist information centers, chambers of commerce, and special-interest organizations conspire to barrage you with an overwhelming amount of free information; it's best to write with specific requests (see Tourist Information).

■■■ DOCUMENTS

All visitors to New York should carry at least two **forms of identification,** one of which should be a photo ID. Banks in particular will require more than one form of identification whenever you cash a traveler's check. Before you leave for a trip to New York, **photocopy** both sides of your important documents as well as your credit cards, and leave these copies with someone you can contact easily. **Students** should bring proof of their status to qualify for any number of discounts. A current university ID card will generally suffice for U.S. students. Foreign students should purchase an **International Student Identification Card (ISIC)** (see Student Travelers below). For info on **passports and visas,** see Visitors From Abroad below.

■■■ MONEY

No matter how tight your budget or how short your trip, you won't be able to carry all your cash with you. Even if you think you can, don't: non-cash reserves are necessary. Unfortunately, out-of-state personal checks aren't readily accepted in NYC.

Before you arrive in New York, you might want to find out if your home bank is networked with any NYC banks; **Cirrus** (800-424-7787) and **Plus** (800-843-7587) are both popular **Automatic Teller Machine (ATM)** networks. If you're here for a while, open a savings account at one of the local banks and get a local ATM card, which you can use 24 hours a day all over the city (see Financial Services below).

New York **banks** are usually open from Monday to Friday 9am to 3:30pm. Some may also be open Saturdays from 9am to noon or 1pm. All banks, government agencies, and post offices are closed on legal holidays (see Holidays below).

TRAVELER'S CHECKS

If you're only passing through the city or if you're on the road a lot, traveler's checks can eliminate the need for a bank account. Most tourist establishments accept them (though some might require a driver's license or major credit card), and almost all banks will cash them. Get your checks in your hometown bank, usually with a 1-2% surcharge; the surcharge may be waived if you have a large enough balance or a certain kind of account. Some travel organizations, such as the **American Automobile Association (AAA),** offer commission-free traveler's checks to their members, but you must go to one of their offices to purchase them.

Refunds on lost or stolen checks can be time-consuming. To accelerate the process and avoid red tape, always hold onto the receipt from the purchase of your

Don't forget to write.

Now that you've said, "Let's go," it's time to say
"Let's get American Express® Travelers Cheques." If they are lost or
stolen, you can get a fast and full refund virtually anywhere you
travel. So before you leave be sure and write.

traveler's checks, a list of their serial numbers, and a record of which ones you've cashed. Keep these in a separate pocket or pouch from the checks themselves, since they contain the information you could need to replace the checks if they're stolen. It's also a good idea to leave a copy of the serial numbers at home.

American Express traveler's checks are perhaps the most widely recognized in the world and the easiest to replace if lost or stolen—you'd just contact the nearest AmEx travel office or call the 800-number below. Other well-known banks market their own brands. Major traveler's check and credit card companies offer a variety of free services when you buy their checks or apply for their cards, including emergency cash advances; travel information hotlines; medical, legal, and interpreter referrals; emergency message relays; guaranteed hospital entry payments; assistance with lost documents and credit card cancellation; travel insurance; and help with travel arrangements.

American Express traveler's checks may be purchased within the U.S. at AmEx Travel Services Offices, banks, and by calling 800-221-7282. Visitors from abroad should contact their local AmEx office. There is a small fee for check purchases. (It is now also possible to purchase traveler's checks from automated American Express Dispensers (AEDs); call 800-CASH-NOW before departing to inquire about this service.) To report lost or stolen checks, call 800-221-7282. AmEx offices cash their own checks commission-free and sell checks that can be signed by either of two people traveling together ("Check for Two"). Checks available in nine currencies. American Automobile Association members can obtain AmEx traveler's checks commission-free at AAA offices.

Barclay's Bank, 800-221-2426. Barclay's sells Visa traveler's checks for a 1-3% commission, depending on the bank at which the checks are purchased. To report lost or stolen checks, in the U.S. call 800-227-6811; in the U.K. (0171) 937 8091; elsewhere call collect (212) 858-8500. Barclay's banks will cash Visa traveler's checks for free.

Citicorp sells both Citicorp and Citicorp Visa traveler's checks for a 1-2% commission, depending on the branch. To place orders and report lost or stolen checks, in the U.S. call 800-645-6556; in the U.K. (0171) 982 4040; elsewhere call collect (813) 623-1709. Citicorp's Travel Assist Hotline (800-523-1199) can connect check holders with an English-speaking doctor and lawyer, as well as provide traveler's check refund assistance. Numerous Citibank branches are located throughout New York; Citicorp's **World Courier Service** guarantees hand-delivery of traveler's checks anywhere in the world.

MasterCard International offers traveler's checks for a 1-2% commission; try ordering through Thomas Cook (see below) for potentially lower commissions. To order, in the U.S. call (800) 423-3630; from abroad, call collect (609) 987-7300. To report lost or stolen checks, in the U.S., Canada, and Mexico, call (800) 223-9920, or collect (609) 987-7300; from abroad, call collect 44 733 502995. Master-Card traveler's checks are also available from participating banks displaying the MasterCard logo.

Thomas Cook sells MasterCard traveler's checks in addition to its own brand. To order, in the U.S. call (800) 223-4030; from abroad, call collect (609) 987-7300. Rates range from low (2%) to nonexistent. To report lost or stolen checks, call the numbers listed above for MasterCard International.

CREDIT CARDS

Even the best-budgeted trip can present unexpected expenses and emergencies; credit cards can save you. American Express is taken at most upscale establishments; most places take both VISA and MasterCard.

American Express (800-528-4800) has a sizable annual fee ($55) but membership has its privileges. AmEx cardholders can cash personal checks at offices abroad (up to $1000, with Goldcard $5000); offices can also help with reservations, lost travel documents, and the provision of temporary IDs. Global Assist, a 24-hour hotline available to cardholders, offers information and legal assistance in emergencies (800-554-2639 in the U.S. and Canada; from elsewhere call collect 202-783-7474).

AmEx members can also have their mail held at one of the 1500-plus AmEx offices around the world. American Express features a free **Express Cash** service, which lets enrolled cardholders access cash from their accounts at any ATM with the AmEx trademark. Each transaction costs between $2.50 and $10, not including conversion fees and interest. Call (800) CASH-NOW (227-4669) to enroll in the program and receive a list of participating machines in the New York City area.

MasterCard (800-999-0454) and **VISA** (800-336-8472) credit cards are sold by individual banks, and each bank offers different services in conjunction with the card. Both cards can be used at ATMs; to obtain a PIN (personal identification number), which is needed to access ATMs, contact the issuer of the card before you travel. For guilt-free consumerism, call **Working Assets** (800-522-7759), a California-based company that has offered VISA cards since 1985 and donates a portion of money from all VISA purchases to 36 different non-profit, save-the-world organizations. (They even print their bills and statements on recycled paper.)

SENDING MONEY

If you run out of money on the road, you can have more mailed to you in the form of **traveler's checks** bought in your name or **certified checks;** another option is **postal money orders,** available at U.S. post offices (75¢ fee for orders under $25; $700 limit per order; cash only). Certified checks are redeemable at any bank, while postal money orders can be cashed at post offices upon display of two IDs (one of which must contain a photo). Keep receipts; money orders are refundable if lost.

American Express cardholders can cash personal checks at any full-service **American Express** office; if necessary, checks can be mailed to AmEx offices and held for recipients. The **American Express MoneyGram** service allows travelers (and the friends and families of travelers) to wire and receive money from over 70 countries. (Bear in mind, however, that some European and Australian AmEx offices can only *receive* MoneyGrams—which won't help you if you're stuck penniless in NY.) Fees are commensurate with the amount of money being sent and the speed of the service being requested—10 minute, overnight, or 3-5 day delivery. Call (800) 543-4080 for information about rates and participating offices.

To take advantage of a classic, time-honored, and expensive service, use **Western Union** (800-325-6000 in the U.S., Mexico, and Canada; in Europe, call the London office at 448 174 13639 or 0 800 833 833). You or someone else can phone in a credit card number, or else someone can bring cash to a Western Union office. Fees depend not on how far the money's going, but on how much is being sent. Charges are $29 for $250, $40 for $500, and $50 for $1000. As always, you need ID to pick up your money. Funds will usually be available within 15 minutes; money sent from some locations overseas (such as Portugal) may take longer, in which case an additional surcharge may apply. Call (800) 325-6000 for the Western Union location nearest you.

Another alternative is **cabling money.** Through **Bank of America** (800-346-7693), money can be sent to almost any bank in the U.S. Just have someone bring cash, a Bank of America check, or possibly a cashier's check (at the individual branch's discretion) to the sending bank, at which neither you nor the sender need have an account. Funds are usually available within one working day at the destination bank of your choice (check with the bank beforehand to make sure it's OK); the money will be paid out to you in U.S. currency. The fee for this service is $30 if the sender deducts the money from an existing account at Bank of America, otherwise $40. Other fees may apply depending on the bank at which you receive the money. Not all Banks of America are sending banks; call (800) 346-7693 for the most convenient location or for more information.

If time is of the essence, you can have money **wired** directly from one bank to another for about $30 (plus the commission charged by your home bank) for sums of less than $1000. Once you've found a bank that will accept a wire, write or telegram your home bank with your account number, the name and address of the bank to receive the wire, and a routing number. Also notify the bank of the form of ID that the second bank should accept before paying the money.

Bank drafts or **international money orders** are cheaper but slower. You pay a commission of $15-20 on the draft, plus the cost of sending it registered air mail. As a last resort for visitors from abroad, **consulates** will wire home for you and deduct the cost from the money you receive. Don't expect them to be happy about it.

■■■ HEALTH

Before you leave, check whether your insurance policy covers medical costs incurred while traveling (see Insurance below). Always have proof of insurance as well as policy numbers with you. If you choose to risk traveling without insurance, you may have to rely on public health organizations and clinics that treat patients without demanding proof of solvency. Call the local hotline or crisis center listed in this book under Help Lines and Medical Care. Operators at these organizations have numbers for public-health organizations and clinics that treat patients without demanding proof of solvency. If you require **emergency treatment,** call **911** or go to the emergency room of the nearest hospital.

If you have a chronic medical condition that requires **medication** on a regular basis, be sure to consult your physician before you leave. Carry copies of your prescriptions and always distribute medication or syringes among all your carry-on and checked baggage in case any of your bags is lost. If you wear glasses or contact lenses, carry an extra prescription and perhaps a spare pair.

Any traveler with a medical condition that cannot be easily recognized (i.e., diabetes, epilepsy, heart conditions, allergies to antibiotics) may want to obtain a **Medic Alert Identification Tag.** The internationally recognized tag indicates the nature of the bearer's problem and provides the number for Medic Alert's 24-hour hotline. Attending medical personnel can call this number to obtain information about the member's medical history. Lifetime membership (tag, annually updated wallet card, and 24-hr. hotline access) begins at $35. Contact Medic Alert Foundation, P.O. Box 1009, Turlock, CA 95381-1009 (800-432-5378 or 800-ID-ALERT). The **American Diabetes Association,** 1660 Duke St., Alexandria, VA 22314 (800-232-3472), provides copies of the article "Travel and Diabetes" as well as diabetic ID cards, which show the carrier's diabetic status. Contact your local ADA office for information.

All travelers should be concerned about **Acquired Immune Deficiency Syndrome (AIDS),** which is transmitted through the bodily fluids of an infected (i.e., HIV-positive) individual. Remember that there is no assurance that someone is not infected; HIV tests show antibodies only after a six-month lapse, and there is no way to determine through physical inspection whether or not a person carries the HIV virus. Do not have sex without using a condom, and don't ever share intravenous needles with anyone. (Latex condoms have smaller pores than sheepskin condoms and are thus more effective in preventing the spread of AIDS and other sexually-transmitted diseases.) The Center for Disease Control's **AIDS Hotline** provides information on AIDS in the U.S. (800-342-2437, TDD 800-243-7889, hours are 8am-2am, 7 days a week).

Although reliable **contraception** is easily obtainable in New York City, women taking birth control pills should bring enough to allow for extended stays. Condoms can be found in any pharmacy, usually right on the shelves; many of the city's pharmacies, conveniently, stay open all the time.

If you are in the New York area and need an abortion, contact the **National Abortion Federation,** a professional association of abortion providers. Call its toll-free hotline for information, counseling, and the names of qualified medical professionals in the area (800-772-9100; Mon.-Fri. 9:30am-5:30pm). The NAF has informational publications for individuals and health-care clinics alike. Clinics they recommend must maintain certain safety and operational standards. In New York the NAF will refer you to the Planned Parenthood clinics. The number for the Manhattan clinic is 677-6474; in Brooklyn, 718-858-1819; in the Bronx, 718-292-8000.

■■■ INSURANCE

Beware of purchasing unnecessary coverage for a trip to New York—your current policies might well extend to many travel-related accidents. **Homeowners' insurance** (or your family's coverage) often covers theft during travel. Homeowners are generally covered against loss of travel documents (passports, plane tickets, railpasses, etc.) up to about $500. **Canadians** are protected by their home province's health insurance plan up to 90 days after leaving the country; check with your provincial Ministry of Health or the Health Plan Headquarters.

ISIC and **International Student** or **Teacher ID Cards** provide $3000 worth of accident and illness insurance and $100 per day for up to 60 days of hospitalization while the card is valid, and give you access to a toll-free Traveler's Assistance hotline (800-626-2427) whose multilingual staff can provide help in medical, legal, and financial emergencies. **CIEE** offers the inexpensive Trip-Safe Plan, with options covering medical treatment and hospitalization, accidents, baggage loss, and even charter flights missed due to illness. If you are ineligible for the cards mentioned above, Trip-Safe extends the coverage of the insurance you have. **STA** offers a more expensive, more comprehensive plan. **American Express** cardholders receive automatic flight and car rental insurance on purchases made with the card. (For addresses for CIEE and STA, see Students and Young Adults below.)

Remember that insurance companies usually require a copy of the police reports for claims involving thefts. Evidence of having paid medical expenses (doctor's statements and/or receipts) is necessary for medical claims to be honored. Don't ignore the time limits on filing for reimbursement that many companies impose, and always carry policy numbers and proof of insurance. Some of the plans listed below offer cash advances or guaranteed bills. If your coverage does not include on-the-spot payments or cash transferals, leave an extra budget for emergencies.

Access America, Inc., 6600 West Broad St., P.O. Box 11188, Richmond, VA 23230 (800-284-8300). Covers trip cancellation/interruption, on-the-spot hospital admittance costs, emergency medical evacuation. 24-hr. hotline.

Globalcare Travel Insurance, 220 Broadway, Lynnfield, MA 01940 (800-821-2488, fax 617-592-7720). Complete medical, legal, emergency, and travel-related services. On-the-spot payments and special student programs.

Travel Guard International, 1145 Clark St., Stevens Point, WI 54481 (800-826-1300 or 715-345-0505, fax 715-345-0525). "Travel Guard Gold" packages: Basic ($19), Deluxe ($39), and Comprehensive (9% of total trip cost) for medical expenses, baggage and travel documents, travel delay, baggage delay, emergency assistance, and trip cancellation/interruption. 24-hr. emergency hotline.

Travel Insured International, Inc., 52-S Oakland Ave. P.O. Box 280568, East Hartford, CT 06128-0568 (800-243-3174, fax 203-528-8005). Insurance against accident, baggage loss, sickness, trip cancellation/interruption, and company default. Covers emergency medical evacuation and automatic flight insurance.

■■■ CLIMATE

City summers are hot and sticky, and New York winters can compete with those seen by Boston and points north. Winter snowfalls are common, but New York usually clears streets within a day due to all the traffic. In the spring and fall, frequent showers make umbrellas a good idea.

MONTH	HIGH	LOW
January	38°	26°
February	40°	27°
March	49°	34°
April	61°	44°
May	72°	53°

June	80°	63°
July	95°	68°
August	90°	67°
September	76°	60°
October	66°	50°
November	54°	41°
December	42°	30°

■■■ TRAVELERS WITH SPECIFIC CONCERNS

STUDENTS AND YOUNG ADULTS

In the world of budget travel, youth has its privileges. In many cases, establishments will offer discounts to holders of ordinary **student IDs** from high schools, colleges, and universities. The **International Student Identity Card (ISIC),** however, is the most widely accepted form of student identification. The card, which is sponsored by the International Student Travel Confederation (ISTC), can get you discounts galore; ask about discounts even when none are advertised. The perks include access to student airfares through **Council Travel,** sickness and accident insurance of up to $3000 as well as $100 per day for in-hospital care for up to 60 days, and a toll-free 24-hour Traveler's Assistance hotline (800-626-2427; outside the U.S. call collect 713-267-2525) whose staff can provide help in medical, legal, and financial emergencies. ISTC also offers an **International Teacher Identity Card (ITIC)** with similar benefits. Many student travel offices issue ISICs and ITICs.

The **GO 25** card is sponsored by the Federation of International Youth Travel Organizations (FIYTO), Bredgade 25 H, DK 1260 Copenhagen K, Denmark (tel. +45 33 33 96 00, telex 31 239, fax +45 33 93 96 76). Like the ISIC, the GO 25 offers a range of discounts on transportation and admissions worldwide. Unlike the ISIC, the GO 25 can be obtained by anyone, including non-students, under age 26.

Both of these cards generally require an application form, one or more passport-type photos, a fee, and proof of student, teacher, or youth status (whichever is relevant). For students, "proof" means something like a declaration (with school seal) from the school, a letter on school stationery from the registrar or dean, a photo-copy of a recent transcript, a bursar's receipt, or a high school report card or letter from the principal. Teachers will need a letter on school stationery from their department chair, principal, or other school official which declares their status as a full-time faculty member. For proof of youth status (a.k.a. "age"), a copy of a driver's license, birth certificate, or personal data page of a passport will usually suffice.

Council on International Educational Exchange (CIEE), 205 East 42nd St., New York, NY 10017 (212-661-1414). A private, not-for-profit organization, CIEE administers work, volunteer, academic and professional programs around the world. They also offer ID cards (including the ISIC and GO 25) and a range of pub-lications, among them the useful magazine *Student Travels* (free, postage $1) and *Going Places: the High School Student's Guide to Study, Travel and Adventure Abroad* ($13.95, postage $1.50). Call or write for further information.

Council Travel, a subsidiary of CIEE, is an agency specializing in student and bud-get travel. They sell charter flight tickets, guidebooks, ISIC, ITIC, and GO 25 cards, hostelling cards, and travel gear. Their **New York City** branch is located at 205 East 42nd St. (661-1450; zip code 10017). Forty other U.S. offices, including: 729 Boylston St., Suite #201, **Boston,** MA 02116 (617-266-1926); 1153 N. Dear-born St., 2nd floor, **Chicago,** IL 60610 (312-951-0585); 6715 Hillcrest, **Dallas,** TX 75205 (214-363-9941); 1093 Broxton Ave., Suite 220, **Los Angeles,** CA 90024 (310-208-3551); 715 S.W. Morrison, Suite 600, **Portland,** OR 97205 (503-228-1900); 530 Bush St., Ground Floor, **San Francisco,** CA 94108 (415-421-3473); 1314 Northeast 43rd St., Suite 210, **Seattle,** WA 98105 (206-632-2448).

FOR $20 YOU CAN STAY HERE OR GET YOUR SHOES SHINED AT THE HOTEL DOWN THE STREET.

Hostelling International - New York offers a clean, comfortable place to spend the night in New York City. . . plus the opportunity to meet and share experiences with travelers from all over the world. And while you may have to do without a few of life's little luxuries, at this price we don't think you'll miss them.
For reservations or more information, call (212) 932-2300.

HOSTELLING INTERNATIONAL

The new seal of approval of the International Youth Hostel Federation.

HOSTELLING
INTERNATIONAL®

Additional U.S. offices include **San Diego,** CA, **Tempe,** AZ, **Miami,** FL, **Ann Arbor,** MI, **Providence,** RI, **Cambridge,** MA, and **Washington, D.C.** Council Travel also has offices in Europe, including: 28A Poland St. (Oxford Circus), **London** WIV 3DB, England ((0171) 437 77 67); 22, Rue des Pyramides, 75001 **Paris,** France ((1) 44 55 55 44); and 18, Graf-Adolph-Strasse, 4000 Dusseldorf 1, **Germany** ((211) 32.90.88).

Let's Go Travel, Harvard Student Agencies, Inc., 53-A Church St., Cambridge, MA 02138 (800-5-LETS-GO or 617-495-9649). The world's largest student-run travel agency, Let's Go Travel is operated by the same happy-go-lucky students who published this book. Let's Go offers railpasses, HI/AYH memberships, ISIC and International Teacher ID cards, FIYTO cards, guidebooks (including every *Let's Go*), maps, bargain flights, and a complete line of budget travel gear. All items available by mail; call or write for a catalog (or see color catalog at the center of this publication).

STA Travel, 5900 Wilshire Blvd., Ste. 2110, Los Angeles, CA 90036 (800-777-0112 nationwide). A student and youth travel organization with over 100 offices around the world offering discount airfares (for travelers under 26 and full-time students under 32), railpasses, accommodations, tours, insurance, and ISICs. In **New York City,** they are located at 48 E. 11th St. (477-7166, zip code 10003). Ten other U.S. offices, including: 297 Newbury St., **Boston,** MA 02116 (617-266-6014); 51 Grant Ave., **San Francisco,** CA 94108 (415-391-8407); and 2401 Pennsylvania Ave. NW, **Washington, D.C.** 20037 (202-887-0912). In the **UK:** 86 Old Brompton Rd., London SW7 3LQ and 117 Euston Rd., London NW1 2SX ((0171) 937 99 21 for European travel, (0171) 937 99 71 for N. American travel, (0171) 937 99 62 for Long Haul travel). In **New Zealand:** 10 High St., Auckland ((09) 398 99 95). In **Australia:** 222 Faraday St., Melbourne VIC 3053 ((03) 349 24 11).

Travel CUTS, 187 College St., Toronto, Ontario M5T 1P7 (416-798-CUTS, fax 416-979-8167). Canada's national student travel bureau and equivalent of CIEE, with 40 offices across Canada. Also in the **UK:** 295-A Regent St., London W1R 7YA ((0171) 637 31 61). Discounted domestic and international airfares available to all; special student fares to all destinations with valid ISIC. Issuing authority for ISIC, FIYTO, and HI hostel cards. Offers free *Student Traveller* magazine, as well as info on Student Work Abroad Program (SWAP).

Campus Travel, 52 Grosvenor Gardens, London SW1W 0AG ((0171) 730 88 32), fax (0171) 730 57 39). 37 branches nationwide in the UK. Puts out booklets including travel suggestions, average prices, dates of local holidays, and other general information for British travelers in Europe and North America. (Also offers a bookings service via telephone: from Europe (0171) 730 34 02, from North America (0171) 730 21 01, worldwide (0171) 730 81 11.)

Educational Travel Center (ETC), 438 North Frances St., Madison, WI 53703 (800-747-5551, fax 608-256-2042). Flight information and HI/AYH cards. Write for their free pamphlet *Taking Off.*

International Student Exchange Flights (ISE), 5010 East Shea Blvd., #A104, Scottsdale, AZ 85254 (602-951-1177). Budget student flights, ISE Identity Cards, and travel guides, including the *Let's Go* series. Free catalog.

WST Charters, 65 Wigmore St., London W1H 9LG ((0171) 224 05 04, fax (0171) 224 61 42). Offers ISICs and bargain flights worldwide.

USIT Ltd., Aston Quay, O'Connell Bridge, Dublin 2, Ireland ((01) 679 88 33, fax (01) 677 88 43). ISICs, discount airfares, the works: Ireland's student travel organization. Branches in Belfast and Cork, among other places.

SENIOR TRAVELERS

Discounts abound for the mature traveler. All you need is ID proving your age. For only $8 you and your spouse can enroll in the **American Association of Retired Persons (AARP),** open to U.S. residents aged 50 and over. Members take advantage of benefits and services such as the **AARP Travel Experience** from American Express (800-927-0111), the **AARP Motoring Plan** from Amoco (800-334-3300), and discounts on lodging, car rental, and sight-seeing. Write to 601 E St. NW, Washington, D.C. 20049 (202-434-2277; Mon.-Fri. 9am-5pm). The following organizations may be of interest to older travelers:

Elderhostel, 75 Federal St., 3rd floor, Boston, MA 02110-1941 (617-426-8056). You must be 60 or over and may bring a spouse. Programs at colleges and universities in over 47 countries focus on varied subjects and generally last one week.

Gateway Books, 2023 Clemens Rd., Oakland, CA 94602 (510-530-0299, fax 510-530-0497). Publishes *Get Up and Go: A Guide for the Mature Traveler* ($10.95) and *Adventures Abroad* ($12.95) which offer recommendations and general hints for the budget-conscious senior. Call 800-669-0773 for credit card orders.

National Council of Senior Citizens, 1331 F St. NW, Washington, DC 20004 (347-8800). Membership ($12/yr., $30 for 3 yrs., or $150 for a lifetime) provides an individual or couple with access to hotel and auto rental discounts, a senior citizen newspaper, a discount travel agency, and supplemental Medicare insurance (if you're over 65).

Pilot Books, 103 Cooper St., Babylon, NY 11702 (516-422-2225). Publishes *The International Health Guide for Senior Citizens* ($4.95, postage $1).

WOMEN TRAVELERS

Women exploring any area on their own inevitably face additional safety concerns. Forgo cheap accommodations in city outskirts—the risks outweigh any savings—and stick to youth hostels, university accommodations, bed and breakfasts, and organizations offering rooms to women only. A woman should *never* hitchhike alone; even in groups it can be dangerous.

If you find yourself the object of catcalls or unwelcome propositions, your best answer is no answer. Always look as if you know where you're going (even when you don't), and maintain an assertive, confident posture wherever you go. If you feel uncomfortable asking strangers for information or directions, it may be easier to approach other women or couples. Always carry enough change for a bus, taxi, or phone call. And in emergencies, don't hesitate to yell for help.

Know the emergency numbers for the area you're visiting; see Safety and Help Lines below. More information and safety tips can be found in Maggie and Gemma Moss's *Handbook for Women Travelers,* available from **Piatkus Books,** 5 Windmill St., London W1P 1HF, England ((0171) 631 0710). The folks who produced *Gaia's Guide* (no longer available) are now publishing *Women Going Places,* a women's travel and resource guide emphasizing women-owned and -operated enterprises. The guide is aimed at lesbians but useful to all women, and is available for $14 from **INLAND Book Company,** P.O. Box 120261, East Haven, CT 06512 (203-467-4257). The latest book on women's travel to hit the market, *A Journey of One's Own* by Thalia Zepatos, provides lots of good advice as well as a specific and manageable bibliography of books and resources. The book is published by Eighth Mountain Press and retails for $14.95.

GAY AND LESBIAN TRAVELERS

New York City has a large, active, and supportive out gay and lesbian population. Gay and lesbian visitors will have no trouble finding bars, clubs, bookstores, and special events in the city. The NYC Gay Pride Parade, in late June of each year, is one of the biggest in the world. In June 1994, the Gay Pride Parade—with the aid of the hugely successful Gay Games athletic competition and a rally marking the 25th anniversary of the Stonewall riots—transformed New York into the undisputed cynosure of the gay and lesbian community. Highlights of the events included an appearance by the newly out Olympic diver Greg Louganis and a mile-long rainbow banner which waved its way up Broadway during the parade. Estimates of attendance at the final rally on the Great Lawn in Central Park ranged widely, from 100,000 to 500,000.

Let's Go lists many information lines, community centers, entertainment, and special services for gays and lesbians. Consult New York's many gay papers, most of which are available at corner newsstands (especially in Greenwich Village), for the most current information. *NY Native* is one of the most useful. *Homo-Xtra,* which bills itself as the "politically incorrect" weekly, directs its readers to all kinds of sexy services. The nationally distributed *Advocate* magazine has a New York section; also check the *Village Voice*, which details events, services, and occasional feature articles of interest to gays and lesbians. The quarterly *Metrosource* covers bars, bookstores, and various gay resources, and is available at most gay bookstores. For a directory of gay and lesbian establishments and services in North America, consult the *Gayellow Pages* ($12). Order a copy from **Renaissance House,** P.O. Box 533, Village Station, New York, NY 10014 (212-674-0120). You can also order the spin-off *NY Gayellow,* which focuses exclusively on establishments in New York City. Two other excellent sources of books for gay and lesbian travelers are **Giovanni's Room,** 345 S. 12th St., Philadelphia, PA 19107 (215-923-2960, fax 215-923-0813), and **Damron,** P.O. Box 422458, San Francisco, CA 94142-2458 (800-462-6654 or 415-255-0404). Many of the following publications are available through Giovanni's Room as well as the address listed; call Giovanni's for a free mail-order catalogue.

Spartacus International Gay Guide: $29.95. International guide for gay men, listing bars, restaurants, hotels, and hotlines throughout the world. Available in the U.S. from Giovanni's Room and Renaissance House. Published by Bruno Gmünder, Postfach 301345, D-1000 Berlin 30, Germany (tel. +49 (30) 25 49 82 00).

The Damron Address Book: $14 plus $4 shipping. Over 8000 listings of bars, restaurants, guest houses, and services catering to gay males. Published by Damron.

Ferrari's Places of Interest ($16), **Ferrari's Places for Men** ($15), and **Ferrari's Places for Women** ($13). Available in bookstores, or by mail order (postage $3.50 for the first item, 50¢ for each additional item). Ferrari Publications, P.O. Box 37887, Phoenix, AZ 85069 (602-863-2408).

Inn Places: USA and Worldwide Gay Accommodations: $14.95. Also available from Ferrari Publications.

The Women's Traveler: $10 plus $4 shipping. A travel guide for lesbians. Maps of 50 major U.S. cities; 6000 listings of bars, restaurants, accommodations, bookstores, and services. Published by Damron.

Women Going Places: $14. A women's travel guide emphasizing women-owned enterprises. Geared towards lesbians, but offers advice appropriate for all women. $14. Published by Inland Book Co., P.O. Box 120261, East Haven, CT 06512 (203-467-4257), but available only in bookstores (such as Giovanni's).

The number for the **Gay and Lesbian Switchboard** in New York is 777-1800 (phone staffed daily 10am-midnight; interactive recording gives info on bars and nightlife, including lists of which places are popular which nights of the week); the number for the **Lesbian Switchboard** is 741-2610. When you first arrive in the city, stop by the **Lesbian and Gay Community Services Center** (620-7310; phones staffed daily 9am-11pm), located at 208 W. 13th St., between Seventh and Eighth Ave. Over 400 meeting groups hold their gatherings in this three-story converted schoolhouse. The center houses a medical walk-in clinic, holds dances, and will refer you to various support groups. The **Gay and Lesbian Visitors Center** (463-9030), at 135 W. 20th St., between Sixth and Seventh Ave., publishes the bi-monthly magazine *The List* ($2.95), which carries advertisements for gay-friendly hotels, restaurants, and cultural events. Membership in the center costs $35 per year; members receive a year-long subscription to *The List*, mailed notices of interest to the gay and lesbian community, and a number of useful discounts.

TRAVELERS WITH DISABILITIES

With a little research and planning ahead, the disabled traveler can gain access to all but the most awkwardly built establishments. Your primary resource should be the brand new *Access for All* guide to New York's cultural institutions, aimed at people with mobility, sight, or hearing impediments. It describes in detail over 180 locations throughout the city. For a free copy, contact **Hospital Audiences, Inc.** (575-7663), Access Department, 220 W. 42nd St., New York, NY 10036. Call restaurants, hotels, and other facilities to find out about ramps, trails, the width of doors, the dimensions of elevators, and so on. Also inquire about restrictions on motorized wheelchairs. *Let's Go* indicates wheelchair access whenever possible.

You can also root around in more general books helpful to travelers with disabilities. One good resource is *Access to the World,* by Louise Weiss ($16.95). Check local bookstores, or contact **Facts on File, Inc.,** 460 Park Ave., New York, NY 10016 (800-829-0500, or 212-683-2244 from AK and HI). **Twin Peaks Press** publishes *Directory for Travel Agencies for the Disabled* ($19.95), *Travel for the Disabled* ($19.95), and *Wheelchair Vagabond* ($14.95), which discusses camping and travel in cars, vans, and RVs. Order from Twin Peaks Press, P.O. Box 129, Vancouver, WA 98666-0129 (order desk 800-637-2256, fax 206-696-3210).

Arrange transportation well in advance to ensure a smooth trip. If you give sufficient notice, some major car rental agencies offer hand-controlled vehicles at select locations. Call **Avis** (800-331-1212), **Hertz** (800-654-3131), or **National** (800-328-4567). Both **Amtrak** and the airlines will accommodate disabled passengers if notified at least 72 hours in advance. Hearing-impaired travelers may contact Amtrak (800-872-7245, in PA 800-322-9537) using teletype printers. **Greyhound** buses will also provide free travel for a companion; if you are without a fellow traveler, call Greyhound (800-752-4841) at least 48 hours before you plan to leave and it will make arrangements to assist you. For information on transportation availability in D.C., contact the **American Public Transit Association,** 1201 New York Ave. NW, Suite 400, Washington, DC 20005 (202-898-4000).

The following organizations offer services and information which may be of interest to travelers with physical disabilities:

Moss Rehabilitation Hospital Travel Information Service, 1200 W. Tabor Rd., Philadelphia, PA 19141 (215-456-9603). A telephone resource center and an excellent source of information on tourist sights, accommodations, and transportation for the disabled. Will refer callers to other agencies if they cannot provide information.

Society for the Advancement of Travel for the Handicapped, 347 Fifth Ave., Suite 610, New York, NY 10016 (212-447-7284, fax 212-725-8253). Publishes quarterly travel newsletter, SATH News, and several information booklets (free for members, $3 for nonmembers). Membership is $45 per year, or $25 for senior citizens and students.

American Foundation for the Blind, 15 W. 16th St., New York, NY 10011 (212-620-2147, open Mon.-Fri. 9am-2pm). Issues ID cards ($10) which provide the legally blind with access to discounts at participating institutions; write for an application or call the Product Center at 800-829-0500. Also call the Product Center to order AFB catalogues in braille, print, or on cassette or disk.

The following organizations arrange tours or trips for disabled travelers:

Directions Unlimited, 720 N. Bedford Rd., Bedford Hills, NY 10507 (800-533-5343; in NY, 914-241-1700, fax 914-241-0243). Specializes in arranging individual and group vacations, tours, and cruises for the physically disabled.

Flying Wheels Travel Service, 143 W. Bridge St., Owatonne, MN 55060 (800-535-6790, fax 507-451-1685). Arranges trips for groups and individuals in wheelchairs or with other sorts of limited mobility.

The Guided Tour, Elkins Park House, Suite 114B, 7900 Old York Road, Elkins Park, PA 19117-2339 (800-738-5841 or 215-635-2637). Organizes year-round travel programs, domestic and international, for persons with developmental and physical challenges (including those requiring renal dialysis). Call or write for a free brochure.

TRAVELERS WITH SPECIAL DIETS

Vegetarians won't have any problem eating cheap and well in New York. *Let's Go* lists the best vegetarian restaurants we could find, but you might want more. Try

Barbara Holmes's *Vegetarian Dining in New York City* ($8.95). Write to P.O. Box 845, Midwood Station, Brooklyn, NY 11230 (718-434-3180).

Travelers who keep **kosher** should contact New York synagogues for information about kosher restaurants; your own synagogue or college Hillel office should have lists of Jewish institutions in New York. The *Jewish Travel Guide* ($11.95 with a $1.75 shipping charge) is available in the U.S. from Sepher-Hermon Press, 1265 46th St., Brooklyn, NY 11219 (718-972-9010), and lists Jewish institutions, synagogues, and kosher restaurants. (The guide is also available in the U.K. from Jewish Chronicle Publications, 25 Furnival St., London EC4A IJT, England, tel. +44 (0171) 405 92 52, fax +44 (0171) 831 51 88.) Muslim travelers seeking **halal** foods should check the local Yellow Pages listings under "halal."

■■■ VISITORS FROM ABROAD

United States Tourist Offices, found in many countries, can provide you with armloads of free literature. If you can't find a U.S. Tourist Office in your area, write the **U.S. Travel and Tourism Administration,** Department of Commerce, 14th St. and Constitution Ave. NW, Rm. 1860, Washington, D.C. 20230 (202-482-4003). Or write or call N.Y. state and city tourist offices (see Tourist Information below). In Canada, contact **Travel CUTS,** 187 College St., Toronto, Ont. M5T 1P7 (416-798-CUTS, fax 416-979-8167).

If you wish to stay in a U.S. home during your vacation, many organizations can help. **Home Exchange,** PO Box 567, Northhampton, MA 01061, offers a registry service, linking homeowners all over the US and UK. Subscribers (US $50 fee) list their homes in a directory that is sent to all subscribers for the purpose of free exchange or rental. **Intervac U.S.,** International Home Exchange, PO Box 590504, San Francisco, CA 94159 (tel. (415) 435-3497, fax (415) 386-6853), is a worldwide network of home-exchange offices that publishes directories in February, April and June, listing over 7000 houses, condominiums and townhouses. **Barclay International Group,** 150 East 52nd Street, New York, NY 10022 (tel. (800) 845-6636 or (212) 832-3777, fax (212) 753-1139) has apartments and private homes available for short-term rentals (one night plus). These apartments are equipped with kitchen, telephones, TV, concierge and include maid service.

DOCUMENTS AND FORMALITIES

Foreign visitors who wish to travel to the United States should plan early so they can complete all the necessary paperwork in time. All foreign visitors are required to have a **passport, visitor's visa,** and **proof of intent to leave** (i.e., a round-trip airline ticket). You should probably file all applications several weeks or months in advance of your planned departure date. Remember—you're relying on (underfunded, overworked) government agencies to complete these transactions.

Passports and Visas

As a precaution in case your passport is lost or stolen, be sure before you leave to photocopy your passport. Carry this photocopy in a safe place apart from your passport, perhaps with a travel companion, and leave another copy at home. Better yet, carry a photocopy of all the pages of the passport, including all visa stamps. These measures will facilitate the issuing of a new passport. If you do need a new passport while in the U.S., go to your consulate or embassy.

To acquire a visa for entrance to the U.S., you will need your passport and proof of intent to leave the U.S. Most visitors obtain a B-2 or "pleasure tourist" visa, valid for six months. Contact the nearest U.S. consulate in your home country to obtain yours. Upon arrival, the I-94 form (an arrival/departure certificate) will be attached to your visa; if you lose this, replace it at the nearest **U.S. Immigration and Naturalization Service (INS)** office. (If you lose your passport in the U.S., you must replace it through your country's embassy.) The INS also grants extensions for visas (max. 6 months), which require form I-539 as well as a $70 fee.

Visitors from certain nations may enter the U.S. without visas through the **Visa Waiver Pilot Program.** Travelers qualify as long as they are traveling for business or pleasure, are staying for 90 days or less, have proof of intent to leave and a completed I-94W form, and enter aboard particular air or sea carriers. Participating countries are Andorra, Austria, Belgium, Brunei, Denmark, Finland, France, Germany, Iceland, Italy, Japan, Lichtenstein, Luxembourg, Monaco, the Netherlands, New Zealand, Norway, San Marino, Spain, Sweden, Switzerland, and the U.K. Contact the nearest U.S. consulate for more information.

Canadian citizens do not need a visa or passport, but must carry proof of citizenship (a passport, birth certificate, or voter registration card). Canadian citizens under 16 need notarized permission from both parents. Naturalized citizens should have their naturalization papers with them; occasionally officials will ask to see them. **Mexican citizens** may cross into the U.S. with an I-186 form.

Non-tourist Visas For Work and Study

Non-U.S. citizens who hope to **work** in this country should be aware of the guidelines and restrictions governing such activity. Working or studying in the U.S. with only a B-2 visa is grounds for deportation; other visas, however, are available based on the duration and nature of your intended stay. Join a USIA-authorized Exchange Visitor Program and get a **J-1** visa. Apply at your nearest U.S. embassy or consulate by first obtaining an IAP-66 eligibility form, issued by a U.S. academic institution or a private organization involved in U.S. exchanges. Alternatively, enroll full-time in a U.S. academic or language program and get an **F-1** visa. Again, fill out an IAP-66 eligibility form issued by the program in which you plan to enroll.

Both the J-1 and F-1 are valid for the full duration of your stay, which includes the length of your particular program and a brief grace period thereafter. In order to extend a student visa, fill out an I-538 form. Requests to extend a visa must be submitted 15 to 60 days before the original departure date.

If you are studying in the U.S. on an F-1 visa, you can take any on-campus job to help pay the bills once you have applied for a social security number and have completed an Employment Eligibility Form (I-9), as long as you do not displace a U.S. resident. On-campus employment is limited to 20 hours per week while school is in session, but you may work full time during vacation if you plan to return to school. For further information, contact the international students office at the institution you will be attending.

Alternatively, you can locate an employer who will sponsor you and get an **H-2B** visa. This is more difficult to obtain, since your employer will have to prove that there are no other Americans or foreign permanent residents with your job skills.

TOEFL/TSE

Almost all institutions accept applications from foreign students directly. If English is not your native tongue, you will likely be required to take the **Test of English as a Foreign Language** and **Test of Spoken English (TOEFL/TSE),** which is administered in many countries. Requirements are set by each school. Contact the TOEFL/TSE Application Office, P.O. Box 6151, Princeton, NJ 08541-6151 (609-951-1100).

International Driver's Permit

If you plan to drive here, consider obtaining an International Driver's Permit (IDP) from your national automobile association before leaving (you can't get one here). Though not required by law in the U.S., an IDP is a good idea for visitors from non-English-speaking countries, whose driver's licenses might be unfamiliar to American authorities. Make sure to have proper **insurance,** required by law in the U.S. You will need a green card, or International Insurance Certificate, to prove that you have liability insurance. The application forms are available at any AAA office or car rental agency.

Members of national automobile associations affiliated with the **American Automobile Association** (800-222-4357) can receive services from the AAA while they are in the U.S. Automobile Associations in 19 countries have full reciprocity agreements with the AAA. Check your country's association for details.

If your home country signed the Geneva Road Traffic Convention, you can legally drive in the U.S. for one year. However, unless you are from Canada or Mexico, your personal cars must exhibit the International Distinguishing Sign, which must be obtained in your home country. Consult the resident sages at your national automobile association before you leave. Remember that the usual **minimum age** for car rental and auto transport services is 21, occasionally 25.

Customs

Customs restrictions should not impose an undue burden on budget travelers. You may bring the following into the U.S. duty free: 200 cigarettes, 50 cigars, or 2 kilograms of smoking tobacco; $100 in gifts; and personal belongings such as clothing and jewelry. Articles imported in excess of your exemption will be subject to varying duty rates, to be paid upon arrival. In general, customs officers ask how much money you're carrying and your planned departure date in order to ensure that you'll be able to support yourself while here. In some cases they may ask about travel companions and political affiliation. Carry prescription drugs in labeled containers and have a written prescription or doctor's statement ready to show the customs officer. Women especially should be aware that certain prescription drugs are illegal in the U.S. For more information, including the helpful pamphlet *U.S. Customs Hints for Visitors (Nonresidents)*, contact a U.S. embassy or write the U.S. Customs Service, P.O. Box 7407, Washington, D.C. 20004 (202-927-2095).

Upon returning home, you must declare all articles acquired in the U.S. and pay a duty on the value of those articles that exceed your country's allowance. Holding onto receipts for purchases made in the U.S. will help establish values when you return.

CURRENCY AND EXCHANGE

In Boston they ask, How much does he know? In New York, How much is he worth?

—Mark Twain

CDN$1 = US$0.73	US$1 = CDN$1.37
UK£1 = US$1.54	US$1 = UK£0.65
IR£1 = US$1.52	US$1 = IR£0.66
AUS$1 = US$0.77	US$1= AUS$1.35
NZ$1 = US$0.60	US$1 = NZ$1.66

U.S. currency uses a decimal system based on the **dollar ($)**. Paper money ("bills") comes in six denominations, all the same size, shape, and dull green color. The bills now issued are $1, $5, $10, $20, $50, and $100. You may occasionally see funny denominations of $2 and $500, which are no longer printed but are still acceptable as currency. Some restaurants and stores may be squeamish about accepting bills larger than $50. The dollar is divided into 100 cents (¢). Pick your favorite notation for values of less than a dollar: 35 cents can be represented as 35¢ or $0.35. U.S. currency uses these coins: the penny (1¢), nickel (5¢), dime (10¢), and quarter (25¢). Half-dollar (50¢) and one-dollar coins are rarely seen (but are both legal tender).

Convert your currency infrequently and in large amounts to minimize exorbitant exchange fees. Try to buy traveler's checks in U.S. dollars so that you won't have to exchange them. Personal checks can be difficult to cash in the U.S. Most banks require that you have an account with them before they will cash a personal check, and opening an account can be a time-consuming affair (see Money above).

U.S. HOLIDAYS

Martin Luther King, Jr.'s Birthday is celebrated on the third Monday in January (Jan. 16 in 1995), **Presidents Day** on the third Monday in February (Feb. 20).

Memorial Day, falling on the last Monday of May (May 29), honors all U.S. citizens who have died in wars and signals the unofficial start of summer. Halfway through summer, **Independence Day** explodes on July 4. Americans celebrate their independence from England with barbecues and fireworks. Summer unofficially ends with another long weekend, **Labor Day,** on the first Monday of September (Sept. 4). **Columbus Day** comes on the second Monday in October (Oct. 9). **Thanksgiving,** the fourth Thursday of November (Nov. 23), celebrates the arrival of the Pilgrims in New England in 1620. The holiday season peaks at **Christmas** (Dec. 25) and runs through **New Year's Day** (Jan. 1). All public agencies and offices and many businesses close on these holidays.

MEASUREMENTS

Although the metric system has made considerable inroads into American business and science, the British system of weights and measures continues to prevail in the U.S. The following is a list of U.S. units and their metric equivalents:

1 inch (in.) =	25.4 millimeters (mm)
1 foot (ft.) =	0.30 meter (m)
1 yard (yd.) =	0.91 meter (m)
1 mile (mi.) =	1.61 kilometers (km)
1 ounce (oz.; mass) =	28.35 grams (g)
1 fluid ounce (fl. oz.; volume) =	29.59 milliliters (mL)
1 pound (lb.) =	0.45 kilogram (kg)
1 liquid quart (qt.) =	0.95 liter (L)
1 gallon (gal.) =	3.78 liter (L)

Electric outlets throughout the U.S., Canada, and Mexico provide current at 117 volts, 60 cycles (Hertz), and American plugs usually have two rectangular prongs; plugs for larger appliances often have a third prong for the purpose of grounding. Appliances designed for the European electrical system (220 volts) will not operate without a transformer and a plug adapter (this includes electric systems for disinfecting contact lenses). Transformers are sold to convert specific wattages (e.g., 0-50 watt transformers for razors and radios, larger watt transformers for hair dryers and other appliances). The U.S. uses the Fahrenheit **temperature scale** rather than the Centigrade (Celsius) scale. To convert Fahrenheit to Centigrade temperatures, subtract 32, then multiply by 5/9. 32°F is the freezing point of water, 212° its boiling point, and room temperature hovers around 70°.

TIME

U.S. residents tell time on the 12-hour, not 24-hour, clock. Hours after noon are *post meridiem* or pm (e.g. 2pm); hours before noon are *ante meridiem* or am (e.g. 2am). Noon is sometimes referred to as 12pm and midnight as 12am; *Let's Go* uses "noon" and "midnight." The Continental U.S. is divided into four **time zones:** Eastern, Central, Mountain, and Pacific. Hawaii and Alaska claim their own time zones as well. When it's noon Eastern time, it's 11am Central, 10am Mountain, 9am Pacific, 8am Alaskan, and 7am Hawaiian-Aleutian. New York City follows Eastern Standard Time (EST) and, like most states, advances its clocks by one hour for **daylight saving time.** In 1995, daylight saving time will begin on Sunday, April 2, at 2am. It will end on Sunday, October 29, at 2am; set your clocks back one hour to 1am then.

ALCOHOL AND DRUGS

You must be 21 years old to purchase **alcoholic beverages** legally. Many bars and stores will want to see a photo ID (a driver's license or other valid government-issued document) before selling you alcohol. On the other hand, many won't—particularly in areas like Morningside Heights (Columbia University's neighborhood) and Greenwich Village (NYU's neighborhood), both of which meet the demands of large populations of underage college students. The more popular drinking spots, as well as the more upscale liquor stores, are likely to card—and ruthlessly, at that.

Possession of marijuana, cocaine, heroin, and most opiate derivatives (among many other chemicals) is punishable by stiff fines and imprisonment. But that doesn't stop New York's thriving **drug trade,** whose marketplaces are street corners and city parks throughout the city, most notably the Village's Washington Square Park and the Lower East Side. As a rule of thumb, it is not a good idea to put much faith in the illicit products of Fun City.

If you carry **prescription drugs** while you travel, it is vital to have a copy of the prescriptions themselves readily accessible at U.S. Customs. In general, possession of illicit drugs during travel is a *very* bad idea. Check with the U.S. Customs Service before your trip (see Customs) for more information on any questionable drugs.

FOREIGN CONSULATES
Australian, 630 Fifth Ave. (245-4000). **British,** 845 Third Ave. (745-0202). **Canadian,** 1251 Sixth Ave. (768-2400). **Israeli,** 800 Second Ave. (351-5200). **Japanese,** 299 Park Ave. (371-8222). **South African,** 333 E. 38th St. (213-4880).

GETTING TO NEW YORK CITY

■■■ BY PLANE

If you're planning to fly into New York, you will have to choose not only a carrier but an airport as well. Three airports serve the New York metropolitan region. The largest, **John F. Kennedy Airport,** or JFK (718-244-4444), is 12 mi. from midtown Manhattan in southern Queens and handles most international flights. **LaGuardia Airport** (718-533-3400), 6 mi. from midtown in northwestern Queens, is the smallest, offering domestic flights and hourly shuttles to and from Boston and Washington, D.C. **Newark International Airport** (201-762-5100 or 201-961-6000), 12 miles from midtown in Newark, NJ, offers both domestic and international flights at budget fares often not available at the other airports (though getting to and from Newark can be expensive). Bi-monthly *Airport Guides* by the Port Authority have comprehensive information on all flights arriving and departing New York's airports. The guides' most useful aspect is that they let you know all the airlines—budget and charter as well as the biggies—flying any particular route into or out of the city and you can then call all these airlines in search of the best deal. The guides do not carry any information on ticket prices themselves. Write to Airport Customer Services, One World Trade Center 65N, New York, NY 10048, or call 435-4877 8am-5pm on weekdays. The guides cost $7 for a year's subscription through the mail but are free if picked up in person. (If you only want one, they'll usually send it to you free.)

For the toll-free phone number of any airline, call 800-555-1212.

FROM WITHIN THE U.S.
When dealing with any commercial airline, buying in advance is always the best bet. To obtain the cheapest fare, buy a round-trip ticket and stay over at least one Saturday; traveling on **off-peak** days (Mon.-Thurs. morning) is usually $30 to $40 cheaper than traveling on the weekends. You will need to pay for the ticket within 24 hours of booking the flight, and tickets are entirely non-refundable. Any change in plans incurs a fee of between $25 (for some domestic flights) and $150 (for many international flights), even if only to change the date of departure or return. Since travel peaks between June and August and around holidays, you may want to reserve a seat several months in advance for these times. When inquiring about fares, be sure

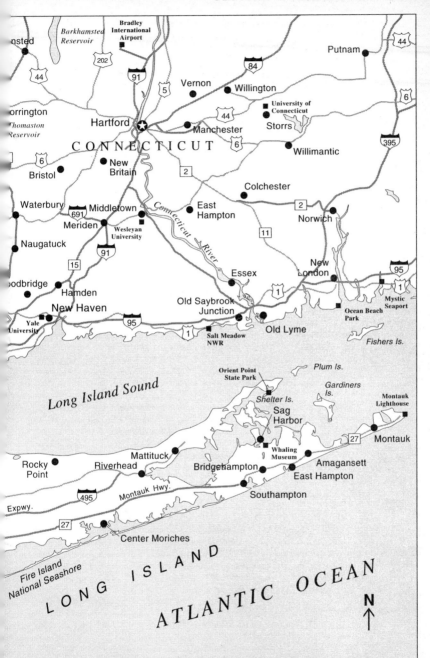

New York Metropolitan Area

to get advance purchase and length of stay requirements, or else you may not be able to buy your ticket in time or be forced to return home sooner than expected.

The commercial carriers' lowest regular offer is the **APEX** (Advanced Purchase Excursion Fare); specials advertised in newspapers may be cheaper, but have correspondingly more restrictions and fewer available seats. APEX fares provide you with confirmed reservations and often allow **"open-jaw" tickets** (landing in and returning from different cities). APEX tickets usually must be purchased two to three weeks ahead of the departure date. Be sure to inquire about any restrictions on length of stay (the minimum is most often 7 days, the maximum 2 months; shorter or longer stays usually mean more money.)

Most airlines allow children under two to fly for free on the lap of an adult. Students and seniors get good deals on the **Delta** and **USAir** Boston-New York and New York-Washington **shuttles.** Travel from 10am to 2pm and after 7pm on weekdays and all day on weekends costs $72 each way for both sets of travelers. No advance purchase is required. The standard fare for adults is generally $145 round-trip but requires a 14-day advance purchase.

Last-minute travelers should also ask about **"red-eye"** (i.e., all-night) flights, which are common on popular business routes. It is unwise to buy from others their **"frequent-flyer" coupons,** which allow the passenger named on them to fly for free; it has become standard policy to check a photo ID against the name on the ticket, and as an impostor you could find yourself paying for a new, full-fare ticket.

Consider **discount travel agencies** such as **Travel Avenue,** 10 S. Riverside Plaza, Chicago, IL, 60606 (800-333-3335), which rebates 4-7% on the price of all airline tickets (domestic and international) minus a $15 ticketing fee. Also try **Last Minute Travel** (800-527-8646). Student-oriented agencies such as **CIEE, Travel CUTS,** and **STA Travel** (see Students and Young Adults above) sometimes have special deals that regular travel agents can't offer. In the summer of 1994, CIEE offered the following round-trip fares to New York: **Los Angeles** $358; **Chicago** $130; **Houston** $287; **Miami** $198; **Washington, D.C.** $101; and **Boston** $62. The weekend travel sections of major newspapers (especially *The New York Times)* are good places to seek out bargain fares from a variety of carriers.

Charter Flights

Charter flights can save you a lot of money if you can afford to be flexible. Many charters book passengers up to the last minute—some will not even sell tickets more than 30 days in advance. However, many flights fill up well before their departure date. You must choose your departure and return dates when you book, and you will lose all or most of your money if you cancel your ticket. Charter companies themselves reserve the right to change the dates of your flight or even cancel the flight a mere 48 hours in advance. Delays are not uncommon. To be safe, get your ticket as early as possible, and arrive at the airport several hours before departure time (the earlier the better, since ticket agents seat passengers in the order that they've checked them in). Many of the smaller charter companies work by contracting service with commercial airlines, and the length of your stay is often limited by the length of the company's contract. Prices and destinations can change (sometimes markedly) from season to season; contact as many organizations as possible in order to get the best deal. Contact **Council Travel** or **Travel CUTS** for more information (see Students and Young Adults, above).

> **Wings of the World,** 404 Park Ave. South, Ste. 200, New York 10016 (725-1314), between 28th and 29th St. Excellent agency offering reserved seats on American Trans Air domestic flights. New York to Chicago $59 each way; New York to Los Angeles or San Francisco $149 each way. Tickets require 7-day advance purchase; you must call to confirm your reservation 48 hrs. prior to the flight. International flights also available; call for info. Open Mon.-Sat. 9am-5pm, Sun. 11am-4pm.

> **Unitravel,** 1177 N. Warson Rd., St. Louis, MO 63132 (800-325-2222, fax 314-569-2503). Specializes in trans-continental flights (mostly from Europe). Most domes-

tic flights are coast-to-coast. Rates vary seasonally; call to find out if the route you want is available. During the summer of 1994, a round-trip flight from L.A. to New York was $370. All payments will be held in a bank escrow until the completion of your trip.

Travac, 989 Sixth Ave., New York, NY 10016 (800-872-8800; fax 212-563-3631). In 1994, Travac ran flights between New York and LA and New York and San Francisco for $403 round-trip. Prices and destinations vary with changing contracts, as do the max. lengths of stay.

Also try **DER Tours,** 9501 West Devon Ave. Ste. 400, Rosemont, IL 60018 (800-782-2424, fax 800-282-7474), and **Travel Charter International,** 1301 W. Long Lake, Ste. 270, Troy, MI 48098 (800-521-5267, fax 800-FAX-3888), both of which offer charter flights to and from a more limited range of cities.

Ticket Consolidators

Ticket consolidators are companies which sell unbooked commercial and charter airline seats; they're both less expensive and more risky than those on charter flights. Companies work on a space-available basis that does not guarantee a seat; you get priority over those flying stand-by but below those who are regularly booked. Although consolidators that originate flights in Europe, Australia, or Asia are scarce, the market for flights within North America is a good one and is growing. Consolidators tend to be reliable on these domestic flights, both in getting you on the flight and in getting you exactly where you want to go. Flexibility is often necessary, but all companies guarantee that they will put you on a flight or refund your money. On the day of the flight, the earlier you arrive at the airport the better, since ticket agents seat passengers in the order of check-in. **Now Voyager,** 74 Varick St. #307, New York, NY 10013 (212-431-1616), books flights as a consolidator, as well as placing people on flights as air couriers. **L.A.** to New York runs $299 round-trip; and flights from **Chicago** are $176 round-trip. Flights run exclusively out of and into NYC. (Phones open Mon.-Fri. 10am-5:30pm, Sat. noon-4:30pm.)

FLIGHTS FROM ABROAD

Many major U.S. airlines offer special **"Visit USA" air passes** and fares to international travelers. You must purchase these passes outside the U.S., paying one price for a certain number of "flight coupons." Each coupon is good for one flight segment on an airline's domestic system within a certain time period; typically, all travel must be completed within 30 to 60 days. Some cross-country trips may require two segments. The point of departure and the destination must be specified for each coupon at the time of purchase, and once in the States, any change in route will incur a fee of between $50 and $75. Dates of travel may be changed once travel has begun at no extra charge. **USAir** offers vouchers good for travel on the east coast for $589-649, or in all 48 states for $649-679. **United, Continental, Delta,** and **TWA** also offer programs. Remember that there is **no smoking** on any flight under six hours within the U.S.

From Europe

Travelers from Europe will experience the least competition for inexpensive seats during the off-season; "off-season" need not mean the dead of winter. Peak season rates generally take effect on either May 15 or June 1 and run until about September 15. You can take advantage of cheap off-season flights within Europe to reach an advantageous point of departure for North America. London is a major connecting point for budget flights to the U.S.; New York City is often the destination. Discount travel agencies offer reasonable rates even during the peak season. In the summer of 1994, CIEE carried round-trip tickets from London for $458 (and as low as $400 off-season).

If you decide to fly with a commercial airline rather than through a charter agency or ticket consolidator, you'll be purchasing greater reliability, security, and flexibility. Many major airlines offer reduced-fare options, such as three-day advance-purchase fares: these tickets can be purchased only within 72 hrs. of the time of the departure, and are restricted to youths under a certain age (often 24). Check with a travel agent for availability. **TWA** and **British Airways** both offer these fares on a variety of international flights. Seat availability is known only a few days before the flight, although airlines will sometimes issue predictions. The worst crunch leaving Europe takes place from mid-June to early July, while August is uniformly tight for returning flights; at no time can you count on getting a seat right away. Call airlines for specific flight restrictions.

Smaller, budget airlines often undercut major carriers by offering bargain fares on scheduled flights. Competition for seats on these smaller carriers during peak season is fierce—book early. Discount transatlantic airlines include **Virgin Atlantic Airways** (800-862-8621) and **Icelandair** (800-223-5500). Virgin Atlantic's fares from London to NYC range between $500-650, depending on the season. Tickets require a 21-day advance purchase with mid-week travel and a Saturday stop-over. Icelandair flies from New York into and out of Luxembourg, with fares ranging from $400 to $700.

From Australia and New Zealand

A good place to start searching for tickets is the local branch of one of the budget-travel agencies listed above. STA Travel is the largest international agency, with offices in Sydney, Melbourne, and Auckland. (See Students and Young Adults.) **Qantas, Air New Zealand, United,** and **Northwest** fly between Australia or New Zealand and the United States. Prices are roughly equivalent among the four (American carriers tend to be a bit less), but the cities they serve differ. Advance purchase fares from Australia have extremely tough restrictions. If you are uncertain about your plans, pay extra for an advance purchase ticket that has only a 50% penalty for cancellation. Many travelers from Australia and New Zealand reportedly take Singapore Air or other Far East-based carriers during the initial leg of their trips; check with STA or another budget agency for more comprehensive information.

TO AND FROM THE AIRPORTS

Travel between each of the airports and New York City without a car of your own becomes simpler as cost increases; you pay in time or money. Though **public transportation** is generally the cheapest option, this mode can be time-consuming and usually involves changing mid-route from a bus to a subway or train (especially tricky if you're loaded with baggage.) **Private bus companies** will charge slightly more, but will take you directly from the airport to any one of many Manhattan destinations: Grand Central Station (42nd St. and Park Ave.), the Port Authority Bus Terminal (41st St. and Eighth Ave.) or the World Trade Center (1 West St.), along with several prominent hotels. Private companies run frequently and according to a set schedule (see below). Some services peter out or vanish entirely between midnight and 6am. If you want to set your own destination and schedule, and if you're willing to pay, you can take one of New York's infamous **yellow cabs.** Heavy traffic makes the trip more expensive: traveling during rush hour (7:30-10am and 4-7:30pm) can devastate a wallet. You are responsible for paying **bridge and tunnel tolls.** For the most up-to-date guide to reaching the airports, call **AirRide,** the Port Authority's airport travel hotline, at 800-247-7433; it is an automated interactive system offering very detailed information on how to reach any of the three airports by car, public transportation, or private bus line. Also try the **MTA/New York City transit center** at 718-330-1234 for similar information. Finally, if you make lodging reservations ahead of time, be sure to ask about limousine services—some hostels offer transportation from the airports for reasonable fares.

From JFK Airport

The cheapest route into the city is on the **subway.** Catch a free brown and white JFK long-term parking lot bus from any airport terminal (every 10-15 min.) to the

Howard Beach-JFK Airport subway station. Non-white travelers should be warned that the Howard Beach area can be hostile. You can take the A train from there to the city (1 hr.); the A stops several times in lower Manhattan, as well as at Washington Sq., 34th St.-Penn Station, 42nd St.-Port Authority, and 59th St.-Columbus Circle ($1.25). Heading from Manhattan to JFK, take the Far Rockaway A train. Or you can take one of the local buses (Q10 or Q3; fare $1.25, exact change required) from the airport into Queens. The Q10 bus heads to Lefferts Blvd. where it connects with the A train, and to Kew Gardens where it connects with the E and F trains. You can then take the subway into Manhattan ($1.25). The Q3 connects JFK with the F train at 179th St.-Jamaica. Ask the driver where to get off, and be sure you know which subway line you want. Although these routes are safer during the day, nighttime travelers should check with the information desk to find the safest way into the city.

Those willing to pay more can take the **Carey Airport Express** (718-632-0500 or -0509), a private line that runs between JFK (also LaGuardia, see below) and Grand Central Station and the Port Authority Terminal. Buses leave every 30 minutes from JFK to Manhattan from 5am to 1am daily (45-75 min., $13). If you want to save a few dollars, Carey will take you to Jamaica station in Queens ($5), from where you can catch the E, J, or Z subway trains into the city ($1.25). If you are heading to JFK from Manhattan, get on the Carey bus at one of six locations, including 125 Park Ave. at Grand Central Station (every 30 min., 6am-midnight, 1 hr.) or at the Port Authority Terminal (1½ hr.). **Students** get half-price tickets, which can be purchased only at the company office in Manhattan at 125 Park Ave. at Grand Central Station; buy two in Manhattan if you plan to take the express back into the city. The **Gray Line Air Shuttle** (757-6840) will drop you off (not pick you up) at any hotel in Manhattan between 23rd and 63rd St. ($16). Inquire at a Ground Transportation Center in JFK. A **taxi** from JFK to mid-Manhattan costs about $35.

From LaGuardia Airport

The journey to LaGuardia takes about two-thirds as long as the trek out to JFK. If you have extra time and light luggage, take the MTA Q33 **bus** ($1.25) to the 74th St.-Broadway-Roosevelt Ave.-Jackson Hts. subway stop in Queens. From there, take the #7, E, F, G, or R train into Manhattan ($1.25). You can catch the Q33 bus from the lower level of the terminal. Allow at least 1½ hours travel time. Be especially careful traveling these routes at night. The **Carey Airport Express** also runs to and from LaGuardia every 30 minutes, stopping in Manhattan at a number of locations in Manhattan, including Grand Central Station and Port Authority (30-60 min., $9). If you can't afford a cab but you still crave door to door service, the **Gray Line Air Shuttle** (757-6840) will take you to any hotel between 23rd and 63rd for $13 (6am-7pm). Be prepared for a long ride: the bus runs the circuit of large midtown hotels before stopping at smaller hotels. A **taxi** to Manhattan costs around $25, a sum not all that unreasonable if split between two or more people; at LaGuardia, it is relatively easy to find someone to share a cab.

From Newark Airport

The trip from Newark Airport, in New Jersey, takes about as long as from JFK. **New Jersey Transit Authority (NJTA)** (201-762-5100 or 212-629-8767) runs a fast, efficient **bus** (NJTA #300) between the airport and Port Authority every 15 minutes during the day, less frequently at night (24 hrs., $7). For the same fare, the **Olympia Trails Coach** (212-964-6233) travels between the airport and Grand Central, Penn Station, or the World Trade Center (daily 5am-11pm, every 20-30 min.; 25-45 min.; $7; tickets may be purchased on the bus). **NJTA Bus #107** will take you to midtown for $3.25 (exact change required), but don't try it unless you have little luggage and lots of time. The NJTA also runs an **Air Link bus** ($4) between the airport and Newark's Penn Station (*not* Manhattan's); and from there **PATH** trains ($1) run into Manhattan, stopping at the World Trade Center, Christopher St., Sixth Ave., 9th St., 14th St., 23rd St. and 33rd St. For PATH information call 1-800-234-7284. A taxi should run you about $45, but be sure to negotiate the price with the driver before departing.

■■■ BY BUS

Getting in and out of New York can be less expensive and more scenic by bus or train than by plane. **Greyhound** (800-231-2222) operates the largest number of lines, departing to New York from Boston (4½ hrs.; $26 one-way, $50 round-trip), Philadelphia (2 hrs.; Mon.-Thurs. $12 one-way, $23 round-trip), Washington, D.C. (4½ hrs.; $26 one-way, $50 round-trip), and Montreal (8 hrs.; $70 one-way, $120 round-trip). The fares listed here require no advance purchase; significant discounts off these fares can be had by purchasing tickets 3, 7, or 14 days in advance. Some buses to these cities take longer (up to 2 hrs. more) due to additional stops or time of travel.

A number of **discounts** are available on Greyhound's standard-fare tickets: senior citizens ride for 15% off, children under 11 ride for 50% off, and children under 2 ride for free in the lap of an adult. A traveler with a physical disability may bring along a companion for free, and active and retired U.S. military personnel and National Guard Reserves (and their spouses and dependents) may take a round trip between any two points in the U.S. for $169.

Greyhound allows passengers to carry two pieces of luggage (up to 45 lbs. total) and to check two pieces of luggage (up to 100 lbs.). Whatever you stow in compartments underneath the bus should be clearly marked; be sure to get a claim check for it, and watch to make sure your luggage is on the same bus as you. As always, keep your essential documents and valuables on you. Take a jacket, too; surprisingly efficient air-conditioning brings the temperature down to arctic levels.

If you plan to tour a great deal by bus within the U.S., you may save money with the **Ameripass,** which entitles you to unlimited travel for 7 days ($250), 15 days ($350), or 30 days ($450); extensions for the 7- and 15-day passes cost $15 per day. The pass takes effect the first day used, so make sure you have a pretty good idea of your itinerary before you start. Before purchasing an Ameripass, total up the separate bus fares between towns to make sure that the pass is indeed more economical, or at least worth the unlimited flexibility it provides. Greyhound offers an **International Ameripass** for visitors from outside North America. A 7-day pass sells for $175, a 15-day pass for $250, and a 30-day pass for $325.

Always check bus schedules and routes personally, and don't rely on old printed schedules since listings change seasonally. Greyhound schedule information can be obtained from any Greyhound terminal, or from the reservation center at 800-231-2222. Greyhound is implementing a reservation system much like that of the airlines, which will allow you to call and reserve a seat or purchase a ticket by mail. If you call seven or more days in advance and want to purchase your ticket with a credit card, reservations can be made and the ticket mailed to you. Otherwise, you may make reservations up to 24 hours in advance.

If you are boarding at a remote "flag stop," be sure you know exactly where the bus stops. Call the nearest agency and let them know you'll be waiting at the flag stop for the bus at a certain time. Catch the driver's attention by standing on the side of the road and flailing your arms wildly—better to be embarrassed than stranded.

The hub of the Northeast bus network, New York's **Port Authority Terminal,** 41st St. and Eighth Ave. (435-7000; Subway: A, C, or E to 42nd St.-Port Authority), is a tremendous modern facility with labyrinthine bus terminals. The Port Authority has good information and security services, but the surrounding neighborhood is somewhat deserted at night, when it pays to be wary of pickpockets and to call a cab. Avoid the terminal's bathrooms at all times.

New this year is **East Coast Explorer,** a bus service connecting the cities of Boston, New York, and Washington, D.C. For $3-7 more than Greyhound, travel all day with 13 other people on back roads, stopping at sites of historic interest—a good bargain for those trying to tour the East Coast for cheap. Trips from Washington to

New York leave Friday mornings, stopping at Newcastle, DE, and Philadelphia. Trips from New York to Washington leave Thursday mornings and visit the Amish countryside of Lancaster, Pennsylvania. From Boston, the bus departs for New York on Tuesday mornings and passes through Massachusetts and Dinosaur State Park. Trips head back to Boston from New York on Monday mornings, with stops at the seaside towns of Mystic, Connecticut and Newport, Rhode Island. The air-conditioned bus makes pick-ups and drop-offs at most hostels and budget hotels; call between one month and one day in advance for reservations (718-694-9667 or 800-610-2680, between 8 and 11pm). Trips between New York and Washington cost $32; $29 between New York and Boston. Costs for all trips include tolls and tour guide (Larry Lustig, the company's founder and operator). Limit two bags per passenger.

■■■ BY TRAIN

The train is still one of the cheapest and most comfortable ways to travel in the U.S. You can stretch your legs, buy overpriced victuals, and shut out the sun to sleep in a reclining chair (avoid paying unnecessarily for a roomette or bedroom). Travel light; not all stations will check baggage and not all trains carry large amounts.

Amtrak, 60 Massachusetts Ave. NE, Washington, D.C. 20002 (800-872-7245), offers a discount **All-Aboard America** fare that divides the continental U.S. into three regions—Eastern, Central, and Western. Amtrak charges the same rate for both one-way and round-trip travel, with three stopovers permitted and a maximum trip duration of 45 days. During the summer, rates are $198 if you travel in one region, $278 to travel in two regions, and $338 for all three (from late Aug. to mid-Dec. and early Jan. to mid-June, rates are $178, $238, and $278). (See below for regular fare information.) Your itinerary, including cities and dates, must be set at the time the passes are purchased; the route may not be changed once travel has begun, although times and dates may be changed at no cost. All-Aboard fares are subject to availability; reserve two to three months in advance for summer travel.

Another discount option, available only to those who aren't citizens of North America, is the **USA Rail Pass,** which allows unlimited travel and unlimited stops over a period of either 15 or 30 days. As with the All-Aboard America program, the cost of the pass depends on the number of regions in which you wish to travel. The pass allowing 30 days of travel nationwide sells for $399 during the peak season and for $319 off-season; the 15-day nationwide pass sells for $318 during the peak season and for $218 off-season. Another discount option on Amtrak is the **Air-Rail Travel Plan,** offered in conjunction with United Airlines, which allows you to travel in one direction by train and then fly home, or vice-versa. The transcontinental plan, which allows coast-to-coast travel originating in either coast, sells for $550 peak-season and $463 off-season. The East Coast plan, which allows travel roughly as far west as Atlanta, is $381 during peak season, $337 off-peak.

Full fares on Amtrak vary according to time, date, and destination. Amtrak seldom places advance-purchase requirements on its fares, although the number of seats sold at discount prices is always limited. These discount tickets are naturally the first to sell, so it's best to plan in advance and reserve early. It's best to call and reserve as soon as your travel dates are set—if you reserve well ahead of your date of departure, Amtrak will often give you a grace period of several weeks or months before requiring you to actually pay for your tickets (e.g., reserve in August for a trip the following June and you'll often be given till November to pay). Amtrak accepts reservations up to 11 months in advance. One-way fares don't vary with the season, but round-trip tickets can be significantly cheaper between late August and late May, with the exception of Christmastime. The *Maple Leaf* connects Toronto with New York for $98 one-way and as little as $86 round-trip; the *Crescent* connects New Orleans with New York for $160 one-way and between $168 and $320 round-trip. From Washington, tickets to New York cost $68 one-way and $92 round-trip.

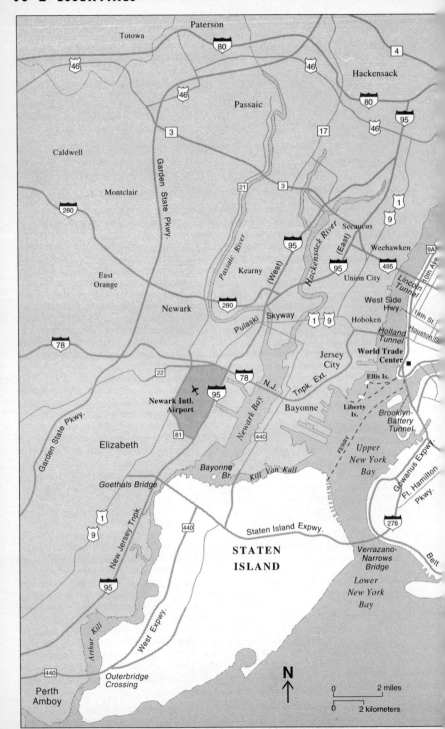

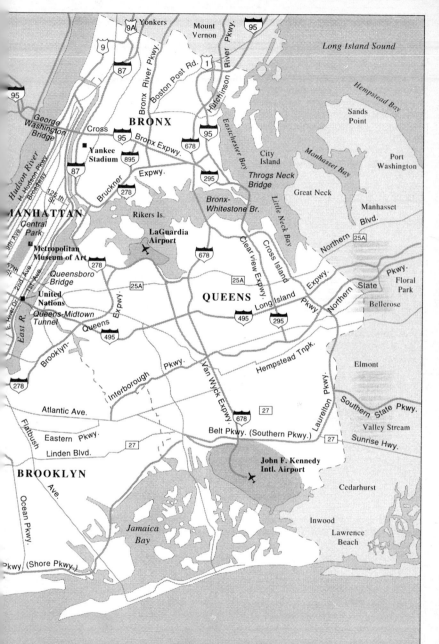

Greater New York

Tickets from Chicago to New York are $128 one-way and between $128 and $256 round-trip.

Amtrak offers several **discounts** off its full fares for certain travelers: children ages two to 15 accompanied by a parent (½-fare); children under age two (free on the lap of an adult); senior citizens (15% off Mon.-Thurs.); travelers with disabilities (25% off); and current members of the U.S. Armed Forces and active-duty veterans (25% off), as well as their dependents (12½% off). Circle trips and special holiday packages can save you money as well. Keep in mind that discounted air travel, particularly for longer distances, may be cheaper than train travel. For up-to-date information and reservations, contact your local Amtrak office or call **800-USA-RAIL** from a touch-tone phone.

TRAIN STATIONS

Grand Central Station, 42nd St. and Park Ave. (subway: #4, 5, 6, 7 or S to 42nd St.-Grand Central), handles more than 550 trains a day. It handles the three **Metro-North** (800-METRO-INFO or 532-4900) commuter lines to Connecticut and the New York suburbs (the Hudson, Harlem, and New Haven lines). Longer train routes run out of the smaller **Penn Station,** 33rd St. and Eighth Ave. (subway: #1, 2, 3, 9, or A, C, E to 34th St.-Penn Station); the major line is **Amtrak** (800-872-7245 or 212-582-6875), which serves upstate New York and most major cities in the U.S. and Canada, especially those in the Northeast (to Washington, D.C., 3¾ hrs., $68 one-way, $92 round-trip; Boston 4-5 hrs., $52 one-way, $72-86 round-trip depending on time of travel). Penn Station also handles the **Long Island Railroad (LIRR)** (718-822-5477; fares range from $3-14 and service is fairly extensive, extending to the eastern tip of the island; see Long Island) and **PATH** service to New Jersey (recorded info. 800-234-7284; travel assistance 435-7000, Mon.-Fri 8am-5pm; all trains always $1).

■■■ BY CAR

The **speed limit** in New York State, as in most other states, is 55 miles per hour; a number of states, or sections of states, have limits of 65 miles per hour. Driving into New York there are several major approaches. From New Jersey there are three choices. The **Holland Tunnel** connects to lower Manhattan, exiting into the SoHo area. From the NJ Turnpike you'll probably end up at the **Lincoln Tunnel,** which exits in midtown in the West 40s. The third option is the **George Washington Bridge,** which crosses the Hudson River into northern Manhattan, giving fairly easy access to either Harlem River Drive or the West Side Highway. Coming from New England or Connecticut on I-95, follow signs for the **Triboro Bridge.** From there get onto the FDR Drive, which runs along the east side of Manhattan and exits onto city streets every 10 blocks or so. Or look for the Willis Avenue Bridge exit on I-95 to avoid the toll, and enter Manhattan farther north on FDR Drive.

For information on renting a car, see Getting Around below.

HITCHHIKING

Hitchhiking is illegal in New York State and the laws tend to be strictly enforced within New York City. Offenders will usually be asked to move on. It's best to take the train or bus out of the metropolitan area; hitching in and around New York City is dangerous. If someone you don't know offers you a free ride, don't take it. *Let's Go* cannot recommend hitchhiking as a safe means of transport. *Do not hitchhike.*

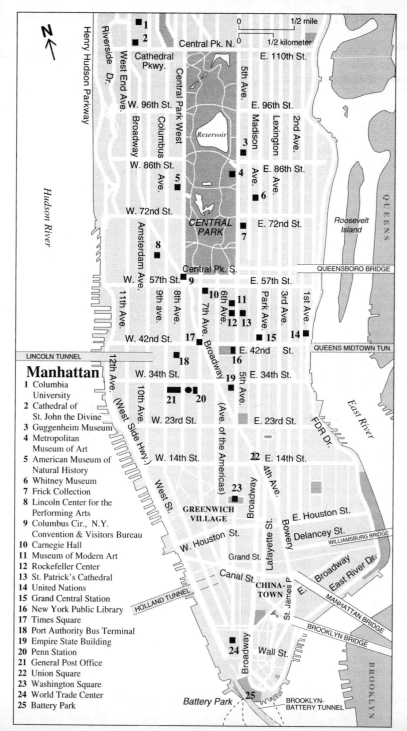

0   1/2 mile

0   1/2 kilometer

Manhattan

1 Columbia
  University
2 Cathedral of
  St. John the Divine
3 Guggenheim Museum
4 Metropolitan
  Museum of Art
5 American Museum of
  Natural History
6 Whitney Museum
7 Frick Collection
8 Lincoln Center for the
  Performing Arts
9 Columbus Cir., N.Y.
  Convention & Visitors Bureau
10 Carnegie Hall
11 Museum of Modern Art
12 Rockefeller Center
13 St. Patrick's Cathedral
14 United Nations
15 Grand Central Station
16 New York Public Library
17 Times Square
18 Port Authority Bus Terminal
19 Empire State Building
20 Penn Station
21 General Post Office
22 Union Square
23 Washington Square
24 World Trade Center
25 Battery Park

ORIENTATION

GETTING AROUND

*I have two faults to find with New York. In the first place, there is nothing
to see; and in the second place, there is no mode of getting about to see
anything.*

—Anthony Trollope, North America, 1862

To be equipped for the New York City navigation experience, you will need more
than an understanding of the logic underlying its streets. You will need to know
how to use the **public transportation system.** Get a free subway or bus map from
station token booths or the visitors bureau, which also has a free street map (see
Tourist Information below). For a more detailed program of travel, find a Manhattan
Yellow Pages, which has detailed subway, PATH, and bus maps. Since bus routes
vary for each of the boroughs, you may want to get other bus maps; send a self-
addressed, stamped envelope to **NYC Transit Authority,** 370 Jay St., Brooklyn, NY
11201. Then wait about a month. The **Transit Authority Information Bureau**
(718-330-1234) dispenses subway and bus info.

■■■ ORIENTATION

New York City is composed of five boroughs: Brooklyn, the Bronx, Queens, Staten
Island, and Manhattan. Nevertheless, plenty of tourists and Manhattanites have been
known to confuse Manhattan with New York. This Manhattancentric perspective
has deep historical roots. The island's original inhabitants, the Algonquin, called it
"Man-a-hat-ta" or "Heavenly Land." The British were the first to call the island "New
York," after James, Duke of York, the brother of Charles II. It was only in 1898 that
the other four boroughs joined the city's government. No matter how often you
hear Manhattan referred to as "The City," each of the other boroughs has a right to
share the name. Flanked on the east by the East River (actually a strait) and on the
west by the Hudson River, Manhattan is a sliver of an island. It measures only 13
miles long and 2½ miles wide. Fatter Queens and Brooklyn look onto their svelte
neighbor from the other side of the East River, and pudgy, self-reliant Staten Island
averts its eyes in the south. **Queens,** the city's largest and most ethnically diverse
borough, is dotted with light industry, airports, and stadiums. **Brooklyn,** the city's
most populous borough (with 2.24 million residents), is even older than Manhattan.
Founded by the Dutch in 1600, the borough today cradles several charming residential neighborhoods along with pockets of dangerous slums. **Staten Island** has
remained a staunchly residential borough, similar to the suburban bedroom communities of eastern Long Island. North of Manhattan sits the **Bronx,** the only borough
connected by land to the rest of the U.S. Supposedly, the whole borough was once
a Dutch estate owned by Jonas Bronck; an excursion to his family's farm was
referred to as a visit to "the Broncks'." Today's Bronx encompasses both the genteel
suburb of Riverdale and New York's most devastated area, the South Bronx.

DISTRICTS OF MANHATTAN

Glimpsed from the window of an approaching plane, New York City can seem a
monolithic jungle of urbania. But up close, New York breaks down into manageable
neighborhoods, each with a history and personality of its own. As a result of city
zoning ordinances, quirks of history, and random forces of urban evolution, bound-
aries between these neighborhoods can often be abrupt.

The city began at the southern tip of Manhattan, in the area around **Battery Park**
where the first Dutch settlers made their homes. The nearby harbor, now jazzed up
with the **South Street Seaport** tourist magnet, provided the growing city with the
commercial opportunities that helped it succeed. Historic Manhattan, however, lies
in the shadows of the imposing financial buildings around **Wall Street** and the
civic offices around **City Hall.** A bit farther north, neighborhoods rich in the ethnic

culture brought by late 19th-century immigrants rub elbows below Houston Street—**Little Italy, Chinatown,** and the southern blocks of the **Lower East Side.** Formerly home to Russian Jews, Delancey and Elizabeth Streets now offer pasta and silks. To the west lies the fashionable **TriBeCa** ("Triangle Below Canal St."). **SoHo** (for "South of Houston"), a former warehouse district west of Little Italy, has transformed into a pocket of gleaming art studios and galleries. Above SoHo huddles **Greenwich Village,** whose lower buildings, jumbled streets, and neon glitz have for decades been home to intense political and artistic activity. To its east the **East Village** and **Alphabet City** are bohemian and anarcho-punk hangouts, with fun streets and an active nightlife.

A few blocks north of Greenwich Village, stretching across the west teens and twenties, lies **Chelsea,** the late artist Andy Warhol's favorite hangout and former home of Dylan Thomas and Arthur Miller. East of Chelsea, presiding over the East River, is **Gramercy Park,** a pastoral collection of elegant brownstones. **Midtown Manhattan** towers from 34th to 59th St., where traditional and controversial new skyscrapers stand side by side, supporting over a million elevated offices. Here department stores outfit New York while the nearby **Theater District** attempts to entertain the world, or at least people who like musicals.

North of Midtown, **Central Park** slices Manhattan into East and West. On the **Upper West Side,** the gracious museums and residences of Central Park West neighbor the chic boutiques and sidewalk cafés of Columbus Ave. On the **Upper East Side,** the galleries and museums scattered among the elegant apartments of Fifth and Park Ave. create an even more rarefied atmosphere.

Above 97th St., the Upper East Side's opulence ends with a whimper where commuter trains emerge from the tunnel and the *barrio* begins. Above 110th St. on the Upper West Side sits majestic **Columbia University** (founded as King's College in 1754), an urban member of the Ivy League. The communities of **Harlem, East Harlem,** and **Morningside Heights** produced the Harlem Renaissance of black artists and writers in the 1920s and the revolutionary Black Power movement of the 1960s. Although torn by crime, **Washington Heights,** just north of St. Nicholas Park, is

nevertheless somewhat safer and more attractive than much of Harlem and is home to Fort Tryon Park, the Met's Medieval Cloisters museum, and a quiet community of Old World immigrants. Manhattan ends in a rural patch of wooded land with caves inhabited at various times by the Algonquin and homeless New Yorkers.

MANHATTAN'S STREET PLAN

The city of right angles and tough, damaged people.

—Pete Hamill

Most of Manhattan's street plan was the result of an organized expansion scheme adopted in 1811, and the major part of the city grew in straight lines and at right angles. Above 14th St., the streets form a grid that a novice can quickly master. In the older areas of lower Manhattan, though, the streets are named rather than numbered. Here, the orderly grid of the northern section dissolves into a charming but confusing tangle of old, narrow streets. Bring a map; even long-time neighborhood residents may have trouble directing you to an address.

Above Washington Square, avenues run north-south and streets run east-west. Avenue numbers increase from east to west, and street numbers increase from south to north. Traffic flows east on most even-numbered streets and west on most odd-numbered ones. Two-way traffic flows on the wider streets—Canal, Houston, 14th, 23rd, 34th, 42nd, 57th, 72nd, 79th, 86th, 96th, 110th, 116th, 125th, 145th, and 155th. Four transverses cross Central Park: 65/66th St., 79th/81st St., 85/86th and 96/97th St. Most avenues are one-way. Tenth, Amsterdam, Hudson, Eighth, Avenue of the Americas (Sixth), Madison, Fourth, Third, and First Ave. are northbound. Ninth, Columbus, Broadway below 59th Street, Seventh, Fifth, Lexington, and Second Avenues are southbound. Some avenues allow two-way traffic: York, Park, Central Park West, Broadway above 59th St., Third below 24th St., West End, and Riverside Dr.

New York's east/west division refers to an address's location in relation to the two borders of Central Park—**Fifth Avenue** along the east side and **Central Park West** along the west. Below 59th St. (where the park ends) the West Side begins at Fifth Ave. Looking for adjectives to describe where you are relative to something else? Uptown is anywhere north of you, downtown is south, and crosstown means to the east or the west. Want to use nouns? Uptown (above 59th St.) is the area north of Midtown. Downtown (below 34th St.) is the area south of Midtown.

Now for the discrepancies in the system. You may still hear **Avenue of the Americas** referred to by its original name, **Sixth Avenue.** Lexington, Park, and Madison Ave. lie *between* Third and Fifth Ave., where there is no Fourth Ave. On the Lower East Side, there are several avenues east of First Avenue that are lettered rather than numbered: Avenues A, B, C, and D. Finally, above 59th St. on the West Side, Eighth Avenue becomes Central Park West, Ninth Avenue becomes Columbus Avenue, Tenth Avenue becomes Amsterdam Avenue, and Eleventh Avenue becomes West End Avenue. **Broadway,** which follows an old Algonquin trail, cavalierly defies the rectangular pattern and cuts diagonally across the island, veering west of Fifth Ave. above 23rd St. and east of Fifth Ave. below 23rd St.

Tracking down an address in Manhattan is easy. When given the street number of an address (e.g. #250 E. 52nd St.), find the avenue closest to the address by thinking of Fifth Ave. as point zero on the given street. Address numbers increase as you move east or west of Fifth Ave., in stages of 100. On the East Side, address numbers are 1 at Fifth Ave., 100 at Park Ave., 200 at Third Ave., 300 at Second Ave., 400 at First Ave., 500 at York Ave. (uptown) or Avenue A (in the Village). On the West Side, address numbers are 1 at Fifth Ave., 100 at Avenue of the Americas (Sixth Ave.), 200 at Seventh Ave., 300 at Eighth Ave., 400 at Ninth Ave., 500 at Tenth Ave., and 600 at Eleventh Ave. In general, numbers increase from south to north along the avenues, but you should always ask for a cross street when you are getting an avenue address. Or you can figure it out for yourself using the following complex but fun formula. Take the address number, cancel its last digit, divide by two, and follow these avenue-specific directions:

First Avenue: Add 3.
Second Avenue: Add 3.
Third Avenue: Add 10.

Fourth Avenue: Add 8.

Fifth Avenue: Up to 108, add 11; 108-200, add 13; 200-400, add 16; 400-600, add 18; 600-775, add 20; 775-1286, eliminate the last digit, do not divide by two, subtract 18; 1286-1500, add 45; above 2000, add 24.

Sixth Avenue: Subtract 12.

Seventh Avenue: Up to 1800, add 12; above 1800, add 20.

Eighth Avenue: Add 9.

Ninth Avenue: Add 13.

Tenth Avenue: Add 14.

Amsterdam Avenue: Add 59.

Broadway: Subtract 30.

Central Park West: Divide number by 10 and add 60.

Columbus Avenue: Add 60.

Lexington Avenue: Add 22.

Madison Avenue: Add 26.

Park Avenue: Add 35.

West End Avenue: Add 60.

Riverside Drive: Divide number by 10 and add 72.

■■■ SUBWAYS

Operated by the New York City Transit Authority (718-330-1234, daily 6am-9pm), the 230-mile New York subway system operates 24 hrs. a day, 365 days a year. It moves 3.5 million people daily, and has 469 stations with 25 free transfer points. The fare for Metropolitan Transit Authority (MTA) subways is a hefty $1.25 (and there are never discounts for bulk purchases), so groups of four may find a cab ride to be cheaper and more expedient for short distances. Long distances are best traveled by subway, since once inside a passenger may transfer onto any of the other trains without restrictions.

Although by far the quickest means of transportation in Manhattan, the subways are much more useful for traveling north-south than east-west, as there are only two crosstown shuttle trains (42nd and 14th St.). In upper Manhattan and in Queens, Brooklyn, and the Bronx, some lines become "El" trains (for "elevated") and ride above street level to the city's nether regions.

"Express" trains run at all hours and stop only at certain major stations; "locals" stop everywhere. Be sure to check the letter or number and the destination of each train, since trains with different destinations often use the same track. When in doubt, ask a friendly passenger or the conductor, who usually sits near the middle of the train. Once you're on the train, pay attention to the often garbled announcements—trains occasionally change mid-route from local to express or vice-versa, especially when entering or leaving Manhattan.

Efforts at aesthetic sterility in the trains have by no means erased the perils of subway crime. In crowded stations (most notably those around 42nd St.), pickpockets find work; violent crimes, although infrequent, tend to occur in stations that are deserted. Always watch yourself and your belongings, and try to stay in lit areas near a transit cop or token clerk. Some stations have clearly marked "off-hours" waiting areas that are under observation and significantly safer. Don't stand too close to the platform edge (some people have been pushed, though others have fallen in of their own accord) and keep to well-lit areas when waiting for a train. When boarding the train, pick a car with a number of other passengers in it.

For safety reasons, try to avoid riding the subways between 11pm and 7am, especially above E. 96th St. and W. 120th St. and outside Manhattan. Try also to avoid rush-hour crowds, where you'll be fortunate to find air, let alone seating—on an average morning, more commuters take the E and the F than use the entire rapid-transit system of Chicago (which has the nation's second-largest system). If you must travel at rush hour (7:30-9:30am and 5-6:30pm on every train in every direction), the local train is usually less crowded than the express. Buy a bunch of tokens at once at the booth or, preferably, at the new and more efficient token-vending machines now at many stations; you'll not only avoid a long line, but you'll be able to use all the entrances to a station (some token booths close late at night). You'll see glass globes outside of most subway entrances. If the globe is green it means that the entrance is staffed 24 hours a day. A red globe indicates that the entrance is closed or restricted in some way; read the sign posted above the stairs.

The subway network integrates the **IRT, IND,** and **BMT** lines, now operated by the NYC Transit Authority. The names of these lines are still used, although they are no longer of functional significance. The IRT (#1-#9) and the IND (A, C, D, E, F, Z) are two groups of lines that run through Manhattan; the BMT (B, J, L, M, N, Q, R) runs mostly from lower Manhattan to Queens and Brooklyn. Certain routes also have common, unofficial names based on where they travel, such as the "7th Ave. Line" or the "Broadway Line" for the #1, 2, 3, or 9; the "8th Ave. Line" for the A and C; the "Lexington Line" for the #4, 5, or 6; and the "Flushing Line" for the #7.

■■■ BUSES

Because buses are often mired in traffic, they can take twice as long as subways, but they are almost always safer, cleaner, and quieter. They'll also get you closer to your destination, since they stop every two blocks or so and run crosstown (east-west), as well as uptown and downtown (north-south). For long-distance travel (over 40 north-south blocks) buses can be a nightmare (except at night and on weekends, when traffic is manageable), but for shorter and especially crosstown trips, buses are often as quick as and more convenient than trains. The MTA transfer system provides north-south travelers with a slip good for a free ride east-west, or vice-versa, but you must ask the driver for a transfer when you board and pay your fare. Make sure you ring when you want to get off. Bus stops are indicated by a yellow-painted curb, but you're better off looking for the blue sign post announcing the bus number or for a glass-walled shelter displaying a map of the bus's route and a schedule of arrival times. A flat fare of $1.25 is charged when you board; either exact change or a subway token is required (dollar bills are not accepted).

Queens is served in addition by five private bus lines: **Metropolitan Suburban Bus Authority** (516-766-6722; covers mainly Nassau Cty., Long Island), **Green Bus Lines** (718-995-4700; covers mainly Jamaica and central Queens), **Jamaica Buses, Inc.** (718-526-0800; covers mainly Jamaica and Rockaway in Queens), **Queens Surface Corp.** (718-445-3100), and **Triboro Coach Corp.** (718-335-1000; covers Forest Hills, Ridgewood, and Jackson Hts.), while the Bronx has two: **Liberty Lines Express** (718-652-8400) and **New York Bus Service** (718-994-5500). All of these companies charge $1.25 and accept MTA tokens, except MSBA, which charges $1.50. Most of these bus routes do not appear on MTA schedules.

■■■ TAXIS

With drivers cruising at warp speed along near-deserted avenues or dodging through bumper-to-bumper traffic, cab rides can give you ulcers. And even if your stomach survives the ride, your budget may not. Still, it's likely that you'll have to take a taxi once in a while, in the interest of convenience or safety. Rides are expensive: the meter starts at $1.50 and clicks 25¢ for each additional fifth of a mile; 25¢ is tacked on for every 75 seconds spent in slow or stopped traffic, a 50¢ surcharge is levied from 8pm to 6am, and passengers pay for all tolls. Don't forget to tip 15%; cabbies need and expect the dough. Before you leave the cab, ask for a receipt, which will have the taxi's identification number (which can be either its meter number or its medallion). This number is necessary to trace lost articles or to make a complaint to the **Taxi Commission** (221-TAXI; 221 W. 41st St., between Times Sq. and the Port Authority Bus Terminal; open Mon.-Fri. 9am-5pm). Since some drivers may illegally try to show the naive visitor the "scenic route," quickly glance at a street map before embarking so you'll have some clue if you're being taken to your

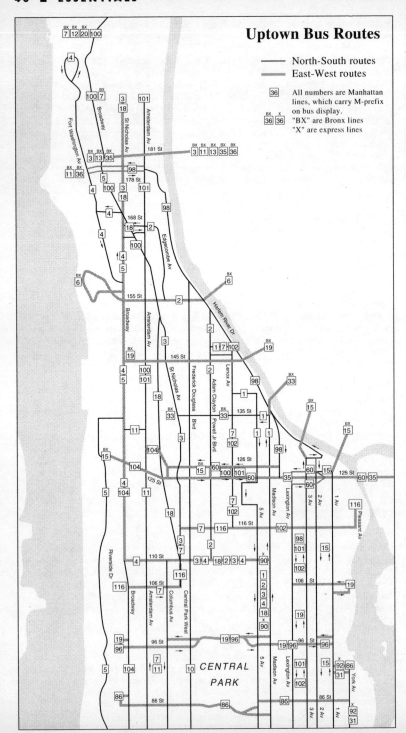

Uptown Bus Routes

— North-South routes

— East-West routes

36 All numbers are Manhattan lines, which carry M-prefix on bus display.

BX 36 X 36 "BX" are Bronx lines
"X" are express lines

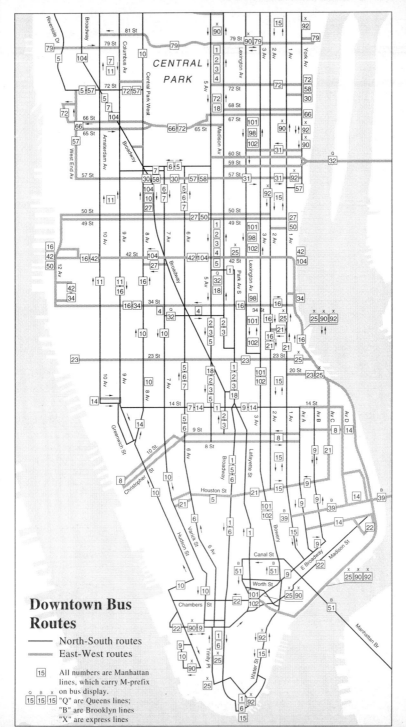

Downtown Bus Routes

—— North-South routes

░░░░ East-West routes

[15] All numbers are Manhattan lines, which carry M-prefix on bus display.

[15] [15] [15] "Q" are Queens lines; "B" are Brooklyn lines "X" are express lines

destination, or just being taken for a ride. Use only yellow cabs—they're licensed by the state of New York. Cabs of other colors are unlicensed and illegal in NYC. If you can't find anything on the street, commandeer a radio-dispatched cab (see the Yellow Pages under "Taxicabs"). Use common sense to make rides cheaper—catch a cab going your direction and get off at a nearby street corner. When shared with friends a cab can be cheaper, safer, and more convenient than the subway, especially late at night. But don't expect to be allowed to cram more than four people into the cab.

■■■ DRIVING

Driving in New York is not something to look forward to. Most New Yorkers only learn to drive in order to escape from the city, and some Manhattanites never learn to drive at all. When behind the wheel in New York, you are locked in combat with aggressive taxis, careless pedestrians, and crazed bicycle messengers. Stopped in traffic, you may have to fight off over-eager windshield washers who expect to be paid either to wash the windshield or not to wash the windshield.

Once in Manhattan, traffic continues to be a problem, especially between 57th and 34th St. The even greater hassle of parking joins in to plague the weary. Would-be parallel parkers can rise to this challenge in one of three ways. **Parking lots** are the easiest but the most expensive. In midtown, where lots are the only option, expect to pay at least $25 per day and up to $15 for two hours. The cheapest parking lots are downtown—try the far west end of Houston St.—but make sure you feel comfortable with the area and the lot. Is it populated? Is the lot guarded? Is it lit?

The second alternative is short-term parking. On the streets, **parking meters** cost 25¢ per 15 minutes, with a limit of one or two hours. Competition is ferocious for the third option, **free parking** at spots on the crosstown streets in residential areas. Read the signs carefully; a space is usually legal only on certain days of the week. The city has never been squeamish about towing, and recovering your car once it's towed will cost $100 or more. Break-ins and car theft are definite possibilities, particularly if you have a radio. The wailing of a car alarm, a noise as familiar to city residents as the crowing of a rooster is to rural Americans, attracts little if any attention.

CAR RENTAL

All agencies maintain varying minimum-age requirements and require proof of age as well as a security deposit. Agencies in Queens and Yonkers are often less expensive than their Manhattan counterparts, especially for one-day rentals. Most auto insurance policies will cover rented cars, and some credit cards like American Express and Chase VISA take care of your rental insurance costs if you've charged the vehicle to their card (but be sure to ask about all the particulars from the companies themselves; as always, "restrictions apply").

Nationwide, 220 E. 9th St. (867-1234), between Second and Third Ave. Reputable nationwide chain. Mid-sized domestic sedan $59 per day, $289 per week, unlimited mileage. Open Mon.-Fri. 8am-6pm. Must be 23 with a major credit card.

Payless, 189-08 Northern Blvd. (718-886-0058), near Utopia Pkwy. in Flushing, Queens. Take the #7 subway to Main St., Flushing, then the Q12 or Q13 bus (toward Bayside) to 189th St. Mon.-Thurs. $39 per day, Fri.-Sun. $50 per day; 100 free mi., 17¢ each additional mi. Weekly $240, 1000 free mi., 17¢ each additional mi. (All rates include insurance.) Open Mon.-Fri. 7am-7pm, Sat. 7am-noon. Must be 25 with a major credit card.

ABC Car Rental, 12 E. 13th St. (989-7260), between Fifth Ave. and University Pl. Current mid-sized sedans available: Mon.-Thurs. $50 per day, Fri.-Sun. $80 per day; 175 free mi. $299 per week with 1000 free mi. Open Mon.-Fri. 8am-6:30pm. Must be 23 with a major credit card.

AAMCAR Rent-a-Car, 323 W. 96th St. (222-8500), between West End Ave. and Riverside Dr. Japanese compacts $50 per day, 200 free mi., 25¢ each additional mi.; $289 per week with unlimited mileage. No one-day rentals Sat.-Sun. Open

Mon.-Fri. 8am-7:30pm, Sat.-Sun. 9am-5pm. Must be 25 with a major credit card, but will rent to cash customers with deposit.

All-Star Rent-A-Car Inc., 325 W. 34th St. (714-0556), between Eighth and Ninth Ave. Mid-sized Dodge sedan $5 per day Mon.-Thurs. with 150 free mi. and 20¢ per additional mi.; weekend rate Fri.-Mon. $179 with 600 free mi. and 20¢ per additional mi.; weekly rate $279 with 800 free mi. and 20¢ per additional mi. Open Mon.-Fri. 7:30am-6:30pm, Sat. 9am-3pm. Must be 25 with a major credit card.

Manhattan Ford, Eleventh Ave. and W. 57th St. (581-7800). Four-door Ford Escorts; Mon.-Thurs. $50 per day with unlimited mi.; weekend rental Fri.-Mon. $170 with unlimited mi.; weekly rental $250 with 1000 free mi. and 30¢ per additional mi. Open Mon.-Fri. 8am-6pm. Must be 21 with a major credit card.

■■■ BICYCLING

Weekday biking in commuter traffic poses a mortal challenge even for veterans. But on weekends, when the traffic thins, cyclists who use helmets and caution can tour the Big Apple on two wheels. From May-Oct., Central Park (except the lower loop) is closed to traffic on weekdays from 10am-3pm and 7-10pm, and from Fri. 7pm-Mon. 6am. Otherwise, Sunday mornings are best. For a challenging and aesthetic traffic-free course, try the 3.5-mile path in Central Park. If you must leave your bike unattended, use a strong "U" lock. Thieves laugh at (then cut through) weaker chain locks. Don't leave quick-release items unattended; you will find them very quickly released. For more information on cycling in and around Manhattan, see Sports.

BICYCLE RENTALS

Pedal Pushers, 1306 Second Ave. (288-5592), between 68th and 69th St. Rents 3-speeds for $4 per hr., $10 per day, $12 overnight; 10-speeds for $5 per hr., $14 per day, $19 overnight; mountain bikes for $6 per hr., $17 per day, $25 overnight. Overnight rentals $12 for 3-speeds, $25 for mountain bikes. Overnight rentals require a $150 deposit on a major credit card, but regular rentals just need ID or a drivers license. Open daily 10am-6pm.

Gene's, 242 E. 79th St. (249-9344), near Second Ave. This discount bike shop rents 3-speeds for $3 per hr., $10.50 per day; mountain bikes and rollerblades for $6 per hr., $21 per day. $20 deposit required for 3-speeds, $40 deposit required for mountain bikes, plus driver's license and credit card. Both available for overnight rentals ($8 plus cash deposit of $100 or $250). 2-hr. minimum. Open Mon.-Fri. 9:30am-8pm, Sat.-Sun. 9am-7pm.

■■■ WALKING, JOGGING, AND ROLLERBLADING

Walking is the cheapest, the most entertaining, and often the fastest way to get around town. During rush hours the sidewalks are packed with suited and sneakered commuters. In between rush hours, sidewalks are still full of street life. Twenty street blocks (north-south) make up a mile; one east-west block from one avenue to the next is about triple the distance of a north-south, street-to-street block. New York distances are short: a walk from the south end of Central Park to the World Trade Center, through all of midtown and downtown Manhattan, for example, should take under 1½ hours.

If you plan to jog along the street, be prepared to dodge pedestrians and to break your stride at intersections. Women may prompt catcalls. A better alternative to the sidewalk are paths along the rivers or in Central Park—most are pavement, but there is a 1.58 mile cinder loop that circles the Reservoir (between 84th and 96th St.). Joggers pack this path from 6-9am and 5-7pm on weekdays and all day on weekends. If you can, run between 9am and 5pm to avoid the night-time crime and rush-hour collisions on the narrow strip. For information on running clubs, call the **New**

Luciano Pavarotti. Photo by Allen Malschick.

Joan Baez. Photo by Melanie Nissen.

Ruth Fuglistaller. Photo by Ruby Levesque.

York Roadrunner's Club (860-4455). The Roadrunner's Club hosts races in Central Park on summer weekends and the New York City Marathon every fall.

For those who prefer speed without pounding the pavement, **Rollerblades** are available at **Peck and Goodie Skates,** 917 Eighth Ave. (246-6123), between 54th and 55th St. They'll hold your shoes while you whiz past your favorite New York sights (Sat.-Sun. $15 per 2 hrs., $25 per 24 hrs.; Mon.-Fri. $15 per day). Rates include all protective gear. $200 deposit or credit card required. As with any rental agreement, be sure to read the details carefully before you sign—you may face hefty repair fees when you come back for your shoes and deposit. Lessons for all levels of skill offered Sat.-Sun. at 11am in Central Park, $6 per hr. (open Mon.-Wed. and Sat.-Sun. 10am-6pm, Thurs.-Fri. 10am-8pm). **Wollman Skating Rink** (517-4800) in Central Park also rents skates and Rollerblades for $15 per 2 hrs., $25 per day. (Open Mon.-Thurs. 10am-9:30pm, Fri.-Sun. 10am-11:30pm.)

GETTING ACQUAINTED

The Americans are justly very proud of it, and its residents passionately attached to it . . . a young New Yorker, who had been in Europe for more than a year, was in the same sleigh with me. "There goes the old city!" said he in his enthusiasm, as we entered Broadway; "I could almost jump out and hug a lamp-post!"
—Alexander Mackay, The Western World, 1849

■■■ TOURIST INFORMATION

Visitor Information: New York Convention and Visitors Bureau, 2 Columbus Circle (397-8222 or 484-1200), 59th St. and Broadway. Subway: #1, 9 or A, B, C, D to 59th St.-Columbus Circle. Multilingual staff will help you with directions, hotel listings, entertainment ideas, safety tips, and "insiders'" descriptions of New York's neighborhoods. Try to show up in person; the phone lines tend to be busy, the maps and brochures worthwhile. Open Mon.-Fri. 9am-6pm, Sat.-Sun. and holidays 10am-3pm.

New York State Department of Economic Development, 1515 Broadway between 44th and 45th St. in Times Sq., on the 51st floor. Subway: #1, 2, 3, 7, 9 or N, R, S to 42nd St./Times Sq. Tourist Division (827-6250) open Mon.-Fri. 9am-5pm. Or call their toll-free *I Love New York* number (800-CALL-NYS or 800-225-5697) for information about sights and events.

Travelers' Aid Society: 1481 Seventh Ave. (944-0013), between 42nd and 43rd St.; and at JFK International Airport (718-656-4870), in the International Arrivals Building. JFK office provides general counseling and referral to travelers, as well as emergency assistance (open Mon.-Thurs. 10am-7pm, Fri. 10am-6pm, Sat. 11am-6pm, Sun. noon-6pm). Times Sq. branch specializes in crisis intervention services for stranded travelers or crime victims (open Mon.-Fri. 9am-6pm, but it's best to call first as they can sometimes close unexpectedly). In an emergency, call the **Victims Service Agency** at 577-7777, a 24-hr. assistance source. Subway: #1, 2, 3, 7, 9 or N, R, S to 42nd St.

■■■ SAFETY

Emergency: Dial 911.
Police: 212-374-5000. Use this for inquiries that are not urgent. 24 hrs.
TDD Police: 374-5911.
Fire: 628-2900 or 999-2222.

In a news conference following the 1993 bombing of the World Trade Center, Governor Mario Cuomo declared New York City to be "one of the safest cities in the country." Although statistics may prove this to be an overstatement (New York's street robbery and mugging statistics are the worst in the country), with some precautions you can emerge from your vacation in the city enriched, unscathed, and maybe even more confident.

ON FOOT

Acting like a native (read: rude) may be your best protection. Petty criminals often attack tourists because they seem naive and hapless. In a recent interview, a city cop told reporters, "They go for the gawkers"—which means that small-time crooks scam the unwary, the wide-eyed, and the slow-moving. The New Yorker walks briskly; the tourist wanders absently. Maintain at all times the fiction that you know where you are going. Be discreet with street maps and cameras and address questions about directions to police officers or store-owners. Consider covering your trusty *Let's Go* with plain brown paper. Stay out of public bathrooms; they tend to be filthy and unsafe. Instead, try department stores, hotels, or restaurants; even those with a sign on the door saying "restrooms for patrons only" will usually allow you to go if you look enough like you're a customer (see Bathrooms below).

If, despite your confident swagger, you suspect you're being followed, duck into a store or restaurant. Some East Side shops near school districts have yellow-and-black signs that say "safe haven" in their windows. The signs mean that shop managers have agreed to let people—especially students—who feel unsafe remain in their stores for long periods of time or call the police.

Rip-off artists seek the rich as well as the unwary, so hide your wealth. Conceal watches, necklaces, and bracelets under your clothing if you're in a dangerous neighborhood. Turn that huge diamond ring around on your finger so jewelry-swipers can only see the band. Grip your handbag tightly and wear the strap diagonally. If you keep the bag and the strap on one side, it can easily be pulled off—or a clever thief with scissors may cut the strap so adeptly that you don't even notice.

Tourists are especially juicy prey because they tend to carry large quantities of cash. Transfer your money into traveler's checks and be careful with it. Don't count your money in public or use large bills. Tuck your wallet into a discreet pocket and keep an extra 10 bucks or so in a more obvious one. Many New Yorkers invest in a cheap extra wallet designated for "mugging money." Keep an extra bill for emergencies in an unlikely place, such as your shoe, sock, inner ear, or esophagus.

New York's streets are rife with con artists. Their tricks are many. Beware of hustlers working in groups. And remember that no one ever wins at three-card monte. If someone spills ketchup on you, someone else may be picking your pocket. Be mistrustful of sob stories that require a donation from you. If you must, chasten yourself for letting the city harden you, but maintain your skepticism at all costs.

Pay attention to the neighborhood that surrounds you. A district can change character drastically in the course of a single block. The haughty Upper East Side, for example, segues into a dangerous bit of Harlem up in the triple digits. Simply being aware of the flow of people on the street can tell you a great deal about the relative safety of the area. Many notoriously dangerous districts have safe sections; look for children playing, women walking in the open, and other signs of an active community. If you feel uncomfortable, leave as quickly and directly as you can, but don't allow your fear of the new to close off whole worlds to you. Careful, persistent exploration will build confidence, undergird your emerging New York attitude, and make your stay in the city that much more rewarding.

At night, of course, it's even more important to keep track of your environment. Avoid poor or drug-ridden areas like the South Bronx, Washington Heights, Harlem, northeastern Brooklyn, and Alphabet City. West Midtown and the lower part of East Midtown, both well-populated commercial centers during the day, can be unpleasant at night. Follow the main thoroughfares; try to walk on avenues rather than streets. Residential areas with doormen are relatively safe even in the twilight. Fifth and Park are the least dangerous avenues in the evening on the East Side, Central Park West and Broadway the safest on the West.

Central Park, land of frisbees and Good Humor trucks by day, becomes dangerous and forbidding after sunset. If you find yourself penniless, tokenless, and on the wrong side of the park, walk around it by Central Park South rather than north of it or through it. If you're uptown, walk through the 85th St. Transverse near the police station. Avoid the woodsy deserted areas far from the main path. If you are visiting the gay bars near the West Side docks along the Hudson River, stay away from the abandoned waterfront area. Although the bars are trendy, the surrounding areas are purported to be unsafe. Bars and clubs in the Village may be a better bet. Further inland, the areas around Times Square and Penn Station are also dangerous.

IN VEHICLES

If you take a car into the city, try not to leave valuable possessions—such as radios or luggage—in it while you're off rambling. Radios are especially tempting. In fact, most thieves in New York actually make their living stealing only radios (note the many "No Radio" or "Radio Already Stolen" signs adorning car windows). If your tape deck or radio is removable, hide it in the trunk or take it with you. If it isn't, at least conceal it under a lot of junk. Similarly, hide baggage in the trunk—although some savvy thieves can tell if a car is heavily loaded by the way it is settled on its tires. Park your vehicle in a garage or well-traveled area. Sleeping in a car or van parked in the city is extremely dangerous—even the most dedicated budget traveler shouldn't consider it an option.

Late at night, take the bus rather than the subway; buses are safer because the driver is in plain view. On weekends, taking the subway in the evening is less dangerous since most major lines are quite crowded then. If a station seems empty, stand near the token counter or look for a Guardian Angel, one of the self-appointed crime-fighters clad in red berets. Or treat yourself to a taxi; although more expensive, they are probably the safest mode of travel at night.

In taxis, the dangers are financial rather than physical. Don't let the driver, er, take you for a ride. Cab fares can be paid only at the end of the ride. New York taxis must drop off individuals and charge a bulk fare at the end; any driver who tries to charge you per person or by location has no business doing so. Take a yellow cab with a meter and a medallion on the hood rather than an illegal "gypsy" cab, which isn't yellow and doesn't have a meter. The driver's name should be posted, and when you get out you can request a receipt with a phone number to call about complaints or lost articles. State your destination with authority and suggest the quickest route if you know it. If you hesitate or sound unsure, the driver will probably know—and possibly care—that you can be taken out of your way without noticing.

When disembarking from a plane or train, be wary of unlicensed taxi dispatchers. At Grand Central or Penn Station, a person may claim to be a porter, carry your bags, hail you a cab, and then ask for a commission or share of the fare. Don't fall for this baggage-carrying scam—give directions to the driver as fast as you can and drive off in style. Official dispatchers do not need to be paid.

■■■ MAIL

Individual offices of the U.S. Postal Service are usually open Monday to Friday from 9am to 5pm and sometimes on Saturday until about noon. All are closed on national holidays. **Postcards** mailed within the U.S. cost 19¢ and **letters** cost 29¢ for the first ounce and 23¢ for each additional ounce. To Canada, it costs 30¢ to mail a postcard, and 40¢ to mail a letter for the first ounce and 23¢ for each additional ounce. It costs 30¢ to mail a postcard to Mexico; a letter is 35¢ for a half-ounce, 45¢ for an ounce, and 10¢ for each additional half-ounce up to two pounds. Postcards mailed overseas cost 40¢, and letters are 50¢ for a half-ounce, 95¢ for an ounce, and 39¢ for each additional half-ounce up to 64 ounces. **Aerogrammes,** printed sheets that fold into envelopes ready to be airmailed, are sold at post offices for 45¢. Most U.S. post offices offer an **International Express Mail** service, which is the fastest way to send

MAIL

an item overseas. (A package under 8 ounces can be sent to most foreign destinations in 40 to 72 hours for around $13.)

Although the rates listed above will remain in effect at least until the end of 1994, the U.S. Postal Service has requested **rate hikes** (33¢ instead of 29¢ for a domestic letter, for instance) which will not be approved or rejected until January or February of 1995. Travelers should check with their local post offices or call a New York City post office (see below) for the latest postal rates.

The U.S. is divided into postal zones, each with a five- or nine-digit **ZIP code** particular to a region, city, or part of a city. Writing this code on letters is essential for delivery. The normal form of address is as follows:

Jenna Morrison (name)
830 Machniak Ave., Suite 301 (address, apartment number)
Nibs Falls, NY 10027 (city, state abbreviation, ZIP)
USA (country, if mailing internationally)

RECEIVING MAIL

Depending on how neurotic your family is, consider making arrangements for them to get in touch with you. Mail can be sent **General Delivery** to a city's main post office branch. Once a letter arrives it will be held for about 30 days; it can be held for longer at the discretion of the Postmaster if such a request is clearly indicated on the front of the envelope. Family and friends can send letters to you labeled like this:

Sid VICIOUS (underline and capitalize last name for accurate filing)
c/o General Delivery
Main Post Office
James A. Farley Building
390 Ninth Ave.
New York City, NY 10001

The envelope should also say "Please hold until <...>," the blank filled in with a date a couple weeks after your correspondent expects you to pick up the letter. When you claim your mail, you'll have to present ID; if you don't claim a letter within two to four weeks, it will be returned to its sender.

American Express offices throughout the U.S. will act as a mail service for cardholders if you contact them in advance. Under this free "Client Letter Service," they will hold mail for 30 days, forward upon request, and accept telegrams. The last name of the person to whom the mail is addressed should be capitalized and underlined, and "Client Letter Service" should be written on the front of the envelope. For a complete list of offices and instructions on how to use the service, call 800-528-4800.

New York's **central post office branch,** at 421 Eighth Ave. (330-2908), occupying the block between Eighth and Ninth Ave. and 33rd and 32nd St., handles General Delivery mail, which should be sent to the Ninth Ave. address above; you must collect your General Delivery mail at the Ninth Ave. entrance as well. The branch is open 24 hrs. C.O.D.s, money orders, and passport applications are also processed at some branches. If you have questions concerning services, branch locations, or hours, call the Customer Service Assistance Center (967-8585; open Mon.-Fri. 8:30am-5pm). For speedier service at any time, dial 330-4000 for the 24-hour automated **Postal Answer Line (PAL),** which provides information on branch hours and locations at ext. 127, first-class surface mail at ext. 319, International Express Mail at ext. 318, Parcel Post at ext. 317, customs at ext. 308, and special services at ext. 142 (a directory of these extensions can be found at ext. 328).

■■■ TELEPHONES

Area Code: 212 (Manhattan); 718 (Brooklyn, Queens, the Bronx, and Staten Island). Dial "1" first when making calls between these area codes. All telephone numbers in this book are area code 212 unless otherwise noted.

Most of the information you will need about telephones—including area codes for the U.S., foreign country codes, and rates—is in the front of the local **white pages** telephone directory. The **yellow pages,** published at the end of the white pages or in a separate book, is used to look up the phone numbers of businesses and other services. Federal, state, and local government listings are provided in the blue pages at the back of the directory. To obtain local phone numbers or area codes of other cities, call **directory assistance** at 411. Calling "0" will get you the **operator,** who can assist you in reaching a phone number and provide you with general information. For long-distance directory assistance, dial 1-(area code)-555-1212. The operator will help you with rates or other information and give assistance in an emergency. Directory assistance or the operator is free from any pay phone.

Telephone numbers in the U.S. consist of a three-digit area code, a three-digit exchange, and a four-digit number, written as 123-456-7890. Only the last seven digits are used in a **local call. Non-local calls within the area code** from which you are dialing require a "1" before the last seven digits, while **long-distance calls outside the area code** from which you are dialing require a "1" and the area code. For example, to call Ray's Pizza in the Village from outside Manhattan, you'd dial 1-212-243-2253. Generally, discount rates apply after 5pm on weekdays and Sunday and economy rates every day between 11pm and 8am; on Saturday and on Sunday until 5pm, economy rates are also in effect. Numbers beginning with area code 800 are **toll-free calls** requiring no coin deposit. Numbers beginning with 900 are **toll calls** and charge you (often exorbitantly) for whatever "service" they provide.

Pay phones are plentiful, most often stationed on street corners and in public areas. Be wary of private, more expensive pay phones—the rate they charge per call will be printed on the phone. Put your coins (25¢ for a local call in NYC) into the slot and listen for a dial tone before dialing. If there is no answer or if you get a busy signal, you will get your money back after hanging up; connecting with answering machines will prevent this. To make a **long-distance direct call,** dial the number. An operator will tell you the cost for the first three minutes; deposit that amount in the coin slot. The operator or a recording will cut in when you must deposit more money. A rarer variety of pay phone found in some large train stations charges 25¢ for a one-minute call to any place in the continental U.S.

If you are at an ordinary telephone and don't have barrels of change, you may want to make a **collect call** (i.e., charge the call to the recipient). First dial "0" and then the area code and number you wish to reach. An operator will cut in and ask to help you. Tell him or her that you wish to place a collect call and give your name; anyone who answers may accept or refuse the call. If you tell the operator you are placing a **person-to-person collect call** (more expensive than a regular, **station-to-station collect call),** you must give both your name and the receiving person's name; the benefit is that a charge appears only if the person with whom you wish to speak is there (and accepts the charges, of course). The cheapest method of reversing the charges is MCI's new **1-800-COLLECT** service: just dial 1-800-COLLECT, tell the operator what number you want to call (it can be anywhere in the world), and receive a 20% to 44% discount off normal rates (discounts are greatest when the rates are already cheapest). Finally, if you'd like to call someone who is as poor as you, simply **bill to a third party** by dialing "0," the area code, and then the number; the operator will call the third party for approval.

In addition to coin-operated pay phones, AT&T and its competitors operate a **coinless** version. Not only can collect and third-party calls be made on this kind of phone, but you can also use a **telephone calling card;** begin dialing all these kinds of calls with "0." Generally, these phones are operated by passing the card through a slot before dialing, although you can always just punch in your calling-card number on the keypad (a desirable alternative if you happen to be traveling in an area where carrying around credit cards is unwise). Many of these phones—especially those located in airports, hotels, and truckstops—accept Visa, MasterCard, and American Express cards as well. The cheapest way to call long-distance from a pay phone is by using a calling card or credit card.

You can place **international calls** from any telephone. To call direct, dial the universal international access code (011) followed by the country code (see below), the city/area code, and the local number. Country codes and city codes may sometimes be listed with a zero in front (e.g., 033), but when dialing 011 first, drop succeeding zeros (e.g., 011-33). In some areas you will have to give the operator the number and he or she will place the call. Rates are cheapest on calls to the United Kingdom and Ireland between 6pm and 7am (Eastern Time); to Australia between 3am and 2pm; and to New Zealand between 11pm and 10am.

The **country code** is 1 for the U.S. and Canada; 44 for the U.K.; 353 for the Republic of Ireland; 61 for Australia; 64 for New Zealand; and 27 for South Africa.

TELEGRAM

Sometimes **cabling** may be the only way to contact someone quickly (usually by the next day). Within the U.S., the minimum cost for a same day, hand-delivered telegram is $30.90 for 15 words. A "Mailgram" is a telegram that arrives on the next mail-day and costs $18.95 for 50 words. For foreign telegrams, **Western Union** (800-325-6000) charges a base fee for the first seven words plus delivery; after seven words, an additional per-word charge is assessed. To Canada, the rate is $12.85 plus 55¢ per additional word; to Great Britain and Ireland, $13.27/61¢; and to Australia, New Zealand, and South Africa, $13.62/66¢.

■■■ FINANCIAL SERVICES

Travelers visiting New York will have no trouble finding a place to exchange foreign currencies and traveler's checks into U.S. dollars. Large banks—including Citibank (627-3999, or 800-627-3999 from outside New York State), Chase Manhattan (800-282-4273), and Chemical (935-9935, or 800-935-9935 from outside NY, NJ, and CT)—blanket the city with subsidiary branches and ATMs, and fall over each other claiming to be the largest, biggest, nicest bank in town. Other companies specialize in providing foreign exchange services up to seven days a week, often quoting rates by phone.

American Express: Multi-task agency providing tourists with traveler's checks, gift checks, cashing services, you name it. Branches in Manhattan include: **American Express Tower,** 200 Vesey St. (640-2000), near the World Financial Center (open Mon.-Fri. 9am-5pm); **Macy's Herald Square,** 151 W. 34th St. (695-8075), at Seventh Ave. inside Macy's (open Mon.-Sat. 10am-6pm); **150 E. 42nd St.** (687-3700), between Lexington and Third Ave. (open Mon.-Fri 9am-5pm); in **Bloomingdale's,** 59th St. and Lexington Ave. (705-3171; open Mon.-Wed. and Fri.-Sat. 10am-6pm, Thurs. 10am-8pm); **822 Lexington Ave.** (758-6510), near 63rd St. (open Mon.-Fri. 9am-6pm, Sat. 10am-4pm).

Bank Leumi, 579 Fifth Ave. (343-5000), at 47th St. Account not required to buy or sell foreign currencies and traveler's checks, issue foreign drafts, or make payments by wire, although Bank Leumi does charge for its services. Latest exchange rates are available by phone (343-5343). Open Mon.-Fri. 9am-5pm.

Cheque Point USA, 551 Madison Ave. (980-6443), between 55th and 56th St., with other branches throughout the city (call for locations). Wire funds to major foreign cities at rates cheaper than American Express's. Open Mon.-Fri. 8am-7:30pm, Sat. 9:30am-7:30pm, Sun. 10am-6pm.

TAXES AND TIPPING

The prices quoted throughout *Let's Go: New York City* are the amounts before sales tax has been added. Sales tax in New York is 8.25%, depending on the item. Hotel tax is 14.25%; there's also a $2 occupancy tax per single room per night and a $4 tax for suites.

Remember that service is never included on a New York tab. Tip cab drivers and waiters about 15%; especially good waiters—or those who work at especially good restaurants—are often tipped 20% of the tab. Tip hairdressers 10% and bellhops around $1 per bag. Bartenders usually expect between 50¢ and $1 per drink.

■■■ LIBRARIES

New York Public Library, 11 W. 40th St. (661-7220, or 869-8089 for a recorded listing of exhibitions and events), entrance on Fifth Ave. at 42nd St. Non-lending central research library. Wide variety of exhibits on display. Open Tues.-Wed. 11am-7:30pm, Mon. and Thurs.-Sat. 10am-6pm. Exhibitions open Mon. and Thurs.-Sat. 10am-6pm, Tues.-Wed. 11am-6pm.

Midtown Manhattan, 455 Fifth Ave. (340-0833), at 40th St. Largest branch of the circulating libraries; specialized sections include Folklore and Women's Studies. Occasional exhibits and presentations; pick up a free events calendar at any NYPL location. Identification and proof of local address required to take out books. Open Mon. and Wed. 9am-9pm, Tues. and Thurs. 11am-7pm, Fri.-Sat. 10am-6pm.

Donnell Library Center, 20 W. 53rd St. (621-0618), between Fifth and Sixth Ave. Central Children's Room for "Curious George" fans. Largest circulation of foreign-language books. Open Mon., Wed., and Fri. noon-6pm, Tues. and Thurs. 9:30am-8pm, Sat. 10am-5:30pm.

Performing Arts Research Center, at Lincoln Center, 111 Amsterdam Ave. (870-1630), entrance at 65th St. Specializes in theater, music, dance, film, and TV. Circulation section (for anybody with a NYC library card) includes CDs, CD-ROMs, tapes, and records. Tour (870-1670) Wed. at 2pm. Open Mon. and Thurs. noon-8pm, Tues.-Wed. and Fri.-Sat. noon-6pm.

Andrew Heiskell Library for the Blind and Physically Handicapped, 40 W. 20th St. (206-5400), near Sixth Ave. between Prince and Spring St. Braille and large-type books. Open Mon. 11am-4pm, Tues. and Sat. 1-5pm, Thurs. 1-6pm. Librarians available by phone Mon.-Wed. and Fri.-Sat. 10am-5pm, Thurs. 10am-6pm.

Schomburg Center for Research in Black Culture, 515 Lenox/Malcolm X Ave. (491-2200), on the corner of 135th St. Largest collection of books by and about African-Americans anywhere in the world. Large, quiet reading rooms on the basement and second floor. Library open Mon.-Wed. noon-8pm, Thurs.-Sat. 10am-6pm; archives dept. open Mon.-Wed. noon-5pm, Fri.-Sat. 10am-5pm.

The other boroughs' head branches are: the **Bronx Reference Center,** 2556 Bainbridge Ave. (718-220-6565); the **St. George Library Center,** 5 Central Ave., Staten Island (718-442-8560); the **Queensborough Public Library,** 89-11 Merrick Blvd., Jamaica, Queens (718-990-0700); and the **Brooklyn Public Library,** Grand Army Plaza, Brooklyn (718-780-7700).

■■■ HELP LINES

Crime Victim's Hotline, 577-7777. 24-hr. counseling and referrals for victims of crime or domestic violence.

Sex Crimes Report Line, New York Police Department, 267-7273. 24-hr. information and referrals.

Poison Control Center, 764-7667 or 340-4494.

Samaritans, 673-3000. 24-hr. suicide prevention. Confidential phone counseling.

Runaway Hotline, 619-6884. 24-hr. counseling and shelter referral.

Helpline Telephone Services, 532-2400. Crisis counseling and referrals. Daily 9am-10pm.

Crisis Counseling, Intervention, and Referral Service, 516-679-1111. Focused primarily on youths, providing information and confidential counseling for all kinds of crises (AIDS, abortion, suicide, etc.). Includes the Gay Peer Counseling Network. 24 hrs.

New York Gay and Lesbian Anti-Violence Project, 807-0197. 24-hr. crisis intervention hotline, counseling, and referrals to support groups and legal services.

Gay and Lesbian Switchboard, 777-1800. Peer counseling and referral for the gay or lesbian traveler. Daily 10am-midnight.

Lesbian Switchboard, 741-2610. Mon.-Fri. 6-10pm. Information on NYC-based activities and general support.

Alcohol and Substance Abuse Information Line, 800-522-5353. 24-hr. information and referrals on all drug-related problems.

Alcoholics Anonymous, 647-1680. Counseling and referrals to local AA meetings. Daily 9am-10pm.

New York City Department for the Aging, 442-1000. Information and referrals. Mon.-Fri. 9am-5pm.

Legal Aid Society, 577-3300. Referrals. Mon.-Fri. 9am-5pm.[CUT]

Consumer's Union, 914-378-2000. Consumer advice. Mon.-Fri. 9:15am-5pm.

Department of Consumer Affairs, 487-4398. Handles consumer complaints. Mon.-Fri. 9:30am-4:30pm.

MLM Talking Yellowbook, 718-921-1400. Quick information on a variety of topics for the cost of a local phone call. Simply punch in the 4-digit code after the initial greeting to access the rich store of available data, such as Today's Top Stories (2277), New York Local Weather Forecast (2777), and Sports Report (1278).

■■■ MEDICAL CARE

Most hospitals will bill you later if you aren't covered by insurance, and most have multilingual (at least Spanish) services as well.

Bellevue Hospital Center, First Ave. and E. 27th. St. (561-4141). Emergency Room 561-4347 (adult), 561-3025 (pediatric).

Beth Israel Medical Center, First Ave. and E. 16th St. (420-2000). Emergency Room 420-2840.

Columbia-Presbyterian Medical Center, Fort Washington Ave. and W. 168th St. (305-2500).

Mount Sinai Medical Center, Fifth Ave. and 100th St. Emergency Room 241-7171. Affiliated with CUNY Medical School.

New York Hospital-Cornell Medical Center, 520 E. 70th St., between York Ave. and FDR Dr. Emergency Room 726-5050.

New York Infirmary Beekman Downtown Hospital, 170 William St. (312-5000).

New York University Medical Center, 550 First Ave., between E. 32nd and E. 33rd St. Emergency Room 263-5550.

Walk-in Clinic, 57 E. 34th St. (683-1010), between Park and Madison Ave. Open Mon.-Fri. 8am-6pm, Sat. 10am-2pm. Affiliated with Beth Israel Hospital.

Kaufman's Pharmacy, 557 Lexington Ave. (755-2266), at 50th St. Free delivery within five blocks, otherwise customer pays two-way taxi fare. Open 24 hrs.

Eastern Women's Center, 44 E. 50th St. (686-6066), between Park and Madison Ave. Gynecological exams and surgical procedures for women, by appt. only.

Women's Health Line, New York City Department of Health (230-1111). Information and referrals concerning reproductive health. Open Mon.-Fri. 8am-6pm.

Planned Parenthood, 677-6474.

AIDS Information, 807-6655. Run by the Gay Men's Health Crisis. Mon.-Fri. 10am-9pm, Sat. noon-3pm.

AIDS Information Hotline, NYC Dept. of Health. 447-8200. Open 9am-9pm.

Venereal Disease Information, NYC Dept. of Health. 427-5120. Mon.-Fri. 8:30am-4:30pm.

Accommodations

If you know someone who knows someone who lives in New York—get that person's phone number. The cost of living in New York can rip the seams off your wallet. Don't expect to fall into a hotel; if you do, odds are it will be a pit. At true full-service establishments, a night will cost around $125. Hotel tax is 14.25%, with an additional $2 occupancy tax per night on a single room and $4 for suites. Many reasonable choices are available for under $60 a night, as well, but it really depends on your priorities. People traveling alone may want to spend more to stay in a safer neighborhood. The young and the outgoing may prefer a budget-style place crowded with students. Honeymooning couples will not.

Hostels offer fewer amenities than more commercial establishments, yet manage to preserve a greater feeling of homeyness and camaraderie. Cheap YMCAs and YWCAs offer another budget option, but young backpackers may miss the intimacy and social life a hostel can offer. All of these places advise you to reserve in advance—even once you get to New York, you should call to make sure there are rooms available before trekking to someplace with your bags. Cheap hotels lasso in hapless innocents and ingenues around the Penn Station and Times Square areas of Midtown, but you should avoid these honky-tonk spots; the hotel rooms often rent by the hour. Another high concentration of budget hotels can be found in the lower part of East Midtown, south of the Empire State Building. These spots, around Park Avenue South in the 20s, vary widely in quality, and the neighborhood changes drastically from block to block.

Crime-free neighborhoods in the city exist only in dreams; never leave anything of value in your room. Most places have safes or lockers available, some for an extra fee. Don't sleep in your car, and never, ever sleep outdoors, anywhere in New York. The city has a hard enough time protecting its vast homeless population—tourists simply would not stand a chance.

■■■ HOSTELS

Hostels offer unbeatable deals on indoor lodging and are great places to meet budget travelers from all over the world. Hostels are generally dorm-style accommodations where the sexes usually sleep apart, often in large rooms with bunk beds. Because most hostelers don't place a huge premium on luxury or privacy, hostel beds can cost as little as $15 per night. Expenses and frills are kept to a minimum as a tradeoff. Guests often must rent or bring their own sheets or "sleep sacks" (two sheets sewn together); sleeping bags are usually not allowed. Many hostels make kitchens and utensils available for their guests, and some provide storage areas and laundry facilities. Some hostels are in former hotels, while others like to call themselves hotels; hybrids may offer private singles and doubles in addition to the communal dorms. In most other hostels, you can get a room with fewer occupants and more conveniences for a little more money. Most hostel guests are young and/or students, often from outside the U.S., but the clientele can be surprisingly mixed. This diversity of backgrounds and experiences leads to many late-night conversations in the common room.

If you're going to be traveling extensively in the rest of the U.S. or Canada, you should consider joining **Hostelling International/American Youth Hostels (HI/ AYH)** the leading organization of U.S. hostels. There are over 300 AYH/HI-affiliated hostels throughout North America; these are usually kept up to a higher standard than most private hostels, though they tend to be more strict and institutional. AYH/ HI runs an excellent hostel in New York, with much space and many amenities (see below). Yearly **HI/AYH membership** is $25 for adults, $15 for those over 54, $10 for those under 18, $35 for families. **Non-members** who wish to stay at an AYH/HI hostel usually pay $3 extra, which can be applied toward membership. For more information, contact AYH/HI, 733 15th St. NW, Ste. 840, Washington, D.C. 20005 (202-783-6161; fax 202-783-6171), or inquire at any HI-affiliated hostel.

Though you may not be as enthusiastic as the Village People, don't overlook the **Young Men's Christian Association (YMCA)** or the **Young Women's Christian Association (YWCA).** The YMCA's and YWCA's rates are often better those of city hotels, and Christianity is neither a requirement nor much of a presence. Singles average $25-42 per night, around $110 per week; rooms include use of a library, pool, and other facilities. You may have to share a room and use a communal bath or shower, however. Some YMCAs in New York (listed below) accept women and families as well as men, while the YWCA in Brooklyn (also below) is for women only. Reserve 2 months in advance, and expect to pay a refundable key deposit of about $5. For information and reservations, write or call **The Y's Way,** 224 E. 47th St., New York, NY 10017 (212-308-2899).

Let's Go lists New York's best hostels and YMCA/YWCAs, ranked in order of value, based on price, safety, and location.

New York International HI/AYH Hostel, 891 Amsterdam Ave. (932-2300, fax 932-2574), at 103rd St. Subway: #1, 9, B, or C to 102nd St. Located in a block-long, landmark building designed by Richard Morris Hunt, this is the largest hostel in the U.S., with 90 dorm-style rooms and 480 beds. Shares its site with the **CIEE Student Center** (666-3619), an information depot for travelers, as well as a Council Travel office. Spiffy new soft carpets, blondewood bunks, spotless bathrooms. Members' kitchens and dining rooms, coin-operated laundry machines ($1), communal TV lounges, and a large outdoor garden. Walking tours and outings. Key-card entry to individual rooms. Secure storage area and individual lockers. 29-day max. stay, 7-day in summer. Open 24 hrs. Check-in any time, check-out 11am (late check-out fee $5). No curfew. Members $22-25 per night, depending on number of beds in room ($3 more for non-members). Family room $60. Groups of 4-12 may get private rooms. Linen rental $3. Towel $2. Excellent wheelchair access.

International Student Center, 38 W. 88th St. (787-7706, fax 580-9283), between Central Park West and Columbus Ave. Subway: B or C to 86th St. Open only to foreigners (but not Canadians) aged 18-30; you must show a foreign passport to be admitted. A once-gracious, welcoming brownstone on a cheerful, tree-lined street noted for frequent celebrity sightings. Single-sex, no-frills bunk rooms. Large basement TV lounge with affable, satisfied guests. 7-day max. stay when full. Open daily 8am-11pm. No curfew. A bargain at $12 a night. Key deposit $5. No reservations, and generally full in summers, but call by 10pm for a bed, and they'll hold it for you for two hours. No wheelchair access; lot of stairs.

International Student Hospice, 154 E. 33rd St. (228-7470), between Lexington and Third Ave. Subway: #6 to 33rd St. Up a flight of stairs in an inconspicuous converted brownstone with a brass plaque saying "I.S.H." Homey hostel with helpful and knowledgeable owner exudes friendliness and community. Populated by a predominantly European crowd of backpackers. Good location in Murray Hill. Twenty very small rooms with bunk beds bursting with crusty bric-a-brac, cracked porcelain tea cups, and clunky oak night tables. The ceilings are crumbling and the stairs slant precariously, but the house is slowly being restored by willing residents. Rooms for 2-4 people and hall bathroom. Large common room, lounge, and enough dusty books to last a summer. Strict midnight curfew. $25 per night, with some weekly discounts.

Banana Bungalow, 250 W. 77th St. (800-6-HOSTEL or 769-2441, fax 877-5733), between Broadway and Eleventh Ave. Subway: #1 or 9 to 79th St. Walk two blocks south and turn right. A vast, continually expanding and renovating hostel, with sun deck on the top floor, a tropical-themed lounge/kitchen, and dorm-style rooms sleeping 4-7, each with its own bathroom. Beds $10-15. Reservations available by fax or writing with your Visa or Mastercard number and expiration date. Wheelchair access.

De Hirsch Residence, 1395 Lexington Ave. (415-5650 or 800-858-4692, fax 415-5578), at 92nd St. Subway: #6 to 96th St. Affiliated with the 92nd St. YMHA/YWHA, de Hirsch has some of the largest, cleanest, and most convenient hostel housing in the city. Huge hall bathrooms, kitchens, and laundry machines on every other floor give this hostel a collegiate feel. Single-sex floors, strictly enforced. A/C available for $3. Access to the many facilities of the 92nd St. Y—free Nautilus and reduced rates for concerts. Organized activities such as video nights in the many common rooms and walking tours of New York. The rates are quite reasonable: Singles $280 per week; beds in doubles $210 per week. 3-day min stay. Long-term stays from 2 mo. to 1 yr. available for $595 per month for singles, $420-500 per month for beds in doubles. Application required at least a month in advance; must be a student or working in the city, and must supply references. Wheelchair access.

Sugar Hill International House, 722 Saint Nicholas Ave. (926-7030, fax 283-0108) at 146th St. Subway A, B, C, or D to 145th St. Located on Sugar Hill in Harlem, across from the subway station. Reassuring, lively neighborhood. Converted brownstone with huge, well-lit, comfortable rooms. 2-10 people per room in sturdy bunkbeds, hand-built by the owners. Staff is stunningly friendly and helpful, with a vast knowledge of NYC and the Harlem area. Facilities include kitchens, TV, stereo, and paperback library. Beautiful garden in back. All-female room available. Check-in 9am-10pm. No lockout. Incredible deal at $12 per person. Call in advance. The owners of Sugar Hill also run the new 4-floor hostel next door at 730 Saint Nicholas Ave., the **Blue Rabbit Hostel** (491-3892, 800-610-2030). Similar to the Sugar Hill, but with more doubles and hence more of a sense of privacy. Backyard garden, friendly kittycats, common room, and kitchen. Amazingly spacious rooms. Check-in 9am-10pm. $12 per person, $14 for a private room. Call in advance.

Gershwin Hotel, 3 E. 27th St. (545-8000, fax 684-5546), between Fifth and Madison Ave. Subway: N or R to 28th St. Bright sculptures and European travellers congregate in this airy hotel, while a rooftop garden beckons to sun-seekers. Passport or ID proving out-of-state or foreign residence required. Free tea and coffee. 20-day max. stay. 24-hr. reception. Check-out 11am. No curfew. Doubles $55. Triples $70. 4-bed dorms $17 per bed. Continental breakfast $2.50. All dorm rooms have lockers.

Chelsea International Hostel, 251 W. 20th St. (647-0010), between Seventh and Eighth Ave. Subway: #1, 9, C, or E to 23rd St. The congenial staff at this new 47-bed hostel offers their guests free beer and pizza on Wed. nights, and free beer (bring your own pizza) on Sun. Cramped but adequate 4-person dorm rooms $18 per bed; private rooms $35. Reservations recommended; call ahead.

Big Apple Hostel, 119th W. 45th St. (302-2603, fax 533-2603) between 6th and 7th Ave. Subway: #1,2,3,9,N, or R to 42nd St.; or B,D, or E to Seventh Ave. Centrally located, this hostel offers clean, comfortable, carpeted rooms, a full kitchen with refrigerator, a big back deck, and laundry facilities. Passport nominally required; Americans accepted with out-of-state photo ID or some other convincing means of proving themselves tourists. Open 24 hrs. Bunk in dorm-style room with shared bath $20. Private room with double bed and bath $45-50. Lockers in some rooms, but bring your own lock. No reservations accepted July-Aug., but they'll hold a bed if you call after 11am on the day you want to arrive. Reservations accepted Sept.-June; make them a few weeks in advance for June.

Mid-City Hostel, 608 Eighth Ave. (704-0562), between 39th and 40th St. on the 3rd and 4th floors. Subway: #1,2,3,9,N, or R to 42nd St.-Seventh Ave.; or A,C, or E to 42nd St.-Ninth Ave. On the east side of Eighth Ave. No sign: just look for the street number on the small door (and the sign advertising the fortune teller who works inside at the base of the stairs). Don't be intimidated by the lively neighborhood and busy streets that surround this comfortable, homey hostel. Brick walls, skylights, and old wooden beams across the ceiling make it feel like a friend's apartment. Caters to an international backpacking crowd—a passport and ticket out of the country are required, and Americans are nominally excluded (although they may be able to talk themselves in). Small breakfast included. 5-day max. stay in summer. Lock-out noon-6pm. Curfew Sun.-Thurs. midnight, Sat.-Sun. 1am.

Bunk in dorm-style room with shared bath $18 ($15 Oct.-late June). Reservations will be taken over the phone and should be made weeks in advance for summer.

Uptown Hostel, 239 Lenox/Malcolm X Ave. (666-0559), at 122nd St. Currently run by the knowledgeable and helpful Gisèle out of the New York Bed and Breakfast (see below). Bunk beds, sparkling clean and comfy rooms, and spacious hall bathrooms. $12 a night. Call 1-2 weeks in advance during the summer.

YMCA—Vanderbilt, 224 E. 47th St. (756-9600, fax 752-0210), between Second and Third Ave. Subway: #6 to 51st St. or E, F to Lexington-Third Ave. Five blocks from Grand Central Station. Convenient and well-run, with reasonable prices and vigilant security. Clean, brightly-lit lobby bustles with jabbering internationals and internal-frame backpacks. Rooms are quite small, and bathroom-to-people ratio is pretty low, but the perks! Lodgers get free run of the copious athletic facilities (Stairmasters, aerobics classes, Nautilus machines, pool, and sauna), safe-deposit boxes, and guided tours of the city. 25-day max. stay; no NYC residents. Check-in 1-6pm; after 6pm must have major credit card to check in. Check-out at noon, but luggage storage until departure ($1/bag). Five shuttles daily to the airports. Singles $45. Doubles $55. Key deposit $10. Make reservations a week or two in advance and guarantee them with a deposit. Wheelchair access.

YMCA—West Side, 5 W. 63rd St. (787-4400, fax 580-0441). Subway: #1, 9, A, B, C, or D to 59th St.-Columbus Circle. Small, well-maintained rooms but dilapidated halls in a big, popular Y with an impressive, Islamic-inspired façade. Free access to 2 pools, indoor track, racquet courts, and Nautilus equipment. Showers on every floor and spotless bathrooms. A/C and cable TV in every room. Check-out noon; lockout at 11pm. Singles $42, with bath $65. Doubles $55, with bath $75. Reservations recommended. A few stairs at entrance; otherwise wheelchair-friendly.

Chelsea Center Hostel, 313 W. 29th St. (643-0214), between Eighth and Ninth Ave. Subway: #1, 2, 3, 9, A, C, E to 34th St. Gregarious, knowledgeable staff will help you out with New York tips in multiple languages (including Irish). Twenty-five bunks in a low-ceilinged room make for a slightly cramped setup. Only one shower. Tiny backdoor garden, replete with ivy and a picnic table. Check in anytime, but lockout 11am-5pm. Dorm beds $20 in summer, $18 in winter, light breakfast included. Be sure to call ahead; usually full in summer.

YMCA—McBurney, 206 W. 24th St. (741-9226, fax 741-0012), between Seventh and Eighth Ave. Subway: #1, 9, C, or E to 23rd St. A working YMCA with a lot of activity on the ground floor. The no-frills rooms upstairs are liveable, but no A/C. Mix of elderly locals, students, and other travelers. Good security. Singles $34-41. Doubles $50. Triples $66. Quads $88. Free access to gym. 25-day limit on stays. Usually has vacancies, but reservations are advisable. Wheelchair access.

YMCA—Flushing, 138-46 Northern Blvd., Flushing, Queens (718-961-6880, fax 718-461-4691), between Union and Bowne St. Subway: #7 to Main St.; the "Y" is about a 10-min. walk, about 40 min. from Manhattan. Walk north on Main St. (the Ave. numbers should get smaller as you walk) and turn right onto Northern Blvd. Men only. The area between the "Y" and Flushing's nearby shopping district is lively and well-populated, but the neighborhood quickly deteriorates north of Northern Blvd. Standard "Y" rooms—clean but worn, with hall bathroom. Daily maid service provided. Gym, Nautilus, squash, and swimming facilities included. $25 per night, $120 per week, 28-day maximum stay. Key deposit $20. Passport or driver's license required.

YMCA—Central Queens, 89-25 Parsons Blvd., Jamaica, Queens (718-739-6600, fax 718-658-7233), at 90th Ave. Subway: E or J to Jamaica Center. Parsons Blvd. joins Archer Ave. right at the subway station; walk north along it across Jamaica Ave. and one block further to 90th Ave. Men only. In a bustling, noisy downtown district. Concrete prevails in the small but neat private rooms. Gym, Nautilus, racquetball, and swimming facilities included. $32 per night; $123.50 per week for students with ID or workers with proof of employment; $164 per week for others. Key deposit $10. Passport or driver's license required. No reservations.

■■■ DORMITORIES

Miss that boxlike dorm ambience? Now you can experience it on vacation, too. Some colleges and universities open their residence halls to conferences and travelers, especially during the summer. You may have to share a bath, but rates are often low and facilities are usually clean and well-maintained. If you hope to stay at a school, contact its housing office before your vacation.

Columbia University, 1230 Amsterdam Ave. (678-3235, fax 678-3222) at 120th St. Subway: #1 or 9 to 116th St. Whittier Hall sets aside some rooms for visitors year-round. Rooms are small but clean. 24-hr. tight security. Not the safest neighborhood, but well populated until fairly late at night. Singles $35. Doubles with A/C, bath, and kitchen $55. Reserve in advance.

New York University, 14a Washington Pl. (998-4621). NYU's Summer Housing Office rents rooms on a weekly basis (3-week min., 12-week max.) from mid-May to mid-August. Rooms available with or without A/C, bath, or kitchenette; boarders without kitchens must join the meal plan for $70 per person per week. Anyone is eligible. Singles without A/C or meal plan $105 per week. Doubles with kitchen and A/C $130 per person per week. Rooms are located in various dorms of NYU's campus in Greenwich Village and vary in size but are all eminently livable. Call after Jan. 1 for more information and reservations; reserve by May 1.

Fashion Institute of Technology, 210 W. 27th St. (760-7885), between Seventh and Eighth Ave. Subway: #1 or 9 to 28th St. Decent neighborhood, but adjacent to the sleazy Penn Station neighborhood; exercise caution at night. Most residents are F.I.T. summer students, but others can rent rooms by the week or month, space permitting. Application required; call or pick one up, but expect to wait a couple of days for processing. Office open Mon.-Fri. 8am-7pm. Spartan dorm-style doubles with communal baths in a fairly modern building, $150 per person per week (1-week min. stay). Double-occupancy suites with kitchen and bath, $750 per person per month (1-month min. stay). Reservations necessary; full payment in advance. Housing offered from 1st week of June until July 31. Some rooms wheelchair-accessible; make advance arrangements.

■■■ HOTELS

No chocolate dainties for you, O budget traveler; count yourself lucky if you've found a reasonably-priced room. A single in a cheap hotel should cost $35-60. Most hotel rooms can be reserved in advance. Ask the hotel owner if you can see a room before you pay for it. You should be told in advance whether the bathroom is communal or private. Most hotels require a key deposit when you register. Check-in usually takes place between 11am and 6pm, check-out before 11am. You may be able to store your gear for the day even after vacating your room and returning the key, but most proprietors will not take responsibility for the safety of your belongings.

If you have a particular fondness for Hiltons and Marriotts beyond your means, consider joining **Discount Travel International,** 114 Forrest Ave. #203, Narberth, PA 19072 (215-668-7184; fax 215-668-9182). For an annual membership fee of $45, you and your household will have access to a wealth of discounts on unsold hotel rooms, airline tickets, cruises, car rentals, etc., which can save you as much as 50%.

Let's Go has found the best budget hotels and ranked them in order of value, based on price, facilities, safety, and location.

Carlton Arms Hotel, 160 E. 25th St. (684-8337, for reservations 679-0680), between Lexington and Third Ave. Subway: #6 to 23rd St. Stay inside a submarine and peer through windows at the lost city of Atlantis, travel to Renaissance Venice, or stow your clothes in a dresser suspended on an astroturf wall. Each room has been designed in a different motif by a different avant-garde artist, not one of whom has left many motel pastels around. "I sought to create a resounding rhythm that echoed wall-to-wall, layer upon layer, to fuse our separate impressions into one existence," writes the artist of room 5B. Hmm. Aggressive adornment doesn't completely obscure the age of these budget rooms, or their lack of air, but it goes a long way toward providing distractions. You won't pay that much, either. Singles $44. Doubles $57, with bath $65. Triples with bath $78. Pay for six nights up front and get the seventh free. Confirm reservations at least 10 days in advance. Discounts for students and foreigners.

Pickwick Arms Hotel, 230 E. 51st St. (355-0300 or 800-PICKWIK, fax 755-5029), between Second and Third Ave. Subway: #6 to 51st St. or E, F to Lexington-Third Ave. Business types congregate in this extremely well-located and well-priced mid-sized hotel. Chandeliered marble lobby filled with the silken strains of "Unforgettable You" contrasts with small rooms and microscopic hall bathrooms. Roof garden and airport service available. Check-in 2pm; check-out 1pm. Singles $45, with shared bath $55. Doubles with one bed and bath $90, two beds $100. Studios (double bed and sofa, with up to four people) $100. Additional person in room $12. Gets very busy, so make reservations.

Roger Williams Hotel, 28 E. 31st St. (684-7500, reservations 800-637-9773, fax 576-4343), at Madison Ave. in pleasant Murray Hill neighborhood. Subway: #6 to 33rd St. You won't be able to cook up a feast on the 2-burner stove in every room, but the spacious, clean rooms are a steal anyway. Small refrigerators will hold leftovers from the many take-out restaurants lining Madison Ave. All rooms with toilet, bath, cable TV, phone, and kitchenette. 24-hr. security. Singles $65, doubles $70, two twin beds $75, triples $80, and quads $90. Approximately 15% off regular rates with student ID, except for June through mid-July.

Portland Square Hotel, 132 W. 47th St. (382-0600 or 800-388-8988, fax 382-0684), between Sixth and Seventh Ave. Subway: B, D, F, Q to 50th St.–Sixth Ave. Rooms are carpeted, clean, and entirely comfortable, with A/C and cable TV, but the hotel's main asset is its great location. Attracts mostly foreigners. Singles with shared bath $40, with private bath $60. Doubles $85. Triples $90. Quads $95.

Herald Square Hotel, 19 W. 31st St. (279-4017 or 800-727-1888, fax 643-9208), at Fifth Ave. Subway: B, D, F, N, or R to 34th St. In the original Beaux Arts home of *Life* magazine (built in 1893). Above the entrance note the reading cherub entitled the "Winged Life," carved by Philip Martiny. The sculpture was a frequent presence on the pages of early *Life* magazines. Work by some of America's most noted illustrators adorns the lobby, halls, and rooms. Tiny, clean, newly renovated rooms with color TV and A/C. Singles with shared bath $40, with private bath $50. Doubles $55, with 2 beds $80. Reservations recommended for the cheaper rooms; without them you may have to take something more expensive.

Hotel Wolcott, 4 W. 31st St. (268-2900, fax 563-0096), between Fifth and Sixth Ave. Subway: B, D, F, N, or R to 34th St. An ornately mirrored and marbled entrance hall leads into this inexpensive, newly renovated hotel. New furniture and carpeting, cable TV, and efficient A/C. Singles $40, with bath $55-60. Doubles $45, with bath $55-65. Triples with bath $65-75. Reservations recommended a month or more in advance for summer.

Washington Square Hotel, 103 Waverly Pl. (777-9515, 800-222-0418, fax 979-8373), at MacDougal St. Subway: A, B, C, D, E, F, or Q to W. 4th St. Fantastic location. Glitzy marble and brass lobby, with a pretty cool medieval gate in front. TV, A/C, and key-card entry to individual rooms. Clean and comfortable; friendly and multilingual staff. Singles $58. Doubles $85. Two twin beds $95. Quads $112. Reservation required 2-3 weeks in advance.

Hotel Iroquois, 49 W. 44th St. (840-3080 or 800-332-7220, fax 398-1754), near Fifth Ave. Subway: B, D, or F to 47th St.-Rockefeller Ctr. Pink and blue, slightly worn but spacious rooms in an old prewar building. This hotel once hosted James Dean and is now the stop of choice for Greenpeace and other environmental activists when in town. Check-out noon. Singles and doubles $75-100. Suites (up to 5 people) $125-150. Student discounts available, and all prices negotiable during winter. Reservations advisable a few weeks in advance during the summer.

Mansfield Hotel, 12 W. 44th St. (944-6050 or 800-255-5167, fax 740-2508), at Fifth Ave. Subway: B, D, or F to 47th St.-Rockefeller Ctr. A dignified establishment housed in a turn-of-the-century building with comfortable leather couches in the lobby and beautiful oak doors in the hallways. Rooms in process of renovation; the new ones have new lighting, paint, and furniture, and some of the larger ones have whirlpool tubs. Be sure to request a renovated room specifically when making reservations (1 month in advance for summer). Check-out noon. Singles $65. Doubles $75. Triples $85. Quads $100. Large suites $120 for 5 people, $140 for 6.

Hotel Remington, 129 W. 46th St. (221-2600, fax 764-7481), between Broadway and Sixth Ave. Subway: B, D, or F to 47th St.-Rockefeller Ctr.; or #1, 2, 3, 9, N, or R to 42nd St.-Times Sq. Centrally located. Plush carpeting, bedspread, and curtains in matching orange hang in reasonably large rooms. All rooms with color TV and A/C. Singles $60, with bath $75. Doubles $60, with bath $80. Triples $65, with bath $85.

Broadway American Hotel, 222 W. 77th St. (362-1100, 800-446-4556, fax 707-9521), at (surprise) Broadway. Subway: #1 or 9 to 79th St. Cool, clean, and ultramodern with few right angles and lots of charcoal-gray; if it were roomier, it'd be a corporate law office. All rooms equipped with refrigerators and TV; kitchen available for all guests. Singles $45, with bath $79. Doubles $65, with bath $89. Triples $75, with bath $99. Reservations recommended.

Riverview Hotel, 113 Jane St. (929-0060, fax 675-8581), near West St. on the Hudson in Greenwich Village, and between W. 12th and W. 14th St. Subway: #1 or 9 to Christopher St. Moderately safe area, particularly for two or more. Clean and friendly, but no frills. Singles are cramp-inducingly small but doubles are decent. No deadbolts on room doors. Shared co-ed bathrooms on the hall. Singles w/TV $25. Doubles $39.

Senton Hotel, 39-41 W. 27th St. (684-5800), at Broadway. Subway: R to 28th St. Comfortable beds in spacious quarters, amidst a bevy of large-print floral wallpapers. TV, including HBO, cable, and dirty movies. Basic accommodations—spartan but newly renovated, with a shockingly incongruous bright-blue paint job. Not the best of neighborhoods at night, but the hotel has 24-hr. security and guests are not allowed. Singles with communal hall bath $40. Doubles $60. Suites (2 double beds) $65.

Hotel Grand Union, 34 E. 32nd St. (683-5890, fax 689-7397), between Madison and Park Ave. Subway: #6 to 33rd St. Centrally located but reasonably priced. big, comfy rooms equipped with cable TV, phone, A/C, a mini-fridge, and full bathroom. Friendly, 24-hr. security. Singles $70. Doubles $90. Will allow extra people in a room. Major credit cards accepted.

Arlington Hotel, 18-20 W. 25th St. (645-3990, fax 633-8952), between Fifth and Sixth Ave. Subway: F or R to 23rd St. Prides itself on hospitality and courteous service. Clean-smelling refurbished rooms, all with TV and A/C. Single or double (with one bed) $68. Double (with two beds) or triple $80. 10% discount with ISIC. No visitors after 11pm.

Malibu Studios Hotel, 2688 Broadway (222-2954, fax 678-6842), at 103rd St. Subway: #1 or 9 to 103rd St. Tropical motif. 2nd and higher floors on a funky block. Brightly-lit blue rooms with refrigerator and hot plate. Variable rates hover around $35 for a single with shared bath, $60 for a private bath; doubles $50, with private bath $70. Unusually clean for a budget hotel. Ask about student, off-season, and weekly and monthly discounts. No wheelchair access.

Madison Hotel, 21 E. 27th St. (532-7373 or 595-9100, fax 686-0092), at Madison Ave. Subway: #6, N, or R to 28th St. Dark, tight hallways with precipitous stairs, but big rooms with color TV, refrigerator sets, and newly-renovated private baths once you get there. 10-day max. stay. $5 key deposit. Singles $65. Doubles $70.

Hotel Stanford, 43 W. 32nd St. (563-1480, fax 629-0043), between Fifth Ave. and Broadway. Subway: B, D, F, N, or R to 34th St. The lobby glitters with sparkling ceiling lights and a well-polished marble floor (and adjoins the *extremely* authentic Gimme OK restaurant, which serves up such delicacies as ox-bone soup, pork bellies, and cow's feet). Rooms well-cooled and impeccably clean, with firm mattresses and plush carpeting. TV, and A/C. Check-out at noon. Reservations strongly recommended. Singles $80. Doubles $90. Twins $100. Triples $120. 10% discount for students with ID

.Milford Plaza, 270 W. 45th St. (869-3600 or 800-221-2690, fax 944-8357), between Eighth Ave. and Broadway. Subway: #1, 2, 3, 9, N, or R to 42nd St.-Times Sq. Smack in the heart of the theater district, this hulking 1300-room hotel's greatest asset is its location. In a process of renovation that will be completed by April

1995. New rooms are comfortable and extremely clean, all with A/C and TV. Fitness center for guests and a deli (open 24 hrs.) in lobby. Check-in 3pm, check-out noon. Singles $95-135. Doubles $110-150. **"Lulla-buy" package,** offered Sun.-Thurs. nights, includes a double room, breakfast, and dinner at the hotel's Honolulu Steamship Co. restaurant for $99. Advance reservations recommended, especially June-Sept. Wheelchair access.

■■■ BED AND BREAKFASTS

Bed and Breakfasts (private homes which rent out one or more spare rooms to travelers) are a great alternative to impersonal hotel and motel rooms. They're hardly your stereotypical B&Bs—no sleepy New England village squares or big front porches—but Manhattan does have a wide selection. Many don't have phones, TVs, or showers with their rooms. Reservations should be made a few weeks in advance, usually with a deposit. Most apartments listed have two-night minimums. Listings are divided into "hosted"—meaning traditional B&B arrangements—and "unhosted," meaning that the people renting you the apartment will not be there. Most agencies offer a wide range of prices, depending on the accommodation's size and quality and the neighborhood's safety. Apartments in the West Village and the Upper East Side cost the most. Most agencies also list accommodations in boroughs other than Manhattan; these can be an excellent budget alternative.

As an alternative to standard B&Bs, contact the **U.S. Servas Committee,** 11 John St., Ste. #407, New York, NY 10038-4009 (212-267-0252; fax 212-267-0292), an international cooperative system of hosts and travelers. This non-profit organization provides travelers with hosts for two nights. Applications with references and an interview are required. Participation in the program costs $55 per year per traveler, with a $25 deposit on host lists, but travelers and hosts do not exchange money.

New York Bed and Breakfast, 134 W. 119th St. (666-0559), between Lenox and Adam Clayton Powell Ave. in Harlem. Subway: #2 or 3 to 116th St. or 125th St. Run by the incredibly warm and friendly Gisèle, this B&B features a double and single bed in every well-kept room, croissants, and the unfriendly black cat Alain. (Alain is restricted to certain rooms, so folks with allergies need not fret.) 2-day min. stay. Gisèle lives in the brownstone, so no lockout time. $20 per room per night. Call 1-2 weeks in advance during the summer. Gisèle runs tours of Harlem, trips to jazz clubs and gospel choirs, and rents bicycles.

Bed and Breakfast of New York (645-8134). 300 listings throughout the city. 25% deposit required when you make your reservations, refundable up to 10 days before your visit, minus $20 booking fee. Deposits payable by personal check, but only cash, certified checks, or traveler's checks accepted for the bill. Hosted accommodations: singles $50-70, doubles $80-90. Unhosted one-bedroom apartments from $80-175. Weekly and monthly rates available.

New World Bed and Breakfast (675-5600 or toll-free from U.S. and Canada, 800-443-3800). About 150 listings, in all parts of Manhattan. When you make your reservation, you must pay with your credit card 25% of the total bill as a deposit; refundable up to five days before your visit, with $15 cancellation fee. Hosted accommodations: singles $55-70 (most around $65), doubles $65-80. Unhosted apartments: singles and doubles $70-100, triples $120-140, quads $150-160.

Urban Ventures (594-5650, fax 947-9320). The oldest and most established agency in the city. A whopping 700 listings covering most neighborhoods in Manhattan. 2-night min. Hosted accommodations: singles $55-80, doubles $65-90, triples from $100. Unhosted accommodations: studio apartments $75-110, one-bedroom $110-140, two-bedroom $165-230.

Eating & Drinking

This city takes its food seriously. For those whose culinary experience has been limited to the classic American strip-mall fast-food joint, New York will dazzle you with its stupendous culinary bounty, serving the needs of its diverse (and hungry) population. Ranging from mom-and-pop diners to elegant five-star restaurants, the food offered here will suit all appetites and pocketbooks.

New York's restaurants do more than the United Nations to promote international goodwill and cross-cultural exchanges. City dining spans the globe, with eateries ranging from relatively tame sushi bars to wild combinations like Afghani/Italian and Mexican/Lebanese. In a city where the melting pot is sometimes less than tranquil, one can still peacefully sample Chinese pizza or a Cajun knish. Just remember to be open-minded: you won't get very far in New York if you eat only what you can pronounce.

Chinese restaurants spice up every neighborhood and even fill up a town of their own. For a taste of bell'Italia, cruise to Mulberry Street in Little Italy. For the most realistic of post-post-revolutionary Russian cuisine, make a trip to Brooklyn's Brighton Beach, where Soviet emigrés have built their community. Many Eastern European dishes have become New York staples. The plump traditional dumplings (*knishes*) make a great lunch; eat potato knishes with mustard or meat knishes with *yoich* (gravy). Fill up on *pirogi,* Polish (or Ukrainian or Russian) dough creations stuffed with fruit, potato, or cheese and garnished with fried onions and sour cream; sample some spicy Polish *kielbasa* (sausage), or pig out on *blintzes,* thin pancakes rolled around sweet cheese, blueberries, and other divine fillings. Grab a *bialy,* a flat, soft, onion-flavored bagel cognate, from a local bakery.

And of course there are always two old favorites: pizza and bagels. New Yorkers like their pizza thin and hot, with no shortage of grease. Warfare between pizzerias has been going on for years; the major issue is not the taste but the name. There are now a full 22 institutions fighting over the right to call themselves the Original Ray's. Who is Ray? Who cares? No-name pizzerias can offer fare as fine as titled competitors. The humble bagel is mighty Brooklyn's major contribution to Western civilization. Bagels come in a rainbow of flavors—the most common being plain, egg, poppyseed, and onion—but only one shape, well suited for a thick layer of cream cheese. Exiles from the city often find bagel deprivation to be one of the biggest indignities of life outside of New York.

Those low on cash can take advantage of the inexpensive lunch specials offered by otherwise unapproachable restaurants—a large Hungarian lunch can be yours for $5. Almost any local coffeeshop will serve you a full American breakfast with eggs, bacon, toast, and coffee for $2-3. Don't expect to find any gargantuan supermarkets in this town; the many bakeries, corner markets, and greengrocers make New York's streets more fruitful than air-conditioned aisles. Atriums and public parks throughout the city provide idyllic urban settings for picnics, and many of the larger museums offer picturesque, artwork-filled cafés to facilitate your digestion. For those who like to eat on the street, pushcart vendors abound. Sidewalk gourmands can stick with the old roving standbys on wheels (hot dogs, pretzels, roasted chestnuts), or try something more adventurous (shish kebabs, felafel, knishes).

New Yorkers dine later than most Americans. In New York you can find a restaurant open and serving dinner almost anytime between afternoon and midnight. Make reservations or arrive before 7pm to beat the crowds to the best tables in the house. Remember to read the daily specials on the wall, and don't judge a restaurant by its façade; good things often come in a dingy package.

ORGANIZATION

We have prefaced the restaurant listings, which are organized by neighborhood, with a list of the same restaurants, categorized by type of food and by features (delivery, open late, outdoor dining, etc.). The "Splurge" category consists of restaurants where a typical entree costs $10-15. Restaurants in the "*Let's Go* Pick" category feature extraordinary combinations of low prices and quality and are denoted in the *By Type of Food*, *By Feature*, and *By Neighborhood* listings with a star (★). Every restaurant listed in the *By Type of Food* and *By Feature* sections is followed by an abbreviated neighborhood label, which directs you to the section within the *By Neighborhood* list where you'll find the restaurant's complete write-up. The abbreviations used are as follows:

EM	East Midtown		CHT	Chinatown
WM	West Midtown		LI	Little Italy
LEM	Lower East Midtown		FD	Financial District
CH	Chelsea		B	Brooklyn
UES	Upper East Side		Q	Queens
UWS	Upper West Side		BX	Bronx
H	Harlem		SI	Staten Island
GV	Greenwich Village		HO	Hoboken, NJ
ST	SoHo and TriBeCa		★	*Let's Go* pick
EV	East Village, Lower East Side, and Alphabet City			

BY TYPE OF FOOD

New American

Aunt Sonia's *B*
★Bubby's *ST*
Coldwaters *EM*
The Cupping Room *ST*
The Ear Inn *ST*
Eighteenth and Eighth *CH*
Elephant and Castle *GV*
Hourglass Tavern *WM*
O'Lunney's *WM*
Prince St. Bar and Restaurant *ST*
Quantum Leap *GV*
Short Ribs *B*
Soups Café *GV*
★Yaffa's Tea Room *ST*

Standard American

Around the Clock *EV*
Diane's Uptown *UWS*
EJ's Luncheonette *UES*
Empire Kosher Chicken Restaurant *Q*
First Edition *Q*
Hamburger Harry's *FD*
Jackson Hole Wyoming *UES*
Jimmy's Famous Heros *B*
Junior's *B*
Moon Dance Diner *ST*
Ottomanelli's Café *UES*
Oysters Bar and Restaurant *EM*

Roll-n-Roasters *B*
Urban Grill *UES*
Utopia-W-Restaurant *CH*
Viand *UES*
Washington Square Diner *GV*

Bakery

Bel Gusto Bagel Smashery and
   Café *HO*
College Bakery *B*
Damascus Bakery *B*
Galaxy Pastry Shop *Q*
★H&H Bagels *UWS*
Hammond's Finger Lickin' Bakery *B*
Hot Bagels and Tasty Bakery *UWS*
The Hungarian Pastry Shop *UWS*
Les Friandises *UES*
New Lung Fong Bakery *CHT*
Ruggieri Pastry Shop *BX*
Sarabeth's Kitchen *UES*
Sea Lane Bakery *B*
Yonah Schimmel Knishery *EV*

Barbecue and Ribs

Brother Jimmy's BBQ *UES*
Brother's BBQ *ST*
Dallas BBQ *UWS*
Jack 'n' Jill's *Q*
Short Ribs *B*

British

Tea and Sympathy *UWS*

Café

Café Gitane
Café Lalo *UWS*
Café Mozart *UWS*
Caffè Biondo *LI*
Caffè Borgia *GV*
Catte del Corso *WM*
Caffè Dante *GV*
Caffè Egidio *BX*
Caffè Margherita *BX*
Caffè Reggio *GV*
Caffè Roma *LI*
The Cloister Café *ST*
Dean and Deluca Espresso *GV*
De Lillo Pastry Shop *BX*
Ferrara *LI*
La Bella Ferrara *LI*
La Petit Café *ST*
Lo Spuntino *LI*
Maria Caffè *EM*
Ottomanelli's Café *UES*
Pink Pony Café *EV*
Sarabeth's Kitchen *UES*

Candy

Philip's Confections *B*

Central and Eastern European

★Primorski Restaurant *B*
Stylowa Restaurant *B*
Teresa's *B*
Ukrainian East Village Restaurant *EV*
Uncle Vanya Café *WM*
Veselka *EV*
Yonah Schimmel Knishery *EV*

Chinese

Dumpling King II *EM*
Empire Szechuan Balcony *LEM*
Empire Szechuan Gourmet *UWS*
Empire Szechuan Restaurant *LEM*
Excellent Dumpling House *CHT*
Fortune Garden *EM*
Hong Fat *CHT*
House of Vegetarian *CHT*
HSF *CHT*
★La Caridad *UWS*
La Favorita *CH*
Mee Noodle Shop and Grill *EV*
New Lung Fong Bakery *CHT*
Ollie's *UWS*
Oriental Palace *B*
Oriental Pearl *CHT*

Peking Duck House *CHT*
★Sam Chinita *CH*
Tibetan Shambala *UWS*
20 Mott St. Restaurant *CHT*
Tang Tang Noodles and More *UES*
Yeun Yeun Restaurant *CHT*
Zen Palate *LEM*

Creole, Cajun, and Caribbean

Daphne's Hibiscus *LEM*
Donna's Jerked Chicken *B*
Hammond's Finger Lickin' Bakery *B*

Deli

Broadway Farm *FD*
Carnegie Delicatessen *WM*
Commodore Gourmet Deli *EM*
Fulton Seaport Deli *FD*
Jimmy's Famous Heros *B*
Katz's Delicatessen *EV*
★Pastrami King *Q*
Second Ave. Delicatessen *EV*

Diner

Bendix Diner *CH*
Bi-Metro *B*
EJ's Luncheonette *UES*
Frank's Papaya *FD*
Jackson Hole, Wyoming *UES*
Moon Dance Diner *ST*
★Tom's Restaurant *B*
Tom's Restaurant *H*
Washington Square Diner *GV*

Ethiopian

★Abyssinia *ST*
The Blue Nile *UWS*

Fast Food

Frank's Papaya *FD*
McDonald's *FD*
Nathan's *B*
Roll-n-Roaster *B*

Greek and Middle Eastern

Cleopatra's Needle *UWS*
Fountain Café *B*
Khyber Pass Restaurant *EV*
Moroccan Star *B*
Olive Tree Café *GV*
Stacy's *B*
Time-Out Kosher Pizza and Israeli Food *H*
Uncle George's *Q*
Yaffa Café *EV*

Indian, Pakistani, and Afghan

★Al Hamra *EV*
Ariana Afghan Kebab *WM*
Indian Café *UWS*
Khyber Pass Restaurant *EV*
Madras Mahat *LEM*
Minar *WM*
Sirtaj *CH*

Italian

Ann & Tony's *BX*
Ballato *LI*
Bella Donna II *UES*
Benito One *LI*
Caffè del Corso *WM*
Caffè Sorrento *LI*
Cola's *CH*
★Cucina Stagionale *GV*
Dominick's *BX*
★ecco'la *UES*
Il Fornaio *LI*
Joe's Luncheonette *B*
La Mela *LI*
La Petit Café *ST*
Mangia é Bevi *WM*
Mappamondo *GV*
Maria Caffè *EM*
Mario's *BX*
Milo's Restaurant *B*
Paninoteca *LI*
Paolucci's *LI*
Pasquale's Rigoletto *BX*
Pietro and Vanessa *LI*
Puglia Restaurant *LI*
Ristorante Taormina *LI*
Rocky's Italian Restaurant *LI*
Taormina Ristorante *BX*
Tutta Pasta *GV*
Two Boots *EV*
Vincent's Clam Bar *LI*
Zigolini's *FD*

Japanese and Korean

Daikichi Sushi *UWS*
★Dosanko *EM*
Mill Korean Restaurant *H*
Obento Delight *UWS*
★Sapporo *WM*
Woo Chon Restaurant *Q*

Kosher

Bi-Metro *B*
Empire Kosher Chicken Restaurant *Q*

Ratner's Restaurant *EV*
Time-Out Kosher Pizza and
    Israeli Food *H*

Latin American and Spanish

★El Castillo de Jagua *B*
El Gran Castillo de Jagua *B*
El Pollo *UES*
Meson Sevilla *WM*
★La Caridad *UWS*
La Favorita *CH*
La Rosita *UWS*
★Las Tres Palmas *B*
★Sam Chinita *CH*
Spain *GV*

Mexican/Tex-Mex

Benny's Burritos *EV*
Buddy's Burrito and Taco Bar *B*
Dallas BBQ *UWS*
El Teddy's *ST*
★Kitchen *CH*
Lupe's East L.A. Kitchen *ST*
Mary Ann's *CH*
Poco Loco *WM*
Viva Pancho *WM*

Pizza

Arturo's Coal Oven Pizza *ST*
John's Pizzeria *GV*
★Louie's Pizza *Q*
Mimi's Pizza and Ristorante *UES*
Original Ray's Pizza and
    Restaurant *UWS*
Ray's Famous Original Pizza *LEM*
★Ray's Pizza *GV*
Sal and Carmine's Pizza *UWS*
Tony's Pizza *BX*

Roughage

Bennie's Café *UWS*

Seafood

Coldwaters *EM*
Cucina di Pesce *EV*
Joe's Clam Bar *B*
Mary Ann's *CH*
Oyster's Bar and Restaurant *EM*
Sidewalker's *UWS*
Vincent's Clam Bar *LI*
Waterfront Crabhouse *Q*

Soul Food and Southern Cookin'

Copeland's *H*

Dallas BBQ *UWS*
Jack 'n' Jill's *Q*
Monck's Corner *WM*
The Pink Teacup *GV*
Ray's Soul Kitchen *HO*
Sylvia's *H*

Southeast Asian
Bali Burma *WM*
Bendix Diner *CH*
BTI East *UES*
Gia Lam *B*
★Jai-ya *LEM*
Kuala Lumpur *Q*
★Mingala West *UWS*
Mueng Thai Restaurant *CHT*
Prince St. Bar and Restaurant *ST*
Road to Mandalay *CHT*
Thai House Café *ST*

Tibetan
Tibetan Kitchen *LEM*
Tibetan Shambala *UWS*

Vegetarian
★Dojo Restaurant *EV*
Eva's *GV*
House of Vegetarian *CHT*
Quantum Leap *GV*
Zen Palate *LEM*

BY FEATURES

Delivery
Ariana Afghan Kebab *WM*
Bali Burma *WM*
Brother's BBQ *ST*
★Bubby's *ST*
Coldwaters *EM*
Daikichi Sushi *UWS*
Dumpling King II *EM*
Empire Szechuan Balcony *LEM*
Fortune Garden *EM*
Hamburger Harry's *FD*
★Louie's Pizza *Q*
Maria Caffé *EM*
Mimi's Pizza and Ristorante *UES*
Minar *WM*
Obento Delight *UWS*
Original Ray's Pizza and
   Restaurant *UWS*
Sirtaj *CH*
Tibetan Kitchen *LEM*
Zen Palate *LEM*

Open Late
Al Hamra *EV*
Around the Clock *EV*
Broadway Farm *FD*
Café Lalo *UWS*
Café Mozart *UWS*
Caffè Borgia *GV*
Caffè Reggio *GV*
Carnegie Delicatessen *WM*
Commodore Gourmet Deli *EM*
Diane's Uptown *UWS*
Empire Szechuan Gourmet *UWS*
First Edition *Q*
Fulton Seaport Deli *FD*
★H&H Bagels *UWS*
Hong Fat *CHT*
Hot Bagels and Tasty Bakery *UWS*
HSF *CHT*
The Hungarian Pastry Shop *UWS*
Moon Dance Diner *ST*
Olive Tree Café *GV*
Original Ray's Pizza and
   Restaurant *UWS*
Philip's Confections *B*
Pink Pony Café *EV*
Tom's Restaurant *H*
Uncle George's *Q*
Veselka *EV*
Washington Square Diner *GV*
Woo Chon Restaurant *Q*
Yaffa Café *EV*

Outdoor Dining
Artura's Coal Oven Pizza *ST*
★Bubby's *ST*
Caffè Sorrento *LI*
The Cloister Café *EV*
Il Fornaio *LI*
Indian Café *UWS*
La Bella Ferrara *LI*
La Mela *LI*
Pietro and Vanessa *LI*

Let's Go Picks
★Abyssinia *ST*
★Al Hamra *EV*
★Bubby's *ST*
★Cucina Stagionale *GV*
★Dojo Restaurant *EV*
★Dosanko *EM*
★ecco'la *UES*
★El Castillo de Jagua *B*
★H&H Bagels *UWS*
★Jai-ya *LEM*
★Kitchen *CH*
★La Caridad *UWS*
★Las Tres Palmas *B*

★Louie's Pizza *Q*
★Mingala West *UWS*
★Pastrami King *Q*
★Primorski Restaurant *B*
★Ray's Pizza *GV*
★Sam Chinita *CH*
★Sapporo *WM*
★Tom's Restaurant *B*
★Yaffa's Tea Room *ST*

Splurge

Aunt Sonia's *B*
Cola's *CH*
Joe's Clam Bar *B*
Le Cirque *UES*
Lutece *EM*
Meson Sevilla *WM*
Spain *GV*
Waterfront Crabhouse *Q*

BY NEIGHBORHOOD

The restaurants listed under each neighborhood have been ranked by *Let's Go* according to our somewhat subjective appraisals of prices, quality, and atmosphere. Restaurants at the bottom of the listings are not necessarily crummy, as we don't list places that we wouldn't recommend. And if you're in the mood for Italian food, don't feel like you have to eat at the great Indian place at the top of our listings. The only restaurants we'll be mad at you for missing are denoted with our *"Let's Go* Pick" stars (★); these places are a true cut above the rest.

■■■ EAST MIDTOWN

East Midtown teems with restaurants. In this area where tycoons run their corporate empires and dine their clients well, prices can run up pretty quickly, but there is no need to despair—the tycoons' underlings all eat cheap lunches in this same area. Around noon to 2pm, the many delis and cafés become swamped with harried junior executives trying to eat quickly and get back to work. The 50s on Second Ave. and the area immediately surrounding Grand Central Station are filled with good, cheap fare. You might also check out grocery stores, such as the **Food Emporium,** 969 Second Ave. (593-2224), between 51st and 52nd, **D'Agostino,** Third Ave. (684-3133), between 35th and 36th, or **Associated Group Grocers,** 1396 Second Ave., between E. 48th and E. 49th St. These upscale supermarket chains, with branches scattered throughout Manhattan, feature reliable, well-stocked delis, fresh fruit and salad bars, ice cold drinks, gourmet ice cream, tons of munchies, and lots more—all at reasonable prices. This part of town has many public spaces (plazas, lobbies, parks) to picnic with your new purchases; try **Greenacre Park,** 51st St. between Second and Third; **Paley Park,** 53rd St. between Fifth and Madison; or the **United Nations Plaza,** 48th St. at First Ave.

★**Dosanko,** 423 Madison Ave. (688-8575), at E. 47th St. Japanese fast food; very cheap, very fast, and very good. The ramen is the dish to get, though not of the five-for-a-buck slacker variety ($5.30-7, depending on the toppings). A more sit-down location up a few blocks at 217 E. 59th St. (752-3936), between Second and Third Ave. Open Mon.-Fri. 11:30am-11pm, Sat.-Sun. noon-8pm.

Fortune Garden, 845 Second Ave. (687-7471, fax 687-3838), between E. 45th and E. 46th St. The prices in the restaurant are sky-high ($15-20), but if you get take-out, it's much cheaper. Weekday lunch is two appetizers and an entree (beef and broccoli, General Gao's chicken, or 16 other choices) for $6. Dinner entrees $7-11. Open daily 11:30am-3am.

Oysters Bar and Restaurant (490-6650), in Grand Central Station. Excellent seafood for the weary traveler. Opened soon after Grand Central itself, the restaurant has hosted celebrities such as Lillian Russell and famous eater Diamond Jim Brady. The prices are a little high, but the chowder is a great deal—$3.25 for a huge bowl. Ask for the sandwich menu, too. Open Mon.-Fri. 11:30am-9:30pm.

Dumpling King II, 986 Second Ave. (759-7070, 759-7553, 759-7554), at E. 53rd St. Small but amazingly tasty dumplings. 8 pork dumplings (steamed or fried) $4.75. The other dishes are great deals too (chicken *lo mein* $4.75), but they don't call it Dumpling King for nothin'. Another location at 1696 Second Ave. Open Mon.-Sat. 11am-midnight.

Maria Caffé, 973 Second Ave. (832-9053, fax 750-7125), between E. 51st and E. 52nd St. Pastries and pizzas made on the premises, and an incredible combo deal—$5 for pasta, salad, roll, and drink (daily 11am-3pm). Pita pizza $1.25, chicken cacciatore $6.50/lb. Small but very filling portions. Open daily 8am-9pm.

Commodore Gourmet Deli, 45 E. 45th St. (986-8692), at Vanderbilt Ave. Round-the-clock $4.29/lb. Mongolian buffet and $3-3.50 deli sandwiches. Also sells sundries and grocery items. Convenient to Grand Central Station. Open 24 hrs.

Coldwaters, 988 Second Ave. (888-2122), between E. 52nd and E. 53rd St. Seafood ($6-11) served under nautical paraphernalia and stained-glass lamps. Lunch is a bargain: two drinks (alcoholic or non), choice of entree, salad, and fries for $7 (daily 11:30am-4pm). Dinner is also a good deal: soup, salad, entree, and dessert for $12 (Mon.-Thurs. 4-7pm). Open daily 11:30am-3:30am.

■■■ WEST MIDTOWN

West Midtown smokes with summer heat, booms with construction, and buzzes with all types of promise, but only rarely does that promise include decent food at reasonable prices. Your best bets are generally along Eighth Ave. between 34th and 59th St. in the area known as **Hell's Kitchen.** Although once deserving of its name, this area has within the past few years given birth to a fantastically diverse array of ethnic restaurants. These places cater to a wide mix of people, many of whom arrive from swankier parts of the city and leave secure in the knowledge that not only have they been to Hell and back, but they've been well-fed and left a tip. Those whose resources reach down a little deeper should take a meal on posh **Restaurant Row,** on 46th St. between Eighth and Ninth Ave., which offers a solid block of elegant dining, often to a pre-theater crowd (arriving after 8pm will make getting a table easier).

The area's cheapest meals can be had along the **fast food** version of Restaurant Row, on the east side of Seventh Ave. between 33rd and 34th St. Besides the requisite McDonald's and Wendy's, you'll find Italian food and pizza, good Chinese food on buffet sold by the pound (only $3.69 at **Chinatown Express**), gyros, and Philly cheesesteaks.

Celebrities occasionally drift over to **Sardi's,** 234 W. 44th St., and take a seat on the plush, red leather, surrounded by caricatures of themselves and their best friends. Traditionally, on the opening night of a major Broadway play, the main star makes an exalted entrance following the show—to hearty cheers for a superb performance or polite applause for a bomb. If this exercise grows tedious, they may head to appealing but expensive Restaurant Row. Follow luminaries into **Joe Allen,** 326 W. 46th St., and marvel at posters of shows that closed in under a week. Farther uptown, near Carnegie Hall, lies the **Russian Tea Room,** 150 W. 57th St., a New York institution where dancers, musicians, and businesspeople meet to down caviar and vodka.

★ **Sapporo,** 152 W. 49th St. (869-8972), near Seventh Ave. A Japanese translation of the American diner, with the grill in full view. A favorite snack spot for Broadway cast members and corporate types alike, as well as many who can converse with the waiters in their native tongue. Menu items listed on the wall in Japanese (but don't worry—the menu explains in English). Portions are huge and flavors astounding. The *Sapporo ramen* special is a big bowl of noodles with assorted meats and vegetables, all floating around in a *miso* soup base ($5.85). Open Mon.-Fri. 11am-1am, Sat.-Sun. 11:30am-11:45pm.

Carnegie Delicatessen, 854 Seventh Ave. (757-2245), at 55th St. One of New York's great delis. Ceiling fans whir gently overhead as photos of famous (and, after eating here, well-fed) people stare out from the walls; you'll find everyone from Willis Reed to Oliver North to "Barney's friends." Eat elbow-to-elbow at long tables, and chomp on the free dill pickles. The "Woody Allen," an incredible pastrami and corned beef sandwich could easily stuff two people ($12.45), but sharing incurs a $3 penalty. First-timers shouldn't leave without trying the sinfully rich (and genuinely gargantuan) cheesecake topped with strawberries, blueberries, or cherries ($5.45). Open daily 6:30am-4am.

Ariana Afghan Kebab, 769 Ninth Ave. (307-1612 or 307-1629), between 51st and 52nd St. With about the dimensions of a shoebox (and possibly the *exact* dimensions of some boxes you'll find at the Big and Tall Store), this place serves up excellent Afghani food at reasonable prices. Check out the ceiling fans modeled on the nose of an old Tiger Shark fighter plane, and don't miss the adoring portrait of Ronald Reagan, supporter of the Afghan rebels against the Soviets. Try the *beef tikka kebab,* chunks of beef marinated and cooked over wood charcoal, served with rice, bread, and salad ($7.50), or the *mushawa* soup, with fresh veggies, lentils, and spices ($3). Open Mon.-Sat. noon-10pm.

Mangia é Bevi, 800 Ninth Ave. (956-3976, fax 977-3754), at 53rd St. Much like those trendy types now wearing platform shoes and other forms of 70s chic, the owners of this restaurant have realized that fashion travels in cycles and have hence positioned themselves on the cutting edge of hipness. The red and white checkered tablecloths and standard ceiling fans, which only a few years ago had been relegated to the worst of Oklahoma-Italian, have recently been labeled "refreshing" by *New York* magazine, and a host of well-dressed gentry crowd themselves in daily (and nightly) to feast on the fine food. The *taglioni al pesto* (pasta in pesto sauce, $6) is great, and the *penette alla vodka* (pasta in vodka sauce, $6.50) is always sure to tempt. Meat and fish entrees run higher ($9.50-14). Open daily 11:30am-midnight.

Bali Burma, 651 Ninth Ave. (265-9868, fax 307-5795), between 45th and 46th St. Sheer white walls, solid blue tablecloths, and the soothing Burmese pipe music that's piped in all contribute to the subdued, relaxing atmosphere of this restaurant. Good food served in plentiful portions. The Rangoon Night Market Noodles ($7) are a favorite, and the lunch specials, served with soup or salad, a shrimp spring roll, and Indonesian red rice ($5, daily 11:30am-4pm) are a great bargain. Open daily 11:30am-10pm.

Viva Pancho, 156 W. 44th St. (944-9747), between Sixth and Seventh Ave. Neon and cactus rule inside this somewhat generic restaurant, which advertises itself as "The Home of the Sizzling Fajitas." Friendly folks guzzle margaritas and sangria by the pitcher. Regular entrees ($9-11) include fajitas, enchiladas, *chile rellenos,* and *flautas,* but the real reason to come is the all-you-can-eat meal ($8) served Mon. 4:30-11:30pm. Otherwise, you're better off with the bar menu, where most items (such as burritos and tacos) run $4.50. Open Mon.-Thurs. 11:30am-11:30pm, Fri. 11:30am-midnight, Sat. 3pm-midnight, Sun. 3-11pm.

Hourglass Tavern, 373 W. 46th St. (265-2060), between Eighth and Ninth Ave. A tiny, theater-crowd-crowded, and dark triangular joint with a limited menu that changes weekly. Waitresses flip an hourglass at your table when you sit down— the 59-min. time limit is strictly enforced when people are waiting. The menu describes this policy as "part of the game we play!" Dramatized in John Grisham's *The Firm* as the covert meeting-place for two cloak-and-dagger types. *Prix fixe* entrees ($12.75) include soup or salad. Lunch entrees, offered a la carte, are less expensive ($7.25-9.50). Full bar and cheap wine. Open daily for lunch 11:30am-2:15pm, for dinner 5-11:15pm.

Poco Loco, 598 Ninth Ave. (765-7626), at 43rd St. Much higher on the *haute cuisine* ladder than most Mexican restaurants—the "Chef de Cuisine" is even credited on the menu. Elegant atmosphere complements complex, delicious main courses ($9-15) like the grilled breast of chicken with poblano mashed potatoes, crispy red onion, and jalapeño cranberry jam ($11). That's one of the simpler ones—burritos and enchiladas ($7-8.50) also available under the somewhat dismissive heading "Other Fare." Sip a papaya or mango frozen margarita ($4.50) while you eat. Open daily 11:30am-midnight.

Monck's Corner, 644 Ninth Ave. (397-1117, fax 262-6517), at 45th St. Although lacking seating and offering only take-out or free delivery, Monck's is the home to truly delectable Southern homestyle cooking. Those new to Southern cooking should opt for the mainstays: Southern fried chicken (with collard greens and potato salad, $7) or the spare ribs (with collard greens and potato salad, $8). Veterans looking for a little adventure might want to sample the oxtail stew ($7) or the vegetarian entree ($7), which includes yams, macaroni and cheese, okra, mixed vegetables, and string beans. The sweet potato pie is a great finish. Open Mon.-Sat. 1-9pm.

Minar, 9 W. 31st St. (684-2199), between Fifth Ave. and Broadway. Although narrow and long like a subway platform and sharing a similar color scheme, this Indian restaurant still manages to pack in many of the neighborhood's South Asians for lunch and dinner. (Hint: it's because of the food.) Tasty, spicy vegetable curries ($4-4.25) and "non-vegetable" curries ($4-5) are served with a small salad and choice of bread (go with the *nan*—an unleavened flour variety—it's delicious). Open daily 10:30am-10pm.

O'Lunney's, 12 W. 44th St. (840-6688), between Fifth and Sixth Ave. The motto on the menu (given in both English and Old Irish) reads "Hunger makes a good sauce," and indicates the kind of plain and hearty hospitality you can expect from this place. Very Irish, with Guiness on tap and many regulars. Try the corned beef with boiled cabbage, potato, and salad ($11.50). Kitchen open Mon.-Fri. 11:30am-11:30pm, Sat. 6-11:30pm. Bar open Mon.-Sat. until 4am.

Uncle Vanya Café, 315 W. 54th St. (262-0542), between Eighth and Ninth Ave. Marionettes hang from the ceiling and the *samovar* reigns in this cheerful yellow café. Delicacies of czarist Russia range from *borscht,* a hot or cold soup of beets, cabbage, and tomatoes served with sour cream and dill ($3) to *teftley,* Russian meatballs in sour cream sauce ($5.50) to caviar (market price—a concession to capitalism). Undiscovered, homey, and very good. Open Mon.-Sat. noon-11pm, Sun. noon-10pm.

Meson Sevilla, 344 W. 46th St. (262-5890), between Eighth and Ninth Ave. Prices may be too high for those on a shoestring budget, but this is one of the best values on Restaurant Row. The pre-theater crowd dines here on white linen, savoring the Continental Spanish and Italian cuisine. The favored choice and house specialty is Spanish *paella,* yellow rice with carefully arranged seafood ($13.50). Pasta dishes ($9-10) are the most affordable. Open daily noon-midnight.

■■■ LOWER EAST MIDTOWN

Straddling the extremes, the lower Midtown dining scene is neither fast-food commercial nor *haute cuisine* trendy. Instead, this slightly gentrified, ethnically diverse neighborhood features many places where an honest meal is wed to reasonable prices. On Lexington in the upper 20s, Pakistani and Indian restaurants battle for customers, some catering to a tablecloth crowd, others serving take-out. Liberally sprinkled throughout are Korean corner shops that are equal parts grocery and buffet bars. You can often fill up on prepared pastas, salads, and hot entrees, paying for them by the pound. The main eating areas are Lexington Ave. and Third Ave., in the upper 20s and low 30s. Delis and Chinese restaurants abound, as do a variety of other ethnic restaurants. On 18th Street and Irving Place, among rows of 19th-century red-brick houses, you'll run into **Pete's Tavern.** Operating since 1864, it claims to be the oldest saloon in New York. Legend has it that O. Henry, who lived nearby, wrote his "The Gift of the Magi" in one of the booths.

★ **Jai-ya,** 396 Third Ave. (889-1330), at 28th St. Thai and Oriental food that the critics rave over, with three different degrees of spiciness, from mild to "help-me-I'm-on-fire." *Pad thai* $8—a definite steal. Another location at 81-11 Broadway in Elmhurst, Queens. Open daily Mon.-Fri. 11:30am-midnight, Sat. noon-midnight, Sun. 5pm-midnight.

Daphne's Hibiscus, 243 E. 14th St. (505-1180 and 505-1247), between Second and Third Ave. Dim lighting and intricate woodwork give this Caribbean restaurant an authentic Jamaican feel. Try the chicken cooked in coconut milk ($11), the jerk pork ($9), or the special meat-filled pastries called "patties." Most entrees $7.50-9.50. The plantains make an excellent side dish. Happy hour Mon.-Fri. 5-7pm. Open Tues.-Thurs. 11am-11pm, Fri. 11am-midnight, Sat. 4pm-midnight, Sun noon-4pm and 6-10pm.

Zen Palate, 34 E. Union Sq. (614-9345, fax 614-9401), across from the park. Gourmet veggie food, with an Asian twist (but not really Asian...maybe Asian-American). Stir-fried rice fettucini ($6.50)? Moo shu, Mexican style ($7.45)? Who knows? It's good, though. Delivery available in limited range. Open Mon.-Sat. 11:30am-3pm and 5-11pm, Sun. 5-10:30pm.

Tibetan Kitchen, 444 Third Ave. (679-6286), between 30th and 31st St. Small place but excellent food. Meatier than Chinese, with a dollop of Indian thrown in, Tibetan food is filling and tasty. *Momo* (beef dumplings, "Tibet's most popular dish," $7.25) and *bocha*, Tibetan buttered and salted tea, should both be tried. Open Mon.-Fri. noon-3pm and 5:30-11pm, Sat. 5:30-11pm.

Empire Szechuan Balcony, 381 Third Ave. (685-6215, 685-6961, 685-6962, or 685-6670), between 27th and 28th St. Mirrored walls and leafy plants rim this purple-trimmed, multi-tiered Chinese food emporium. Well-cooked, tasty Chinese fare, refreshingly free of goo, oil, and MSG. Entrees $6-10. Open Mon.-Fri. 10:30am-midnight, Sat.-Sun. 11:30am-midnight.

Madras Mahat, 104 Lexington Ave. (684-4010), between 27th and 28th St. In a paean to multicultural correctness, this vegetarian Indian restaurant is owned by a Catholic and has been approved as strictly kosher. $7 all-you-can-eat veggie chowdown Mon.-Fri. 11:30am-3pm, entrees $6-9, combination platter $14. Open Mon.-Fri. 11:30am-3pm and 5-10:30pm, Sat.-Sun. noon-10:30pm.

Ray's Famous Original Pizza, 77 Lexington Ave. (686-2349 and 686-2299), at 26th St. One of the 22 "Original" Ray's Pizzas in NYC. Lovely grease-dripping, cheese-laden, crusty-doughed pizza. Don't look for atmosphere here—just pizza at small fiberglass tables, serve-yourself-please-style. Slice $1.55, large pepperoni pie $13.35. Open daily 10am-11pm.

■■■ CHELSEA

Finding food in Chelsea isn't always easy. Good food tends not to be cheap, and cheap food is rarely good. The neighborhood is dotted with fake-retro diners that offer unexceptional $6 hamburgers and $7 omelettes. These establishments are ideologically corrupt, and thus should be eschewed. The best offerings are the products of the large Mexican and Central American community in the southern section of the neighborhood. From 14th Street to 22nd Street, restaurants offer combinations of Central American and Chinese cuisine as well as varieties of Cajun and Creole specialties. Eighth Avenue provides the best restaurant browsing. Pool sharks willing to pay a little more for their meal for the chance to play a game of eight-ball should check out the echoing, cavernous **Billiard Club,** 220 W. 19th St. (206-7665), where you can get lunch for two and an hour on a table for $17 (pool table alone $5/hr.).

★ **Kitchen,** 218 Eighth Ave. (243-4433), near 21st St. A real kitchen specializing in Mexican food, with hot red peppers dangling from the ceiling. All food to go; there's no dining room. Burrito stuffed with pinto beans, rice, and green salsa ($5.70). Open Sun.-Thurs. 11:30am-9:30pm, Fri.-Sat. 11:30am-10pm.

★ **Sam Chinita Restaurant,** 176 Eighth Ave., at 19th St. A red '50s diner with turquoise curtains serves up Spanish-and-Chinese cuisine. Dozens of deals under $6. Try the yellow rice with chicken Latin-style ($6). Daily lunch specials $3-6 (noon-4pm). Open daily 11:45am-11pm.

Bendix Diner, 219 Eighth Ave. (366-0560), at 21st St. A new hybrid—the Thai greasy spoon. Try the stir-fried noodles with vegetables ($7) or play it safe with a burger ($3.75). Pies and sandwiches, too. Open Mon.-Sat. 7am-1am, Sun. 7am-11pm.

Cola's, 148 Eighth Ave. (633-8020), near 17th St. Classic Italian cuisine in a simple setting. Restaurant critic Jeff LeBeau calls it one of the best Italian places in the city. Try *linguine alla vongole,* with baby clams, parsley, and garlic ($9.50). BYOB. Open for dinner only Sun.-Thurs. 4-11pm, Fri.-Sat. 4-11:30pm.

Mary Ann's, 116 Eighth Ave. (633-0877), at 16th St. Benevolent waiters serve up huge portions in this white-walled, wood-finished restaurant hung with *piñatas* and slung with lights. Inventive and unusual Mexican cuisine, often in surprising marriages with seafood. Try the enchilada stuffed with shrimp and snowcrab served in *tomatillo* sauce ($9.25) or the tuna tacos ($11). Most entrees $9-11. Popular and crowded. Open Mon.-Sat. 11:30am-11pm, Sun. noon-10pm.

Eighteenth and Eighth, Eighth Ave. (242-5000), at 18th St. (duh). Between the artsy-looking regular customers and the photography display, this slightly cramped room has the feel of a downtown gallery. The masterpiece is the constantly changing menu, which does wonderful things to chicken, fish, vegetables, and tropical fruit. Curry-mango chicken, $9; other entrees $7-15. Desserts $3-5. Open daily 8am-midnight.

La Favorita, 114 Eighth Ave. (243-1736), near 16th St. Another example of that inexplicable culinary hybrid: Latin American and Chinese. Wild chicken rice Dominican-style glows fluorescent yellow ($5). Lunch specials $3.50-4. Open daily 11am-midnight.

Sirtaj, 36 W. 26th St. (989-3766 or 989-6492), between Broadway and Sixth Ave. A pink-walled, slightly grungy establishment serving dirt-cheap, decent Indian and Pakistani foods. The samosas (2 pieces for $1.25) make a satisfying light meal, and the curries ($3.50-5) make a satisfying heavy meal. Free delivery. Open daily 10:30am-8pm.

Utopia-W-Restaurant, 338 Eighth Ave. (807-8052), at 27th St. in the boxy shadow of the Fashion Institute of Technology. The school's chic diner. Heavy-duty meaty burgers on toasted buns (cheeseburger with fries $4.80). Dinner comes with a complimentary glass of wine. Open daily 6am-9:30pm.

Galaxy Diner, 174 Eighth Ave. (463-7460), near 19th St. Neither the decor nor the food is out of this world, but the waiters are funny, and it's a real neighborhood hangout. French toast and other breakfasts $3-4, sandwiches $4-5. Open daily 6am-1:30am.

■■■ UPPER EAST SIDE

Unless you feel like eating a large bronze sculpture or an Armani suit, you won't find many dining opportunities on Museum Mile along Fifth and Madison Ave., aside from some charming cappuccino haunts, brunch breweries, and near-invisible ritzy restaurants. You will find mediocre food at extraordinary prices in posh and scenic museum cafés where you can languish among ferns and sip espresso between exhibits.

For less glamorous and more affordable dining, head east of Park Ave. Costs descend as you venture toward the lower-numbered avenues, though many do not escape the Madison pricing orbit. Hot dog hounds shouldn't miss the 100% beef "better than filet mignon" $1.50 franks and exotic fruit drinks at **Papaya King,** 179 E. 86th St. (369-0648), off Third Ave. (open Sun.-Thurs. 8am-1am, Fri.-Sat. 9am-3am). Free, unlimited wine is served with meals at **Szechuan Hunan Cottage,** 1433 Second Ave. (535-1471), between 74th and 75th St. (open Sun.-Thurs. 11:30am-11pm, Fri.-Sat. 11:30am-11:30pm.) For a classic New York bagel, try **H&H East,** 1551 Second Ave. (734-7441), between 80th and 81st St., which bakes them round-the-clock, still using its original formula. Impervious to fads, H&H continues to deliver on its promise to put you in heaven. Don't feel confined to restaurant dining; grocery stores, delis, and bakeries speckle every block. You can buy your provisions here and picnic in honor of frugality in Central Park.

★ **ecco'la,** 1660 third ave. (860-5609), corner of 93rd st. if you don't mind waiting with the rest of the neighborhood, you're in for a lowercase fantasy. sit at hand-painted tables and eat fresh pasta pockets filled with lobster, mushrooms, scallions, and parsley in an avocado cream sauce ($9). pizza $8, pastas $8-9. open sun.-thurs. noon-11:45pm, fri.-sat. noon-12:30am.

Tang Tang Noodles and More, 1328 Third Ave. (249-2102/3/4), at 76th St. Cheap, hot, tasty Chinese noodles and dumplings. Not one noodle dish over $5.75—most around $5. Dense crowds but quick service, and very authentic food. Open Sun.-Thurs. 11:30am-11pm, Fri.-Sat. 11:30am-midnight.

El Pollo, 1746 First Ave. (996-7810), between 90th and 91st. This secret Peruvian dive has mastered the practice of cooking chicken and potatoes, which they serve with complimentary wine in their cramped bowling alley of a restaurant. Plump chickens are marinated and spit-roasted, topped with a variety of sauces. The *Menudencias Fritas* (sauteed gizzards' necks and hearts, $6) demonstrate the restaurant's waste-conscious preparation. The corkscrew fries ($2.50) alone make it worth the trip. The *quinoa* pudding is quite a taste treat for dessert. Half chicken $5. BYOB. Open daily 11:30am-11pm.

EJ's Luncheonette, 1271 Third Ave. (472-0600), at 73rd St. Diner extravaganza; Eternally crowded, but there's a good reason for it—huge portions of good food. The various combos of fruit toppings on pancakes have defeated many a diner. Blueberry-strawberry on buttermilk pancakes $6.50, plain buttermilk pancakes $4.75. Hamburgers also a great deal ($5.75, fries included). Chow down. Open Mon.-Thurs. 8am-11pm, Fri.-Sat. 8am-midnight, Sun. 8am-10:30pm.

BTI East, 1712 Second Ave. (427-1488), between 88th and 89th St. BTI stands for Burmese, Thai, and Indonesian, and that's what you get. As Hong Kong pop music bops along in the background, try as much as you can. Early bird dinner special ($7) includes entree, soup, and salad (Mon.-Fri. 4:30-6:30pm). Noodles $7 (*pad thai* $8), entrees $8-9.50. Open Mon.-Fri. noon-11pm, Sat.-Sun. noon-midnight. Complimentary wine with dinner.

Bella Donna II, 1663 First Ave. (534-3261), between 86th and 87th St. Also at 307 E. 77th St. (535-2866), between First and Second Ave. The mood isn't Venice or romantic violins and Lady and the Tramp, but the food is good enough that it doesn't matter that half of the Upper East is eavesdropping on you and your significant other's fight-*cum*-"discussion." Pasta in many configurations $6.75-11. The odor of garlic and olive oil oozes around you as you work your way through the food. Open daily 4-11pm.

Viand, 673 Madison Ave. (751-6622), between 61st and 62nd St. A real New York-style joint. The food is all pricey, except for the exceptional burgers. Cheeseburger $3.85, with fries, cole slaw, and toppings $5.65. Great atmosphere and nice staff. Open daily 6am-10pm.

Sarabeth's Kitchen, 1295 Madison Ave. (410-7335), at 92nd St. Well-dressed parents and children masticate in grand style in this erstwhile local bakery, now a bustling glossy duplex. Dinner prices are steep, but brunch addicts should join the masses, put their names down an hour early, stroll around the neighborhood, and return to sink their teeth into Dr. Seussian "green and white" eggs scrambled with cream cheese and scallions ($6.75). Budget-conscious sweet teeth can sample the amazingly delectable assortment of pastries, custards, and muffins while sipping cappuccino in the small café. Also at 423 Amsterdam Ave. (496-6280), at 81st St. Open Mon.-Thurs. 8am-3:30pm, Fri.-Sun. 9am-4pm and 6-11pm.

Ottomanelli's Café, 1662 York Ave. (772-7722), between 85th and 86th St., and many other locations on the Upper East Side, including 439 E. 82nd St. at York Ave. (737-1888), 1518 First Ave. at 79th St. (734-5544), 1370 York Ave. at 73rd St. (794-9696), 1315 Second Ave. at 69th St. (249-5656), and 1199 First Ave. at 65th St. (249-7878). Outposts of the vast and powerful Ottomanelli Empire that has supplied New York with meat and baked goods since 1900. No-frills setting but extraordinary fresh-baked goods. An impressive selection of bagels, breads, danish, and muffins 50¢-$1.25. After 5pm, buy a danish or muffin and get a 2nd for free. Open daily 6:30am-6:30pm.

Brother Jimmy's BBQ, 1461 First Ave. (545-RIBS), at 76th St. The sign proclaims "BBQ and booze, the stuff that makes America strong," and this greasy-chops kitchen serves up plenty of both under the watchful eyes of boars' heads nailed to the walls. Kids ride bareback on Jimmy's life-sized plastic promo-cow, which is wheeled around Upper East Side playgrounds every afternoon. Ribs $13, with 2 side dishes and corn bread. Sandwiches, for the less strong, $6-7. Kitchen open Sun.-Thurs. 5pm-midnight, Fri.-Sat. 11am-1am. Bar open "until you finish your last drink" or until around 4am (whichever comes first, presumably).

Urban Grill, 1613 Second Ave. (744-2122), between 83rd and 84th St. Straightforward grill food at reasonable prices and doodle-it-yourself tablecloths. Burgers $3.50-8 (bacon, cheese, mushroom, onion, with fries, lettuce, and tomato). Open daily 11am-1am.

Les Friandises, 972 Lexington Ave. (988-1616), between 70th and 71st St. *Une patisserie plus enchantée.* Pastries and baked goods; a bit pricey, but some of the best French pastries this side of the Atlantic. Muffins and croissants $1.50, slice of quiche $3, and many tempting desserts. Open Mon.-Sat. 8am-7pm.

Jackson Hole Wyoming, 1270 Madison Ave. (427-2820), at 91st St. This culinary institution, like its geographical namesake, attracts tan and lively urbanites on the romantic prowl. Half-pound burgers served in 37 variations amidst gleaming chrome for $4-8, $6.50-10 for a platter. Also at 64th St. between Second and Third Ave., and on Second Ave. between 82nd and 83rd St. Open daily 7am-11pm.

Mimi's Pizza and Ristorante, 1248 Lexington Ave. (861-3363), at 84th St. Pizza the way it should be: thin, crispy crust, spicy sauce, and the perfect amount of not-too-greasy cheese. Craved by New Yorkers, copied by impersonators (Mimmo's and Mimma's), and the favorite of at least one Englishman in New York—Paul McCartney. The pizza's not incredibly different from all the other first-name pizza joints, but the rickety seats and crowded counter make the mood here feel like a legit pizza parlor. Large pie $11.75, slice $1.50, spaghetti with meatballs $6, veal parmigiana $7.50. Unusual array of toppings, including spinach and sun-dried tomatoes, complements such standbys as pepperoni and peppers. Take-out and free delivery. Open daily 11am-11pm.

■■■ UPPER WEST SIDE

Unlike many other New York neighborhoods, the Upper West Side lacks a definitive typology of restaurants. Cheap pizza joints often neighbor chic eateries; street vendors hawk sausages in the shadow of pricey specialty stores. If browsing in Laura Ashley or Charivari makes you grumpy, go haggle at the Columbus Avenue Street Fair; if it makes you hungry, wander down the tempting aisles of **Zabar's,** 2245 Broadway (787-2002), the deli *cum* grocery that never ends. The vast array of restaurants in the area offers meals for the solitary as well as the social.

★ **La Caridad,** 2199 Broadway (874-2780), at 78th St. One of New York's most successful Chinese-Spanish hybrids. Feed yourself and a pack of burros with one entree. *Arroz con pollo* (¼-chicken with yellow rice) $5.55. Other entrees of the Americas, including *chop suey de cerdo ahumada*, $5-7. Fast-food ambience, but so what? Often crowded; beware of lines during lunch- and dinner-time rush. Open Mon.-Sat. 11:30am-1am, Sun. 11:30am-10:30pm.

★ **Mingala West,** 325 Amsterdam Ave. (873-0787), at 75th St. Burmese cooking uses rice noodles, peanut sauces, coconuts, and curries, yet tastes nothing like Thai or Indonesian food. With its lavender walls, ebony elephants, and photo of 1991 Burmese Nobel laureate Aung San Soo Kyi (still under house arrest in Burma), the place makes for a friendly introduction to a new cuisine. Generous $5 lunch specials (soup or salad, plus your choice of among twenty tantalizing entrees with rice or noodles) Mon.-Fri. noon-4pm; $6-9 "light meal" samplers 4:30-6:30pm. Glass noodles and beef dishes on the main menu ($7-13). Open Mon.-Thurs. noon-11pm, Fri.-Sat. noon-midnight.

Empire Szechuan Gourmet, 2574 Broadway (663-6004/5/6), at 97th St. A favorite of Upper West Siders (hence the 3 telephone numbers). Airy restaurant with modern decor—a nice contrast to the dingier Chinese places that line Broadway. Exhaustive menu features "revolution diet" section of low-calorie entrees, hors d'oeuvres (mostly $1), and *dim sum* ($1-6, Mon.-Fri. 10:30am-3:30pm and Sat.-Sun. 10am-3:30pm), as well as a sushi bar and Japanese dishes. Cold sesame noodles $4. Pint of soup $1.30. Beef with hot chili sauce $8.25. Generous lunch specials $5 (Mon.-Fri. 11:30am-3pm). Dinner coupons on take-out menus handed out in front of the restaurant. Free delivery. Open Mon.-Tues. 10:30am-midnight, Wed.-Sun. 10:30am-2am.

★ **H&H Bagels,** 2239 Broadway (595-8000), at 80th St. 65¢ bagels with a string of awards behind 'em; stop in if only to *smell* this bagelry. Call 1-800-NY-BAGEL to ship them anywhere in the world. Always open.

The Hungarian Pastry Shop, 1030 Amsterdam Ave. (866-4230), at 111th St. The West Side's worst-kept secret: plain, friendly, Boho pastry shop with *hamen-tashen* ($1.30). Eclairs, cake slices, and other goodies all around $2. Fine coffee too ($1.30). Write or read in the outdoor garden, or watch passersby on Amsterdam from the outdoor tables. Open Mon.-Fri. 8am-11:30pm, Sat. 9am-11:30pm, Sun. 9am-10pm.

Sal and Carmine's Pizza, 2671 Broadway (663-7651), between 101st and 102nd St. In a neighborhood dotted with hit-or-miss pizza shops, the $1.50 slices here will delight you with their exquisitely tangy cheese and tomato sauce. Large pie around $11. Open daily 11am-11pm.

Dallas BBQ, 27 W. 72nd St. (873-2004), between Columbus and Central Park West. Georgia O'Keefe-ish horse skulls and Navajo rugs have migrated to the walls of this kitschy NY eatery. Authentic Texas-style chicken and ribs on the same bill as tasty tempura and homey chicken soup. Big breakfast featuring 50¢ coffee. Early bird special (Mon.-Fri. noon-6:30pm, Sat.-Sun. noon-5pm) features soup, ½ chicken, cornbread, and potato for each member of a dining duo for $8 apiece. ½-lb. burger $5, Texas-style chili $4 per bowl. Greenwich Village location at 21 University Pl. (674-4450), at 8th St. Open Sun.-Thurs. noon-midnight, Fri.-Sat. noon-1am.

Hot Bagels & Tasty Bakery, 2079 Broadway (699-5611), between 71st and 72nd St. Tired of expensive, precious cafés? 4am and you've got the munchies? Seek refuge in this tiny bakery, which serves up all manner of delicious Italian pastries ($1-3), sandwiches ($2-4), coffee, and other delights. Take out or eat in at the counter or one of the few small tables. Open 24 hrs.

Indian Café, 2791 Broadway (749-9200), at 108th St. and West End Ave. Cozy Indian joint with pleasant outdoor and patio seating. Lunch specials $5-6, vegetarian entrees $6-9. Seafood dishes include shrimp *muglai* (sauteed with fresh ginger and garlic in a creamy curry sauce with almonds), $9-10. Treat yourself to a mango shake for $2.25. Open daily 11:30am-midnight.

The Blue Nile, 103 W. 77th St. (580-3232), between Columbus and Amsterdam Ave. No etiquette worries here; the waiter brings one tray and no silverware to your table. Sop up fine Ethiopian entrees with *injera,* a spongy pancake. Entrees from $7.25. Try the *doro wat,* a stewy blend of chick peas and chicken, which the menu describes as "NY's spiciest dish" ($11). Open Mon.-Thurs. 5-11pm, Fri. 5pm-midnight, Sat. noon-11pm, Sun. noon-midnight.

Cleopatra's Needle, 2485 Broadway (769-6969), between 92nd and 93rd St. Crackling jazzy vocals eerily reminiscent of Woody Allen soundtracks suit the snappy decor. Floor-to-ceiling windows open on Broadway. Roast cornish hen $8.25, various Middle Eastern entrees $7-10. The $2.75 felafel sandwich is a good lunch bet. Deli/takeout open daily 8am-11pm; restaurant open daily noon-midnight. Jazz piano Fri.-Sat. nights.

Diane's Uptown, 251 Columbus Ave. (799-6750), near 71st St. Large portions and reasonable prices make this popular, brass-railed, inexplicably dark café a student hangout. Spice up a 7-oz. burger ($4.50) with chili, chutney, or your choice of seven cheeses (85¢ per topping). Sandwiches $3-5, omelettes $3.90, onion rings and lots of fries $3. Frequently, burgers and omelettes are $1 off. Open daily 11am-2am.

Ollie's, 2315 Broadway (362-3111 and 362-3712), at 84th St. The requisite whole chickens hang inside the window, but the real marks of quality here are the wonderful smells of the noodle soups, most in the $5 range and the size of a meal. Come early to avoid the movie-going crowd. Brunch Sat.-Sun. 11:30am-4pm. Open Sun.-Thurs. 11:30am-midnight, Fri.-Sat. 11:30am-1am. Other locations (same hours and menus): 2957 Broadway at 116th St., and 190 W. 44th St. between Sixth and Seventh Ave.

Original Ray's Pizza and Restaurant, 462 Columbus Ave. (873-1134/5), between 82nd and 83rd St. Every branch of Ray's claims to be the original one; this one's claims appear no more authentic than most others'. But the pizza is outstanding, made with tender loving care using Neapolitan tomatoes, Wisconsin cheese, and fresh meat supplied by Neapolitan butchers. Large plain pie $12, with 1 topping $14.50. Just $1.75 for a slice the size of Manhattan. Tasty calzone $3-3.50. Take-out and free delivery. Open Mon.-Thurs. 10am-3am, Fri.-Sun. 10am-4am.

Daikichi Sushi, 2345 Broadway (362-4283), between 85th and 86th St. Ultra-cheap sushi served in plasticware. Selections like the Manhattan Special (8 pcs., $5.25) will satisfy your raw fish cravings so long as you don't demand the pinnacle of freshness. Eat in at the small counter, take out, or have it delivered free. Other locations throughout the city. Open daily 11am-10pm.

Café Lalo, 201 83rd St. (496-6031), at Amsterdam Ave. Fabulously popular and new-looking dessert café attracts struggling artists, young people, and loaded professionals; it's worth the short wait to join them all at their high tables and antique chairs amid the strains of the Baroque top 40. More than 60 different pastry and cake desserts, most of them excellent, $3-6; try any fruit tart. Not the best value for your café dollar, but probably the best food. Cappuccino $1.75. Peach, pear, or apricot nectar $1.25. Wine and beer from $2.75. Open Sun.-Thurs. noon-2am, Fri.-Sat. 11am-4am.

La Rosita, 2823 Broadway (663-7804), between 108th and 109th St. A bustling restaurant serving no-frills Dominican and Cuban food. Breakfast $2.50-4. Hamburgers $1.75, fried kingfish $6.75. Many dishes come with gigantic helpings of black beans and yellow rice. For dessert, have the famed Spanish flan (a caramel custard, $1.40). Open daily 7am-1am.

Tibet Shambala, 488 Amsterdam Ave. (721-1270), between 83rd and 84th St. Tasty Tibetan food, including many vegetarian dishes. $5.50 lunch specials Mon.-Fri. noon-4pm, dinner entrees $5.50-9. Reincarnation not included. Open daily noon-11pm.

Sidewalker's, 12 W. 72nd St. (799-6070), between Columbus Ave. and Central Park West. One of the best places in the city to enjoy hard-shell crabs. Order six Maryland spiced crabs and attack them with a wooden mallet and a sharp knife (price is seasonal, hovering around $18). Unique visceral pleasure, though not for the faint of heart. Open Mon.-Thurs. 5-11pm, Fri.-Sat. 5-11:30pm, Sun. 4-10pm.

Obento Delight, 210 W. 94th St. (222-2010), between Amsterdam Ave. and Broadway. Eating in? Consider sending out for fresh Japanese food at low prices. Drab battleship-gray decor and styrofoam cartons might rub some the wrong way, but the fish is fresh. *Miso* soup $1, *yakitori* (2 skewers of chicken and onion) $3, sashimi $7.50. Sushi a la carte from under $2. Electrify your senses with flamed eel in tantalizing sauce grounded in a heaping bowl of rice ($9). Lunch special (daily 11:30am-3:30pm) $4.25-8. Free delivery with a $7 min. Open daily 11:30am-11pm.

Bennie's Café, 321 Amsterdam Ave. (874-3032), at 75th St. Extensive selection of gourmet and homemade salad entrees $5 each. Open daily 11am-11pm.

Café Mozart, 154 70th St. (595-9797), between Broadway and Columbus Ave. Dainty, mock-sophisticated café featuring floral motifs, chairs a bit too small, and ever-poignant classical music. Good selection of Italian desserts (*cannoli, zabaglione,* etc.) $2.50-4.75. Lunch special (Mon.-Fri. 11am-2pm) is sandwich, quiche, or omelette, with soda or coffee and dessert ($6). The perfect spot to drink tea and read *Alice in Wonderland* after a hard day at Lincoln Center. Live classical music Mon.-Sat. 9pm-midnight, Sun. 3-6pm and 7-10pm. Open Mon.-Thurs. 11am-2am, Fri. 11am-3am, Sat. 10am-3am, Sun. 10am-2am.

■■■ HARLEM AND WASHINGTON HEIGHTS

Cheap food abounds in Harlem and Washington Heights. Ethnic food is everywhere, with Jewish food in Washington Hts., various Latino and Cuban foods in the Hispanic communities, collegiate fare around Columbia (small cafés, delis, pizza, and other Ivy League date food), and of course, all kinds of African-American cuisine—East and West African food, Caribbean and Creole, and some of the best soul food north of the Mason-Dixon Line. Try Lenox Ave., 125th St., or 116th St. in Harlem, the Columbia area, or the Yeshiva/Fort Washington area.

Sylvia's, 328 Lenox/Malcolm X Ave. (996-0660), at 126th St. Subway: #2 or 3 to 125th St. This touristy place has magnetized New York for over 20 years with enticing soul food dishes. Sylvia highlights her "World-Famous talked-about BBQ ribs special" with "sweet spicy sauce" (served with collard greens and macaroni and cheese, $10.50). Lunch special is a pork chop, collard greens, and candied yams for $6. Gospel Brunch Sun. 1-7pm with live music and soul food. Live music (Wed.-Fri. 7-9pm; no cover) features jazz and R&B.

Copeland's, 547 W. 145th St. (234-2357), between Broadway and Amsterdam Ave. Subway: #1 or 9 to 145th St. Sylvia's without the tourists; excellent soul food without the slick presentation. Smothered chicken $6.50; fried pork chop $7.20. Smorgasbord next door—cafeteria-style but just as good. Open Tues.-Thurs. 4:30-11:30pm, Fri. 4:30pm-midnight, Sat. noon-midnight, Sun. noon-9:30pm.

Time-Out Kosher Pizza and Israeli Food, 2549 Amsterdam Ave. (923-1180), between 185th and 186th St. on the campus of Yeshiva University. Subway: #1 or 9 to 181st St. The name says it all. Slice of kosher pizza $1.50. Kosher felafel $4.75. Bagel with lox $2.25. Open Sun.-Fri. 7am-7pm.

Tom's Restaurant, 2880 Broadway (864-6137), at 114th St. near Columbia. Subway: #1 or 9 to 116th St. "Doo-doo-*doo*-doo..." Suzanne Vega wrote that darn catchy tune about this diner. Greasy burgers for $3-5, dinner under $6.50. Open Mon.-Wed. 6am-1:30am and from Thurs. 6am-Sun. 1:30am. "Doo-doo-*doo*-doo..."

Mill Korean Restaurant, 2895 Broadway (666-7653), between 112th and 113th St. near Columbia. Subway: #1 or 9 to 110th St. Traditional, freshly prepared Korean food. Lunch specials Mon.-Fri. 11am-3pm ($5-7). Complete dinners with side dishes $7-10. Try the fiery stir-fried squid ($8 at dinner, $5.50 at lunch). Open daily 10:30am-10:30pm.

■■■ GREENWICH VILLAGE

Whatever your take on the West Village's bohemian authenticity, it's undeniable that all the free-floating artistic angst does result in many creative (and inexpensive) food venues. The aggressive and entertaining street life makes stumbling around and deciding where to go almost as much fun as eating.

Try the major avenues for cheap, decent food. The European-style bistros of **Bleecker Street** and **MacDougal Street,** south of Washington Square Park, have perfected the homey "antique" look. Bleecker St. between Sixth and Seventh Ave. offers so much food you won't know what to do with yourself. You can't eat inside the **Murray Cheese Shop,** 257 Bleecker St. (243-3289), at Cornelia St., but the 400-plus kinds of cheese justify a picnic. Try the camembert in rosemary and sage ($4), and get the bread to eat it on from **A. Zito Bread,** next door at 259 Bleecker St. (Cheese Shop open Mon.-Sat. 8am-7pm, Sun. 9am-5pm.)

Late night in the Village is a unique New York treat: as the sky grows dark, the streets quicken. Don't let a mob at the door make you hesitant about sitting over your coffee for hours and watching the spectacle—especially if the coffee is good. Explore twisting side streets and alleyways where you can drop into a jazz club or join Off-Broadway theater-goers as they settle down over a burger and a beer to write their own reviews. Or ditch the high life and slump down 8th St. to Sixth Ave. to join the freak scene and find some of the most respectable pizzerias in the city. The crucial question: John's or Ray's?

★ **Ray's Pizza,** 465 Sixth Ave. (243-2253), at 11th St. Half of the uptown pizza joints claim to be the "Original Ray's," but any New Yorker will tell you that this is the real McCoy. People have been known to fly here from Europe just to bring back a few pies—it's the best pizza in town. Well worth braving the lines and paying upwards of $1.75 for a cheese-heavy slice. No seating; slices only. Open Sun.-Thurs. 11am-2am, Fri.-Sat. 11am-3am.

★ **Cucina Stagionale,** 275 Bleecker St. (924-2707), at Jones St. Unpretentious Italian dining in a clean, pretty environment. Packed with loyals on weekends—the lines reach the street at times. Sample the soft *calimari* in spicy red sauce ($6) or the pasta *putanesca* ($7) to realize why. Pasta dishes all under $8, meat dishes under $10. Sneer at the folks in line and get a dessert too; it still won't be over $15. Open Sun.-Thurs. noon-midnight, Fri.-Sat. noon-1am.

Mappamondo, 11 Abingdon St. (675-3100), at W. 8th St. Small, cozy, and filled with globes, this place serves pasta with a range of creative toppings, as well as antipasti and meat dishes. Get the saffron and squid *farfalle* ($7). When this place gets crowded, go kitty-corner across Abingdon Sq. to **Mappamondo Due,** 581 Hudson St. (675-7474), with the same menu and slightly more food. Open Mon.-Fri. noon-midnight, Sat.-Sun. 11am-1am.

Elephant and Castle, 68 Greenwich Ave. (243-1400), near Seventh Ave. Their motto is *"j'adore les omelettes,"* and boy, are those omelettes adorable ($5-7). The apple, cheddar, and walnut creation is weird but good. The non-omelette options are just as good; main entrees involve intriguing toppings on chicken or pasta for $9-10.50. Open Mon.-Thurs. 8:30am-midnight, Fri. 8:30am-1am, Sat. 10am-1am, Sun. 10am-midnight.

John's Pizzeria, 278 Bleecker St. (243-1680), at Jones St. Loud NYU hangout caters to fratboys, freaks, and even U.S. presidents, if you believe the handwriting on the wall. The pizza's cooked in a brick oven and has thin, crispy crust and just enough cheese. Pizza for two or three costs $9. If the place is full, they'll find room for you at **John's Too** next door. No slices; table service only. Open Mon.-Sat. 11:30am-11:30pm, Sun. noon-midnight.

Tea and Sympathy, 108 Greenwich Ave. (807-8329), between Jane and W. 13th St. An English tea house—high tea, cream tea, and good old-fashioned British cuisine. Filled with kitschy teacups and salt shakers, fading photos of obviously English families, and beautiful chipped china. The waitresses all have the best accents, too. Afternoon tea (the whole shebang—sandwiches, tea, scones, rarebit) $11, cream tea (tea, scones, and jam) $6, shepherd pie $6.75. Open daily approximately 11:30am-8:30pm.

Soups Café, 210 W. 10th St. (727-7499), near Bleecker St. Soups are, obviously, the main focus of this small restaurant, and they're all really good. They're also all $2.50. Try the chicken-like *augolemono* soup. The lunch special is great, too; $6 for soup or salad, and a hiply garnished sandwich such as spinach feta or mango salad. Dinner is soup with a main entree like veal marsala for $9. Open daily noon-11pm.

The Pink Teacup, 42 Grove St. (925-3065), between Bleecker and Bedford St. Soul food in a small, pink, and friendly environment. Moon over the photos of Brooke Shields, Pee-Wee Herman, and New Kids On The Block as you swoon over the fried chicken. Pretty expensive, but the $6 lunch special includes choice of fried chicken, stew, or barbecued anything; soup or salad; two vegetables; and dessert (served 11am-2pm). Coffee, eggs, and fritters can feed two well for under $10. Dinner prices are steep. BYOB. Open Sun.-Thurs. 8am-midnight, Fri.-Sat. 8am-1am.

Quantum Leap, 88 W. 3rd St. (677-8050), between Thompson and Sullivan St. Brown rice galore at this aggressively veggie restaurant. Exotic ways to save the planet, including BBQ Teriyaki Tofu ($8.50) and the lunch special—spaghetti and wheat ball ($6). For dessert, try the "no cholesterol, no fat, brown rice syrup" treats. It's all very good. Open Mon.-Thurs. 11:30am-10:45pm, Fri. 11:30am-11:45pm, Sat. 11am-11:45pm, Sun. 11am-9:45pm.

Olive Tree Café, 117 MacDougal St. (254-3630), north of Bleecker St. Standard Middle Eastern food offset by seemingly endless stimulation. If you get bored by the old movies on the wide screen, rent chess, backgammon, and Scrabble sets ($1), or doodle with colored chalk on the slate tables. Felafel $2.50, chicken kebab platter with salad, rice pilaf, and vegetable $7.50. Delicious egg creams only $1.75. Open Sun.-Thurs. 11am-3am, Fri.-Sat. 11am-5am.

Spain, 113 W. 13th St. (929-9580), between Seventh and Eighth Ave. This restaurant offers enormous tureens of traditional Spanish food for $11-16. The entrees can easily satisfy 2 or even 3 people (sharing incurs an extra $2 charge). Try the *paellas* or anything with garlic. You even get a tantalizing selection of free appetizers such as *chorizo*. Open daily noon-1am.

Washington Square Diner, 150 W. 4th St. (533-9306), at Sixth Ave. All-American dining fare to satisfy your cravings. Power ballads on the radio and large booths, ideal for eavesdropping on the too-glam Villagers eating pancakes ($3-5) at 8pm. Sandwiches and burgers $5-6. Open 24 hrs.

Tutta Pasta, 26 Carmine St. (463-9653), south of Bleecker. A modern establishment with glass doors that slide open in summer. The treat here is the fresh homemade pastas, including tortellini, manicotti, and linguine ($7.25). Offers a 10% discount for students and seniors with ID. Open Mon.-Thurs. 11:30am-10:30pm, Fri.-Sat. 11:30am-11:30pm. Another location at 504 La Guardia Pl. (420-0652), between Bleecker and Houston St.

Eva's, 11 W. 8th St. (677-3496), between MacDougal St. and Fifth Ave. Refreshing fast-service health food with a seating parlor. Massive meatless combo plate with felafel, grape leaves, and eggplant $5.35. Open daily 11am-11pm.

CAFÉS

Dean and Deluca Espresso, 75 University Pl. (473-1908), at E. 11th St. The coffee (90¢) is amazing here, and so are the pastries ($2-3) at this coffee shop run by the gourmet food shop. The seating area is a bit yuppie-warehouse (20 faux-granite tables and 40 sleek, black chairs?), but just sip on a good cup of joe and you'll have reached nirvana. Open Mon.-Thurs. 8am-10pm, Fri.-Sat. 8am-11pm, Sun. 9am-8pm.

Caffè Reggio, 119 MacDougal St. (475-9557), south of W. 3rd St. Celebs and wanna-bes crowd the oldest café in the Village. Open since 1927, this place showcases Renaissance paintings on the wall and fine, fine cappuccino ($2.25) and pastries ($2.50-3.50). You'll be ping-ponging off the walls. Open Sun.-Thurs. 10am-2am, Fri.-Sat 10am-4am.

Caffè Borgia, 185 Bleecker St. (673-2290), at MacDougal St. Moody, dark café has the look and feel of mother Italy. Cult figures who frequent the place include Pacino and De Niro. Stick with the virtually endless coffee list ($1.50-2.75) and the delicious desserts. Open Sun.-Thurs. 10am-2am, Fri. 10am-4am, Sat. 10am-5am.

Caffè Dante, 79 MacDougal St. (982-5275), south of Bleecker St. A Village staple. If you can't find a seat at Caffè Reggio, you'll be just as happy here. Try the *frutta di bosco* ($4.50) and beware the espresso: it bites back. Coffee-based liquids $2-6. Nice gelati and Italian ices ($4.50). Open daily 10am-2am.

■■■ SOHO

In SoHo, food, like life, is all about image. Down with the diner: food here comes in a variety of exquisite and pricey forms, none of it fried or served over a counter. Most of the restaurants in SoHo tend to demonstrate a strong preoccupation with decor, and most aim to serve a stylishly healthful cuisine which, like Life cereal, is both good and good *for* you. Expect a lot of lean meats and fresh vegetables, prepared with wonderful and unusual sauces, served in sizable portions. With the image lifestyle, of course, comes money, so don't be surprised if you find it hard to get a cheap meal. Often the best deal in SoHo is brunch, when the neighborhood shows its most cozy and good-natured front (and puts the calorie-counter away for a while). You can down your omelette or pancakes and coffee in any number of café/bar establishments.

Even more than its restaurants, SoHo's grocery stores tend to champion the organically gourmet way of eating. At **Dean and Deluca,** 560 Broadway (431-1691), at Prince St., gallery quality art surrounds a huge selection of gourmet coffees, pastas, produce, and seafood (open Mon.-Sat. 8am-8pm, Sun. 9am-7pm). Much less chic and more budget-friendly, the **Gourmet Garage,** 453 Broome St. (941-5850), at

Mercer St., is more organic-intensive in its stock of pastas, produce, fresh salads, and teas; in summer be sure to try some of Grandma Koslowski's Home-made Summer Fruit Jam ($2.50/lb.). (Open Mon.-Fri. 10am-8pm, Sat. 9am-8pm, Sun. 9am-7pm.)

Arturo's Coal Oven Pizza, 106 W. Houston St. (677-3820). While the decor seems guided by a definite "Old and Dark" motif (the brightest thing in the back room is the orange and blue poster instructing on aid to choking victims), the coal-oven pizza is truly delicious. You'll find artsy types and other regulars here along with a full bar. Pianist plays dinner jazz nightly 8pm-1am. A number of tables outside allow outdoor dining. Pizzas $10-16, pasta $8-10, other Italian entrees $10-14, wine $7-9 by the carafe. Open Mon.-Thurs. 4pm-1am, Fri.-Sat. 4pm-2am, Sun. 4pm-midnight.

Brother's BBQ, 228 W. Houston St. (727-2775), near Varick St. Friendly service, delicious ribs, and mashed potatoes—what a combo. Bring a bib. Most entrees roll in at $8. Sandwiches $6.25-7.25. Mon. nights all-you-can-eat BBQ $11. During lunch (Mon.-Fri. 11:30am-5pm) all prices about $2 less. Open Mon.-Thurs. 11:30am-11pm, Fri. 11:30am-2am, Sat. 5pm-2am, Sun. 5-11pm; kitchen closes at midnight Fri.-Sat.

The Cupping Room, 359 West Broadway (925-2898), near Broome St. Drinks, dinner, and coffee in a low-key atmosphere. A great choice for a weekend brunch ($10), but arrive early or be prepared to wait. On the bright side, brunch is served from 7am to 6pm and therefore difficult to miss. During the week, the Cupping serves a full breakfast and dinner menu. Sandwiches ($7-12), salads ($7-11), burgers ($7-9), and entrees (about $15) available. At breakfast, all waffles and pancakes served with pure Quebec maple syrup. Open Mon. 7:30am-midnight, Tues.-Thurs. 7:30am-1am, Fri. 7:30am-2am, Sat. 8am-2am, Sun. 8am-midnight. Kitchen closes at midnight.

The Ear Inn, 326 Spring St. (226-9060), near the Hudson. Once a big bohemian/activist hangout, this bar now tends to the SoHo stubble-and-baseball-cap crowd (not to be confused with the gallery crowd). Dark wood, mellow blues, and tables with crayons. Back room functions as restaurant during lunch and dinner hours, serving examples of all styles which have been appropriated into the dominant American cultural hegemony. (If you're now thinking, "How random!", that's what you'll think when you see the menu.) From leek and potato soup to BBQ'd ribs to baked ziti to spinach salad. Try the rich and delicious mud pie ($3). Appetizers and salads $2-6, specials and entrees $5-9. Restaurant open Mon.-Thurs. noon-4:30pm and 6pm-2am, Fri.-Sat. noon-4pm and 6pm-3am, Sun. noon-4:30pm and 6pm-1am. Bar open until 4am.

Prince St. Bar and Restaurant, 125 Prince St. (228-8130), at Wooster St. High ceilings, spare decor, and a wall of large windows exemplify the SoHo style; hardwood floors and a couple of cacti complete the effect. Buy hey, Prince St. has been here since 1975, so at least it can say it got here first. An excellent selection of Indonesian specialties ($6-11)—try the stir-fry noodles with steamed vegetables and choice of sauce (peanut, garlic, or ginger) for dinner, or the challah bread French toast for breakfast. Burgers also available ($6-8.50). Full bar with a selection of microbrews (pints $3-4). Open Sun.-Mon. 11:30am-11pm, Tues.-Wed. 11:30am-midnight, Fri.-Sat. 11:30am-1am. Kitchen closes ½-hr. earlier.

Lupe's East L.A. Kitchen, 110 Sixth Ave. (966-1326), at Watts St. Small, downscale, and diner-esque; not elegant but one of the cheaper and tastier spots around. Burritos ($7-8), enchiladas ($7-7.75), and beer are standard. Super Vegetarian Burrito ($7) and the Taquito Platter ($7.25) are super-tasty; a selection of four types of bottled hot-pepper sauce are on every table in case you need a little more fire. Brunch ($3.75-7.25) served Sat.-Sun. 11:30am-4pm. Better atmosphere than East L.A. Do you think they put themselves on Watts St. on purpose? Open Sun.-Tues. 11:30am-11pm, Wed.-Sat. 11:30am-midnight.

La Petit Café, 156 Spring St. (219-9723). Atypical SoHo dining—small, unpretentious, inexpensive, zero modern art quotient. Fro yo available. Large and tasty fresh mozzarella sandwich with avocado and tomato ($5.75). Italian specialties such as veggie lasagna and cheese ravioli change daily (about $6.75). Wonderful strawberry lemonade made of pink lemonade plus strawberry juice, minus the sugar. Open Sun.-Thurs. 9am-11pm, Fri.-Sat. 9am-2am.

■■■ TRIBECA

Dining in TriBeCa is generally a much funkier (and blessedly cheaper) experience than in chic SoHo. It's not that restaurants here don't put a lot of though into style, but that the style of choice has a dressed-down, folksy, flea marketish flavor. TriBeCa is much more industrial than SoHo, and restaurants are often hidden like little oases among the hulking warehouses and decaying buildings.

★ **Yaffa's Tea Room,** 19 Harrison St. (274-9403), near Greenwich St. Situated in a pleasingly uncommercial and hidden corner of TriBeCa, Yaffa's is one of the few places in Manhattan that serves high tea—and definitely the coolest. The decor is straight out of flea markets and used furniture stores—not ratty, just stylishly "unusual." Wide selection of healthful sandwiches ($7.50) and entrees ($6-10)—the spinach and cheese ravioli with tomatoes and artichoke hearts is typical of the menu and very good. Brunch served daily 8:30am-5pm (omelettes and main selections $4.50-6.50, pastries $1-2). High tea ($15, reservations required) served daily 2-6pm, and includes a "savory course," fresh baked scones, dessert sampler, and a pot of tea. Open daily 8:30am-midnight. The attached bar/restaurant, at the corner of Greenwich St., is a little less subdued, with a mostly different menu (including tapas ($2-3) like marinated mushrooms or mozzarella with sundried tomatoes) to complement its small tables covered with bright green, corrugated aluminum. Bar/restaurant open nightly until 1am.

★ **Bubby's,** 120 Hudson St. (219-0666), between Franklin and N. Moore St. The rough brick walls with white woodwork, unupholstered wooden window benches, and the two walls of windows all add to the stylish simplicity of this small café/restaurant. Great scones, muffins, and pies keep this place packed with locals, but lunch and dinner are excellent as well; try the half spicy jerk chicken with homemade mashed potatoes and greens ($8.75), or the mushroom ravioli with plum tomato and basil sauce ($8.75). Also a number of soups ($2.75-3.75), salads ($2.75-7.50), and sandwiches ($6.75-7.75), as well as a full breakfast menu. A number of comfortable tables line the uncrowded sidewalk. Expect a wait on weekend mornings. Open Mon.-Wed. 7am-10:30pm, Thurs.-Fri. 7am-11pm, Sat.-Sun. 9am-11pm.

★ **Abyssinia,** 35 Grand St. (226-5959), at Thompson St. Terrific Ethiopian restaurant which seats you on low-to-the-ground, hand-carved stools at tables made of woven fibers akin to wicker. Couple this decor with the fact that most dishes require you to eat with your hands, scooping up the food with pieces of dense and spongy *injara* bread, and you get a very comfortable, communal atmosphere. Vegetarian entrees $6-8, meat dishes $8.50-12. The *azefa wot*—lentils, red onions, garlic ginger, and hot green peppers, served cold—is great in the summer (as is a St. George, the Ethiopian-style beer served here). Open Mon.-Thurs. 6-11pm, Fri. 6pm-midnight, Sat. 1pm-midnight, Sun. 1-11pm.

Thai House Café, 151 Hudson St. (334-1085), at Hubert St. Small and cozy in its spot just across from a park, this inconspicuous little place serves up the Thai standards in fine fashion. *Pad thai* ($6), chicken red curry ($7), and roast duck hot basil ($8) are all excellent. Open Mon.-Sat. 11:30am-11pm.

El Teddy's, 219 West Broadway (941-7070), between Franklin and White St. First-rate, creative Mexican cuisine (yes, cuisine) conceived with a strong dose of California-healthful. Baby artichoke and sundried tomato quesadilla ($7) and the shrimp tostada with jalapeños, avocados, and refried beans ($9) are both excellent. And you'll definitely have no trouble finding it—the huge, colorful awning made in stained glass window fashion from many colors of paper is *nada* if not obvious. Step back to see the points of Lady Liberty's crown poking up over the top of the building. Open for lunch Mon.-Fri. noon-3pm. Open for dinner Mon.-Sat. 6-11:30pm, Sun. 6-11pm; abridged "supper" menu available Thurs.-Sat. 11:30pm-1am.

Moon Dance Diner, Sixth Ave. and Grand St. (226-1191). The real thing—an authentic old diner car replete with curved ceilings and counter service. Excellent short-order breakfasts served all day—cheese omelette with toast and home fries ($3.50) is mighty tasty. Wed. nights offer all-you-can-eat pasta (with a big selection pastas and sauces) for $8. Dollar draft beers all day every day. Sandwiches $6.50-9. Open Mon.-Tues. 8am-midnight; Wed.-Sat. 24 hrs, closing Sun. night at midnight.

■■■ EAST VILLAGE, ALPHABET CITY, AND LOWER EAST SIDE

Culinary cultures clash on the lower end of the East Side, where pasty-faced punks and starving artists dine alongside an older generation conversing in Polish, Hungarian, and Yiddish. The neighborhood took in the huddled masses, and, in return, got lots of cool places to eat; immigrant culture after immigrant culture has left its residue in the form of cheap restaurants. As Chinatown gradually dissipates along East Broadway, you can still find kosher Jewish eateries. Farther north, the Ukrainians made their mark in the form of cheap places serving *borscht, pirogi,* and other inexpensive, hearty foods.

Lately, the most noticeable immigrant culture in the East Village has been that of young, artsy white people; they too brought their restaurants and cafés, although these are not always cheap. The East Village thus provides a hodgepodge of eating choices. First and Second Avenues are the best for restaurant-exploring, and sidewalk cafés and bars line Avenue A. Check out 6th St. between First and Second Ave., a block composed of several Indian restaurants offering $2.95 lunch specials.

★ **Dojo Restaurant,** 24 St. Mark's Pl. (674-9821), between Second and Third Ave. One of the most popular restaurants and hangouts in the East Village, and rightly so. Offers an incredible variety of healthful, delicious, and inexplicably inexpensive food in a comfortable brick and darkwood interior. Tasty soyburgers with brown rice and salad $3.20. Spinach and pita sandwich with assorted veggies $2.15. Outdoor tables allow for interaction with slick passers-by, though the loud chaos of St. Mark's might give you a headache. New location (same menu) on Washington Square South. Open Sun.-Thurs. 11am-1am, Fri.-Sat. 11am-2am.

★ **Al Hamra,** 203 First Ave. (505-6559), between 12th and 13th St. This phenomenally cheap and undiscovered restaurant serves huge plates of Indian and Pakistani food, all for under $5. Try the spicy chicken *vindaloo* ($5) or lamb curry ($3.50), or make a light meal out of the *pakoras* ($1.50). Top it all off with a mango *lassi* ($1.50). No decor to speak of, but who cares. Open 24 hrs. Free delivery from noon-midnight.

Pink Pony Café, 174 Ludlow St., between E. Houston and Stanton St. Ultra-friendly café/ice cream parlor/bookshop catering to the Lower East Side artist set. A great place to study, read, or write over an espresso ($1.30). Several shelves of secondhand books for sale or perusal, tending towards the trashy spy thriller genre. Lots of hip magazines to read and even a comfy couch and a pool table in the back room. Open Sun.-Thurs. 10am-midnight, Fri.-Sat. 10am-4am.

Two Boots, 37 Ave. A (505-2276), at E. 2nd St. The two boots are Italy and Louisiana, both shaped remarkably like footwear. It may be Cajun Italian or Italian Cajun, but it sure is tasty. Menu changes twice a year, but pasta is $6-9, and the shrimp pizza ($7) is a mainstay. Weekend brunch (noon-4pm) includes sangria and muffins with a choice of entree ($7.50). Open daily noon-midnight. **Two Boots to Go,** across the street at 36 Ave. A (505-5450), and at 60 Bleecker St. just off Broadway (777-1033), serve great pizza too ($1.35 for a plain slice); both open noon-1am.

Ukrainian East Village Restaurant, 140 Second Ave. (529-5024), between 8th and 9th St. Pleasantly decorated, complete with chandeliers and large plants; excellent food at amazingly low prices. More genuine Ukranians and fewer young non-Slavs than in the other East Village borscht-houses. Potato *pirogi* $4.75, cheese or meat *pirogi* $5, stuffed cabbage with potato and mushroom gravy $6, *kielbasa* with sauerkraut and potato $5.75, hot *borscht* with vegetables $1.60 a cup. Open Sun.-Thurs. noon-11pm, Fri.-Sat. noon-midnight.

Mee Noodle Shop and Grill, 219 First Ave. (995-0333/0396/0563), at 13th St. There are over 200 items on the menu at this friendly, efficient Chinese restaurant. Try one of the noodle soups ($2.75-5; be sure to follow the amusingly ungrammatical ordering instructions) or go for the *dan-dan* noodles ($4.25). Other entrees $4-8.50. Open daily 11am-11pm.

Veselka, 144 Second Ave. (228-9682), at 9th St. Down-to-earth, soup-and-bread, Polish-Ukrainian joint. Enormous menu includes about 10 varieties of soups, as well as salads, blintzes, meats, and other Eastern European fare. Blintzes $3.25, soup $1.95 a cup (try the sumptuous chicken noodle). Combination special gets you soup, salad, stuffed cabbage, and 4 melt-in-your-mouth *pirogi* ($7.75). Open 24 hrs.

Benny's Burritos, 93 Ave. A (254-2054), at 6th St. This colorful, shiny Cal-Mex hot spot is dirt-cheap and always hoppin'. Plump, tasty burritos with black or pinto beans around $5. Locals swear by it. Open Sun.-Wed. 11am-midnight, Thurs.-Sat. 11am-1am.

Khyber Pass Restaurant, 34 St. Mark's Pl. (473-0989), between Second and Third Ave. A dainty place on the central artery of the East Village serving Afghani food. The unusual cuisine served here recalls more familiar Middle Eastern foods, but with surprising twists and turns. Try one of the unusual vegetarian selections, such as steamed pumpkin dumplings ($3 for 4). Sit on pillows and enjoy *bouranee baunjaun,* eggplant with mint yogurt and fresh coriander ($7.50), or *phirnee,* a delicate rice pudding with pistachios and rosewater ($2.25). Open daily noon-midnight.

Yaffa Cafe, 97 St. Mark's Place (674-9302), between First Ave. and Ave. A. The highest decor-to-price ratio in the Village. Diners peruse a 5-page menu offering all sorts of salads ($5-6), sandwiches ($3.50-6), and Middle Eastern specialties ($2-6) in an interior right out of I-Dream-of-Jeannie's bottle. The outdoor garden in the back is open all summer, complete with abandoned bathtubs, a working fountain, and random Duchamps-inspired sentence fragments spray-painted on the walls. Open 24 hrs.

The Cloister Café, 238 E. 9th St. (777-9128), between Second and Third Ave. Not a top choice for full meal—the food is expensive and unmemorable—but you'll feel like the Pope as you drink your hefty bowl of cappucino ($2.75) amidst more stained glass than you could shake a stick at in the café's jaw-dropping interior. Lounge in a gorgeous outdoor garden complete with fish and a fountain. Lunch platters $6-10, dinner $10-14. Open daily 11am-midnight.

Cucina di Pesce, 87 E. 4th St. (260-6800), between Second and Third Ave. Fish warrants the longish wait and highish prices. Friendly Italian seafood-and-pasta joint. Grilled tuna served with a side of pasta $9. Entrees $6-10. Open Sun.-Thurs. 5pm-midnight, Fri.-Sat. 5pm-1am.

Second Ave. Delicatessen, 156 Second Ave. (677-0606), at 10th St. The definitive New York deli, established in 1954. People come into the city just to be snubbed by the waiters here. Have pastrami (reputed to be the best in the city) or tongue on rye bread for $7.50, a fabulous burger deluxe for $7, or chicken soup for $3. Note the Hollywood-style star plaques embedded in the sidewalk outside: this was once the heart of the Yiddish theater district. But while their art form is all but forgotten, such personages as Moishe Oysher and Bella Meisel have gained a fragile foothold on immortality—metallic tributes sunk in pocked pavement. Open Sun.-Thurs. 8am-midnight, Fri.-Sat. 8am-2am.

Around the Clock, 8 Stuyvesant St. (598-0402), between 9th and 10th St. Pleasant, wood-panelled restaurant serving a large menu replete with burgers, omelettes, and specialty sandwiches. Try the Lafayette ($5), a grilled chicken sandwich with lots of melted mozzarella, pesto sauce, and tomato. Entrees $4-7.

For kosher eating, hold on to your yarmulke and head on down to the Lower East Side around and south of East Houston St. **Kossar's Hot Bialys,** 367 Grand St. at Essex St. (473-4810; open 24 hrs.), makes bialys that recall the heyday of the Lower East Side. Here are some more of the most famed establishments.

Katz's Delicatessen, 205 E. Houston St. (254-2246), near Orchard. Classic informal deli established in 1888. The fake-orgasm scene in *When Harry Met Sally* took place here. You'd better know what you want, because the staff here doesn't fool around. Have an overstuffed corned beef sandwich with a pickle for $6.65. Mail-order department enables you to send a salami to a loved one (or, perhaps, an ex-loved one). With testimonial letters from Carter and Reagan, how could it be bad? Open Sun.-Wed. 8am-9pm, Thurs. 8am-10pm, Fri.-Sat. 8am-11pm.

Ratner's Restaurant, 138 Delancey St. (677-5588), just west of the Manhattan Bridge. The most famous of the kosher restaurants, partly because of its frozen-food line. Despite the run-down surroundings, this place is large, shiny, and popular. Jewish dietary laws are strictly followed and only dairy food is served; you will have to go elsewhere for a pastrami sandwich with Swiss and mayo. But there's no better place to feast on fruit blintzes and sour cream ($9) or simmering vegetarian soups ($4). Potato pancake to go $6. Open Sun.-Thurs. 6am-midnight, Fri. 6am-3pm, Sat. sundown-2am.

Yonah Schimmel Knishery, 137 E. Houston St. (477-2858). Rabbi Schimmel's establishment, around since the heyday of the Jewish Lower East Side (around 1910), has honed the knish to an art. A dozen varieties available for $1.10-1.60. Try yogurt from a 71-year old strain (no, really) for $1.25. Open daily 8am-7pm.

■■■ LITTLE ITALY

Immortalized by Billy Joel, who used to have dinner in the local *ristoranti,* Mulberry Street is the main drag and the appetite avenue of Little Italy. Here, among the strings of tiny Italian flags that fly above the street, restaurants and caffès fall into line one after another. Daylight during the work week finds Little Italy quieter than most districts of New York; at night and on weekends, though, tourists and natives released from their jobs come here to stroll and feast and finally relax in the sidewalk caffès. Arrive here after 7pm to catch street life but come a little earlier to get one of the better tables. For the sake of variety and thrift, dine at a restaurant and then move to a caffè to get your just desserts. The caffè atmosphere is more conducive to lingering (and the coffee's usually better to boot). Beginning with the second Thursday in September, Mulberry Street goes wild as Little Italy toasts the Saint of Naples during the raucous 10-day **Feast of San Gennaro.** To get to Little Italy, take the #4, 5, or 6, the N or R, or the J, M, or Z to Canal St.; or take the B, D, F, or Q to Broadway-Lafayette.

Ballato, 55 E. Houston St. (274-8881), at Mott St. Gracefully stemmed wine glasses and glistening chocolate-covered cherries greet you. As much a child of SoHo as of Little Italy, Ballato serves its impeccable southern Italian cooking to a thankful crowd of artsy types, tourists, and college students. Pasta $9-11.50, trout in olive oil $12.50. *Antipasti* $5.50-8. Two-course, *prix fixe* lunch (Mon.-Fri. noon-4pm; $7.50) includes choice from a wide selection of entrees, and either an appetizer or dessert. *Prix fixe* dinner (Sun.-Fri. 4-6:30pm, Sat. 5-6:30pm; $14.50) includes all three courses. Open daily noon-11pm; closed Sun. noon-5pm June-Aug.

Pietro & Vanessa, 23 Cleveland Pl. (941-0286), near Spring and Lafayette St. Removed from the main fray of Mulberry St.; the large, relaxing patio out back is a welcome change from the crowded and hectic outdoor tables along Mulberry St. A *trattoria* with a menu of very good standards. Baked clam *antipasto* $5.25; pasta such as *fusilli primavera* (with fresh vegetables) $8-9; chicken entrees $9-11; fish and veal $10. Open Mon.-Fri. noon-11pm, Sat. 4-11pm, Sun. 4-10pm.

La Mela, 167 Mulberry St. (431-9493), between Broome and Grand St. If Little Italy believed in cult restaurants, La Mela would be the kingpin. Kitschy pictures, paintings, and postcards dot the walls haphazardly; tables and chairs shift and merge to accommodate the large groups and families who come here to feast. People travel from as far as Rapid City to sink their teeth into the famed chicken *scarpariello.* Equally rambunctious outdoor seating in their backyard, complete with a guitar-touting bard, the final mark of "authenticity." A wide assortment of pasta and *gnocchi* ($6.50-10), along with a large number of entrees ($12-15).

Always specials; the waiters love to talk you through your order. Open daily noon-11pm.

Rocky's Italian Restaurant, 45 Spring St. (226-8121), at Mulberry St. This Italian stallion punches out primo dishes a few blocks away from the heart of the action. Billy Crystal and his uncle are regulars in this place that's been cooking up consistently good Italian fare for over 20 years. Signed portraits of stars hung throughout. For lunch try a pizza hero ($4) or sandwiches ($4-7), which are served until 5pm. Pastas $8-11, entrees $9-13. For dessert, try their homemade Italian cheesecake, made with fresh ricotta tinted with anise ($3). Open Mon.-Sat. 11am-11pm.

Paninoteca, 250 Mulberry St. (219-1351), at Prince St. Different from most Little Italy restaurants in that it doesn't seem afraid of sunlight. Two walls of windows and lots of light woods; this lighter, simpler decor complements a lighter, simpler, more healthful menu. Salads $4-7, pastas $6-9, entrees $9-13. The *carbonara alla panna* ($9), cheese-filled tortellini with bacon, ham, peas, and onions, will leave you smiling. Open Sun.-Thurs. 11am-midnight, Fri.-Sat. 11am-1am.

Puglia Restaurant, 189 Hester St. (966-6006), at Mulberry St. Long tables mean fun and rowdiness. Venture into 3 separate dining rooms, ranging from diner-like to batcave-like (it's lined with stones and a little bit cavernous). A favorite of New Yorkers and bold tourists. Pastas $7-10, entrees $8.25-14. Monstrous plate of mussels $9.25. Live music nightly beginning at 7pm. Open Sun.-Thurs. 11:30am-midnight, Fri.-Sat. 11:30am-1am.

Caffè Sorrento, 132 Mulberry St. (219-8634), between Broome and Grand St. What you probably think of when you think Little Italy: uninspired decor set off by a colorful Italian wait-staff which still dons the obligatory black pants, vest, and bow tie with a white tuxedo shirt. Pasta from $8.50; entrees $10-13. *Capelli d'angeli primavera* (angel hair pasta with vegetables in cream) $9.50, *costata e salsicce di maiale alla calabrese* (pork chop and sausage with vinegar peppers) $10.75. Open daily noon-midnight.

Paolucci's, 149 Mulberry St. (226-9653), between Grand and Hester St. Family-owned restaurant with a penchant for heaping portions. The boss watches you from the front wall. Chicken *cacciatore* with salad and spaghetti $12. Pastas $8-10, house "favorites" $10-17, other entrees $12.50-22. Daily lunch specials (11:30am-5pm) $5-9.50. Open Sun. 11:30am-10pm, Mon.-Thurs. 11:30am-10:30pm, Fri.-Sat. 11:30am-11:30pm.

Vincent's Clam Bar, 119 Mott St. (226-8133), at Hester St. A New York institution. Archaic photos line the walls of the restaurant that Giuseppe and Carmela Siano established in 1904 and named after their son. Small and unimposing; all the energy goes into the food. Ravioli with Vincent's famous sauce $8, pasta from $6.50. Entrees are mainly seafood ($6.50-17); Vincent's Famous Shrimp Balls $8.50. Open Sun.-Thurs. 11:30am-1:30am, Fri.-Sat. 11:30am-3:30am.

Ristorante Taormina, 147 Mulberry St. (219-1007/8/9), between Grand and Hester St. Upscale and right in the heart of Mulberry Street's restaurant row. No linoleum here; just large windows, graceful green plants, exposed brick walls, and blondewood fittings. Dressy but comfortable clientele enjoys gourmet food and bottles of wine. *Penne arrabiate* $10, *saltinbocca alla romana* (veal with *prosciutto,* white wine, and sage) $12.50. Pastas $10-16, entrees $12-18. Open Mon.-Thurs. noon-11:30pm, Fri. noon-12:30am, Sat. noon-1am, Sun. noon-10:30pm.

Benito One, 174 Mulberry St. (226-9171). A small no-nonsense *trattoria* churning out a menu of excellent standard dishes. For a memorable appetizer, order *mozzarella in carozza* ($6), and follow it up with *pollo scarpariello,* a chicken on the bone with garlic, olive oil, and fresh basil ($11). Open Sun.-Thurs. noon-11pm, Fri-Sat. noon-midnight.

Il Fornaio, 132A Mulberry St. (226-8306), between Broome and Grand St. A clean and simple white-tiled interior, with perfectly symmetrical jars and tins of olive oil. Upbeat, reasonable menu; the excellent thin-crust pizzas ($4-10) are a specialty. Hot sandwiches start at $4.50, pasta dinners at $6. Rumored to have the best *antipasti* in town ($5-6). Open Sun.-Thurs. 11:30am-11:30pm, Fri.-Sat. 11:30am-midnight.

Caffè

La Bella Ferrara, 110 Mulberry St. (966-1488). Named after the city that brought you turbo power, La Bella Ferrara maintains the dual imperatives of power and grace in its dynamic production of *dolci.* One of the largest selection of pastries around. Sleek glass and checkered tile. Pastries $1.50-2, desserts $3-4.50, cappuccino $2.50. Breakfast special (served 9am-noon; $2.75) includes cappuccino or espresso, juice, and croissant, bagel, or muffin. Lunch special (soup and sandwich; until 5pm) $5.50. Definitely worth a visit on a nice day or evening, as it's one of the few places on Mulberry St. that gives you outdoor seating without putting you right in the middle of the sidewalk pedestrian flow. Open Sun.-Thurs. 9am-1am, Fri.-Sat. 9am-2am.

Caffè Biondo, 141 Mulberry St. (226-9285). Chic Euro-atmosphere of rough brick walls, long black tables, and stone reliefs. Strike a pose and sip espresso ($1.75). Or try *caffè corretto* (espresso with Sambucca, $2.70), *caffè alla panna* (with whipped cream, $1.75). *Cannoli* $2.50; *spumoni* $2.50. Open daily noon-1am.

Caffè Roma, 385 Broome St. (226-8413), at Mulberry St. A good *caffè* gets better with time. A full-fledged saloon in the 1890s, Roma has kept its original furnishings intact: dark green walls with polished brass ornaments, chandeliers, and darkwood cabinets where liquor bottles used to roost. Since its saloon days, Roma has removed the imbibery and installed several elegant Tuscan landscapes. The pastries and coffee, Roma's *raison d'être,* prove as refined as the setting. Try the neapolitan *cannoli* or the *baba au rhum* ($1.50 to take out, $2.25 to eat in). Potent espresso $1.60; obligatory cappuccino, with a tiara of foamed milk, $2.40. Open daily 8am-midnight.

Café Gitane, 242 Mott St. (334-9552), at Prince St. Trendy but very relaxed café which caters to the young and bohemian. Inside it's small, retro, and diner-esque, with chairs upholstered in vinyl, tables topped with linoleum, and full counter service. Hang out with a book or over conversation; a magazine rack invites you to linger. Creative, healthful salads $6.50-9. Sandwiches $5.25-7.50. Espresso $1.75, café au lait $2.75, cheesecake $3.75, chocolate torte $4. Selection of tears $1.75-2. Open daily 10am-11pm.

Ferrara, 195-201 Grand St. (226-6150). A slick emporium where hundreds of tempting pastries vie for your attention. The espresso bar has become one of the city's most popular places for cappuccino and its creamy siblings. In good weather the bar extends onto the sidewalk, where a counter dispenses authentic Italian *gelati. Cannoli* $2.85, *tiramisu* $4.50, strawberry shortcake $4.25. Excellent sandwiches like the *focaccia imbottita,* with broccoli, artichoke, provolone, roasted peppers, and pesto ($4.50). Open daily 8am-midnight.

Lo Spuntino, 117 Mulberry St. (226-9280), between Hester and Canal St. Small and simple, but gorgeous desserts compensate for lackluster decor. Lengthy list of mousses includes pumpkin mousse (in season). Pear mousse with raspberry puree $5, chocolate mousse $4.50, espresso $2. Open Mon.-Fri. 5pm-1am, Sat.-Sun. 11:30am-1am.

■■■ CHINATOWN

If you're looking for cheap, authentic Asian fare, join the crowds that push through the narrow, chaotic streets of one of the oldest Chinatowns in the U.S. A trip to this large and rapidly expanding district is sure to result in at least a little bit of culture shock; the streets here are trafficked almost excluvely by Chinese and other Asians, and the businesses which line them are guided by (and cater to) a sensibility that shows little influence of mainstream America. In the numerous small stores that operate here, you can find rare items like Chinese housewares, hermetically sealed whole fish, roots, and spices of all stripes. If you decide you're up to doing some cooking of your own, head to **Kam Kuo Food Corp.,** 7 Mott St. (349-3097), just north of Chatham Sq. Multitudinous wonders occupy this local supermarket. In the frozen meats section, London broil is supplanted by pork toes, chicken feet, and duck wings. The produce section features Chinese versions of broccoli and eggplant. Look out for the sweetened, dried cuttlefish (80¢-$2). Upstairs, an entire floor of chinaware and cooking utensils rivals Zabar's. (Open daily 9am-8:30pm.)

The neighborhood's 200-plus restaurants cook up some of the best Chinese, Thai, and Vietnamese cooking around. And they don't make dumplings for Trumplings either—compared to prices in French and Italian eateries, these restaurants are remarkably inexpensive. This is probably due to the fierce culinary competition. The great Vietnamese place you ate in last year may now be serving Malaysian cuisine under a different name. Such competition has been a boon for palates; once-predominantly Cantonese cooking has now burgeoned into different cuisines from the various regions of China: hot and spicy Hunan or Szechuan food, the sweet and mildly spiced seafood of Soochow, or the hearty and filling fare of Beijing. This competition has not diminished the popularity of Cantonese *dim sum,* however. In this Sunday afternoon tradition, waiters roll carts filled with assorted dishes of bite-sized goodies up and down the aisles. To partake, you simply point at what you want (beware of "Chinese Bubblegum," a euphemism for tripe). At the end of the meal, the number of empty dishes on your table is tallied up.

For dessert (especially in summer), check out the Chinatown Ice Cream Factory, 65 Bayard St. (608-4171), at Mott St. Many of the flavors here you probably wouldn't be surprised to find at the Häagen-Dazs down the street, but authentic homemade ice cream flavors like lychee, mango, ginger, red bean, and green tea are unique. One scoop $1.80, two $3.20, three $4.15. (Open Mon.-Thurs. 11:30am-11pm, Fri. and Sun. 11:30am-11:30pm, Sat. 11:30am-midnight.) Also try the May May Gourmet Bakery, 35 Pell St. (267-0733), between Mott and Bowery, with its countless interesting pastries (all under 75¢). Make the familiar seem unfamiliar with a black bean paste or lotus seed pastry (each 50¢), or a coconut tart (60¢). (Open daily 9am-8:30pm.) To reach Chinatown, take the #6, the J, M, Z, or the N, R to Canal St., walk east on Canal to Mott St., go right on Mott, and follow the curved street toward the Bowery, Confucius Plaza, and E. Broadway.

Excellent Dumpling House, 111 Lafayette St. (219-0212 or 219-0213), just south of Canal St. If this restaurant's name is at all misleading, it's only because it's too modest. Terrific vegetarian and meat dumplings fried, steamed, or boiled ($4 for 8 sizeable pieces). Also great pan-fried noodles ($5-6.50) and huge bowls of noodle soups (mostly $3.50-4). Lunch specials (served Mon.-Fri. 11am-3pm) include entree such as shredded pork with garlic sauce or chicken with black bean sauce, choice of soup, and fried rice and a wonton (all specials $5.50). Small and unassuming, but the food is splendid and the service fast. Open daily 11am-9pm.

HSF (Hee Sheung Fung), 46 Bowery (374-1319), just south of Canal St. Tasteful, large, and crowded. Well-known for its fantastic *dim sum* (served daily 7:30am-5pm) and for its "Hot Pot buffet." The Hot Pot is a sort of Asian equivalent to fondue, in which a huge pot of boiling broth is placed in the center of your table with a platter of more than 50 raw ingredients spread around it. Ingredients range from fresh scallops, squid, shrimp, clams, mussels, and periwinkles to spinach, watercress, and Chinese cabbage; you dip each piece into the flavored broth, and then into one of several sauces. All ingredients are unlimited ($18 per person). Range of other entrees ($7.50-17) as well, including delicacies like prawns in Yushan garlic sauce ($13). Open daily 7:30am-5am.

House of Vegetarian, 68 Mott St. (226-6572), between Canal and Bayard St. Faux chicken, faux beef, faux lamb, and faux fish comprise the huge menu; all the animals are ersatz here, made from soy and wheat by-products. Try *lo mein* (with 3 kinds of mushrooms, $6.75) or gluten with black bean sauce ($7). Most entrees $6-10. An ice-cold lotus seed or lychee drink ($2) really hits the spot on hot summer days. Open daily 11am-11pm.

Road to Mandalay, 380 Broome St. (226-4218), at Mulberry St. A rare Burmese pearl washed up on the Italian shores of Mulberry St. Refined Burmese cuisine served in a cozy setting enhanced by baskets overflowing with fruit and vegetables. Start with the coconut noodle soup ($3.50) and the 1000-layered pancake, a delicate Burmese bread ($2.50). Entrees range from $8-11.50, with chili chicken checking in at $8. Lighter fare features street-market noodles fried with duck and garlic $5.50-7. Open Mon.-Fri. 4-11pm, Sat.-Sun. 11am-11pm.

Yeun Yeun Restaurant, 61A Bayard St. (406-2100). Chinese food in an American diner atmosphere—shoebox-shaped, full of booths, and downscale. Small menu that'll probably seem straight out of the '50s: chicken chop suey ($6.50) and shrimp chow mein ($4.25). Entrees $3.50-7. For dessert try a lychee ice—a milkshake with syrup and fresh lychees at the bottom ($1.50).

Hong Fat, 63 Mott St. (962-9588), near Bayard St. No-frills meals in formica heaven, with a small, hot Szechuan menu. Try the Szechuan-style *kung po* beef ($7.50), or go straight for the fat noodles, a.k.a. *chow fon* ($5.50). Entrees $6-11.25. With massive air-conditioned support, Hong Fat stays chilly all night long. Open daily 10am-5am.

Peking Duck House, 22 Mott St. (227-1810), at Park St. This is the place that won seven stars from the *Daily News* and that former mayor Ed Koch called "the best Chinese restaurant in the world." If someone else is paying, order the Peking Duck Extravaganza ($29). If not, you'll probably want to stick with one of the entrees ($5.50-13), like the shrimp in garlic sauce ($12.25). *Dim sum* ($2.40-7 per dish) served Sat.-Sun. 11:30am-3pm. Open Sun.-Thurs. 11:30am-10:30pm, Fri.-Sat. 11:30am-11:30pm.

Oriental Pearl, 103-105 Mott St. (219-8388), between Hester and Canal St. Huge, garishly red, and family-filled—the decor may tend to turn you away ("Where am I? Omaha? A mall on Long Island?"), but the food is worth staying for. Try the orange beef Hunan-style ($9), or the shrimp fried rice ($6). Entrees $8-18, fried rice and noodle dishes $5-9. Open daily noon-11pm.

20 Mott St. Restaurant, 20 Mott St. (964-0380), near Pell St. This very red two-story restaurant is generally crowded (often with tourists), but the *dim sum* served daily from 8am-4pm more than makes up for the atmosphere (or the lack of it). Try the excellent jasmine tea, too. Entrees $7-13 (except for the abalone dishes, which run about $40). Open Sun.-Thurs. 8am-midnight, Fri.-Sat. 8am-1am.

Mueng Thai Restaurant, 23 Pell St. (406-4259), near Mott St. The curry comes in 4 different colors—good luck to those who choose hot green. Try the Matsuman curry ($9) or the chicken in coconut milk soup ($3). Extensive selection of meat and seafood entrees (most $8-11). Lunch special (Tues.-Fri. 11:30am-3pm): rice and your choice of curry for $5. Open Sun. and Tues.-Thurs. 11:30am-10pm, Fri.-Sat. 11:30am-11pm.

New Lung Fong Bakery, 41 Mott St. (233-7447), at Bayard St. Unlike many other bakeries around here, a clean, spacious, airy place. The "New" refers to the eating area installed toward the back. An amazingly cheap selection of pastries (all 40-75¢ each). Almond cookies 50¢, pineapple sponge cake 50¢, chicken rolls 60¢, ham and cheese or sausage buns 50¢. Open daily 8am-9pm.

■■■ LOWER MANHATTAN

Lower Manhattan is luncheon heaven to sharply-clad Wall St. brokers and bankers; it offers cheap food (often "heart smart" to fend off nasty stress and cholesterol) prepared lightning-fast at ultra-low prices, always available as take-out and sometimes with free delivery. Bargain-basement cafeterias here can fill you up with everything from gazpacho to Italian sausages. Fast-food joints pepper Broadway near Dey and John St. just a few feet from the overpriced offerings of the Main Concourse of the World Trade Center. In the summer, food pushcarts form a solid wall along Broadway between Cedar and Liberty St., wheeling and dealing in a realm beyond hot dogs. Vendors sell felafel and eggplant plates ($2.75), burritos ($3), and chilled gazpacho with an onion roll ($3). You can sup in Liberty Park, across the street.

At the pedestrian plaza at Coenties Slip, between Pearl and South William St., you can choose among the small budget restaurants. Grab an *empanada* (turnover) for $2.75 at **Ruben's** (509-3825) (which has another outlet near the South Street Seaport at 64 Fulton St.); select from a bounteous buffet at the **Golden Chopsticks** (825-0314) for $4 per pound; or venture into the adjacent Indian or fish-'n'-chips restaurants. North of City Hall, food kiosks fill St. Andrew's Plaza, a no-frills alternative for the local crowd of office workers doing lunch.

Two food courts near South Street Seaport also take a stab at providing every imaginable type of ethnic cuisine in a single, convenient location. **The Promenade,** on the third floor of Pier 17 at South Street Seaport (732-7678) juxtaposes the Wok-'n'-Roll (sweet-'n'-sour pork, egg roll, and fried rice $5.22) with the Athenian Express (gyro or souvlaki $4.70) with The Salad Bowl (pita sandwich with tuna, chicken, or hummus $4.50), and a cornucopia of other eateries. (Promenade open Mon.-Sat. 10am-9pm, Sun. 11am-8pm; some bar/restaurants open later.) **The Topside Shops and Cafés,** in Fulton Market, at the corner of Fulton and Front St., offers a similarly diverse if smaller selection, mainly centered around pizza, hamburgers, and Chinese food. (Topside restaurants open same hours as Promenade.)

Zigolini's, 66 Pearl St. (425-7171), at Coenties Alley. One of the few places in the area where indoor air-conditioned seating abounds, this authentically Italian restaurant serves huge and filling sandwiches ($5-7), as well as some great pasta dishes. Try the tomato spirals with sundried tomatoes, artichokes, roasted peppers, and parsley ($6.50). Come up with an appealing combination of your own and they just might add it to the menu—it's happened before. Open Mon.-Fri. 7am-7pm.

Frank's Papaya, 192 Broadway (693-2763), at John St. Excellent value, quick service. Very close to the World Trade Center. Jumbo turkey burger $1.10, all-beef hot dog 70¢. Breakfast (egg, ham, cheese, coffee) $1.50. Stand and eat at one of the counters inside. Open Mon.-Sat. 5:30am-10pm, Sun. 5:30am-5:30pm.

Broadway Farm, 181 Broadway (587-1105 or 227-0701), between John and Cortlandt St. A salad bar the size of a Winnebago—choose your favorite greens and fruit, along with lots of hot pasta and Chinese dishes ($4 per lb.). Small amount of seating in rear. Open 24 hrs.

Hamburger Harry's, 157 Chambers St. (267-4446), between West and Greenwich St. Gourmet burgers for the connoisseur: 7-oz. patty broiled over applewood with exotic toppings like avocado, alfalfa sprouts, chili, salsa, and bearnaise sauce ($6, with red slaw and fries or potato salad $8). You can have chicken breast done similarly for the same price. Regular burger $4, nacho cheese fries $3. Open daily 11am-10pm.

Fulton Seaport Deli, 52 Fulton St. (393-1137). More like a convenience store than a deli (especially since there aren't any actual tables here), but still you can select from the massive, high-quality salad bar at $4 per lb., or try a triple-decker sandwich for $4.25, then munch back at the seaport. Open 24 hrs.

McDonald's, 160 Broadway (385-2063), at Liberty St. For the Wall St. McPower lunch. A $3 million double decker McPalace that seats 250 at marble tabletops. A doorman in a tux and the strains of a baby grand piano greet you if you come during peak hours, but you may have to fight through the hordes that sometimes arrive on tour buses. Pick at grapes and strawberries ($2.25) with your breakfast, or down a fruit tart ($2.50) and espresso ($1.75). Fruit nectar ($1.50) and herbal tea ($1) to quench that Big McThirst. Plus the super-sizable standard menu. Prices run about 25% higher than the usual McDonald's fare. Open Mon.-Fri. 6am-10:30pm, Sat-Sun. 7:30am-9pm.

■■■ BROOKLYN

Ethnic flavor changes every two blocks in Brooklyn. Brooklyn Heights offers nouvelle cuisine, but specializes in pita bread and *baba ghanoush*. Williamsburg is dotted with kosher and cheap Italian restaurants, Greenpoint is a borscht-lover's paradise, and Flatbush serves up Jamaican and other West Indian cuisine. For those who didn't get enough in Manhattan, Brooklyn now has its own Chinatown in Sunset Park.

■DOWNTOWN AND NORTH BROOKLYN

★ **Las Tres Palmas,** 124 Court St. (718-596-2740, 624-9565), near Atlantic Ave. Subway: #2, 3, 4, 5, M, or R to Borough Hall, then down 3½ blocks on Court St. What this small, clean restaurant lacks in polish it makes up for with excellent food at reasonable prices. Local Latinos come to the self-proclaimed "best Spanish restaurant in downtown Brooklyn" to enjoy hefty bowls of soup ($2.15-3) as well as meat dishes like chicken fricasse ($5.95) and Palomilla steak with onions ($7). Entrees served with rice and beans, green plaintains and salad, or sweet plantains and salad. Open daily 10am-10pm.

Moroccan Star, 205 Atlantic Ave. (718-643-0800), in Brooklyn Heights. Subway: #2, 3, 4, 5, M, or R to Borough Hall, then down 4 blocks on Court St. Ensconced in the local Arab community, this restaurant serves delicious and reasonably cheap food. Try the *pastello*, a delicate semi-sweet chicken pie with almonds ($8.75, lunch $6). Open Sun. noon-10pm, Tues.-Thurs. 10am-11pm, Fri.-Sat. 11am-11pm.

Joe's Luncheonette, 349 Court St. (718-624-3223), between Union and President St. in Carroll Gardens. Subway: F or G to Carroll St., one block west on Carroll St., then right 1½ blocks. Come to this crowded neighborhood hangout for wholesome, substantial Italian lunches such as fried calamari ($6). Avoid the tepid-looking gyros, but you probably can't go wrong with the daily specials ($5-6). Open Mon.-Sat. 5am-5pm, Sun. 5am-4pm.

Stylowa Restaurant, 694 Manhattan Ave. (718-383-8993), between Norman and Nassau Ave. in Greenpoint. Subway: G to Nassau Ave. Polish cuisine at its best and cheapest. Sit among Polish-speakers and sample *kielbasa* (Polish sausage) with fried onions, sauerkraut, and bread ($4) or roast beef in homemade gravy with potatoes ($4). Excellent potato pancakes $3. All other entrees ($2.75-7.25) served with a glass of compote (pink, apple-flavored fruit drink). Open Mon.-Thurs. noon-9pm, Fri. noon-10pm, Sat. 11am-10pm, Sun. 11am-9pm.

Stacy's, 85 Broadway (718-486-8004), at Berry St. in Williamsburg. Subway: J, M, or Z to Marcy St., then walk four blocks west on Broadway to Berry St. This small, bohemian eatery offers friendly service and a small, eclectic menu including stick-to-your-bones fare such as Moroccan vegetable stew ($6). Entrees $5-8. Open Mon.-Fri. 7am-10pm, Sat. 11am-10pm.

Teresa's, 80 Montague St. (718-797-3996), in Brooklyn Heights. Subway: #2, 3, 4, 5, M, or R to Borough Hall; Montague St. is right there. Good, cheap Polish food in a pleasant wood and off-white interior. Two pieces of stuffed pepper ($6.50) or some *pierogi* ($3.50) stuffed with cheese, potatoes, meat, or sauerkraut and mushrooms make a filling meal. Try the weekday lunch specials (Mon.-Fri. 11am-4pm)—entree, soup and beverage for $6 . Open daily 7am-11pm.

Damascus Bakery, 195 Atlantic Ave. (718-855-1456), in Brooklyn Heights. Subway: #2, 3, 4, 5, M, or R to Borough Hall, then down 4 blocks on Court St. Friendly bakery serving up all kinds of baked goods, Middle Eastern and otherwise. Superior *baklava* $1.50, others $1-2. Open daily 7am-7pm.

College Bakery, 239 Court St. (718-624-5534), between Baltic and Kane St. in Carroll Gardens. Subway: F or G to Bergen St., west one block to Court St., then left 3 blocks. Yummy Italian pastries around $1-2. Open Tues.-Sat. 7am-8pm.

Buddy's Burritos and Taco Bar, 260 Court St. (718-488-8695), between Kane and Douglass St. in Carroll Gardens. Subway: F or G to Bergen St., west one block to Court St., then left 4 blocks. You should probably eat Italian food in this neighborhood, but if you want a well-stuffed burrito made with fresh ingredients ($5-6), this is the place. Open Mon.-Sat. 11:30am-11pm, Sun. 11:30am-10pm.

Fountain Café, 183 Atlantic Ave. (718-624-6764), in Brooklyn Heights. Subway: #2, 3, 4, 5, M, or R to Borough Hall, then down 4 blocks on Court St. This place, named for a rumbly little fountain in the center of the restaurant, serves up inexpensive and more-than-edible Middle Eastern food. *Shwarma* $4, shish kebab $3.75, felafel sandwich $2.85, Syrian spinach pie $1.50. Open daily 10:30am-10:30pm.

Junior's, 986 Flatbush Ave. Extension (718-852-5257), across the Manhattan Bridge at De Kalb St. Subway: #2, 3, 4, 5, B, D, M, N, Q, or R to Atlantic Ave. Lit up like a jukebox, Junior's feeds classic roast beef and brisket to hordes of loyals. Brisket sandwich $6.25, dinner specials $10. Suburbanites drive for hours to satisfy their cheesecake cravings here (plain slice $3.50). Open Sun.-Thurs. 6:30am-12:30am, Fri.-Sat. 6:30am-2am.

Milo's Restaurant, 559 Lorimer St. (718-384-8457), near Metropolitan Ave. in Williamsburg. Subway: G to Lorimer St.-Metropolitan Ave. or L to Metropolitan Ave.-Grand St. In a neighborhood packed with Italian food, this place stands out with its Sinatra-special jukebox (19 of his greatest!). Antipasto $3, several choices of pasta for less than $5. Don't miss the Neapolitan specialty *capozzelle*, which consists of an entire lamb's head, garnished with lemon wedges, that resembles one of Georgia O'Keefe's skulls before the sea and sand got to it ($5.50). Open Wed.-Sun. 11am-9pm.

■ CENTRAL BROOKLYN

In Central Brooklyn, good ethnic fare abounds. Despite its recent yuppification and growing chic, the Park Slope area remains a haven for international specialties at reasonable prices. Eighth Avenue in Sunset Park is the heart of Brooklyn's Chinatown, and Church Ave. in Flatbush is the place to go for Jamaican and other West Indian cuisine.

★ **El Castillo de Jagua,** 148 Fifth Ave. (718-783-9743), at Douglass St. in Park Slope. Subway: D or Q to 7th Ave., south 2 blocks on 7th Ave, then right on St. Johns St. two blocks to Fifth Ave. The deafening jukebox pumps out the newest Latino rhythms. Excellent, cheap food with great breakfast specials. Try the *pasteles,* meat-filled green bananas, for $1.50. Full meals (such as the succulent fried chicken for $5.50) run $5-12 and include beans and rice, plantains, or (if you're a lame-o) french fries. Open daily 7am-midnight.

★ **Tom's Restaurant,** 782 Washington Ave. (718-636-9738), at Sterling Pl. Subway: #2 or 3 to Brooklyn Museum. Walk a ½-block east to Washington St. and then 1½ blocks north. The best breakfast place in Brooklyn—an old-time luncheonette complete with a soda fountain and 50s-style hyper-friendly service. Two eggs with fries or grits, toast, and coffee or tea $1.95. Famous golden challah french toast $2.75. Breakfast served all day. Open Mon.-Sat. 6:30am-4pm.

El Gran Castillo de Jagua, 345 Flatbush Ave. (718-622-8700), at Carlton St. near Grand Army Plaza. Subway: D or Q to 7th Ave. A terrific place for cheap, authentic Latino food. Meat dinners with rice and beans or plantains and salad $5-7. Try the *mofungo* (crushed green plantains with roast pork and gravy), $3.50. Open daily 7am-midnight.

Donna's Jerked Chicken, 3125 Church Ave. (718-287-8182), between 31st and 32nd St. in Flatbush. Subway: #2 or 5 to Church Ave. and 2 blocks east. Jerked chicken is a Jamaican specialty—crispy chicken roasted with a sweet and very peppery marinade. It's good; try it here, or sample one of the many other enticing entrees ($5-9). Open daily 11am-midnight.

Aunt Sonia's, 1123 Eighth Ave. (718-965-9526) at 12th St. near Park Slope. Subway: F to Seventh Ave.-Park Slope. Walk east one block to 8th Ave. and then south three blocks. A tiny, very classy haven for the budget gourmand. Besides providing daily specials, the chef unveils a new menu every two months to loyal crowds. Entrees $9-18. Open Mon.-Thurs. 5:30-10pm, Fri.-Sat. 5:30-11pm, Sun. 11am-3:30pm, 5:30-10pm.

Gia Lam, 5402 Eighth Ave. (718-854-8818), at 54th St. in Sunset Park. Subway: N to 8th Ave. This popular Vietnamese restaurant serves large portions at low prices. The squid with lemongrass on rice ($3.50) is an excellent lunch choice. Lunches $3-5, dinner entrees $6-9. Open Mon.-Thurs. 11am-10:15pm, Fri. 11am-10:30pm, Sat.-Sun. 10:30am-10:30pm.

Short Ribs, 9101 Third Ave. (718-745-0614), in Bay Ridge. Subway: R to 86th St. Walk one block west and south a few blocks. The best barbecue around—especially if someone else foots the somewhat hefty bill. Try the French onion soup served in a round loaf of semolina bread ($4.50). A solid meal with onion rings costs $10-15. Incredibly popular; this two-story joint fills at mealtimes. Open daily noon-2am.

Hammond's Finger Lickin' Bakery, 5014 Church Ave. (718-342-5770), at Utica Ave. in Flatbush. Subway: #2 or 5 to Church Ave., then 20 blocks east. Jamaican and other West Indian pastries all $1-2, including juicy fruit turnovers ($1.60). Open daily 9am-7pm.

Oriental Palace, 5609 Eighth Ave. (718-633-6688), near 56th St. in Sunset. Subway: N or R to 59th St. Authentic and inexpensive. *Dim sum* $1.50 per piece, including chicken feet and bird's nest (daily 7:30am-4pm). Lunch around $3, roast pork bun 50¢. Juicy roasted meats on rice $3-4. Open daily 7:30am-midnight.

■ SOUTH BROOKLYN

The shores of Brooklyn present a welcome culinary quandary: the choices are endless. Try authentic Eastern European knishes (heated, flaky dough with a choice of filling) on Brighton Beach Avenue, Italian *calamari* (fried squid) in spicy marinara sauce along Emmons Avenue in Sheepshead Bay, or tri-colored candy on Coney Island. Eat until you feel ill—it still won't make a dent in your wallet.

★ **Primorski Restaurant,** 282 Brighton Beach Ave. (718-891-3111), between Brighton Beach 2nd St. and Brighton Beach 3rd St. Subway: D or Q to Brighton Beach, then four blocks east on Brighton Beach Ave. Populated by Russian-speaking Brooklynites, this vaguely nautically-themed restaurant serves the best Ukrainian borscht ($2.25) in the Western hemisphere in an atmosphere of gritty Slavic decadence. Many of the waiters struggle with English, but every dish is tasty. Eminently affordable lunch special (Mon.-Fri. 11am-5pm, Sat.-Sun. 11am-4pm; $4) is the best lunch deal in NYC—your choice of among three soups and about 15 entrees, bread, salad, and coffee or tea. At night, prices rise as the disco ball begins to spin. Nightly entertainment, including "live disco music." Open daily 11am-2am.

Bi-Metro, 107 Brighton Beach Ave. (718-714-5996). Subway: D or Q to Brighton Beach, then one block east on Brighton Beach Ave. A kosher diner with excellent prices: try the lunch special, which includes a choice of soup, entree, side dish, and fruit ($5). Sandwiches start at $4. Open daily 7am-10pm.

Jimmy's Famous Heros, 1786 Sheepshead Bay Rd. (718-648-8001), near Emmons Ave. Subway: D or Q to Sheepshead Bay, then southeast on Sheepshead Bay Rd. a little ways. Heros—New Yorkese for subs or grinders—cost about $5 and can be shared by two. Never mind what it entails; always ask for "the works" on whatever you order. Open Mon.-Fri. 7am-6pm, Sat. 7am-7pm, Sun. 7am-5pm.

Joe's Clam Bar, 2009 Emmons Ave. (718-646-9375), across the street from the bay. Subway: D or Q to Sheepshead Bay, then Sheepshead Bay Rd. southeast to Emmons Ave. and left to 21st St. Pricey, but the fish hail from the Atlantic rather than the toxic bay. Try the fried *calamari* and dip the chunks of chewy squid in hot or mild sauce ($12). Raw clams served on the half-shell ($5 for 6) are especially good smothered in lemon juice and crackers. Open Sun. 11am-midnight, Mon.-Thurs. 11am-1am, Fri.-Sat. 11am-2am.

Roll-n-Roaster, Nostrand Ave. and Emmons Ave. (718-769-6000). Subway: D or Q to Sheepshead Bay. Take Sheepshead Bay Rd. southeast to Emmons Ave. and go left about ½-mi. Twenty years of remarkable roast beef ($3.30) have earned this semi-fast food joint a loyal following despite the plastic gas lamps and hollow stone walls. Cheese fries a perennial favorite ($1.70). Open Sun.-Thurs. 11am-11pm, Fri.-Sat. 11am-1am.

Sea Lane Bakery, 615 Brighton Beach Ave. (718-934-8877). Subway: D or Q to Brighton Beach, then about 5 blocks east on Brighton Beach Ave. The best Jewish bakery in Brighton. Try a little of everything (9 kinds of pastry cost 85¢ each) or buy a loaf of honey cake with almonds and cherries ($4). Open daily 7am-9pm.

Nathan's, Surf and Stillwell Ave. (718-946-2206), in Coney Island. Subway: B, D, F, or N to Coney Island. Seventy-four years ago, Nathan Handwerker became famous for underselling his competitors on the boardwalk: his hot dogs cost a nickel; theirs were a dime. His crunchy dogs have since become nationally famous, sold in franchises of the restaurant and in supermarkets. A classic frank at this crowded place—the original Nathan's—sells for $1.79. Unique, absurdly plump crinkle-cut french fries ($1.59). Open Sun.-Thurs. 8am-4am, Fri.-Sat. 8am-5am.

Philip's Confections, 1237 Surf Ave. (718-372-8783), at the entrance to the B, D, F, or N train in Coney Island. Sate your inner child. Famous salt-water taffy (95¢ for a ¼-lb.). Candy or caramel apple 75¢. Cotton candy $1. Lime rickeys (60¢) are one of the cheapest and best Coney Island refreshment sources on hot summer days. Open Sun.-Thurs. 11am-3am, Fri.-Sat. 11am-4am.

■■■ QUEENS

With nearly every ethnic group represented in Queens, this often overlooked borough offers visitors authentic and reasonably priced international cuisine away from Manhattan's urban neighborhoods. **Astoria** specializes in discount shopping and cheap eats. Take the G or R train to Steinway St. and Broadway and start browsing— the pickings are good in every direction. The number of Greek and Italian restaurants increases right around the elevated station at Broadway and 31st St., where you can catch the N train north to Ditmars Blvd. for still more Astorian cuisine. In **Flushing,** excellent Chinese, Japanese, and Korean restaurants flourish. Restaurants here often make use of authentic ingredients, such as skatefish, squid, and tripe, that more Americanized Asian restaurants tend to shy away from. Always check the prices; an identical dish may cost half as much only a few doors away. **Bell Boulevard** in Bayside, out east near the Nassau border, is the center of Queens nightlife for the young, white, and semi-affluent; on most weekends you can find crowds of natives bar-hopping here.

In **Jamaica** and the other African-American and West Indian neighborhoods to its southeast, you can try fast food like Jamaican beef pattie or West Indian *rito* (flour tortilla filled with potatoes, meat, and spices). Jamaica Avenue in downtown Jamaica and Linden Blvd. in neighboring St. Albans are lined with restaurants specializing in this type of cuisine. Jamaica also holds a **farmer's market** at 159-15 Jamaica Ave. (718-291-0282; open Mon.-Fri. 7am-7:30pm, Sat. 7am-7pm), where a few farmers offer their bounty indoors, next to a food court that offers Caribbean and Carolina-Southern restaurants, among others. To get to Jamaica, take the E or J train to Jamaica Center; from there the Q4 bus goes to Linden Blvd. in St. Albans. The **St. Albans West Indian Bakery,** 187-17 Linden Blvd. (718-525-2078), just west of Farmers Blvd., serves great Jamaican beef patties ($1) and a huge selection of fresh-baked breads. (No seating; open Mon.-Fri. 8am-8pm, Sat.-Sun. 8am-9:30pm.)

★ **Pastrami King,** 124-24 Queens Blvd. (718-263-1717), near 82nd Ave., in Kew Gardens. Subway: E or F to Union Tpke./Kew Gardens. Exit station following sign that says "Courthouse" and "Q10 bus;" then go left following the sign to the north side of Queens Blvd.; it's 2 blocks ahead and across the street. Everything here, from the meats to the coleslaw to the pickles, is made on the premises. The home-cured pastrami and corned beef are among the best in New York. Take out a sprawling, 3-inch-thick pastrami on rye for $6 or eat in at one of the back tables. Open Sun.-Fri. 11am-9pm, Sat. 11am-10pm.

★ **Louie's Pizza,** 30-79 Steinway St., Astoria (718-626-9800), between 30th and 31st Ave. Subway: G or R to Steinway St., then walk north 1½ blocks. The standard, small-parlor decor might not seem too inviting, but Louie makes a quality pie for cheap. (Pick up a delivery menu at the counter to see a picture of Louie with his family.) Regular or Sicilian slice $1.25. 14" large pizza $7 (a great deal). Calzones and strombolis $3. Open Mon.-Sat. 11am-10pm, Sun. noon-8pm.

Uncle George's, 33-19 Broadway, Astoria (718-626-0593), at 33rd St. Subway: N to Broadway, then 2 blocks east; or G or R to Steinway St., then 4 blocks west. This popular Greek restaurant, known as *"Barba Yiogis O Ksenihtis"* to the locals, serves inexpensive and hearty Greek delicacies around the clock. Almost all entrees are under $10; try the roast leg of lamb with potatoes ($8), or, if you're feeling intrepid, the octopus sauteed with vinegar ($7). Excellent Greek salad with feta cheese ($6). The hanging plants and flowers on the table lend the diner a cheery greenhouse effect. Open daily 24 hrs.

Jack 'n' Jill's, 187-29 Linden Blvd., St. Albans (718-723-9344), near Mexico St. Subway: E, J, or Z to Jamaica Ctr., then the Q4 bus to St. Albans and Linden Blvd.; ask to be let off at Farmers Blvd. and then backtrack 1 block. Small and sparely decorated, the BBQ here will give you a good dose of Southern harmony. 4-piece BBQ rib dinner $8.30; half BBQ'd chicken $6—both served with choice of 2 sides such as greens, string beans, black-eyed peas, or candied yams. Try the peach cobbler ($1.50) for dessert. Open daily noon-9pm.

Kuala Lumpur, 135-31 40th Rd., Flushing (718-353-8333), just off Main St. Subway: #7 to Main St., then go south on Main St. one block to 40th Rd. and take a right. Malaysian cuisine (basically Chinese crossed with a little bit of Indian) for breakfast, lunch, and dinner at extremely reasonable prices. The lunchtime special (Mon.-Fri. 11am-3pm) features 3 small dishes of your choice, soup, and fresh fruit for $3.75—a great deal. Karaoke nightly in basement starting around 8pm. Open daily 6am-midnight.

First Edition, Bell Blvd. at 41st Ave., Bayside (718-428-8522). Subway: #7 to Main St.-Flushing, then the Q12 bus (catch it in front of Stern's Department Store, next to the station) along Northern Ave. to Bell Blvd., then walk north 3 blocks. This bar/restaurant tries to lure you in with cheap, filling food specials and then stick it to you with costly drinks. If you can control your thirst, you'll eat for cheap. Mon. 25¢ wings and half-price chicken fingers; Tues. half-price pizzas and pastas; Wed. half-price ribs and supersalads; Thurs. half-price fajitas and heroes; Sun. 25¢ wings and half-price burgers. Specials run all day. Crowded, lively, and meat-marketish at night. Open daily 11am-4am.

Galaxy Pastry Shop, 37-11 30th Ave., Astoria (718-545-3181). Subway: N to 30th Ave. (Grand Ave.) Make a right on 30th Ave. and walk east to 37th St. The deliciously gooey baklava ($1) and fried dough are among the best in the neighborhood, if not anywhere. Gorge yourself at a squeaky-clean table inside the slickly mirrored shop, or lounge in the ample outdoor seating area. Open daily 6:30am-2am.

Woo Chon Restaurant, 41-19 Kissena Blvd., Flushing (718-463-0803). Subway: #7 to Main St., then walk south 2 blocks to where Kissena Blvd. forks off to your left; it's just ahead on the left. Duck behind the waterfall for some of the finest Korean food in Flushing. Abandon the safety of Korean-style "barbecue" ($14-17) and experiment with selections like *gop dol bibimbab* ($9), an obscure and ancient rice dish served in a superheated stone vessel; mix immediately, or the rice will be scorched by the bowl. For lunch, try a filling bowl of *sulrong tang* ($6.50), fine rice noodles in a beef broth with assorted Oriental veggies. An unlimited supply of *kim-chi* (spicy marinated vegetables) accompanies every meal. Open 24 hrs.

Empire Kosher Chicken Restaurant, 100-19 Queens Blvd. (718-997-7315), in Forest Hills. Subway: G or R to 67th Ave.; when leaving the station, head right following the sign that says "67th Ave.-North Side Queens Blvd." Turn around at the top of the stairs, and it's right behind you. Cheap chicken prepared according to Jewish law by one of the major kosher meat manufacturers. Fried, roasted, nuggetized, or barbecued birds served quickly, cafeteria-style. Dinners ($6-8.50) include a fresh-baked muffin and two sides. Sandwiches ($3-3.75) range from an excellent chicken salad ($3.70) to the exotic "fried fillet of chicken breast" ($3.25). Open Sun.-Thurs. 11am-9:30pm, Fri. 11am-2:30pm (take-out until 4pm), Sat. from 1 hr. after Shabbat until 10:30pm.

Waterfront Crabhouse, 2-03 Borden Ave. Long Island City (718-729-4862). Subway: #7 to Vernon Blvd./Jackson Ave., then south on Vernon; turn right on Borden Ave. and walk all the way to the river. Perhaps better named the "Across-the-Street-from-the-Waterfront" Crabhouse, this is the former home of the turn-of-the-century "Miller's Hotel," through which the rich and famous passed as they escaped to Long Island by ferry. Theodore Roosevelt, Grover Cleveland, and Lillian Russell all dined in this building, which lost its 3rd floor in a fire in 1975. Today the likes of Paul Newman and Ed Asner dine in the Crabhouse's wooden booths, which are decorated with the requisite antiques and touches of stained glass. Kindle a romance with the "Loveboat," a stuffed lobster floating in an ocean of shrimp scampi ($19). Beef steaks $7-14. Daily entertainment. Reservations recommended. Open Mon.-Wed. noon-10pm, Thurs. noon-11pm, Fri. noon-midnight, Sat. 1pm-midnight, Sun. 1-10pm.

■■■ BRONX

When Italian immigrants settled the Bronx, they brought their recipes and a tradition of hearty communal dining. While much of the Bronx is a culinary disaster zone, the New York *cognoscenti* soon discovered the few oases along Arthur Avenue and in Westchester where the fare is as robust and the patrons as rambunctious as their counterparts in Naples. The neighborhood of **Belmont,** which centers around the intersection of Arthur Ave. and 187th St. brims with pastry shops, streetside *caffè,* pizzerias, restaurants, and mom-and-pop emporiums vending Madonna 45s and battalions of imported espresso machines—all this without the schmaltzy tourist veneer of Little Italy. Revel in elaborate French and Italian pastries to the tune of a warm cappuccino at **Egioio Pastry Shop,** 622 E. 187th St. An octogenarian with modern flair, a trim, sexy interior, and inviting outdoor tables, Egioio makes the best *gelato* in the Bronx. To get to Arthur Ave., take the #2 train to Pelham Pkwy., then Bronx bus #BX12 two stops west; alternatively, take the C or D train to Fordham Rd. and walk five blocks east.

Ann & Tony's, 2407 Arthur Ave. (718-933-1469), at 187th St. Typical of Arthur Ave., this bistro has not only an understated and comfortable decor but excellent food as well. Unlike most restaurants in the area, however, Ann & Tony's has specials for dinner that run as low as $6, salad included. For lunch, sandwiches begin at $5. Open Tues.-Thurs. 11:30am-10pm, Fri. 11:30am-11pm, Sat. noon-midnight, Sun. 2-9pm.

Mario's, 2342 Arthur Ave. (718-584-1188), near 186th St. Five generations of the Migliucci *famiglia* have worked the kitchen of this celebrated southern Italian *trattoria.* The original clan left Naples in the early 1900s and opened the first Italian restaurant in Egypt, then came to the U.S. and cooked themselves into local lore: Mario's appears in the pages of Puzo's *Godfather.* Celebrities pass through, among them the starting lineups for the Yankees and the Giants. A room-length couch embraces patrons with familial arms. Try *spiedini alla romana,* a deep-fried sandwich made with anchovy sauce and mozzarella ($8). Notorious for pizza too. Traditional pasta $9-11, *antipasto* $5.50, eggplant stuffed with ricotta $6.25. Open Sun. and Tues.-Thurs. noon-10:30pm, Fri.-Sat. noon-midnight.

Dominick's, 2335 Arthur Ave. (718-733-2807), near 186th St. Small authentic Italian eatery. Vinyl tablecloths and bare walls but great atmosphere nonetheless. Waiters won't offer you a menu or a check—they'll recite the specials of the day and bark out what you owe at the end of the meal. Try the linguine with marinara sauce ($7) and the special veal *francese* ($12). Arrive before 6pm or after 9pm, or expect at least a 20-min. wait. Open Mon. and Wed.-Sat. noon-10pm, Sun. 1-9pm.

Pasquale's Rigoletto, 2311 Arthur Ave. (718-365-6644). A relative newcomer to the Arthur Ave. pasta scene, Pasquale's cooks with the best of them. As the name suggests, they do soothe you with potent arias; if you have a favorite in mind, they'll gladly play it. Favorite customer Joe Pesci's pictures adorn the front door. *Antipasto* $8.50, pasta $12.50, poultry $14.50. Open Tues.-Fri. noon-10pm, Sat.-Sun. noon-1am.

Taormina Ristorante, 1805 Edison Ave. (718-823-1646). Subway: #6 to Buhre Ave. Hearty Italian fare in the shadow of the subway tracks. Combine any pasta with any sauce to suit your fancy. Pasta $9.50-10, sandwiches $5-8. Chicken dishes from $10, veal from $12. Open Mon.-Thurs. noon-10:30pm, Fri.-Sat. noon-11:30pm, Sun. noon-10pm.

Tony's Pizza, 34 E. Bedford Park Blvd. (718-367-2854). Subway: #4 to Bedford Park Blvd. Pizza so good that students from nearby Bronx High School of Science will skip class to grab a slice. Crisp crust slathered with generous amounts of cheese. Slice $1.30, extra topping 65¢. Open Mon.-Sat. 11am-8pm.

Ruggieri Pastry Shop, 2373 Prospect Ave., at E. 187th St. Established in 1910, and now under the dynamic leadership of Sam and Lurdes, this shop produces mountains upon mountains of classic Italian pastries, though they're especially proud of their sfogliatella, a flaky Neapolitan pastry stuffed with ricotta. Those nostalgic for the groovy golden '50s will be glad to know that Ruggieri operates one of the last authentic ice cream fountains in New York. Drag your sweetheart here for a real malted ($4) or an egg cream ($1.25). Open daily 8am-10pm.

Caffè

Caffè Egidio, 622 E. 187 St. (718-295-6077), near Arthur Ave. In addition to *gelati*, cappuccino, espresso, and a fascinating interior complete with oversized portraits of the Borgias, this *caffè* has one of the largest selections of jellybeans in the city with flavors from blueberry and lemon meringue to banana and cranberry. Also has inexpensive lunch and dinner specials. Open daily 7am-10pm.

Caffè Margherita, 689 E. 187 St., near Arthur Ave. In the late '70s the *New York Times* called Margherita's cappuccino the "best in the world." On hot summer nights, retreat from the city into the fantasies offered by this *caffè*, complete with an outdoor jukebox with tunes ranging from Sinatra and Madonna to Italian folk music. Also serves pizza. "Cold" espresso $2. Alcohol served but no desserts. Open daily 8am-midnight.

De Lillo Pastry Shop, 606 E. 187 St. (718-367-8198), near Arthur Ave. Although this small shop is often crowded, it's worth your while to sit here and sample the excellent baked goods ($1-2) along with a cappuccino ($1.75) or espresso ($1.25). Open daily 8am-7:30pm.

■■■ HOBOKEN, NJ

The food in Hoboken is pretty uniformly mediocre. Then again, one comes to Hoboken not to eat, but to drink (see Bars below). Many of the hottest bars have restaurants attached—snag your munchies there instead. To get to Hoboken, take the B, D, F, N, Q, or R train to 34th St., then the PATH train ($1) to the 1st stop in Hoboken. (The PATH train also leaves from the 23rd and 14th St. stations of the F train, as well as from its own stations at 9th St./Sixth Ave. and Christopher St./Greenwich St.) To get to the main drag of Washington St. from the PATH station, walk along Hudson Pl. to Hudson St., up one block to Newark St., left two blocks to Washington St., and right onto Washington St.

Ray's Soul Kitchen, 1039 Washington St. (201-798-4064), at 11th St. in Maxwell's. Southern-style soul food most notable for its tantalizing proximity to luminary underground rock types. Platter o' food $11. Open Fri.-Sun. 4pm-1am.

Bel Gusto Bagel Smashery and Café, 718 Washington St. (201-217-9119), between 7th and 8th St. They claim to attack your food with hammers here. A "potato smash" with cheese $2.50, a "pizza bagel smash" $3.25. Say hello to the friendly calico kitty (if she doesn't say hello first), and if you're feeling frisky order an erotic cake for your next party ($45 and up). Open Mon.-Fri. 7:30am-4pm, Sat.-Sun. 8am-3pm.

BARS

New York soaks in bars. Every major street has a couple of dark holes where the locals burrow on weeknights. Most keep prices tied down and music pumped up. To capture the essence of a particular New York subset, venture into the wild Venn diagram of the city's bar life. Many music and dance clubs (see Entertainment and Nightlife) are also festive places to quaff; the following listings are for places where the focus is on conversing and imbibing.

■■■ GREENWICH VILLAGE

Automatic Slims, 733 Washington St. (645-8660), at Bank St. Subway: A, C, or E to 14th St. Simple bar in the West Village with the best selection of blues and screamin' soul, complemented by the pensive faces of South-side stars. Twenty-something Villagers sit at tables with classic 45s under the glass top. Packed on weekends with a more diverse crowd. American cooking served 6pm-midnight. Entrees $7.50-14. Open Sun.-Mon. 5:30pm-2:30am, Tues.-Sat. 5:30pm-4:30am.

Barrow Street Ale House, 15 Barrow St. (206-7302), near Seventh Ave. and W. 4th St. Ignore the paintings on the wall and enjoy this roomy neighborhood bar. Don't miss the tremendous deals: $1 drafts all day Sun. and Mon. and between 5:30-9:30pm on Tues. and Wed. You'll be laughing and stumbling all the way to the bank. Pool and pinball downstairs. Have a black and tan. Open Sun.-Thurs. 3pm-2am, Fri.-Sat. 3pm-4am.

Julius's, 159 W. 10th St. (929-9672), at Waverly Pl., between Sixth and Seventh Ave. This bar has been a hot spot for gay men since 1966, when gays staged a protest against the laws denying service to homosexuals. Today commemorative plaques explain the event in garbled prose as unruffled men drink legally amidst the rainbow flags.

Peculier Pub, 145 Bleecker St. (353-1327). Subway: #6 to Bleecker St. Over 300 kinds of beer from 43 countries. A neighborhood crowd during the week but packed with tourists and the "bridge-and-tunnel" crowd on weekends. Beer can get a little pricey: domestic beers $3-4, imports $5-6. Open Mon.-Wed. 5pm-2am, Thurs. 5pm-3am, Fri. 4pm-4am, Sat. 2pm-4am, Sun. 5pm-1am.

Polly Esther's, 21 E. 8th St. (979-1970), near University Pl. Grab those bell-bottoms and funky platform shoes—it's a bar dedicated to the 1970s! Brady Bunch reruns, discomania, psychedelic decor (complete with those weird rice-curtain things), and drinks like the Sonny and Cher special ($4.75)! Beer $3. Two-for-one happy hour 1-9pm on weekdays and 1-7pm on weekends. Open Mon.-Fri. 11am-2am, Sat.-Sun. 11am-4am. Another location at 249 W. 26th St. (929-4782).

The Slaughtered Lamb Pub, 182 Bleecker St. (627-LAMB), at Jones St. A rather sinister-looking English pub dedicated to the werewolf, although Jack Nicholson has not been sighted recently. Eighty types of beer ($5-20 per bottle), yards of ale, darts and billiards downstairs in the "dungeon." Check out the skeleton at the front door and try not to howl at the moon. Open 4pm-4am.

The Whitehorse Tavern, 567 Hudson St. (243-9260), at W. 11th St. Dylan Thomas drank himself to death here, pouring 19 straight whiskies through an already tattered liver. Boisterous students (and waiters) pay a strange and twisted homage to the poet. Beer $4, ½-off during happy hr. Open Sun.-Thurs. 11am-2am, Fri.-Sat. 11am-4am.

■■■ EAST VILLAGE, ALPHABET CITY, AND LOWER EAST SIDE-

Sophie's, 507 E. 5th St. (228-5680), between Ave. A and B. Subway: F to Second Ave. or #6 to Astor Pl. Packed with leather jackets, T-shirts, jeans, and baseball-caps on weekends. Cheap cheap cheap. Draft beer $1 for a large mug (imported draft $2). Mixed drinks start at $2.50. Pool table and soulful jukebox. Open daily noon-4am.

Max Fish, 178 Ludlow St. (529-3959), at Houston St. in the Lower East Side. Subway: F to Delancey St. or J, M, Z to Essex St. Wall covered with found art and original cartoons. Plastic skulls line the wall-ceiling juncture. The crowd is hip, if a bit pretentious, and the all-CD jukebox is easily the best in town: The Fall, The Minutemen, Superchunk, and the Gordons. Beer $2.50 per glass. Open daily 5:30pm-4am.

Ludlow St. Café, 165 Ludlow St. (353-0536), right below E. Houston St. in the Lower East Side. Subway: F to Delancey St. or J, M, Z to Essex St. Fashionable downtown bag ladies and men with shorn hair and nerdy glasses come here for loud live music. Music varies in quality and tends toward folk, rock, and strange;

the schedule is painted fluorescent on the wall. Dinner 6pm-midnight ($4-9). Draft beer $1.50, free with dinner. Open daily 6pm-3am. Cover Fri.-Sat. $3.

Siné, 122 St. Mark's Pl. (982-0370), between First Ave. and Ave. A. Subway: #6 to Astor Pl. Name means "That's it" in Gaelic. Down-to-earth, folksy crowd comes here after a long day at the farm. Live folk, blues, and Irish music at 8pm and 10pm nightly. No cover. Open daily 11am-1am.

The International Bar, 120½ First Ave. (777-9214), between 7th St. and St. Mark's Pl. This long and skinny bar has only two tables in the back, but the large, friendly counter seats many. Christmas lights and yellow-sponge-painted walls give this bar a fiery glow. Grimy and authentic East Village. Clientele includes immigrants, lost youths, and college kids. Lots of regulars and history. Open Mon.-Fri. 11am-4am, Sat.-Sun. noon-4am.

10th Street Lounge, 212 E. 10th St. (473-5252), between Second and Third Ave. A chic, new East Village hotspot where the artsy twentysomething set sip $4 beers on over-stuffed couches or around the circular bar. Dim red lighting and all kinds of music from reggae to hip-hop lure all types to this inconspicuous, unmarked hole-in-the-wall. Open daily until 3:30am.

■■■ SOHO

The Ear Inn, 326 Spring St. (226-9060), near the Hudson. Established in 1817 and once a big bohemian/activist hangout, this bar now tends to the TriBeCa young-and-wistful crowd. Dark woods, an uneven ceiling that's done some settling, and dusty old bottles behind the bar. Mellow jazz and blues at low volume so as not to stem the flow of conversation. Very comfortable; tables are covered with paper and stocked with crayons. Good American food served from 11am-4:30pm and 6pm-1am every day. Appetizers and salads $2-6, specials and entrees $5-9. Bar open till 4am.

Fanelli's, 94 Prince St. (226-9412), at Mercer St. Established in 1972, with a beautiful bar of black cast iron. A very mellow neighborhood hangout, where it always feels like late at night. Standard bar fare and cheap brew ($2.50 for domestic drafts, $3 for imports and micro-brews). Open Sun.-Thurs. 10am-2am, Fri.-Sat. 10am-3am.

Milano's, 51 E. Houston (226-8632), between Mulberry and Mott St. The celebrity crowd drifts in here on the weekends; Madonna stopped here with Sean in happier days. Long and so narrow that the bar almost divides the room in half, Milano's is dark, low-key, and full of kitschy comfort. Witness the Superman doll, the wall-painting of Bogart, and the photo of Marciano about to deck Joe Louis. Fine selection of drafts, including Harp, Guinness, Bass, New Amsterdam, and Watney's ($3.75 per pint). Happy Hour daily 4-7pm (pints $2.50). Open Mon.-Sat. 8am-4am, Sun. noon-4am.

Lucky Strike, 59 Grand St. (941-0479), at W. Broadway. Favorite hunting ground of the SoHo ultra-magna-beautiful, but $3.50 Budweisers with similarly scaled food prices in the back make this more of a sight than a watering hole. Expect to be stared at (rudely) as you walk in the door; if you're prepared to stare right back, then you'll have a good time. Open daily noon-4am.

■■■ UPPER WEST SIDE

The Bear Bar, 2156 Broadway (362-2145), at 76th St. A bit removed from the Amsterdam Ave. yupbar scene—thus cheaper and less boring. Stuffed black bears beside and over the door. Terrific beer selection with over 75 microbrews. Lots of cheap drink promotions, like a "drink early" scheme whereby beer starts at 50¢ at 5pm and goes up 25¢ every hour and "Ladies Drink Lite" nights Mon.-Wed. 8pm-close, where women drink all the lite beer they can for free. Open Mon.-Fri. 5pm-3am, Sat.-Sun. noon-3am.

The Westend Gate, 2911 Broadway (666-8687), between 113th and 114th St. Subway: #1 or 9 to 116th St. Once frequented by Kerouac, now a hangout for the Columbia University and prep-school set. Huge sitting areas, indoors and outdoors, give way to the small dance room with rock and funk bands in the back—6 bands every Fri.-Sat. night (cover $5 and up). Cheap pitchers with a great beer selection. Comedy club and theater downstairs (no cover for comedy, theater tickets around $10; 2-drink min.).

Lucy's Retired Surfers Bar and Restaurant, 503 Columbus Ave. (787-3009), at 85th St. Subway: B or C to 86th St. Loud and packed to frothing with young Upper West Siders and people who heard it was fun. Surfers and surfboards on the walls and on TV screens. Happy hour 3-7pm daily. Open 24 hrs.

The Shark Bar, 307 Amsterdam Ave. (874-8500), between 74th and 75th. High-class, enjoyable bar and soul-food restaurant; possibly the only truly interracial establishment on the Upper West Side below 110th St. Well-dressed after-work crowd nurses stiff drinks. Live jazz on Tues. with a $5 cover; "gospel brunch" Sat. 12:30pm and 2pm (no cover). Reasonable drink prices (bottled beer from $3). Entrees from $11. Open Mon.-Fri. 11:30am-2am, Sat.-Sun. 11:30am-4:30pm and 6:30pm-4am.

■■■ UPPER EAST SIDE

American Trash, 1471 First Ave. (988-9008), between 76th and 77th St. Cavernous barroom hung with "trash" oddities from Christmas stockings to prize ribbons. Baby busters having a wild-'n'-crazy time. Drink specials change every night; call for details. Women drink free Tues. 4-11:30pm. Happy hour daily 4-7pm. Pints $2. Open daily noon-4am.

Manny's Car Wash, 1558 Third Ave. (369-BLUE), between 87th and 88th Ave. Done up like a drive-thru car wash, this place host some smokin' blues. Come before 9pm and drink all you want for $5. Women drink free Mon. night. Happy hour Wed.-Sat. 5-10pm. Open daily 5pm-3:30am.

Electric Café Bar, 1608 Third Ave. (360-6036), between 90th and 91st St. Psychedelic posters pulsate on the walls and planets swirl in color on the ceiling. Locals of all ages from around the neighborhood play '90s tunes on a glistening '60s jukebox. Pinball and a garden for those who aren't glued to the bar. Pints $2, pitchers $6. Open 2pm-4am.

■■■ MIDTOWN AND CHELSEA

Coffee Shop Bar, 29 Union Sq. West (243-7969), facing Union Sq. Park. Subway: #4, 5, 6, L, N, or R to Union Sq. A chic diner for fashion victims, owned by three models. Sure, it's a bar, but more importantly, it's a spectacle. Go for a very late dinner, or to watch others have dinner. Open daily 23 hrs.

Old Town Bar and Grill, 45 E. 18th St. (473-8874), between Park Ave. and Broadway. Subway: #4, 5, 6, L, N, or R to Union Sq. A quieter hideaway with wood and brass, as seen on the old "Late Night" opening montage. Beer on tap $4, Heineken $3.50. Open Mon.-Fri. 11:30am-3pm and 5-11:30pm, Sat. 1-11:30pm, Sun. 3-10pm.

O'Flaherty's, 334 W. 46th St. (246-8928), between Eighth and Ninth Ave. Subway: A, C, or E to 50th St. Although located on ritzy Restaurant Row, this small bar manages to keep the feel of a true neighborhood pub. Great selection of beers on tap, including Murphy's ($4 per pint). Live music Tues.-Sat. at 10:30pm ranges from rock-and-roll to blues unplugged to bluegrass. Call for schedule.

Peter McManus, 152 Seventh Ave. (929-9691), at 19th St. Made famous by a *New York Times* article on the timeless appeal of ordinary bars, of which this is the epitome. Ordinary drinks, ordinary clientele, ordinary prices, and ordinary bathrooms. The carved mahogany bar and leaded glass windows add to the charm. $1.75 drafts. Open daily 11am-4am.

■■■ THE OUTER BOROUGHS

Adobe Blues, 63 Lafayette Ave. (718-720-2583) at Fillmore St., in Staten Island. Take the Staten Island Ferry, then the S40 bus to Lafayette Ave. A lively mix of beer and chili-lovers fill this bar, which is styled after the saloons of the Old West. Features the second-largest selection of beers in all of NYC—more than 230. Bottles arrive from the Czech Republic, Korea, Columbia, and France, as well as much of the rest of our Global Village. And the prices aren't bad either: a 20-oz. glass of Newcastle Brown runs $3.25 (but selection of drafts changes frequently). Also sample one (or two or three) of their 35 brands of tequila. Ask the bartender to give you a look at Jake the one-eyed king snake—he lost his eye in an unfortunate shedding accident. Lunch entrees $5-7, dinner entrees $8-13. Live jazz Wed., Fri., and Sat. nights with no cover. (Lunch served Mon.-Sat. 11:30am-5pm; dinner nightly 5-10:30pm; late-night menu available. Bar open Sun.-Thurs. 11:30am mid night, Fri.-Sat. 11:30am-2am.)

Teddy's, N. 8th St. and Berry St. (718-384-9787), in Greenpoint, Brooklyn. Subway: L to Bedford Ave. and one block west. The new artiste crowd starts drinking here, and only you can find out where they end up. Cheap drinks ($1-3). Jazz on Thurs. from Nov.-March. Open daily 11am-1am.

■■■ HOBOKEN, NJ

Hoboken swims in alcohol. Everywhere you go, there's bound to be a raucous bar in earshot. Go down the mile of Washington St. (1st to 14th St.), the area from Newark St. to 4th St. in the south of town, and the region surrounding the PATH station. PATH runs 24 hours, so even Manhattanites can come and drink 'til they drop. Remember to bring your 21+ ID.

In June 1994 the City Council, worried about rampant drunkenness and potential World Cup fervor, ruled that all bars in Hoboken must close at 1am. They then ruled that bars could stay open until 3am, but with a "one-way" policy of no admittance or re-admittance after 1am. The situation is still working itself out.

To get to Hoboken, take the B, D, F, N, Q, or R train to 34th St., then the PATH train ($1) to the 1st stop in Hoboken. (The PATH train also leaves from the 23rd and 14th St. stations of the F train, as well as from its own stations at 9th St./Sixth Ave. and Christopher St./Greenwich St.)

Scotland Yard, 72 Hudson St. (201-222-YARD). From the PATH station, walk along Hudson Pl. to Hudson St. and up two blocks. A dim, smoky place with little seating but a huge bar. Beers $2.50-3. Open daily 11:30am-1am.

Miss Kitty's Saloon and Dance Hall Floozies, 94-98 Bloomfield St. (201-792-0041), at 1st St. From the PATH station, walk along Hudson Pl. to Hudson St., up three blocks to 1st St., left four blocks to Bloomfield St. A sit-down bar/restaurant featuring occasional musical entertainment and a lively clientele. Beers $3-3.50. Open daily 4pm-1am.

Fabian's, 110 1st St. at Bloomfield St. From the PATH station, walk along Hudson Pl. to Hudson St., up three blocks to 1st St., left four blocks to Bloomfield St. This small, dark, fortress-like bar offers a welcome respite from the frat-boy chug-a-lug atmosphere so rampant in the other bars in town. Ol' Blue Eyes Frank Sinatra (a former Hoboken resident) croons on the jukebox here, where the more angstful members of the Hoboken slacker set come to relax.

Bahama Mama's, 215 Washington St. (201-217-1642). From the PATH station, walk along Hudson Pl. to Hudson St., up one block to Newark St., left two blocks to Washington St., and right a few blocks. Frat-boy heaven. From the bitter invective against the City Council ordinance to the festively Caribbean-themed decor, this place drips with *Animal House*-style antics. Pay-what-you-weigh schtick ("if your [sic] 300 lbs. or more, keep walkin'"). Open daily 8pm-3am.

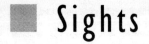

Sights

Far below and around lay the city like a ragged purple dream, the
wonderful, cruel, enchanting, bewildering, fatal, great city.

—O. Henry

The classic sightseeing quandary experienced by New York tourists is finding the Empire State Building. They've seen it in dozens of pictures and drawings, captured in sharp silhouettes or against a steamy pink sky as a monument of dreams. They've seen it towering over the grey landscape as their plane descends onto the runway, or in perspective down long avenues or from a river tour. But they can't see it when they're standing right next to it.

This optical illusion may explain why many New Yorkers have never visited some of the major sights in their hometown. When you're smack in the middle of them, the tallest skyscrapers seem like a casual part of the scenery. In this densely-packed city, even the most mind-boggling sights are awash in the endless combination of environments that serve as backdrops for everyday life. Not all sights are as glaringly obvious as the Statue of Liberty. Sometimes you'll enter a modest doorway to find treasures inside, and sometimes you'll need to take a long elevator ride to see what everybody's raving about. If it's your first time in the big city, you'll notice even more subtle attractions—the neighborhoods and personalities jumbled together on shared turf, the frenzy of throngs at rush hour, the metropolitan murmur at dusk. And if it's your hundredth time in the city, there will still be parts of town you don't know too well, architectural quirks you've never noticed, and streetscapes you've never appreciated. Seeing New York takes a lifetime.

■■■ SIGHTSEEING TOURS

The best way to discover New York City is on foot. Stare at a map, learn the layout of the city, and hit the streets. **Walking tours** offer the inside scoop on neighborhoods and sights you might overlook, as knowledgeable New Yorkers share their love for the city with you. Many of these tours are thematic or highly specialized. Call around to get a sense of what's being offered on the days you plan to be in the city (and see Walking Tours below).

Standard **bus tours** whisk you around Manhattan in cushy splendor, often stopping at a pre-printed list of sights and directing you to a slew of souvenir stands. These tours are good for an overview of the city but offer little to those willing to use the subway and do some legwork. More specialized bus tours are usually more rewarding, though there are probably better walking tours of the same areas. **Boat tours** offer breathtaking views of the cityscape, but don't expect to see much more.

A number of New York landmarks offer tours of their inner workings. Imperial **Lincoln Center** sponsors guided tours of its theaters: The Metropolitan Opera House, New York State Theater, and Avery Fisher Hall. There are four to eight tours every day, from 10am to 5pm, and they last about an hour (admission $7.50, students and seniors $6.50, children $4.25). For information, and to make a reservation, call 875-5351. In addition, a free tour every Wednesday at 2pm instructs the curious in the art of locating items in the library's mammoth collection of musical soundtracks and movie scores. The tour passes through the center's three art galleries. For information, call 870-1670.

Historic **Carnegie Hall,** at Seventh Ave. and 57th St., opens its doors to tourists Mondays, Tuesdays, Thursdays, and Fridays at 11:30am, 2pm, and 3pm. The tour grants entrance to the main hall itself, discusses the history and architecture of the building, visits other performance spaces in the building, and lasts about an hour.

Tours cost $6, seniors and students $5, children under 10 $3. For information, call 903-9790.

A true shrine to an era long past, **Radio City Music Hall,** 1260 Sixth Ave. (632-4041), between 50th and 51st St., gives behind-the-scenes tours every day between 10am and 5pm, leaving every 30 to 45 minutes. Billed as "the one-hour tour that will last you a lifetime," the tour grants access to the Great Stage, the 6000-seat auditorium, and the mighty Wurlitzer; lets you talk with a current member of the Rockettes; and fills you in on the full history of the place. Admission is $9 for adults and $4.50 for children under 7. Check out "Late Night" arrival Conan O'Brien on the **NBC Studio Tour,** where you'll also see **Saturday Night Live's** famous Studio 8H. (Tours given daily 9:30am-4:30pm, leaving every 15 minutes. Extended hours for summer months and holidays. Each tour is limited to 17 people, and tickets go on a first-come, first-served basis. No one under 6 admitted. Admission $8.25.)

Madison Square Garden (465-5800), on Seventh Ave. between 31st and 33rd St., also offers a tour of its inner workings. Tours include a trip into the 20,000 seat arena and the Paramount (the Garden's concert stage), visits into the locker rooms of the 1994 Stanley Cup-winning Rangers and the 1994 almost-NBA title-winning Knicks, and a step up into the luxury suites. (Tours offered on the hour Mon.-Fri. 10am-2pm, Sat. 10am-1pm, and Sun. 11am-1pm. Admission $7.50.)

A visit to the world's financial capital wouldn't be complete without a trip to the **New York Stock Exchange,** on 20 Broad St. (656-5168). A tour of the building—including the zoo-like main trading floor—is free but tickets are required (open Mon.-Fri. 9:15am-4pm). Check out the **Commodities Exchange Center** at the World Trade Center (938-2018) where gold, silver, sugar, coffee, and cotton change hands. Free guided tours are offered to groups of between 15 and 49 people, but at least two weeks' advance notice is required.

Housing a quarter of the world's gold reserves in a vault sinking five stories below street level, the immense **Federal Reserve Bank of New York,** 33 Liberty St. (720-6130), conducts hour-long free tours of the premises from Monday to Friday at 10am, 11am, 1pm, and 2pm. A minimum of seven working days' prior notification is required. Behind-the-scenes tours of the **Fulton Fish Market** are given on the first and third Thursdays each month between 6am and 8am, June through October (admission $8; advance reservations required; call 669-9416 or 748-8590).

WALKING TOURS

92nd Street Y, 1395 Lexington Ave. (996-1100). The Y leads an astounding variety of walking tours covering all boroughs and many aspects of New York life, from Beaux Arts Fifth Avenue, the Botanical Gardens, and the Brooklyn Navy Yards to literary tours, museum visits, even a murder mystery. Tours are given on Sun., last about 3 hrs., and cost $15-25. Call for the latest tours.

City Walks (989-2456). Run by the friendly and knowledgable John Wilson, a Yalie and a New Yorker for over 35 years. Walking tours of Manhattan cost $12 and usually last 2 hrs., although he'll arrange for private trips. Covering all parts of the city, from Battery Park City to Greenwich Village to the Upper West Side, Mr. Wilson's excursions focus on history and architecture. Call to confirm schedule and make reservations; meeting places vary according to the area on which the tour is focusing.

Adventure on a Shoestring, 300 W. 53rd St. (265-2663). Walking tours of all parts of Manhattan, all the boroughs, and even the more interesting parts of northern New Jersey (e.g. Hoboken). 90-minute tours incorporate chats with members of the various communities. In Manhattan, the Millionaire's Tour of Fifth Ave. (between 59th and 59th St.) and the tour of Greenwich Village are especially entertaining. (Tours cost $5; the price has never increased during the organization's 31 years of existence.) Some excursions—like touring backstage at the Met, or chatting with those who claim to have had out-of-body experiences—are open only to members ($3 per event; membership $40 per year).

Sidewalks of New York (517-0201 for a recorded schedule; 662-5300 to reach the office). Anecdotal, amusing, and offbeat walking tours with titles like "The

Hundred-and-One-Year-Old Broadway Baby" and "All in the Family," a survey of popular Mafia hangouts in Little Italy. All tours cost $10 and last 2 hrs. No reservations required. Call to find out about the next few forays.

Museum of the City of New York, Fifth Ave. and 103rd St. (534-1672). In spring and early fall the museum sponsors popular walking tours ($15) every other Sun., starting at 1pm and lasting for a leisurely 1-2 hrs. Areas covered include Chelsea, the Lower East Side, and Greenwich Village, with foci on the history and architecture of the particular district. Call to sign up a few days beforehand.

Joyce Gold's Tours, 141 W. 17th St. (242-5762). The devoted Ms. Gold has read over 900 books on Manhattan, the subject she teaches at NYU and at the New School. Forty Sundays per year she and a company of intrepid adventurers set out on tours focusing on architecture, history, and the movements of ethnic groups within the city. Tours last 3-3½hrs., depending on the subject, and cost $12.

Municipal Art Society, at the Urban Center, 457 Madison Ave. (935-3960) near 50th St., leads guided walking tours ($10 during the week, $15-30 on weekends); destinations change with the seasons but include most major districts of Manhattan, such as SoHo, Greenwich Village, and Times Square. Their free tour of Grand Central Station meets every Wed. at 12:30pm, in front of the Chemical Commuter Bank. Call in advance with an idea of where you'd like to go, or ask for a schedule of their tentatively-planned future tours.

Times Square Exposé, Seventh Ave. at 42nd St. (768-1560), in the Times Square Visitors Center. This free, 2-hr. walking tour unfolds the theatrical history of Times Square, along with its celebrated scandals and electronic "miracles." Tours given every Fri. at noon.

BOAT TOURS

The Petrel (825-1976), a 70-ft. pecan mahogany yacht, leaves from Battery Park and will take 40 passengers around New York Harbor, visiting Governor's Island, Ellis Island, the Brooklyn Bridge, or the Verrazano-Narrows Bridge—depending on Mother Nature's whims. On weekdays, the Petrel makes 45-min. trips at 1pm (45 min.), 5:50pm (90 min.), and 7:30pm (2 hrs.); weekends at 3, 5:30, and 8pm (all 2 hrs.). Sails cost $8-20 per person. Make reservations in advance.

Circle Line Tours, Pier 83, W. 42nd St. (563-3200), at the Hudson River and Twelfth Ave. Boats circumnavigate Manhattan island during a 3-hr. tour. Eight cruises run daily 9:30am-4:30pm from mid-June to early Sept.; call for specific times and to hear the reduced off-season schedule. (Admission $18, seniors $16, children under 12 $9.) Also conducts romantic, 2-hr. "harbor lights" tours around Manhattan in the lovely light of sunset. You'll hear the sirens singing if you're not careful. (Daily at 7pm early May-early Oct.; weekends only throughout the off-season. Same rates as daytime tour. Light snacks and cocktails served.) All boats operate late March-Dec. 24. No reservations necessary.

Pioneer, Pier 16, South Street Seaport Museum (669-9417). This 109-yr.-old sailing schooner was originally built to carry cargo but will now carry you around the harbor south of Manhattan—you can help hoist the mainsail or take a turn at the wheel. Fantastic views of the skyline and Statue of Liberty. Two-hr. cruises Mon.-Fri. at 3:30pm; Sat. at 12:30, 3:30 and 7pm; and Sun. at 12:30, 3:30, and 6:30pm ($16, seniors $13, students $12, children under 13 $6). One-and-a-half-hour lunchtime cruises sail Mon.-Fri. at 12:30pm ($12). Reservations recommended, especially for weekend cruises.

Staten Island Ferry, on South St. near Battery Park (718-390-5253). Offers one of the best deals in Manhattan, and 'round the clock to boot. Amazing views of the lower Manhattan skyline, Ellis Island, the Statue of Liberty, and Governor's Island. Don't miss the trip at night, but exercise caution around the Staten Island terminal. Fare 50¢ round-trip (!!!). No reservations required.

BUS TOURS

Lou Singer Tours (718-875-9084), offers tours of the "Twin cities of Brooklyn and Manhattan." The tours, now in their 23rd year, are still led by the colorful Mr. Singer, who regales his audience with zesty little nuggets while driving from place to place. The 6-hr. Manhattan Noshing Tour ($25 plus $18 food charge) is a multi-ethnic food-sampling extravaganza, with 12 food stops peppered with Lou's intriguing commentary on the history and architecture of the Lower East Side. Also offered is a tour of Brooklyn Brownstones ($25 plus $2 admission charges), which includes a jaunt through an historic house and a visit to a church with Tiffany windows. Advance reservations are required; reserve 2 wks. in advance during the summer. Bus departs from 325 E. 41st St., between First and Second Ave.

Rock and Roll Tour NY (807-ROCK). Created by Danny Fields, currently manager of the Ramones and Iggy Pop and long-time music industry insider, this 2½-hr. bus tour takes you to over 50 places where rock history was made in New York from the mid-'50s to the present. The tour covers everything from where Dylan and Zappa lived to where John Lennon was murdered and where Sid and Nancy wrote the script of their demise. (Tours depart from and conclude at the Hard Rock Café, 221 W. 57th St. between Broadway and Seventh Ave. Operates weekends only, but call for schedule. Tickets $25. Reservations recommended. Tickets may be purchased through Ticket Master (307-7171), but you'll be charged an extra $4.25 per ticket; they're also available on the bus.)

Gray Line Sight-Seeing, 900 Eighth Ave. (397-2600), between 53rd and 54th St., or 166 W. 46th St. (397-2620), near Seventh Ave. Huge bus-tour company offering more than 20 different trips, including jaunts through Manhattan and gambling junkets to Atlantic City. The tour of the lower half of Manhattan ($17) runs about 2½ hrs. and visits Times, Herald, and Madison Squares, Greenwich Village, the World Trade Center, the United Nations, Park Ave., and Rockefeller Center. Other good bets include a 2-hr. trip through Harlem ($17), and the grand, 4-5-hr. NYC-immersion tour ($28). The launder-your-money voyage to Atlantic City costs $26. Reservations aren't required, but arrive at the terminal ½ hr. in advance.

Harlem Spirituals, 1697 Broadway (757-0425), at 53rd St. Offered are tours of upper Manhattan (in English, French, German, Spanish, and Italian) including the "Spirituals and Gospel" tour, which includes trips to historic homes and participation in a Baptist service ($30 for 3½ hrs., leaves Sun. at 8:45am). The "Soul Food and Jazz" tour ($65, offered Thurs.-Sat. 7pm-midnight) features a short tour of Harlem and filling meal at a Harlem restaurant (usually Sylvia's). Tickets should be purchased in advance; call for info.

Harlem Renaissance Tours (722-9534). The 4-hr. "Sunday Gospel Tour" features the history of Harlem and includes 1 hr. at a gospel-church service and lunch or brunch at a local restaurant ($35). Call ahead for a schedule and to make reservations, as tours are often offered to groups and will not accept individuals.

■■■ EAST MIDTOWN

East of Sixth Ave., from about 34th St. to 59th St., lies the bulk of East Midtown. This is the land of fast-talking, high-stakes business deals, where it always seems dark because the buildings are so tall. But this part of town showcases some of New York's finest architecture, as well as some of its most amazingly active people and places. East Midtown gives New York its most common stereotypes—business-women in Ann Taylor suits and white Keds, architecturally challenging buildings, chic boutiques, and rude cabbies. Don't let it frighten you; let yourself be swept away in the frenzy.

■ THE EMPIRE STATE BUILDING

New York impressed me tremendously because, more than any other city in the world, it is the fullest expression of our modern age.
—Leon Trotsky

Consuming the southwest corner of 34th St. and Fifth Ave. is the heart of Manhattan—nay, of the capitalist universe itself—the Empire State Building (slurred together by any self-respecting New Yorker into "Empire Statebuilding"). This icon retains its place in the hearts and minds of New Yorkers even though it is no longer the tallest building in the U.S. (an honor now held by Chicago's Sears Tower), nor

Upper Midtown

Lincoln Center

W. 62nd St.

W. 61st St.

CENTRAL PARK

St. Paul the Apostle

W. 60th St.

W. 59th St.

Maine Monument

Central Park South

W. 58th St.

COLUMBUS CIRCLE

New York Convention & Visitors Bureau

W. 57th St.

Russian Tea Room

W. 56th St.

Carnegie Hall

W. 55th St.

Eleventh Ave.

Tenth Ave.

W. 54th St.

Ninth Ave.

Eighth Ave.

Seventh Ave.

W. 53rd St.

W. 52nd St.

W. 51st St.

W. 50th St.

W. 49th St.

W. 48th St.

W. 47th St.

Guardian Angels Headquarters

THEATER DISTRICT

W. 46th St.

W. 45th St.

Shubert Theater

W. 44th St.

DUFFY SQUARE

W. 43rd St.

Sardi's

W. 42nd St.

Central Synagogue

TIMES SQUARE

W. 41st St.

Port Authority Bus Terminal

W. 40th St.

Broadway

Lincoln Tunnel

W. 39th St.

Dyer Ave.

W. 38th St.

Eighth Ave.

Seventh Ave.

W. 37th St.

Jacob K. Javits Convention Center

W. 36th St.

W. 35th St.

W. 34th St.

Macy's

Eleventh Ave.

Tenth Ave.

W. 33rd St.

Ninth Ave.

General Post Office

Madison Square Garden

W. 32nd St.

Penn Station

W. 31st St.

W. 30th St.

GARMENT DISTRICT

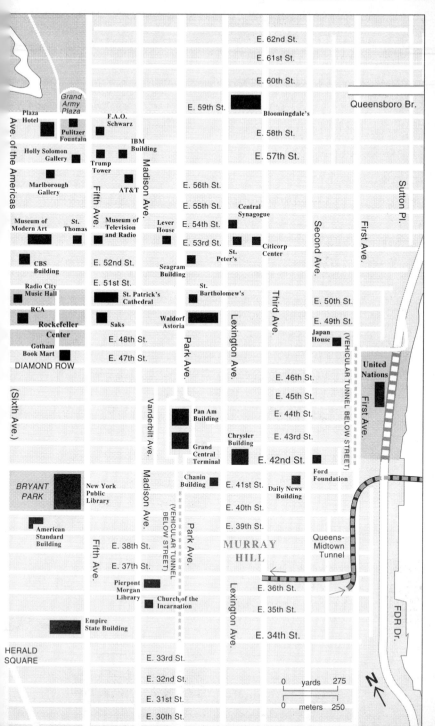

E. 62nd St.

E. 61st St.

E. 60th St.

E. 59th St.

Bloomingdale's

Queensboro Br.

E. 58th St.

E. 57th St.

Grand Army Plaza

Plaza Hotel

Pulitzer Fountain

F.A.O. Schwarz

IBM Building

Holly Solomon Gallery

Trump Tower

AT&T

Marlborough Gallery

Ave. of the Americas

Fifth Ave.

Madison Ave.

E. 56th St.

E. 55th St.

Central Synagogue

Museum of Modern Art

St. Thomas

Museum of Television and Radio

Lever House

E. 54th St.

E. 53rd St.

St. Peter's

Citicorp Center

CBS Building

E. 52nd St.

Seagram Building

Second Ave.

First Ave.

Sutton Pl.

Radio City Music Hall

E. 51st St.

St. Patrick's Cathedral

St. Bartholomew's

RCA

Rockefeller Center

Saks

Waldorf Astoria

Gotham Book Mart

DIAMOND ROW

(Sixth Ave.)

E. 48th St.

E. 47th St.

Park Ave.

Lexington Ave.

Third Ave.

E. 50th St.

E. 49th St.

Japan House

(VEHICULAR TUNNEL BELOW STREET)

First Ave.

United Nations

E. 46th St.

E. 45th St.

E. 44th St.

Vanderbilt Ave.

Pan Am Building

Grand Central Terminal

Chrysler Building

E. 43rd St.

E. 42nd St.

Ford Foundation

BRYANT PARK

New York Public Library

Chanin Building

E. 41st St.

Daily News Building

E. 40th St.

American Standard Building

Madison Ave.

(VEHICULAR TUNNEL BELOW STREET)

Park Ave.

E. 39th St.

Queens-Midtown Tunnel

Fifth Ave.

E. 38th St.

E. 37th St.

MURRAY HILL

Lexington Ave.

Pierpont Morgan Library

Church of the Incarnation

E. 36th St.

E. 35th St.

FDR Dr.

Empire State Building

E. 34th St.

HERALD SQUARE

E. 33rd St.

E. 32nd St.

E. 31st St.

E. 30th St.

0   yards   275

0   meters   250

N

even the tallest building in New York (now the upstart twin towers of the World Trade Center). It doesn't even have the best looks (the Chrysler building is more delicate, the Woolworth more ornate). But the Empire State remains New York's best-known and best-loved landmark and dominates the postcards, the movies, and the skyline.

The limestone and granite structure, with glistening mullions of stainless steel, stretches 1454 ft. into the sky; its 73 elevators run on two miles of shafts. The Empire State was among the first of the truly spectacular skyscrapers, benefiting from innovations like Eiffel's pioneering work with steel frames and Otis's perfection of the "safety elevator." In Midtown it towers in relative solitude, away from the forest of monoliths that has grown around Wall St. The upper 30 floors of the building are illuminated nightly until midnight, in appropriate color schemes for holidays or special events; they turned red, white, and blue after the Rangers' victory in the 1994 Stanley Cup hockey finals.

The Empire State was built on the site of two famous 19th-century mansions belonging to the prominent Astor clan. In the 1880s, William Waldorf Astor tore down one of the mansions to build the Waldorf Hotel, and in 1897 his cousin John Jacob demolished the other, building the Astoria Hotel. These hotels operated here until 1929, when they consolidated and moved uptown to make way for the Empire State Building.

The sleek, gray building, with graceful setbacks and light Art Deco ornamentation, seems appropriate for the city—tall, not too garish, but masterfully impressive. The formula, though, came about more by chance timing than by one man's vision. In 1929 the Art Deco style was in vogue, and zoning ordinances required setbacks on tall buildings; had it been built a few years later, with the International style and a different set of zoning laws in full swing, the Empire State might have been just another dull box of a building.

The Empire State has always been in the limelight. It co-starred in the film classic *King Kong,* along with the jumbo-sized ape and his ravishing hostage. It has also played a part in several tragedies, beginning in 1933 with a rash of suicides. Twelve years later, a disoriented but earnest army pilot crashed his B-25 into the 79th floor. A plaque on the observation deck commemorates his mishap.

When you enter the building, check out the lobby, a shrine of Art Deco interior decorating right down to the mail drops and the elevator doors. Don't miss the singularly tacky series of 1963 illustrations depicting the Seven Wonders of the Ancient World (plus you-know-which New York skyscraper), done in "textured light." Take the escalator down to the Concourse Level, where you can purchase tickets to the observatory. A sign here indicates the visibility level. On a day with perfect visibility you should be able to see 80 mi. in any direction, but even on a day with a visibility of only five mi. you'll still spot the Statue of Liberty. The nighttime view will leave you gasping. (Observatory open daily 9:30am-midnight, tickets sold until 11:30pm. Admission $3.75, children under 12 and seniors $1.75. Call 736-3100 for observatory information.)

If lines get long, you can also purchase observatory tickets at the **Guinness World's Records Exhibit Hall, Inc.** (947-2335), located on the Concourse Level, but they must be bought in conjunction with exhibition tickets (see Museums).

Once on the main observatory, 1050 ft. above Gotham, you can venture onto the windswept outdoor walkways or opt to stay in the temperature-controlled interior. Whip out your map and get your bearings straight; you are pretty much in the center of the Manhattan street grid. Quiver at the gorgeous view to the north, which gives a feel for the monumental scale of Central Park. That's right—quiver. Go ahead. We dare you.

■ MURRAY HILL

Once you've managed to pull your head out of the clouds, head up and over to the Murray Hill area, east of Fifth Ave. between 34th and 42nd St. The late 19th-century "robber barons," who amassed fortunes to rival those of the European monarchs while transforming the U.S. from a rural backwater into the world's leading industrial nation, lived in posh homes here. In this neighborhood, warm brownstones and condos lie in the shadow of the glass-and-steel business citadels further uptown. At 205 Madison Ave. and 35th St. is the **Church of the Incarnation.** A comprehensive collection of late 19th-century art fills its sanctuary. Built in 1864, the church contains stained glass by Tiffany, and sculptures and memorials by Augustus Saint Gaudens and Daniel Chester French in the nave. A handy pink pamphlet near the entrance can guide you to the church's art. (Open Mon.-Fri. from about 11:30am-2pm, but the times are variable—try your luck at the church door.)

The highlight of Murray Hill is the **Pierpont Morgan Library,** 29 E. 36th St. (685-0610), at Madison Ave., where the J. Pierpont Morgans developed the concept of the book as fetish object. With regular exhibitions and lots and lots of books inside, this Low Renaissance-style *palazzo* should not be missed (see Museums).

■ 42ND STREET

Back on Fifth Ave., head north past the upscale shopping of **Lord and Taylor** (See Shopping: Department Stores) to the hubbub of 42nd Street. The **New York Public Library** reposes placidly on the west side of Fifth Ave. between 40th and 42nd St. On sunny afternoons, throngs of people perch on the marble steps, which are dutifully guarded by the mighty lions Patience and Fortitude. Grecian urns, sculptural groups, and fountains (the one on the right represents Truth, the other Beauty) all reflect the importance attached to making this structure worthy of housing one of the world's great libraries. The free brochure offered inside ("A Building to Celebrate") will guide you through all the facets of its interior and exterior architecture.

Carrère and Hastings erected the building in 1911 with the resources of two privately funded libraries—John Jacob Astor's general reference library (the first in the New World) and James Lenox's collection of literature, history, and theology. Samuel J. Tilden added a generous $2 million bequest, and Andrew Carnegie gave an even more generous $5.2 million donation for the establishment of the Public Library's 80 citywide branches. Free tours of the library take place Tuesday through Saturday at 11am and 2pm starting from the Friends Desk in Astor Hall. For a recorded announcement of exhibitions and events, call 869-8089. (Library open Mon. and Thurs.-Sat. 10am-6pm, Tues.-Wed. 11am-7:30pm.) Note that this library, devoted entirely to research, doesn't lend a thing. If you wish to borrow a book or just read outside the intimidating shadow of leonine Virtue, you're better off across the street at the Midtown Manhattan branch (see Practical Information: Libraries).

Spreading out against the back of the library along 42nd St. to Sixth Ave. is soothing **Bryant Park.** Site of the World's Fair in 1853, the park has recently undergone renovations, and in the afternoon people of all descriptions crowd into the large, grassy, tree-rimmed expanse to talk, relax, and sunbathe. The stage that sits at the head of the park's big, grassy field plays host to a variety of free cultural events throughout the summer, including screenings of classic films, jazz concerts, and live comedy. Call the New York Convention and Visitors Bureau (397-8222) for an up-to-date schedule of events.

To the east along 42nd St., **Grand Central Terminal** sits where Park Ave. would be, between Madison and Lexington Ave. A former transportation hub where dazed tourists first got a glimpse of the glorious city, Grand Central has since been partially supplanted by Penn Station and the Wright Brothers, but it maintains its dignity nonetheless. The massive Beaux Arts front, with the famed 13-ft. clock, gives way to the Main Concourse, a huge lobby area which becomes zebra-striped by the sun falling through the slatted windows. Constellations are depicted on the sweeping, arched expanse of green roof, while egg-shaped ribbed chandeliers light the secondary apses to the sides. Mysteriously benchless, though, Grand Central most certainly does not countenance contemplation; people hustle and bustle, rarely stopping to reflect on the monumentality of their location.

Stores take up most of the arcades, which snake their way underground to many of the surrounding buildings. Buy some newspapers here and people-watch as specimens of all descriptions hobble, stride, meander, and dash across the marble floor, but keep your eyes peeled for the bag-snatchers and pickpockets who also roam the halls. Free tours are given at 12:30pm on Wednesdays from the Chemical Bank in the Main Concourse, and Fridays from the Phillip Morris building across the street. The bathrooms here are grungy but functional.

Growing out of the back of Grand Central, the **Pan Am Building** looms above like a stern parent, occupying most of 44th and 45th St. You can't miss this one; it's the 59-story blue monolith that slices Park Ave. in half and—at least according to some gimlet-eyed savants—resembles an airplane-wing section. (The once-familiar Pan Am logo atop the building has been replaced by that of Met Life, but the old name remains.) The obstruction of the view down Park Ave. by this building has evoked huge uproars and inspired recent photographers to employ alternative-process photos to show us how the street would look unblocked. The largest commercial office building ever built, it contains 2.4 million sq. ft. of corporate cubicles. It also has swankier stores than in Grand Central, pink rather than white marble, and a nice but unfortunately benchless atrium. Deep inside the lobby, right above the escalators, hangs an immense Josef Albers mural. In the building's other lobby, at E. 44th and Vanderbilt, an intriguing wire-and-light sculpture encloses what appears to be an energized atom. Right across E. 45th St. sits the **Helmsley Building,** which also truncates Park Ave. but which gives the thoroughfare a very impressive appearance if you look down from the streets further uptown.

The New York skyline would be incomplete without the familiar Art Deco headdress of the **Chrysler Building,** at 42nd St. and Lexington Ave., which appears to charleston madly in a flapper dress (23 skiddoo!) even as the latest postmodern constructions go up nearby. The Chrysler is topped by a spire modeled on a radiator grille, and many other details evoke the romance of the automobile in the Golden Age of the Chrysler Automobile Company: a frieze of idealized cars in white and gray brick on the 26th floor; flared gargoyles at the fourth setback styled after 1929 hood ornaments and hubcaps; and stylized lightning-bolt designs symbolizing the energy of the new machine. During construction, the Chrysler building engaged in a race with the Bank of Manhattan building for the title of the world's tallest structure. Work on the bank was stopped when it seemed as if it had already won. The devious Chrysler machinists then brought out and strapped on the spire that had been secretly assembled inside. And so, when completed in 1929, this elegantly seductive building stood as the world's tallest. The Empire State topped it a year later.

Walk east on 42nd St. about 1½ blocks; between Park and Second Ave. the **Daily News Building** delivers itself with smug, self-important pomp. Home to the country's first successful tabloid, the building may have been the inspiration for the *Daily Planet* of Superman fame. Though the *Daily News* caters to an exclusively New York readership, the lobby is dominated by a gigantic rotating globe and a clock for every time zone in the world. An inexplicable tribute to our solar system graces the walls, as do the paper's photographs of distraught evacuees from the World Trade Center bombing.

After admiring the glories of the Milky Way and tabloid journalism, go farther east to 320 E. 43rd St., between First and Second Ave., to find the much more moderate **Ford Foundation Building.** Glass and rust-colored steel enclose a 12-story garden atrium dense with vegetation. Despite the slightly unsettling zoo-creature sensation that the atrium engenders, this is an incredibly soothing place to take a break from the rigors of East Midtown.

In fact, the intimidatingly man-made jungle setting of East Midtown is interrupted quite frequently with oases from steel and pavement (though they are just as man-made). Many corners have small public areas, and there are also several parks of note. **Tudor Park,** between 42nd and 43rd St. on Tudor Pl. (which is itself between First and Second Ave.), has a European charm, with its gravel paths, metal benches, ornate fence, and outsized oaks congregating in a refreshingly uncluttered silence (open daily 7am-midnight). Down a flight of curved stairs from Tudor Park lies **Ralph J. Bunche Park,** right in front of the U.N. A tall sculpture and carved faces grace this small area, as does an inspirational quote from Isaiah.

Why don't you leave the country for a little bit? The **United Nations Building** (963-4475) is actually not located along New York's First Ave. between 42nd and 48th St.—this area is international territory and thus not subject to the laws and jurisdiction of the U.S. You can tell because the 184 flags that fly outside all fly at equal height, in flagrant violation of Americanism. An understated skyscraper and kicky little lobby make up the bulk of the place. Outside, a multicultural rose garden and a statuary park provide a lovely view of the East River (and a rather un-lovely one of Queens). Relish the muscle-bound Socialist Realist statue showing a man beating a sword into a plowshare. The buff guy was a gift of the former U.S.S.R., which sent it to the U.N. in 1959.

Once inside, go through security check and work your way to the back of the lobby for the informative tours of the very '60s-style **General Assembly.** The tours last about 40 minutes, leaving every 15 minutes from 10am to 4:15pm daily, and are available in 20 languages if there is sufficient demand. Make sure to buy the special U.N. postage stamps, which can only be mailed from the U.N., but which will ship that postcard to Dubuque all the same. (Tours $6.50, seniors over 60 and students $4.50, children under 16 $3.50. Visitor's Entrance at First Ave. and 46th St.) You must take the tour to get past the lobby. Sometimes free tickets to G.A. sessions can be obtained when the U.N. is in session (Oct.-May); call 963-1234 in advance to see.

Just up the street at First Ave. and E. 44th St. is the **UNICEF House,** devoted to advocacy for children in the international arena. The Danny Kaye Visitors Center opened in July 1994, with exhibits and explanations of UNICEF's mission. A gift shop also sells cards and other paraphernalia, with all profits going to the UNICEF Children's Fund.

Located a few blocks north of the U.N. at 333 E. 47th St. and First. Ave. is the deceptively modernist **Japan House** (832-1155), the first building of contemporary Japanese design in New York City. The designer, Junzo Yoshimura, sought to integrate Western with Asian style, and the result is half-Japanese, half-American—Western on the outside but completely Asian on the inside. The mission of the **Japan Society,** headquartered within, is similar. An association dedicated to bringing the people of Japan and America closer together, it sponsors Japanese language courses, conferences, lectures, meetings with notable leaders, a film series, and various performers. In the spirit of a traditional Japanese home, there is an interior pool garden on the first floor, complete with stones and bamboo trees, and a gallery on the second floor exhibits traditional and contemporary Japanese art. (Open Mon.-Fri. 9:30am-5:30pm. Gallery open Sept.-May 11am-5pm; $3 suggested donation.)

■ LEXINGTON, PARK, AND MADISON

The area between First and Third Ave. is mostly residential, with embassies thrown in for good measure. Further west, though, skyscrapers and ritzy hotels take over. At 570 Lexington Ave. and 51st St., the **General Electric Building** was originally the headquarters of the Radio Corporation of America (RCA) when it was completed in 1931. General Electric moved in a year later when RCA shifted to the Rockefeller Center, but some RCA executives moved back in 1986 when G.E. swallowed RCA. The famous orange-and-buff eight-sided brick tower is alive with bolts and flashes that crackle off the surface, an allegorical reference to the power of radio. G.E. keeps tight security, but the elegantly designed Art Deco lobby and elevators are worth a quick peek.

On Park Ave. around the high 40s and low 50s, posh hotels pamper the elite. Though the rooms may be unaffordable, the security guards will most likely let you have a look around; plus, these hotels have excellent bathrooms. The *crème de la crème* of these hotels is the **Waldorf-Astoria Hotel,** at 301 Park Ave. between 49th and 50th. Cole Porter's piano sits in the front lounge, while a huge chandelier and an actual red carpet greet you as you slink humbly down the hallways. The Duchess of Windsor, King Faisal of Saudi Arabia, and the Emperors Hirohito and Akihito of Japan all have stayed here (as have about a million business travelers), and every U.S. President since Hoover has spent a night or two away from the White House at the hotel.

To see the more garish end of the hotel spectrum, walk one block west to 451-455 Madison Ave. and 50th St. The **Helmsley Palace Hotel** has incorporated the six powerful, graceful brownstones that comprise the former **Villard Houses,** which date from 1884. The carpet is a bit too red, and the frighteningly large chandelier gleams a little too conspicuously; the brass is too shiny, the grandeur too forced. Leona and Harry have since fallen from their heady days at the top, but their real estate legacy lives on.

Up Park Ave., between 50th and 51st St., stands the Byzantine **St. Bartholomew's Church** (751-1616), whose design is reminiscent of medieval European ecclesiastical architecture. The church was completed in 1919. Inside, a large mosaic of the Resurrection glitters with golden halos, while less subtle paper flames dangle from the quilt-like dome.

One of the monuments to modern architecture, Ludwig Mies Van der Rohe's dark and gracious **Seagram Building,** is further up at 375 Park Ave., between 52nd and 53rd St. Pure skyscraper, with no frills or silly froufrou like the buildings near Grand Central, the Seagram stands as a paragon of the austere International Style. Van der Rohe envisioned it as an oasis from the tight canyon of skyscrapers on Park Ave. He set the tower back 90 ft. from the plaza and put two great fountains in the foreground. This design has inspired many other nearby plazas and atriums, and the building itself has certainly inspired many of the steel and glass enclosures in the immediate vicinity.

East one block at 619 Lexington Ave. and 53rd St., **Saint Peter's Church** (935-2200) foregoes the classical religious architectural styles and instead creates a more contemporary and urban space of worship. This funky church sponsors services, jazz vespers, musical concerts, social groups, and off-Broadway theater. (See Entertainment and Nightlife: Music and Theater.) Built as a modern-day equivalent of the medieval church as social center, St. Peter's was developed in conjunction with the Citicorp Building behind it and works to fuse the corporate with the corporeal.

The shiny, slanted **Citicorp Center** stands on four 10-story stilts at Lexington and 53rd St. in order to accommodate St. Peter's Church below. The entire structure is sheathed in reflective grayish aluminum; at sunrise and sunset, the entire building radiates warmly. The 45-degree-angled roof was originally intended for use as a solar collector, but this plan has not come to light. Instead the roof supports an intriguing gadget, the so-called TMD, or Tuned Mass Damper, which senses and records the tremors of the earth and warns of earthquakes.

Leave modernity behind and head across the street for the **Central Synagogue** at 652 Lexington Ave. and 55th St. Built in 1870 by Henry Fernbachn, its Moorish-revival architecture combines a lavish façade of onion domes and intricate trim with an exquisite display of stained glass within. It is the oldest continuously operating synagogue in the city.

The stylish **Madison Lexington Venture Building,** up a few blocks at 135 E. 57th St., is just a little over six years old, but it has already garnered quite a few awards. The front of the main building curves inward, creating an arc around four pairs of green Italian marble columns arranged in a Stonehenge circle and highlighted by a fountain. The ironically hip references that this building compresses into one amalgamated postmodern structure make New York architecture critics squirm with foam-flecked joy.

Philip Johnson's postmodern **AT&T Building** stands farther west, on Madison Ave. between 55th and 56th St. Sony has recently leased out the building and renamed it **Sony Plaza.** It now features two massive Sony superstores featuring hands-on interaction with the products and free movie screenings on Sony TVs of releases by Sony-owned Columbia. Sony has also answered its charge to provide free education for the children of New York with its new **Sony Wonder** museum, an interactive introduction to communications technology which should not be missed. It's free!

One block up and across the street, at 590 Madison Ave. between 56th and 57th St., the green granite **IBM Building** sits in stolid waiting, as it has recently been sold by IBM. It features a fine atrium with comfortable chairs as well as a dense bamboo jungle for the panda in you.

One more block up on Madison Ave., between 57th and 58th St., the **Fuller Building** is a big, black, shiny Deco building that looks like it just came off the set of *Dick Tracy.* Completed in 1929, it was one of the first office buildings to be situated this far north in Manhattan and served as the headquarters of America's leading construction firm during the Great Depression. Inside, the Fuller contains 12 floors of art galleries (see Galleries).

■ ROCKEFELLER CENTER

Between 48th and 51st St. and Fifth and Sixth Ave. stretches Rockefeller Center, a monument to the conjunction of business and art. Raymond Hood and his cohorts aspired to that all-American credo "bigger is better" in their attempt to glorify business through architecture. Rockefeller Center is the world's largest privately owned business and entertainment complex, occupying 22 acres of midtown Manhattan.

On Fifth Ave. between 49th and 50th St., the famous gold-leaf statue of Prometheus sprawls out on a ledge of the sunken **Tower Plaza** while jet streams of water pulse around it. The Plaza serves as an overpriced open-air café in the spring and summer and as an ice-skating rink in the winter. Over 100 flags from the member nations of the U.N. flap in simultaneous obedience to the winds. Inside, hulking Social-realist workers heave and strain on a heroic mural, a mute and ironic testament to the idealized glory of manual labor. The 70-story **RCA Building,** seated at Sixth Ave., remains the most accomplished artistic creation in this complex. Every chair in the building sits less than 28 feet from natural light. The **NBC Television Network** makes its headquarters here, allowing you to take a behind-the-scenes look at their operations. The hour-long tour traces the history of NBC, from their first radio broadcast in 1926 through the heyday of TV programming in the 50s and 60s. The tour visits the studios of *Donahue* and 8H, the hallowed halls of *Saturday Night Live.* (For times and prices, see Sights: Sightseeing Tours. For information on becoming an audience member for an NBC show, see Entertainment & Nightlife: Television.)

Despite possessing an illustrious history and a wealth of Art Deco treasures, **Radio City Music Hall** was almost demolished in 1979 to make way for new office high-rises. The public rallied, however, and the music hall was declared a national landmark; it received a complete interior restoration (which, incredibly, took only a month to complete). Today, it thrives again as a multi-format entertainment venue. First opened in 1932, at the corner of Sixth Ave. and 51st St., the 5874-seat theater remains the largest in the world. The 144-ft.-wide stage is equipped with a revolving turntable comprising three separate sections, each of which can be elevated or dropped 40 ft. The hydraulic stage elevator system was so sophisticated that during World War II, the U.S. Navy borrowed its design while developing aircraft carriers. The brainchild of Roxy Rothafel (originator of the Rockettes), the hall was originally intended as a variety showcase, yet it functioned primarily as a movie theater; over 650 feature films debuted here from 1933 to 1979, including *King Kong, Breakfast at Tiffany's, To Kill a Mockingbird,* and *Doctor Zhivago.* The Rockettes, Radio City's chorus line, still dance on. The current dancers range in stature from 65½ to 68½ in., but seem to be of equal height onstage thanks to the marvels of perspective. People are blown away to this day by their complicated routines and eye-high kicks, a cut above the little waist-high kicks of their competitors. Tours of the great hall are given daily 10am-5pm. (See Sights: Sightseeing Tours for more information, or call 632-4041. See Entertainment and Nightlife: Music for information on concerts and performances in the hall.)

■ FIFTH AVENUE

The section of Fifth Avenue between 42nd and 59th St., once the most desired residence of New York's elite, has now been taken over by the stores and institutions that originated to serve them. The grand scale of the establishments here and the centrality of Fifth Avenue itself combine to make this stretch of street the most famous avenue in the U.S. Protestors and celebrators of all types choose this thoroughfare for their parade routes, and parading consumers and tourists revel in the unsurpassed opportunities for window-shopping. Fascinating stores and boutiques line the streets here—don't be afraid to go in and poke around. Just don't break anything.

Just off Fifth Ave., on 44th St. between Fifth and Sixth Ave., is the **Algonquin Hotel,** which in the 1920s hosted Alexander Woollcott's "Round Table," a regular gathering of the brightest luminaries of the theatrical and literary world. The hotel's major attraction was proximity to the offices of *The New Yorker.* The Oak Room still serves tea every afternoon, but now exclusively to Algonquin guests (and their friends). On the southeast corner of Fifth Ave. and 51st St. stands **St. Patrick's Cathedral** (753-2261), New York's most famous church and the largest Catholic cathedral in America. Construction began on the Gothic Revival structure in 1858 and took 21 years to complete. Designed by James Renwick, the structure captures the essence of great European cathedrals like Reims and Cologne yet retains its own spirit. The twin spires on the Fifth Ave. façade, captured in countless photos and postcards, streak 330 ft. into the air. Artisans in Chartres and Nantes created most of St. Patrick's stained-glass windows, under which the controversial Cardinal O'Connor communes with God. The combined effect of both the windows and O'Connor is unfortunately disrupted by the midday crush of summertime tourists. Today High Society intermarries at the cathedral.

Up one block and just west of Fifth Ave. at 25 W. 52nd St. is the newly relocated **Museum of Television and Radio** (621-6800), formerly the Museum of Broadcasting. The museum spent $50 million on its recent move and expansion, and the new building is quadruple the size of its predecessor. It has only one small gallery of exhibits, though; it works almost entirely as a "viewing museum," allowing visitors to attend schedules screenings in one of its theaters or to choose and enjoy privately a TV or radio show from its library of 60,000 (see Museums). Down the block at 51 W. 52nd St., the **CBS Building** (975-4321), a virtual cross between a skyscraper and a black hole, maintains a cold but fervid watch over arch-enemy NBC. For greatest dramatic effect, view Eero Saarinen's smoke-colored granite tower from Sixth Ave. (For information on tickets to CBS shows, see Entertainment: Television.)

St. Thomas's Church (757-7013), with its famously heavy, lopsided left tower, anchors down the northwest corner of Fifth Ave. and 53rd St. This Episcopal institution has occupied the site since 1911, and maintains among its treasures the statues of 50 saints, apostles, and missionaries on huge stone reredos reaching up to overhead vaults. The walking-tour brochure just inside the door (suggested donation 25¢) will help you to spot St. Stephen, the first Christian martyr, St. Sebastian, the hopeless voluptuary, and Daniel Sylvester Tuttle, the presiding bishop in 1923. Guided tours are offered Sundays following the 11am service. Continue down W. 53rd St. towards Sixth Ave. and take in a handful of masterpieces in the windows of the **American Craft Museum** and the **Museum of Modern Art** (see Museums). If you have some time (and the money for admission), rest your tired feet with a visit to the sculpture garden of the MoMA, featuring the works of Rodin, Renoir, Miró, Lipschitz, and Picasso. And if you have a few days, you can see all there is to see of the museum's masterpieces.

The imposing **University Club,** on the northwest corner of Fifth Ave. and 54th St., is a turn-of-the-century McKim, Mead, and White creation. This granite palace, with its lavish interior, was one of the first men's clubs that required its members to hold college degrees. Try to pick out the crests of over 20 prestigious universities carved above its windows (or at least the few along the front of the building). In June of 1987, the previously all-male club voted to admit women in accordance with a city ordinance.

New York's most influential congregation, including the Walcotts, the Livingstons, and Theodore Roosevelt, once prayed in the pews of **Fifth Avenue Presbyterian Church,** at the northwest corner of Fifth Ave. and 55th St. Built in 1875 by Carl Pfeiffer, it is the largest Presbyterian sanctuary in Manhattan, seating 1800. The old clock which is visible on three sides of the steeple still runs on its own gravity weight—a huge box of rocks. For a view of an even more elaborate top, check out the **Crown Building,** 730 Fifth Ave. at 57th St. Originally designed by Warren and Wetmore in 1924, the upper façade has now been overlaid with over 85 lbs. of 23-carat gold leaf. At sunset, the reflected light results in a crown of fire.

Just across Fifth Ave. is the magic block: Trump and Tiffany. The **Trump Tower,** at 56th St., shines like a beacon to excess. Was it really necessary to put those plants on the side of the building? Inside, a ludicrous five-story waterfall-on-a-wall washes down the atrium. There are enough fashion boutiques here to satisfy even the most depraved world leader, and for the world leader who drinks a bit too much water, the bathrooms here are some of the nicest in New York.

Marla Maples and Donald Trump named their daughter Tiffany after their glittery neighbor at 727 Fifth Ave. between 56th and 57th St. At **Tiffany & Co.** (755-8000), everything is beautiful. Nervous (and rich) couples pick out rings and jewelry on the first floor and register for housewares on the second. Go up to the third floor and see which famous people have registered for what. New York-related exhibitions show regularly, and the window displays are art in themselves, especially around Christmas. (Open Mon.-Wed. and Fri.-Sat. 10am-5:30pm, Thurs. 10am-7:30pm.)

Two blocks north, reclaim that inner child at **F.A.O. Schwarz,** 767 Fifth Ave. (644-9400) at 58th St. It's *Babes in Toyland* for real; automated toys greet you and talk (endlessly). Complex Lego constructions, environmentally-responsible toys, adorable huggy bears, and a separate annex exclusively for Barbie dolls. "If you loved me, you'd buy it for me." (Open Mon.-Wed. and Fri.-Sat. 10am-7pm, Thurs. 10am-8pm, Sun. noon-6pm.)

On Fifth Ave. and 59th St., at the southeast corner of Central Park, sits the legendary **Plaza Hotel,** built in 1907 by Henry J. Hardenberg. Built at the then-astronomical cost of $12.5 million, its 18-story, 800-room French Renaissance interior flaunts five marble staircases, countless ludicrously named suites, and a two-story Grand Ballroom. Past guests and residents have included Frank Lloyd Wright, the Beatles, F. Scott Fitzgerald, and, of course, the eminent Eloise. When Donald Trump bought this national landmark in 1988, locals shuddered; so far, there has been little to fear. Flash the doorman a charming smile as he opens the door for you and head in to have a look. The wealth inside is amazing—marble, glass, brass, and gold—but more to the point, it's extremely well-cooled and will always provide a great break from summer heat and humidity. *Let's Go* recommends the $15,000-per-night suite.

Double-billing as a forecourt to the Plaza Hotel and as an entrance to Central Park, the **Grand Army Plaza** absorbs the Pulitzer Memorial Fountain, along with Karl Bitter's Statue of Abundance and an Augustus Saint-Gaudens gaudy, gilt equestrian statue of General William Tecumseh Sherman, the Union general who coined the ringing phrase "war is hell."

■■■ WEST MIDTOWN

Decidedly more grungy than its eastern counterpart, West Midtown offers a break from the high-society boutiques, corporate wonderworlds, and neck-craning tourists that clutter East Midtown. This area, west of Sixth Ave. between 31st and 59th St., shines in a more neon-signed, less gold-foiled way, with Broadway theaters, countless hotels, and peep shows all beckoning through the grime. This is not the "grunge" of teenage fashion that collects in the clubs downtown, but if you want to see the city of James Dean, with the Broadway lights splashing on the dingy canvas of old warehouses and steamy streets, shuffle through the west side.

■ HERALD SQUARE AREA AND THE GARMENT DISTRICT

Pennsylvania Station, at the corner of 33th St. and Seventh Ave., is one of the less engrossing pieces of architecture in West Midtown, but, as a major subway stop and train terminal, it can at least claim to be highly functional. The original Penn Station, a classical marble building modeled on the Roman Baths of Caracalla, was gratuitously demolished in the 60s. The railway tracks were then covered with the equally uninspiring **Madison Square Garden** complex. The venue hosts a fine array of top entertainment, including both the Knicks and the Rangers. Behind-the-scenes tours of the complex, including looks into the locker rooms and luxury boxes, are offered daily (see Sights: Sightseeing Tours). Facing the Garden at 421 Eighth Ave., New York's immense main post office, the **James A. Farley Building,** sits complacently in its primary 10001 ZIP code. Completed in 1913, it mirrored the neoclassical magnificence of Penn Station across the street until the original station's destruction. A huge stretch of Corinthian columns shoulders broadly across the front, and a 280-ft. frieze on top of the broad portico bears the often-quoted motto of the U.S. Postal Service: "Neither snow nor rain nor heat nor gloom of night stays these couriers from the swift completion of their appointed rounds." Step inside during business hours to see the small poster featuring the mugshots and fingerprints of the real-life "America's Most Wanted."

East on 34th St., between Seventh Ave. and Broadway, stands monolithic **Macy's.** This giant, which occupies a full city block, was recently forced to relinquish its title as the "World's Largest Department Store" and change its billing to the "World's Finest Department Store" when a new store in Germany was built one square foot larger. With nine floors (plus a lower level) and some two million sq. ft. of merchandise, Macy's has come a long way from its beginnings in 1857, when it grossed $11.06 on its first day of business. Recently, however, it was forced to revisit its humble roots when it filed for bankruptcy, and its fate still remains uncertain. The store sponsors the **Macy's Thanksgiving Day Parade,** a New York tradition buoyed by helium-filled 10-story Snoopies and other such cultural-icon blobs, marching bands, floats, and general hoopla. Santa Claus always marches last in the parade, signaling the arrival of the Christmas shopping season and joy to kids (and merchants) everywhere. If you're in town in August, be sure to catch the store's "Tapamania," when hundreds of tap-dancers cut loose on the sidewalks of 34th St.

Further east along 34th St., at the convergence of Broadway and Sixth Ave., lies hectic **Herald Square.** Here a bronze statue of Minerva presiding over bellringers sits at the center of a small triangle of asphalt, ringed by park benches which seem to have attracted a crowd of regulars.

To the north is the **Garment District,** which extends along Seventh Ave. (also known as Fashion Ave. in this area) from 34th St to 42nd St. The Garment District gained its name by once housing the bulk of the city's often inhumane clothing manufacturers. Today a small statue titled "The Garment Worker," depicting an aged man huddled over a sewing machine, sits near the corner of 39th St. to commemorate that era.

■ TIMES SQUARE AND THE THEATER DISTRICT

Just north of the Garment District is **Times Square,** which centers around the intersection of 42nd St., Seventh Ave., and Broadway. Although probably still considered the dark and seedy core of the Big Apple by most New Yorkers, the Square has worked hard in the past few years to straighten its laces and improve its image. The prime mover in this effort at urban renewal has been the Times Square Business Improvement District (BID), which began operations in 1992, funded by area residents and businesses. The BID began by putting 45 cherry-red jumpsuited sanitation workers on the streets daily, along with 40 public safety officers. According to the Mayor's Sanitation Scorecard, the rating of sidewalks alone jumped from 54% to 94.4% clean in just over a year. Robberies are down by 40%, pick-pocketing and purse-snatching by 43%, and the number of area porn shops has plummeted by more than 100 from its late-70s climax of 140. The historic Victory Theater is undergoing restoration and will be the site of a new children's theater, and Disney has big plans for the aging New Amsterdam Theater, where the Ziegfeld Follies performed their original chorus line routine for more than twenty years.

Still, Times Square is Times Square. Teens continue to roam about in search of fake IDs, and hustlers are still as eager as ever to scam suckers. One-and-a-half million people pass through Times Square every day. The carnival excitement here—the sense of bustle and chaos—is unique, and perhaps endangered. Be sure to stop by the **Visitor Center** at the northwest corner of 42nd St. and Seventh Ave. for all kinds of information and suggestions (open daily 10am-7pm). The center offers a free, two-hour walking tour of the area every Friday at noon.

Just west of Times Square, at 229 W. 43rd St., are the offices of the **New York Times** (556-1600), founded in 1857, for which the square was named in 1904 (although the *Times* was then housed at One Times Square—the big, triangular building at the head of the square on which the huge Sony Jumbotron screen now roosts). A short trip south down Eighth Ave. to 41st St. parks you in front of the multi-storied **Port Authority Bus Terminal,** the departure point for a volley of buses. Despite high-profile police presence, this area and the terminal itself are a little seedier than the area north of 42nd St. and can be dangerous, especially at night; stay on the major thoroughfares and try not to look like a tourist.

Further west, on 42nd St. between Ninth and Tenth Ave., lies **Theater Row,** a block of renovated Broadway theaters. The nearby **Theater District** stretches from 41st to 57th St. along Broadway, Eighth Ave., and the streets which connect them. Some of the theaters have been converted into movie houses or simply left to rot as the cost of live productions has skyrocketed. Approximately 37 theaters remain active, most of them grouped around 45th St., and 22 of them have been declared landmarks in testament to their historical importance (see Entertainment: Theater). Between 44th and 45th St., a half-block west of Broadway just in front of the Shubert Theater, lies **Shubert Alley,** a private street for pedestrians originally built as a fire exit between the Booth and Shubert Theaters. After shows, fans often hover at stage doors, generally labeled and several yards to the side of the main entrance, to get their playbills signed. Behind the scenes of every show are the playwrights, composers, and lyricists; protecting their interests is the **Dramatists Guild,** 234 W. 44th St. (398-9366), located in the former penthouse suite of J.J. Schubert, the Broadway mogul who popularized theater in the 1920s and 30s. Members of the guild include luminaries such as Stephen Sondheim, Peter Stone, and Mary Rodgers. According to the Guild's charter, "producers, directors, agents, students, academicians, and patrons of the arts" can all become members for $50 per year. Hard-core autograph hunters prey outside.

A few blocks uptown, at the helm of Restaurant Row (a strip of posh eateries catering to the free-spending pre-theater crowd), the **Guardian Angels Headquarters** (397-7822), work out of a small space off the corner of Eighth Ave. and W. 46th St. Wearing red berets rather than halos, these angels are self-declared vigilantes and martial artists who have taken city crime into their own hands. They carry no weapons, yet rarely hesitate to make a citizen's arrest. Angels are renowned for their stamina; controversial founder Curtis Sliwa managed to strike fear into his attackers even after being shot twice and thrown out of a taxi. The Angels have launched a preemptive graffiti strike against the corrugated metal front door of their headquarters, spray-painting a beautiful scene there in order to keep anyone else from doing so in a less appealing fashion.

Up several blocks at 130 W. 55th St. between Sixth and Seventh Ave., a former Muslim mosque was converted into the **City Center Theater** in 1943. Sickles and crescents still adorn each doorway, four tiny windows face Mecca from the limestone upper stories, and a Moorish dome caps the roof. Venture inside the lobby to see the elaborate tile mosaics surrounding the elevators.

How do you get to **Carnegie Hall?** Practice, practice, practice. This institution at 57th St. and Seventh Ave. was established in 1891 and remains New York's foremost soundstage. Over the years, Carnegie Hall has become synonymous with musical success. During its illustrious existence, the likes of Tchaikovsky, Caruso, Toscanini, and Bernstein have played Carnegie; Dizzy Gillespie, Ella Fitzgerald, and Charlie Parker all took the stage in 1957; and the Beatles and the Rolling Stones performed here within five months of each other in 1964. Other notable events from Carnegie's playlist include the world premiere of Dvořák's Symphony No. 9 (*From the New World*) on December 16, 1893, Winston Churchill's landmark lecture *The Boer War as I Saw It* in 1901, an energetic lecture by Albert Einstein in 1934, and Martin Luther King, Jr.'s last public speech on February 28, 1968.

Apparently suffering from the same "Great Music Hall Syndrome" as Radio City, Carnegie Hall was in danger of being demolished in the 1950s and being replaced by a large office building. Luckily, outraged citizens managed to stop the impending destruction through special state legislation in 1960. In 1985, in commemoration of the 25th anniversary of the rescue, a $50 million restoration and renovation program gave the worn façade a face-lift, enlarged the street-level lobby, and modernized the backstage. During renovations, the stage ceiling, which had been damaged during the filming of "Carnegie Hall" in 1946 (and subsequently covered with only some canvas and a curtain), was finally repaired. Legend has it that it was actually this hole that gave Carnegie Hall its better-than-perfect acoustics. Tours are given Mondays, Tuesdays, Thursdays, and Fridays at 11:30am, 2pm, and 3pm ($6, students and seniors $5, children under 9 $3; call 903-9790 for more information). Carnegie Hall's **museum** displays artifacts and memorabilia from its illustrious century of existence (open daily 11am-4:30pm; free).

■ COLUMBUS CIRCLE AND HELL'S KITCHEN

Columbus Circle, at Eighth Ave. and Central Park South, marks the northern end of West Midtown, the southwest corner of Central Park, and the beginning of the Upper West Side. A smirking Christopher Columbus postures atop his pedestal, unmindful of the hubbub his anniversary celebration in 1992 generated. The **Maine Monument,** on the northeast side of Columbus Circle, pays tribute to the seamen who died on the *USS Maine* in 1898. The sinking of the ship sparked the Spanish-American War. The **New York Convention and Visitors Bureau,** Two Columbus Circle, assists tourists with all manners of brochures, discount coupons, and suggestions (397-8222; open Mon.-Fri. 9am-6pm, Sat.-Sun. 10am-3pm).

Nearby, on the west side of the circle, is the **New York Coliseum,** built in 1954 by the Triborough Bridge and Tunnel Authority to serve as the city's convention center. Nowadays, the **Jacob K. Javits Convention Center,** which sits along Twelfth Ave. between 34th and 38th St., has stolen the spotlight, leaving the Coliseum somewhat empty and its future uncertain, especially now that Mort Zuckerman has dropped his multimillion dollar bid to develop the site into a huge office complex. Its front has become an unofficial shelter for the homeless, protecting them from the winds whipping across the circle. The city periodically evicts these homeless people in order to clean up the area in preparation for special events, like the 1992 Democratic National Convention.

Hell's Kitchen, west of Ninth Ave. between about 34th and 59th St., was formerly a violent area inhabited by impoverished immigrants. Until the turn of the century, gangs, coppers, and pigs roamed its swarming streets. Now, the district's overcrowded tenements have been replaced with an artsier crowd, through the encouragement of those authorities who are trying to give this area the less ominous (though still loaded) name **Clinton.** Ninth and Tenth Ave. are loaded with restaurants, delis, and pubs, The low-slung Gothic brownstone **Church of St. Paul the Apostle** sits placidly amid the action at 415 W. 59th St., between Ninth and Tenth Ave. A high-relief above a sky-blue mosaic rests above an impressive front door of carved wood, and dioramas of Christ's Passion flank the interior. Be sure to heed the sign warning you not to throw coins into the Baptismal Font which sits just inside the entrance—it does resemble a wishing well, and the temptation will be there. Services are given in both English and Spanish (entrance on Ninth Ave.).

Student protests over tuition hikes culminated in a two-week takeover of CUNY's **John Jay College of Criminal Justice,** 899 Tenth Ave. at 58th St., in May 1990; the turmoil ended in a violent reinstatement of power by administration officials. Renovations have given the 1903 neo-Victorian building, formerly the DeWitt Clinton High School (attended by Calvin Klein), a postmodern atrium and extension. Statues in niches, somber gargoyles, fretful nuthatches, and grape leaves adorn the building's white façade, while the American eagle stares blankly overhead.

■■■ LOWER MIDTOWN: MADISON SQUARE, UNION SQUARE, AND GRAMERCY PARK

Neither coldly commercial nor hotly trendy, lower Midtown, like the third little bear's bowl of porridge, seems just right. Neoclassical architecture and generous avenues create an aura of refinement. At the 23rd St.-Madison Square intersection, for example, four of the earliest skyscrapers form a sub-skyline, one of the city's hidden visual treasures.

To escape the roar of the midtown crowds, walk downtown from the Empire State Building area. On 29th St., between Fifth and Madison Ave., is the **Church of the Transfiguration,** better known as "The Little Church Around the Corner." This has been the home parish of New York's theater world ever since a liberal pastor agreed to bury Shakespearean actor George Holland here in 1870, when no other church would. The diminutive Victorian brick structure features peculiar green roofs, cherub-like gargoyles, and a tangled garden out front. Check out the stained-glass windows: they may look like a scene from the Bible, but look again—the vignette is from *Hamlet.* Open daily 8am-6pm.

Madison Avenue ends, appropriately enough, at **Madison Square Park.** The park, opened in 1847, originally served as a public cemetery. Check out the statuary of your favorite Civil War generals. Since developers have only just started to sink their cranes into this area, a number of the landmark buildings from years past remain, forming a miniature skyline. The area near the park sparkles with funky architectural gems.

The first of the old-but-tall buildings you will encounter, the **New York Life Insurance Building,** is located northeast of the park, occupying the northeast corner of 26th St. and Madison Ave. Built by Cass Gilbert (of Woolworth Building fame) in 1928, it wears its distinctive golden pyramid hat with an aplomb that should give modern box buildings pause. The building is located on the former site of P.T. Barnum's "Hippodrome," which was rebuilt by Stanford White and renamed Madison Square Garden in 1879. It soon became the premier spot for New York's trademark entertainment spectacles, including the 1906 rooftop shooting death of Stanford White by his reputed mistress. The Garden's present-day descendant and namesake now squats on top of Penn Station.

One block south, at the corner of Madison Ave. and 25th St., sits the **Appellate Division of the Supreme Court.** Check out the allegorical statuary which decorates the outside, including the mild men Wisdom and Force. Civil and criminal defendants from the upstate counties plead their cases inside, and the courthouse also hosts a small exhibition pertaining to court-related notables. It's free, but the bailiff and the intimidating "Be Prepared to be Frisked at Any Time" sign may discourage you from lingering excessively. Next door are the clock faces of the 700-ft. **Metropolitan Life Insurance Tower,** which survey Madison Square Park from the corner of Madison Ave. and 23rd St. The tower, a 1909 addition to an 1893 building, also belongs to New York's I-used-to-be-the-tallest-building-in-the-world club. The annex on 24th St., connected by a walkway, features an eye-catchingly neo-Gothicist façade.

Just west, off the southwest corner of the park, is yet another distinguished club member—the eminently photogenic **Flatiron Building,** often considered the world's first skyscraper. It was originally named the Fuller Building, but its dramatic wedge shape, imposed by the intersection of Broadway, Fifth Ave., 22nd St., and 23rd St., quickly earned it its current *nom de plume*. St. Martin's Press, publisher of such fine books as *Let's Go: New York City*, currently occupies roughly half the impressive building's space (the other half of the building goes to another publishing company).

Until he was 15, Teddy Roosevelt lived in the 1840s brownstone at 28 E. 20th St., between Broadway and Park Ave. South. The **Theodore Roosevelt Birthplace** (260-1616) consists of five elegant period rooms from Teddy's childhood. While not the original rooms, they have been reconstructed along virtually the same lines. (Open Wed.-Sun. 9am-5pm. Guided tours 9am-3:30pm. Admission $1.)

Further east along 20th St. is proof that not all New York real-estate developers are as craven as The Donald. **Gramercy Park,** located at the foot of Lexington Ave. between 20th and 21st St., was built in 1831 by Samuel B. Ruggles, a developer fond of greenery. He drained an old marsh and then laid out 66 building lots around the periphery of the central space. Buyers of his lots received keys to enter the private park; for many years, the keys were made of solid gold. Residents of the buildings now pay annual maintenance fees for the upkeep of the park and can obtain keys to the park's heavy iron gate from their buildings' doormen.

Ruggles believed that the park would not only improve the quality of life of residents, but also increase property values and city tax revenues over the years. Ruggles's idea was a glorious one; over 150 years later, little has changed, as the park, with its wide gravel paths, remains the only private park in New York, immaculately kept by its owners. The surrounding real estate is some of the choicest in the city. The tree-lined sidewalks with conveniently placed stoops offer a breather from the traffic and noise dominating the neighborhoods east and west of the park. With its full-fledged foliage, nearby 19th Street is known as "Block Beautiful" and boasts most of the one-family homes in the neighborhood.

The **Brotherhood Synagogue** faces the park at No. 28. It was formerly a Friends Meeting House, commissioned in 1859 by the Quakers. They asked the firm of King and Kellum to design "an entirely plain, neat, and chaste structure of good taste, but avoiding all useless ornamentation." This tan building—constructed in the Anglo-Italianate style with simple cornices, pediments, and arched windows—fits the bill.

Just east, between Second and Third Ave., is the **Police Academy Museum,** 235 E. 20th St. (477-9753), located on the second floor of the NYC Police Academy (see Museums). Up Lexington Ave. at 26th St. is the **69th Regiment Armory,** notable for having hosted the infamous art exhibition in 1913 that brought Picasso, Matisse, and Duchamp to the shores of America; Teddy Roosevelt called these artists "a bunch of lunatics." Henry James also lived here one winter.

It's just a few increasingly offbeat blocks to **Union Square,** between Broadway and Park Ave. South, and 17th and 14th St. So named because it was a "union" of two main roads, Union Square and its surrounding area sizzled with High Society intrigue before the Civil War. Early in this century, the name gained dual significance when the neighborhood became a focal point of New York's large Socialist movement, which held its popular May Day celebrations in **Union Square Park.** Later, the workers united with everyone else in abandoning the park to drug dealers and derelicts, but in 1989 the city attempted to reclaim it. After some rebuilding and de-toxing, the park has improved somewhat, although it retains an unsavory after-taste. Now homeless and sunbather nap cheek by jowl on a blanket of pigeons.

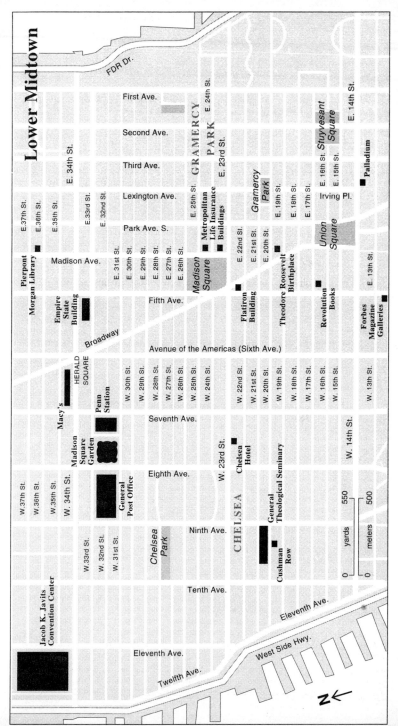

Lower Midtown

FDR Dr.

First Ave.

Second Ave.

Third Ave.

Lexington Ave.

Park Ave. S.

E. 34th St.

E. 37th St.
E. 36th St.
E. 35th St.

E. 33rd St.
E. 32nd St.

GRAMERCY PARK

E. 24th St.
E. 23rd St.

E. 14th St.

Stuyvesant Square

Gramercy Park

Irving Pl.

E. 16th St.
E. 15th St.
E. 17th St.
E. 18th St.
E. 19th St.

E. 25th St.
E. 22nd St.
E. 21st St.
E. 20th St.

Palladium

Union Square

Pierpont Morgan Library

Madison Ave.

E. 31st St.
E. 30th St.
E. 29th St.
E. 28th St.
E. 27th St.
E. 26th St.

Metropolitan Life Insurance Buildings

Madison Square

Empire State Building

Fifth Ave.

Broadway

Flatiron Building

Theodore Roosevelt Birthplace

Revolution Books

Forbes Magazine Galleries

E. 13th St.

Avenue of the Americas (Sixth Ave.)

HERALD SQUARE

Macy's

Penn Station

W. 30th St.
W. 29th St.
W. 28th St.
W. 27th St.
W. 26th St.
W. 25th St.
W. 24th St.

W. 22nd St.
W. 21st St.
W. 20th St.
W. 19th St.
W. 18th St.
W. 17th St.
W. 16th St.
W. 15th St.

W. 13th St.

Seventh Ave.

Madison Square Garden

W. 23rd St.

Chelsea Hotel

W. 14th St.

Eighth Ave.

General Post Office

CHELSEA

General Theological Seminary

W. 37th St.
W. 36th St.
W. 35th St.
W. 34th St.

Chelsea Park

Ninth Ave.

Cushman Row

550

500

yards

meters

0

0

W. 33rd St.
W. 32nd St.
W. 31st St.

Tenth Ave.

Jacob K. Javits Convention Center

Eleventh Ave.

Eleventh Ave.

West Side Hwy.

Twelfth Ave.

N

Check out the sculpture of George Washington, which is said to be the finest equestrian statue in the country. A farmers market sells fresh homegrowns on the east side of the park, while dirt-cheap lycra and lace are for sale in the surrounding stores, which are perennially "going out of business" but never seem to actually close.

On the east side of the park stands the old neo-classical **American Savings Bank;** although designed by Henry Bacon, architect of the Lincoln Memorial in Washington, D.C., the building was never declared an historical landmark. The bank was sent into receivership by New York regulators in 1992, and was purchased in August 1993 (for a whopping $2 million) to become the newest **House of Blues** restaurant and blues bar. The building will be renovated to hold a 300-seat dining room and a hall for live music, and will open sometime in 1995. Although some critics fear that the new restaurant will attract a noisy, touristy "Hard Rock Café crowd," many locals hail the sale as a much-needed step in revitalizing the square. Indeed, the House of Blues franchise (begun in Cambridge, Massachusetts in 1992) is the brainchild of Isaac Tigrett, co-founder of the Hard Rock chain.

Overlooking the ruckus, a number of modern apartment buildings wear levitating party hats that glow at night. The **Zeckendorf Towers,** built in 1987, are at One Irving Pl., between W. 14th and 15th St. The triangular caps and four-sided clock faces seem to gently parody Cass Gilbert's pyramid-topped buildings, including the nearby New York Life.

Make a left onto 14th St. to reach the **Palladium,** at 126 E. 14th St. between Third Ave. and Irving Pl. This former movie palace, converted into a disco in 1985 by Japanese designer Arata Isozaki, contains a mural by Keith Haring and a staircase with 2400 round lights. Once, Madonna and her friends used to party inside while fans waited for hours to get in; since then, the Material Girl has brought her show elsewhere and the bridge-and-tunnel crowd has taken over. Still, the nightclub hosts huge parties and special events and boasts the world's largest dance floor. (See Entertainment & Nightlife: Dance Clubs.)

■■■ CHELSEA

Clement Clark Moore (of "Twas the Night Before Christmas" fame) was more than just a long-winded poet with visions of sugarplums. He also owned and developed most of Chelsea during the mid-1800s. This relatively uniform development resulted in an architecturally consistent residential neighborhood in the Greek Revival and Italianate styles, instead of the architectural stew that characterizes other neighborhoods. Strangely named after the Chelsea Hospital in London, the original Chelsea estate stretched from Eighth Ave. west to the Hudson River, and from 14th to 23rd St. Present-day Chelsea extends a few blocks farther to the north and east. Home to some of the most fashionable clubs, bars, and restaurants in the city, Chelsea has lately witnessed something of a rebirth. A large and visible gay and lesbian community and an increasing artsy-yuppie population have given Chelsea the flavor of a lower-rent West Village.

At 356 W. 20th St., between Eighth and Ninth Ave., **St. Peter's Church** towers imposingly. This is the oldest Gothic revival church in the U.S. An example of Clement Moore's architectural work lives on at **Cushman Row,** 406-418 W. 20th St., a terrace of Greek Revival brownstones, complete with wrought-iron railings. These posh homes face the brick cathedral and the grounds of the **General Theological Seminary,** a grassy oasis that blooms with roses in the summer (243-5150; entrance at 125 Ninth Ave. between 20th and 21st). Dean Eugene Hoffman erected this peaceful gateway in 1883 and called it "The Great Design." If you're lucky, you may catch some monks playing tennis. (Grounds open Mon.-Fri. noon-3pm, Sat. 11am-3pm.) Take in the wonder of the fancy co-op housing of the **London Terrace Apartments,** spanning an entire block; it has occupied the area between 22nd and 23rd St. and Ninth and Tenth Ave. since 1929. A fine Greek revival-style mansion can be found at 414-16 W. 22nd St., also between Ninth and Tenth Ave.

Present-day Chelsea bears the marks of past industrialism. To the west, along Tenth and Eleventh Ave., Chelsea transforms from a residential neighborhood into a burnt-out-looking industrial district. The **Chelsea Piers,** once a transatlantic travel port, sit more or less idle and decaying along the Hudson River from 12th to 21st St. The central stores of the **Terminal Warehouse Company** tower along Eleventh and Twelfth Ave. between 27th and 28th St., and the once-grand and still-fetching **Starett-Lehigh Building** sits at Eleventh Ave. and 26th St. Exercise caution in this somewhat deserted area at night.

The historic **Hotel Chelsea,** 222 W. 23rd St. between Seventh and Eighth, has sheltered many a suicidal artist, most famously Sid Vicious of the Sex Pistols. Edie Sedgwick made pit stops here between Warhol films and asylums before lighting the place on fire with a cigarette. Countless writers, as the plaques outside attest, spent their final days searching for inspiration and mail in the lobby. Arthur Miller, Vladimir Nabokov, and Dylan Thomas all made use of the abundant flat surfaces. Many over-zealous fans beg the management to let them spend a couple of nights in their superstar's former chamber.

Chelsea's **flower district,** on 28th St. between Sixth and Seventh Ave., blooms most colorfully during the wee hours of the morning. Later in the day, if you wander around 27th St. and Broadway, you can witness the wholesale trading of cheap imports ranging from porn videos to imitation Barbie dolls to wigs made from 100% human hair.

■■■ UPPER EAST SIDE

Until the end of the Civil War, 19th-century jet-setters chose this part of town for their summer retreats, building elaborate mansions in garden settings. By the late 1860s, simply summering uptown would not suffice. Landowners converted their warm-weather residences into year-round settlements. Then, the building of ele-vated railroads brought an influx of the urban proletariat, and the East was won. In 1896, Caroline Schermerhorn Astor built a mansion on Fifth Avenue at 65th St., and the rest of high society soon followed. The Golden Age of East Side society flour-ished until the outbreak of World War I. The old-money crowd took advantage of improvements in technology to produce sumptuous mansions outfitted with eleva-tors, intercoms, and theatrical plumbing devices. Scores of the wealthy moved into the area and refused to budge, even during the Great Depression when armies of the unemployed pitched their tents across the way in Central Park.

So it was that select hotels, mansions, and churches first colonized the former wil-derness of the Upper East Side. The lawns of Central Park covered the land where squatters had dwelt; **Fifth Avenue** rolled over a stretch once grazed by pigs. These days parades, millionaires, and unbearably slow buses share Fifth Avenue. Its **Museum Mile** includes the Metropolitan, the Guggenheim, the International Center of Photography, the Cooper-Hewitt, the Museum of the City of New York, and the Jewish Museum, among others. **Madison Avenue** means advertising: this is where artists, market psychologists, and salespeople conspire to manipulate America's buying habits. But these jingle factories are well concealed above the unbroken façade of expensive boutiques and superb galleries. The high-art and high-fashion windows of Madison afford endless hours of aesthetic bliss and materialistic glee.

The stately, dreary boulevard **Park Avenue** was constructed according to strict building codes. Equipped with every conceivable luxury but air and light, the archi-tecturally unimaginative apartment blocks were termed "super-slums" in the 1930s. Landscaped green islands now smother Park Avenue where railroad tracks once lac-erated the thoroughfare. Admire the view down the avenue to the hazy indigo out-line of midtown's starscraping silhouettes. Grittier **Lexington Avenue** injects a little reality into the East Side. Here and on Third, Second, and First Ave., you'll find the area's most vibrant crowds, a happening singles scene, and quick, reliable public transportation. Farther north, highrise projects and grimmer urban settings replace the party atmosphere of the streets in the 70s and 80s.

A walk through the Upper East Side, land of decadence, might as well be kicked off at 59th St. and Third Ave., where **Bloomingdale's** sits in regal splendor (see Shopping: Department Stores). Try on designer clothes with no price tags, get sprayed with a little perfume—get ready for the Upper East Side.

Reeking of the latest Calvin Klein scent, waft over to 60th St. and Madison Ave. to see where the "old boys" cavort and establish their networks of power. The infamous **Copacabana Club,** where Sammy Davis Jr. and Jerry Vale crooned in the 40s and "Copa girls" like Lola danced with music and passion, was here until just recently, when it moved across Central Park. Men in suits with cigars still convene at the stodgier clubs nearby. The **Metropolitan Club,** at 1 E. 60th St., was built by the dynamic trio of McKim, Mead and White on a commission from J.P. Morgan for his friends who had not been accepted at the **Union Club** (101 E. 69th St.). The **Knickerbocker Club,** 2 E. 62nd St., was founded by disgruntled Union men: Knickerbockers wanted to keep the club of pure Colonial stock.

Down the block from the Metropolitan Club, at 47 E. 60th St. between Madison and Park Ave., stands the less snooty (but no less exclusive) **Grolier Club.** Built in 1917 in honor of 16th-century bibliophile Jean Grolier, this Georgian structure houses a collection of fine bookbindings and a specialized research library. Though built and decorated in the 1930s, **Christ Church,** 520 Park Ave. at 60th St., manages to appear quite ancient. Ralph Adams Cram ornamented this Byzantine-Romanesque hybrid on the outside with Venetian mosaics and marble columns. Note the iconic panels (taken from an old Russian church) inside, above the altar. (Open daily 9am-5pm for meditation, prayer, and respectful viewing. Occasional concerts of classical church music given; call 838-3036 for information.) Just around the corner, at 22 E. 60th St., the **French Institute** (355-6100), the cultural mission of the French Embassy, offers a variety of Gallic lectures and films (open Mon.-Thurs. 10am-8pm, Fri. 10am-6pm).

Did we mention the old-boy network and dead white males already? They (and their blonde wives) get dressed at **Barneys New York** at 660 Madison Ave. between 60th and 61st St. Designers such as Calvin Klein, Vera Wang, Jean-Paul Gaultier, Armani, and many more all sell here at extraordinary prices. Celeb-spotting is a sport here—shoot for JFK, Jr.; he's reputed to show up a lot.

Between Lexington and Park Ave., at 128 E. 63rd St., you'll find the **Society of American Illustrators** (838-2560) and its **Museum of American Illustration** (see Museums). If you can draw the little animal inside the matchbook, you too might be able to become a member.

Over on Third Ave. at 62nd St. is part of the Trump real estate empire—the **Trump Plaza.** Less aggressively tacky than its Towering big brother, it nonetheless bears the brass which evidently runs in Trump genes. Over on 62nd St. is a small public park with a smaller version of the water wall in the Trump Tower. At 1190 Second Ave. and 63rd St., check out the **Elizabeth Street Garden Galleries.** A gallery devoted to garden statuary, this outdoor exhibition features a large fountain and young marble giants.

Walking back west to Fifth Ave., examine the building at 63rd St. Past residents of **810 Fifth Avenue** include publisher William Randolph Hearst and a pre-presidential Richard Nixon. Dick could go upstairs to borrow butter, eggs, and wire-taps from Nelson Rockefeller, a former shoeshine boy and anxious owner of New York's only fully equipped bomb shelter. At the corner of Fifth Ave. and 65th St. stands **Temple Emanu-El** ("God is with us"), the largest synagogue in the U.S. Outside, Eastern details speckle the limestone and otherwise Romanesque structure. Inside, the nave bears Byzantine-style ornaments and seats 2500 worshippers—more than St. Patrick's Cathedral (744-1400; open daily 10:30am-4:30pm).

Richard Hunt designed the **Lotos Club,** on E. 66th St. between Madison and Fifth, an organization of actors, musicians, and journalists. Red brick rises from a base of rusticated limestone. The building is capped by a two-story mansard roof in a style perhaps best described as Second Empire meets wedding cake. East 67th and 68th

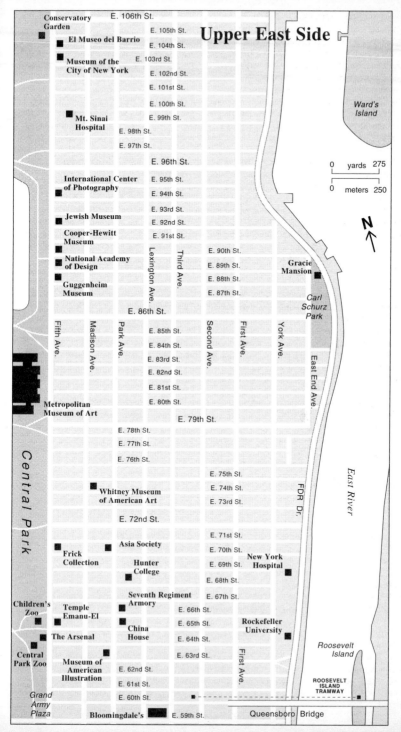

Conservatory Garden
El Museo del Barrio
Museum of the City of New York
Mt. Sinai Hospital
International Center of Photography
Jewish Museum
Cooper-Hewitt Museum
National Academy of Design
Guggenheim Museum
Metropolitan Museum of Art
Whitney Museum of American Art
Frick Collection
Asia Society
Hunter College
Seventh Regiment Armory
Temple Emanu-El
China House
The Arsenal
Museum of American Illustration
Children's Zoo
Central Park Zoo
Grand Army Plaza
Bloomingdale's
Gracie Mansion
Carl Schurz Park
New York Hospital
Rockefeller University
Roosevelt Island
ROOSEVELT ISLAND TRAMWAY
Queensboro Bridge

Upper East Side

UPPER EAST SIDE

Ward's Island

Central Park

East River

E. 106th St.
E. 105th St.
E. 104th St.
E. 103rd St.
E. 102nd St.
E. 101st St.
E. 100th St.
E. 99th St.
E. 98th St.
E. 97th St.
E. 96th St.
E. 95th St.
E. 94th St.
E. 93rd St.
E. 92nd St.
E. 91st St.
E. 90th St.
E. 89th St.
E. 88th St.
E. 87th St.
E. 86th St.
E. 85th St.
E. 84th St.
E. 83rd St.
E. 82nd St.
E. 81st St.
E. 80th St.
E. 79th St.
E. 78th St.
E. 77th St.
E. 76th St.
E. 75th St.
E. 74th St.
E. 73rd St.
E. 72nd St.
E. 71st St.
E. 70th St.
E. 69th St.
E. 68th St.
E. 67th St.
E. 66th St.
E. 65th St.
E. 64th St.
E. 63rd St.
E. 62nd St.
E. 61st St.
E. 60th St.
E. 59th St.

Fifth Ave.
Madison Ave.
Park Ave.
Lexington Ave.
Third Ave.
Second Ave.
First Ave.
York Ave.
East End Ave.
FDR Dr.
First Ave.

0 yards 275
0 meters 250

N

Streets between Fifth and Madison Ave. furnish examples of turn-of-the-century mansion architecture with a distinct French accent.

The Sarah Delano Roosevelt Memorial House, actually a pair of identical buildings executed by Charles Platt in 1908, sweeps 45-47 E. 65th St. between Madison and Park Ave. The Roosevelt matriarch commissioned the construction on the occasion of her son Franklin's wedding. The bedroom on the fourth floor kept Roosevelt during his recovery from polio in the early 1920s. He launched his political career in these buildings, now a community center for Hunter College students.

Occupying virtually an entire block, the **Seventh Regiment Armory** makes its stand between 66th and 67th St. on Park Ave. The Seventh Regiment fought in every major U.S. campaign from 1812 on, including a valiant outing for the Union in the Civil War. Much of the armory's original 19th-century decoration and furnishing remain in place today. Notable rooms were designed by the Associated Artists under the baton of Louis Comfort Tiffany. Quite remarkable are the Veterans' Room and the adjoining former library, now a display room for the Regiment's silver. The front hallway boasts a gargantuan staircase sheathed in venerable red plush, as well as a whole host of decomposing flags. The eerily impenetrable gloom makes it impossible to see the portraits, but they can see you. Since the Armory still serves as an active military facility, you should call ahead if you'd like a tour (744-8180).

Hunter College, part of the City University of New York, presents its unsightly modernist façade to Park Ave. and its even less attractive posterior to Lexington Ave., between 67th and 69th St. **Hunter College High School,** located much further uptown at Park Ave. and 94th St., is housed in a former armory; its sheer, windowless walls have inspired the nickname "the brick prison" among the school's smart-ass, gifted 'n' talented students. The courtyard façade looks impressive from Madison Ave.—it has been used in a number of films, most recently *The Fisher King*—but is actually nothing more than a free-standing wall, a stage set backdrop for the cement courtyard. Students from the ritzy private schools that clutter the neighborhood come here to slum it, but Hunter is one of a kind, a public school which is also supported by the City University of New York. Founded at the turn of the century as an all-female teacher-training school, H.C.H.S. went co-ed in the 70s when a few parents sued the city for the right to give their sons a Hunter education. Famous alums include Young MC and Adam "SANE" Smith, the late graffiti artist, number one on the NYPD's wanted list, who tagged up the Brooklyn Bridge.

Three galleries of foreign art stand on Park Ave. at 69th St.: the Americas Society at 680 Park Ave., the Spanish Institute at 684 Park Ave., and the Italian Institute at 688 Park Ave. The **Asia Society,** 725 Park Ave. at 70th St., increases cultural awareness of Asia with lectures, films, and an impressive art collection assembled by John D. Rockefeller III (see Museums). Capitalist running-dog Henry Clay Frick's marvelous mansion, home of the **Frick Collection,** stands poised at 1 E. 70th St. at Fifth Ave., kicking off the southern end of Museum Mile (see Museums).

Speaking of marvelous mansions, the contrived ambience of fake-English luxury as interpreted by a New Yorker named Ralph has been conveniently summarized in the **Polo–Ralph Lauren** boutique (606-2100), in a French Renaissance-style mansion at 867 Madison Ave., between 71st and 72nd St. The store's atmosphere—complete with a live string quartet—has been so meticulously orchestrated that you may feel you're on location for the shoot of *The Great Gatsby*. They'll be glad to dress you up, for a price (open Mon.-Sat. 10am-6pm, Thurs. 10am-8pm).

On Madison Ave. at 75th St., box-shaped and brutal, stands the **Whitney Museum of American Art** in a shape as aloof as some of the art you'll find inside. You don't even have to enter the lobby to enjoy Alexander Calder's whimsical wirefest of acrobatics; peek through the window and let Calder convince you that all the world's a circus (see Museums).

Slightly removed from the mayhem of Madison where it once stood, **Sotheby Park Bernet Inc.** (606-7000) conducts its affairs and auctions at 1334 York Ave. at 72nd St. Viewings are open to the public, although admission to a few of the biggest auctions requires tickets. On the corner of Lexington Ave. and 76th St. sits the multidomed **Church of St. Jean Baptiste.** Currently undergoing renovations on the largest dome over the altar (God smote the cross off the top in a thunderstorm), St. Jean still displays Italianate style and swagger. Inside, examine the sculpture in the shrine to St. Anne, as well as the Vatican-esque altar pieces.

The front door of **900 Park Ave.,** at 79th St., may look familiar: the once-wholesome cast of *Diff'rent Strokes* drove up in a limousine to Mr. Drummond's penthouse residence at the beginning of every episode. No, the naked female statue on the pedestal up front is not Kimberly.

Even after passing on to the Grand Ballroom in the sky, celebrity New Yorkers manage to uphold their status and maintain their coteries. The grave roll call of the **Frank E. Campbell Chapel,** a prestigious funeral chapel (1076 Madison Ave. at 81st St.), reads like Who Was Who on the American Mount Olympus: Elizabeth Arden, James Cagney, Jack Dempsey, Tommy Dorsey, Judy Garland, Howard Johnson, Robert Kennedy, Mae West, John Lennon, and Arturo Toscanini.

The **Metropolitan Museum of Art** lies at 1000 Fifth Ave., near 82nd St.; fountains and sore-footed museum-goers flank its majestic presence. The largest in the Western hemisphere, the Met's art collection encompasses some 33 million works (see Museums). Across the street at 1014 Fifth Ave., **Goethe House** (439-8700) offers a Germanic cultural respite from the *Sturm und Drang* of New York through films and lectures (library open Tues. and Thurs. noon-7pm, Wed. and Fri.-Sat. noon-5pm; see Movies).

East of Lexington Ave. between 77th and 96th St. is the **Yorkville** area. Originally settled by Germans, Yorkville continued to welcome immigrants from the Rhine Valley over the first half of this century. The heavy German flavor that once marked local restaurant menus, beer gardens, pastry shops, and deli counters has been diluted in the wake of newer chain stores and pizza parlors, but it hasn't vanished. A few of the old faithfuls remain, especially along 86th St. and Second Ave., keeping the *Bratwurst* basting and the tradition going.

Starting on 82nd St. and East End Ave. is the **John Finley Walk,** a sidewalk overlooking the East River and the speeding cars on FDR Drive. Stroll down the path which leads to the **Carl Schurz Park,** between 84th and 90th St. along East End Ave., named in honor of a many-hatted German immigrant who served as a Civil War general, a Missouri senator, President Rutherford B. Hayes's Secretary of the Interior, and finally as editor of the *New York Evening Post* and *Harper's Weekly.* The park, overlooking the East River, is a haven of greenery with many nooks for asphalt-weary metropolites. Dogs abound and bark. The park sponsors free jazz concerts on Wednesdays from 7pm to 9pm. **Gracie Mansion,** at the northern end of the park, has been the residence of every New York mayor since Fiorello LaGuardia moved in during World War II. Rudy Giuliani presently occupies this hottest of hot seats. To make a reservation for a tour of the colonial mansion, call 570-4751 (tours Wed. only; suggested admission $3, seniors $2).

Henderson Place lines East End Ave. near 86th St.; this series of Queen Anne-style houses—decorated with multiple turrets, parapets, and dormers—could have been fashioned from red Lego blocks. Ghostbusters beware: rumor has it that some of these houses are haunted. All done up in reds, golds, and browns, the fanciful **Church of the Holy Trinity** all but hides from view at 316 E. 88th St. between First and Second Ave. Behind this late-19th-century church lies a small, heavenly garden.

Truckin' on down Museum mile, at Fifth Ave. and 88th St., the toilet-bowl-shaped **Guggenheim Museum,** designed by Frank Lloyd Wright, spirals away (see Museums). Down the street, the **National Academy Museum**, 1083 Fifth Ave. at 89th St., serves as both a school and a museum for the academy, which dates back to 1825. Works by 11 of the 30 founding members lodge at the Metropolitan Museum (see Museums).

When Andrew Carnegie requested that Babb, Cook, and Willard construct "the most modest, plainest, and most roomy house in New York" on 91st St. at Fifth Ave., he received a large but formulaic Renaissance-Georgian combination of red brick and limestone, situated in a luxurious garden. Within, dark oak paneling, textured wallpaper, and demure atriums create the perfect setting for a society ball. When Carnegie moved out, the Smithsonian moved in, relocating their National Museum of Design here as the **Cooper-Hewitt Museum** (see Museums).

The **Jewish Museum,** at 92nd St. and Fifth Ave., a French Renaissance structure with a modern wing added in 1962, contains the country's largest collection of Judaica (see Museums). The **International Center of Photography,** 130 Fifth Ave. at 94th, maintains a rich permanent collection and operates workshops, photolabs, and a screening room (see Museums).

Wandering off the Museum Mile, you can see the **Synod of Bishops of the Russian Orthodox Church Outside Russia,** inhabiting the 1917 Georgian mansion at Park Ave. and 93rd St. The bishops scattered a few icons about but left the interior decoration virtually unchanged, save a former ballroom converted into a cathedral.

The **Islamic Cultural Center,** at Third Ave. and 96th St., New York's most prominent mosque, was precisely oriented by computer to face the holy city of Mecca. Meanwhile the tenacious Russians continued their conquest of the Upper East Side with the construction of the **Russian Orthodox Cathedral of St. Nicholas** at 15 E. 97th St. The cathedral has a polychromatic Victorian body with a strong dose of authentic Russia, manifested in its five onion domes.

Museum Mile finally ends up in East Harlem with the **Museum of the City of New York,** on Fifth Ave. and 103rd St., and **El Museo del Barrio,** on Fifth Ave. and 104th St., the only museum in the U.S. specializing in Latin American and Puerto Rican art (see Museums).

■■■ ROOSEVELT ISLAND

"New York's Island Paradise," as the ad for the luxury apartments here croons, has had a long and complicated history. This minute strip of land floating in the East River between Manhattan and Queens was originally occupied by the Canarsie Indians and known as Minnahannock ("It's nice to be on the island"). After the Canarsie sold the land to the Dutch in 1637, it changed hands many more times, from Dutch hog farmers to an English farmer named Robert Blackwell to New York City in 1828. The city then used the island as a dumping ground for people, establishing jails, hospitals, and a lunatic asylum here. Boss Tweed of the politically murky Tammany Hall was incarcerated here, as was the hardened criminal Mae West (for her role, prefiguring Madonna, in a play called "Sex"). Finally, in 1969, architects Phillip Johnson and John Burgee redesigned the island as a state-sponsored utopia of mixed income housing, safety, and handicapped-accessibility. In 1986 the island's name was changed from Welfare Island to Roosevelt Island, in honor of FDR, and a park in memorial to him is presently under construction on the south end of the island.

Most of Roosevelt Island's action is on the north end. Here, people seem to live one of the most idyllic suburban existences, not even 300 yards away from the hustle and bustle of East Midtown. Aided by state funding and extensive planning, the past 25 years have seen the construction of residential complexes for a variety of income groups, with a concerted effort at racial diversity. The community here runs a communal garden (open May-Sept. Sat.-Sun. 8am-6pm), and, as the great number of running tracks, tennis courts, soccer fields, and softball diamonds attests, they keep in shape as well. Apartments in this model community are hard to come by, except for the luxury apartments ($2400/month). With the completion of Southgate, the final housing complex, in 1995, the residential projects will be complete, so get your name on the rental waiting-list now. The Roosevelt Island community has its own public services, stores, restaurants, and public school, as well as cheerfully-colored buses and garbage trucks—Disneyland comes to Manhattan.

To add to this Wonderland effect, a bright orange tram shuttles residents and tourists across the East River. Featured in the action movie *Nighthawks* (which starred Sylvester Stallone), the tram ride is both terrorist- and Rambo-free, but it does offer the relatively safer excitement of a great view. As you hover almost 250 feet above the river, you can see the United Nations complex and the distinctive hats of the

Chrysler Building and the Empire State Building to your right. Don't forget to wave gleefully to the cars stuck in traffic on the bridge below. One of the only publicly operated commuter cable cars in the world, it operates at an annual deficit of $1 million, and its future is especially uncertain now that the subway line has been extended to the island.

You can pick up the tram at 59th St. and Second Ave. Look for the big red cable rotors next to the Queensboro Bridge. Round-trip fare costs $2.80 and the ride takes about four minutes each way. (Cars run every 15min., Sun.-Thurs. 6am-2am, Fri.-Sat. 6am-3:30am; twice as frequently during rush hour.) For those with a fear of heights, you can take the Q and N subway line, which was finally extended here in 1989. The Q102 bus also makes the trip.

Once on the island, take the mini-bus (10¢) up Main St. and roam around a bit. A walking/rollerblading path encircles the island, and gardens and playgrounds are abundant on the northern half of the island. At the northernmost tip, Lighthouse Park is an especially pleasant place to lie in the grass and make out animal shapes in the clouds floating over Manhattan. With the aid of a 25¢ map, you can also wander among the shops on Main St. and dream of making enough money to live in one of the nearby postmodern apartment buildings.

■■■ CENTRAL PARK

Beloved Central Park has certainly had its moments in the sun: from Simon and Garfunkel's historic 1981 concert, to Dustin Hoffman's refuge here in *Marathon Man,* to the annual meeting of stars in Joe Papp's summertime Shakespeare-in-the-Park festival. New York's enormous metropolitan oasis has set the verdant stage for these and many other concerts (such as Paul Simon's hugely successful 1991 return) and comedies (such as Art Garfunkel's unsuccessful 1993 return). From ardent suitors proposing marriage on horse-drawn carriages to huge Stonewall gay-and-lesbian rallies, 843-acre Central Park brings out the natural, poetic side of the urban creature that is New York (and helps clean the air as well).

Despite its pastoral appearance, Central Park has never been an original wilderness: the landscaped gardens were carved out of the city's grid, between 59th and 110th St. for more than two blocks west of Fifth Ave. The campaign for a public park in New York began in the mid-1840s with William Cullen Bryant, the vociferous editor of the *New York Evening Post,* and received support from the acclaimed architect Andrew Jackson Downing in his magazine *The Horticulturist.* The creation of the park became a unifying issue in the mayoral campaign of 1851—both candidates were strongly in favor of the project. In 1853, the state authorized the purchase of land from 59th to 106th St. (The 106th-110th St. addendum was purchased in 1863.) Alas, Downing met his death by drowning and was unable to design his dream project. The city held a competition to determine the new designer.

The winning design, selected in 1858 from 33 competing entries, came out of a collaboration between Frederick Law Olmsted and Calvert Vaux. Because Olmsted had a day job heading the construction crews that cleared the debris and edifices from the proto-park, most of the plans for Central Park were drawn at night. Olmsted and Vaux transformed 843 acres of bogs, cliffs, glacial leftovers, bone-boiling works, and pig farms into a living masterwork they called Greensward. The whole landscape took 15 years to build and 40 years to grow.

The Park may be roughly divided between north and south at the main reservoir; the southern section of the Park affords more intimate settings, serene lakes, and graceful promenades, while the northern end has a few ragged edges. Nearly 1400 species of trees, shrubs, and flowers grow here, the work of distinguished horticulturist Ignaz Anton Pilat. When you wander amidst the shrubbery, you need not get lost. Look to the nearest aluminum lamppost for guidance, and check the small metal four-digit plaque bolted to it. The first two digits tell you what street you're nearest (89, for example), and the second two whether you're on the east or west side of the Park (an even number means east, an odd west). In an emergency, call the **24-hour Park Line** (570-4820; call boxes located throughout the Park).

Along Central Park South (also known as 59th St.), horses chew contemplatively on oats as children and couples clamor for carriage tours of the Park ($34 first ½-hr., $10 each additional ½-hr.; 246-0520 for information). Try to be better-behaved than some radical activists, who, in their misguided zeal to support animal rights, recently punched out one hapless driver.

Start off a tour of Central Park at the **Central Park Zoo** (recently renamed the Central Park Wildlife Center) at E. 65th St. and Fifth Ave. (861-6030). Built in 1934, it has been attracting flocks of visitors ever since. Roving herds of sugar-hyped children make even the drowsy reptiles of the Tropical Rainforest pavilion tremble in fear, and solitary tourists find a safe haven from sweat in the deliciously chilly Penguin room. The insouciant sea lions flip and spin in their tank, and recently an obsessively-backstroking polar bear was treated for depression. (Open April-Oct. Mon.-Fri. 10am-5pm, Sat.-Sun. 10:30am-5:30pm; Nov.-March daily 10am-4:30pm, last entry ½-hr. before closing. Admission $2.50, seniors $1.25, children 3-12 50¢.) Above the archway, north of the main zoo, hangs the **Delacorte Musical Clock,** made in 1965 by Andrea Spaldini. Every half-hour from 8am to 6pm, bears, monkeys, and other bronze creatures perform a ritual hop-and-skip routine. North of the 65th St. transverse lies the Children's Zoo, currently undergoing renovation.

In front of the Zoo at Fifth Ave. and E. 64th St. sits the dumpy, ivy-covered **Arsenal,** which holds the Park's administrative offices. The third-floor **Arsenal Gallery** (315-0385) hosts free exhibitions related to the Park. (Open Mon.-Fri. 9am-4:30pm.)

Walking west from the Arsenal (to the left, if you're facing the clock), you'll reach the Children's District. The area south of 65th St. was specifically designated by Vaux and Olmsted for the young (and the young-at-heart), where they could play, ride rides, and get good, clean food. The food was distributed at the **Dairy,** built by Vaux in 1870 so that purity-tested milk could be distributed to poor families susceptible to food poisoning. The building now houses the **Central Park Reception Center** (794-6564). Brochures and calendars are available here, as are exhibitions on Park history. Pick up the free map of Central Park and the seasonal list of events. (Open Tues.-Thurs. and Sat.-Sun. 11am-5pm, Fri. 1-5pm; Nov.-Feb. Tues.-Thurs. and Sat.-Sun. 11am-4pm, Fri. 1-4pm.)

Next to the Dairy is what Olmsted and Vaux called the *kinderberg* (children's mountain). At the **Chess and Checkers House** (794-6564), a striped, red-brick concoction created by Robert Moses, grandmasters and spunky amateurs square off at the 24 outdoor boards and 14 indoor boards. (Indoor tables available Sat.-Sun. 11:30am-4:30pm; equipment available at the Dairy.)

Follow the techno beat to the **Wollman Skating Rink** (517-4800), which features children doing their best Tonya Harding on rollerskates (ow! my knee!) and adults clinging cautiously to the railing. When it gets cold enough at this outdoor rink, wheels turn to blades for ice-skating. The rink also offers the mysterious "bankshot," which appears to be a half-court game of pseudo-basketball, and miniature golf, complete with amusing props on the putting greens. (Whole complex open Mon. 10am-5pm, Tues. 10am-9:30pm, Wed.-Thurs. 10am-6pm and 7:30-9:30pm, Fri. 10am-11pm, Sat. 11am-11pm, Sun. 10am-9:30pm. Ice- or roller-skating $6, children under 13 and seniors over 55 $3, plus $3 skate rental or $6 rollerblade rental; Tues. and Wed. cheapskate nights $6, children and seniors $4, includes skate rental; credit card required. "Bankshot" $6, children and seniors $3; 9-hole mini-golf $5, $2.50 children and seniors. Discounts available for combinations.) A nice addition to the roller rink is the railed ledge overlooking it, from which an unparalleled view of midtown can be had free of charge. Wollman also rents skates and rollerblades for use throughout the park ($15 for 2 hr., $25 all day; includes helmet and pads; deposit required.)

If you enjoy going in circles while listening to calliope renditions of easy-listening hits, visit the **Friedsam Memorial Carousel** (879-0244), located at 65th St. west of Center Dr. The 58-horsepower carousel was brought from Coney Island and fully

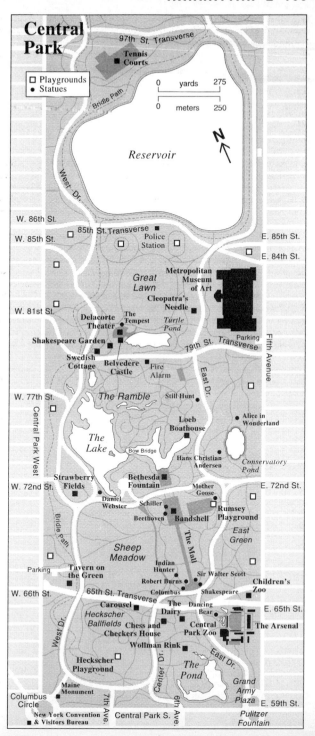

Central Park

□ Playgrounds
• Statues

97th St. Transverse

Tennis Courts

Bridle Path

0   yards   275
0   meters   250

N

Reservoir

West Dr.

W. 86th St.
W. 85th St.   85th St. Transverse
Police Station   E. 85th St.
E. 84th St.

Metropolitan Museum of Art

Great Lawn

Cleopatra's Needle

W. 81st St.

Delacorte Theater   The Tempest   Turtle Pond

Shakespeare Garden

Parking

Fifth Avenue

79th St. Transverse

Swedish Cottage

Belvedere Castle   Fire Alarm

East Dr.

W. 77th St.

The Ramble   Still Hunt

Central Park West

Alice in Wonderland

Loeb Boathouse

The Lake   Bow Bridge

Hans Christian Andersen

Conservatory Pond

Strawberry Fields   Bethesda Fountain

Mother Goose

W. 72nd St.   E. 72nd St.

Daniel Webster   Schiller

Rumsey Playground

Beethoven   Bandshell

East Green

Bridle Path

Sheep Meadow

Indian Hunter

The Mall

Parking   Tavern on the Green

Sir Walter Scott

Robert Burns

Children's Zoo

W. 66th St.   65th St. Transverse   Columbus   Shakespeare

Carousel   The Dairy   Dancing Bear

E. 65th St.

Heckscher Ballfields   Chess and Checkers House

Central Park Zoo   The Arsenal

West Dr.

Wollman Rink

Heckscher Playground

Center Dr.

6th Ave.

East Dr.

The Pond

Maine Monument

Grand Army Plaza

Columbus Circle   E. 59th St.

New York Convention & Visitors Bureau   7th Ave.   Central Park S.   Pulitzer Fountain restored in 1983. (Open Mon.-Fri. 10:30am-5pm, Sat.-Sun. 10:30am-6pm. Thanksgiving to mid-March Sun. 10:30am-4:30pm. Admission 90¢.)

Directly north of the Carousel lies **Sheep Meadow,** from about 66th to 69th St. on the western side of the Park. This is the largest chunk of Greensward, exemplifying the pastoral ideals of the Park's designers and today's teenage crowds. Sheep did graze here until 1934, but after that the Park could afford lawn mowers and so terminated the flock. Inside "The Meadow," legions of the young and beautiful (and their friends) play frisbee and drink beer. Directly north of the meadow, the crowd instantly ages about 50 years. Complexions turn noticeably less bronzed under the broad straw hats and white clothes of the lawn bowlers and **croquet** players who gather in shady hedge-rimmed patches from May through November (call 360-8133 for permits).

West of Sheep Meadow, between 66th and 67th St., is **Tavern on the Green** (873-3200), said to be New York's most profitable restaurant, specializing in overpriced food with a view of greenery and horse excrement. Watch out or your fresh-brewed coffee may be surreptitiously replaced with Folgers crystals. (Lunch $11-25.50, dinner $13-29. Open Mon.-Fri. noon-3pm and 5:30pm-1am, Sat.-Sun. 10:30am-3:30pm and 5pm-1am.)

Along West Drive, at 67th St., stands the **Seventh Regiment Civil War Monument,** sculpted by John Quincy Adams Ward in 1870. Although bureaucrats deemed the Park "too chipper" for "sepulchral monuments," someone somewhere pushed the statue design through. In subsequent years it became a prototype for Civil War monuments throughout the country.

To the east of Sheep Meadow lies the cool dark path of the **Mall.** Along this tree-lined thoroughfare, bronze statues of literary lions sit stolidly, appearing as if they need to go the bathroom very badly. Off the southwestern end of the Mall is the first American statue placed in the Park: **The Indian Hunter** (1869), by J.Q.A. Ward.

At the north end of the Mall is the **Rumsey Playground** and a bandshell. The Dairy can give you calendars for the **'95 Central Park Summerstage** program (assuming its funding comes through), which is held here. In years past Summerstage has sponsored free concerts by big names in genres from opera to punk rock. Past performers include Sonic Youth, Sarah McLachlan, and Sun Ra, among others. (For recorded Summerstage info., call 360-2777.)

North of the 72nd St. Transverse is the **Terrace,** linking the Mall with the Lake and boasting elaborate, ornamental carvings of plants, birds, and park animals. The bas-reliefs along the grand central staircase depict the four seasons. The centerpiece of the Terrace and the Park as a whole is **Bethesda Fountain,** containing the 1865 statue of the **Angel of the Waters,** sculpted in Rome by Emma Stebins. Benches in the sun and the pleasant sound of running water against the ubiquitous drone of New York crowds make this an ideal picnic spot—so bring your sandwich or buy your (overpriced) hot dog here.

On the northern edge of the Terrace and spreading out to the west from underneath the Bow Bridge is the **Lake,** green with algae but still a very dramatic sight in the heart of the City. The 1954 **Loeb Boathouse** (517-2233), a late but indispensable addition to the Park, supplies all necessary romantic nautical equipment. Its mighty rental fleet includes rowboats, swanboats, and even gondolas. (Open daily late March-Nov. Mon.-Fri. noon-5pm, Sat.-Sun. 10am-5:30pm, weather permitting. Rowboats $10/hr., refundable $20 deposit; gondola rides $25 per ½-hr. per group and require reservations.)

Aquaphobes can rent a bike from the boathouse and make their own journeys on *terra firma.* (Bike rental late March-Nov. Mon.-Fri. 10am-6pm, Sat.-Sun. 9am-6pm, in clement weather. $6/hr. for 3-speeds, $8/hr. for 10-speeds, $12/hr. for tandems; credit card, ID or $100 deposit required for all bikes; 10-speeds require additional $20 deposit. Call 861-4137.)

To the east of the Terrace and the Lake, model boats set sail daily on the pacific swells of **Conservatory Water.** This formal basin, site of the yacht race in E.B. White's *Stuart Little,* vibrates in summertime with the careless joy of children and the plodding progress of their intrepid vessels (races and regattas on weekends; call 360-8133 to sign up). A statue of **Hans Christian Andersen,** a gift from Copenhagen in 1956, stands near dreamchild **Alice in Wonderland** and several of her friends—another gift of the Danes in 1959. The Andersen statue has become a prime storytelling spot in the summer; tales are spun Saturdays at 11am and in July on Wednesdays (sponsored by the New York Public Library; call 340-0906 for information). More stories for the 3- to 8-year-old set are told on the playgrounds in July and August; check the schedules posted in the playgrounds.

Strawberry Fields, sculpted as Yoko Ono's memorial to her late husband, is located to the west of the Lake at 72nd St. and West Dr., directly across from the Dakota Apartments where John Lennon was assassinated and where Ono still lives with their son. Ono battled valiantly for this space against city-council members who had planned a Bing Crosby memorial on the same spot. Picnickers and 161 varieties of plants now inhabit the rolling hills around the star-shaped "Imagine" mosaic on sunny spring days. And on John Lennon's birthday in October, in one of the largest unofficial Park events, thousands gather here to remember—or as time passes, to "imagine"—what the legend was really like.

North of the Lake, the **Ramble** features forestry and greenery, as well as bird-watching adventures on Thursdays and Fridays at 3pm (772-0210; meet at Belvedere Castle). The high point of the Park, literally, is **Belvedere Castle,** a whimsical fancy designed by the restless Vaux in 1869. The castle rises just off the 79th St. Transverse from the **Vista Rock,** commanding a view of the Ramble to the south and the **Great Lawn** to the north. For many years a weather station, Belvedere Castle has been reincarnated as an education and information center and serves as the stronghold of the green knights—the **Urban Park Rangers** (772-0210), who provide visitor and emergency services for the Park.

The **Swedish Cottage Marionette Theater,** at the base of Vista Rock, puts on regular puppet shows; 1994's was *The True Story of Rumpelstiltskin.* (Shows Sat. at noon and 3pm. $5, children $4. Call 988-9093 for information and reservations.)

Up the hill from the Cottage Theater lies the round wooden space of the **Delacorte Theater,** hosting the wildly popular **Shakespeare in the Park** series each midsummer. These plays often feature celebrities and are always free. Come early: the theater seats only 1936 lucky souls (see Entertainment & Nightlife: Theater).

North of the theater and the reptile-packed **Turtle Pond** lies the **Great Lawn,** where large concerts often take place. Paul Simon sang here, the Stonewall 25 marchers rallied here, and the New York Philharmonic and the Metropolitan Opera Company frequently give free summer performances here (see Entertainment and Nightlife: Theater and Classical Music). Unless something is going on, though, the Lawn tends to be dusty and a bit forlorn.

Encircled by joggers and larger than many towns, the shiny, placid **Reservoir** may be the most tranquil sight in Manhattan. Runners trot about the 1.58-mile track and small, annoying insects congregate in their eyes. North of the Reservoir at the 97th St. Transverse are the basketball courts of the **North Meadow Recreation Center** (348-4867), which also sponsors board games, pool, wall climbing, baseball, tennis, and kite-flying.

Further up at 105th St. and Fifth Ave. is the attractive **Conservatory Garden** (860-1382; gates open spring-fall daily 8am-dusk). Free tours of the Garden are offered every Saturday through the summer at 9am. Up at the northeast corner of the Park lies the recently reopened **Harlem Meer.** The **Dana Discovery Center** here at 110th St. and Fifth Ave. (860-1370) features exhibitions and activities presenting Central Park as an environmental (as opposed to historical or cultural) space. The "Fragile Forest" permanent exhibition is open Tues.-Sun. 11am-5pm. The Center also leads tours and loans out fishing rods for use in the Meer (you have to release your savory catches, though).

Central Park is fairly safe during the day, but less so at night. Don't be afraid to go see the shows or Shakespeare in the Park at night, but stay on the path and try to go with someone else. Do not go wandering on the darker paths at night. Women especially should use caution after dark.

For general Central Park **information** call 794-6564 (TDD: 800-281-5722). For information about wheelchair accessibility, call 360-2766.

■■■ UPPER WEST SIDE

Along Central Park West the well-to-do residents can look down at doormen or across the park to their soul mates on the Upper East Side. The fancy apartment buildings here date mostly from before the Depression, some from the aptly named Gilded Age of the 1880s. But the rest of the West Side is much less daunting; the white-collar takeover that began in the 1950s with the construction of Lincoln Center hasn't wiped out all the ethnic enclaves, though plenty of the antique stores, clothing emporiums, and fern-colored singles bars attest to the comfortable West-Siders' tastes.

The original plan slated Broadway for residences and West End Ave. for business, but no one paid attention. Before long Broadway had become the principal, most colorful street on the West Side. The thoroughfare today is crammed with delis, theaters, and boutiques; on the sidewalk desperate hawkers peddle everything from bun dumplings to worn copies of *Juggs* magazine to the kitchenware of yesteryear.

Columbus Circle, on Broadway at 59th St., is a bustling nexus of pedestrian and automobile traffic, marking the end of Midtown and the symbolic entrance to the Upper West Side (see Sights: West Midtown). At 1865 Broadway near 61st St., the **Bible House** (408-1200), run by the American Bible Society, distributes the Good Book in nearly every tongue. Its exhibition gallery showcases rare and unorthodox Bibles, plus a smattering of Gutenberg pages and an on-line *Good News Bible*. (Gallery open Mon.-Fri. 9:30am-4:30pm; free. Library open Mon.-Fri. 9am-4:30pm. Bookstore open Mon.-Fri. 9am-5pm.)

■ LINCOLN CENTER

Broadway intersects Columbus Ave. at Lincoln Center, the cultural hub of upper-crust New York. The seven facilities that constitute Lincoln Center—Avery Fisher Hall, the New York State Theater, the Metropolitan Opera House, the Library and Museum of Performing Arts, the Vivian Beaumont Theater, the Walter Reade Theater, and the Juilliard School of Music—accommodate over 13,000 spectators at a time and take up the space between 62nd and 66th St., and Amsterdam and Columbus Ave. Power broker Robert Moses masterminded this project in 1955 when Carnegie Hall seemed fated for destruction.

The **plaza** is especially lively on weekend afternoons. The main entrance on Columbus Ave. between 63rd and 64th St. features the fountain where Cher and Nicholas Cage were *Moonstruck* and where the cast of *Fame* danced at the beginning of the show (before the first commercial). This open area is also a favorite spot for fashion photographers; watch as models sweat under faux fur coats in August. Marvel at the uniform white monumentality of the eight-block complex. On your left, with your back to Columbus Ave., is an automated information booth.

Keeping your back to Columbus Ave., you will see **Avery Fisher Hall** on your right. The hall was designed in 1966 by Max Abramovitz and houses the New York Philharmonic under the direction of Kurt Masur, who recently inherited the baton from conductor Zubin Mehta. Previous Philharmonic directors include Leonard Bernstein, Arturo Toscanini, and Leopold Stokowski (see Entertainment & Nightlife: Classical Music). To your left with your back to Columbus Ave. is the monolithic **New York State Theater,** which plays host to the New York City Ballet and the New York City Opera. December is *Nutcracker* month.

Straight ahead and beyond the fountain is the centerpiece of Lincoln Center, the **Metropolitan Opera House.** This 1966 work by Wallace K. Harrison echoes behind a Mondrian-inspired glass façade. Chagall murals span the lobby, and a grand, many-

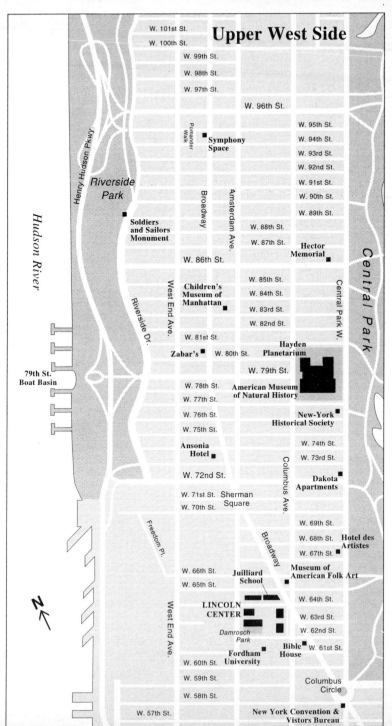

Upper West Side

W. 101st St.
W. 100th St.
W. 99th St.
W. 98th St.
W. 97th St.
W. 96th St.
W. 95th St.
W. 94th St.
W. 93rd St.
W. 92nd St.
W. 91st St.
W. 90th St.
W. 89th St.
W. 88th St.
W. 87th St.
W. 86th St.
W. 85th St.
W. 84th St.
W. 83rd St.
W. 82nd St.
W. 81st St.
W. 80th St.
W. 79th St.
W. 78th St.
W. 77th St.
W. 76th St.
W. 75th St.
W. 74th St.
W. 73rd St.
W. 72nd St.
W. 71st St.
W. 70th St.
W. 69th St.
W. 68th St.
W. 67th St.
W. 66th St.
W. 65th St.
W. 64th St.
W. 63rd St.
W. 62nd St.
W. 61st St.
W. 60th St.
W. 59th St.
W. 58th St.
W. 57th St.

Pomander Walk
Symphony Space
Riverside Park
Soldiers and Sailors Monument
Hector Memorial
Children's Museum of Manhattan
Zabar's
Hayden Planetarium
American Museum of Natural History
New-York Historical Society
Ansonia Hotel
Dakota Apartments
Sherman Square
Hotel des Artistes
Museum of American Folk Art
Juilliard School
LINCOLN CENTER
Damrosch Park
Fordham University
Bible House
Columbus Circle
New York Convention & Vistors Bureau

Hudson River
79th St. Boat Basin
Henry Hudson Pkwy.
Riverside Dr.
West End Ave.
Broadway
Amsterdam Ave.
Central Park W.
Central Park
Columbus Ave.
Freedom Pl.
West End Ave.

N

tiered staircase curves down to the humble opera buff. The gift shop here sells books, posters, libretti, and boxes of cough drops endorsed by Caruso. Mmm. The shop also broadcasts performances live on house monitors; sneaky budgeteers can get a quick opera fix just browsing in the shop at performance time. (Shop open Mon.-Sat. 10am-5:30pm or until 2nd intermission of performance; Sun. noon-6pm.)

To your left as you face the opera house, in the southwest corner of Lincoln Center, is **Damrosch Park,** which hosts frequent outdoor concerts at its **Guggenheim Bandshell.** On the north side of the opera house, Henri Moore's 1965 *Lincoln Center Reclining Figure* sits gloomily in the reflecting pool. Across the pool squats the **Vivian Beaumont Theater,** a tidy glass box under a heavy cement helmet, built by Eero Saarinen in 1965. The **New York Public Library for the Performing Arts** (870-1630) joins the opera house and the theater and holds over eight million items, from videotapes to manuscripts, available for loan to anyone with a NYC library card. (Library open Mon. and Thurs. noon-8pm, Wed. and Fri.-Sat. noon-6pm. See Essentials: Getting Acquainted: Libraries.)

The combined terrace and bridge leads across 66th St. to the halls of the prestigious **Juilliard School of Music,** Pietro Belluschi's brutalist-inspired building. Here Itzhak Perlman and Pinchas Zukerman fine-tuned their skills, and a drama major by the name of Robin Williams tried out his first comedy routines. For information on student concerts, call 769-7406. Within the Juilliard building complex is the intimate **Alice Tully Hall,** where the Chamber Music Society of Lincoln Center resides (see Entertainment and Nightlife: Classical Music). To your left as you face Juilliard and about 200 ft. away, a beige office building conceals Lincoln Center's newest offering, the **Walter E. Reade Theater.** Scan the schedule in the front window; the theater often features foreign films and special festivals (see Entertainment and Nightlife: Movies).

Guided tours of Lincoln Center's theaters and galleries are offered daily. For information and to make reservations, see Sights: Sightseeing Tours.

■ REST OF THE UPPER WEST

Directly across from Lincoln Center, on a triangular plot just south of the intersection of Broadway and Columbus Ave., is **Dante Park,** designed in 1921 to commemorate the 600th anniversary of the poet's death. Presiding over the minuscule park is an imposing bronze of the man himself. Juilliard students often play jazz or chamber music here on Tuesdays at 6:30pm during the summer.

The undistinguished modern façade of the **Museum of American Folk Art,** across from Lincoln Center, on Columbus Ave. between 65th and 66th St., gives way to a cool interior, where you can rest on a bench when you've had your fill of 18th-century quilts (see Museums).

Edging Central Park, the mammoth, Moorish-inspired **West Side Y** hulks at 5 W. 63rd St. A block up Central Park West at 2 W. 64th, the **New York Ethical Culture Society** (874-5210) gives sporadic lectures, readings, classical recitals, and schedules for the foregoing. This venerable organization helped found many others, including the American Civil Liberties Union. One of New York City's armories holds the fort down at 56 W. 66th St., between Central Park West and Broadway; the one-time turrets and battlements of the **First Battery of the New York National Guard** now defend the ABC television studios hidden behind the Fisher-Price castle.

At 1 W. 67th St., poised between Central Park West and Columbus Ave., stands the stately **Hotel des Artistes,** a mass of luxury co-ops originally designed to house bohemians who had moved beyond their romantic garret stage. Built by George Mort Pollard in 1913, the building has quartered Isadora Duncan, Alexander Woollcott, Norman Rockwell, and Noel Coward. The opulence is mostly on the inside, but dig the ivy-shaped exterior stonework. Here you will also find the chic **Café des Artistes.**

The stone-hewn glory of Imperial Egypt meets the principles of streamlined design at **135 W. 70th St.,** between Columbus and Amsterdam Ave. This apartment house, the original home of the Knights of Pythias club, flaunts sapphire-blue columns with bearded men for capitals, as well as hawks whose lengthy wingspans any Grateful Dead fan will immediately recognize.

Constructed in 1970, the curvaceous, sunken **Lincoln Square Synagogue** at 69th St. and Amsterdam is a travertine cousin of Lincoln Center. The bow-tie-shaped **Sherman Square** knots at 72nd St. and Broadway. On the north half of the cravat, **Verdi Square,** Giuseppe stares into space hailed by four characters from his operas.

At 2109 Broadway between 73rd and 74th St., the famed **Ansonia Hotel,** grande dame of Belle Apartments, bristles with heavy ornaments, curved Verona balconies, and towers. Its soundproof walls and thick floors proved most enticing to illustrious tenants like Enrico Caruso, Arturo Toscanini, and Igor Stravinsky. Theodore Dreiser did his own composing here while Babe Ruth, just a few doors away, meditated on his pinstripes.

A few blocks east are the stately apartment buildings that line Central Park West and contrast with the lively businesses of Broadway and Columbus Ave. As Manhattan's urbanization peaked in the late 19th century, wealthy residents sought tranquility in the elegant **Dakota Apartments,** 1 W. 72nd St. at Central Park West. When the apartment house was built in 1884, someone thought it so remote from the heart of the city that "it might as well be in the Dakota Territory." In a rare convergence of real estate and humor, the idea caught on and became the building's official name. Henry J. Hardenburg designed the luxury complex, which featured the first passenger elevators in the city. John Lennon's streetside murder here in 1981 brought new notoriety to the mammoth building.

Secure in their block-long neoclassical building, the staff of the **New-York Historical Society,** at 77th St. and Central Park West (873-3400), will help you uncover obscure facts about the past or provide pop trivia about the present. By the time you read this, the galleries should have re-opened after an economically-necessitated hiatus. The research library is still open for scholarly pursuits (open Mon.-Fri. 10am-5pm).

The **American Museum of Natural History** looks as unwieldy as a prehistoric mastodon at Central Park West between 78th and 81st St. Built in 1899 by J.C. Cady and Co.—and since added to by like-minded architects—the rectilinear stonework reeks of Romanesque. The museum's patron saint Teddy Roosevelt is honored at the main entrance on Central Park West by a Beaux Arts triumphal arch and a somewhat racist bronze sculpture. The recent success of *Jurassic Park* has sparked dinosaur mania that is bound to last at least until early 1995, when the museum will unveil the renovated fourth floor with its extensive dinosaur collection. Holden Caulfield used to hang out at the museum's **Hayden Planetarium.** (See Museums and J.D. Salinger.)

Over on West End Ave. between 76th and 77th St. is a block of Victorian townhouses designed by master masons Lamb and Rich in 1891. It is rumored that graft king and former mayor Jimmy "Gentleman Jim" Walker's mistress once occupied a flat at 76th and Broadway above the townhouses, and that the doting mayor had the block zoned off to stop construction on high-rises that might obscure the lovely view.

In 1637, Dutch settlers constructed the **West End Collegiate Church and School,** 370 West End Ave. at 77th St., as a reproduction of a market building in Holland. Robert Gibson overhauled it in 1893, using characteristically Dutch stepped gables and elongated bricks; with its one enormous stained-glass window, the church looks a little like a dyspeptic cyclops.

With ornate iron gates and a spacious interior courtyard, the **Apthorp Apartments,** 2207 Broadway at 79th St., have starred in a number of New York-based films: *Heartburn, Network, Eyewitness, The Cotton Club, The Changeling,* and *The Money Pit.* The apartments were built by Clinton and Russell in 1908 on a commission from William Waldorf Astor, who named them after the man who owned the site in 1763. Try to persuade the guard to let you take a peek at the courtyard. Across 79th St., the **First Baptist Church's** lopsided spires cavort asymmetrically.

The **West Park Presbyterian Church** has been a fixture at Amsterdam Ave. and 86th St. since 1890. It exhibits fine Romanesque styling, with a rough-hewn red sandstone surface that makes it look as if it just popped out of a clay oven. Strangely, Byzantine doorways and capitals top off the Romanesque half-baked look. On ever-ecclesiastical 86th St., at West End Ave., you'll also find the **Church of St. Paul and St. Andrew,** which dates from 1897. Check out the octagonal tower and the angels in the spandrels.

Central Park creator Frederick Law Olmsted's other green contribution to Manhattan, **Riverside Park,** blooms down the stretch from 72nd to 145th St. along the Hudson River. As in the case of Central Park, Olmsted had a little help from Calvert Vaux. Directly across the intersection of Riverside Drive and 89th St., the **Soldiers and Sailors Monument,** more tomb than memorial, mourns the Union lives lost in the Civil War. The **Carrére Memorial,** a small terrace and plaque at 99th St., honors one of the city's great architects, John Merven Carrére, who died in an automobile accident. His partner Thomas Hastings designed the monument. Back east at 87th St. between Columbus Ave. and Central Park West is another memorial: a brightly colored and moving mural entitled **"In Memory of Hector"** (by "Chico").

Next to a vacant lot, at 175 W. 89th St. and Amsterdam Ave., stands the only surviving stable in Manhattan: the multi-story **Claremont Stables,** which serves as equine condos for high-pedigree horses and also offer riding lessons (see Sights: Central Park). The appropriately named **Eldorado Apartments,** on Central Park West between 90th and 91st, showcase flashy Art Deco detailing in a full array of golds.

Originally a skating rink, **Symphony Space,** 2537 Broadway at 95th St. (864-5400), has distinguished itself with brilliant if wacky programming. Their **Wall to Wall Bach** took a walk on the wild side, as did their gala birthday salute to the late avant-garde composer John Cage. Every Bloomsday (June 16) they celebrate James Joyce's *Ulysses* with readings, lectures, and parties. The space also hosts a giant foreign-film fest each summer to complement its classical-music, world-beat, and literary programs during the year; stop in for a monthly program (or ask to be added to their mailing list). (See Entertainment and Nightlife: Music, and Entertainment and Nightlife: Movies.)

From the masters Carrére and Hastings comes the English Renaissance-style **First Church of Christ, Scientist,** on location at the corner of 96th St. and Central Park West. The exterior of the **Cliff Dwellers' Apartments** at Riverside and 96th St. features a syncretic marriage of Art Deco and Native American styles.

Throughout the Upper West Side, if not all over the City, apartment-dwellers have conspired to break the city's colorless monotony by planting and maintaining cozy, informal public gardens. Especially verdant, varied, and flowerful is the **Lotus Garden** (580-4897), up a flight of stairs on 97th St. between Broadway and West End Ave. You can sit on the benches and admire the fat tulips on Sundays from 1-4pm.

If the antique barbershop window display of the Polo boutique has left you craving the real McCoy, check out the **Broadway Barber Shop** at 2713 Broadway, between 103rd and 104th St. The gilt lettering on the windows has faded but the 1907 trappings, such as the antique barber chairs and the storefront swizzle stick, remain.

■■■ HARLEM

Half a million people are packed into the three square miles that make up greater Harlem. On the East Side above 96th St. lies **Spanish Harlem,** known as El Barrio ("the neighborhood"), and on the West Side lies Harlem proper, stretching from 110th to 155th St. West of Morningside Ave. and south of 125th St. is the Columbia University area, known more commonly as **Morningside Heights** than as a part of Harlem. All these neighborhoods heat up with street activity, not always of the wholesome variety; visit Harlem during the day or go there with someone who

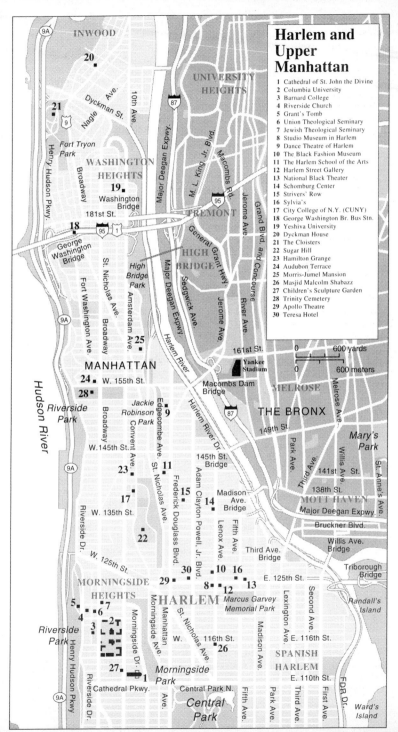

Harlem and Upper Manhattan

1 Cathedral of St. John the Divine
2 Columbia University
3 Barnard College
4 Riverside Church
5 Grant's Tomb
6 Union Theological Seminary
7 Jewish Theological Seminary
8 Studio Museum in Harlem
9 Dance Theatre of Harlem
10 The Black Fashion Museum
11 The Harlem School of the Arts
12 Harlem Street Gallery
13 National Black Theater
14 Schomburg Center
15 Strivers' Row
16 Sylvia's
17 City College of N.Y. (CUNY)
18 George Washington Br. Bus Stn.
19 Yeshiva University
20 Dyckman House
21 The Cloisters
22 Sugar Hill
23 Hamilton Grange
24 Audubon Terrace
25 Morris-Jumel Mansion
26 Masjid Malcolm Shabazz
27 Children's Sculpture Garden
28 Trinity Cemetery
29 Apollo Theatre
30 Teresa Hotel

0   600 yards
0   600 meters

knows the area. If you lack the street wisdom or can't find your own guide opt for a commercial tour (see Sights: Sightseeing Tours).

Yet it is a colossal misconception to consider Harlem merely a crime-ridden slum, devoid of worth. Although poorer than most neighborhoods, it is culturally rich; and, contrary to popular opinion, some of it as safe as the rest of New York. Known as the "city within the City," Harlem is considered by many to be the black capital of the Western world. Over the years Harlem has entered the popular consciousness as the archetype of America's frayed cities, but you won't believe that hype after you've visited the place.

Harlem's rich history contributes to its prominence and attraction today. During most of the 19th century, West Harlem held the large country estates of affluent Manhattanites. When subway construction began in the 1890s, speculators built expensive housing in Harlem, anticipating an influx of middle-class residents. They never came. The owners rented the empty buildings to people who for the first time could obtain respectable New York housing. Over the next 30 years blacks flocked to Harlem by the thousands, more than doubling its population of 80,000 between 1920 and 1930 alone. With this increase in population came an unparalleled cultural flourishing. The 1920s were Harlem's Renaissance; a thriving scene of artists, writers, and scholars lived fast and loose, producing cultural masterworks in the process. The Cotton Club and the Apollo Theater, along with numerous other jazz clubs, were on the musical vanguard. Harlem also supported a flourishing gay and lesbian underground in the '20s and '30s; they flocked to the clubs here, which were more tolerant than those downtown.

After the Depression and World War II, Harlem continued to thrive culturally, if not economically. Music fans of the 1950s could easily find themselves paralyzed by the diversity of offerings. In one bar Charles Mingus would be strumming on his dancing bass; next door Charlie Parker would be blowing solos over the newest bebop tune from a hocked horn, while across the street Billie Holiday would be mellifluously reducing her audience to pools of tears. Many small jazz clubs still exist. Ask around and you won't be sorry.

In the 1960s, some blacks began to feel that whites courted them only for their contributions to entertainment rather than out of any feeling of true respect of equality, and the radical Black Power movement flourished here. The Revolutionary Theater of LeRoi Jones performed consciousness-raising one-act plays in the streets, and Malcolm X, Stokely Carmichael, and H. Rap Brown spoke eloquently against racism and injustice. Recognizing the need for economic revitalization as a route to empowerment, members of the community began an attempt at redevelopment in the 1970s. This attempt continues today as the City pumps money into the area and communities bond together to beautify their neighborhood and actively resist crime. There is a definite strand of "We don't need Whitey" in the current Harlem philosophy, as Malcolm X's teachings of self-empowerment gain increasing popularity, but it would be an exaggeration to say whites are wholly unwelcome here.

In fact, today's Harlem is home to a population that is increasingly diverse, both ethnically and socioeconomically. In recent years an influx of Dominicans has changed the culture of much of the western part of Harlem. Hamilton Heights, concentrated around St. Nicholas and Convent Ave. in the 140s, is home to professionals of all types. The stereotypical Harlem which attracts all the negative publicity is largely represented south of 125th St. in the Manhattan Valley, particularly along Frederick Douglass Ave. and Adam Clayton Powell Blvd.; you will want to avoid these avenues after dark. For more information on Harlem call the Uptown Chamber of Commerce at 996-2288.

■ MORNINGSIDE HEIGHTS AND COLUMBIA U.

Morningside Heights, south of 125th St. and west of Morningside Park, is a good place to start a tour of the Harlem area (Subway: #1 or 9 to 110th St. or 116th St.). The **Cathedral of St. John the Divine,** between 110th and 113th St. along

LET'S GO
TRAVEL

C A T A L O G

1 9 9 5

WE GIVE YOU THE WORLD... AT A DISCOUNT

Discounted Flights, Eurail Passes,
Travel Gear, Let's Go™ Series Guides,
Hostel Memberships... and more

Let's Go Travel

a division of

Harvard Student
Agencies, Inc.

**Bargains
to every
corner of
the world!**

Travel Gear

A Let's Go T-Shirt...$10

100% combed cotton. Let's Go logo on front left chest. Four color printing on back. L and XL. Way cool.

B Let's Go Supreme..........$175

Innovative hideaway suspension with parallel stay internal frame turns backpack into carry-on suitcase. Includes lumbar support pad, torso, and waist adjustment, leather trim, and detachable daypack. Waterproof Cordura nylon, lifetime gurantee, 4400 cu. in. Navy, Green, or Black.

C Let's Go Backpack/Suitcase.....................$130

Hideaway suspension turns backpack into carry-on suitcase. Internal frame. Detachable daypack makes 3 bags in 1. Waterproof Cordura nylon, lifetime guarantee, 3750 cu. in. Navy, Green, or Black.

D Let's Go Backcountry I..$210

Full size, slim profile expedition pack designed for the serious trekker. New Airflex suspension. X-frame pack with advanced composite tube suspension. Velcro height adjustment, side compression straps. Detachable hood converts into a fanny pack. Waterproof Cordura nylon, lifetime guarantee, main compartment 3375 cu. in., extends to 4875 cu. in.

E Let's Go Backcountry II.............................$240

Backcountry I's Big Brother. Magnum Helix Airflex Suspension. Deluxe bi-lam contoured shoulder harness. Adjustable sterm strap. Adjustable bi-lam Cordura waist belt. 5350 cubic inches. 7130 cubic inches extended. Not pictured.

800-5-LETSGO

Discounted Flights

Call Let's Go now for inexpensive airfare to points across the country and around the world.

EUROPE • SOUTH AMERICA • ASIA • THE CARRIBEAN • AUSTRALIA •
AFRICA

Eurail Passes

...urailpass (First Class)

...days......................................$498
...nonth (30 days)....................$798
...ionths (60 days).................$1098

Unlimited rail travel anywhere on Europe's 100,000 mile rail network. Accepted in 17 countries.

Eurail Flexipass (First Class)

A number of individual travel days to be used at your convenience within a two-month period.

Any 5 days in 2 months.............$348
Any 10 days in 2 months...........$560
Any 15 days in 2 months...........$740

...urail Youthpass (Second Class)

...days......................................$398
...nonth (30 days)....................$578
...ionths (60 days)...................$768

All the benefits of the Eurail Pass at a lower price. For those passengers under 26 on their first day of travel.

Eurail Youth Flexipass (Second Class)

Eurail Flexipass at a reduced rate for passengers under 26 on their first day of travel.

Any 5 days in 2 months.............$255
Any 10 days in 2 months...........$398
Any 15 days in 2 months...........$540

...uropass (First & Second Class)

...st Class starting at................$280
...cond Class starting at............$198
...r more details......................CALL

Discounted fares for those passengers travelling in France, Germany, Italy, Spain and Switzerland.

Hostelling Essentials

F **Undercover Neckpouch............$9.95**
Ripstop nylon with soft Cambrelle back. Three pockets. 6 x 7". Lifetime guarantee. Black or Tan.

G **Undercover Waistpouch.........$9.95**
Ripstop nylon with soft Cambrelle back. Two pockets. 5 x 12" with adjustable waistband. Lifetime guarantee. Black or Tan.

H **Sleepsack................................$13.95**
Required at all hostels. 18" pillow pocket. Washable poly/cotton. Durable. Compact.

I **Hostelling International Card**
Required by most international hostels. For U.S. residents only. Adults, $25. Under 18, $10.

J **Int'l Youth Hostel Guide.......$10.95**
Indispensable guide to prices, locations, and reservations for over 4000 hostels in Europe and the Mediterranean.

K **ISIC, ITIC, IYTC..........$16, $16, $17**
ID cards for students, teachers and those people under 26. Each offers many travel discounts.

800-5-LETSGO

Order Form

Please print or type — Incomplete applications will not be processed

| Last Name | First Name | Date of Birth |

| Street | (We cannot ship to P.O. boxes) |

| City | State | Zip |

| Country | Citizenship | Date of Travel |

( )   -

| Phone | School (if applicable) |

Item Code	Description, Size & Color	Quantity	Unit Price	Total Price
			SUBTOTAL:	

Domestic Shipping & Handling		Shipping and Handling (see box at left):	
Order Total:	Add:	Add $10 for RUSH, $20 for overnite:	
Up to $30.00	$4.00	MA Residents add 5% tax on books and gear:	
$30.01 to $100.00	$6.00		
Over $100.00	$7.00	**GRAND TOTAL:**	
Call for int'l or off-shore delivery			

MasterCard / VISA Order

CARDHOLDER NAME _____

CARD NUMBER _____

EXPIRATION DATE _____

Enclose check or money order payable to:
Harvard Student Agencies, Inc.
53A Church Street
Cambridge, MA 02138

Allow 2-3 weeks for delivery. Rush orders guaranteed within
one week of our receipt. Overnight orders sent via FedEx the same afternoon.

Missing a Let's Go Book from your collection?
Add one to any $50 order at 50% off the cover price!

Let's Go Travel
1-800-5-LETSGO

(617) 495-9649   Fax: (617) 496-8015
53A Church Street
Cambridge MA 02138

Amsterdam Ave., promises to be the world's largest cathedral when finished. Construction, begun in 1892, is still going on and is not expected to be completed for another century or two. At a stoneyard nearby, artisans carve blocks much as they would have in the age of the great Medieval cathedrals. The original design called for a Byzantine church with some Romanesque ornamentation. Twenty years and several bishops later, Ralph Adams Cram drew up new designs that betrayed his admiration for the French Gothic. The façade resembles Notre Dame, with its centerpiece rose window, symmetrical twin towers, and heavy arched portals. The nave measures 601 ft. long, the towers will be 300 ft. high, and the width will span 320 ft. The bronze door of the central portal was cast in Paris by M. Barbedienne, who also cast the Statue of Liberty (which would fit underneath the central dome of this church).

A "living cathedral," St. John's features naves dedicated not only to the sufferings of Christ, but to the beauty of abstract geometry and the experience of immigrants. Stained glass windows portray TV sets and George Washington as well as the usual religious scenes. Amble down the overwhelming central nave to see the altar dedicated to AIDS victims, a 100 million-year-old nautilus fossil, a modern sculpture for 12 firefighters who died in 1966, and a 2000-lb. natural quartz crystal. Don't forget to look at the beautiful rose window right above. The church currently maintains an extensive secular schedule, hosting concerts, art exhibitions, lectures, theater, and dance events (for information call 316-7540). The complex also has a homeless shelter, a school, and countless other community services. Vertical tours of the church are given on the first and third Saturday of the month at noon and 2pm ($2); regular horizontal tours Tues.-Sat. by appointment ($2; call 932-7314). (Church open daily 7am-5pm; suggested donation $2; wheelchair access.)

Next to the cathedral, the **Children's Sculpture Garden,** at 111th St. and Amsterdam Ave., is crowned by a huge, grotesque fountain of a winged warrior on a smiling disc and explodes with spiraling jets of water. The Ring of Freedom surrounds the fountain, topped with small bronze sculptures created annually by schoolchildren. Enter to the right of the main entrance to see the impressive stone-yard where raw marble is chiseled. Currently undergoing renovation, the winged warrior sits in a ring of plywood on which people lounge about. (Open 24 hrs.)

To the east of St. John's, down the cliffs from Morningside Dr., lies **Morningside Park,** a bit of greenery stretching from 110th to 123rd St. Featured in *When Harry Met Sally,* this sloping park offers a recreational space and rambling paths where you too can discuss your sexual dreams. The wooded park is not very safe, however, especially at night.

New York City's member of the Ivy League, **Columbia University,** chartered in 1754, is tucked between Morningside Dr. and Broadway, stretching from 114th to 120th St. Now co-ed, Columbia also has cross-registration with all-female **Barnard College** across Broadway. This urban campus occupies the former site of the Bloomingdale Insane Asylum. The centerpiece of the campus is the magisterial **Low Library,** named after Columbia president Seth Low. Daniel Chester French's statue of the Alma Mater, stationed on the front steps of the building, became a rallying point during the riots of 1968. Prospective students get group tours starting in late fall and continuing to spring, but there are no regularly scheduled tours for the public during the year (you must call ahead to make an appointment). Call 854-2842 for information or to schedule a tour.

Near Columbia, at 120th St. and Riverside Dr., is the **Riverside Church.** Its well-known pastor, William Sloane Coffin, uses his pulpit to champion the struggle for civil rights and the fight against AIDS (he was once a leading crusader against the war in Vietnam). The observation deck in the tower commands an amazing view of the bells within and the expanse of the Hudson River and Riverside Park below. You can hear concerts on the world's largest carillon (74 bells), the gift of John D. Rockefeller, Jr. (Open Mon.-Sat. 9am-4:30pm, Sun. service 10:45am. Tours of the tower given Sun. 12:30pm; call for tickets.)

Diagonally across Riverside Dr. lies **Grant's Tomb** (666-1640). Once a popular monument, it now attracts only a few brave souls willing to make the hike. The massive granite mausoleum rests in peace atop a hill overlooking the river. Inside, the black marble sarcophagus of ("who's buried in Grant's tomb?") Ulysses S. Grant and his wife Julia is surrounded by bronze casts of the general's cronies. (Open daily 9am-5pm. Free.) Take a rest on the Gaudí-inspired tile benches around the monument, added in the mid-70s.

■ CENTRAL HARLEM

125th Street, also known as Martin Luther King Jr. Boulevard, spans the heart of traditional Harlem. (Subway: #2, 3, A, B, C, or D to 125th St.) Fast-food joints, jazz bars, and the **Apollo Theatre,** at 253 W. 125th St. (222-0992, box office 749-5838), keep the street humming day and night. 125th has recently resurged as a center of urban life; street vendors, small shops, families with children, and an increasing vogue have combined to make this part of Harlem a lively community center.

Most of the streets around here have been renamed. Sixth Ave. is now Lenox Ave. but is also known as Malcolm X Blvd. Seventh Ave. is Adam Clayton Powell, Jr., Blvd., and Eighth Ave. is Frederick Douglass Blvd.

The recently built **Adam Clayton Powell, Jr., Office Building,** at 163 W. 125th St., between Lenox and Powell Ave. has brought bureaucratic life (an oxymoron?) to 125th St. The **Studio Museum in Harlem** displays at 144 W. 125th St. (see Museums). The former **Teresa Hotel,** at the northwest corner of 125th St. and Powell Ave., has housed Malcolm X and Fidel Castro, who once preached solidarity and brotherhood to the people of Harlem from these balconies. An unconventional tourist, Castro felt safer in Harlem than in other parts of New York; still, charmingly paranoid, he transported live chickens from Cuba for his meals. Off 125th St., at 328 Lenox Ave., **Sylvia's** (966-0660) has been the "Queen of Soul Food" for over 20 years (see Eating and Drinking). The silver dome of the **Masjid Malcolm Shabazz,** where Malcolm X was once a minister, glitters on 116th St. at Lenox Ave. (Visit Fri. at 1pm and Sun. at 10am for services and information, or call 662-2200.)

Walk up Lenox Ave. for a slice of life in Harlem. Teenagers, families, and older professionals all mingle on the wide sidewalks. Older residents sit on stoops and watch the world whiz by. Check out the **Liberation Bookstore,** 421 Lenox Ave. at 131st St., which has a great selection of African and African-American history, art, poetry, and fiction. (Open Mon.-Fri. 11am-7pm, Sat. 11:30am-6:30pm.) Nearby at 132nd and Lenox Ave. is the Lenox Terrace Apartment complex where many black politicians live, including Percy Sutton. On 135th St. and Lenox Ave., the **Schomburg Center,** a branch of the public library, houses the city's African archives and presents exhibits of local artists' work (see both Museums and Practical Information: Libraries). The #2 and 3 subway line also runs up Lenox Ave. from 125th to 135th St.

Just north, at 132 W. 138th St. between Lenox and Powell Ave., is New York's oldest African-American church, the **Abyssinian Baptist Church.** It was at one time presided over by the ubiquitous congressman Adam Clayton Powell, Jr. The church has 14,000 members and the pastor, Calvin Butts, is a well-known local political leader. A notable upper-class Harlem neighborhood is a one block west, on 138th St. between Powell and Douglass Blvd. **Striver's Row,** consisting mainly of brownstones, was built by David King in 1891. Three different architects designed these buildings, now part of the St. Nicholas Historic District. Spike Lee filmed *Jungle Fever* here, and Bob Dylan owns a house on this street.

Further west, across St. Nicholas Park, is the **City College,** at 138th St. and Convent Ave. (650-5310). This is the northernmost outpost of the City University of New York, and it sports an odd mix of Gothic and '70s-esque architecture. Founded in 1849 as a free college, it accepted everyone who wanted to go and was populated primarily by Jewish students until after World War II. Today, the school, which has no dorms, educates mostly commuter students from the city. Over 50 languages are spoken on campus. The less-appealing south campus lies between 130th and 135th St. The college can be reached by walking up Morningside/Convent Ave. from 125th St. or by taking the #1 or 9 subway to 137th St. and walking two blocks east.

Just north of the college, along Convent Ave. between 140th and 145th St., is **Hamilton Heights,** home to many upper-middle-class black families living in some of the city's most intricately designed brownstones. Walk down Hamilton Terrace, which is between Convent and St. Nicholas Ave., for a good example of these homes. Alexander Hamilton built his two-story Colonial-style country home, **Hamilton Grange,** at what is now 287 Convent Ave. (283-5154), at 141st St. (Open Wed.-Sun. 9am-4pm. Free.) If funding comes through, the house will be moved to nearby St. Nicholas Park; the National Parks Service wants to restore the house to its original state and make it a bona fide national landmark. Up a couple blocks, **Sugar Hill** (which stretches from 143rd to 155th St. between St. Nicholas and Edgecombe Ave.) was at one time home to some of the city's wealthiest and most important gangsters. Today the neighborhood is better known for the Sugarhill Gang, the rap act that emerged from its streets in 1979 to release the first rap crossover success, "Rapper's Delight." These areas can be reached by the A, B, C, or D subway to 145th St. West of Amsterdam Ave., the neighborhood shifts to one which is predominantly Dominican. Spanish (obviously) is spoken here, and a business here even runs a $60 express bus to Miami.

Farther north at Broadway and 155th St. are the four buildings in **Audubon Terrace,** the Beaux Arts complex that houses the **Numismatic Society Museum,** the **Hispanic Society of America,** the **National Museum of the American Indian,** the **American Academy of Arts and Letters** (see Museums), and **Boricua College,** a private Hispanic liberal arts college. The neo-Italian Renaissance courtyard has huge reliefs and sculptures. Diagonally across Broadway, you can wander around the **Trinity Cemetery,** between 153rd and 155th St., and Amsterdam Ave. and Riverside Dr. The grave of John James Audubon is near the Church of the Intercession. John Jacob Astor and former mayor Fernando Wood are also rumored to be buried here. Exercise caution visiting the cemetery, especially if alone. The #1 subway to 157th St. or the A or B subway to 155th St. will get you to this area.

Further west and across the West Side Hwy. is the newly-opened **Riverbank State Park.** In 1993 the state decided to put a sewage plant here, an act which many members of the black community considered racist, so Governor Cuomo decided that a state-run park would be built over the new plant. The park, with year-round ice-skating, an indoor pool, tennis, tracks, roller rinks, baseball diamonds, and picnic fields, is extremely popular. Munch on sandwiches on the green lawn and try not to think about what lies directly under you. The funny odor you detect is tidewater—honest. Call 694-3643 or 694-3610 for times and rates of the various activities. The M11 bus runs directly into the park, as does the Bx11, which also runs to the Bronx zoo. The #9 subway to 145th St. and the #1 or 9 subway to 157th St. also take you near the park.

■ SPANISH HARLEM

East Harlem, better known as **Spanish Harlem** or El Barrio ("The Neighborhood"), hugs the northeast corner of Central Park and extends to the 140s, where it is framed by the Harlem River. At the main artery on 116th St., the streets bustle with people selling fruit, shirts, and diverse sorts of chow. The famous "ice man" flavors ground-up ice with mango, papaya, coconut, or banana syrup to save you from the summer heat. Anti-crack murals and memorials to the drug's victims adorn the walls. Spanish Harlem north of 110th St. is not safe unless you know which streets to stay on; areas below 110th are usually safe during the day. The northern tip of Fifth Avenue's Museum Mile stretches up to the **Museum of the City of New York** at 103rd St. and **El Museo del Barrio** at 105th St. (see Museums).

■■■ WASHINGTON HEIGHTS

Once upon a time the area north of 155th St. was an all-Irish enclave, but the sounds of rhumba and calypso soon drowned out those of the drum and bagpipes as Puerto Ricans and Latin Americans began to claim the neighborhood for their own. Blacks, Greeks, and Armenians, as well as a large Jewish community, subsequently moved in. Unfortunately, the newest sound is the police siren; crack, cocaine, and other drugs litter the urban blightscape here, near the frontline of the war on drugs.

Come here during the day for a taste of urban life with a thick ethnic flavor. On the same block, you can eat a Greek dinner, buy Armenian pastries and vegetables from a South African, and talk Talmud with a student at nearby Yeshiva University.

Bargain-shop along trinket-filled St. Nicholas Avenue or Broadway. Street vendors sell swimwear, Italian shoes, and household items for half the going rate. You'll find discount electronics stores here too. Prices go down as the street numbers go up.

The Georgian **Morris-Jumel Mansion,** in Roger Morris Park at W. 160th St. and Edgecombe Ave. (923-8008), was built in 1765 and is one of Harlem's oldest buildings. Washington lived here while planning his successful (but little-known) Battle of Harlem Heights in the autumn of 1776. In 1810 Stephen and Eliza Jumel bought the house; Eliza seems to have spent most of her time primping, as seen by the vast numbers of parlors and dressing rooms in the house. Stephen died in 1832, and in 1833 Eliza up and married Aaron Burr in the front room. Don't be afraid to knock if the house seems closed. (Open Tues.-Sun. 10am-4pm; $3, seniors and students $1, children under 12 free. Tours Mon.-Fri.) The gardens are exceptional as well, with a great view of the Harlem River. Nearby, at St. Nicholas Ave. and 161st St., more brownstones with architecturally varied façades vie for your attention on **Sylvan Terrace,** at 161st St. The A or B subway to 163rd St.will get you in the vicinity of all these sights.

Columbia University recently started a controversy when it decided to buy the abandoned **Audubon Ballroom,** on 165th St. between St. Nicholas Ave. and Broadway. The ballroom was the site of Malcolm X's assassination and protesters have covered the doorway with plaques calling for a memorial to the Black Power advocate. Nonetheless, all that remains now is the front façade.

You can either walk to Broadway and up to 178th St. or take the A train to 181st St. to view the **George Washington Bridge Bus Station,** on 178th St. between Broadway and Fort Washington Ave. It resembles a huge Christmas tree cookie-cutter. The **George Washington Bridge** heads west and across the Hudson from the station. Constructed in 1931 by Othmar Amman, this 14-lane, 3500-ft. suspension bridge was once pronounced "the most beautiful bridge in the world" by Le Corbusier. Then again, Le Corbusier designed some of the more hideous buildings in architectural history. Just beneath the bridge, accessible by steps from the intersection of 181st St. and Pinehurst, lies **Fort Washington Park,** home to the **Little Red Lighthouse** and the remnants of the original fort. Originally constructed to steer barges away from Jeffrey's Hook, the lighthouse became the thinly disguised subject of Hildegarde Hoyt Swift's obscure children's book *The Little Red Lighthouse and the Great Grey Bridge.*

Back on Amsterdam Ave., from 182nd to 186th St., you'll find **Yeshiva University,** surrounded by kosher bakeries and butcher shops. This is the oldest Jewish-studies center in the U.S., dating from 1886. The **Yeshiva University Museum** (960-5390) on 185th St. features exhibitions concerning the Jewish community. (Open Tues.-Thurs. 10:30am-5pm, Sun. noon-6pm, or call for appointment. $3, seniors and children under 17 $1.50.) **Tannenbaum Hall** is the centerpiece of the campus at 186th St., featuring Romanesque windows and colorful minarets. Take the #1 or 9 train to 181st or 190th St.

Five blocks west along 181st St. will lead you to the gently (and not-so-gently) sloping hill that is Fort Washington Ave. The journey north along Fort Washington Ave. takes you past a succession of mid-rise apartment buildings (ca. 1920) home to Jewish and Hispanic families. At 190th St. and Ft. Washington Ave., the **St. Francis**

Xavier Cabrini Chapel shelters the remains of Mother Cabrini, the patron saint of immigrants. Her fleshy body lies in a crystal casket under the altar, but her smiling face is made of wax—Rome's got her head. Gross. Legend has it that shortly after her death, a lock of her hair restored the eyesight of an infant who has since grown up to be a Texas priest (open Tues.-Sun. 9am-4:30pm). One more block down is Margaret Corbin Circle and the official entrance to **Fort Tryon Park,** lovingly landscaped by Central Park's Frederick Law Olmsted. John D. Rockefeller donated this land to the city in exchange for permission to construct Rockefeller University. You can still see the crusty remains of Fort Tryon, a Revolutionary War bulwark. The park also contains a magnificent expanse of gardens and **The Cloisters,** the Met's sanctuary for Medieval art (see Museums). To get to the Cabrini Chapel or Ft. Tryon Park by subway, take the A train to 190th St., then take the elevator up from the station; otherwise, you'll end up at the base of a less lovingly landscaped mountain.

Huff and puff your way down the mini-mountain (but not before admiring the beautiful view of the Hudson) and get back on Broadway. Then you can walk up to Broadway and 204th St. to visit a modest but charming 18th-century Dutch dwelling. Donated to the city as a museum in 1915, **Dyckman House** (304-9422) has been restored and filled with period Dutch and English family furnishings. (Open Tues.-Sun. 11am-noon and 1-4pm. Free. Subway: A to Dyckman or 207th St.)

■■■ GREENWICH VILLAGE

In "The Village," bordered by 14th St. to the north and Houston to the south, bohemian cool meets New York neurosis, resulting in the "downtown" approach to life. The buildings here do not scrape the skies, the street grid dissolves into geometric whimsy, and the residents revel in countercultural logics. Village people wear their slogans on their crotches and hang underwear in their galleries. Pop culture and P.C. politics thrive here, but both are the secret slaves to the real arbiter of cool: fashion.

The Village's prominence began with Tom Paine, who in 1808 had the derring-do to live on Bleecker St. Herman Melville and James Fenimore Cooper wrote American masterworks here, and Mark Twain and Willa Cather explored the U.S. heartland from their homes near Washington Square. Henry James was born on the square during the Village's High Society days, and Edith Wharton lived nearby. John Reed, John Dos Passos, and e.e. cummings all made the Manhattan transfer straight from Harvard, followed by James Agee. Village rents were low then, and many writers came to this American Bohemia to begin their careers in poverty and obscurity. Eugene O'Neill created the Provincetown Playhouse in the West Village, and it created him in turn. Theodore Dreiser wrote here, as did Edna St. Vincent Millay and Thomas Wolfe. Tennessee Williams, James Baldwin, and William Styron found their way to small apartments in the area, and Richard Wright lived in the same building as Willa Cather, 35 years later.

"Greenwich Village" used to refer to the entire strip of Manhattan between Houston and 14th Streets but now refers primarily to the West Village (from Broadway west to the Hudson River), while the area east of Broadway is now called the "East Village." And if you hear anyone refer to "The Village," they probably mean the West Village, though bohemians to the east would argue that true "Village" life has shifted to the East Village. Got it?

Today there are fewer and fewer aspiring artists in the Village as young professionals take over one of the liveliest neighborhoods in Manhattan. But the Village has not entirely sold out its old bohemian sense of fun—every year the wild **Village Halloween Parade** winds its way through the streets. If you ever wanted to see people dressed as toilets or carrots or giant condoms, this is your chance; if you're lucky, you may even receive a personal benediction from Rollerina, the city's crossdressing fairy godmother on wheels.

The Village stays lively all day and most of the night. People with various pierced body parts share the street with NYU business students, an amazing panoply of dogs and the owners who love them, and awfully rich families who can afford a two-bedroom here. Sit at one of the sidewalk cafés and watch the human drama unfold before you.

■ WASHINGTON SQUARE PARK AREA

Washington Square Park has been the universally acknowledged heart of the Village since the district's days as a suburb. The marshland here served first as a colonial cemetery (around 15,000 bodies lie buried here) and then as a Revolutionary hanging-grounds (people swung from trees that still stand today), but in the 1820s the area was converted into a park and parade ground. Soon high-toned residences made the area the center of New York's social scene.

Society has long since gone north, and **New York University** has moved in. The country's largest private university and one of the city's biggest landowners (along with the city government, the Catholic Church, and Columbia University), NYU is most notable for its hip students, its takeover of historic buildings, and some of the most amazingly ugly architecture in the Village. As if proud of this, many of the most unattractive buildings around the Square are festooned with the purple NYU flag.

At the north end of Washington Square Park stands the majestic **Washington Memorial Arch,** marking the end of Fifth Ave. Some nostalgics built it in 1889 to mark the centennial of Washington's inauguration as President. The statues on top depict multi-talented George in poses of war and peace. The arch is actually hollow—every year the NYU band opens the door at the base and trudges up the 110 stairs to *Pomp and Circumstance* the NYU commencement in the Park.

In the late 1970s and early '80s Washington Square Park became a base for low-level drug dealers, and a rough resident scene came along with the culture. The mid-80s saw a noisy clean-up campaign that has made the park fairly safe and allowed a more diverse cast of characters to return. Today concerts play, defiant punks congregate, homeless people try to sleep, pigeons strut in the lawn, and children romp in the playground. In the southwest corner of the park, a dozen perpetual games of chess wend their ways toward ultimate checkmate. The fountain in the center of the park provides an amphitheater for comics and musicians of widely varying degrees of talent. Judge for yourself how well Beethoven's *Moonlight Sonata* translates to the steel drum. A statue of Italian revolutionary Giuseppe Garibaldi, rather mysteriously, is also in the park.

The north side of the park, called the **Row,** showcases some of the more renowned architecture in the city. Built largely in the 1830s, this stretch of elegant Federal-style brick residences soon became an urban center roamed by 19th-century professionals, dandies, and novelists. No. 18, now demolished, was the home of Henry James's grandmother and the basic setting for his novel *Washington Square.* Today the Row is mostly NYU administration buildings. The Admissions Office at #22 (998-4500) offers tours of NYU (Mon.-Fri. at 11am and 2:30pm). At the west end of the street, at 29 Washington Sq. West, is the house where Eleanor Roosevelt lived after FDR's death.

A few steps north up Fifth Ave. on the east side, you'll find **Washington Mews,** a quirky, cobblestoned alleyway directly behind the Row. The boxy little brick houses, originally constructed as stables for the houses facing the park, are now NYU faculty housing. Yes, NYU owns everything.

Walking up Fifth Ave. another half-block, you'll reach **Eighth Street.** Lined with offbeat shops and stores, this is the punk hangout in the West Village. Famous residents have included Jimi Hendrix, whose Electric Lady studio was located at 52 W. 8th St. Take a quick detour from your tour of the Village and buy a skull earring or something.

Farther up Fifth Ave., at the corner of 10th St., rises the **Church of the Ascension,** a fine 1841 Gothic church with a notable altar and stained-glass windows. Former President John Tyler consummated a secret elopement with his second wife here in 1844. (Open daily noon-2pm and 5-7pm.) Many consider the block down

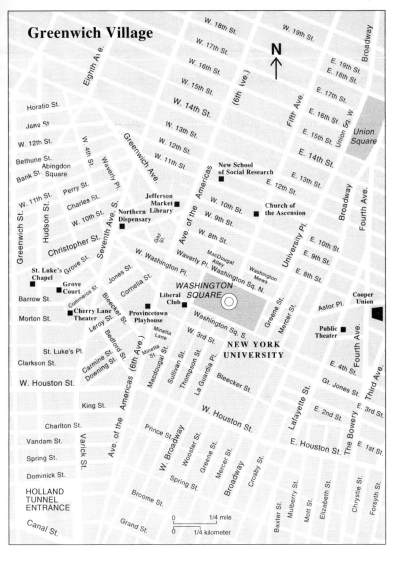

Greenwich Village

10th St. between Fifth and Sixth Ave. the most beautiful residential stretch in the city. This short strip plays out innumerable variations in brick and stucco, layered with wood and iron detailing. Ivy clothes the façades of many of the buildings, while window boxes brighten others. **The Pen and Brush Club,** located at 16 E. 10th St., was founded to promote female intelligentsia networking; it has counted as members such notables as Pearl Buck, Eleanor Roosevelt, Marianne Moore, and muckraker Ida Tarbell.

The next block up on Fifth Ave., 11th St., features more turn-of-the-century architecture. That is, except for 18 W. 11th St., where a striking new building has replaced the house destroyed in 1970 by a bomb-making mishap of the Weathermen, a radical group residing in the basement. At Fifth Ave. and 11th St. is the **Salmagundi Club,** New York's oldest club for artists. Founded in 1870, the club's building is the only remaining mansion from the area's heyday at the pinnacle of New York society. (Open during exhibitions. Call 255-7740 for details.)

The corner of Fifth Ave. and 12th St. is dominated by the eccentric **Forbes Magazine Galleries** (206-5548), Malcolm Forbes's vast collection of random *stuff* (see Museums). Up one more block, off Fifth Ave. at 2 W. 13th St., lies the **Parsons School of Design,** with its own exhibition galleries and cigarette-wielding, black-garbed *artistes.*

Over one avenue to the east is **University Place.** At 12th St. and University Pl. is the **New School for Social Research,** dedicated to adult continuing education. John Dewey and W.E.B. DuBois once taught here, and the New School made itself famous during WWII when it offered positions to European intellectuals fleeing the Nazis.

One more block east is Broadway. At 12th St. and Broadway lies the **Forbidden Planet,** the world's largest science fiction store. You can browse through European space toys, vintage Superman comics, hundreds of science-fiction paperbacks, and a complete line of "Dungeons & Dragons" fantasy paraphernalia. Across the street is one of the world's most famous bookstores—the **Strand,** which bills itself as the "largest used bookstore in the world" with over two million books (arranged according to no identifiable scheme) on eight miles of shelves. (See Shopping: Bookstores.) **Grace Church,** constructed in 1845, asserts its powerful Gothic presence at 800 Broadway between 10th and 11th. The church used to be *the* place for weddings. The dark interior has a distinctly Medieval feel. (Open Mon-Thurs. 10am-5pm, Fri. 10am-4pm, Sat. noon-4pm.) Antique stores flock around the church, especially on 10th and 11th St. Most specialize in large, high-priced pieces of furniture or architectural elements (Greek-style columns and eagle-shaped statues).

Walking back down Broadway to the south can be exciting; a strange conglomeration of cheap futon stores, "antique" (read: used yet expensive) clothing outlets, bars, and health food markets line the street Here the trendy styles are usually a few steps behind the truly avant-garde and a few dollars above the truly bohemian. At Broadway and 4th St., you'll find another of the Village's spiritual landmarks, **Tower Records,** a store with an enormous musical inventory (but no actual records—only CDs and cassettes). Open late (and often a privileged site for drug-induced meanderings), Tower has become not only a popular hangout, but also a sudden bonding ground for people of similar musical taste: "Wow, you're into Velvet Crush? I *love* Velvet Crush! Were you at their last concert?" Lots of models have been "discovered" here. (See Shopping: Record Stores.)

Back up a block, at 721 Broadway and Washington Pl., NYU's **Tisch School of the Arts** churns out principled indie-style filmmakers like Spike Lee and Martin Scorcese. At this point, it's all NYU. Walking back towards Washington Square Park, note those ubiquitous purple banners.

At Greene St. and Waverly Pl., one block up from Washington Pl., lies NYU's **Brown Building,** the former site of the Triangle Shirtwaist Company. In 1911 the Triangle caught fire, and because the owners had so thoughtfully locked and chained all the doors shut to prevent the workers from theft and dilly-dallying, most of the primarily female staff was killed. This mobilized the cause of worker safety and led to new workplace regulations.

One block west, Washington Sq. East is lined with NYU classrooms and administrative offices; the **Main Building** is located at Waverly Pl. Go through the building to the **Grey Art Gallery** (998-6780), or enter at 33 Washington Pl. The gallery features both student work and that of community artists, as well as works directly concerning the Village. (Open Mon.-Fri. 11am-6pm; Sept.-May Tues. and Thurs.-Fri. 11am-6:30pm, Wed. 11am-8:30pm, Sat. 11-5pm; closed Aug.) Further down Washington Sq. East, at the southeast corner of the park, is **NYU Information** at 70 Washington Sq. South. Come here for free maps and any questions you might have.

One block east at Greene St. and W. 4th St. is a red-rust architectural don't—NYU's **Tisch Hall,** home to the Stern Business School. The vast space before it and the brown cinderblock Courant Institute of Mathematical Sciences is known as **Gould Plaza.** A shiny aluminum Dadaist sculpture by Jean Arp, which bears an uncanny resemblance to a bunny rabbit, often reflects light straight into your eyes, blinding you temporarily. Two blocks west at Washington Sq. South and LaGuardia Pl. looms another rust-colored monstrosity, the **Elmer Holmes Bobst Library.** The university for a time wanted all of its buildings to look like this, so that the campus would have a common theme. Luckily, NYU ended up opting for the cheaper, more discreet, but no less tacky purple flags instead. Across the street is the **Loeb Student Center,** festooned with pieces of scrap metal that purport to represent birds in flight.

Further west, at 55 Washington Sq. South and Thompson St., you'll see the **Judson Memorial Baptist Church,** built in 1892 by the indomitable trio of McKim, Mead, and White. Stained glass by John LaFarge panels the sanctuary. Known for its liberal stance on religion, Judson hosted much avant-garde art activity in the '50s and '60s and nowadays prides itself as a positive force for tolerance in the Village. Further west along Washington Sq. South, across the street from the park's chess players, stands NYU's brick-arched **Vanderbilt Law School.** Inside the arch lies a surprisingly pleasant courtyard, filled with people nervously cramming for contract law.

The area directly south of Washington Square Park, from W. 4th to Houston St., is in many ways the most heavily touristed area of the Village. On MacDougal St., Sullivan St., Thompson St., and Bleecker St., you could spend days or weeks sipping cappuccinos, flipping through records, going to small clubs, emulating bohemia. Just south of Washington Square Park, at 133 MacDougal St., is the **Provincetown Playhouse,** a theatrical landmark. Originally based on Cape Cod, the Provincetown Players were joined by the young Eugene O'Neill in 1916 and brought here that same year to perform his successful play *Bound East for Cardiff.* The playhouse went on to premiere many of O'Neill's works, as well as the work of other Village writers such as Edna St. Vincent Millay. Farther south on **MacDougal Street** are the Village's finest (and most tourist-trampled) coffeehouses, which had their glory days in the 1950s when Beatnik heroes and coffee-bean connoisseurs Jack Kerouac and Allen Ginsberg attended jazz-accompanied poetry readings at **Le Figaro** and **Café Borgia** (see Eating & Drinking). These sidewalk cafés still provide some of the best coffee and people watching in the city.

By all means, don't restrict yourself to MacDougal St. **Sullivan Street** is home to the **Sullivan St. Theater** and its Fantastiks (see Entertainment and Nightlife: Theater). **Bleecker Street** features a number of jazz clubs and bars, as well as lively people and places. On the corner of Bleecker St. and LaGuardia Pl. are three 30-story apartment buildings (once again, NYU faculty housing; apparently no one else can live in the Village). The buildings surround a Picasso sculpture, proclaimed by the *New York Times* to be the ugliest piece of public art in the city. It is pretty nasty. Continuing down LaGuardia Pl. to E. Houston St., you'll find the **Time Sculpture,** purporting to depict the way Greenwich Village looked some 30,000 years ago. The effect, however, is severely curtailed by the fence surrounding it, not to mention the cars zipping along behind you.

■ WEST OF SIXTH AVE.

The bulk of Greenwich Village lies west of Sixth Ave., thriving on the new and different. In spite of rising property prices, the West Village still boasts an eclectic summer street life and excellent nightlife. As Bleecker and W. 4th St. cross Sixth Ave., they begin to twist crazily. W. 4th will cross W. 10th and W. 11th St.—roads will even appear to cross themselves. No matter how well you did in high school geometry, you should enlist the help of a map.

Walk up Sixth Ave. and watch cars desperately trying to negotiate the non-rectilinear driving patterns, created when the uptown avenues plowed through the preexisting Village streets. This also made for very large intersections; exercise caution crossing the streets, or follow the crowds.

At the intersection of Sixth Ave. and W. 8th St., flee to the northeast corner and check out **Balducci's,** the legendary Italian grocery at 424 Sixth Ave. It has grown over the years from a Sixth Ave. sidewalk stand to a gourmand's paradise. Marvel at its orgy of cheese barrels, bread loaves, and chilled vegetables, and get into a staring contest with the live, bug-eyed lobsters (hint: they'll win).

Across the street at 425 Sixth Ave. stands the landmark **Jefferson Market Library** (243-4334) a Gothic structure complete with detailed brickwork, stained-glass windows, and a turreted clocktower. Built as a courthouse in 1874, it occupies the triangle formed by the intersection of W. 10th St., Sixth Ave., and Greenwich Ave. In the 1880s, architects voted it one of the 10 most beautiful buildings in the country. Changing tastes then threatened the site: in the early 1960s the remarkable structure faced a demolition plot. Carefully restored in 1967, the building reopened as a public library. Inside, the original pre-Raphaelite stained glass graces the spiral staircase. The brick-columned basement now serves as the Reference Room. An excellent pamphlet details the history of the site and the restoration. (Open Mon. and Thurs. noon-6pm, Tues. 10am-6pm, Wed. noon-8pm, Sat. 10am-5pm.)

Make a left out of the library onto 10th St., cross the street, and you'll see an iron gate and a street sign that says "Patchin Place." Behind the gate lies a tiny courtyard, little more than a paved alley. The buildings here, constructed around 1850, housed writers e.e. cummings, Theodore Dreiser, and Djuna Barnes.

Back on Sixth Ave., walk down to Bleecker St. and check out the stretch between Sixth and Seventh Ave. This area features a huge array of cheap Italian (and Italianate) restaurants. Get knee-deep in pasta, and wander through the spaghetti pattern of the little side roads.

Seventh Ave. is another crossroads of sorts. Walking up to the next huge snarl of roads will lead you to **Sheridan Square,** the intersection of Seventh Ave., Christopher St., W. 4th St., and Grove St. Rioters against the Civil War draft thronged here in 1863 during some of the darkest days in New York City's history; some protesters brutally attacked freed slaves. **Christopher Street** and the West Village proper is well-known for its large and very visible gay community. This is the native territory of the Guppie (Gay Urban Professional), although all kinds of gay males and lesbians shop, eat, and live here. Same-sex couples can walk together openly (see also Entertainment and Nightlife: Gay and Lesbian Clubs). The area of Christopher St. that runs near Sheridan Sq. has been renamed Stonewall Place, alluding to the **Stonewall Inn.** Police raids at this club in 1969 prompted the riots that sparked the U.S. Gay Rights Movement. A plaque marks the former site of the club at 53 Christopher St.; the bar that resides there now is not the same one of 26 years ago. Sheridan Square holds two sculptures of same-sex couples as celebration of the vibrant gay community here, as well as a rather forlornly single General Sheridan.

Christopher St. runs into **Bedford Street,** a remarkably narrow old-fashioned strip. **Chumley's** bar and restaurant, at No. 86 between Grove and Barrow St., became a speakeasy in Prohibition days, illegally serving alcohol to literary Johns (Dos Passos and Steinbeck). As if in honor of its surreptitious past, no sign of any kind indicates that the neglected structure might be a commercial establishment.

One of the oldest buildings in the city, No. 77 Bedford St. at the corner of Commerce St., dates from 1799. Its handsome brick has tastefully faded. Next door, run-down and boarded up No. 75½, constructed in a former alley, is the narrowest building in the Village; it measures a mere 9½ ft. across. Edna St. Vincent Millay lived here until 1950. In 1924 Millay founded the **Cherry Lane Theater** at 38 Commerce St. (989-2020), which has showcased important Off-Broadway theater ever since.

Across the way at 39-41 Commerce St. and Bedford St. stand a pair of identical houses separated by a garden, known as the **"Twin Sisters."** Completely unsubstantiated legend has it that they were built by a sea-captain for his spinster daughters, who were not on speaking terms. One block up Bedford St. is more twin action— 102 Bedford St. at Grove St. is **Twin Peaks.** Don't bust in and demand to see Laura Palmer; just check out the two-roofed structure.

At the western end of Grove St. is the **Church of St. Luke's in the Fields,** 179-485 Hudson St. The third-oldest church in Manhattan, it got its name because of the remote location at which it was built in 1821. Walking up Hudson St. will lead you to the **meat-packing district,** around W. 12th and Gansevoort St. It's still used for this purpose—watch slabs of meat get loaded onto large trucks, if that turns you on.

From Hudson St., it's just a few blocks over to the docks along West St., which used to handle a great deal of New York's freight traffic, as well as a few ocean liners. Recently, gay teenagers have been hanging out in this area, and Mayor Giuliani has begun to enforce "quality of life" laws against these young ruffians. So if you're here late at night, don't drink outside, and try not to urinate on the street.

Look across the water to Hoboken, or down the island at the World Trade Center. Just don't get run over by the cars on the highway.

■■■ SOHO

Artist Barbara Kruger's statement "Your are where you are shown" is a sentiment widely shared in SoHo, the diminutive district SOuth of HOuston St. (pronounced "HOW-ston"), north of Canal St., west of Broadway, and east of Sullivan St., which has become as much a style of life as a place to live. While established artists may not splatter paintings of city monuments to wafting strains of Puccini and Bob Dylan in their mega-lofts (à la Scorcese's film *New York Stories),* many do inhabit the area and thrive on the energy of its image-intensive bars, galleries, boutiques, and restaurants. This is a great place for star-gazing, too, so bring your autograph book and a bright flash for your camera. Celebrities like that.

The architecture here is American Industrial (1860-1890), notable for its cast-iron façades. Architects used iron to imitate stone, often painting it to look like limestone, and they laced the columns and pediments with ornate detail (you can still see an 1861 building made by James Bogardus, the inventor of iron buildings, at 85 Leonard St.). The iron frames made heavy walls unnecessary and allowed for the eventual installation of vast windows. The sweatshops and factories that filled the structures were outlawed in time, and in 1962 the City Club called the area "the wasteland of New York." Redevelopment plans were hatched soon afterwards, and residents fought against the construction of an intruding expressway. In 1973 the city declared the neighborhood an historic district.

The huge open spaces of these building proved strongly attractive to New York's artistic community, and the past two decades have seen SoHo transformed into the City's high-priced gallery mecca. Here, art is nothing if not for sale. Every block has its own set of galleries (dozens line the streets between Broadway and West Broadway), usually offering obsequious smiles to those serious about buying but only nasty glances to the riff-raff who want only to ogle. Don't be put off by snooty gallery-owners; unless you're interrupting a private showing to a visiting head of state, visitors short on cash are always allowed, if not entirely welcome. Most close Sundays and Mondays from September to June and often close altogether through the heat of July and August (see Galleries).

Greene Street offers the best of SoHo's lofty architecture. Note the classic roof of No. 28-30, a faded blue building known as the Queen of Greene St. Its neighbor up the block, No. 72-76, the King of Greene St., is actually two buildings designed to look like one, its detailed Corinthian portico spread across five stories of painted metal. It's striking to realize that gaudy iron palaces such as these once contained inhuman sweatshops; the buildings' current tenants seem much more appropriate (especially since you can't escape the feeling that these rich-and-snooty have always secretly dreamt of living in something that could be called a "palace").

A few real museums make their home amid the SoHo galleries. **The Alternative Museum** (966-4444) claims a space on the fourth floor of 594 Broadway, a building which also houses nine commercial galleries. Across the street is **The Museum for African Art,** 593 Broadway (966-1313), which exhibits a stunning variety of African and African-American art. At 583 Broadway, just north of Prince St., you'll find the **New Museum of Contemporary Art** showing the newest and latest on the art scene. At 575 Broadway, the Guggenheim's new downtown branch, the **Guggenheim Museum SoHo** (423-3500), fills two spacious floors of an historic 19th-century building with selections from the museum's permanent collection of modern and contemporary works. (See Museums.)

When you're in the mood to buy (and believe us, you won't be buying the art), browse through SoHo's extensive selection of international goods. A surprising number of good buys await in the district's vintage clothing stores and streetside stands. Be sure to check out the daily "fair" which sets up shop on a lot on Wooster at Spring St. The bargain hunt continues on Broadway with a wide selection of used clothing stores. Flea market devotees should check out the outdoor **Antiques Fair and Collectibles Market** (682-2000), held from 9am to 5pm on Saturdays and Sundays on the corner of Broadway and Grand St.

■■■ TRIBECA

If you're looking for genuine starving artists, you probably won't find them in SoHo—unless they're looking with envied longing through dark, plate-glass gallery windows. But you may find a few in **TriBeCa** ("TRIangle BElow CAnal St."), an area bounded by Chambers St., Broadway, Canal St., and the West Side Highway. Lacking the Rodeo Drive-ish feel of SoHo, TriBeCa seems much more akin to the rest of the city—a visit won't leave you wondering whether the graffiti you see really *is* graffiti or just an artist's subtle attempt to create something that resembles graffiti but which will really confront you with your secret prejudices and thus open your eyes.

The SoHo style is spreading, though, and while the upstairs lofts here are still flanked by butter and egg warehouses, they have undergone art gentrification similar to those in SoHo. That building you see that seems old and decaying is more likely than not home to a number of beautifully restored lofts and studios. Today Robert DeNiro owns a grill and a film company in the neighborhood, and rents are already high.

Admire the cast-iron edifices lining White Street, Thomas Street, and Broadway. The decrepit, crumbling building at 77 White St., just east of Broadway, was once home to the **Mudd Club,** a punk rock venue from the late '70s. West along White St., at 2 White St. and West Broadway, stands an anachronistic 1809 Federal house, a small brick structure whose paint is aged and peeling but whose interior has been completely refurbished and now houses a stylish and comfortable (although nameless) bar. Southwest of here, on Harrison St. between Greenwich and West St., stands a row of beautifully restored 18th-century townhouses. Pretty as they are, they look as if they'd be more at home in a Midwestern condominium complex than in the urban-industrial district which they do inhabit. Just to the south, in an open triangular space bounded by Greenwich, Chambers, and West St., is **Washington Market Park,** which holds a surprisingly big and green spread of grass, as well as a killer playground/sandbox which attracts kids of all ages. The park hosts Thursday-evening concerts each week from late June to early August; performances include every type of music, from jazz to R&B to country (call the Parks Dept. at 408-0100 for info., or just visit the bulletin board by the main gate to the park, where a schedule is always posted). Between Chambers and N. Moore St. stands **Manhattan Community College,** part of the City University system.

For commercial goods, residents roam the streets of Canal, Hudson, and West Broadway. You'll find a number of discount shops selling many kinds of clothing, luggage, jewelry, and electronics. Both West Broadway and Duane Street have good food, if not great prices.

The avant-garde art world has migrated south from SoHo; new galleries offer exhibitions by less-established artists. Art lovers should look to the **Franklin Furnace,** 112 Franklin St. (925-4671), which battles fire regulations in its continuing quest to display the most alternative of alternative art. The Institute for Contemporary Art's **Clocktower Gallery** (233-1096) stands at 108 Leonard St., between Broadway and Lafayette, as TriBeCa recedes into Chinatown. The avant-garde gallery and studio space resides in the former home of the New York Life Insurance Company, on the 13th floor. Although the gallery and exhibition space will be closed to the public

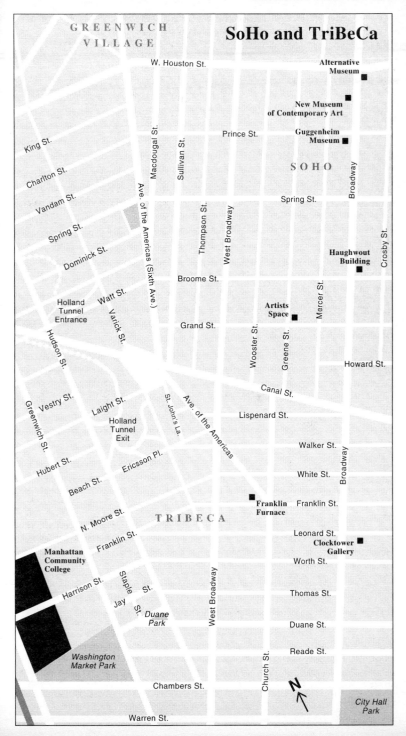

GREENWICH
VILLAGE

SoHo and TriBeCa

W. Houston St.

Alternative
Museum

New Museum
of Contemporary Art

Macdougal St.

Sullivan St.

Prince St.

Guggenheim
Museum

King St.

S O H O

Broadway

Charlton St.

Vandam St.

Spring St.

Thompson St.

West Broadway

Spring St.

Dominick St.

Ave. of the Americas (Sixth Ave.)

Crosby St.

Haughwout
Building

Holland
Tunnel
Entrance

Watt St.

Varick St.

Broome St.

Mercer St.

Artists
Space

Grand St.

Hudson St.

Wooster St.

Greene St.

Howard St.

Vestry St.

Laight St.

St. John's La.

Ave. of the Americas

Canal St.

Greenwich St.

Holland
Tunnel
Exit

Lispenard St.

Hubert St.

Ericsson Pl.

Walker St.

Broadway

Beach St.

White St.

N. Moore St.

Franklin
Furnace

Franklin St.

T R I B E C A

Franklin St.

Leonard St.

Clocktower
Gallery

Manhattan
Community
College

Franklin St.

Worth St.

Harrison St.

Staple St.

Jay St.

West Broadway

Thomas St.

Duane
Park

Duane St.

Washington
Market Park

Reade St.

Church St.

N

Chambers St.

City Hall
Park

Warren St.

until 1996 (the gallery will be exclusively an artists' studio space until then while its sister gallery, P.S. 1 in Long Island City, Queens, undergoes renovations), on Thursday afternoons (after 2pm) you can still climb inside the clocktower to observe its eye-boggling mechanism and fine view of lower Manhattan.

■■■ EAST VILLAGE

The old Lower East Side, once home to Eastern European immigrants, extended from East Broadway to 14th St. Now this area has developed a three-way split personality, encompassing the part south of Houston and east of the Bowery (now considered to be the whole of the Lower East Side), the section east of Broadway and north of Houston (known as the "East Village"), and the part of the East Village east of First Ave. (known as "Alphabet City").

The East Village, a comparatively new creation, was carved out of the Bowery and the Lower East Side as rents in the West Village soared and its residents sought accommodations elsewhere. Allen Ginsberg, Jack Kerouac, and William Burroughs all eschewed the Village establishment to develop their junked-up "beat" sensibility east of Washington Square Park. Billie Holiday sang here; more recently, the East Village provided Buster Poindexter and Sonic Youth with their early audiences. The transfer of population has recaptured much of the gritty feel of the old Village, and the population here is less homogeneous than in the West, with older Eastern European immigrants living alongside new Hispanic and Asian arrivals. But it has been a difficult compromise, and many poorer denizens of the East Village feel they have been pushed out by the newcomers. These tensions have not been helped by glimmers of gentrification and rising rents in the East.

A fun stretch of Broadway marks the western boundary of the East Village and the eastern edge of the Greenwich Village/NYU area. Everyone and their grandmother know about this browser's paradise. (See Sights: Greenwich Village for more on Broadway.) From the NYU area, walk one block east of Broadway on E. 4th to reach Lafayette St. To your right will be **Colonnade Row,** with the Public Theater across the street. Colonnade Row consists of four magnificently columned houses, built in 1833, once the homes of New York's most famous 19th-century millionaires: John Jacob Astor and Cornelius "Commodore" Vanderbilt, as well as the Delano family (as in Franklin Delano Roosevelt). There used to be nine of these houses; the ones that remain, at 428-434 Lafayette St., are a tad on the grubby side. The **Joseph Papp Public Theatre,** a grand brownstone structure across the street at 425 Lafayette St. (598-7150), was constructed by John Jacob Astor in 1853 to serve as the city's first free library. After its collection moved uptown, the building became the headquarters of the Hebrew Immigrant Aid Society, an organization dedicated to assisting thousands of poor Jewish immigrants who came to New York in the early years of this century. In 1967, Joseph Papp's "New York Shakespeare Festival" converted the building to its current use as a theatrical center. (See Entertainment & Nightlife: Theater.)

Up Lafayette St., Astor Place, both a small street and a large intersection, simmers with street life. The street signs were recently covered with the words "Peltier Place," in honor of a Native American man currently in prison for allegedly killing two FBI agents in 1985, and in protest of John Jacob Astor, whose fur trading is seen by some as exploitation of the Native American population.

At 2 Astor Pl. and Broadway you can complement your new Village wardrobe with a distinctive trim at the largest haircutting establishment in the world, **Astor Place Hair Stylists** (475-9854), which is famous for its low-priced production-line approach to style. Scissors are passé here; expect to be mechanically clipped. Stay away if you are finicky—Astor is suited to those who enjoy living dangerously. A total of 110 people (including a DJ) are employed in this three-story complex (open Mon.-Sat. 8am-8pm, Sun. 9am-6pm; men's cuts $10, women's cuts $12; Sun. and holidays $2 extra).

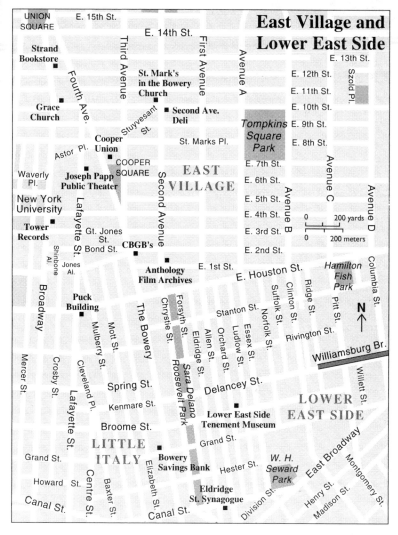

East Village and Lower East Side

UNION SQUARE

E. 15th St.
E. 14th St.
E. 13th St.
E. 12th St.
E. 11th St.
E. 10th St.
E. 9th St.
E. 8th St.
E. 7th St.
E. 6th St.
E. 5th St.
E. 4th St.
E. 3rd St.
E. 2nd St.

Third Avenue
First Avenue
Avenue A
Avenue B
Avenue C
Avenue D
Szold Pl.

Strand Bookstore
Grace Church
Fourth Ave.
St. Mark's in the Bowery Church
Second Ave. Deli
Stuyvesant St.
St. Marks Pl.
Cooper Union
Astor Pl.
COOPER SQUARE
Joseph Papp Public Theater
Waverly Pl.
New York University
Tower Records
Shinbone Al.
Jones Al.
Lafayette St.
Gt. Jones St.
Bond St.
CBGB's
Second Avenue

Tompkins Square Park

EAST VILLAGE

0   200 yards
0   200 meters

Anthology Film Archives
E. 1st St.
E. Houston St.
Hamilton Fish Park
Columbia St.

Puck Building
Broadway
Mulberry St.
Mott St.
Cleveland Pl.
Lafayette St.
Mercer St.
Crosby St.
The Bowery
Chrystie St.
Forsyth St.
Eldridge St.
Allen St.
Orchard St.
Ludlow St.
Essex St.
Norfolk St.
Suffolk St.
Clinton St.
Ridge St.
Pitt St.
Rivington St.
Stanton St.
Sara Delano Roosevelt Park

N

Williamsburg Br.
Willett St.

Spring St.
Kenmare St.
Broome St.
Delancey St.

LOWER EAST SIDE

Lower East Side Tenement Museum
Grand St.

LITTLE ITALY
Grand St.
Howard St.
Canal St.
Centre St.
Baxter St.
Elizabeth St.
Bowery Savings Bank
Hester St.
Eldridge St. Synagogue
Canal St.
Division St.
W. H. Seward Park
East Broadway
Henry St.
Madison St.
Montgomery St.

Astor Place, the intersection (at the juncture of Lafayette, Fourth Ave., Astor Pl., and E. 8th St.) is distinguished by a sculpture of a large black cube balanced on its corner. If you and your friends push hard enough the cube will rotate, but somebody sleeping underneath may complicate the process. "The Cube" is a frequent meeting point for rallies, marches, demonstrations, and site-specific performance art pieces. Note the subway kiosk, a cast-iron Beaux Arts beauty that was built—believe it or not—in 1985 as part of a reconstruction of the station (the #6 train stops here).

Astor Place prominently features the rear of the **Cooper Union Foundation Building,** 41 Cooper Sq. (254-6300), built in 1859 to house the Cooper Union for the Advancement of Science and Art, a tuition-free technical and design school founded by the self-educated industrialist Peter Cooper. The school's free lecture series has hosted practically every notable American since the mid-19th century. Cooper Union was the first college intended for the underprivileged, the first co-educational college, the first racially open college, and the first college to offer free adult-education classes. The American Red Cross and the NAACP were founded here. It's also the oldest standing building in the U.S. incorporating steel beams. Appropriately enough, its namesake founder first laid down the steel rails that sped up railroad construction. On the second floor, the **Houghton Gallery** hosts changing exhibits on design and American history, as well as displays of student-produced work, but usually not during the summer. (Open daily noon-7pm. Free.)

Stuyvesant Street angles off to the northeast from Astor Place, cutting north over 9th St. and terminating at Second Ave. and 10th St., right in front of the pretty **St. Mark's-in-the-Bowery Church,** 131 E. 10th St. (674-6377). The church was built in 1799, on the site of a chapel that was on the estate of Peter Stuyvesant, the much-reviled last Dutch governor of the colony of New Amsterdam. He lies buried in the small cobblestone graveyard here. Restored in the mid-'70s, the church building burned to a near-crisp in a 1978 fire, and re-restoration was not completed until a few years ago.

Across from the church at 156 Second Ave. stands a famous Jewish landmark, the **Second Avenue Deli** (677-0606). This is all that remains of the "Yiddish Rialto," the stretch of Second Ave. between Houston and 14th St. that comprised the Yiddish theater district in the early part of this century. The Stars of David embedded in the sidewalk in front of the restaurant contain the names of some of the great actors and actresses who spent their lives entertaining the poor Jewish immigrants of the city. Order sublime chicken soup or splash out on a pastrami sandwich while you watch a schedule of Broadway shows flash by on what used to be an electronic stock-ticker. (See Eating & Drinking.)

St. Mark's Place, running from Third Ave. to Ave. A where E. 8th St. would be, is the geographical and spiritual center of the East Village. In the 1960s, the street was the Haight-Ashbury of the East Coast, full of pot-smoking flower children waiting for the next concert at the Electric Circus. In the late 1970s it became the King's Road of New York, as mohawked youths hassled the passers-by from the brownstone steps off Astor Place. Today things are changing again: a Gap store sells its conventional color-me-matching combos across the street from a shop stocking "You Make Me Sick" T-shirts. St. Mark's is the East Village's answer to a small town's Main Street. People know one another here—sometimes they even stop to talk to each other. Dark little restaurants and cafés elbow for space with leather boutiques and trinket vendors. Though many "Village types" now shun the commercialized and crowded street, St. Mark's is still central to life in this part of town and a good place to start a tour of the neighborhood.

Farther east, First and Second Avenues are filled with restaurants, cafés, and bars. A few remnants of old New York remain. The **New York Marble Cemeteries,** on Second Ave. between 2nd and 3rd St., and on 2nd St. just east of Second Ave., are the city's first two non-sectarian graveyards. Gaze through the fences at the dilapidated tombstones. Many prominent New Yorkers have been buried here, including (at the 2nd St. yard) the improbably named Preserved Fish, a prominent merchant.

■■■ ALPHABET CITY

East of First Ave., south of 14th St., and north of Houston, the avenues run out of numbers and take on letters. This part of the East Village has so far escaped the escalating yuppification campaign that has claimed much of St. Mark's Place. In the area's heyday in the '60s, Jimi Hendrix and the Fugs would play open-air shows to bright-eyed Love Children. Rent is still relatively reasonable; here you'll find the stately residences of the East Village's deadbeatniks and hard-core anarchists (including girl-noise terrorists God Is My Co-Pilot), as well as artists, students, and regular people. There has been a great deal of drug-related crime in the recent past, but the community has done an admirable job of making the area livable again. Alphabet City is generally safe during the day, and the addictive nightlife on Avenue A ensures some protection there, but try to avoid straying east of Avenue B at night.

Alphabet City's extremist Boho activism (and the brutish behavior of the NYPD) has made the neighborhood chronically ungovernable in the last several years, a little kernel of Amsterdam or old West Berlin set deep in the bowels of Manhattan. A few years ago, police officers set off a riot when they attempted to forcibly evict a band of the homeless and their supporters in **Tompkins Square Park,** bordered by E. 10th and E. 7th St., Ave. A and Ave. B. An aspiring video artist recorded scenes of wanton police depravity, setting off a public outcry and a further round of police-inspired violence. Today, the park is no longer a glum testament to the progress of gentrification—it has recently re-opened after a two-year hiatus, and officials have high hopes for the area. The park still serves as a psycho-geographical epicenter for many a churlish misfit; one of the many riots that erupted in New York City following the Rodney King verdict in 1992 was led by the "East Side Anarchists," who humped down to Tompkins Square after tearing through St. Mark's Place. There are basketball courts and a playground in the northwest section of the park (quite popular with the younger, less politically-concerned East Village set), and the park hosts free outdoor concerts during the summer. A water fountain near the 9th St. entrance advises "Temperance," but Alphabet City has never been known for "keeping the straight edge."

East of the park, countless memorial murals attest to the scars left by drugs on this area. A mural on an old burned-out crack house on Ave. C between 8th and 9th pleads for action against drugs at home rather than on the streets, and a mural on the northwest corner of 8th St. and Ave. C hangs "in memory of Cesar." Less solemn projects include the community gardens that bloom next to some of these murals and blasted buildings, including one on 9th St. between Ave. B and Ave. C. At the corner of Ave. B and 2nd St., the "Space 2B" is surrounded by a fence made of pipes and car parts and serves as an outdoor gallery and performance space. For information on current issues and events, check for free local papers at St. Mark's Bookshop and other stores in the area. The often extravagant street art and neighborhood posters can also give you an update on some of the current issues. Or just sit at one of the sidewalk cafés that line Ave. A between 6th and 10th St. and watch for yourself.

■■■ LOWER EAST SIDE

Down below Houston in the somewhat deserted Lower East Side you can still find some excellent kosher delis and a few old-timers who remember the time when the Second Ave. El ran from the power station at Allen and Pike St. Two million Jews arrived on the Lower East Side in the 20 years before World War I. Today the Lower East Side continues to be a neighborhood of immigrants, now mostly Asian and Hispanic. Chinatown has expanded across the Bowery and along the stretch of East Broadway, one of the district's main thoroughfares. A substantial number of East Village-type artists and musicians have recently moved in as well, especially near Houston St. The Lower East Side is presently the heroin capital of New York; the drug has lately acquired a bohemian trendiness.

Despite the population shift, remnants of the Jewish ghetto that inspired Jacob Riis's compelling work *How the Other Half Lives* still remain. New York's oldest synagogue building, the red-painted **Congregation Anshe Chesed** at 172-176 Norfolk St., just off Stanton St., now houses a Hispanic social service organization. Further down Norfolk, at #60 between Grand and Broome St. sits the **Beth Hemedash Hagadol Synagogue,** the best-preserved of the Lower East Side houses of worship. From Grand St., follow Essex St. three blocks south to **East Broadway.** This street epitomizes the Lower East Side's flux of cultures. You will find Buddhist prayer centers next to (mostly boarded up) Jewish religious supply stores, and the offices of several Jewish civic organizations. At 175 East Broadway, across from Seward Park, the **Forward Building** stands watch. Now occupied by an Asian church, this tower once housed the offices of the Yiddish daily newspaper that bore its name and was once the bastion of Yiddish intellectual culture. The *Forward* still publishes weekly from its midtown offices. Further down at 197 East Broadway and Jefferson St. is the

Educational Alliance, displaying photographs of early 20th-century Jewish education in its lobby windows. Near East Broadway, at 15 Pike St., sits the dilapidated **Congregation Sons of Israel Kalwarie.** Graffiti covers this once-grand temple. At 12-16 Eldridge St., another synagogue in disrepair, the **Eldridge St. Synagogue,** is being restored.

The area around Orchard and Delancey Streets is one of Manhattan's bargain shopping centers. On Sundays, Orchard Street fills up with salesmen hawking their discount goods to multitudes of potential customers. Stop in at **Schapiro's House of Kosher Wines,** 126 Rivington St. (674-4404), for a tour of the only operational winery left in NYC, famous for once giving a bottle of "the wine you can cut with a knife" to every immigrant family. (Tours Sept.-June only, Sun. 11am-4pm.) At 97 Orchard St., between Broome and Delancey St., you can visit the **Lower East Side Tenement Museum** (431-0233), a preserved tenement house of the type that proliferated in this neighborhood in the early part of the century. Buy tickets at 90 Orchard St. at the corner of Broome St. ($3, seniors $2, students $1, free Tues.) The museum gallery at 90 Orchard St. offers slide shows, exhibits, and photographs documenting Jewish life on the Lower East Side (included in admission price). Guided historical tours are offered on Sundays (call for information; open Tues.-Fri. 10am-2pm, Sun. 11am-5pm).

■■■ LITTLE ITALY & CHINATOWN

Little Italy, a touristy pocket of Naples and Sicily nestled in the lower spine of Manhattan, is roughly bounded by Houston St. to the north, Canal St. to the south, the Bowery to the east, and Broadway to the west. Raging Bull Robert DeNiro stalked the *Mean Streets* here in 1973 and then returned a year later to cut a few slice-of-life scenes for the 1918 segments of *The Godfather II* (you can still see the remnants of the set). Although once worthy of its name, the neighborhood has been in definite decline in recent years—not in terms of cleanliness or quality of life (or food), but just in terms of space—Little Italy's borders have begun to collapse and recede as it gives way to an aggressively expanding Chinatown. Walk a few blocks in any direction from the main, Italian flag-flying section of Mulberry St. and you're almost certain to encounter a number of Chinese-language shops and signs. Many young Italians are moving out; meanwhile, more authentic Italian neighborhoods flourish in Bensonhurst, Brooklyn, and in Belmont, the Bronx. Until he landed in prison, alleged Mafia kingpin John Gotti still made his way around here to the few remaining social clubs for a deal or meal. Between about Broome and Canal St. on Mulberry St., the flavor of the old Little Italy lives on.

The Little Italy experience revolves primarily around food. Most restaurants are reasonable, but some can be horrendously overpriced—a full meal could run $60-70 (remember: it's important to keep that wine under control). Save money by dining on appetizers or grabbing a snack at one of the many shops and groceries. (See Eating & Drinking: Little Italy.)

A walk up Mulberry Street will have you ducking under the umbrellas of sidewalk cafés. At **Umberto's Clam House,** 129 Mulberry St., at Hester St. in the heart of Little Italy, "Crazy Joey" Gallo was slain in 1972 while celebrating his birthday; allegedly he offended a rival "family." Further north, at 264 Mulberry St., at Prince St., you'll find **St. Patrick's Old Cathedral,** finished in 1815. One of America's earliest Gothic Revival churches, the façade was damaged in an 1866 fire. The Cathedral offers marriages and baptisms (by appt. only; call 226-8075).

The well-kept **Engine Co. 55** stands at 363 Broome St., between Mott and Elizabeth St., dating from 1898. You can continue your tour of historic buildings devoted to civil protection by walking west on Broome St. a few blocks to Centre St. At this corner looms the massive and elegant **former police headquarters** of the city; since 1909, it's been a private residence. Step inside to escape an extreme of climate (inside it's climate-controlled) and check out the beautiful polished marble and

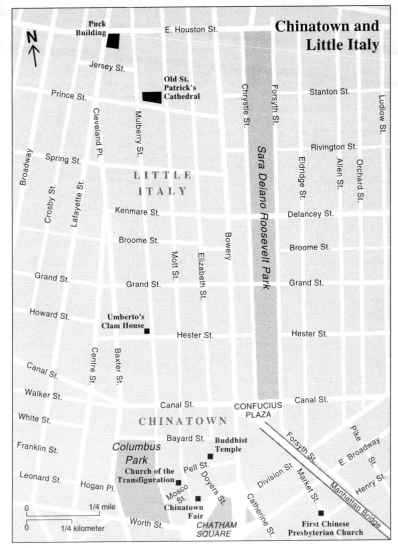

Chinatown and Little Italy

N

Puck Building

E. Houston St.

Jersey St.

Old St.
Patrick's
Cathedral

Prince St.

Chrystie St.

Forsyth St.

Stanton St.

Ludlow St.

Cleveland Pl.

Mulberry St.

Broadway

Spring St.

Lafayette St.

LITTLE
ITALY

Rivington St.

Eldridge St.

Allen St.

Orchard St.

Crosby St.

Kenmare St.

Sara Delano Roosevelt Park

Delancey St.

Broome St.

Bowery

Broome St.

Grand St.

Mott St.

Elizabeth St.

Grand St.

Grand St.

Grand St.

Howard St.

Umberto's
Clam House

Hester St.

Hester St.

Canal St.

Centre St.

Baxter St.

Walker St.

Canal St.

CONFUCIUS
PLAZA

Canal St.

White St.

CHINATOWN

Franklin St.

Columbus
Park

Bayard St.

Buddhist
Temple

Forsyth St.

Pike

E. Broadway

Leonard St.

Hogan Pl.

Church of the
Transfiguration

Pell St.

Doyers St.

Division St.

Market St.

St.

Henry St.

0   1/4 mile

Mosco
St.

Chinatown
Fair

Catherine St.

Manhattan Bridge

0   1/4 kilometer

Worth St.

CHATHAM
SQUARE

First Chinese
Presbyterian Church

chandeliers in the main lobby. The guard just inside the door will probably ask you to leave fairly quickly, though, so don't plan an extended stay.

At the corner of Lafayette St. and E. Houston St. stands the **Puck Building,** appropriately enough the former home of the monthly humor magazine *Spy.* This beautiful red-brick building was constructed in 1889 to house the *Spy's* humor-magazine forebear *Puck*; a cute golden Puck stands over the Lafayette St. door.

Dotted with stores selling low-cost electronics and plastics, commercial **Canal Street** divides Little Italy and Chinatown. Stepping south across Canal St., the *caffè* and *gelaterie* of Little Italy give way to pagoda-topped phone booths, steaming tea shops, and firecracker vendors. New York's **Chinatown** has seven Chinese newspapers, over 300 garment factories, innumerable food shops, and houses the largest Asian community in the U.S. outside San Francisco. Vaguely bounded by Worth St. and Canal St. to the south and north, and Broadway and the Bowery to the west and east, Chinatown spills out further into the surrounding streets every year, especially to the north and east. The Chinese population here is estimated at nearly 300,000.

Mott Street and Pell Street are full of commercial activity, as is East Broadway, the former center of Lower East Side Jewish life, on the other side of the Bowery. Street life and businesses flourish here. Don't be snookered by the low prices on merchandise; creative labelling abounds. Just because those Walkmans say Sony doesn't mean they're made in Japan. Gift shops line the streets, hustling to peddle their overpriced miniature Buddhas and dragon-shaped clogs. During the Chinese New Year (in late Jan. or early Feb.), the area's frenetic pace accelerates. Be careful down here around the Fourth of July. You can buy fireworks of all stripes, but most are illegal, and dealing with the crafty sales techniques of fire-hawkers can be intimidating.

For a trippy freak of a hybrid religion, check out the **Ling Liang Church,** 173-175 East Broadway, the resting place of a postmodern Christ surrounded by biblical blessings on a bed of red Chinese characters. Head southwest along East Broadway and go left (south) on Market St. One block down, on the corner at 61 Henry St., stands the **First Chinese Presbyterian Church,** a large dark stone building built in 1817. Back to East Broadway and one block further southwest is Chatham Square and its **Kimlau War Memorial.** The Memorial, a large Chinese-style stone arch, was erected in memory of those Chinese-Americans killed in pursuit of "freedom and democracy." Just north on the Bowery, secular Confucius stands firm and wise on the plaza dedicated to him at the corner of Division St. South of Chatham Square, on St. James Pl. between James and Oliver St., is the **First Shearith Israel Graveyard.** This site served as the cemetery for New York City's first Jewish congregation, the Spanish-Portuguese Shearith Israel Synagogue; the gravestones here date from 1683.

Head northwest back across Chatham Square and you'll reach Chinatown proper, west of the Bowery. Scholars should ascend to the **Oriental Enterprises Company,** 13 Elizabeth St. (2nd floor), a bookstore serving those literate in Chinese. Its extensive collection includes books, tapes, CDs, and newspapers, as well as some interesting calligraphy equipment (open daily 10am-7pm). At the **Buddhist Temple,** 16 Pell St., off Mott St., commercialism comes together with religion (move over L. Ron Hubbard). The devout are invited to kneel and give offerings in front of a porcelain statue, while the less devout can browse through the gift shop in the rear of the same room.

The **Chinatown Fair,** 8 Mott St., features video games and two woeful chickens. For 50¢ one of the chickens is forced to "play" tic-tac-toe (a sign claims she's appeared on the TV show "That's Incredible.") For 75¢, another chicken "dances" over what appears to be a spinning hot plate (a sign above this hen claims the hen went to school to learn her steps, and asserts that she does not suffer). The manager may ask you to "save your money; she's getting old."

Early-rising ornithologists (or those who are just curious) should take an early morning stroll over to Sara Delano Roosevelt Park, west of the Bowery, at the corner of Chrystie and Delancey St. There, between about 7 and 9am, a number of older Chinese men gather each morning from spring through fall to give sun to their songbirds—an old tradition intended as a distraction from vice. The men arrive with caged birds in hand, the cages still covered in cloth so that their occupants don't wake too early. After positioning their cages in a small, grassy area at the park's northern edge, the men gingerly remove the cages' coverings, speaking to their songbirds and bidding them good morning. The men do some stretching exercises and socialize as they wait for their birds to warm to the sun and begin singing. The birds' songs are indeed amazingly loud and melodic, easily heard over the roar of the heavy morning traffic.

■■■ LOWER MANHATTAN

Many of the city's superlatives congregate at the southern tip of Manhattan. The Wall Street area is the densest in all New York; Wall Street itself measures less than a ½-mile long. This narrow state of affairs has driven the neighborhood into the air, creating one of the highest concentrations of skyscrapers in the world. Along with density comes history: lower Manhattan was the first part of the island to be settled by Europeans and many of the city's historically significant sights lie buried in the concrete canyons here. Omnipresent **Heritage Trail** markers indicate the most significant spots.

Touring lower Manhattan won't cost much. Parks, churches, and temperature-controlled cathedrals of commerce such as the New York Stock Exchange and City Hall charge no admission. Visit during the work week, when suspendered and high-heeled natives brandishing *Wall Street Journals* rush around between deals. After hours, these titans of trade loosen ties and suck in the ocean breeze (and a few drinks) at the South Street Seaport.

■ THE FINANCIAL DISTRICT

Battery Park, named for a battery of guns that the British stored there from 1683 to 1687, is now a chaotic chunk of green forming the southernmost toenail of Manhattan Island. The #1 and 9 trains to South Ferry terminate at the southeastern tip of the park; the #4 and 5 stop at Bowling Green, just off the northern tip. You can take your morning constitutional here, admiring plaques and monuments along the way or just inhaling some sea air as you sit by the Hope Garden. Beware, though, that on weekends the park is often mobbed with people on their way to the Liberty and Ellis Island ferries, which depart from here.

As you enter the park from the north, walk past the **Netherlands Memorial Flagpole** toward Castle Clinton and the water. On the way is **Hope Garden,** a living AIDS memorial dedicated in 1992 where 100,000 roses bloom and fade each year. Off to the right as you face the water stands the affecting **Korean War Memorial,** dedicated in 1991. The memorial presents a large block of black granite from which the shape of an infantry soldier has been cut out.

Just east of the memorial, **Castle Clinton,** the main structure in the park, contains an information center and a circular pavilion where you can purchase tickets for the Liberty or Ellis Island ferries (see Sights: Liberty Island and Ellis Island). More than a glorified ticket booth, this structure was completed just before the War of 1812, as tensions between Britain and the newly independent United States were coming to a boil. It then stood in 35 ft. of water, connected by a drawbridge to the shore 200 ft. away. Not a single shot was ever fired from the fort and by 1824 the city felt safe enough from British invasion to lease the area for public entertainment. First it was a theater for outdoor events: balloon ascents, scientific demonstrations, and fireworks. Later, in the 1840s, the castle was roofed over and turned into a concert hall. By 1855, enough landfill from nearby construction had accumulated to connect Castle Clinton to the mainland, and it became New York's immigrant landing-depot. Between 1855 and 1889, more than seven million immigrants passed through these walls. In later years, when Ellis Island had assumed this function, Castle Clinton turned into the site of the beloved New York Aquarium; then the aquarium moved to Coney Island and the building was left vacant. When the city declared the fort a National Historic Site in 1950, wreckers had already removed the second story, the roof, and other expansions, leaving the building at its present dimensions, the same as those of 1811. The fort is now under the care of the National Park Service and attended by Park Rangers. The Rangers lead one- to one-and-a-half-hour walking tours of Castle Clinton (Mon.-Fri. 10:35am, 11:35am, 1:05pm, 4:05pm; Sat.-Sun. 10:35am, 1:05pm, 4:05pm), Wall Street (Sat.-Sun. and holidays 11:30am and 3pm), and the skyline (Mon.-Fri. 11am, 12:30pm, 2pm, 3:30pm; Sat.-Sun. 12:30pm, 2pm, 3:30pm). All tours are free and leave from the castle. (Castle Clinton open daily 8:30am-5pm.)

As you look out at the water from Castle Clinton, you'll have a clear view of lush New Jersey (on your right), Ellis Island (dominated by a large brick building), Liberty Island (she's waving at you), Staten Island (directly behind the Statue of Liberty), and Governor's Island, a command center for the U.S. Coast Guard (on your left). A

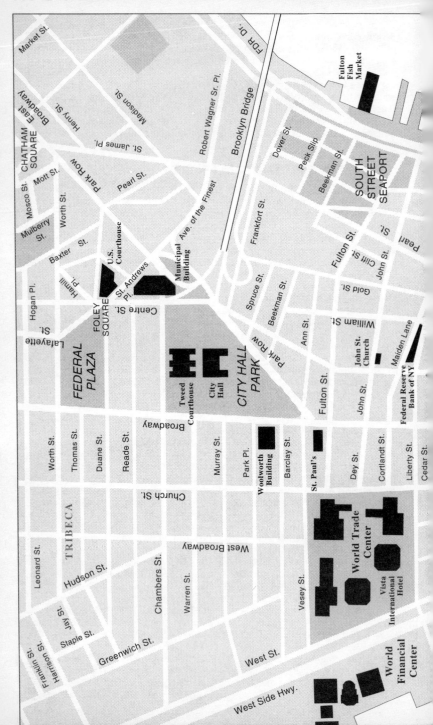

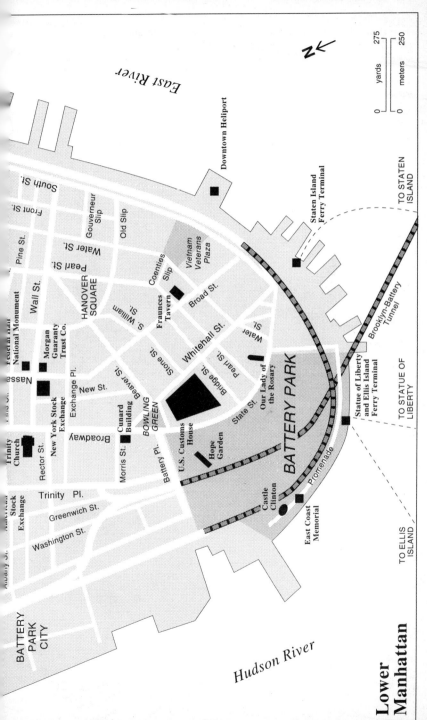

Lower
Manhattan

East River

Hudson River

BATTERY
PARK
CITY

Washington St.

Greenwich St.

Trinity Pl.

American
Stock
Exchange

Trinity
Church

Rector St.

New York Stock
Exchange

Broadway

Exchange Pl.

New St.

Nassau

Morgan
Guaranty
Trust Co.

Federal Hall
National Monument

Wall St.

Pine St.

Front St.

South St.

Morris St.

Beaver St.

Battery Pl.

Cunard
Building

BOWLING
GREEN

Stone St.

S. William St.

HANOVER
SQUARE

Pearl St.

Water St.

Gouverneur
Slip

Old Slip

Coenties
Slip

Fraunces
Tavern

Broad St.

Vietnam
Veterans
Plaza

U.S. Customs
House

Hope
Garden

State St.

Whitehall St.

Bridge St.

Pearl St.

Water
St.

Our Lady of
the Rosary

BATTERY PARK

Castle
Clinton

East Coast
Memorial

Promenade

Downtown Heliport

**Staten Island
Ferry Terminal**

**Statue of Liberty
and Ellis Island
Ferry Terminal**

Brooklyn-Battery
Tunnel

TO STATEN
ISLAND

TO STATUE OF
LIBERTY

TO ELLIS
ISLAND

N

0   yards   275

0   meters   250

short walk to your left as you face the water, east from Castle Clinton, brings you to the **East Coast Memorial,** a monument to those who died in coastal waters in World War II. A large sculpture of a swooping eagle stands in front of two rows of granite monoliths engraved with the names of the dead. The huge green buildings on the water just east of the park are hard to miss even if you try: the **Coast Guard Building** and the **Staten Island Ferry Terminal** are painted in that odd shade of aqua-green which automatically recalls the 1950s and the bottoms of old YMCA swimming pools.

Just north lies State Street, which forms the northeast border of the park. Before this area was filled with land, State St. was the shorefront, and by the 1790s it had become the most fashionable residential street in Manhattan. State Street's domestic glamor has vanished today, but you can still feel its former elegance in the **Church of Our Lady of the Rosary** and the adjoining **Shrine of St. Elizabeth Ann Seton,** at 7-8 State St. (269-6865). They stand out like brick and wooden ghosts against an expanse of streamlined glass and steel. The shrine, originally the James Watson House, was built in stages from 1792 to 1805 in the Federal style and retains its original façade, with columns supposedly cut from ship masts. St. Elizabeth Ann Seton, canonized in 1975 as the first U.S.-born saint, lived here with her family from 1801 to 1803. The adjoining church, to the left as you face it, dates from 1883, when it served as a shelter for Irish immigrant women.

Just north up State St., at the rear of the courtyard adjacent to the church, you can explore the quirky museum **New York Unearthed** (363-9327), which, under the sponsorship of the South Street Seaport Museum, features artifacts from Manhattan. Excavators discovered most of the items here during preparations for new construction in the downtown area. The small collection runs from clay pipes dated AD 1250 to small displays depicting "Meetings at the Tavern, ca. 1700" and "Lunch at the Counter, ca. 1950." Visitors can also enjoy the opportunity to view archaeologists at work in the basement conservation laboratory as they preserve and prepare artifacts for the South Street Seaport Museum. (Open Mon.-Sat. noon-6pm; closed Sat. Jan.-March. Free.) Right next to the museum stands the sheer, elegant—and largely empty—wedge of **17 State St.** Built in 1989, this leviathan of a building stands on the site of the house where Herman Melville was born in 1819. Melville soon left to pen his masterpiece *Moby Dick* as well as "Bartleby the Scrivener," an endearing story of the uncompromising life of a clerk in the 19th-century financial district.

A walk up State St. along the edge of Battery Park leads to the **U.S. Custom House,** which is off the northeastern corner of the park. This majestic building, designed by Cass Gilbert, was completed in 1907, when the majority of U.S. revenues came from customs duties and the majority of customs duties came from New York. Come inspect this palace of trade. Fort Amsterdam stood here in 1626, facing out at the harbor and defending the Dutch colony. In 1790, a Georgian mansion was built here as the presidential residence, but George Washington never moved in because the United States capital moved to Philadelphia the very same year (Washington, D.C., didn't become the nation's capital until 1803).

The Beaux Arts masterpiece that stands here now combines Baroque and Renaissance inspiration with aggressive decoration. All of the sculpture and artwork on the building relates directly to its function. The 12 statues on top of the façade represent the 12 great trading centers of the world. On the ground level, four large sculptures of enthroned women represent four continents: Africa sleeps, her arms resting on a sphinx and a lion, while a self-satisfied Europe sits stately and dignified. America seems ready to leap forward out of her chair, carrying the torch of Liberty (although a Native American peeps ominously over her shoulder), and a dozing Asia rests on her throne of skulls. The four women were seated there by Daniel Chester French, the same sculptor who placed Lincoln in his memorial in Washington, D.C., and John Harvard in his high chair in Cambridge, MA. On the façade, observe the window arches, which are adorned with the heads of the six "races" of the world.

When the Customs Department moved to the World Trade Center in 1973, the building closed to the public. The federal government's General Services Administration has decided to re-occupy the building and plans to re-open it to the public; after four years of extensive restorations to be completed in late 1994 or early 1995, the **Smithsonian Museum of the American Indian** will move in. In the meantime, the building's only functional department is, ironically, the Bankruptcy Court.

The Custom House faces egg-shaped **Bowling Green,** the city's first park. It was rented out as a bowling green in 1733 for the price of one peppercorn a year— hence the oddball name. Here, colonists rioted in the 1760s against the taxes imposed by George III's Stamp Act. When George repealed the act in 1770, forgiving New Yorkers commissioned an equestrian statue of the king and in 1771 protected the park with a gold-crowned fence made in England. But after the Declaration of Independence was read on July 9, 1776, in front of City Hall, the joyous (if fickle) populace raced to Bowling Green and tore down the statue as well as the crowns on the fence. Bits of the statue were later used as bullets in the revolution. The 1771 fence still surrounds the park today.

Poised to run from the tip of Bowling Green right up Broadway is the **Bull,** whose massive head is lowered as he paws the ground. As the symbol of a good market, the bull was the gift of an Italian artist who mischievously planted it in front of the New York Stock Exchange in the middle of the night a few winters back. Unamused brokers had it promptly removed; as a compromise, it now stands here, at a distance.

A modest stone building across Broadway from Bowling Green advertises itself merely as "United States Post Office–Bowling Green Station." This is the **Cunard Building,** built in 1921 as the central headquarters of the fleet of great transatlantic ocean liners which departed from nearby piers. The humble post office facilities are dwarfed by the vast classical rotunda in the grand booking hall. Antiquated maps, winged cherubs, acres of tubage, and frescoes of Viking ships adorn the walls. (Building open Mon.-Fri. 6am-7pm, Sat. 6am-1:30pm.)

Cross Broadway at the post office and walk back down the east side of Bowling Green on Whitehall Street. At Whitehall and Pearl St. stands the **Broad Financial Center,** with one of the most whimsical lobbies in New York. Tapering pylons with revolving metal globes on top balance on surreal spheres of marble, and a wall-sized clockface stares over a sloping pool of water. Exit onto Pearl St.; walking northeast one block leads to Broad St. Dutch colonists trying to recreate their homeland dug a canal here that ran through their settlement, but it soon became putrid. The disappointed Dutch filled in the filthy canal to create the present street. The million-sq.-ft. monster which looms at the corner at 85 Pearl St. is the headquarters of **Goldman Sachs.** Just across Pearl St. from Goldman Sachs, also at the corner of Broad St., lies the pseudo-historic Fraunces Tavern block, an island of traditional and rather ordinary architecture in the sea of modern self-aggrandizement that is the financial district. The block contains structures built between 1719 and 1883, with many 20th-century additions and reconstructions. The **Fraunces Tavern** museum (425-1778), at 54 Pearl St., is a reconstruction of one of George Washington's favorite New York hangouts. It was on the second floor of this tavern that he said his final farewell to the officers of his victorious revolution (see Museums).

Continue up Pearl St. to Hanover Square, a paved-over intersection that provides benches for the weary. Note the statue of the Dutch goldsmith Abraham De Peyster, moved to this spot in the 1970s from Bowling Green. Once the northern border of the New Amsterdam settlement, **Wall Street** takes its name from the wall built here in 1653 to shield the Dutch colony from a British invasion from the north. By the early 19th century, it had already become the financial capital of the United States, and many a populist reformer used its name to refer to the entire financial district and its baleful menace to the nation. Its mystique endures today—Wall Street means big business, big money, loose lips, and lost illusions.

Although it is currently behind locked gates, take note of historic **55 Wall St.** This building once housed the Second Merchants' Exchange (1836-1854), the predecessor of the modern stock exchange. Its 16 Ionic columns, each weighing 41 tons and cut from a single slab of stone, were dragged here by teams of oxen. In 1863, it became the U.S. Custom House. Across the street at No. 60 hovers the unmistakable headquarters of the **Morgan Bank,** 52 stories of bizarre but eye-catching 1980s neo-neoclassicism. Some quick-witted critics have pointed out that the building itself resembles a column. Wander through the vast public atrium of white and gray marble and gaze at the mirrored, white-latticed ceiling—a gazebo gone wild (open daily 7am-10pm).

Just a bit farther down Wall St., at its intersection with Broad St. (which turns into Nassau St. to the north), cluster a mass of sights. Meet **Federal Hall** (264-8711) with its larger-than-life statue of a tightly pantalooned George Washington on its steps (several historians have commented on the heft of Washington's rump). After 1703, this classical building housed the original City Hall, where the trial of John Peter Zenger helped to establish freedom of the press in 1735, and where the Stamp Act Congress met in 1765. It also served as the first seat of the constitutional government adopted in 1789; it was here that Washington was first sworn in (roughly on the spot where he stands today), that James Madison submitted the Bill of Rights to Congress, and that the House of Representatives and the Senate first met. Unfortunately, the original building was demolished in 1812. Its 1842 replacement functioned as a customs house (which building hasn't?) until 1862, when a branch of the U.S. Treasury Department moved there. In 1955 it became a national memorial, and its exhibits now include the illustrated Bible used by Washington at his inauguration, a 10-minute animated program called "Journey to Federal Hall," and models of the building's predecessor. Tours and the animated film by request. (Open Mon.-Fri. 9am-5pm; disabled entrance at 15 Pine St.)

Walk across Wall St. from Federal Hall to the **Morgan Guaranty Trust Company,** built in 1913. On the Wall St. side of the building, underneath the fourth window, pockmarks in the stone wall bear witness to a lunch-hour explosion on September 16, 1920, when a bomb in a pushcart went off. Conspiracy theorists and assorted experts disagree on whom to blame, but the consensus fingers an anarchist trying to destroy Morgan and his bank. The explosion killed 33 and injured 400 but the bank itself was left unscathed—as was Morgan, who happened to be abroad at the time.

South on Broad St. between Wall St. and Exchange Pl. stands the current home of the **New York Stock Exchange** (656-5168). The main building, constructed in 1903, has a relief sculpture on its pediment titled *Integrity Protecting the Works of Man,* made by J.Q.A. Ward, the man responsible for the statue of Washington outside Federal Hall. The Stock Exchange was first created as a marketplace for handling the $80 million in U.S. bonds that were issued in 1789 and 1790 to pay Revolutionary War debts. In the course of the 19th century, the exchange became increasingly formalized, and the 1867 invention of the stock ticker revolutionized the market; the ticker recorded every sale of stock and made transaction information instantly available to the public (and, of course, provided the necessary material for New York's famous "ticker tape" parades). The stock market cooked throughout the 1920s, only to collapse suddenly like a cheese soufflé on Black Monday, October 7, 1929, leading many brokers to bolt or go over the edge. The early 1980s saw another impressively "bullish" market, but its nosedive on October 19, 1987, recalled to broken traders an unpleasant history lesson. Fortunately, though, these traders found consolation awaiting them outside the NYSE doors, as ice cream manufacturer Ben & Jerry's was quick to arrive in a mobile truck and begin giving away free scoops of its new, just-for-the-occasion flavor, "That's Life."

To get to the Stock Exchange's visitors' entrance, walk to the left, down Broad St. to the main doors at No. 20, where someone should be distributing free admission tickets, each labeled with a session time. A limited number of tickets are available for each session, and the later in the day you arrive the more likely it is that only tickets for sessions several hours away will be left. Tickets often run out entirely by 1pm, and it's preferable to arrive around 9am to ensure a convenient admission time. On crowded days, you'll be forced to wait in a long line for the elevator once you are admitted to the building. (Open to public Mon.-Fri. 9:15-4pm, with last session beginning at 3:15pm.)

Upstairs, you can see exhibits detailing the workings and history of the stock market, along with a wide-screen "experience theater," which shows an 11-minute video on the history of the exchange (narrated in logical fashion by Leonard Nimoy). But the real draw is the observation gallery that overlooks the zoo-like main trading floor of the exchange. From the glass-enclosed gallery, you can observe the frenzy that fills all 37,000 sq. ft. of the room (which claims 50-ft. ceilings). Recorded introductions to the floor activity are available in any of a number of languages. The visitors' gallery has been enclosed ever since the '60s, when leftist hooligans invented creative ways to disrupt trading activity, like throwing dollar bills at the traders.

Observe the chaos of murmuring and milling in this paper-strewn pen, as people huddle around honeycombed banks of green video screens. The TV monitors, grouped in clusters called "trading posts," nearly outnumber the people. More than 2000 companies deal on the New York Stock Exchange, the world's largest with 79 billion shares of stock valued at $3 trillion. Note the color-coded jackets sported by the folks on the trading floor; brokers are clad in yellow, reporters in navy, and pages in light blue. To your left, at the rostrum, the bell rings for opening at 9:30am and closing at 4pm.

Around the corner, at the end of Wall St., rises the seemingly ancient **Trinity Church** (602-0800). Its Gothic spire was the tallest structure in the city when it was first erected in 1846. Two other churches have stood on this site; the Episcopal congregation here dates from 1696. The vaulted interior feels positively medieval. Behind the altar is a small **museum** (602-0773; open Mon.-Fri. 9-11:45am and 1-3:45pm, Sat. 10am-3:45pm, Sun. 1-3:45pm; daily tours given at 2pm). The church's 2½-acre yard, dating from 1681, houses the graves of both Alexander Hamilton and Albert Gallatin, successive Secretaries of the Treasury. Hamilton, who served under Washington, committed himself to the development of the United States as a financial power, while Gallatin dedicated himself to the Jeffersonian vision of an agrarian republic. They now lie together in a churchyard appropriately consumed by the vast financial establishment that is the legacy of their age. From September through June, Trinity Church, with St. Paul's Chapel, presents the **Sundays at Four** classical-concert series (see Entertainment & Nightlife: Classical Music). The church also hosts changing exhibitions of contemporary sculpture in both its north and south courtyards; the church commissions these works in an attempt to combine contemporary art with venerable architecture (Courtyards open Mon.-Fri. 8am-4pm, Sat.-Sun. 8am-3pm).

■ WORLD TRADE CENTER AND BATTERY PARK CITY

Walk up Broadway to Liberty Park, and in the distance you'll see the twin towers of the **World Trade Center.** The main plaza, on Church and Dey, contains two sculptures, a large fountain, ample seating space, daily lunchtime entertainment, and front-row views of the 1377-ft.-tall towers. Bosom companions at 110 stories each, the sleekly striped shafts (constructed in 1973) dwarf every other building in the city. They provide 10 million sq. ft. of office space for their creator, the Port Authority of New York and New Jersey. The bombing of the complex in 1993 has left no visible scars other than the ubiquitous "All visitors must carry ID" signs, though for the thousands of employees who had to escape down dark, smoke-filled flights of stairs, the memory likely remains vivid.

Two World Trade Center has the **observation deck** (435-7377), and a banner indicating as much hangs outside. When you enter the lobby from Liberty St., take an escalator to the ticket booth on the mezzanine. (Open daily June-Sept. 9:30am-11:30pm, Oct.-May 9:30am-9:30pm. Admission $4.75, seniors $2.75, children 6-12 $2.) A branch of the Visitor Information Center is also located on the mezzanine, dispensing all the maps, brochures, and schedules that make it worthy of its name (open Mon.-Fri. 9am-5pm; also Sat. in summer). Also on the mezzanine you'll find a TKTS booth which sells half-price, same-day tickets to Broadway and off-Broadway shows (see Entertainment and Nightlife: Theater).

Once you've stood in line for observation deck tickets and had your bag searched, ride the elevator up to the 107th floor, where everyone ignores exhibits on trade history and economics to enjoy the best view in New York. Unfortunately, looking out the window can be a little bit frustrating, since the stainless steel stripes on the building walls preclude any panoramic picture-window views. The architects opted to place much of the skeleton of the building on the outside, in order to leave large, unbroken spaces inside the building. You may want to use the coin-operated telescopes or the diagrams of landmarks distributed throughout the observatory. From the north, the Citicorp Building looks particularly impressive, a little like the neck of one of Jamie Reid's guitar swastikas, while the Citibank branch in Queens looks astray and diminutive. The green-capped Woolworth Building stands a bit to the north of the World Trade Center and still appears attractive, even though its architects could scarcely have imagined that it would ever be appreciated from this angle. Note the gold-crowned federal court-house and the hulking Municipal building astride the traffic of Chambers Street, topped off in a delicate wedding-cake fashion. And of course you'll see (as always) the pencilly Chrysler Building and the chunky Empire State Building flaunting their fancy outlines amid the more mundane edifices of Midtown.

To the west glimmers the golden-hued World Financial Center, obviously designed to be seen from above. Its crisp, glinting angles and smooth curves look more like an architect's model than a real building. Across the river, a flat New Jersey stretches into the distance on a glorious plane of radon. To the south, you can see (from right to left) Ellis Island, Liberty Island, and Governor's Island, with Staten Island in the distance behind them. You can also see the entrance to the Brooklyn-Battery Tunnel; look for the red paved area just north of Battery Park where cars seem to disappear and re-appear from inside a boxy structure. To the east, the faraway Manhattan and Brooklyn bridges steal the show. It's hard to believe that the arches of the Brooklyn Bridge once overshadowed the rest of the New York skyline.

In good weather, the **rooftop observatory** opens. Unless you're terrified of heights, take the escalator up for an extraordinary experience. The top of the neighboring twin seems only a few feet away (though really it's farther away at the top than at the bottom due to the curve of the earth). You might have the distinct feeling of violating the divine order of things as you stand there, exposed to the elements, more than a half-mile up in the sky. You can't get much higher than this without hopping a jet or climbing the Himalayas—it's the world's tallest outdoor platform.

At Four World Trade Center, the **Commodities Exchange Center** (938-2018) does its thing on the eighth floor. The glass-enclosed visitors' gallery on the floor above overlooks the trading floor where gold, silver, sugar, coffee, and cotton change hands from 9am to 3pm on weekdays. The "floor show" can actually get more entertaining than the one at the Stock Exchange, since you're much closer to the action—you can hear the traders screaming and see them using a bizarre dialect of sign language which must be seen to be believed. Screen the Murphy-Aykroyd classic *Trading Places* for an introduction to the frenzy. (Open Mon.-Fri. 9:30am-3pm. Free. Guided tours available for groups, but two weeks' advance notice required. Call 938-2000 for more information on tours.)

The World Trade Center hosts a series of free lunchtime concerts called **"Centerstage"** weekdays throughout July and August. The concerts are held on the mezzanine-level plaza at Five World Trade Center. (Call 435-4170 or see Entertainment and Nightlife: Music for more information.)

One level below ground at the Trade Center lurks an underground shopping mall—the largest (and arguably the most boring) in New York. If subterranean shopping fazes you, skip out of Hades and follow the signs directing you to the **World**

Financial Center and **Battery Park City.** Whatever the city tore up to construct the towering World Trade Center, it dumped west of West St. The 100 new acres were recently developed to form Battery Park City. Reached via the pedestrian overpass or a suicidal dash across West. St., the area lies less than a mile from Wall Street. With the stock market a few blocks away and the Statue of Liberty in full view, this neighborhood maintains the spirit of capitalism.

Cesar Pelli's **World Financial Center** rises in a pleasingly geometric fashion. Each of its 40 story towers is more spacious than the 102-story Empire State Building because the buildings were built for computers requiring huge windowless rooms—not people who need a view to survive. The Center's main public space is the vaulted and glass-enclosed **Winter Garden,** an expanse of sixteen 40-ft.-tall palm trees and numerous expensive cafés and shops. The space regularly hosts free concerts, dance programs, poetry readings, and other art and cultural events, including disco dancing, jazz concerts, and a Cowboy Jubilee. (Call 945-0505 or see Entertainment and Nightlife: Music for more information.) The garden looks out on the esplanade, which takes you right out to the water. A **ferry** makes an eight-minute crossing from here to Hoboken and back on weekdays. (Fare $2; call 908-GO-FERRY for more information.)

Head onto the Battery Park City **promenade** and stroll past a series of postmodern residences. Sculptures by Fischer, Artschwager, Ned Smyth, Scott Burton, and Mary Miss line the esplanade. The loyal and insightful sentiments of two New York poets have been inscribed on the terrace here.

The best way to get back to the street is to return the way you came, back through the Winter Garden to the walkway and the plaza.

■ CITY HALL AND THE CIVIC CENTER

The aura of 19th-century New York, bulldozed out of existence elsewhere, still dominates this district. A number of magnificent municipal buildings stand in the neighborhood surrounding City Hall, nearly all housing some branch of city, state, or federal government, and most of them set back atop a huge flight of stone steps. Munching a hot dog and belching loudly as you sit high on one of these flights of steps is sure to put some happiness in your heart.

At 111 Centre St., between Leonard and White St., sits the **Civil Court Building,** which now actually serves mainly as a venue for criminal hearings and proceedings. You can sit in on every kind of trial from misdemeanor to murder here—just visit the clerk's office in Room 927 for a schedule of what's taking place where, or, better yet, call the Expeditor (374-8076) before you come to make sure you'll find something of interest.

As you proceed south down Centre to its intersection with Lafayette St., you can observe a group of sizable office buildings housing anonymous parts of the city bureaucracy. The pillared **United States Courthouse,** at 40 Centre St., while unremarkable at street level, bears a gold roof that crowns the skyline. Next door, to the left on St. Andrew's Place and past a group of inexpensive food kiosks, the **Church of St. Andrew** (962-3972) stands in the shadow of the Municipal Building. Enter the serene space of the church, built in 1938, to see the dark wood crucifix set against a crimson background and framed by dark pillars. (Open daily 7am-6pm.)

Its towering neighbor, One Centre Street, also known as the **Municipal Building,** was completed in 1914. A bizarre free-standing colonnade distinguishes its enormous façade, and its enormous base actually straddles Chambers St. Across Centre St. on the north side of Chambers St., you'll find the former Hall of Records, which now houses the **Surrogate's Court.** Two terribly municipal sculpture groups—*New York in Its Infancy* and *New York in Revolutionary Times*—grace the turn-of-the-century Beaux Arts exterior. Twenty-four statues of notable New Yorkers also enliven the building. Come into the subdued marble entrance hall and step up to the balcony to get closer to the unique curvy ceiling. In the lobby, the ceiling is covered with Egyptian tile mosaics and the 12 signs of the Zodiac.

This building faces the infamous **Tweed Courthouse,** across Chambers St. and west a few steps, on the northern edge of City Hall Park. Builders laid the foundations of the courthouse on a $150,000 budget in 1862 and finished it a decade and $14 million later. Pop mythology has it that $10 million of this money was actually embezzled into the corrupt Tweed political machine, leading to a public outcry that marked the beginning of the end of the Tweed party's rule. Politics aside, today you can admire the building's Victorian reinterpretation of the classical rotunda, if that kind of thing suits you. (Open Mon.-Fri. 9am-4:30pm.)

Exit from the other side of the Tweed Courthouse and you'll find yourself in City Hall Park, facing the rear of **City Hall** itself. Go around to the other side to observe the front of the building, which still serves as the focus of the city's administration. The Colonial chateau-style structure, completed in 1811, may be the finest piece of architecture in the city. It illustrates the idea that good things come in little packages, a concept foreign to those phallic skyscrapers which are so obsessed with size. During its restoration in 1956, a durable limestone façade replaced the original marble, and the northern side was refinished and improved (originally left rough in the belief that the city would never expand north of this point anyway). The vaulting rotunda here, while minuscule compared to the grand public spaces of lower Manhattan, wields a more restrained power. The winding stairs lead to the **Governor's Room,** which was originally intended for the use of that official during his trips to the city. The room is now used to display a number of important early portraits, including ones of Jefferson, Monroe, Jackson, Hamilton, Jay, and Washington (who hated sitting for portraits because his rickety false teeth caused him so much pain). On one side of the Governor's Room sits the **City Council Chamber;** on the other side, down the short hallway to the right, are the **Mayor's Offices,** which are closed to the public. There is no admission fee to the building, officially open to tourists on weekdays from 10am to 4pm, but public meetings here often run later (sometimes through the night) and can be interesting.

City Hall Park has been a public space since 1686—home to an almshouse, a jail, a public-execution ground, and a barracks for British soldiers. On July 9, 1776, George Washington and his troops encamped on the park to hear the Declaration of Independence. Today it is prettily landscaped with colorful gardens and a fountain.

Towering at 233 Broadway, off the southern tip of the park, is the Gothic **Woolworth Building,** one of the most sublime and ornate commercial buildings in the world. Erected in 1913 by F.W. Woolworth to house the offices of his corner-store empire, it stood as the world's tallest until the Chrysler Building opened in 1930 and was during that time known as the "Cathedral of Commerce." The lobby of this five-and-dime Notre Dame is littered with Gothic arches and flourishes, its glittering mosaic ceilings complemented by carved caricatures high up in the four corners of the lobby; note the one of Woolworth himself counting change and the one of architect Cass Gilbert holding a model of the building.

A block and a half farther south on Broadway, near Fulton St., **St. Paul's Chapel** was inspired by London's St. Martin-in-the-Fields. Constructed in 1766, with a spire and clocktower added in 1794, St. Paul's is Manhattan's oldest public building in continuous use. Gaze at the green churchyard and the surprising shades of the interior—baby blue, soft pink, and cream, with gold highlights. You can see George Washington's pew, where the first President worshiped on Inauguration Day, April 30, 1789. Above the pew hangs an oil painting of the nation's Great Seal—the first such rendition of the Seal, which was adopted in 1782. Below the east window outside the church is a memorial to Major General Richard Montgomery, killed in the famous 1775 attack on Quebec. The chapel presents classical music concerts from September through June (see Entertainment & Nightlife: Classical Music). For information on the chapel, call the office of the Trinity Museum (602-0773; chapel open Mon.-Fri. 8am-4pm, Sun. 7am-3pm).

Head across Broadway again, then east on Ann St., to the **Nassau Street pedestrian mall,** a little-known and slightly seedy shopping district characterized by fabulous 19th-century architecture and cheesy ground-level clothing stores. Packed with shoppers during the day, the area has acquired a nice gritty feel (in spite of the one large restored building painted pastel pink and green); like many places in New York, it's worth avoiding at night.

South on Nassau St. and cross Maiden Lane, the **Federal Reserve Bank of New York** (720-6130) occupies an entire block. Built in 1924, this neo-Renaissance building was modeled after the Palazzo Strozzi of a 15th-century Florentine banking family. More than 200 tons of iron went into the decorative treatment. This building stores more gold than Fort Knox, since many nations store their gold reserves here in a vault sinking five levels below the street. The interior of the vault is a cell-block of 121 triple-locked compartments, each a separate storehouse, most containing the gold of a single nation. When the balance of trade shifts between nations, the gold is physically moved from one country's compartment to another's. Free one-hour tours of the building and vault are offered by the Fed, but reservations are required at least seven working days in advance. (Tours scheduled Mon.-Fri. 1am, 11am, 1pm, and 2pm.)

A trip one block back up Nassau St. and right onto John St. will bring you to **John Street United Methodist Church** (269-0014). Established in 1766, the church houses the oldest Methodist society in the country (sanctuary and museum of Colonial and 19th-century memorabilia both open Mon., Wed., Fri. 11:30am-3pm).

Fulton St. is one block further north on Nassau St. Turn right on Fulton St. and head toward the East River. The southwest corner of Pearl and Nassau St. was Thomas Edison's first generating station, a site now consumed by an office tower. It was from a building on this site that Edison first produced and sold electricity to the businesses in his "First District," a one-square-mile area in lower Manhattan. Edison chose location because even then, in 1882, the area housed a high concentration of financial, banking, and commercial activities; he knew that he would have to convince investors such as those who ran the activities of this area that his revolutionary system of lighting was practical and profitable before they would back its development and growth.

■ SOUTH STREET SEAPORT

Walking east on Fulton St. toward the river leads you past a large strip of moderately priced restaurants and ultimately to the **South Street Seaport.** New York's shipping industry thrived here for most of the 19th century, when New York was the nation's prime port and shipping was one of its leading commercial activities. Like many other waterfront areas of lower Manhattan, its size has increased considerably through the use of landfill. At the beginning of the 18th century, Water Street marked the end of Manhattan. Soon landfills had stretched the island to Front Street, and by the early 19th century they stretched it to its present dimensions, with South Street bordering the water.

Zoning and development decisions made in the early '80s rescued the neighborhood from its seedy state of decay, steering it in the alternative direction of homogenized commercialization. If you get a feeling of déjà vu as you tread the cobbled streets or wander among the overpriced novelty shops, that may be because the Rouse Corporation, which designed the rejuvenated area, sponsored similar gentrification at Boston's Quincy Market and Baltimore's Harborplace.

The process succeeded and the historic district, in all its fishy and foul-smelling glory, became a ritzy Reagan-era playground. The fresh-fish market became a yuppie meat market. Now the South Street Seaport complex has an 18th-century market, graceful galleries, and seafaring schooners. After 5pm, masses of crisply attired professionals—sneakers lurking under their skirts and ties trailing over their shoulders—flee their offices and converge here for much-anticipated cocktails. The whole complex recalls a semi-formal frat party. And make sure to use the free and clean public toilets, if you have the wherewithal.

The seaport begins at the intersection of Fulton, Pearl, and Water St., as car traffic gives way to street performers. To your left stands the ironically miniature **Titanic**

Memorial Lighthouse. To the left, on Water St., a number of 19th-century buildings have been restored and now house some interesting shops. Maritime buffs will like the **Chandlery,** 207 Water St. (748-8667; open Mon.-Sat. 10am-6pm, Sun. 11am-7pm), which displays several interesting (and expensive) photography prints of maritime ships from the late 19th century. Lovers of the printing process can be gratified at **Bowne & Co.,** 211 Water St., a restored 19th-century printing shop where employees teach you to use a working letterpress (669-9400; open Mon. by appointment, Tues.-Sat. 10am-5pm, Sun. noon-4pm). On the Fulton St. side of this block, you can enter **Cannon's Walk,** a sparklingly clean alley around the back of these shops.

Back on Fulton St., to the right as you face the water, huddles a row of novelty shops housed in famous **Schermerhorn Row,** the oldest block of buildings in Manhattan, constructed mostly between 1811 and 1812. When Peter Schermerhorn purchased this tract in the 1790s as an investment, it was a "water lot" and the city sold him the right to fill it in with solid surface. Schermerhorn's just-add-landfill purchase proved to be profitable, for this spot rapidly became the focus of much of New York's sea-related commerce. At the **Seaport Museum Visitors' Center** (669-9400 or 748-8600), you can buy tickets to many of the attractions at the Seaport (open daily 10am-6pm; Sept.-May daily 10am-5pm). You can also purchase tickets at Pier 16 (see below).

Across Fulton St. from Schermerhorn Row stands one of the focuses of the seaport, the **Fulton Market Building.** On the ground floor, you can smell the wonders of "Market Hall," a collection of bakeries and exotic, expensive grocery-type establishments, while upstairs you'll find a selection of ethnic fast-food restaurants that'll make you feel a part of the Global Village. At the end of Fulton St., the river rises suddenly into view—and so does the smell, as the spirits of dead fish assault your nostrils. The stench comes from the **Fulton Fish Market,** the largest fresh-fish market in the country, hidden to the left on South St. under the overpass. The city has tried to dislodge the market, but it has been there for over 160 years, still opens at 4am, and resists all efforts at displacement. New York's store and restaurant owners have bought their fresh fish here by the East River since the Dutch colonial period. Between midnight and 8am you can see buyers making their pick from the gasping catch, just trucked here in refrigerated vehicles. Those who can stomach wriggling scaly things might be interested in the behind-the-scenes tour of the market given some Thursday mornings June to October (see Sightseeing Tours).

Further on toward the river on Fulton St., you'll find the **Pier 17 Pavilion** to your left, the **Pier 16 Ticketbooth** straight ahead, and a number of sailing ships docked to your right. At Pier 17 you can play on a three-story, glass-enclosed "recreation pier" filled with small, upscale specialty shops, restaurants, and food stands. The top-floor eating complex here takes the "It's-a-Small-World" theme even farther than Fulton Market and has a seating area with striking views of the Brooklyn Bridge (marketplace information 732-7678).

The Pier 16 kiosk, the main ticket booth for the seaport, stays open from 10am to 7pm (open one hour later on summer weekends). You can buy tickets here for several cruises, with predictably overstarched company aboard. The **Seaport Line** offers 90-minute day cruises, one-hour cocktail cruises, and evening cruises with live music (see Sightseeing: Tours).

An admission ticket, sold at both the Pier 16 booth and the Museum Visitors Center, serves as a full-day pass to many small galleries, ships, and tours. The ticket includes entrance to **The Seaport Museum Gallery** (Water St.), which is devoted to the city's evolution; **The Children's Center** (John St.), which hosts craft workshops for kids; the **Norway Galleries** (John St.), which has exhibitions on the history of New York's seamen; and the ships *Ambrose, Wavertree,* and *Peking* (see below). Take a "Hard Tack and Hard Times Ship Tour" which explores both the *Ambrose* and the *Peking* (Wed.-Sun. 2pm) or board a "Ships Restoration Tour" (daily 1pm). For recorded information about the museums, call 669-9424. (Admission $5, seniors $4, students $3, children 4-12 $2.) Finally, if you want to take a cruise as well as visit the museums (and line the seemingly bottomless pockets of the Rouse Corporation while you're at it), you can pay a combination fare ($14, seniors $13, students $12, children $7).

Harbored at Pier 16, next to the ticket kiosk, you'll find the **Peking,** the second-largest sailing ship ever built. You can get in with your museum ticket or by paying a suggested donation of $2 between 1pm and 2pm. The *Peking,* built in 1911 by a Hamburg-based company, spent most of its career on the "nitrate run" to Chile, a route that passes around Cape Horn, one of the most dangerous stretches of water in the world. Powered purely by shifting winds and brute force, ships like the *Peking* are the culmination of 2000 years of sailing history.

On board, don't miss the 10-minute 1929 film of the ship during an actual passage around Cape Horn (shown daily 10am-closing). Also on board, you can see reconstructed living quarters and a photo exhibit about sailing life. Help the current crew raise one of the ship's 32 sails (Wed.-Sun. 3:30pm) after half-hour tours beginning at 2pm.

Several other ships have been docked for good in the seaport. Smaller ones include the *Wavertree,* an iron-hulled, three-masted ship built in 1885. In addition, you can see the *Ambrose,* a floating lighthouse built in 1907 to mark an entrance to the New York harbor. The *Pioneer* sailing ship gives two- and three-hour cruises on which you can assist with sailing duties (see Sightseeing Tours).

The Seaport also hosts a number of concerts and performances outdoors on the Ambrose Stage throughout the summer. The "Twilight Dance Series" brings such notable companies as Paul Taylor II and the Dance Theatre of Harlem School Ensemble. Past events have also included "NHL Street Hockey at the Seaport," a crafts fair, and a Gospel Night. (For information, call 732-7678.)

■■■ LIBERTY ISLAND:
THE STATUE OF LIBERTY

From its conception the Statue of Liberty has been a repository for America's fantasies, an oversized icon of the creed called "The American Dream." The list of famous names attached to these national fantasies includes sculptor and conservative republican Frédéric-Auguste Bartholdi, publisher and yellow journalist Joseph Pulitzer, and auto tycoon Lee Iacocca on one side; U2, Lou Reed, and Andy Warhol on another; and the films *Escape from New York, Working Girl, Splash, Planet of the Apes,* and *Brother from Another Planet* on yet another. But it's the chance to dream *oneself* onto the list—not merely to witness but to partake of the myth—that makes the statue such a tourist draw.

The statue began as French self-aggrandizer Bartholdi's idea for a lighthouse at the Suez Canal, but he dropped the Africa plan when the prospect of building a monument to the Franco-American friendship was mentioned. The new statue was to commemorate the victory of the Union in the Civil War and the constitutional extension of liberty to black slaves; more pragmatically, the gift would improve the chances that America would oppose the government of Napoleon III in France. The reference to liberation was reduced over time as the project was stalled, and it now remains only as a set of broken manacles (invisible from the ground) at the statue's feet. Bartholdi finally came to America to line up support for his plan in 1871, when the Paris Commune made things inhospitable for him in France. While his compatriots were plotting against the establishment of the worker's paradise in Paris, Bartholdi, along with President Grant and others, was plotting *Liberty Enlightening the World,* the biggest statue the world had ever seen.

Bigness was the thing. Bartholdi was convinced that, in America, size mattered. He wrote to his mother that everything was bigger here, "even the peas." Liberty is the embodiment of Kant's idea of the colossal—"the presentation of a concept almost too large for any presentation, bordering on the relatively monstrous." At 151 ft. tall (300 with pedestal), with Bartholdi's moderate talents to serve it, and with a face modeled on Bartholdi's mother's, Liberty might understandably be described as somewhat monstrous. What Bartholdi had going for him was the publicist's eye for location—and Bedloe's (now Liberty) Island is arguably the best piece of real estate in the New World.

Even before its inauguration on October 28, 1886, the monument to Franco-American relations (something few Americans, then or now, get all that choked up about) had begun to acquire symbolic significance: immigrants, and not just French ones, had made a claim to the statue. Publishing magnate Joseph Pulitzer, a Hungarian immigrant made rich by the new journalism, raised the money for the pedestal by guilt-tripping ordinary New Yorkers into giving whatever they could. Natives of all ages responded to the fervent efforts with words (and hard-earned pennies) of generosity—"A lonely and very aged woman with limited means wishes to add her mite"; "Enclosed please find five cents as a poor office boy's mite to the pedestal fund"; and "We send you $1.00, the money we saved to go to the circus with." Emma Lazarus gave this new Liberty voice when she wrote *The New Colossus* as part of an artists-for-Liberty campaign in 1883. The socialist-Zionist poet forever captured that monumental solidity Bartholdi envisioned in a call for mass migration and a liberation movement. In "Mother of Exiles," the New Colossus declaims the celebrated lines,

> Give me your tired, your poor,
> Your huddled masses yearning to breath free,
> The wretched refuse of your teeming shore.
> Send these, the homeless, tempest-tossed to me.
> I lift my lamp beside the golden door!

America's destiny as the home of the homeless, a nation of settlers, was sealed.

The movement of a colossus is from carnivalesque crescendo to grinding monotony. The latest spasm occurred in 1986—the statue's centennial—with the monstrous Liberty Weekend (critic Paul Fussell cited Liberty Weekend as an example of everything *bad* about American culture). Chrysler Chairman and migrant-son-made-good Lee Iacocca was put in charge of efforts to restore the statue and Ellis Island as well as of planning the blow-out party. It was the pinnacle of Reaganaut bread-and-circus extravaganzas—over budget, corrupt, dirty, televised, and riddled with Elvis impersonators—but at least it had an official snack food. And at least women could attend this celebration. (Women were officially barred from the opening ceremonies in 1886, but a group of determined suffragettes chartered a boat and sailed themselves over to the statue, interrupting speakers by pointing out the irony of a female embodiment of Liberty in a country where women could not vote.) Iacocca's fund drive was riven with political and administrative arguments, and Lee was eventually fired from one of his jobs for a conflict of interest. But the restoration did fix the torch and some structural problems, making the statue newly attractive. This improvement has not been lost on the public, which pays court to Lady Liberty in the form of interminable lines.

You will live with the legacy of Liberty Weekend particularly in the summer—standing in line for up to three hours. Winter is a good time to visit; spring, on the other hand, is dominated by howling packs of schoolchildren who each year refine the art of spitting on the heads of those below them climbing the statue. If you do try to go in the summer get there on the first or second ferry, or forget it. The hotter and sunnier the day, the longer the line (and greater the number of heat-exhaustion cases). Eat before you go; the climb is harder than you think and food on the island is priced according to international-monopoly rules: in other words, whatever foreign tourists can bear.

An ideal summer trip will have you on the boat for Liberty at 9am, off the island by 10:30am, and over to the air-conditioned comfort of Ellis Island by 11am. Ferries run in two loops, Manhattan-Liberty-Ellis and Manhattan-Ellis-Liberty; listen for your stop. The ticket costs the same no matter how long you stay and regardless of whether you want to see only the statue or the immigration station, so you might as well do both.

The ferry ride is one long photo-op, with jaw-dropping views of the lower Manhattan skyline, the Brooklyn Bridge, and, of course, Ms. Liberty. Geared as it is to give you the best shots of the statue, the boat will lean dramatically toward the island so that the camera-ready can snap away by the rail.

Lady Liberty's copper sheeting (2.5mm thick) has acquired its green patina over the last 100 years as a form of self-protection. The symbols of the statue were chosen to promote the ideals of rational republicanism as Bartholdi saw it. Liberty was to enlighten the world; the seven points of the crown stand for the seven seas and seven continents. The toga recalls the ancient republics of Rome. The tablet in her left hand is the keystone of liberty and bears the inscription "July 4, 1776." More obscurely, each window in the visor represents one of the "natural minerals" of the earth. Finally, the torch is a symbol of the Masonic ideal—Enlightenment.

Once you're on the island, head straight for the entrance at the back of the statue. Enter through Fort Wood, part of the system of New York Harbor defenses during the War of 1812. The line on your left is the only way to get to the crown. It is all stairs: 22 stories' worth, or 300-plus of them, many narrow and spiraling (and especially burdensome in the 110°F summertime heat). There are only two reasons to go to the crown: 1) like Mt. Everest, because it's there, or 2) because you dig engineering. Gustave Eiffel, of French tower fame, designed the internal support-system, which is a thing of beauty and elegance. It was also one of the first curtain-wall constructions and inaugurated the skyscraper era. The only way to see the intricate and web-like structure is to clamber to the crown. Don't make the climb for the view: the windows at the top are small and look out not on Manhattan but on the Brooklyn dockyards. One of the restorers wrote that the architectural team felt that a "grueling climb was an integral part of the visitor's experience" and should be preserved. Senior citizens, young children with a propensity to whine or spit, and anyone with a heart, respiratory, or leg ailment should avoid the climb. For those who back down midway, there are plenty of chances to stop climbing and return to the bottom.

The line at the right as you enter is for the elevator. It goes to the top of Richard Morris Hunt's pedestal and its observation decks, where you can admire the beautiful views of New York, Ellis, and the statue above you. You cannot take the elevator halfway up and climb to the top. People with mobility problems can go to the lower observation decks and the museums. An exhibit on the history of the torch is located over the entrance doors on the second level. The torch has been closed to the public since 1916, when anti-American terrorists blew up a munitions barge in New Jersey and threatened to hinder U.S. policies in those early days of World War I. Once a summer, without fail, something equally exciting happens at the statue. A protest, a parachuter, a bomb threat, a takeover—life in the big city.

Rangers are a friendly and knowledgeable lot and are surprisingly willing to answer any question you have, even though you know they've been asked it too many times already (with three million visitors each summer, they have been asked everything too many times already). If they do occasionally appear testy, rattled, or preoccupied with medical cases, it's only because they are so outnumbered: 15 of them to 10,000 tourists on a busy day. (Overheard: "How big are her boobies?")

The Statue of Liberty exhibit is well worth your time (it takes only about 20 min.), but the immigration exhibit on the third floor is useless; if you want immigration, go to Ellis.

If you have some time before the next ferry departs and you're tremendously bored, stop in at the gift shop and cafeteria. In the former you can buy useful things like $70 Liberty hologram watches and 50¢ Statue of Liberty erasers. In the latter, see food names jumbled in a variety of languages by an indifferent staff (fried fish and french fries $4).

Buy tickets for the ferry at Castle Clinton in the southwest corner of Battery Park, the "toe" of Manhattan Island (see Sights: Lower Manhattan). Ferries leave for

Liberty Island from the piers at Battery Park every half hour from 9am to 4pm, and the last ferry back normally runs at 5:15 pm, in July and August at 7pm. (Ferry information 269-5755. Tickets $6, seniors $5, children 3-17 $3, under 2 free.)

■■■ ELLIS ISLAND

Ellis Island re-opened to huddled masses—just tourists this time—in 1990 after an infusion of hundreds of millions of dollars. During its heroic period (1890-1920), approximately 15 million people came through, many winding up with new names in the process.

The exhibits on the island are divided between Ellis's history proper and the history of the peopling of America in general. Most of the first-floor "Baggage Room" has been turned over to exhibits of America's roots and a study of its remarkable diversity— rivaled only by the diversity of tourists you will see milling about. Kodak sponsors "America's Family Album," which attracts mostly the self-obsessed who seek people who have their names or look like them. But it's the exhibit of photos by immigration worker Augustus Sherman that is truly worth seeing. Sherman took all the famous moving images of newly arrived people, and his documentary style clashes provocatively with the real pathos of the newcomers.

Ellis was known as the "Island of Tears," and almost everything about its history speaks of the arrival of the modern bureaucratic state's border control. There were physical and mental tests, quick exams for fitness, financial and criminal checks, and, of course, files. The volume of people at Ellis was so large and required such efficient processing that immigrants in effect became their own files, with their status (possible disease or acceptance) marked right on their bodies in chalk. The exhibit "Through America's Gate" on the second floor chronicles all this. Also on the second floor is the overwhelming Registry Room, also known as the "great hall," where the majority of processing took place. The great windows flood the room with light, making it an ideal place to rest up on a hard day of touring.

The third floor houses the dormitory room, restored to its 1908 state. Triple-hung canvas cots, narrow enough for a thin adolescent, with about 3 ft. of air space between the pancake stacks, supported detainees while they were under examination. While some saw Liberty upon arrival, those given free room and board here most likely conjured up images of prison. Offices and the extensive immigration library, open to researchers who have received advance permission, fill the third floor.

One of the real achievements of the restoration of Ellis Island was an oral history program, which attempted to have immigrants describe their experiences in their own words. These moving words now serve as narration for the exhibits throughout the main hall. They are also the main text for the film *Island of Hope, Island of Tears,* presented twice an hour in one of the two theaters (check for frequency) on the island. The film is free, but tickets must be picked up at the information desk near the entrance in advance of the showing. Do this as soon as you arrive if you want to see the film.

One of the lesser achievements of the restoration was a taped guided tour narrated by Tom Brokaw. It rushes you through everything and costs money besides. Read the signs for yourself. The restaurant is better than the one over on Liberty Island, but it too is overpriced and bland.

Most of the 27½-acre island remains closed to the public. It was originally the site of a hospital complex—contagious-disease wards and staff housing—and has not been restored. Iacocca wanted to tear it down and build an "ethnic Williamsburg"; someone then pointed out that Epcot Center was an ethnic Disneyland, so he scrapped the plan. The Park Service, to its discredit, wanted to build an international business conference center with a swimming pool, racquetball courts, and first-class hotel accommodations. This proposal has also been rejected, and the hollowed-out old buildings remain a silent reminder of the two million people turned away at America's golden door.

Two ferries bring you to and from Liberty and Ellis islands. One runs Battery Park-Manhattan-Liberty-Ellis, and the other Liberty State Park-Jersey City, NJ-Ellis-Liberty. Both run daily every half hour from 9:15am until 4:30pm; on weekends and holidays the last boat might leave as late as 5pm. (Ferry information 269-5755. Tickets $6, seniors $5, children 2-17 $3, children under 2 free.)

■■■ BROOKLYN

When romantics ponder Brooklyn, they conjure up images of the rough stickball players who grew up to become the Brooklyn Dodgers, or think of Woody Allen's boyhood home, presided over by his raucous mother and stubby aunt under the roller coaster in *Annie Hall*. To many Manhattanites, Brooklyn remains elusive—a hodgepodge of ethnic communities, each with its own residential area and commercial zone. What goes on in Brooklyn tends to happen on the streets and out of doors, whether it's neighborhood banter, baseball games in the park, ethnic festivals, or gang violence.

Brooklyn's pride in its distinct culture has deep historical roots. The Dutch originally settled the borough in the 17th century. Although Brits shared the land, Dutch culture flourished well into the early 19th century. When asked to join New York in 1833, Brooklyn refused, saying that the two cities shared no interests except common waterways. Not until 1898 did Brooklyn decide, in a close vote, to become a borough of New York City.

ORIENTATION

Brooklyn's main avenues dissect the borough. The Brooklyn-Queens Expressway pours into the Belt Parkway and circumscribes Brooklyn. Ocean Parkway, Ocean Avenue, Coney Island Avenue, and diagonal Flatbush Avenue run from the beaches of southern Brooklyn to Prospect Park in the heart of Brooklyn. Flatbush Ave. continues on and eventually leads to the Manhattan Bridge. The streets of western Brooklyn (including those in Sunset Park, Bensonhurst, Borough Park, and Park Slope) are aligned with the western shore and thus collide at a 45-degree angle with central Brooklyn's main arteries. In northern Brooklyn, several avenues—Atlantic Avenue, Eastern Parkway, and Flushing Avenue—travel from downtown far east into Queens.

Brooklyn is spliced by subway lines. Most lines serving the borough pass through Atlantic Ave. Station downtown. The D and Q lines continue southeast through Prospect Park and Flatbush to Brighton Beach. The #2 and 5 trains head east to Brooklyn College in Flatbush. The B and N trains travel south through Bensonhurst, terminating in Coney Island. The J, M, and Z trains serve Williamsburg and Bushwick and continue east and north into Queens. The Brooklyn-Queens crosstown G train shuttles from southern Brooklyn through Greenpoint into Queens. For maps and other material on Brooklyn, visit the **Fund for the Borough of Brooklyn,** 16 Court St. near Montague St. (subway #2, 3, 4, 5, M, or R to Borough Hall; 718-855-7882).

■ BROOKLYN BRIDGE

You can stroll for a mile across the **Brooklyn Bridge** in the company of ambitious commuters in Reeboks. From Manhattan, to get to the entrance on Park Row, walk a couple of blocks west from the East River to the City Hall area. Here a stairway leads to the promenade; make sure to walk on the left side, as the right is reserved for bicycles. Once on the bridge, you can do what you've always wanted to do while driving, but couldn't for fear of careening out of control—look straight up at the cables and Gothic arches. On the walkway, you can observe the sun weaving through the constantly shifting cobweb of cables. Suspended above traffic, close your ears and imagine the bridge when only horse-powered vehicles took its path over the East River.

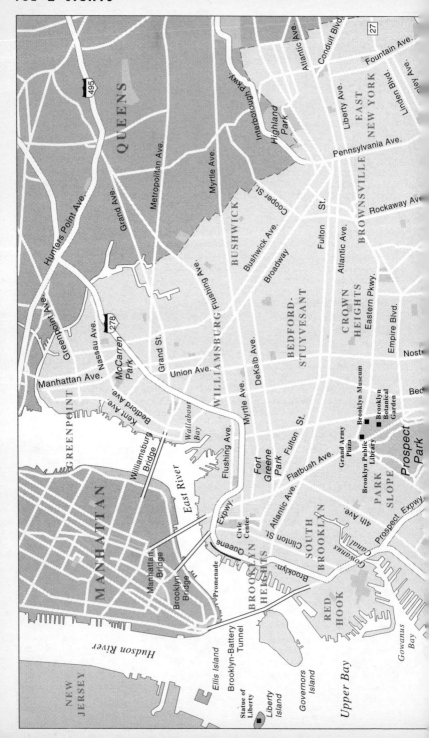

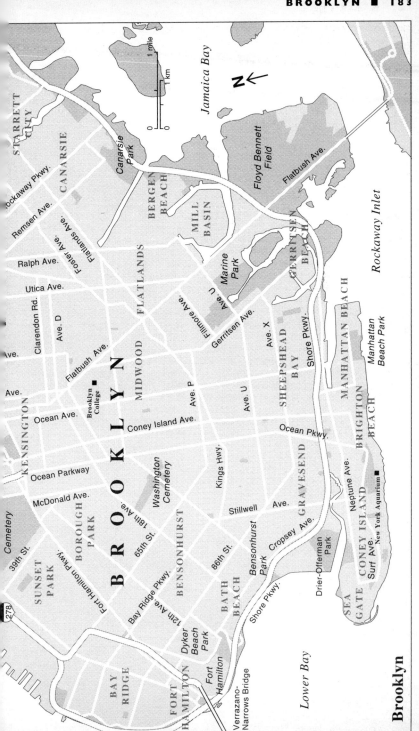

Brooklyn

Back in the present, you'll notice the piers and warehouses of Brooklyn's water-front stretching ahead; behind sits the cityscape that puts all others to shame. The Gothic arched towers of New York's suspended cathedral, the greatest engineering achievement of their age, loomed far above the rest of the city when completed in 1883, the product of engineering wizardry and 15 years of steady work. After chief architect John Augustus Roebling crushed his foot in a surveying accident and died of gangrene, Roebling's son Washington (and subsequently Washington's wife Emily Warren after he succumbed to the bends) took over the management of the job. In the end, the trio achieved a combination of delicacy and power that made other New York bridges look cumbersome or flimsy. Plaques at either end of the walkway commemorate the Roeblings and 20 workers who died during construction.

Like all great bridges, this one has had its share of post-construction death as well. A Mr. Brody leaped off the bridge in 1920, marking the first suicide. Locals say if only he had tucked and rolled, dived and not belly flopped, he might have lived.

■ DOWNTOWN BROOKLYN

Start a tour of downtown Brooklyn at the Atlantic Ave. subway station (#2, 3, 4, 5, D, and Q) or the Pacific Street station (B, M, N, and R). The **Williamsburgh Savings Bank,** at the corner of Flatbush Ave. and Hanson Place, is Brooklyn's tallest building at 512 ft. The building was completed in 1929 and has a splendid Romanesque interior with arches, pillars, patterned marble floors, and a gold and green tiled ceiling. There is also a huge painting of the sun shining down on Brooklyn while a black-ened Manhattan lurks in the shadows (open Mon. and Thurs.-Fri. 8:30am-9pm, Tues.-Wed. 9am-3pm). Walk up Flatbush Ave. a few blocks to Fulton St. and take a left. The stretch of Fulton St. to Borough Hall is now called **Fulton Mall.** The eight blocks were renamed in the '70s in an effort to spark investment in the disintegrating street that had been Brooklyn's main commercial thoroughfare in the '30s and '40s. Instead of the department stores of yesteryear, Fulton Street is now known for smaller, cheaper stores with bargains galore on clothes, shoes, and electronics.

The **Dime Savings Bank,** 9 DeKalb Ave. at the junction of Fulton, presents a grand classical front, with monumental Ionic columns beneath a triangular pediment, two reclining figures, and a majestic domed roof. Pass through the relief-set bronze doors—one of which displays a cubist vision of the New York skyline—and enter a marble interior filled with the building's original turn-of-the-century furniture (open Mon.-Wed. 9am-3pm, Thurs.-Fri. 9am-6pm, Sat. 10am-3pm).

While a meal at **Gage and Tollner,** 372 Fulton St., would be out of the budgeteer's range, the restaurant's 1892 landmark interior—decorated with cherry wood paneling, mirrors, and imitation leather called Lincrusta (invented by the guy who brought you linoleum)—is worth a peek. The original gas lamps still light up every evening.

At the end of Fulton Mall, Fulton St. turns into Joralemon St. **Borough Hall** sits to your right at 209 Joralemon St. This eclectic Victorian/Greek Revival hulk was built in 1851, once housed the city hall of an independent Brooklyn, and is now the oldest building in Brooklyn (tours Tues. at 1pm). If you walk to the opposite side of the building, into **Columbus Park**, you can see that the figure Justice, standing firmly with scales and sword on top of the hall, isn't wearing a blindfold. Cynics may find this peculiarity significant.

Just north of Borough Hall, past the statue of Columbus and a bust of Robert Kennedy, is the **New York State Supreme Court**. The building lies at the southern end of **Cadman Plaza Park,** a long stretch of greenery extending from Columbus Park to the Brooklyn Bridge. The Romanesque Revival lives on at the granite **Brooklyn General Post Office,** 271 Cadman Plaza East, between Tillary and Johnson St. At the northern end of the park is the **Brooklyn War Memorial.**

As Cadman Plaza Park ends at the entrance to the Brooklyn Bridge, Cadman Plaza West becomes Old Fulton St. and runs down to the waterfront, where you can catch a throat-parching view of Manhattan. The **Eagle Warehouse and Storage Co.,** 28 Old Fulton St. at Front St., once housed Walt Whitman's Brooklyn Eagle and has been converted into apartments. The entrance was once a passageway for delivery wagons. **Franklin House,** 1-5 Old Fulton St. at Water St., is another 19th-century building—originally a hotel, now housing the Harbor View Restaurant.

This neighborhood is known as **"DUMBO"** (Down Under the Manhattan Bridge Overpass) and consists largely of industrial warehouse spaces with "For Lease or Sale" signs on their doors. Some of these spaces have been taken over by Brooklyn's volunteer artist militias, who have converted them into galleries. For example, the building at 135 Plymouth St. and Anchorage St. houses several makeshift galleries, including the **Ammo Exhibitions Space.** The **Brooklyn Anchorage** is housed within the bridge suspension cable storage chambers at Front St. (Open mid-May to mid-Oct. Thurs.-Tues. noon-8pm, Wed. noon-7pm. Performances of various sorts Wed. at 8pm; call 718-619-1955.) At the northern end of Main St., between the Manhattan and Brooklyn Bridges, you will find **Empire-Fulton-Ferry State Park,** a pleasant, grassy, waterfront are. The DUMBO neighborhood is largely deserted, even during the day, except for a steady stream of slow, lumbering trucks; after dark, this is probably not a neighborhood to dwell in.

■ BROOKLYN HEIGHTS

In 1814, when the invention of the steamboat made development in Brooklyn Heights possible, rows of now-posh Greek Revival and Italianate houses sprang up. The shady lanes of New York's first suburb were later targeted for preservation, and Brooklyn Heights became New York's—and the nation's—first Historic District, in 1965. Brooklyn Heights is just west of Cadman Plaza Park and south of Old Fulton St. Today the brownstones of the 19th century house the young, upwardly mobile set and a diverse collection of families.

After supping on Middle Eastern food on Atlantic Ave., take a right onto Hicks St. for a stroll through the heart of historic Brooklyn. A few blocks down, **Grace Church,** 254 Hicks St. at Grace Ct., is bedecked with Tiffany windows depicting the life of Christ. Across from the church **Grace Court Alley,** a cul-de-sac intended for the motorless transport of the well-to-do, is flanked by elegant apartments that recall a time when the pleasures of the bourgeois were simpler.

Take a right onto Remsen St. from Hicks St., and head to **Our Lady of Lebanon Maronite Cathedral,** at the corner of Remsen and Henry St. The bronzed doors are decorated with boats and churches that seem eerily prophetic: the doors originally stood at the entrance to the main dining room of the *Normandie,* a grand French oceanliner that sank to the bottom of the Hudson River in 1942.

A left on Henry St., followed by a right on Montague St., will take you to **St. Ann and the Holy Trinity Episcopal Church** (718-875-6960), on the corner of Clinton St. The church is currently undergoing extensive restoration; call about the availability of tours. This is the first church in America to have painted and stained-glass windows; at present, it contains over 4000 sq. ft. of glass. **Arts at St. Ann's** (718-858-2424) is based here and brings performers like Lou Reed and Marianne Faithfull to the acoustically superb church.

Take a left on Clinton St. to get to Pierrepont St., which is parallel to Montague St. and Remsen St. At 128 Pierrepont St. stands the **Brooklyn Historical Society,** housed in a striking building lined with spooky gargoyle-busts of Shakespeare, Beethoven, and others. There is a museum and a research library here for those interested in the esoterica of the borough. (718-624-0890; museum open Tues.-Sat. noon-5pm; admission $2, seniors and children under 12 $1, Wed. free.)

Pierrepont St. leads directly to the **Promenade** (also known as the Esplanade). This waterfront walkway, which spans from Remsen St. to Orange St., also serves as the roof of the toxic Brooklyn-Queens expressway. The view of lower Manhattan exceeds the descriptive and evocative powers of all puny adjectives. To the left, the Statue of Liberty can be seen peeping out from behind Staten Island. In fair weather,

Ellis Island appears in full view, to the right of Liberty Island. The large green protrusion at the southernmost tip of Manhattan is the Staten Island Ferry terminal. The bright orange ferry can be seen crossing back and forth regularly (see Sights: Staten Island for more information). Only the twin tops of the World Trade Center are visible, but they are close enough to get a good look. Walk along the Promenade for a refreshing breath of sea air mixed with less invigorating carbon monoxide from the cars zipping beneath you. During the day, you can continue on to the Brooklyn Bridge for the mile-long walk into Manhattan. Many commuters prefer exercise, a view, and extra pocket change—they walk to work across the bridge.

Parallel to the Promenade, between Montague and Pierrepont St., is **Pierrepont Place.** The addresses begin with No. 2 and end with No. 3. This exclusive street did have a No. 1, but it was deemed too plebeian for a street to have three houses. The two remaining Renaissance Revival brownstones overlook the water. You can see their large rear garden from the wrought-iron fence on the Promenade.

To see the potpourri of 19th-century styles that developed in Brooklyn and that have come to represent U.S. architecture of that period, check out **Willow Street** between Clark and Pierrepont St. Numbers 155-159, in the Federal style, were the earliest houses here (c. 1825), with dormer windows punctuating the sloping roofs. The hand-hammered leadwork and small glass panes date the original doorways. Greek Revival fans should rally to the stone entrances of No. 101 and 103 (c. 1840) and the iron railings on No. 118-22. Numbers 108-12, built by William Halsey Wood in 1884, are Queen Anne-style houses where stone, stained glass, and slate have been pushed to their limits.

Continue along Willow and take a right on Orange St. to the **Plymouth Church of Pilgrims** (718-624-4743). The simple red-brick church is set with stained-glass windows by Lamb Studios, the oldest glass studio in America. The church was the center of abolitionist sentiments before the Civil War under the leadership of its first minister, Henry Ward Beecher. His statue sits in the courtyard alongside a bas-relief of Abraham Lincoln, who visited the church. The Tiffany windows from an earlier church now reside in the modern church's Hillis Hall.

To get to Brooklyn Heights, head down Atlantic Ave. from the Borough Hall station (#2, 3, 4, 5, M, R), or take the A or C train to High St.-Brooklyn Bridge, then walk across Cadman Plaza Park.

■ CARROLL GARDENS AND RED HOOK

Just south of Atlantic Ave., centered around Court St., is a thriving Italian neighborhood. Cobble Hill, whose sidestreets are lined with gorgeous brownstones, stretches a few blocks down and segues into Carroll Gardens. The high Italian population here is evidenced by the numerous pasta and pastry shops lining Court St. Check out the **old Italian guys** who sit in lawn chairs and chew the fat in their native tongue. Carroll Park, a tiny postage stamp of a park, overflows with frolicking children on Court St. between President and Carroll St.

To the west, on the other side of the expressway, is the industrial waterfront area of **Red Hook.** Those in cars can head west on Atlantic Ave. to the docks. On your right hovers one of the **Watchtower buildings,** which house the world headquarters of the Jehovah's Witness organization. Head south (left) on Columbia St. over trolley tracks and cobblestones. Follow the truck route signs one block west to Van Brunt St. At the end of this street, deep in Red Hook, take in a dazzling view of the harbor and the Statue of Liberty. To the right stands a turn-of-the-century warehouse. If you turn around and take a right on Beard St., you will pass a number of lovely decaying industrial complexes. An ensuing left on Columbia St. followed by a right on Bay St. will bring you to a football field that draws young crowds for pick-up soccer games and white-clad Haitian immigrants for cricket. The Red Hook housing projects are just north of here. Avoid these sidestreets at night.

■ NORTH BROOKLYN

Nestled at the northern border with Queens, **Greenpoint** is the seat of an active Polish community (Subway: E or F to Queens Plaza, then G to Greenpoint Ave.). Manhattan Avenue intersects Greenpoint Avenue at the subway station and is at the heart of the neighborhood's bustling business district. Just west of Manhattan Ave.—bounded by Java St. to the north, Meserole St. to the south, and Franklin St. to the west—is the **Greenpoint Historic District.** The Italianate and Grecian houses were built in the 1850s, when Greenpoint was the home of a booming shipbuilding industry. The Union's iron-clad *Monitor*, which defeated the Confederacy's *Merrimac*, was built here.

If you take Manhattan Ave. south to Driggs Ave. and make a right, you will go through McCarren Park and meet up with the copper-covered domes and triple-slashed crosses of the **Russian Orthodox Cathedral of the Transfiguration of Our Lord,** at N. 12th St. Four blocks up N. 12th St. is Kent Ave., which runs through a seedy industrial zone and under the Williamsburg Bridge to the monstrous Brooklyn Naval Yard.

South of Greenpoint is **Williamsburg** (Subway: J, M, or Z to Marcy Ave.), home to a large Hasidic Jewish population, mainly of the Satmar sect. In this part of town, which is bounded by Broadway, Bedford, and Union Avenues, men wear long black coats and hats, dress which dates to early modern Eastern Europe. North of Broadway is a primarily Hispanic neighborhood. In recent years young artists have moved into old industrial complexes here and converted them into lofts, and a hip SoHo-like bar scene has followed in their wake.

If you venture southeast into the neighborhoods of **Bushwick, Bedford-Stuyvesant,** and **Brownsville,** be cautious. Low public funding, high unemployment, and inadequate public works have created a high-crime ghetto. Major sights here are burnt-out buildings, patches of undeveloped land, and stagnant commercial zones. Still, social consciousness and political activism emerge from every pothole in these neglected streets. Wall murals portraying Malcolm X, slogans urging patronage of Black businesses, Puerto Rican flags, and leather Africa medallions all testify to a growing sense of racial and cultural empowerment. Spike Lee's explosive *Do the Right Thing* is set on the streets of "Bed-Stuy."

Every year on the Fourth of July weekend, an African cultural celebration is held in Brownsville on the grounds of the **Boys and Girls School,** 1700 Fulton St. From noon to midnight for several days, you can hear rocking reggae bands and the slamming beats of local rap musicians. The Boys and Girls School is a community-controlled public school which grew out of the 1969 attempt to hand over control of the Ocean Hill-Brownsville School District to the community; the plan was derailed by a teacher strike.

At 770 Eastern Pkwy. in Crown Heights is the **world headquarters of Chabad,** (also known as the Lubavitchers), a Hasidic Jewish sect whose Grand Rebbe, Menachem Mendel Shneerson, died at the age of 92 in June 1994. Prior to his death, many believed that the Rebbe was in fact the Messiah; even after his death some followers claim he will rise again. Shneerson was the last in a hereditary line of Grand Lubavitcher Rebbes; he did not have any children, nor did he name a successor. The future of this sect, which controls millions of dollars of property throughout the U.S. and Israel, and which by most estimates commands the allegiance of hundreds of thousands of Jews worldwide, is presently uncertain. Friday night and Saturday are celebrated as the day of rest, *shabbat.* All of the many sects that coexist here strictly observe the Sabbath; if you intrude, you may feel unwelcome and conspicuous. You will likely feel unwelcome and conspicuous on days other than the Sabbath, unless you are dressed conservatively and, if you are male, wear a yarmulke or some other head covering.

■ INSTITUTE PARK

Brooklyn's cultural focus, **Institute Park,** lies between Flatbush Ave., Eastern Parkway, and Washington Ave. (Subway: #2 or 3 to Eastern Parkway-Brooklyn Museum.) The **Brooklyn Public Library** (718-780-7700) has its main branch here, in a 1941 Art Deco building on the **Grand Army Plaza,** at the corner of Eastern Pkwy. and Flatbush Ave. The library has spawned 53 branches and contains 1,600,000 volumes. There are changing exhibits on the second floor (open Mon. 10am-6pm, Tues.-Thurs. 9am-8pm, Fri.-Sat. 10am-6pm, Sun. 1-5pm; closed Sun. June-Sept.). The **Brooklyn Museum** (718-638-5000), at the corner of Eastern Pkwy. and Washington Ave., has a large permanent collection and special exhibitions that regularly draw Manhattanites out of their borough. The building itself is a neoclassical wonder, with huge stone pillars and sculptures of 30 famous prophets and scholars (see Museums).

The **Brooklyn Botanic Garden** (718-622-4433) flowers next to the museum, at 1000 Washington Ave. This 52-acre fairy-land was founded in 1910 on a reclaimed waste dump by the Brooklyn Institute of Art and Sciences. Throughout the garden are little knolls of wonder. The **Fragrance Garden for the Blind** is an olfactory carnival—in mint, lemon, violet, and more exotic flavors. All are welcome. More formal, the **Cranford Rose Garden** crams in over 100 blooming varieties of that flower. Every spring, visitors can take part in the Sakura Matsuri (Japanese cherry blossom festival) at the Cherry Walk and Cherry Esplanade. The woodsy **Japanese Garden** (admission 25¢) contains weeping willows and a viewing pavilion, grouped around the turtle-stocked pond. Although artificial, the scenery here is realistic enough to fool the many water birds that flock to the site. The **Shakespeare Garden** displays 80 plants mentioned in the Bard's works. Toward the rear of the gardens are two cement pools of flowering lily-pads. The lilies create an intriguing combined effect: some come straight out of a Monet painting, while others are eerily reminiscent of the seed pods in *Invasion of the Body Snatchers.* (Open April-Sept. Tues.-Fri. 8am-6pm, Sat.-Sun. and holidays 10am-6pm; Oct.-March Tues.-Fri. 8am-4:30pm, Sat.-Sun. and holidays 10am-4:30pm. Free, except for the conservatory of tropical plants which costs $2 for the general public and $1 for seniors, students, and children. Donations for entry to other parts of the park are appreciated.)

■ PARK SLOPE AND PROSPECT PARK

The neighborhood called **Park Slope,** bounded by Flatbush Ave. to the north, 15th St. to the south, 5th Ave. to the west, and Prospect Park to the east, combines a thriving business district with magnificent brownstone residences. Restaurants and stores line the north-south avenues, especially 7th Ave., and east-west streets like Carroll St. are lined with beautiful homes. The entire neighborhood is starting to bulge with yuppies and young artists. On the corner of Sixth Ave. and Sterling Pl., owls and angels adorn the graceful brownstone **St. Augustine Roman Catholic Church,** built in 1888. The attached academy has one entrance for "boys," on Sterling Pl., and one entrance for "girls," on Park Pl.

Just east of Park Slope, adjoining the southern border of Institute Park, is **Prospect Park** (718-965-8951). Take the #2 or 3 train to Grand Army Plaza, then head toward **Memorial Arch,** built in the 1890s to commemorate the North's victory over the South. The charioteer atop the arch is an emblem of Columbia, the Union—not of Victory, as is commonly believed. You can climb up to the top of the arch for free on weekends from noon to 4pm.

You can enter Prospect Park's northern corner through Grand Army Plaza. Frederick Law Olmsted designed the park in the mid-1800s and supposedly liked it even more than his Manhattan project, Central Park. The park's largest area is the sweeping, 90-acre **Long Meadow,** the longest open urban parkland in North America. The **Friend's Cemetery,** a Quaker burial ground dating from 1846, remains intact in the western section of the park. Natural glacial pools and man-made Prospect Lake lie south of Long Meadow. **Lookout Hill** overlooks Prospect Lake and marks the site of a mass grave where the British army buried American casualties during the Revolutionary War.

In the eastern part of the park, at Flatbush and Ocean Ave., you can see old Brooklyn preserved in **Leffert's Homestead** (718-965-6505), a Dutch farmhouse burned by George Washington's troops and rebuilt in 1777. The **Children's Historic House Museum** inside the homestead is open weekends and holidays noon-4pm (free). Nearby, saddle a horse taken from Coney Island on the **1912 Carousel**, which plays an odd version of the Beatles' "Ob-La-Di, Ob-La-Da" (open Tues. and Fri. 10am-2pm, Sat.-Sun. noon-5pm; 50¢). The recently re-opened **Prospect Park Wildlife Center** features live animal exhibits mainly aimed at children. (Open daily 10am-5:30pm. Adults $2.50, seniors $1.25, children 3-12 50¢.) In late summer, concerts are held at the bandshell in the northwestern corner of the park (events hotline 718-788-0055, park tours 718-287-3400).

Just southeast of Prospect Park is the neighborhood of **Flatbush,** home to significant Jamaican and other West Indian populations. Reggae music and exotic fruit stands fill major avenues such as Church Ave., Nostrand Ave., and Ave. J on summer days. At the corner of Flatbush Ave. and Clarkson St., down from Avi's Discount Center, you can spot the distinctive "tags" of graffiti artists Rock, Alan, Jew, and Picolo. At Flatbush and Church Ave. (subway: D to Church Ave.), you can see the oldest church in Brooklyn, **Flatbush Dutch Reformed Church** (c. 1654). A few of the sanctuary windows are Tiffany stained glass, including one of Samson. The church has tolled the death of every U.S. president. Next door stands the second-oldest high school in North America, **Erasmus Hall Academy.** Not a single brick can be moved from the school's center building or the Dutch Reformed Church will repossess it. (Founding-father figures Aaron Burr, John Jay, and Alexander Hamilton all contributed to the building of the school.) Although a strange concept today, the turn-of-the-century Manhattan aristocracy maintained summer homes in Victorian Flatbush (bounded by Coney Island and Ocean, Church and Newkirk Ave.). You can wander around Argyle St. and Ditmas Ave. to see some of the old mansions, but be careful to avoid the crack houses on Church Ave. **Brooklyn College** (subway: #2 or 5 to Flatbush Ave./Brooklyn College), founded in 1930, includes the prestigious **Brooklyn Center for the Performing Arts** (718-951-4522; see Entertainment & Nightlife: Classical Music for information on performances).

■ SOUTH BROOKLYN AND CONEY ISLAND

Greenwood Cemetery (768-7300), a vast, hilly kingdom of ornate mausoleums and tombstones, sits directly south of Park Slope and makes for a pleasant, if morbid, stroll (open daily 8am-4pm). Horace Greeley and Boss Tweed both slumber here. The main entrance is at 5th Ave. and 25th St. (Subway: N or R to 25th St.) South of the cemetery, on the southwest flank of Brooklyn, lies **Sunset Park,** a predominantly Latino neighborhood. Recently, Chinese immigrants have begun to establish a community on 8th Ave. between 54th and 61st St., alongside a well-established Arab population. The unique egg-shaped towers of **St. Michael's Roman Catholic Church** rise above the sidewalk on 42nd St. and 4th Ave. Nearby, on the southwest corner of 44th St. and 4th Ave., you can check out a famous graffiti piece by the infamous artist Dare. Between 41st and 44th St., up the hill from 4th Ave. to 6th Ave., is Sunset Park proper, the park for which the neighborhood is named. Here you'll find a sloping lawn with an extraordinary view of the Upper New York Bay, the Statue of Liberty, and lower Manhattan. Avid consumers flock to Fifth Avenue, which is lined with discount stores and odd hybrid restaurants. On the northwest corner of 5th Ave. and 54th St. is a colorful mural (presumably painted by children) of happy people in front of the Manhattan and Brooklyn skyline. On 59th St. and 5th Ave. stands an immense gray-stoned church, **Our Lady of Perpetual Help.** If you're in a car, you can head down to First Ave. and explore the trolley-scarred streets, the setting for Vli Wedel's *Last Exit to Brooklyn.* Near 39th St., 19 huge, white warehouses make up the 6 million sq. ft. of **Bush Terminal,** the largest industrial park in Brooklyn. Exploring this desolate area by foot can be fun, but be extremely cautious.

Bay Ridge, south of Sunset, centers on Third Avenue, also called "Restaurant Row." If you're driving, venture down Shore Road and check out the mansions overlooking the Verrazano-Narrows Bridge and New York Harbor. **Bensonhurst** became a household word and rallying cry in the fight against racism, following the brutal murder of Yusef Hawkins in 1989. The predominantly Italian neighborhood centers around 86th Street, which hosted the dancing feet of John Travolta in the opening scene of *Saturday Night Fever.* This birthplace of disco is chock full of Italian bakeries, pizza joints, rowdy youths, and discount stores, especially around 17th Ave.

North of Bensonhurst and east of Sunset Park, centered around 13th Ave. north of 65th St., is **Borough Park,** the largest Hasidic Jewish neighborhood in Brooklyn. In contrast to the more visible Crown Heights Lubavitchers, the Bobovers of Borough Park eschew, for the most part, the political and secular worlds, preferring to maintain an insular community. The main synagogue sits at 15th Ave. and 48th St. As in the other Hasidic neighborhoods of Brooklyn, visitors will feel more welcome if they are dressed conservatively. East of Ocean Parkway is the traditionally Jewish neighborhood of **Midwood** (subway: D or Q to Kings Hwy.). Once the home of the largest Sephardic Jewish community outside of Israel, the neighborhood has lately seen increasing numbers of Arabs, Italians, and non-Sephardic Jews. Nonetheless, kosher eateries still dot the major arteries such as Kings Hwy and Ocean Ave., along with Halal markets and pizza joints.

The B, D, F, and N trains all plug into the Stillwell Ave. station in **Coney Island,** attesting to South Brooklyn's historic importance as a resort spot for the rest of the city. In the early 1900s, only the rich could afford the trip here. Mornings, they bet on horses at the racetracks in Sheepshead Bay and Gravesend; nights, they headed to the seaside for fifty-dollar dinners. The introduction of nickel-fare subway rides to Coney Island made the resort accessible to the entire population. Millions jammed into the amusement parks, beaches, and restaurants on summer weekends. In the late '40s, the area became less attractive. Widespread car ownership allowed people to get even farther away from the city, and a few devastating fires in Coney Island soon cleared the way for urban housing projects throughout the area.

Some vestiges of the golden era linger. The **Cyclone,** at 834 Surf Ave. and W. 10th St., built in 1927, remains the most terrifying roller coaster ride in the world (718-266-3434; open daily mid-June to Labor Day noon-midnight; Easter weekend to mid-June Fri.-Sun. noon-midnight). Enter its 100-second-long screaming battle over nine hills of rickety wooden tracks—the ride's well worth $3. The 1920 **Wonder Wheel** ($2.50), in Astroland on Surf Ave., has a special twist that surprises everyone; make sure you get in a colored car. The **El Dorado** bumper car ($2.50), 1216 Surf Ave., still plays thumping '70s disco tunes and invites you to "bump, bump, bump your ass off!" The **Hellhole** ($2.50), on 12th St. between Bowery and the Boardwalk, is about as scary as a Munsters rerun, but has some fun, campy moments.

On the boardwalk at 12th St. is the **Coney Island Circus Sideshow** (open Fri. noon-sundown, Sat.-Sun. noon-10:30pm; admission $3, children $2). The Sideshow is run by a bunch of NYC hipsters who sponsor the annual **Coney Island Mermaid Parade** (usually the last Sat. in June), a huge costume and float parade with prizes at the end. Come watch, or even register from 10am-noon on the day of the parade at Steeplechase Park, and join the festivities. The Sideshow also hosts numerous cultural events throughout the summer and fall, including great indie rock shows on most Friday nights (see Entertainment and Nightlife: Music). Call 718-372-5159 for information on all Sideshow happenings.

The **New York Aquarium** (718-265-3400 or 718-265-FISH) on Surf and West 8th St. offers a ride-free environment. The first beluga whale born in captivity was raised in these tanks. Watch a solitary scuba diver be immersed in a tank full of feeding sharks. (Open daily 10am-5pm, holidays and summer weekends 10am-7pm. Admission $6.75, children and seniors $2.)

You can head west on Surf Ave. or take the boardwalk to the corner of W. 16th St., where the **Thunderbolt** coaster stands in ruins, with overgrown weeds and mongrel dogs. The tall, rusted skeleton of the **Parachute Jump,** relocated to the edge of the boardwalk in 1941, once carried carts to the top and then dropped them for a few seconds of freefall before their parachutes opened. Once a year, on Puerto Rican National Day, a flag somehow gets tied to the top. The pier that juts out into the water from here makes a good place for fishing or taking a stroll.

East of Coney Island, Ocean Parkway runs on a north-south line through half of Brooklyn. An extension of Olmsted's Prospect Park, this avenue was constructed to channel traffic to the seaside. Beyond the parkway lies **Brighton Beach** (subway: D or Q to Brighton Beach), nicknamed "Little Odessa by the Sea" because of the steady stream of Russian immigrants who moved there in the early 80s. Take a stroll down Brighton Beach Ave. or the parallel boardwalk along the sea. In late June and early July, old Eastern Europeans complaining about their bodily ailments, Spandex-clad girls listening to Top 40 music on their Walkmans, and middle-aged couples drowning sunburns in Noxzema are all wowed by the Blue Angels air shows. On the weekend of the Fourth of July, parachutists land near cheering seaside crowds. Throughout the summer, Brighton Beach residents sit in lawnchairs or on the benches, with the hot sun wrapped around them like a shroud of tranquility.

To the east lies **Sheepshead Bay** (subway: D or Q to Sheepshead Bay), named after the fish that has since abandoned its native waters for the cleaner Atlantic. Emmons Avenue runs along the bay and faces **Manhattan Beach,** a wealthy residential section of doctors and mafioso just east of Brighton Beach. In Sheepshead Bay, you can go after some blues (the fish, not the music) on any of the boats docked along Emmons Ave. (Boats depart 6am-8am; some also have evening trips leaving 5:30-6:30pm; $25-30.) Traditionally, a couple of dollars is collected from each passenger and the wad goes to the person who lands the biggest fish.

If you have a car, you can drive east along the Belt Parkway, which hugs Brooklyn's shores. Stop off at **Plumb Beach** for a more intimate sun and sand experience. At night, the parking lot here fills with big green Cadillacs and loving couples. Exit the Belt at Flatbush Ave., which leads south to the Rockaway beaches of Queens. Turn left just before the bridge and you can drive around the immense abandoned air strips of Floyd Bennett Field. Here, you will find information about **Gateway National Park** (718-338-3687; open daily dawn till dusk).

Continuing on the Belt will take you to **Starrett City**, based around Pennsylvania Ave. This development has its own schools, its own government, and its own source of electricity and heat. Originally, rent here was based on how much each resident's salary allowed. State legislators soon revoked this "un-American" policy. The complex was also famous for enacting a cap on the number of minority residents in an effort to achieve racial balance; this policy was overturned as well.

■■■ QUEENS

Archie and Edith Bunker now share the brick houses and clipped hedges of their "bedroom borough" with immigrants from Korea, China, India, Greece, and the West Indies. In this urban suburbia, the American melting pot bubbles away with a foreign-born population of over 30%. Immigrant groups rapidly sort themselves out into neighborhoods where they try to maintain the comforting memory of their homelands while living out "the American Dream."

This rural colony was baptized in 1683 in honor of Queen Catherine of Braganza, wife of England's Charles II. At the beginning of the 19th century, the small farms began to give way to industry, and by the 1840s the area along the East River in western Queens had become a busy production center. In 1898 Queens officially became a borough of the City of New York. With political linkage, and the Long Island Railroad's construction of train tunnels under the East River in 1910, came physical growth. Between 1910 and 1930, the population of the borough quadrupled to one million; in 1938, Queens accounted for almost three-quarters of all new building in the city. The building boom of the '50s effectively completed the urbanization of Queens, establishing it as the new Lower East Side, home to a wave of late-20th-century immigrants. Today, in this medley of distinct neighborhoods, you can trace the history of ethnic settlement from block to block.

Although the home of New York's two airports, LaGuardia to the north and JFK to the south, much of Queens feels like a wholly separate city. It has even styled itself one; in response to ongoing concerns about taxes and city benefits (Queens maintains that it pays too much of the former and receives almost none of the latter), some uptight natives have lately called for secession. The city, meanwhile, has made noises about prioritizing outerborough tourism. A Dinkins-inspired "New York: Yours to Discover" advertising blitz was supposed to divert flows of funds and people to Queens and other "neglected treasures," but a few fiscally lean years and cries for more crime-fighters on Manhattan's streets have shifted priorities (Mayor Giuliani's campaign could basically be summed up in two words: Safety First). Until this program gets underway and Queens establishes its own tourism council, places like the **Queens Historical Society** (143-35 37th Ave., Flushing, NY 11354; 718-939-0647) pick up the slack. The society can suggest self-guided tours of historically important neighborhoods (such as the "Freedom Mile") and leads its own free guided tours.

ORIENTATION

Queens is geographically New York's largest borough, comprising over a third of the city's total area. Just across the East River from Manhattan lies the Astoria/Long Island City area, the northwest region of Queens. **Long Island City,** spliced with subway lines and covered in grime, has long been Queens's industrial powerhouse. In the 1930s, 80% of all industry in the borough was based here; Newtown Creek saw as much freight traffic as the Mississippi River. The area has lately acquired a reputation as a low-rent artists' community, though it remains to be seen whether the avant-garde will cross the river. **Astoria,** known as the Athens of New York, has by some estimates the second-largest Greek community in the world. The area is also home to a sizable Italian community.

Southeast of this section, in the communities of Woodside and Sunnyside, new Irish immigrants join more established ones. **Sunnyside,** a remarkable "garden community" built in the 1920s, gained notoriety during the Great Depression when over half the original owners were evicted because they weren't able to pay their mortgages. The neighborhood now commands international recognition as a model of middle-income housing. Southeast of Sunnyside lies **Ridgewood,** a neighborhood founded by Eastern European and German immigrants a century ago. More than 2000 of the distinctively European, attached brick homes there receive protection as landmarks, securing Ridgewood a listing in the National Register of Historic Places, but the adjacent Brooklyn ghetto of Bushwick has frayed its edges.

East of Ridgewood, **Forest Hills** and **Kew Gardens** contain some of the most expensive residential property in the city. The Austin Street shopping district imports the luxury of Manhattan. New York State Governor Mario Cuomo has a home in Forest Hills, as does former Vice Presidential candidate Geraldine Ferraro. Originally called Whitepot, the land of Forest Hills was bought from the Indians for some white pots—a deal almost as unreal as Peter Minuit's Manhattan purchase. Just north of this area, **Flushing Meadows-Corona Park,** site of the World's Fair in both 1939 and 1964, still attracts crowds both for its museums and for its collection of open-air attractions. To the west, **Corona, Jackson Hts.,** and **Elmhurst** have a large Hispanic population. To the east of the park, **Flushing** has become a "Little Asia" with a large Korean, Chinese, and Indian population, as well as a sizable number of Central and South American immigrants. **Bayside,** east of Flushing, is a popular spot for bar-hopping in a relaxed, north shore atmosphere. **Jamaica,** located in the central part of the borough, and many of the middle- and upper-class neighborhoods to its southeast are primarily West Indian and African-American. Along the south shore of Queens, the site of mammoth Kennedy Airport, you can find the **Jamaica Bay**

QUEENS

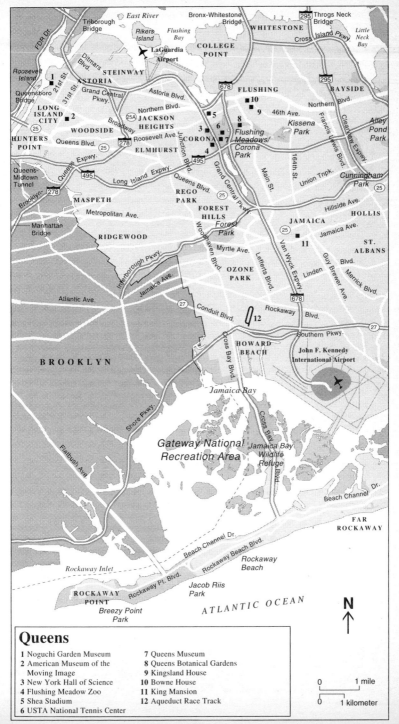

East River
Triborough Bridge
Rikers Island
Flushing Bay
Bronx-Whitestone Bridge
WHITESTONE
Throgs Neck Bridge
Cross Island Pkwy.
Little Neck Bay
LaGuardia Airport
COLLEGE POINT
295
FDR Dr.
Ditmars Blvd.
STEINWAY
Roosevelt Island
21st St.
ASTORIA
31st St.
Grand Central Pkwy.
Astoria Blvd.
FLUSHING ■ 10
Northern Blvd.
BAYSIDE
295
Queensboro Bridge
LONG ISLAND CITY ■ 2
Northern Blvd.
JACKSON HEIGHTS
25A
46th Ave.
9
Kissena Park
Francis Lewis Blvd.
Clearview Expwy.
Alley Pond Park
HUNTERS POINT
WOODSIDE
Broadway
Roosevelt Ave.
■ 5
8 ■
Junction Blvd.
■ 3 ■ 6
CORONA ■ 7
Flushing Meadows/ Corona Park
164th St.
Union Tnpk.
Cunningham Park
25
Queens Blvd.
25
278
ELMHURST
■ 4
495
Main St.
Queens-Midtown Tunnel
278
Queens Expwy.
Long Island Expwy.
Queens Blvd.
Grand Central Pkwy.
Hillside Ave.
Brooklyn
MASPETH
REGO PARK
25
JAMAICA
HOLLIS
Manhattan Bridge
Metropolitan Ave.
FOREST HILLS
Forest Park
25
11 ■
Jamaica Ave.
ST. ALBANS
RIDGEWOOD
Woodhaven Blvd.
Myrtle Ave.
Van Wyck Expwy.
Guy Brewer Blvd.
Blvd.
Linden
Merrick Blvd.
Interborough Pkwy.
OZONE PARK
Lefferts Blvd.
678
Atlantic Ave.
Jamaica Ave.
27
Conduit Blvd.
Rockaway Blvd.
27
Ⓠ 12
Southern Pkwy.
Cross Bay Blvd.
HOWARD BEACH
John F. Kennedy International Airport
BROOKLYN
Jamaica Bay
Gateway National Recreation Area
Jamaica Bay Wildlife Refuge
Cross Bay Blvd.
Flatbush Ave.
Shore Pkwy.
Beach Channel Dr.
FAR ROCKAWAY
Rockaway Inlet
Beach Channel Dr.
Rockaway Beach Blvd.
Rockaway Beach
ROCKAWAY POINT
Rockaway Pt. Blvd.
Jacob Riis Park
ATLANTIC OCEAN
Breezy Point Park
N
↑

Queens

1 Noguchi Garden Museum
2 American Museum of the Moving Image
3 New York Hall of Science
4 Flushing Meadow Zoo
5 Shea Stadium
6 USTA National Tennis Center
7 Queens Museum
8 Queens Botanical Gardens
9 Kingsland House
10 Bowne House
11 King Mansion
12 Aqueduct Race Track

0   1 mile
0   1 kilometer

Wildlife Refuge. The eastern parts of Queens have the same easy feel as adjacent Nassau County.

Queens suffers from neither the monotonous grid of Upper Manhattan nor the slipshod angles of the streets in the Village. Most neighborhoods here developed independently, without regard for an overriding plan. Nevertheless, streets generally run north-south and are numbered from east to west, from 1st St. in Astoria to 271st St. in Glen Oaks. Avenues run perpendicular to streets and are numbered from north to south, from 2nd Ave. in the north to 165th Ave. in the south. The address of an establishment or residence usually tells you the closest cross-street; for example, 45-07 32nd Ave. is near the intersection with 45th St. But named streets sometimes intrude into the numerical system, and sometimes two different numbering systems collapse into one another. For added fun, Roads and Drives are frequently inserted between consecutive Avenues (as in these consecutive thoroughfares in Long Island City: 31st Road, 31st Drive, Broadway, 33rd Avenue), while Places are sometimes inserted between consecutive Streets.

■ FLUSHING

Flushing offers a perfect picture of present-day Queens: here large and active immigrant populations (especially Asians) are transforming and revitalizing an area whose history extends back to colonial times. Getting here by subway couldn't be easier; the #7 Flushing line runs straight from Times Square.

Landmarks from before the American Revolution commingle with a downtown where the signs outside most stores are bilingual (and those signs which aren't are unlikely to be in English). Up Main St. toward Northern Blvd., between 38th and 39th Ave., stands **St. George's Episcopal Church.** The present structure was built in 1853 to replace the original, where Francis Lewis, a signer of the Declaration of Independence, had once been a vestryman. Past the church about four blocks up and to the right, on Northern Blvd., sits a conspicuously shingled building at #137-16. This **Friends Meeting House** (718-358-9636), a national historic landmark, went up in 1694 and still serves as a place of worship for local Quakers. Meetings are held here at 11am every Sunday, and the main room, a severe and simple hall, is open on the first Sunday of every month. Across the street at 137-35 Northern Blvd., the **Town Hall** (718-463-7700), built in 1862, has recently been restored in the Romanesque Revival tradition. Inside await art and historical exhibitions (suggested donation $2, students and seniors $1). Live jazz is offered here every Thurs. during July and August (shows at 8 and 10pm; $15 each show, students and seniors $10.)

For other points of historical interest, continue down Northern Blvd., past the Gothic monstrosity known as Flushing High School, to Bowne St., and make a right. About two blocks down, at #37-01, is **Bowne House** (718-359-0528). This low, unassuming structure, built in 1661, is the oldest remaining residence in New York City. Here, John Bowne defied Dutch governor Peter Stuyvesant's 1657 ban on Quaker meetings—and was exiled for his efforts. Back in Holland, Bowne persuaded the Dutch East India Company to demand of the colony tolerance for all religious groups. This helped to establish the tradition of religious freedom that Buddhist and Hindu newcomers to Flushing enjoy today. The house preserves such interesting antiques as a beehive oven, clay peace pipes, bone-handled utensils, and a walking stick Old Man Bowne used to kill wandering bears. (Open Tues. and Sat.-Sun. 2:30-4:30pm. Admission $2, seniors and children under 14 $1.)

Next to Bowne House lies a small park; head through it and past a playground on your left to the **Kingsland Homestead,** 143-35 37th Ave. (718-939-0647). This large, decrepit house, built in 1775, is currently being restored and holds a permanent collection of antique china and memorabilia that belonged to the early trader Captain Joseph King. There is also a permanent collection of antique dolls and a fully furnished "Victorian Room." Don't be embarrassed to take a peek into "Aunt Marie's Secret Closet." As home of the **Queens Historical Society,** the Homestead displays three or four temporary exhibits each year concerning aspects of the borough's history. It also serves as an archival and genealogical research center for Queens. Pick up a brochure here to guide you through the Flushing Freedom Mile Historic Tour. (Open Tues. and Sat.-Sun. 2:30-4:30pm. Admission $2; admission to archives free with permission.) Behind the house stands New York's only living landmark, a weeping beech tree planted in 1849 by nurseryman Samuel Parsons upon his return from Belgium. The first of its species in North America, it has a height of 65 ft. and a circumference of 14 ft. The venerably twisted patriarch has spawned eight more of its kind around it, all "sons of beeches," and is also the father of every other tree of its species on this continent.

Five blocks down Main St. toward Corona Park from the #7 subway station is the regal **Queens Botanical Garden** (718-886-3800). (The Q44 bus toward Jamaica stops right in front of the Garden.) Begun as a part of the 1939-40 World's Fair in nearby Flushing Meadows-Corona Park, the garden had to move when the park was being redesigned for the 1964-65 World's Fair. With the help of state-planning mastermind Robert Moses, the garden was relocated to its present site, where it now boasts a 5000-bush rose garden (the largest in the northeast), a 23-acre arboretum, and more than nine acres of "theme gardens." (Open mid-April to mid-Oct. Tues.-Sun. 10am-6pm; mid-Oct. to mid-April Tues.-Sun. 9am-4:30pm. Suggested donation $1, children 50¢.)

Kissena Park, on Rose Ave. and Parsons Blvd., preserves nature on a more modest scale. The **Historic Grove** was planted here in the 19th century as part of Parson's Nursery and contains many exotic foreign tree species. As you enter from Rose Ave., pass tennis courts and a nature center; down the hill is beautiful Kissena Lake, circled by picnickers, cyclists, and even a few fisherfolk. Urban park rangers give walking tours (718-699-4204); you can call the **Kissena Park Nature Center** for more information (718-353-2460). (Open Wed.-Fri. 10am-4pm, Sat.-Sun. 11am-5pm.) From the #7 subway stop at Main St., take the Q17 bus from in front of Model's to Rose Ave., and get out in front of Kissena Park.

To the east of Flushing, the 600-acre **Alley Pond Park/Environmental Center,** 228-06 Northern Blvd. (718-229-4000), just off the Cross-Island Pkwy., offers miles of nature trails through the park—a greenbelt of wetlands, woodlands, and marshes. A small exhibit in the back room of the center features live snakes, snapping turtles, frogs, and guinea pigs. (Open Tues.-Sat. 9am-4:30pm.) To get there, take the #7 to Main St., Flushing. Then take the Q12 bus from Stern's department store on Roosevelt Ave., along Northern Blvd. to the center.

▨ FLUSHING MEADOWS-CORONA PARK

Queens has hosted a pair of World's Fairs, both of them in Flushing Meadows-Corona Park, a 1255-acre former swamp sliced out of the middle of the borough. The park, developed during the 1939 Fair, was cultivated on the tip of a huge rubbish dump. Most of the park's present-day attractions were originally built for use at the 1964-65 Fair; their somewhat shabby condition bears witness to better days. Like downtown Flushing, the park is on the #7 subway line from Times Square; you can get off at the 111th St. elevated station. (The next stop over, now known as the Willets Point/Shea Stadium station, was called the World's Fair Station in 1939.) Before leaving the platform, take a look at the huge, pale box of a building on stilts in the distance which reads "Terrace on the Park." Walk straight toward this along 111th St., and after five blocks you will come to a parking lot.

The building that houses the **New York Hall of Science** sits back across this parking lot, near the corner of 111th St. and 48th Ave. (718-699-0675 or 718-699-0005). Futuristic when it was constructed in 1964, it now stands on a neglected site, surrounded by rusty rockets. Its vision of the future may not have aged well on the outside, but the museum does a good job of making sure that its exhibits inside are current, engaging, and make use of such neato technology as an electron microscope and powerful Macintosh computers. This "museum" certainly deserves a visit, especially if you bring children. Over 150 hands-on displays demonstrate a range of scientific concepts and encourage participation. Although the exhibits change with some frequency, recent hits have included "Sound Sensations—The Inside Story of Audio," which let you record and distort your own voice to comic effect, and "Seeing the Light," which demonstrated the principles behind lasers and prisms. If you time your visit just right, you may witness one of the regularly scheduled cow's-eye dissections performed by one of the young and spirited "explainers" on the staff. (Open Wed.-Sun. 10am-5pm. Admission $3.50, seniors and children under 18 $2.50. Free Wed.-Thurs. 2-5pm.)

East of the building, following the walking path across the overpass and then turning right, you will come to the heart of the park and the **New York City Building.** The south wing houses winter ice skating (718-271-1996 for hours and prices; season runs Oct.-March), and the north wing is home to the **Queens Museum of Art** (718-592-5555). In the museum, you can see the "Panorama of the City of New York"—at 1800 sq. ft. the world's largest-scale model of an urban area. One hundred feet of New York correspond to one inch on the model, which re-creates over 865,000 buildings in miniature. As you exit the museum you might notice a 380-ton steel globe in the pavilion to your right. It's the **Unisphere,** the centerpiece of the 1964 World's Fair. The fountain is drained and the foundation decayed, but the globe remains a sight to behold. You can imagine what this place must have looked like 30 years ago, when women in wigged-out hairstyles and miniskirts and men in polyester turtlenecks and beads did little pagan dances around it.

The rest of the park's grounds are fun, too. Just south of the Hall of Science is a restored **Coney Island carousel** (718-592-6539) that pipes out mischievously off-key music at ear-splitting volume (85¢ a ride; open daily 10:30am-7pm). The **Queens Wildlife Center and Zoo** (718-271-7761) next door features North American animals like elk, bison, and bear, along with more exotic species such as sea lions, pumas, and sandhill cranes. A petting zoo features sheep, goats, cows, and the rest of the standard petting zoo crew. (Open Mon.-Fri. 10am-5pm, Sat.-Sun. 10am-5:30pm; Nov.-March 10am-4:30pm daily. Tickets sold until ½-hr. before closing. Admission $2.50, seniors $1.25, children under 13 50¢.)

Also in the park, you can try your hand at a full (but short) course of pitch-'n'-putt golf (718-271-8182), which has 18 par-3 holes (open daily 8am-7pm; greens fee $7.50, Mon.-Fri. $6.50; club rental $1 each), or cavort in a playground accessible to disabled children. In the southern part of the park, **Meadow Lake** offers paddle boating, rowboating, and duck-dunking, while **Willow Lake Nature Area** offers an occasional free tour; call the Urban Rangers at 718-699-4204 for more information.

Shea Stadium (718-507-8499 or 718-699-4220), to the north of the park, was built for the 1964 Fair, though the Mets now slug it out here. Nearby, the **USTA National Tennis Center** (718-592-8000) holds the U.S. Open tennis championship each year (see Sports).

■ ASTORIA AND LONG ISLAND CITY

In Astoria, Greek-, Italian-, and Spanish-speaking communities mingle amidst safe, lively shopping districts and top-flight cultural attractions. Astoria lies in the upper west corner of the borough, and Long Island City is just south of it, across the river from the Upper East Side. A trip on the N train from Broadway and 34th St. in Manhattan to Broadway and 31st St. at the (pseudo-) border between the two cities should take about 25 minutes. As you get off the train you will find yourself in the middle of the Broadway shopping district, a densely packed area where an average block includes three specialty delis, a Greek bakery, and an Italian grocery. Those for whom shopping is an aerobic exercise should go east eight blocks on Broadway to Steinway St., where the stores stretching block on block in both directions form a panoramic vista.

For those whose shopping appetites are satiated, two sculpture gardens provide a remarkable diversion from consumerism. From the Broadway station at 31st St., walk west along Broadway eight blocks toward the Manhattan skyline, leaving the commercial district for a more industrial area. At the end of Broadway, cross the intersection with Vernon Boulevard. The **Socrates Sculpture Garden** (718-956-1819) is located next to the steel warehouse. The sight is stunning, if somewhat discomfiting: modern day-glo and rusted metal abstractions *en masse* in the middle of nowhere, on the site of what was once an illegal dump. The 20-odd sculptures on this five-acre waterfront plot challenge the viewer's interpretive skills. Don't miss the "Sound Observatory" right on the edge of the East River. You could spend hours pitty-pat pattering on the tin drums and honking into the "vocal amplifier," which faces out onto the water. (Open daily 10am-sunset.)

To your left as you face the river, two blocks south on Vernon Blvd. at 32-37, stands the **Isamu Noguchi Garden Museum** (718-204-7088 or 718-721-1932), established in 1985 next door to the world-renowned sculptor's studio. Noguchi (1904-88) designed and built this space, one of the few world-class museums that present a comprehensive survey of the work of a single sculptor. Inside, 12 galleries display Noguchi's breadth of vision. Head upstairs and take a look at the model of his proposed "Sculpture to Be Seen From Mars," a 2-mi.-long face to be carved in the dirt next to Newark International Airport as a monument to man in the post-atomic age. His most inspired works, the smaller stone sculptures, find fantastic display in the indoor/outdoor galleries downstairs. Noguchi once said that he wanted "to look at nature through nature's eyes, and so ignore man as a special object of veneration;" he worked with stones to help them reveal their true souls, not to reshape them. In "The Well," which rests outside, Noguchi left large parts of the boulder uncut, but bored a large circular "belly button" into the top; water perpetually wells over and shimmers down the sides of the stone. Touch its moving surface. The curators at the Metropolitan Museum liked this work so much, they commissioned one of their own. (Open April-Nov. Wed. and Sat.-Sun. 11am-6pm. Suggested contribution $4, students and seniors $2. A shuttle from Manhattan (718-721-1932; $5) leaves from the Asia Society on Park Ave. and 70th St. on Sat. and Sun. every hr. on the half-hr. from 11:30am to 3:30pm. It returns every hr. on the hr. until 5pm. An informative but long guided tour kicks off at 2pm; free.)

Astoria is also the home of the **Kaufman-Astoria Studio**; part of a 13-acre plant with eight sound stages, it is the largest studio in the U.S. outside of Los Angeles. Paramount Pictures used these facilities to make such major motion pictures as *Ragtime, Arthur*, and *Secret of My Success*. The studios are closed to the public, but the complex contains the **American Museum of the Moving Image**, at 35th Ave. and 36th St. To get to the museum from the elevated N-line stop on Broadway, walk five blocks on Broadway away from Manhattan to 36th St.; make a right and walk two blocks through the residential neighborhood. Galleries of wacky film and TV memorabilia, interactive games, and daily screenings serve up a hearty dose of pop culture (see Museums).

More than anything else in the borough, the **Steinway Piano Factory**, at 19th Rd. and 77th St. in northern Astoria (718-721-2600), puts Queens on the map. The Steinways moved their famous operation out to Astoria in the 1870s and had the place to themselves for quite some time. The area was named after pioneering William Steinway, who built affordable housing for his workers around the factory in the 19th century. The thoughtful and considerate Mr. Steinway threw in a library, a kindergarten, and athletic grounds. You can still see some of the rowhouse-style "piano houses" that he constructed on 20th Ave. between Steinway and 41st St.

The world-famous Steinway pianos continue to be manufactured in the same spot, in the same way. The 12,000 parts of the piano range from a 340-lb. plate of cast iron to tiny bits of the skin of a small Brazilian deer. Over 95% of public performances in the U.S. are played on Steinway grands. (Tours Sep.-April on Fri. only; call for more information.) If you're in the area, you can also take a look at the **Steinway House,** 18-33 41st St., the spacious mid-19th-century mansion that belonged to William Steinway, now protected by junkyard dogs.

Heading south of Astoria to Long Island City, you can gain some perspective on Manhattan from **Hunter's Point** on the East River. There, the brand-new **Citicorp**

Building, the tallest building in New York outside of Manhattan, was completed in 1989. (From Astoria, the best option is to take the N line south to Queensboro Plaza and then walk 5 blocks southwest along Jackson Ave. to the Citicorp Bldg. From Manhattan, take the E or F train to 23rd St.-Ely Ave.; you'll come up right in front of the building on 44th Dr.) Its sleek glass exterior hulks over diminutive brick row houses, as if a butter-fingered planning official slipped somewhere, plopping a midtown monolith down on the wrong side of the river.

From the Citicorp Building, go one block south to 45th Ave., turn toward the Manhattan skyline, and walk two blocks. These two blocks, between 23rd and 21st St., are home to the well-kept brownstones of the **Hunter's Point Historic District.** Check out the facing of Westchester stone on the 10 Italianate row houses, rare examples of late 19th-century architecture.

Make a left on 21st St., go three blocks, and you will come to a huge, red, stone Victorian building, at 46-01 21st St. This is the **Institute for Contemporary Art/ PS1** (718-784-2084). The building housed the first public school in Queens; you can still see the word "Girls" cut into the stone lintel above the entrance. To enter the unconventional museum you must be buzzed (in). The partially restored, partially decayed hallways form a maze of empty rooms and makeshift exhibition spaces—sometimes it's hard to tell them apart. The studios of PS1 give homes to artists from all over the world as part of its national and international residence exhibition program. Recent major shows have included "Stalin's Choice," an exhibit of Soviet Social Realist paintings in the USSR from the 1930s, '40s, and '50s, and "Farewell to Bosnia," an exhibition of photographs recently taken in that country. There are three permanent exhibits in the studio wing of the building. Ask a curator to take you up to the roof, where Richard Serra created an untitled piece for the 1976 institute opening. He took an unusual room of exposed beams and bricks and left it completely intact, constructing only a channel in the floor that runs from one corner of the room to the other. Today pigeon droppings complement the piece. Alan Saret's contribution, also designed for the opening, is more accessible (though also somewhat difficult to distinguish from the general decay of the building). Called *Fifth Solar Chthonic Wall Temple,* after an old Blue Öyster Cult song, its walled excavation records the movement of the sun as shadows move around the inside of the third-floor hallway. In James Turrell's well-known *Meeting,* you can sit on high-backed benches in a room where the ceiling rolls back, then watch the skies shift colors at sunset. The design celebrates the interplay between natural and artificial light. The piece reflects Turrell's Quaker background, and, like a Quaker meetinghouse, provides a simple environment for contemplation. *Meeting* opens only at prime sunsetting time for two hours between 5pm and 9pm on weekends. Open by appointment only; call a day ahead. (Museum open Wed.-Sun. noon-6pm. Suggested donation $2.)

Long Island City commands an outstanding view of Manhattan and the East River. To get to the shorefront, walk toward the skyline along 45th Ave. Go right on Vernon Blvd., and then make a left onto 44th Dr. Follow it to the public pier which juts into the river. To your right as you face the river lies the Queensboro Bridge, better known to Simon and Garfunkel fans as the 59th St. Bridge. Directly in front of you, on the southern tip of Roosevelt Island, you can see the romantically turreted ruins of 19th-century hospital facilities. Besides the conventional highlights of the Manhattan skyline (the Art Deco Chrysler Building and the twin towers of the World Trade Center), there is a fine view of the United Nations Complex—the wide gray tower facing out into the river, connected to a smaller domed annex with a satellite dish. The Citicorp Building stands out boldly directly behind you.

■ CENTRAL QUEENS: JAMAICA, ST. ALBANS, AND FOREST PARK

Jamaica, named for the Jameco Indians, lies in the center of Queens and is the heart of the borough's African-American and West Indian community. To get here, take the E, J, or Z train to Jamaica Center. The main strip on Jamaica Ave., stretching between 150th and 168th St., is constantly bustling with activity. The **pedestrian mall** on 165th St. is lined with restaurants selling succulent Jamaican beef patties, stores peddling Malcolm X baseball caps and African clothing, and 30-ft.-tall metal men with arms outstretched.

Like most other northeastern locales, Jamaica has its share of colonial history. The **King Manor Museum,** Jamaica Ave. and 150th St. (718-206-0545), recently renovated, was the colonial residence of King Rufus, signer of the Constitution, one of New York's first senators and the first U.S. ambassador to Great Britain. His son was governor of New York. The house, set in 11-acre King Park, dates back to 1733 and combines examples of Georgian and Federal architecture.

The **Jamaica Arts Center,** 161-04 Jamaica Ave. (718-658-7400) at 161st St., offers changing workshops, as well as frequent visual art exhibitions dealing with aspects of African-American or urban life. Recent exhibits have included the photography collection "African-Americans: A Self-Portrait," and "Interweavings: The Art and Culture of Kenya," by a New York artist who spent six months studying basket weaving in that country. In 1990 the Center was awarded the New York State Governor's Arts Awards by Governor Mario Cuomo, who grew up in Jamaica. (Exhibition space open Mon.-Sat. 9am-5pm. Free.) Next door, the **Jamaica Savings Bank,** at 161-02 Jamaica Ave., is regarded by some as "the finest Beaux Arts building in Queens." Down a few blocks at Jamaica Ave. and 165th St. is the former **Valencia Theater,** now the "Tabernacle of Prayer." It was built in 1929 as one of several atmospheric "Wonder Theaters." While the elders of most religious institutions would probably treat the huge marquee in front with reserve, the Tabernacle's current occupants seem to feel quite lucky to have it. Building open (for the most part) only on Sundays, but a peek into the front lobby will give you the idea.

While the area directly south of downtown Jamaica is fairly barren except for food-processing factories and criminal activity, the middle- and upper-class African-American communities to its southeast are well-kept residential areas with a fair amount of interesting history. After WWII **St. Albans,** the area centered on Linden Blvd. just east of Merrick Blvd., became the home of newly mobile African-Americans, many of whom were empowered by the GI Bill and the work of the NAACP. St. Albans in the 1950s recalled Harlem in the 1920s; jazz greats Count Basie and Fats Waller, as well as James P. Johnson and baseball stars like Jackie Robinson and Roy Campanella, all lived here—mostly in the Addisleigh Park area of western St. Albans. Today, wealthier African-Americans have moved southeast to communities like Laurelton, leaving behind St. Albans's beautiful homes and the West Indian bakeries and restaurants that now flourish in the lively shopping district along Linden Blvd. To get to St. Albans, take the E or J train to Jamaica Center, then the Q4 bus to Linden Blvd.

To the west of Jamaica, **Forest Park** (718-235-0635) is a densely wooded area with miles of park trails, a bandshell, a golf course (718-296-0999), a carousel, baseball diamonds, tennis courts, and horseback riding. If you'd like to rent horses, both Lynne's Riding School (718-261-7679) and Dixie Do Stables (718-263-3500) will oblige you with a guided trail ride. (Both open roughly 8am-7pm; $20/hr.) For information on upcoming park events, call the number above or 718-520-5941. Take the J or Z train to Woodhaven Blvd., or else take the L or M train to Myrtle/Wyckoff Ave., then the Q55 bus.

You can get a little taste of Old New York at the **Queens County Farm Museum** (718-347-3276), 73-50 Little Neck Parkway, in Floral Park on the border of Nassau County. Built by Jacob Adriance in 1772 on 50 acres of land, this is the only working farm of its era that has been restored. Cows, ducks, chickens, and sheep graze here. Take the E or F train to Kew Gdns./Union Turnpike, then the Q46 bus to Little Neck Pkwy. Walk three blocks north. (Farmhouse/museum open Sat.-Sun. noon-5pm. Grounds open 9am-5pm daily. Donations requested.)

■ SOUTHERN QUEENS

The **Jamaica Bay Wildlife Refuge** (718-318-4300), near the town of Broad Channel in Jamaica Bay, is about the size of Manhattan and 10 times the size of Flushing Meadows-Corona Park. The refuge's western half dips into Brooklyn, and the entire place constitutes one of the most important urban wildlife refuges in the U.S., harboring more than 325 species of shore birds, water fowl, and small animals. Lined with benches and birdhouses, the miles of paths around the marshes and ponds resonate to the roar of planes leaving from nearby JFK. Beached wooden rowboats, a trout-mask replica, and the frequent egret or swan make this place a real oasis. Environmental slide shows and tours are available on weekends. (Nature Center open Mon.-Fri. 8:30am-5pm, Sat.-Sun. 8:30am-6pm; free.) To get to the refuge, take the A train to Broad Channel. Walk west along Noel Rd. (which is just in front of the station) to Crossbay Blvd., then turn right and walk about one mile to the center. Alternatively, take the E, F, G, or R line to 74th St.-Roosevelt Ave. in Jackson Heights, then the Q53 express bus to Broad Channel, and follow the walking directions above.

Just south of the refuge lies Rockaway Peninsula, named after a Native American word for "living waters." Here you'll find **Rockaway Beach**, immortalized by the Ramones in one of their formulaic pop-punk tributes. A public beach (718-318-4000) extends from Beach 3rd St. in Far Rockaway to Beach 149th St. in the west, lined by a boardwalk from Beach 3rd St. all the way to Beach 126th St. Between Beach 126th St. and Beach 149th St., the beach is divided between public and smaller, private waterfront areas; no street parking is allowed here during the summer so that the residents of million-dollar homes in Belle Harbor and Neponsit can avoid the riff-raff like us who come to the beach for a little fun and sun. To get to Rockaway Beach, take the A or S train to Beach 105th or 116th St.

Just west of Rockaway Beach (and separated from it by a huge chain-link fence) is **Jacob Riis Park**, part of the 26,000-acre **Gateway National Recreation Area** (718-338-3338), which extends into Brooklyn, Staten Island, and New Jersey. The park was named for Jacob Riis, a photographer and journalist who brought attention to the need for school playgrounds and neighborhood parks in the early 1900s; he persuaded New York City to turn this overgrown beach into a public park. Today the park is lined with its own beauteous beach and boardwalk and contains basketball and handball courts, a golf course, and concession stands. Adjoining the park to the west is **Fort Tilden**, also a part of Gateway, where you can walk through the sand dunes past old Nike missile sites from the Cold War days, as well as the sites of 16-in. shore guns from WWI and WWII, when this was a naval base. To get to Riis Park and Fort Tilden, take the #2 or 5 train to Flatbush Ave., then pick up the Q35 bus on Nostrand Ave. The Q22 bus connects Riis Park to the Beach 116th subway station in Rockaway Park.

■ ■ ■ THE BRONX

The Bronx? No thonx.

—Ogden Nash

The Bronx has long exercised an unhealthy attraction on the American imagination, joined to Detroit, Watts, and Anacostia as a dark specter of urban decay, an apocalyptic city of doom. The reality here sometimes seems to warrant the grim outlook: exiting the subway, one looks out on the far from pacific sight of the bombed-out skeletal remains of cars plastered over with imitation windows—the half-baked efforts of urban planners anxious to conceal obvious systemic decay. The South Bronx *is* a misbegotten tribute to the delusional ambition of the postwar urban empire-builders, who succeeded in providing thousands of units of low-income housing, but only by creating nightmarish prisons of concrete and steel, dense, airless blocks projected upwards into space. But the Bronx is more than the sum of its representations, more than mere blight and phantasmagoric decadence. While the

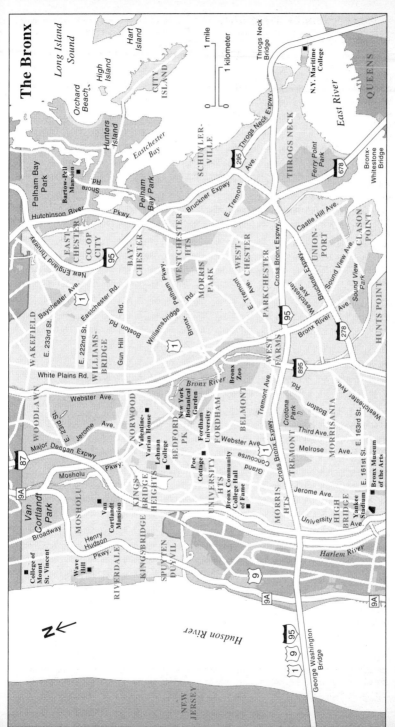

The Bronx

Long Island Sound

Hart Island

High Island

Orchard Beach

CITY ISLAND

Hunters Island

Eastchester Bay

1 mile
1 kilometer

Throgs Neck Bridge

SCHUYLER-VILLE

N.Y. Maritime College

Pelham Bay Park

Bartow-Pell Mansion

Shore Rd

Pelham Bay Park

295 Throgs Neck Expwy

THROGS NECK

Ferry Point Park

678

East River

QUEENS

Hutchinson River Pkwy

Bruckner Expwy

E. Tremont

Bronx-Whitestone Bridge

EAST CHESTER CO-OP CITY

WESTCHESTER HTS

WEST-CHESTER

Castle Hill Ave.

UNION-PORT

CLASON POINT

New England Thruway

95

BAY CHESTER

MORRIS PARK

PARKCHESTER

Cross Bronx Expwy

Bruckner Expwy

Sound View Ave.

Sound View Park

Baychester Ave.

1

Eastchester Rd.

E. Tremont Ave.

Westchester Ave.

HUNTS POINT

WAKEFIELD

E. 233rd St.

E. 222nd St.

Williamsbridge Pelham Pkwy.

Bronx Rd.

95

Bronx River

278

WILLIAMS-BRIDGE

Boston Rd.

Gun Hill Rd.

1

WEST FARMS

895

White Plains Rd.

Webster Ave.

Bronx River

Bronx Zoo

Tremont Ave.

Rd.

Boston

WOODLAWN

NORWOOD

New York Botanical Garden

BELMONT

Crotona Park

Westchester Ave.

Jerome Ave.

E. 233rd St.

Valentine-Varian House

BEDFORD PK

Fordham University

FORDHAM

Webster Ave

Third Ave.

E. 163rd St.

Major Deegan Expwy

87

Lehman College

Poe Cottage

1

Melrose

MORRISANIA

Mosholu Pkwy.

KINGS-BRIDGE HEIGHTS

UNIVERSITY HTS

Grand Concourse

Cross Bronx Expwy

Jerome Ave.

9A

Mosholu

Bronx Community College Hall of Fame

TREMONT

Bronx Museum of the Arts

E. 161st St.

Van Cortlandt Park

MOSHOLU

Van Cortlandt Mansion

MORRIS HTS

HIGH BRIDGE

University Ave.

Yankee Stadium

Broadway

Henry Hudson Pkwy.

KINGSBRIDGE

SPUYTEN DUYVIL

Harlem River

College of Mount St. Vincent

Wave Hill

RIVERDALE

9

9A

9A

N

Hudson River

NEW JERSEY

1 9 95

George Washington Bridge

media presents the Bronx as a crime-ravaged husk, the borough offers its few tourists over 2000 acres of parkland, a great zoo, turn-of-the-century riverfront mansions, and thriving ethnic neighborhoods, including a Little Italy to shame its counterpart to the south.

The only borough on the U.S. mainland, the Bronx took its name from the Bronx River, which in turn took its name from early Dutch settler Jonas Bronck, who claimed the area for his farm in 1636. Until the turn of the century, the area consisted largely of cottages, farmlands, and wild marshes. Then the tide of immigration swelled, bringing scores of Italian and Irish settlers. The flow of immigrants (now Hispanic and Russian) has never stopped.

ORIENTATION

If you're not heading for Yankee Stadium, stay out of the South Bronx unless you're in a car and with someone who knows the area. The northern and eastern parts of the borough are largely middle-class, with single-family houses and duplexes on peaceful, tree-lined streets. Pelham Bay Park, in the northeastern part of the Bronx, is the city's largest park and used to be a private estate owned by the Pell family. In the center of the Bronx, on the banks of the Bronx river, Bronx Park contains the Bronx Zoo and the excellent New York Botanical Garden, with the campus of Fordham University at its western edge. Van Cortlandt Park, in the northwest of the borough, completes the trio of major open spaces. The subway will take you from Manhattan to the Bronx's attractions. The #1, 9, and 4 reach up to Van Cortlandt Park; the C and D lines serve Fordham Rd. and Bedford Park Blvd., near the Botanical Garden; the #2 and 5 skirt Bronx Park and the zoo; and the #6 stretches into Pelham Bay Park. The C, D, and #4 trains whisk fans in and out of Yankee Stadium in the south of the borough. Scarce transfer stations make subway travel within the Bronx often time-consuming. You're usually better off travelling by bus; ask for a bus map at a subway station.

■ BRONX ZOO

The most obvious reason to come to the Bronx is the **Bronx Zoo** (718-367-1010 or 718-220-5100), also known as the New York Zoological Society. The largest urban zoo in the United States, it houses over 4000 animals. While it has some architecturally sound buildings, the animals (and their fans) prefer the 265-acre expanse of natural habitats created for their dwelling pleasure. While the timber rattlesnake has been sentenced to life in the Reptile House, more benign beasts have been loosed into the Zoo's "protected sanctuary;" Indian elephants inhabit the Wild Asia exhibit and white-cheeked gibbons tree-hop in the JungleWorld.

Noteworthy natural habitats include the Himalayan Highlands, home to endangered snow leopards and fiery red pandas; Wild Asia, stalked by rhinoceroses, muntjacs, sambars, nilgais, and rare sika deer; South America, roamed by guanacos, babirusas, and pygmy hippos; and the World of Darkness, which swarms with scores of bats and bushbabies. Kids imitate animals at the hands-on Children's Zoo, where they can climb a spider's web or try on a turtle shell. If you tire of the children, the crocodiles are fed Mondays and Thursdays at 2pm.

You can explore the zoo on foot or ride like the king of the jungle aboard the **Safari Train,** which runs between the elephant house and Wild Asia ($1). Soar into the air for a funky cool view of the zoo from the **Skyfari** aerial tramway that runs between Wild Asia and the Children's Zoo ($2). The **Bengali Express Monorail** glides round Wild Asia (20 min.; $2). If you find the pace too hurried, saddle up a camel in the Wild Asia area ($3). **Walking tours** are given on weekends by the Friends of the Zoo; call 718-220-5142 three weeks in advance to reserve a place. Pamphlets containing self-guided tours are available at the Zoo Center for 75¢. Parts of the zoo close down during the winter (Nov.-April); call for more information. (Open Mon.-Fri. 10am-5pm, Sat.-Sun. 10am-5:30pm; Nov.-Jan. daily 10am-4:30pm.

Admission free on Wednesdays, otherwise $5.75, seniors and children $2. For disabled-access information, call 718-220-5188.)

To reach the zoo by car, take the Bronx River Pkwy. or (from I-95) the Pelham Pkwy. By subway take the #2 or 5 to E. Tremont Ave.-West Farms Sq. and walk four blocks north up Boston Rd. to the zoo entrance. Alternatively, take the D express to Fordham Rd., then the Bx12 bus to Southern Blvd. Walk east on Fordham Rd. to the Rainey Gate entrance. The express BxM11 bus leaves from Madison Ave. in Midtown for the Bronxdale entrance to the zoo ($3.75 each way) and runs back down the east side of Manhattan; call 718-652-8400 for details.

■ CENTRAL BRONX: NEW YORK BOTANICAL GARDEN AND ENVIRONS

North across East Fordham Rd. from the zoo sprawls the labyrinthine **New York Botanical Garden** (718-817-8705). Snatches of forest and virgin waterways allow you to imagine the area's original landscape. The 250-acre garden, one of the world's outstanding horticultural preserves, serves as both a research laboratory and a plant and tree museum. Scope out the 40-acre hemlock forest kept in its natural state, the Peggy Rockefeller Rose Garden, the T.H. Everett Rock Garden and waterfall, the Native Plant Garden, and a Snuff Mill reincarnated as a café. At the westernmost tip of the garden stands the **Enid A. Haupt Conservatory,** built in 1902 to resemble the Great Palm House at Kew Gardens in England. (Conservatory open Tues.-Sun. 10am-5pm. Admission $3.50, seniors, students, and children $1.25. Free Sat. 10am-noon.) Tours of the conservatory take place year-round on weekends from 11am to 4pm, departing from the Palm Court. On weekends from April through October, tours sweep the garden grounds at 1pm and 3pm, departing from the steps of the Visitor Information Center. If you go exploring by yourself, get a garden map; it's a jungle out there for the mapless. The three-mile perimeter walk skirts most of the major sights. (Garden grounds open Tues.-Sun. 10am-7pm; Nov.-March 10am-6pm. Suggested donation $5, seniors, students, and children $3. Parking $4. Call 718-817-8705 for information.) If you're driving, the garden is easily reached via the Henry Hudson, Bronx River, or Pelham parkways. By subway, take the D or #4 to Bedford Park Blvd. Walk eight blocks east or take the Bx26 bus to the garden. The Metro-North Harlem line goes from Grand Central Station to Botanical Garden Station, which lies right outside the main gate (call 718-532-4900 for details).

Fordham University (718-817-1000), begun in 1841 by John Hughes as St. John's College, has matured into one of the nation's foremost Jesuit schools. Robert S. Riley built the campus in classic collegiate Gothic style in 1936. It spans 80 fenced acres on Webster Ave. between E. Fordham Rd. and Dr. Theodore Kazimiroff Blvd. (Subway: C or D to Fordham Rd.)

Traditional immigrant cultures thrive in the Bronx, away from Manhattan's fervid glare. One of the more celebrated communities lies south of Fordham U. in **Belmont,** the uptown "Little Italy." In this neighborhood of two-story rowhouses and byzantine alleyways you'll find some of the best Italian food west of Naples. Outside the **Church of Our Lady of Mt. Carmel,** at 187th St. and Belmont Ave., stand a pair of ecclesiastical shops where you can buy a statuette of your favorite saint. The portable martyrs come in all sizes and every color of the rainbow. Arthur Avenue itself is home to some of the best homestyle southern Italian cooking in the world. At **Dominick's,** between 186th and 187th, boisterous crowds at long communal tables put away pasta without recourse to ordering, prices, or menus. For the same dish on three different days you may pay three different prices, but you'll never leave kvetching (see Eating & Drinking: Bronx). (Subway: C or D to Fordham Rd.)

The enthusiastic Bronx Historical Society maintains the **Edgar Allan Poe Cottage** (718-881-8900), built in 1812 and furnished in the 1840s. The morbid writer and his tubercular wife lived spartanly here at 2640 Grand Concourse off Kingsbridge Rd. (5 blocks west of Fordham U.) from 1846 until 1848. Here Poe wrote *Annabel Lee, Eureka,* and *The Bells,* a tale about the neighboring bells of Fordham. The museum displays a slew of Poe's manuscripts and other macabrabilia. (Open Wed.-Fri. 9am-5pm, Sat. 10am-4pm, Sun. 1-5pm. Call in advance for a tour. Admission $2. Subway: D or #4 to Kingsbridge Rd.)

The **Herbert H. Lehman College** (718-960-8000), is at Jerome Ave. and E. 198th St., three blocks west and two long blocks north of the Poe House. Founded in 1931 as Hunter College, it is a fiefdom in the CUNY empire. The U.N. Security Council met in the gymnasium building in 1946. In 1980, the Lehmans endowed the first cultural center in the Bronx, the **Lehman Center for the Performing Arts,** on the Bedford Park Blvd. West side of campus; the center is a 2300-seat concert hall, experimental theater, recital hall, library, dance studio, and art gallery in one. (Subway: #4 to Bedford Park Blvd.-Lehman College.) One block up through Harris Park, the **Bronx High School of Science** is an unlikely center of academic excellence. The school has produced several Nobel Prize-winning scientists.

At Bronx Community College's **Hall of Fame for Great Americans,** at Martin Luther King Jr. Blvd. and W. 181st St. (718-220-6003), gape at the granite busts of 102 great Americans set on beds of granite and weeds. Predictably, the ubiquitous McKim, Mead, and White designed this turn-of-the-century hall, owned of the City University of New York. (Open daily 9am-5pm. Free. Subway: #4 to Burnside Ave. See Museums.)

■ NORTHERN BRONX: VAN CORTLANDT PARK

Van Cortlandt Park (718-430-1890), the city's third-largest jolly green giant, spreads across 1146 acres of ridges and valleys in the northwest Bronx. The slightly grungy park contains golf courses, tennis courts, baseball diamonds, soccer, football, and cricket fields, kiddie recreation areas, and a large swimming pool. The park's **special-events office** (718-430-1848) can tell you about the many concerts and sports activities that take place during the warmer months. Van Cortlandt Lake teems with bemused fish; big rocks and stone formations speak volumes about the park's fiery prehistoric origins. Hikers have plenty of clambering options. The **Cass Gallagher Nature Trail** in the park's northwestern section leads to rock outcroppings from the last ice age and to damp corners with an assortment of the park's little creatures. The **Old Putnam Railroad Track,** once the city's first rail link to Boston, now leads past the quarry that supplied the marble for Grand Central Station. The **Indian Field recreation area** was laid on top of the burial grounds of pro-rebel Stockbridge Indians ambushed and massacred by British troops during the Revolutionary War.

In the southwest of the park stands the **Van Cortlandt House** (718-543-3344), a national and city landmark built in 1748 by the prominent political clan that divided their time between politics and farming. It's the oldest building in the Bronx. George Washington made frequent visits here, including his 1781 meeting with Rochambeau to determine the final strategy of the Revolutionary War. George began the triumphant march into New York City from here in 1783. Vague British nobility, aristocratic French, solitary Hessians, and continental Americans all showed up with their forces for the brief, historic sojourn. Musty masonry and peeling paint add a few flakes of authenticity to this repeatedly restored mansion. The strange *gorbels* above the windows reveal the Dutch heritage of the builder; grimacing countenances like these showed their faces frequently in Holland but rarely in the New World. The house also has the oldest dollhouse in the U.S. (Mansion open Tues.-Fri. 10am-3pm, Sat.-Sun. 11am-4pm. Admission $2, students and seniors $1.50. The park and the mansion can both be reached by subway—#1 or 9 to 242nd St.)

En route to Van Cortlandt Park stop off at **Manhattan College** (718-920-0100), a 100-year-old private liberal arts institution that began as a high school. Starting from the corner of Broadway and 242nd St. (Subway: #1 or 9 to 242nd St.), take 242nd up, up, *up*hill. As you scale the tortuous mound past Irish pubs and Chinese laundromats, watch for the college's pseudo-Federalist red-brick buildings and chapel. The campus sprawls over stairs, squares, and plateaus like a life-sized game of

Chutes and Ladders. The second staircase on campus brings you to a sheer granite bluff crowned with a kitsch plaster Madonna, a likely kidnapping victim for a suburban garden. Hardy souls who attain the campus peaks can take in a cinemascopic view of the Bronx. Continue up the hill to the sheltered **Fieldston School,** featured in Francis Ford Coppola's short film in *New York Stories.*

Wave Hill, 675 W. 252nd St., a pastoral estate in Riverdale, commands an astonishing view of the Hudson and the Palisades. Samuel Clemens (a.k.a. Mark Twain), Arturo Toscanini, and Teddy Roosevelt all resided in the Wave Hill House. Donated to the city over 20 years ago, the estate currently offers concerts and dance amidst its greenhouses and spectacular formal gardens. Picnic on the splendid lawns. (Gardens open June to mid-Oct. Tues. and Thurs.-Sun. 9am-5:30pm, Wed. 9:30am-dusk; mid-Oct. through May Wed.-Sun. 10am-4:30pm. Weekend admission $4, seniors and students $2.) Wave Hill is a hilly but pleasant half-hour walk from the 242nd St. subway. Alternatively, take the Amtrak Metro North line to Riverdale Station.

The 1758 **Valentine-Varian House** (718-881-8900), the second-oldest building in the Bronx (Van Cortlandt got there first), saw light action during the Revolution. It has since become the site of the **Museum of Bronx History,** which is run by the Bronx County Historical Society. The museum, at Bainbridge Ave. and E. 208th St., functions as the borough archive, profiling its heritage. The house has retained a few period furnishings but negligible Revolutionary ambience. (Open Sat. 10am-4pm, Sun. 1-5pm, otherwise by appointment. Admission $2. Subway: D to 205th St., or #4 to Mosholu Pkwy.)

■ NORTHEAST BRONX: PELHAM BAY PARK

Pelham Bay Park has over 2100 acres of green saturated with playing fields, tennis courts, picnic spaces, wildlife sanctuaries, a beach, and even training grounds for the city's mounted police force. The omniscient Park Rangers lead a variety of history- and nature-oriented walks for creatures great and small (call 718-430-1890 for a schedule). Inside the park, the Federalist **Bartow-Pell Mansion Museum** (718-885-1461) sits among prize-winning formal gardens landscaped in 1915. The interior decorator doted on the Empire/Greek-Revival style. (Open Wed. and Sat.-Sun. noon-4pm. Closed three weeks in Aug. Admission $2, seniors and students $1. Subway: #6 to Pelham Bay Park.)

For a whiff of New England in New York, visit **City Island,** a community of century-old houses and sailboats complete with a shipyard. The **North Wind Undersea Museum** (718-885-0701) can chart a tour better than Julie McCoy any day. The ancient mariner's heart will be warmed at this museum at the sight of a 100-year-old tugboat, antiquated diving gear, exotic sea shells, and bundles of whale bones. The Museum is also home of "Physty the Whale," a life-size replica of the first beached whale ever to be saved by humankind (open Mon.-Fri. 10am-5pm). Take #6 to Pelham Bay Park and then board the #21 bus outside the station. Get off at the first stop on City Island; the museum is on your left.

■ SOUTH BRONX

Sports fans and stair-master freaks will enjoy a visit to historic **Yankee Stadium,** on E. 161st St. at River Ave. Built in 1923, frequent remodeling has kept the aging stadium on a par with more recent constructions. The Yankees played the first night game here in 1946, and the first message scoreboard tallied points here in 1954. Inside the 11.6-acre park (the field measures only 3.5 acres), monuments honor Yankee greats Lou Gehrig, Joe DiMaggio, and Babe Ruth. Besides dispensing pleasure to sports fans, Yankee Stadium provides much-needed income to area merchants struggling to stay afloat in the nation's poorest Congressional district. Controversial Yankees owner George Steinbrenner has announced a possible abandonment of The-House-That-Ruth-Built in the South Bronx for the more convenient and tourist-friendly confines of Midtown Manhattan. Needless to say, the migration would hurt more than just a classic stadium and those who love it. (Subway: C, D, or #4 to 161st St.)

The **Bronx Museum of the Arts** (718-681-6000), at 161th St. and Grand Concourse near Yankee Stadium, is another good reason to go south. Set in the rotunda of the Bronx Courthouse, the museum exhibits works by old masters as well as local talent. (Open Wed.-Fri. 10am-5pm, Sat.-Sun. 1-6pm. Suggested admission $3, students $2, seniors $1; Sundays free.)

■■■ STATEN ISLAND

In 1524, 32 years after Columbus patented the New World, a Florentine named Giovanni Da Verrazano sailed into New York Harbor and made history as the godfather of what would later be known as Staten Island. The name (originally Staaten Eylandt) comes courtesy of Henry Hudson, who plied his sail in the neighboring waters while on a voyage for the Dutch East India Company in 1609. In 1687, the sportive Duke of York sponsored a sailing contest, generously offering Staten Island as the prize. Manhattan won and has since called the island its own.

For the first 440 years after it was settled by Europeans, the only way to get from the island to New York proper was by boat. In 1713, a public ferry started running from Staten Island to the rest of the city. In spite of the new link, Staten Islanders still tended to look west to New Jersey, just a stone's throw away across the Arthur Kill, rather than north and east to the city. In 1964, builder Othmar "George Washington Bridge" Amman spanned the gap between Staten Island and Brooklyn with a 4260-ft. suspension baby, the **Verrazano-Narrows Bridge.** Visible from virtually everywhere on the island, the bridge has the distinction of being the world's second-longest suspension bridge, outspanned only by the Humber Bridge in England. Amman's construction narrowly beats out San Francisco's Golden Gate Bridge for the honor by 60 ft.

Even though traffic now flows more easily between Manhattan and Staten Island (via Brooklyn), the two boroughs exchange little save the barest cordiality. In recent years Staten Islanders have unsuccessfully lobbied borough, city, and state governments to have Staten Island declared an independent municipality. Many resent the higher taxes they pay to subsidize the poorer neighborhoods in New York's other boroughs. Manhattanites tend to lump Staten Island with New Jersey; most only go to there in order to ride the ferry round-trip (without getting off) or to take driving tests (the waiting list for appointments is shorter than in Manhattan and the driving substantially less frenetic). And it's not that they're wrong, exactly—much of the island is depressed, dirty, and in a sad state of decay—but that only makes the few fine attractions the island does offer seem even better for being undervalued. Snug Harbor is an oasis, the Tibetan Museum truly serene, and the Staten Island Mall belongs so solidly to the great American tradition of mall-dom that it's bound to make anyone visiting from the nation's heartland feel right at home.

To get to the **ferry terminal** (718-390-5253 for ferry info.) in Manhattan, take the #1 or 9 train to South Ferry (or take the N or R to Whitehall, then walk west about 3 blocks). Don't stop to wonder why the ferry ride to Staten Island is free and the ride back costs 50¢ (apparently they're not worried that you'll rent a car and drive back through Brooklyn just to spite them). Instead, take in the splendid breeze and the famous views that the ferry ride affords. Look at the lower Manhattan skyline, Ellis Island, the Statue of Liberty, and Governor's Island. The views here might be the best in the city, the frequent prey of postcard photographers and tourism bureaus. New York's scale is imprinted even on the boats and tankers, which are *huge*, and on the giant industrial structures lining the horizon, shaped like headless giraffes. If you can arrange it, don't miss the 30-minute ride at night; the ferry runs 24 hrs.

The **Tourist Information Center** recently burned down and has yet to be replaced. For now, call the **Staten Island Chamber of Commerce,** 130 Bay St. (718-727-1900), for assistance (open Mon.-Fri. 8:30am-5pm). You can also call the Staten Island Institute of Arts and Sciences Arts Hotline (727-1135) to learn about

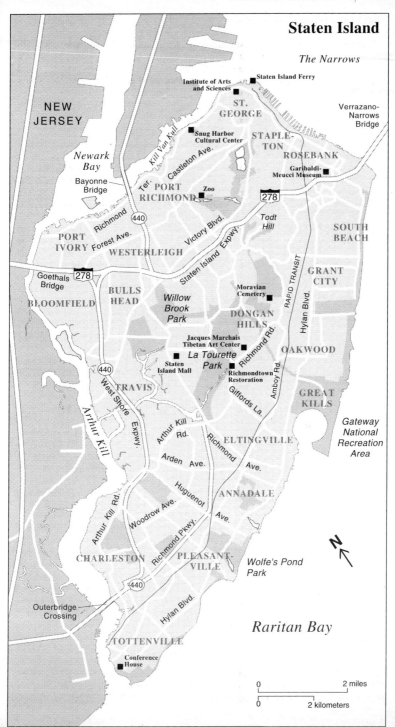

STATEN ISLAND

Staten Island

The Narrows

NEW JERSEY

Institute of Arts and Sciences

Staten Island Ferry

ST. GEORGE

Verrazano-Narrows Bridge

Snug Harbor Cultural Center

STAPLE-TON

Newark Bay

Castleton Ave.

ROSEBANK

Kill Van Kull

Bayonne Bridge

Ter.

PORT RICHMOND

Zoo

Garibaldi-Meucci Museum

278

Todt Hill

Victory Blvd.

SOUTH BEACH

Richmond

Forest Ave.

440

PORT IVORY

WESTERLEIGH

Staten Island Expwy.

RAPID TRANSIT

GRANT CITY

Goethals Bridge

278

BULLS HEAD

Willow Brook Park

Moravian Cemetery

DONGAN HILLS

Hylan Blvd.

BLOOMFIELD

Jacques Marchais Tibetan Art Center

Richmond Rd.

OAKWOOD

440

Staten Island Mall

La Tourette Park

Richmondtown Restoration

Amboy Rd.

GREAT KILLS

TRAVIS

West Shore Expwy.

Arthur Kill Rd.

Giffords La.

Richmond

ELTINGVILLE

Gateway National Recreation Area

Arthur Kill

Arden Ave.

Ave.

Huguenot

ANNADALE

Woodrow Ave.

Ave.

Richmond Pkwy.

CHARLESTON

PLEASANT-VILLE

Wolfe's Pond Park

440

Hylan Blvd.

Outerbridge Crossing

Raritan Bay

TOTTENVILLE

Conference House

N

| 0 | 2 miles |
| 0 | 2 kilometers |

regional art and exhibitions. Because of the hills and the distances (and some potentially dangerous neighborhoods in between), it's a bad idea to *walk* from one site to
the next. Make sure to plan your excursion with the bus schedule in mind; it's available at the New York Convention and Visitor's Bureau (see Practical Information),
or at the South Ferry subway stop in Manhattan.

Just up the hill from the terminal, the second street on the right is Stuyvesant
Place; follow it as it wraps up to the right, leading to the site of the imposing Federalist **Town Hall** and its clocktower. Next door you will find the **College of Staten
Island,** the local colony of the City University of New York system. Its main building, a white institutional construction in the style of a Florentine *palazzo,* makes an
attractive landmark inside and out. The terraced garden in back offers an eye-widen-
ing view of the harbor (as well as the chance to tweak the cheeks of Frank D. Paulo,
depicted there in a sculpture bearing the ambiguous inscription "A Public Man").

One block further west at 75 Stuyvesant Pl., on the far corner of Wall St., are the
galleries of the **Staten Island Institute of Arts and Sciences** (718-727-1135), which
feature displays of natural history and fine arts as well as nifty dioramas on Native
American life. The upstairs galleries feature temporary exhibits whose subjects vary
widely, from the Staten Island Juried Art Exhibition to the "Fantastic World of Butterflies." Guided tours of galleries are offered on the third Monday of each month at
2pm (free with suggested donation). (Open Mon.-Sat. 9am-5pm, Sun. 1-5pm. Suggested donation $2.50; seniors, students, and children under 12 $1.50.)

At 1000 Richmond Terrace lies the **Snug Harbor Cultural Center** (718-448-
2500), 83 sprawling, green, and amazingly well-kept acres of national Historic Landmark District. Founded in 1801, Sailors's Snug Harbor was the first maritime hospital
and home for retired sailors in the U.S. It was purchased by the City of New York in
1976 and now includes 28 historic buildings scattered over wonderfully placid and
unpopulated parkland. The Center provides space for contemporary art, theatre,
recitals, outdoor sculpture, and concerts. Get here by taking the S40 bus from the
ferry terminal.

Once on the grounds, head toward the main cluster of buildings and follow the
signs pointing you to the Visitor's Center, where you can pick up a map of the
grounds and a schedule of the day's exhibitions and events (free tours of the
grounds offered Sat.-Sun. 2pm). At the **Newhouse Center for Contemporary Art,**
you'll be privy to the work of emerging and mid-career artists working in all media
(open Wed.-Sun. noon-5pm; suggested donation $2). The **Staten Island Botanical
Garden** (718-273-8200), also at the Center, tends a striking Butterfly Garden among
the other beds of lilies, lilacs, sunflowers, and snapdragons on its 28 peaceful acres
(open daily dawn to dusk; tours available by appointment). Another of the Center's
tenants is the **Staten Island Children's Museum** (718-273-2060), which offers funky
interactive exhibits. The recent "Living with Water" exhibit was so encouraging of
the hands-on ethic that it offered kids-sized rubber raincoats and rainpants for protection. "Science on Stage" performances by staff members run on weekends
throughout the year. (Open July to mid-Sept. Tues.-Sun. 11am-5pm; mid-Sept. to July
Tues.-Sun. noon-5pm. Admission $3.) Also be sure to call for information regarding
outdoor performances in the Center's South Meadow; 1994 performances included
a Benny Goodman Tribute Orchestra, as well as Arlo Guthrie (tickets $15 each
show). Free family concerts are also held each Sunday at the Gazebo.

· Hungry? Grab a bite at **Melville's Cafe** (718-816-0011), located down the hall
from the Visitors Center (open Wed.-Fri. 11am-2pm, weekends noon-3pm), which
serves cafeteria-style lunch for under $5. Or walk out of the Harbor, down Rich-
mond Terr. less than ¼-mile, and try eating outdoors at **R.H. Tugs Restaurant,**
1115 Richmond Terr. (718-447-6369). Enjoy a waterfront lunch with flowers on the
tables. Stick to the tasty sandwiches and salads ($4-7), or try the crab cakes ($5.25).
Entrees are pricier at $9-15, but alcohol from the bar is surprisingly cheap (12-oz.
domestic draft $1.50). (Open Sun.-Thurs. 11am-midnight, Fri.-Sat. 11am-1am.) Bud-
geteers with only spare change should opt for the **Getty Mart Gas Station and
Convenience Store,** right next door to Tugs, which contains a deli dear to the

locals and serves only Boar's Head cold cuts. Sandwiches under $5, outdoor tables with a splendid view of the parking lot. (Open daily 6am-10pm.)

For something a little more entertaining, head three blocks back toward the ferry from Snug Harbor and turn right on Lafayette Ave. One block up you'll find **Adobe Blues,** 63 Lafayette Ave. at Fillmore St. (718-720-2583), which features Southwestern cuisine and the second-largest selection of beers in all of NYC—more than 230 (see Eating and Drinking: Bars). Lunch entrees are $4-7, and dinner entrees are $8-13. (Lunch served Mon.-Sat. 11:30am-5pm; dinner nightly 5-10:30pm; late-night menu available. Bar open Sun.-Thurs. 11:30am-midnight, Fri.-Sat. 11:30am-2am.)

The **Staten Island Zoo** (718-442-3101), in Barrett Park at Broadway and Clove Rd., has moved all of its big animals permanently to Mexico (recent visitors have remarked on a giant sucking sound). You can still toy with some of the world's finest reptiles for $3, $2 for children under 11. (Open daily 10am-4:45pm.) To reach the zoo, take the S48 bus from St. George Terminal to Broadway, and then walk 2½ blocks south.

Designed like a small Tibetan mountain temple, the **Jacques Marchais Museum of Tibetan Art,** 338 Lighthouse Ave. (718-987-3500, 718-987-3478 for recorded schedule) displays one of the finest collections of Tibetan art in the Western hemisphere (see Museums). To reach the Museum, take the S74 bus from the ferry to Lighthouse Ave., walk up Lighthouse Ave. and follow it as it bends to the right up the fairly steep hill; the Museum rests a few yards beyond the hill's crest.

Historic Richmond Town, 441 Clarke Ave., a huge museum complex, documents three centuries of Staten Island and its culture and history. Reconstructed 17th- to 19th-century dwellings are populated by "inhabitants," costumed master craftspeople and their apprentices. Thanks to budget cuts, only 10 of these buildings, spread over 100 acres, are permanently open to the public. Head for the **Voorlezer's House** (1695), the oldest surviving elementary school in the U.S. (also a church and home), the **General Store** (1840), and an 18th-century farmhouse. The buildings are open to the public rotate, so call in advance to find out what is open, as well as to find out about the "living history" events, which take place on weekends throughout the summer. Tours of Richmond Town are sometimes available with advance notice. Call 718-351-1611 for tours or information on special events. (Open July-Aug. Wed.-Fri. 10am-5pm, Sat.-Sun. 1-5pm; Sept.-Dec. Wed.-Sun. 1-5pm. Admission $4; seniors, students, and children 6-18 $2.50.) To get here, take a 40-min. ride on the S74 bus from the ferry terminal.

The Vanderbilt saga comes to an end at the **Moravian Cemetery,** on Richmond Rd. at Todt Hill Rd. in Donegan Hills. Commodore Cornelius Vanderbilt and his clan lie in this ornate crypt, built in 1886 by Richard Morris Hunt. Central Park creator Frederick Law Olmsted contributed the landscaping. Alas, the crypt can be viewed only from the outside. Adjacent to the cemetery is the 72-acre **High Rock Park Conservation Center** (718-667-6042), with miles of well-marked trails perfect for an afternoon stroll. (Center open daily 9am-5pm; grounds open dawn to dusk; tours Sunday at 2pm. Call in advance.) To get to the Center, take the SIRTOA subway train (takes MTA tokens) from the ferry terminal station to the New Dorp station; walk northwest up New Dorp four blocks and make a left on Richmond Rd.; bear right and stay on Richmond a few blocks ahead where it forks; at the next light, go right onto Rockland Ave.; walk two blocks and go right onto Nevada; follow Nevada all the way to its end. The walk should take 20-25 minutes.

In the mid-1800s, Giuseppe Garibaldi, an Italian patriot and mastermind of Italy's reunification, took refuge on the island following his defeat at the hands of Napoleon III. He settled in an old farmhouse in Rosebank and proceeded to amass enough memorabilia to make the place into a museum: the **Garibaldi-Meucci Museum,** 420 Tompkins Ave. (718-442-1608; open Tues.-Sun. 1-5pm; free). At one time the house belonged to Antonio Meucci, the less-than-celebrated inventor of the telephone (he had developed his first working model by 1851 and finally received a U.S. patent caveat in 1871, but died before being recognized as the inventor—luckily for Alexander Graham Bell). To get here, take the SIRTOA subway train from the ferry terminal station three stops to Clifton Station. Walk west three blocks on Vanderbilt Ave. to Tompkins Ave. and turn left; the museum is a few blocks ahead.

The only peace conference ever held between British forces and American rebels took place in Staten Island in the **Conference House** (718-984-2086). At the summit on Sept. 11, 1776, British commander Admiral Lord Howe met with three Continental Congress representatives—Benjamin Franklin, John Adams, and Edward Rutledge. Located at the foot of Hyland Blvd. in Tottenville, the house has become—what else?—a National Historic Landmark. Inside, you can see period furnishings and refresh your knowledge of Revolutionary War minutiae. (Admission $2, seniors and children under 13 $1. Guided tours by appointment Wed.-Sun. 1-4pm.) To reach the Conference House, take the S78 bus to the last stop on Craig Ave. and walk west one block farther on Hylan Blvd.; make a right on Satterlee St.; the Conference House is about 100 ft. ahead on the left.

■■■ HOBOKEN, NJ

Hoboken could in some ways be called the sixth borough of Manhattan, or even an extension of downtown Manhattan. Its linkage to the downtown scene is both physical, with the 10-minute, $1 PATH train ride across the Hudson, and cultural, with its shelter for the artsy, bohemian, 20-something set. Right across the river from downtown Manhattan, Hoboken boasts a beautiful view of the New York skyline; when Jerry Brown made his ill-fated run for President, he purposely came to Hoboken to announce his candidacy so that he could have the skyline behind him. Hoboken also boasts a bit of historical significance: Frank Sinatra and baseball were both born here. But Hoboken is presently very much an icon of the '90s—famous for being the home of a young, hip, urbane slacker crowd ("hussies"?) that followed Greenwich Village artists here from Manhattan because of the lower rents and close proximity to downtown. Following the cycles of urban cultural ecology, yuppies have started to crowd out the bohemians, but the gentrification is far from complete.

Hoboken's contributions to the alternative music scene are well-known in the New York area. Maxwell's (see Entertainment and Nightlife: Music) often features the best of the indie scene, and Pier Platters, on the other end of town, hawks its wares (see Shopping: Record Stores).

Today Hoboken is faced with unique problems, primarily centered around its increasing reputation as a party town for Generation X. Many of the residents move out once they de-slack, to counties with better schools and more suburban amenities (the average age here is 25). And the bar scene that emerged to serve the local crowd has recently begun to attract hordes of heavy-drinking frat-boy types, seen as a nuisance by many 'Bokenites. The City Council, tired of hearing long-time residents complain of rowdiness and public urination, and ostensibly worried about incoming World Cup crowds, ruled in June 1994 that all bars must close at 1am. But those crowds never appeared, and businesses all over felt the harsh blow. This may affect the scene dramatically; many bars, including the venerable Maxwell's, have been talking about moving out. The City Council promptly responded with a "one-way" policy, allowing bars to stay open until 3am but forbidding them to allow entry after 1am. The long-term equilibrium between the old and new Hoboken has yet to be worked out. For now, though, Hoboken is a great place to be 25 and disaffected—to drink and rent until you get bored.

Hoboken is home to 33,000 people, a good majority of whom are from 25 to 30 years old. The city is laid out in a grid; the east-west streets are (from south to north) Newark St., 1st St., 2nd St.—all the way up one mile to 14th St. The cross streets of note are River Rd. (a.k.a. Frank Sinatra Rd.), Hudson St., Washington St., Bloomfield St., and Willow St. Traipse up Washington St. for most of the action in Hoboken, but the streets around the PATH station and from 1st to 4th St. bustle with activity as well. Be careful crossing the streets, though, as there are no crosswalks, and drivers here are even less friendly than those in the City.

To get to Hoboken, take the B, D, F, N, Q, or R train to 34th St., then the PATH train ($1) to the 1st stop in Hoboken. (The PATH train also leaves from the 23rd and 14th St. stations of the F train, as well as from its own stations at 9th St./Sixth Ave. and Christopher St./Greenwich St.)

From the PATH station, turn to your right, and you'll see the **Erie-Lackawanna Plaza.** This station has been in a number of movies (no doubt because of the spectacular view), including *On the Waterfront* and Woody Allen's *Stardust Memories.* In the summer, the plaza features free movies.

From here, walk the other direction along Hudson Pl. to Hudson St., take a right, then take a quick left onto Newark St. This area is littered with bars because of its PATH proximity. Two blocks down Newark St., stop by **Pier Platters** and pick up some records. Try the local Bar/None label, where They Might Be Giants got their first deal and where Yo La Tengo started out. (See Shopping: Record Stores.)

Washington Street, the main drag of the city, is just down Newark St. Bars, restaurants, cafés, and realtors make up the bulk of the action here. At 1st and Washington St. sits the **Hoboken City Hall,** which often hosts exhibitions by the Hoboken Historical Society. If you find Hoboken history intriguing, take a peek (201-656-2240; open Mon.-Fri. 9am-4pm).

Cruise on up Washington St. to 4th St. For those exhausted by punk rock and fraternity drinking antics ("Shotgun!"), take a left and walk two blocks to Garden St., and **Church Square Park.** Summer concerts here are much more sedate than the screaming at Maxwell's or the grunting in the bars.

Back on Washington St., walk up to 8th St. and take a right up the very large hill which leads to the campus of the **Stevens Institute of Technology.** Cut through the lawn (pay no mind to the awfully graphic statue of the torch-bearer), and walk to the big cannons overlooking the edge of the hill. This is **Castle Point,** where the view of Manhattan's west side is truly awe-inspiring. You can't see the scurrilous corporate types from this far away, but their buildings look pleasant enough.

Descend the hill, with the frat-houses to your right, and keep on truckin' down Washington St. Brownstones in various shades line the street from 8th St. on up. On the right-hand side at 11th St. is the vaunted **Maxwell's** (see Entertainment and Nightlife: Music). On the left-hand side is a monument to baseball, which was supposedly first played in Hoboken, between the New Yorks and the Knickerbockers in 1846. Down 11th St. to the east, past Maxwell's, lies **Elysian Park,** the field where that legendary game was played. Keep walking north and you'll end up in Weehawken—it's probably best to circle back at around 14th St.

■ NEAR HOBOKEN: JERSEY CITY

Artists, further frustrated by the rising rent rates in Hoboken, recently seem to have found refuge in the urban squalor of Jersey City, conveniently located on the PATH line from the World Trade Center. Jersey City's "scene" manages to stay off the streets; the city is in an economic depression, and most of the artistic settlement is near the Grove St. PATH station. To get to **The Art Center on First,** 111 First St. (201-659-7629), walk up Grove/Manila St., go two blocks past Newark St., and take a left onto First St. The Center features local artists, with an emphasis on hip gender-related stuff. **The Cathedral Art Gallery,** 39 Erie St. (201-451-1074), located in the Grace Church Van Voorst, can also be found a few blocks from the station; walk up Grove/Manila St. past Newark St. to 2nd St., go left one block to Erie St., then go left another block. The gallery features rising artists and music-fests; hours change with the exhibitions. The **Jersey City Museum,** 472 Jersey Ave. (201-547-4514), two blocks up Newark St. from the Grove St. station, shows strong selections from the local scene. (Open Tues., Thurs., and Fri. 10:30am-5pm, Wed. 10:30am-8pm.)

Liberty State Park (201-915-3411) is south of the Grove St. station. It contains a lot of state-run greenery, a science museum, and good views of Ellis Island and the Statue of Liberty. Take the #81 bus from the Hoboken Terminal (check for "Liberty State Park" on the LED board; $1).

Museums

New York has accumulated more stuff in more museums than any other city in the New World. Come witness a culture collecting itself. Swoon under a life-sized replica of a great blue whale at the American Museum of Natural History. Control a 900-ft. aircraft carrier at the Intrepid Sea-Air-Space Museum. Slip into the world of the 2000-year-old Egyptian Temple of Dendur or of Van Gogh's 100-year-old *Café at Arles* at the Metropolitan Museum of Art. Relax alongside Monet's *Water Lilies* at the Museum of Modern Art. Or analyze the question of engendered identity in the contemporary art at the Whitney.

Many New York museums request a donation instead of a fixed admission charge. No one will throw you out or even glare at you for giving less than the suggested donation; more likely, you'll feel slightly cheap and maybe guilty. Enjoy that sneaky feeling. Recently the Met has extended its hours so you can stay longer or take a break and come back for more (always keep your pin). Some museums have weekly "voluntary contribution" (read: free) times.

During the annual **Museum Mile Festival** in June, Fifth Ave. museums keep their doors open until late at night, stage engaging exhibits, involve city kids in mural painting, and fill the streets with music and strolling dog-walkers.

■■■ METROPOLITAN MUSEUM OF ART

In 1866, a group of eminent Americans in Paris enthusiastically received John Jay's proposal to create a "National Institution and Gallery of Art." Under Jay's leadership, the New York Union League Club rallied civic leaders, art collectors, and philanthropists and launched the 1870 opening, where the museum showed its first collection, containing 174 paintings (mostly Dutch and Flemish) and assorted antiquities. A decade later, the Metropolitan Museum settled at its present location in Central Park, on Fifth Ave. and 82nd St. This tiny project has since become a monster, spanning 1.4 million sq. ft. and housing 3.3 million works of art. The Met is a high-culture empire—constantly seeking, seducing, and seizing art objects from everyone and everywhere to display them for its enormous audience.

The museum's building, like the art it holds, is a sort of bridal composite; the old and the new, the borrowed and the blue (-blooded) meet here, in a single structure. Though Frederick Law Olmsted, the designer of Central Park, was peeved at the intrusion of the building onto his landscape, different stages of construction continued for over a century. The original, Gothic-style façade, which can now be seen only over the Lehman Wing on the western side, was replaced 20 years later with a more neoclassical construction. The trend continues today as demands for more space are met and walls are erected in the style of the moment. Recent additions include the glass-enclosed Lila Acheson Wallace Wing and the Cantor Roof Garden, which contains changing sculpture exhibitions in open air.

PRACTICAL INFORMATION AND ORIENTATION
The Met (879-5500) is located at Fifth Ave. and 82nd St. (Subway: #4, 5, or 6 to 86th St.) **Hours** are Sun. and Tues.-Thurs. 9:30am-5:15pm, Fri.-Sat. 9:30am-8:45pm. Due to budget cuts, some of the galleries are open only half-days on Tuesdays, Wednesdays, and Thursdays (call ahead). **Admission** is free to members, as well as to children under 12 accompanied by an adult. Suggested donation is $6 for adults, $3 for seniors and students; if you can stomach the shame, disregard their suggestion and plunk down as little as you like. You do have to pay something, though.

Before subjecting yourself to the moral debate of pay-what-you-wish, stop by the **Visitors Center,** located at the information desk in the Great Hall. Stock up on brochures, and be sure to grab a copy of the floor plan. In the Great Hall, the **Foreign Visitors Desk** distributes maps and brochures and gives assistance in a number of languages. For information on **disabled access,** call Disabled Visitors Services (535-7710); for services for **hearing-impaired visitors,** call 879-0421. **Wheelchairs** are available upon request at coat-check areas.

If you feel like you need special direction, you can rent **recorded tours** of the museum's exhibitions or follow the multilingual tour guides. For tour information go to the Recorded Tour Desk in the Great Hall. **Gallery tours** in English roam daily. Inquire at the Visitors Center for schedules, topics, and meeting places. For recorded information on upcoming **concerts** and **lectures,** call 535-7710. Single tickets go on sale one hour before the event.

The museum's holdings sprawl over three floors. The **ground floor** houses the Costume Institute, European Sculpture and Decorative Arts, the Robert Lehman collection, and the Uris Center for Education, where public lectures, films, and gallery talks take place.

The **first floor** contains the extensive American Wing; the Arms and Armor exhibit; Egyptian Art; more European sculpture and decorative arts; Greek and Roman art; Medieval Art; Art of the Pacific Islands, Africa, and the Americas; the Lila Acheson Wallace Wing with its footloose collection of 20th-century art; plus all the information facilities, shops, and restaurants.

The **second floor** brings you more of the American Wing; Ancient Near Eastern Art; Asian Art; a collection of drawings, prints, and photographs; yet another dose of European painting, sculpture, and decorative arts; a Greek and Roman Art encore; more Islamic art; musical instruments; the second installment of 20th-Century Art; and the R.W. Johnson Recent Acquisitions Gallery.

Don't rush the Metropolitan experience; you could camp out in here for a month. (Two children lived here, in fact, in the children's book *The Mixed-Up Files of Mrs. Basil E. Frankweiler.*) No one ever "finishes" the Met. If you only have a few hours, the Greeks and Egyptians should keep you occupied. Or dip into one of the funkier, smaller collections. If you plan to be in the city for a while, you may want to plan on several short trips to the Met. After a couple hours of nonstop aesthetic bombardment, all the paintings start to look alike anyway.

COLLECTIONS

Many critics have asserted that the Met is nothing more than a homage to Eurocentric imperialism; with the European gallery right smack-dab in the middle, the Americans right next to them, and the non-Western art relegated to the back or the sides. Right as you enter the non-Western wings, poised above the great hall, Perseus hoists the hacked-off head of Medusa (Perseus being your typical dead white male, Medusa hailing from Africa) as a not-so-veiled warning to the less pasty. The European collection is one of the world's best, but take this opportunity to spit in the eye of the oppressor and check out the outstanding non-Western galleries first. Of course, these galleries close Tuesday through Thursday, but don't be thwarted; these collections are possibly even better than the pink and fleshy females being ravaged at the hands of brutal men and beasts in the Euro gallery.

After receiving that M lapel pin, fasten it securely onto your clothing (or the guards won't let you in), and hang a left and cruise by the **Greek and Roman Gallery.** The collection spans several millennia and the sweep of both empires. Cypriot sculpture, Greek vases, Roman busts, and Roman wall-paintings fill the rooms. Don't miss the tiny *Seated Harp-Player,* a simple Cycladic statuette that influenced modern styles. Remarkable amid the virile Greek youths is the second-century BC statue of an old, tired woman strolling to the market—a notable reminder that life in Ancient Greece was not a constant Olympiad.

There will be another museum shop as you leave the Greeks and Romans (there are about five altogether—Hans Haache has done some scathing art works about the Met's shameless marketing of its "priceless" wares), and the museum café (open roughly during museum hours). Pay no mind to the blue-haired ladies sipping coffee ($1) and eating lunch ($13-16); take a right and check out the next set of galleries.

The arts of **Africa,** the **Pacific Islands,** and the **Americas** populate the **Michael C. Rockefeller Wing.** The extensive collection features one of the largest collections of non-Western art in the West, and the view from the windows is lovely as well. Totem poles, boats, ceremonial masks, musical instruments, and sculptures ranging from religious to secular uses fill this spacious and light gallery. The African collection has bronze sculpture from Nigeria and wooden sculpture by the Dogan, Bamana, and Senufo of Mali. From the Pacific comes sculpture from Asmat, the Sepik provinces of New Guinea, and the island groups of Melanesia and Polynesia. Inuit and Native American artifacts tell the other story of the arts of America.

Next door is the **Lila Acheson Wallace Wing** of 20th-century art. Since its inception, the museum has been reluctant to invest in controversial modern art—the Museum of Modern Art (see below) was built to house works that the Metropolitan would not accept. But in 1967, the Met relented, establishing the **Department of 20th-Century Art,** which has since welcomed Picasso, Bonnard, Rothko, and Kandinsky. The Americans flex the most muscle here, with paintings by The Eight, the Modernist Stieglitz Circle, Abstract Expressionists, and color field artists. You may or may not catch the big names, as the displays from the permanent collection are always changing, but the wing always has engaging works.

Going around the crowds (and yet another shop), you should then hit the **European Sculpture Garden.** Marble people and animals in various states of repose and anxiety stand among children and parents in similar states of repose and anxiety.

Through another door is the **European Sculpture and Decorative Arts** department. Containing about 60,000 works, ranging from the early labors of the Renaissance to the early 20th century, the collection covers nine areas: sculpture, woodwork, furniture, ceramics, glass, metalwork, tapestries, and textiles. The Italian sculptures feature della Robbia's blue and white, glazed terra-cotta relief *Madonna and Child* hanging by the admission desk in the Great Hall. French sculptor Carpeaux stands out with *Voolino and his Sons* (1865-67), which illustrates the story of Dante's *Inferno.*

Further inside the department, the **Jack and Belle Linsky Galleries** emphasize precious and luxurious objects. Highlights of the collection include canvases by Lucas Cranach the Elder, Rubens, and Boucher; more than 200 Rococo porcelain figures from such renowned factories as Meissen and Chantilly; and exquisite 18th-century French furniture.

The **Medieval Art** collection is housed in dark and mysteriously damp environs, featuring church paraphernalia, including paintings, stained glass, and a set of gates. The collection is not as large as it could be; the rest of the Met's medieval collection is housed at **The Cloisters,** the Washington Heights branch of the Met (see below).

Straight back from those impressive gates, exit the old Met and enter a new gallery (the old brick exterior is now encased in an elaborate glass space). This little sarcophagus houses the **Robert Lehman Wing.** Opened to the public in 1975, it showcases an extraordinary collection assembled by the acquisitive Lehman clan. Italian paintings from the 14th and 15th centuries flank canvases by Rembrandt, El Greco, and Goya. French painters from the 19th and 20th centuries include Ingrès, Renoir, standard Impressionists, and frivolous Fauves.

From here, head back through Medieval Art, swing over to the left, and start humming the *Battle Hymn of the Republic.* The **American Wing** houses one of the nation's largest and finest collections of American paintings, sculptures, and Native decorative crafts. The paintings cover almost all phases of the history of American art from the late 18th to the early 20th century. You can get some celebrated glimpses of early America in Matthew Pratt's *The American School,* Gilbert Stuart's regal portrait of George Washington, Bingham's pensive *Fur Traders Descending the Mississippi,* and the heroic, if precariously perched, *George Washington Crossing the Delaware* by Emanuel Gottlieb Leutze. Of the 19th-century paintings, the pearl of the collection is Sargent's *Madame X,* a stunning portrait of the notorious

French beauty Mme. Gautreau, who allegedly consumed small doses of arsenic in the fashion of the time to give her skin that delicious, classical, marble-like pallor.

The samples of decorative art date from the early Colonial period to the beginning of the 20th century. Twenty-five period rooms document the history of American interior design. Note the especially fun, sinuously curved Victorian *tête-à-tête*—an "S"-shaped love seat that looks like a pair of Siamese armchairs. Art Nouveau fans will gush at the ample selection of Louis Comfort Tiffany's glasswork, while admirers of American Modernism can pay their respects at the Frank Lloyd Wright Room. The room was ingeniously designed to be an integral and organic part of the natural world outside the windows, an example of Wright's concept of total design.

If you feel like re-enacting Bill and Ted's excellent adventure, you can romp around in the **Arms and Armor** collection, nested just off the American collection. The many sharp, pointy objects (and the glare of the guards) may make you nervous, though.

Around the corner, the **Department of Egyptian Art** occupies the entire northeast wing of the main hall, spanning thousands of years—from 3100 BC to the Byzantine Period (AD 700)—and containing a galaxy of artifacts, from earrings to whole temples. Sun gods now smile upon the Temple of Dendur through a shrine of glass. It looks much as it did back when Isis was worshiped inside. Preserved in its entirety, the temple was a gift from Egypt to the United States in 1965 in recognition of U.S. contributions to the preservation of Nubian monuments. Tons of mummies provide spooky fun for kids young and old. Downstairs is the **Costume Institute.** The wittiest people at the Met work here—in exhibitions about the bra and the waistline, the Institute shows how fashion and society are inextricably intertwined.

Back in the Great Hall, you can go up the huge flight of stairs and read the names of especially rich folks who have endowed $10,000 and over to the Met. Go around the upstairs gift shop and the special exhibition rooms to the Perseus statue and examine the extensive collection of Chinese ceramics lining the Great Hall Balcony. To one side is more Greek and Roman art; on the other, the under-appreciated **Ancient Near Eastern** and **Islamic Art** departments await. The collection of Ancient Near Eastern Art, located on the second floor, features artwork from ancient Mesopotamia, Iran, Syria, Anatolia, and a smattering of other lands, all produced during the period from 6000 BC to the Arab conquest in AD 626. Note that the *Human-Headed Winged Lion,* an Assyrian limestone palace gateway piece, has five legs. Viewed from the front, the beast stands firmly in place; viewed from the side, it appears to stride forward. The model Near Eastern house and the rugs are also eye-catching. In the Islamic Art room behind, you can see an intact mid-14th-century Iranian *mihrab* (a niche in a house of worship that points in the direction of Mecca) covered entirely in blue, glazed ceramic tiles. The tasteful exhibition space enhances the geometric intrigue of the tiles and panel designs.

Back on the Great Hall Balcony, on the right (facing Perseus—don't look at Medusa) lies the **Asian Art** department, with the best collection outside of Asia. Walk through to the new South Asia gallery. The **Florence and Herbert Irving Galleries for the Arts of South and Southeast Asia** opened in April 1994 and feature the rhythmic and contortionist sculpture of Buddhas and *bodhissatras* that this region is known for. Encompassing the entire Southeast Asian peninsula from antiquity to the present, the gallery is arranged chronologically, with a Cambodian Khmer courtyard. Running parallel is the **Ancient Chinese** gallery, with a cute Han-dynasty funerary statuary. Check out the little farmhouse with the pigs.

Down the hall, you can either go straight and examine one of the most extensive collections of Chinese painting in the world, take a left for Japanese prints and paintings (the *ukiyo-e* prints shouldn't be missed), or shop at yet another kiosk. The Chinese department will be putting on a once-in-a-lifetime exhibition in the summer of 1995: Chinese paintings from antiquity to the present, with some of the world's oldest and most treasured works, never before seen together.

Finally, taking up the rest of the second floor, comes the "jewel in the crown" of the Met. Bring along your art anthologies to compare the illustrations with the originals, nearly 3000 of which congregate here in the museum's astounding collection of **European Paintings.** The Italian, Flemish, Dutch, and French schools dominate the collection, but British and Spanish works make cameo appearances.

The Italian collection is particularly strong in paintings from the early Renaissance. A later gem is Bronzino's *Portrait of a Young Man,* one of the greatest works by this master of the Mannerist style. The Spaniards are less numerous, but El Greco and Goya are well represented. Take notice of Goya's allegorical portrait of Don Manuel, a dough-eyed boy in red vestments.

In the Flemish quarters, you'll find Van Eyck's *Crucifixion* and the macabre *Last Judgment,* in which an undernourished Christ presides over the heavens as reptiles munch on writhing sinners in Hades below. The enigmatic Hieronymus Bosch makes a rare American appearance with his *Adoration of the Magi.*

The Dutch make a strong showing, led by Rembrandt, whose most emblematic chiaroscuro canvases converge at the Met: *Flora,* the *Toilet of Bathsheba, Aristotle with a Bust of Homer,* and a *Self Portrait* are all here. The Met is also one of the foremost repositories for the works of the Dutch master of light, Johannes Vermeer. Of fewer than 40 widely acknowledged Vermeer canvases, the Museum can claim five, including the celebrated *Young Woman with a Water Jug,* the *Allegory of Earth,* and the vaguely fetal *Portrait of a Young Woman.*

The French contingent of the European collection may be the most comprehensive section of the museum, spanning the 16th to 19th centuries. The Post-Impressionist trio makes a bang with Cézanne's landscapes and *Card Players,* Van Gogh's *Cypresses* and multi-million-dollar *Irises,* and Gauguin's familiar Tahitian canvases, one of which has an unusual twist. In *La Orana Maria,* Gauguin paints a tropical version of the Annunciation. The name of the painting means "I hail thee, Mary"— the first words of the angel Gabriel at the Annunciation.

Despite the warehouse/showroom feel of the place, the Met is one of the few sights that absolutely must be seen during a trip to New York City. The permanent collection is amazing, and the special exhibitions are also some of the best around.

■■■ MUSEUM OF MODERN ART

The MoMA commands one of the world's most impressive collections of Postimpressionist and 20th-century art. Founded in 1929 by scholar Alfred Barr in response to the Met's wariness of cutting-edge work, the museum originally took a maverick stand. It first took up quarters in a Fifth Ave. office building, and the artists on whom its first exhibit focused—Cézanne, Gauguin, Seurat, Van Gogh—were virtually unheard of in the U.S. But as the ground-breaking works of 1900 to 1950 have become accepted masterpieces, the MoMA has shifted from revolution to institution, telling the more or less completed story of the Modernist revolt against Renaissance ways of seeing. Temporary exhibits keep the museum-goer posted on current developments, but little can overshadow the permanent displays.

Cesar Pelli's 1984 glass additions to the 1939 museum building doubled the gallery space and now flood the halls with natural light. The information desk, straight ahead as you enter, dispenses interesting free brochures as well as two printed guides ($2) that connect and contextualize the works in the permanent collection. Past the admission desk lies the Abby Aldrich Rockefeller Sculpture Garden, an expansive patio with a fountain, a drooping willow, and a world-class assemblage of modern sculpture, featuring works by Matisse, Picasso, and Henry Moore. Rodin's tormented, ultramasculine Balzac overshadows its neighbors; the roughly finished, oversize bronze was rejected by Parisians, who expected a more conventionally heroic statue. **Summergarden,** a museum tradition in which Juilliard School affiliates use the garden to present free avant-garde music, is presented here every July and August (see Classical Music).

To the right as you come in from the sculpture garden, a small space presents changing exhibitions by contemporary artists. Works on display have included the singular greeting cards of Erika Rothenberg ("SURPRISE! Our nation has just declared war on your nation!") and, more recently, an exhibit entitled "Masterpieces from the David and Peggy Rockefeller Collection: Manet to Picasso," which featured works by Derain, Braque, and Matisse, as well as the two eponymous artists. To the left of the sculpture garden as you face it from the main hall, the glass-walled **Education Center** shows a few films and posts a schedule of gallery talks. Of greatest interest are the educational videos shown in conjunction with current special exhibitions. On the opposite side of the sculpture garden is the overpriced but crowded **Garden Café.** Take the escalator downstairs to still more temporary shows in the Theater Gallery and to foreign and domestic art films in the **Roy and Niuta Titus theaters.** (For information on screenings, free with the price of admission, see Entertainment and Nightlife: Movies.)

The permanent display of paintings and sculptures, MoMA's core and *raison d'être,* begins on the second floor. The sequence of works in the numbered galleries follows the basic chronology of artistic production in the West from the origins of so-called Modernism—seen in the works of Paris Post-Impressionists—to the cold masterworks of 1970s New York minimalism. The slide-show-quality comprehensiveness of MoMA's collections can provoke an open-mouthed *déjà vu;* these are the originals that inspire virtually all lectures on modern art, and viewers will probably recognize at least one work in each room. Especially strong are the stunning one-artist rooms, like the one containing only Monet's water lilies (adjoining Gallery 6) and another full of enormous Pollocks (Gallery 22).

The museum's **second floor** houses its collection of photography and drawings, and a sizable portion of its collection of painting and sculpture, which is housed in a series of numbered galleries that flow sequentially by period and continue up to the third floor.

To begin at the beginning, with Gallery 1, go in through the large opening to the left of the escalator. **Galleries 1-3** focus on Post-Impressionism, where the flourishing of the modern aesthetic is on full display in works by Cézanne, Seurat, Van Gogh, Rousseau, and Ensor. The Post-Impressionists tried to find new and more individual ways of seeing the world while still producing representations of what actually existed. Van Gogh's well-loved *The Starry Night* is covered by layers of paint so thick that some say patches near the bottom of the frame are still wet.

By the 1900s a painting's content—trees, people, whatever—had become more and more of an excuse to investigate colors, forms, and emotions; for the painting of objects to stay interesting, some new way of seeing them had to be invented. Pablo Picasso and his pal Georges Braque came up with one—Analytical Cubism, which tried to show people and things on canvas from more than one angle at once, making paintings at once disturbingly fractured and mysteriously three-dimensional. The painting that ushered in Cubism is now the star of **Gallery 4:** Picasso's giant *Demoiselles d'Avignon*, which he kept hidden for years until he felt Paris was ready to understand it. Gallery 4 also spotlights Fauvism, which flourished in Paris during 1906-7. The "Fauve" school (the name means "Wild Beast") turned faces orange, apples blue, and gallery owners purple.

At the far end of Gallery 6, in the **Water Lilies Room,** Claude Monet's enormous screens depict the pond flora in dreamy, rough, and unmasked brushstrokes. Each of Monet's studies in light was colored by the sun's slant and the air quality. Monet would put aside a painting until the light and haze he wanted came back. His late style, like Matisse's, was partly a symptom of failing health. Picture windows overlook the sculpture garden and douse you, and the screens, in natural light; show up in early afternoon, and the screens seem perversely washed-out. At other times, the effect can be magical.

Gallery 7 showcases Russian Futurism, with works by Chagall (*I and the Village*), Kandinsky, and Kupka. The next several galleries cover de Chirico (an Italian who explored dreams, mannequins, dark green skies, and classical architecture), works of collage by Dada, and the career of Piet Mondrian. If the vague, tan grids of Mondrian's earliest work in **Gallery 10** resemble vertical slums, the crisp lines, primary colors, and right angles to which he later confined himself suggest that design, precision, and harmony ought to drive out conflict and emotion. His more populated last works, like 1944's *Broadway Boogie-Woogie,* are sometimes read as celebrations of his adopted country and city (guess which). Past the stairwell, in airy **Gallery 12,** you can follow Henri Matisse's 1909 bacchanal *Dance (First Version)* or fear the hidden teacher in his disturbing *Piano Lesson.*

Much of the work in the remaining five galleries on this floor plumbs the Surrealist depths. **Galleries 13 and 15** present the elaborate, 1890s-inspired Max Ernst and the early works of high-concept prankster Marcel Duchamp, whose obsession with mathematics eventually led him out of painting and sculpture and into incessant games of chess. Duchamp painted and signed some works as his female alter ego, Rose Selavy; sometimes he also dressed the part. **Gallery 14** devotes itself to the giggly squiggles and improvisational geometry of Swiss painter and etcher Paul Klee, and **Gallery 16** returns to the Surrealism of Dalí and Belgian René Magritte.

To the left as you exit Gallery 17 is the museum's display of **modern drawings**—some sketches for masterworks, some masterworks themselves. Seek out Kupka's *Girl with Ball.* Past the stairs and to the left after you exit the drawing exhibit are the MoMA's exhibits of **photography.** With hundreds of photos in under 10 rooms, the arrangement is rather daunting: temporary exhibits are in the front, parts of the permanent photo collection in back. The photography in the permanent collection, much of it from the world of journalism, has a stronger social and political dimension than most of the rest of the MoMA.

Escalate to the **third floor** to continue seeing painting and sculpture. This time, enter the gallery directly in front of the escalator. The nine galleries on this floor track American and European painting from the end of World War II to the late 60s. They feature works by Mark Rothko and Jackson Pollock (who created his gigantic "all-over" canvasses by pouring and flinging industrial-quality paint); by Robert Motherwell, Franz Kline, and Barnett Newman (whose vertically striped paintings hang here like large, mystically resonant Universal Price Code tags); and by Jasper Johns, Roy Lichtenstein, and pop-art demagogue Andy Warhol (whose gold Marilyn Monroe rests in Gallery 26).

The MoMA owns tons more 20th-century art than it will ever have space to display; an ever-changing assortment of works cavorts past the third-floor stairwell. Continue on to find a chamber full of work from the past 15 years; the selection here also changes rapidly, but there will surely be plenty to interest. To the right of the exit from the **contemporary art** room is a small room containing video compositions. Directly above the photography exhibits and to the left of the escalator on the third floor is MoMA's **prints** department; again, there are lots of works and they rotate frequently. A "reading room" lets you investigate old catalogs and defunct exhibitions.

Rise up to the **design exhibits** on the fourth floor. Scale models and blueprints for **Bauhaus** buildings accompany up-to-this-decade displays of elegant **furniture,** Finnish tableware, and enough *chaise longues* to outfit every psychoanalyst in New York.

The **bookstore** on the first floor (708-9702) sells art books, 50¢ postcards, and cool posters (open Sat.-Wed. 11am-5:45pm, Thurs.-Fri. 11am-8:45pm). The **MoMA Design Store,** across the street at 44 W. 53d St., sells high-priced objects like those on the fourth floor, along with some interesting housewares such as environmentally sound bowls, plates, and glasses stitched together from whole tropical leaves (open Sat. and Mon.-Wed. 10am-6pm, Thurs.-Fri. 10am-9pm, Sun. 11am-6pm).

The Museum of Modern Art is located at 11 W. 53d St., between Fifth and Sixth Ave. (708-9400, information and film schedules 708-9480. Subway: E or F to Fifth Ave.-53rd St. or B, D, Q to 50th St. Open Sat.-Tues. 11am-6pm, Thurs.-Fri. noon-8:30pm. Admission $7.50, seniors and students $4.50, children under 16 free. Pay what you wish Thurs. and Fri. 5:30-8:30pm. Films require free tickets obtained in advance from the information desk.)

■■■ COOPER-HEWITT MUSEUM

Since 1976 Andrew Carnegie's regal Georgian mansion has been the setting for the Smithsonian Institution's National Museum of Design. Pieces from the museum's vast permanent collection are culled for topical, fascinating shows on aspects of contemporary or historical design.

The museum itself is one of the more impressive design projects on the site. Cast-iron archways alternate with intricately carved ceilings and an operatic staircase; and everything basks in the pale, gilded glow of muted candelabras. You can pick out the Scottish bagpipes, an homage to Carnegie's heritage, in the moldings of the music room. An unusually low doorway leads to what was once 5'2" Carnegie's west library.

The collection dates back to 1859, when Peter Cooper opened the Cooper Union for the Advancement of Science and Art. Cooper's granddaughters opened a museum in 1897, which was donated to the Smithsonian in 1963. In 1972, the collection found a new home in the Carnegie mansion. The largest group of holdings contains drawings and prints, primarily of architecture and design. Glass, furniture, porcelain, metalwork, stoneware, and textiles complete the catalogue.

Exhibitions at the Cooper-Hewitt are often sly and provocative. The museum has staged such playful offerings as a show of doghouses and a history of the pop-up book. Recent guest-curated shows have featured intricate cups and saucers from Denmark and a review of designer fabrics. With over two million volumes, the museum's library is one of the largest and most accessible scholarly resources in America for design.

The museum is located at 2 E. 91st St., at Fifth Ave. (860-6868. Subway: #4, 5, or 6 to 86th St. Open Tues. 10am-9pm, Wed.-Sat. 10am-5pm, Sun. noon-5pm. Admission $3, seniors and students with ID $1.50, under 12 free. Free Tues. 5-9pm.)

■■■ FRICK COLLECTION

Pittsburgh steel magnate and robber baron Henry Clay Frick left his house and art collection to the city, and the museum retains the elegance of his French "Classic Eclectic" white marble *château*. It showcases old masters and decorative arts in an intimate setting—a refreshing break from the warehouse ambience of New York's larger museums. The written guide to the Frick can lead you informatively from room to room ($1); paintings have not been comprehensively labeled in this most private of collections.

The Frick Corporation suggests that you go through the house in the order they suggest, to get the maximum effect of the museum, which remains much as it was when Mr. Frick originally arranged the works. As you fork over the $5 admission fee ($3 for seniors and students), examine the bust of Frick behind you. As you check your bags and coat in the room to your left, examine the two busts, the vase, and the Chinese vases, as well as the outdoor garden. Look in every corner, nook, and cranny; the house is stuffed full of art.

Some of the world's finest Old Masters are on display here, as well as exquisite *objets d'art* such as vases, sculptures, and bronzes—even the furniture. Two of the 35 existing Vermeer paintings hang in the **South Hall:** *Officer and Laughing Girl* and *Girl Interrupted at Her Music,* as does a sassy and flirtatious portrait of Madame Boucher by Monsieur Boucher. The **Octagon Room** features a 15th-century altarpiece by Fra Filippo Lippi, and the anteroom showcases other early pieces, such as a Van Eyck and several religious paintings.

On the way to the dining hall, stop by the **Boucher Room;** this relentlessly cheerful Rococo artist exemplifies frivolity and froufrou in this series entitled *The Arts and Sciences.* The entire room is furnished in 18th-century French style. The **Dining Hall** (yes, you can walk on the carpet) features several noted 18th-century British portraitists—Romney, Reynolds, and Gainsborough—all of whom hated each other. Here icily glamorous women with titles stare at you.

Moving through the numbered galleries, stop by more Rococo foolishness and pink pink pink in the **Fragonard Room,** with the eponymous artist's *Progress of Love.* In the **Living Room,** El Greco's *St. Jerome* clasps his Latin translation of the Bible next to Titian's pensive *Portrait of a Man in a Red Cap* and Giovanni Bellini's extraordinary 15th-century masterpiece *St. Francis in the Deser*t. In the next room, the **Library** walls display Gainsborough and Reynolds portraits, a Constable landscape, a Turner seascape, a Gilbert Stuart likeness of George Washington, and a portrait of a benign, club-footed Henry Clay Frick surveying his domain. Go into the **North Hall** on your way to the next room and try to stare down the defiantly level-eyed Ingres portrait of the *Countesse d'Hansonville.*

The largest room in the Frick, the **West Gallery,** has some stunning natural lighting from the skylight. Here, you can get more eye-candy with no less than three works of Rembrandt: the *Polish Rider,* owned by the last king of Poland; *Nicholaes Ruts,* one of Rembrandt's earliest portrait commissions; and his sensitive 1658 *Self-Portrait,* one of many (over 60) such meditations painted during his lifetime. Also note the works by Van Dyck (an elegant 1620 portrait of a close friend), Vermeer (an unfinished rendering of the opening of a letter), and Velázquez (a famous portrait of King Philip IV of Spain, painted in the town of Fraga following his military victories there against the French). Goya's depiction of blacksmiths at work in *The Forge* seems strangely out of place—perhaps these workers managed to sneak their way into this predominantly aristocratic collection on account of their esteemed previous owner, King Louis-Philippe of France. Over at the head of the West Gallery, the **Enamel Room** contains a collection of Limoges enamels from the 16th and 17th centuries, as well as a penetrating evocation of Satan in Duccio di Buoninsegna's 1308 *The Temptation of Christ on the Mountain.*

The **Oval Room** features two Gainsborough women and 2 Van Dycks, all avoiding eye contact with each other (and you). Try to stand in a pose like theirs—these portraits are life-size. Also note the frisky bronze *Diana* (also avoiding eye contact with the women), executed in 1776 by Jean-Antoine Houdon. The **East Gallery** holds several Whistlers with characteristically musical names: *Symphony in Flesh Color and Pink, Harmony in Pink and Grey,* and *Arrangement in Black and Brown.* They should be easy to tell apart. A fine Goya portrait of a young *Officer* pouts here. Downstairs, basement galleries added in 1977 feature special exhibits.

After walking through the least exhausting museum in New York, you can relax in the cool Garden Court and watch fountains of water burble up from the mouths of little stone frogs. The museum (288-0700) is located at 1 E. 70th St. at Fifth Ave. (Subway: #6 to 68th St. Open Tues.-Sat. 10am-6pm, Sun. 1-6pm. Admission $5, students and seniors $3. No children under 10 admitted; children under 16 must be accompanied by an adult. Group visits by appointment only.)

■■■ GUGGENHEIM MUSEUM

The Guggenheim's most famous exhibit is surely the building itself: the original, seven-story corkscrew of a museum dates to 1959 and is one of the only New York edifices that Frank Lloyd Wright deigned to design. Sleek yet blunt, futuristic yet outdated, it's a 3-D memento of a design style that survives mostly in science-fiction illustration (right down to the *sans-serif* letters of the museum's name out front). But despite how cool it looks, Wright's design offered insufficient space as the museum's programmers tried for more and better exhibits; so from 1990 to 1992, the museum shut down for restoration and expansion. Offices moved out of the corkscrew, skylights and windows were replaced, and a new 10-story "tower gallery" sprouted behind the original structure, nearly doubling potential exhibit space. When the Guggenheim reopened in summer 1992, wags compared the new building to a Modernist toilet while the *Village Voice* blasted the museum's fundraising methods. Gallery-goers, however, voted with their feet, mobbing the museum, the patio, the elevators, the restaurant, and the street outside.

The huddled masses were treated to a dazzling, if uneven, sample of the permanent collection in the tower galleries, and to the work of "minimalist" sculptor Dan Flavin, who has decorated the display spaces (called "bays") along the spiral ramp with nothing but a repeating pattern of colored fluorescent tubes. Despite the chain of pastel lights from floor to ceiling (surely one of New York's tallest sculptures), visitors seem to prefer the new building, with its 20th-century paintings. Most of the museum's space now holds temporary and touring exhibits, like the current spiral show of sculptures by Picasso, Calder, Giacometti, and Smith that replaces today's neon tubes with the wrought iron of yesteryear.

Every Manhattan-bred child dreams of skateboarding down the Guggenheim's spiralling hallway. Despite Wright's wish that visitors ride the elevator to the top of the spiral and "waft" down, exhibitions are sometimes (inexplicably) arranged in ascending chronological order; you might consider trudging *up* the ramp instead. Each ramp bay holds one sequence or exhibit, while Tower Galleries 4, 5, and 7, each accessible by the ramp or by clevator, may present a different sequence or show. (Because these tower rooms to the side have higher ceilings than the ramp levels, there is no Tower Gallery 3 or 6.) Tower Gallery 2, near the bottom, holds the Thannhauser Collection of pre-1920s work. The rest of the permanent collection is especially strong on cerebral, geometric art, showcasing Mondrian and his Dutch *De Stijl* school, the Bauhaus experiments of Hungarian Moholy-Nagy, and the Russian modernists. The collection also holds an amazing Barnett Newman, Miró's well-known *Tilled Field,* and some mind-bending collage/paintings from Jim Dine and Robert Rauschenberg; you might ask if any of these happen to be on display. Tower Gallery 5 adjoins a puny (900-sq.-ft.) outdoor terrace from which you can look over Central Park or study a sculpture or two.

The museum spirals away at 1071 5th Ave. and 89th St. (recording 423-3500, human being 423-3600, TDD 423-3607). There is also a new **Guggenheim Museum SoHo** (see below). The Fifth Ave. Guggenheim is open Sun.-Wed. 10am-6pm, Fri.-Sat. 10am-8pm. Admission $7, students and seniors $4, children under 12 free; Fri. 6-8pm "pay what you wish." 2-day pass to both Guggenheim museums $10, students and seniors $6; if you buy one in SoHo on Wednesday, it remains valid uptown for Fri. And don't forget to stare at the building for a while.

■■■ WHITNEY MUSEUM

When the Metropolitan Museum of Art declined the donation of over 600 works from Gertrude Vanderbilt Whitney in 1929, Ms. Whitney, a wealthy patron and sculptor, decided to form her own museum. Opened on 8th St. in 1931, the Whitney museum has since moved twice, most recently in 1966 to an unusual and forbidding futuristic fortress designed by Bauhauser Marcel Breuer. The museum's collection is devoted solely to American art, including some 8500 sculptures, paintings, drawings, and prints.

Turn right as you enter and stop short before the playful shapes of Calder's *Circus,* one sculptor's fantasy world. A videotape allows you to see these many-hatted dolls put on a three-ring sword-swallowing extravaganza with a little help from their creator. The first and second floors cover a wide range of changing exhibitions including theme shows, retrospectives, and contemporary work by avant-garde artists. The theater periodically shows films and videos from independent American artists. Check *This Week at the Whitney,* posted on a kiosk near the entrance, or call about special events, lectures, and guided tours.

The museum has assembled the largest collection of 20th-century American art in the world; if the varied (and often controversial) temporary exhibits don't float your boat, something in the permanent collection is bound to. Be warned, though; although the museum has dozens of American masterworks (including Ad Reinhardt's *Abstract Painting, Number 33,* Jasper John's *Three Flags,* Frank Stella's famous *Brooklyn Bridge,* Robert Rauschenberg's *Satellite,* Willem De Kooning's *Woman on Bicycle,* and Georgia O'Keefe's *Flower Collection*), don't expect to see them all. The Whitney's permanent collection is shown in bits and pieces; some selection of it is always on display, but specific works are called in and out of hibernation on a rotating basis. Contemporary works by Cindy Sherman, Barbara Kruger, Nam Juin Paik, Kiki Smith, and many others will probably satisfy your aesthetic cravings, even if you can't see your favorites.

Blasted by the Guerilla Girls ("the conscience of the art world") for failing to present women artists, the museum is making an effort to include more women in its shows even as it takes heat on the right from Hilton Kramer and the neo-con art crowd for abandoning time-honored High Modernist standards. The 1993 Biennial Exhibition, for example, showcased the paintings, sculptures, and installations of both famous and relatively unknown artists, all of whom considered cutting-edge issues of "community" and "identity." It was savaged by the left for its condescending attitudes towards minority artists, while the right attacked it for its topical nature. 1995 will host yet another Biennial, so be sure to be part of the firestorm. Despite the denunciation by the NY press, the Biennial features some of the most exciting and engaging contemporary art out there.

There is expensive food downstairs and expensive museum souvenirs next door. Resist the temptation ($10 min. for lunch) and go to Third Ave. for food instead.

The Whitney is located at 945 Madison Ave. (570-3676), at 75th St. (Subway: #6 to 77th St. Open Wed. 11am-6pm, Thurs. 1-8pm, Fri.-Sun. 11am-6pm. Admission $7, students and seniors $5, children under 12 free; Thurs. 6-8pm $3.50.)

Another **branch** of the Whitney is in the **Philip Morris** building, 120 Park Ave. at 42nd St., where a sculpture court features a changing array of installation pieces. Admission is free. Gallery talks, which occur frequently, are also free. Call 878-2453 for updates. (See below.)

■■■ PIERPONT MORGAN LIBRARY

In the **Pierpont Morgan Library,** you can see a stunning collection of rare books, sculpture, and paintings gathered by the banker and his son, J.P. Morgan, Jr. This Low Renaissance-style *palazzo* was constructed with white marble bricks laid, in true Greek fashion, without mortar. Completed in 1907, the library remained private until 1924, when J.P. Morgan graciously opened it to the public. Its permanent collection, not always on display, includes drawings and prints by Blake and Dürer, illuminated Renaissance manuscripts, Napoleon's love letters to Josephine, a manuscript copy of Dickens's *A Christmas Carol,* and music handwritten by Beethoven and Mozart.

After taking in the exhibit in the front room, walk through the hall lined with medieval paraphernalia to a circular room, which once served as the main entrance and which often features exhibitions. To the right, the West Room, Morgan Sr.'s opulent former office, has a carved ceiling made during the Italian Renaissance and stained glass taken from 15th and 17th century Switzerland. It was common (well, not really *common*) in the early days of the century to physically import large parts of European buildings for incorporation into domestic architecture.

To the left of the rotunda is the library, a book lover's dream. Stacked with mahogany-colored bound volumes and encircled by two balconies, this room is often the setting for additional exhibitions. Among the more notable items in the room: one of three existing likenesses of John "Lady of Christ" Milton, a fabulous 12th-century jewel-encrusted triptych believed to contain fragments from the Cross, and one of 11 surviving copies of the Gutenberg Bible, the first printed book.

The museum is located at 29 E. 36th St. (685-0610), at Madison Ave. (Subway: #6 to 33rd St. Open Tues.-Sat. 10:30am-5pm, Sun. 1-5pm. Suggested contribution $5, seniors and students $3. Free tours on various topics Tues.-Fri. 2:30pm.)

■■■ AMERICAN MUSEUM OF NATURAL HISTORY

The largest science museum in the world broods in a suitably imposing Romanesque structure. The building, four blocks long, holds 36 million items of varied appeal. Charm your toddler friends with a stop at the dinosaur fossils and the poignant preserved-mammal dioramas; impress your partner by nonchalantly stomaching the explicit display on the biology of invertebrates. Or play hide-and-seek in the delightfully dark and confusing rocks-and-minerals section.

The original building, constructed in 1877, has been almost entirely walled in by 21 additions. A statue of Theodore Roosevelt—on horseback and in uniform, flanked by a naked African man and a feather-clad Native American, both on foot—stands near the newer Central Park West entrance. Efforts to ditch or alter this flagrantly racist monument have been frustrated by its status as a national landmark. In the cavernous rotunda, just inside, a 40-ft. barosaurus skeleton fights for her life against the fierce, predatory, but fossilized allosaurus. Grab a map from the **information desk** to the left of the entrance. The quotations and murals along the walls were issued from or depict Teddy Roosevelt. His interests, background, and hunting hats are displayed on the first floor, in Hall 12.

Teddy's distant ancestors can be seen in the "Ocean Life and Biology of Fishes" display in Hall 10. A two-story replica of a blue whale casts shadows on the black-lit fish in the surrounding tanks. Admire the largest unexploded Pop Rock on earth in Hall 6—the 34-ton *Ahnghito,* the biggest meteorite ever retrieved.

Also on the first floor, the newest permanent exhibition—the **Hall of Human Biology and Evolution**—boasts skeletons that trace the last three million years. Command your own computerized archaeological dig with "Hominid Hunter," or peruse the anatomically correct re-creations of our hirsute ancestors.

Stuffed stuff representing thousands of species can be discovered on floors one to three. (The fourth floor, future home of the dinosaurs, will reopen in the spring of 1995.) A modest King Kong beats his breast in the Hall of African Mammals (Hall 13). A herd of Indian elephants runs riot through Hall 9, Asiatic Mammals. Toward the back of the second floor dwell huge and colorful anthropology exhibits; don't miss the costumed mannequins of "African Dance and Belief," and try not to wince at the more dated placards. The Primates Wing, on the third floor, demonstrates the evolutionary chain from a tree shrew to you. On the fourth floor, the "Mammals and Their Extinct Relatives" exhibit offers many large skeletons and fossils of, well, mammals and their extinct relatives. See the special display of my Aunt Gertrude.

This dino-centric museum will reopen the doors to its star attraction—the dino-bones themselves—in 1995, and the world will see interactive videos and the dinosaur mummy along with the beloved fossil reconstructions. In the meantime, check out a small dinosaur display in the Roosevelt Rotunda.

The **Alexander White Natural Science Center,** the museum's only room holding live animals, explains the ecology of New York City to kids, while the **Discovery Room** gives them artifacts they can touch. (Hours hover around 2-4:30pm Tues.-Fri., 1-4:30pm Sat.-Sun.; closed September; call ahead to check.) The **People Center** hosts scholarly talks and demonstrations of traditional peoples' arts at scheduled times during the academic year.

The museum is located on Central Park West, at 79th to 81st St. (769-5100). (Subway: B or C to 81st St. Open Sun.-Thurs. 10am-5:45pm, Fri.-Sat. 10am-8:45pm. Suggested donation $5, seniors and students $3, children under 12 $2.50; Fri.-Sat. 5-8:45pm free. Excellent wheelchair access.)

The museum also houses **Naturemax** (769-5650), a cinematic extravaganza on New York's largest movie screen, 4 stories high and 66 ft. wide. Catch "Search for the Great Sharks" and "To the Limit" (about athletes) in a double-feature. (Admission $5, students and seniors $4, children under 12 $2.50; Fri.-Sat. double features $7, students and seniors $5.50, children under 12 $3.50.) The **Hayden Planetarium** (769-5100) offers outstanding multi-media presentations. Seasonal celestial light shows twinkle in the dome of the **Theater of the Stars,** accompanied by astronomy lectures. (Admission $5, seniors and students $4, children under 12 $2.50.) Electrify your senses on Fri.-Sat. nights with 3-D **Laser Grunge,** featuring music of Nirvana and Mudhoney, at 7pm and 8pm, or 3-D Pink Floyd at 10pm. (Admission $8.50). Tickets available through Ticketron (307-7171).

■■■ OTHER MAJOR COLLECTIONS

Alternative Museum, 594 Broadway, 4th floor (966-4444), near Houston St. in SoHo. Subway: B, D, F, or Q to Broadway-Lafayette St., or N or R to Prince St. Founded and operated by artists for non-established artists, the museum advertises itself as "ahead of the times and behind the issues." New visions and social critique are the name of the game, with an emphasis on the international, the unusual, and the socially conscious. Open Tues.-Sun. 11am-6pm. Suggested donation $3.

American Craft Museum, 40 W. 53rd St. (956-3535), across from the MoMA. Subway: E or F to Fifth Ave.-53rd St.; or B, D, or Q to 50th St. Not the old-fashioned quilts and Shaker furniture you might expect. This museum revises received notions of crafts, showing modern pieces in wood, glass, metal, clay, plastic, paper, and fabric. Regular, ingenious exhibitions are shaped around particular subjects or materials. Past shows include "Made with Paper," "Glass Installations," which evokes memories of Superman's home planet Krypton, and the outrageous "Plastic as Plastic." Open Tues. 10am-8pm, Wed.-Sun. 10am-5pm. Admission $4.50, seniors and students $2, children under 12 free.

American Museum of the Moving Image, 35th Ave. at 36th St., Astoria, Queens (718-784-0077 for exhibition and screening information, 718-784-4777 for travel directions). Subway: N to 36th Ave. (Washington Ave.) at 31st St. Walk north along 31st St. one block to 35th Ave. and go right; walk five blocks east to 36th St. The museum promises a dedication to "the art, history, and technology of motion picture and television," but luckily it doesn't take itself quite that seriously. A gallery on the ground floor hosts somewhat bizarre changing exhibitions, such as the recent "Changing Faces," a show on Hollywood hair and makeup design, and a let-you-play display of the newest in interactive CD-Rom video games. In the museum's permanent collection upstairs you can look in a Magic Mirror to see yourself as Marilyn Monroe, or gaze at a wall of Bill Cosby's sweaters (he never wears the same one twice). The video avalanche of cultural icons and entertainment buzz clips is a reminder of how much cultural baggage we lug around with us, as is the memorabilia collection, which includes Mork and Mindy lunch boxes, Fonzie paper dolls, and the Leave it to Beaver "Ambush" game. Also upstairs is "King Tut's Fever Movie Palace," which shows flicks like "Batman and Robin" and "What Made Pistachio Nuts?" while the screening room downstairs regularly plays vintage films and rare collections of film shorts. Tours by appointment (718-784-4520). (Open Tues.-Fri. noon-4pm, Sat.-Sun. noon-6pm. Admission $5, seniors $4, students and children under 12 $2.50.)

The Asia Society, 725 Park Ave. (288-6400), at 70th St. Subway: #6 to 68th St. Exhibitions of Asian art are accompanied by symposia on related topics, musical performances, film screenings, and an acclaimed "Meet the Author" series. The art comes from all over Asia, from Iran to southeast Asia to Japan to China to Korea to Asian America. Particularly well-thought-out exhibitions on topics such as the Asian-American quest for identity in the diaspora, and "the object in context," a series which places one piece amidst others on loan and from the permanent collection to show the influences on and of that one piece. Open Tues.-Wed. and Fri.-Sat. 11am-6pm, Thurs. 11am-8pm, Sun. noon-5pm. Admission $2, seniors and students $1; Thurs. 6-8pm free. Tours Tues.-Sat. 12:30 pm, Thurs. also at 6:30pm, Sun. 2:30pm.

Audubon Terrace Museum Group, at Broadway and 155th St. in Harlem. Subway: #1 to 157th St. Once part of John James Audubon's estate and game preserve, the terrace now contains a number of museums and societies:

National Museum of the American Indian (283-2420). Part of the Smithsonian Institution, with the world's largest collection of Native American artifacts. In

recent years, the museum has been faced with demands by Native American groups seeking the return of many exhibits; for now at least, you can still see Geronimo's warrior cap and cane, Sitting Bull's war club, and Crazy Horse's headdress. Treaty belts given to William Penn are here, as well as a full array of masks, dolls, clothes, and weapons, all presented in surprisingly un-P.C. and rather condescending style. Has this place been renovated since the '60s? The museum will move to the old U.S. Custom House in lower Manhattan at some point in 1995, so call ahead. Open Tues.-Sat. 10am-5pm, Sun. 1-5pm. Admission $1.50, seniors and students with ID $1; free for Smithsonian members.

Hispanic Society of America (926-2234). A museum devoted to Spanish and Portuguese arts and culture, including paintings, mosaics, and ceramics. Works by Spanish greats El Greco, Velázquez, and Goya. Spanish scholars will enjoy the 100,000-volume research library. Open Mon.-Sat. 10am-4:30pm, Sun. 1-4:30pm. Free.

American Numismatic Society (243-3130). Come learn about the fascinating history of the penny! An extraordinary collection of coinage and paper money from prehistoric times to the present. Open Mon.-Sat. 9am- 4:30pm, Sun. 1-4pm. Free.

American Academy of Arts and Letters (368-5900). Honors American artists, writers, and composers; also offers occasional exhibits of manuscripts, paintings, sculptures, and first editions. Call for current exhibition details and times.

Black Fashion Museum, 155-157 W. 126th St. (666-1320), between Adam Clayton Powell Jr. Blvd. and Lenox/Malcolm X Ave. Subway: #2 or 3 to 125th St. Founded in 1979, the B.F.M. maintains a permanent collection and mounts 2 yearly exhibits devoted to garments designed, sewn, or worn by black men and women from the 1860s to the present. Alongside the creations of popular contemporary black designers you'll find two slave dresses, a dress made by Rosa Parks, costumes from Broadway musicals like *The Wiz,* and a tribute to designer Ann Lowe, who designed the wedding dress for Jackie O's wedding to JFK. Open by appointment Mon.-Fri. noon-8pm; call 996-4470 at least one day in advance. Suggested donation $2, students $1.50.

Bronx Museum of the Arts, 165th St. and Grand Concourse (718-681-6000). Subway: C or D to 167th St. and south 3 blocks along Grand Concourse. Set in the rotunda of the Bronx Courthouse. The museum focuses on young talent, collecting works on paper by minority artists and sponsoring twice-yearly seminars for local artists; the seminars culminate in group showings. Open Wed.-Fri. 10am-5pm, Sat.-Sun. 1-6pm. Suggested donation $3, students $2, seniors $1; Sun. free.

Brooklyn Museum, 200 Eastern Pkwy., at Washington Ave. (718-638-5000). Subway: #2 or 3 to Eastern Pkwy. The little sibling of the Metropolitan Museum—but not that little. Check out the outstanding Ancient Greek, Roman, Middle Eastern, and Egyptian galleries on the 3rd floor; larger Egyptian collections are found only at London's British Museum and in Cairo. Crafts, textiles, and period rooms on the 4th floor provide respite from "higher" pursuits; the Moorish Room, a lush bit of exotica from John D. Rockefeller's Manhattan townhouse, is especially amusing. Gems from Sargent and the Hudson River School shine in the American Collection on the 5th floor. Nearby, the small, unusual contemporary gallery contains noteworthy works by Bacon. On the same floor is European art from the early Renaissance to Post-Impressionism, including works by Rodin, Renoir, and Monet. Multi-media Asian art fills the 2nd floor; note the McMullan rugs in the Islamic gallery. The enormous Oceanic and New World art collection takes up the central 2-story space on the 1st floor; the towering totem poles covered with human/animal hybrids could go nowhere else. The impressive African art collection here was the first of its kind in an American museum when it opened in 1923. Galleries downstairs put on temporary exhibits. Due to budget constraints, the museum is open only Wed.-Sun. 10am-5pm. Gift shop with fine jewelry and large art and travel-book collection open same hours. Gallery talks Wed.-Fri. at 2pm. Museum café open 10am-4pm. Suggested donation $4, students $2, seniors $1.50, children under 12 free.

China House Gallery, 125 E. 65th St. (744-8181), between Park and Lexington Ave. Subway: #6 to 68th St. This minute gallery within the China Institute showcases a broad spectrum of Chinese art, including calligraphy, ceramics, and bronzes, as well as occasional cultural-anthropological exhibits. Open Mon. and Wed.-Fri. 10am-5pm, Tues. 10am-8pm, Sat. 10am-1pm. Suggested contribution $3.

The Cloisters (923-3700), Fort Tryon Park in upper Manhattan. Subway: A to 190th St.; from the train station take a right onto Ft. Washington Ave. and head through Ft. Tryon Park. Or take the #4 bus from Fifth Ave. to the Cloisters' entrance (buses leave regularly from the Metropolitan Museum's main building on Fifth). In 1938, Charles Collen brought the High Middle Ages to the edge of Manhattan. Building a monastery from pieces of 12th- and 13th-century French and Spanish cloisters, he established this tranquil avatar of the Met. John D. Rockefeller, never short of a few bob, donated the entire site and many of the contents. Retreat to the air-conditioned Treasury to admire the Met's rich collection of Medieval art. Examine countless books drawn by neurotic monks; when healthy people were off rampaging through the countryside looking for dragons, the monks were carving intricate 3-D biblical scenes in boxwood miniature. Follow the allegory told by the priceless Unicorn Tapestries, and wander through airy archways and manicured gardens bedecked with European treasures like the ghoulish marble fountain in the Cuxa Cloister. Open March-Oct. Tues.-Sun. 9:30am-5:15pm, Nov.-Feb. Tues.-Sun. 9:30am-4:45pm. Museum tours March-Oct. Tues.-Fri. at 3pm, Sun. at noon; Nov.-Feb. Wed. at 3pm. Suggested donation $6, students and seniors $3. Donation includes, and is included with, admission to the Metropolitan Museum's main building in Central Park.

Equitable Gallery, Equitable Center (554-4818), at Seventh Ave. and 51st St. Subway: N or R to 49th St. This small gallery presents 4 free exhibitions per year covering an eclectic array of subjects. An exhibition is always showing, save for the week or so of inter-exhibitional downtime; it's best to call ahead. Open Mon.-Fri. 11am-6pm, Sat. noon-5pm.

Forbes Magazine Galleries, 62 Fifth Ave. (206-5548), at 12th St. Subway: #4, 5, 6, L, N, or R to 14th St.-Union Sq. The holdings here, like those at the Frick Collection and the Morgan Library, were acquired by a multi-millionaire financier for his own pleasure and then turned over to the public. The late Malcolm Forbes's irrepressible penchant for the offbeat permeates this 20th-century collection. Eclectic exhibits occupy the ground floor of the late magnate's publishing outfit: 12,000 toy soldiers assuming various battle positions in the military-miniatures collection; a rotating exhibit of Presidential paraphernalia; the world's largest private collection of Fabergé Easter eggs; a completely random collection of trophies known as "The Mortality of Immortality," including the prized trophy for the best White Leghorn chicken of the Northampton Egg Laying Trial; and the urn of the ashes of Marion Hanbury Stewart (no relation whatsoever). Open Tues.-Sat. 10am-4pm. Free, but entry is limited to 900 persons per day; children under 16 must be accompanied by an adult. Thurs. is reserved for advance-notice group tours; call 206-5549.

Fraunces Tavern, 54 Pearl St. (425-1778) on 2nd and 3rd floors. Subway: #4 or 5 to Bowling Green, #1 or 9 to South Ferry, or N or R to Whitehall St. While some exhibits in the museum convey the spirit of old New York, the building itself is neither a restoration nor a genuine reconstruction of the original Fraunces Tavern—no one knows what it looked like. Instead, the structure, built between 1904 and 1907, is a reconstruction of the typical tavern of the period. The second floor features two period rooms, along with the room where George Washington said goodbye to his troops after the Revolutionary War. The third floor features exhibits on the culture and history of early America, such as "The Changing Image of George Washington." Open Mon.-Fri. 10am-4:45pm, Sat. noon-4pm. Admission $2.50; seniors, students, and children $1.

Guggenheim Museum SoHo, 575 Broadway (423-3500) at Prince St. This branch of the Guggenheim occupies two spacious floors of an historic 19th-century building with selections from the museum's mammoth permanent collection of modern and contemporary works. The neighborhood and the breezy, stylish layout lends the place a gallery atmosphere (much unlike the corkscrew uptown). Special exhibitions are often exceptional: in 1994 these included a selection of watercolors by Kandinsky, and John Cage's "Rolywholyover: A Circus" which was a unique "composition for museum." Open Sun. and Wed.-Fri. 11am-6pm, Sat. 11am-8pm. Admission $5, students and seniors with ID $3, and children under 12 free. A seven -day pass is available for admission to both the Guggenheim Museum and the SoHo branch, $10, students and seniors with ID $6.

Guinness World of Records, 350 Fifth Ave. (947-2335), located on the Concourse level of the Empire State Building at 34th St. Subway: N or R to 34th St.-Herald Sq., or #6 to 33rd St.-Park Ave. Synthesizer pop and enthusiastic recorded voices lure the unwary into the goofy world of Guinness. Primary colors exemplify the level of sophistication. See plastic replicas of the world's tallest man, heaviest man, and longest neck. Open daily 9am-8pm, longer hours in summer. Admission $7, students with ID and seniors $6, children $3.50. Combination tickets available to Guinness and the Empire State Building Observatory (these can save you a wait in line): $9.70, students $8.70, seniors $7.20, children $4.75.

Hall of Fame for Great Americans (718-220-6003), 181st St. and Martin Luther King Jr. Blvd. Subway: #4 to Burnside Ave. Walk 6 blocks west along Burnside Ave. as it becomes 179th St., then walk a block north. Located on the grounds of City University of New York in the Bronx. Spurning the flimsiness of wax, this poignant though decrepit hall features nearly 102 bronze busts of America's immortals, among them Alexander Graham Bell, George Washington Carver, Abraham Lincoln, Booker T. Washington, and both (!) Wright brothers. Open daily 10am-5pm. Free.

International Center of Photography, 1130 Fifth Ave. (860-1777), at 94th St. Subway: #6 to 96th St. Housed in a landmark townhouse built in 1914 for *New Republic* founder Willard Straight. The foremost exhibitor of photography in the city and a gathering-place for its practitioners. Historical, thematic, and contemporary works, running from fine art to photo-journalism. The bookstore sells the bi-monthly booklet *Photography in New York*, a comprehensive guide to what is shown and where ($2.95). Midtown branch at 1133 Sixth Ave. (768-4680), at 43rd St. Both open Tues. 11am-8pm, Wed.-Sun. 11am-6pm. Admission $4, seniors and students $2.50, Tues. 6-8pm pay what you wish.

Intrepid Sea-Air-Space Museum, Pier 86 (245-0072), at 46th St. and Twelfth Ave. Bus: M42 or M50 to W. 46th St. One ticket admits you to the veteran World War II and Vietnam War aircraft carrier *Intrepid,* the Vietnam War destroyer *Edson,* the first and only publicly displayed guided-missile submarine, *Growler,* and the lightship *Nantucket.* On the main carrier, Pioneers Hall shows models, antiques, and film shorts of flying devices from the turn of the century to the 30s. A breathtaking wide-screen flick puts the viewer on a flight deck as jets take off and land. You can also climb aboard the Intrepid's 900-ft. flight deck. Don't miss the Iraqi tanks parked near the gift shop; they were captured in the Gulf War. The museum offers a schedule of temporary and new exhibits and events; call for details. Open Memorial Day-Labor Day daily 10am-5pm; Labor Day-Memorial Day Mon.-Fri. 10am-5pm. Admission $7, seniors and veterans $6, children 6-11 $4, children under 6 free.

The Jewish Museum, 1109 Fifth Ave. (423-3200, 423-3230 for exhibition and program information), at 92nd St. Subway: #6 to 96th St. The permanent collection of over 14,000 works details the Jewish experience around the house and throughout history, ranging from antiques and ceremonial objects to contemporary masterpieces by Marc Chagall and Frank Stella. The permanent exhibition on the third and fourth floors, *Culture and Continuity: The Jewish Journey,* examines Jewish history and culture through art and artifacts. The other two floors host temporary exhibitions. Open Sun.-Mon. and Wed.-Thurs. 11am-5:45pm, Tues. 11am-8pm. Admission $6, seniors and students $4, children under 12 free; Tues. pay what you wish after 5pm.

Lower East Side Tenement Museum, 97 and 90 Orchard St. (431-0233), near Broome St. Subway: B, D, or Q to Delancey St.; or J, M, or Z to Essex St. From Delancey St., walk 4 blocks east to Orchard St. and 1 block south. From Essex St., walk 2 blocks west to Orchard and 1 block south. A preserved, early 20th-century Lower East Side tenement house, along with slideshows, documentaries, and displays about Lower East Side history. Also offers Sun. tours of the neighborhood; call for info. Admission $3, seniors $2, students $1.

Jacques Marchais Museum of Tibetan Art, 338 Lighthouse Ave., Staten Island (718-987-3500, 718-987-3478 for recorded schedule). Take bus S74 from Staten Island Ferry to Lighthouse Ave., then turn right and walk up the fairly steep hill as it winds up to the right. Almost 2 hrs. from Manhattan but worth the trip for one of the largest private collections of Tibetan art in the West. Bronzes, paintings, and sculpture from Tibet and other Buddhist cultures. The museum, which roosts atop a secluded hillside, is designed to resemble a small Tibetan mountain temple with its terraced sculpture gardens and view of the distant Lower Bay. Sunday programs ($2 in addition to regular admission) are offered throughout the museum's season and cover topics ranging from photographs of Mongolia to origami "made easy" to afternoons of Tibetan chanting. Call for current schedule. Open April-Nov. Wed.-Sun. 1-5pm. Admission $3, seniors $2.50, children $1.

El Museo del Barrio, 1230 Fifth Ave. (831-7272), at 104th St. Subway: #6 to 103rd St. El Museo del Barrio is the only museum in the U.S. devoted exclusively to the art and culture of Puerto Rico and Latin America. Begun in an East Harlem classroom, the project has blossomed into a permanent museum that features video, painting, sculpture, photography, theater, and film. Permanent collection includes pre-Columbian art and *Santos de Palo,* hand-crafted wooden saint-figures from Latin America. In celebration of El Museo's 25th anniversary, a special exhibition featuring Latin American artists' reconceptions of their ethnic identity and history will be shown until Jan. 1995. Open Wed.-Sun. 11am-5pm. Suggested contribution $4, students and seniors $2.

The Museum for African Art, 593 Broadway (966-1313), between Houston St. and Prince St. in SoHo. Subway: N or R to Prince and Broadway. Formerly called the Center for African Art, the museum has recently changed its name and expanded to feature two major exhibits a year along with several smaller exhibitions of stunning African and African-American art, often with special themes. Open Tues.-Fri. 10am-5:30pm, Sat.-Sun. noon-6pm. Admission $4, students and seniors with ID $2.

Museum of American Folk Art, 2 Lincoln Center (595-9533, 977-7298 for recording), on Columbus Ave. between 65th and 66th St. Subway: #1 or 9 to 66th St. Three bright, white rooms devoted to crafts, from European-influenced quilts, needlepoint, and folk portraits to Navajo rugs and Mexican polychrome wooden animals. The museum provides special programs for children and crafts demonstrations for everyone, often enlivened by folk dancers and storytellers (call the administrative office at 977-7170 for information). Museum open Tues.-Sun. 11:30am-7:30pm. Wheelchair access. Suggested donation $2.

Museum of American Illustration, 128 E. 63rd St. (838-2560), between Park and Lexington Ave. Subway: #4, 5, or 6 to 59th St. or N or R to Lexington Ave. Changing exhibitions of illustrations from such diverse fields as *Mad Magazine* cartoonists, children's books, and advertising. Open Tues. and Thurs. 10am-8pm, Wed. and Fri. 10am-5pm, Sat. noon-4pm. Free.

Museum of Bronx History (718-881-8900), at Bainbridge Ave. and 208th St. Subway: D to 205th St., or #4 to Mosholu Pkwy. Walk 4 blocks east on 210th St. and then south a block. Run by the Bronx Historical Society on the premises of the landmark Valentine-Varian House, the museum presents historical narratives of the borough of the Bronx. Exhibits change regularly; call for schedule. Open Sat. 10am-4pm, Sun. 1-5pm, or by appointment. Admission $2.

Museum of the City of New York (534-1672), 103rd St. and Fifth Ave. in East Harlem next door to El Museo del Barrio. Subway: #6 to 103rd St. Now that the New York Historical Society galleries are closed, very probably the premier museum about New York City. Originally located in Gracie Mansion, the museum moved to its own roomy neo-Georgian quarters in 1932. It tells the story of the city from the 16th century to the present through historical paintings, Currier and Ives prints, period rooms and furnishings, and exquisitely made toys and dolls. Lectures, symposia, and walking tours for adults. Open Wed.-Sat. 10am-5pm, Sun. 1-5pm. Contribution requested. Wheelchair accessible.

Museum of Television and Radio, 25 W. 52nd St. (621-6600, 621-6800 for daily activity schedule), between Fifth and Sixth Ave. Subway: B, D, F, Q to Rockefeller Center, or E, F to 53rd St. Formerly the Museum of Broadcasting, this museum has only one small gallery of exhibits and works primarily as a "viewing museum." With a collection of more than 60,000 TV and radio programs, the museum's library has a specially designed computerized cataloging system that allows you to find and select a program through the database, request it from a librarian, and privately watch or listen to it at one of the 96 TV and radio consoles. You can watch or listen to anything from a 1935 broadcast of *La Traviata* to a 1976 *Saturday Night Live.* The museum also hosts a number of film series that focus on topics of social, historical, popular, or artistic interest; see the daily schedule at the front counter. Special screenings can be arranged for large groups. Open Tues.-Wed. and Fri.-Sun. noon-6pm, Thurs. noon-8pm. Hours extended until 9pm on Fri. for theaters only. Suggested donation $6, students $4, seniors and children under 13 $3.

National Academy Museum, 1083 Fifth Ave. (369-4880), between 89th and 90th St. Subway: #4, 5, or 6 to 86th St. Founded in 1825 to advance the "arts of design" in America: painting, sculpture, architecture, and engraving. Currently the academy hosts exhibits, trains young artists, and serves as a fraternal organization for distinguished American artists. The collection includes paintings, sculptures, drawings, prints, and architectural designs. Winslow Homer, Frederic Edwin Church, John Singer Sargent, Thomas Eakins, and others represent the 19th century in the permanent collection. The impressive assortment of contemporary artists and architects includes Isabel Bishop, Richard Estes, Robert Rauschenberg, Robert Venturi, and Philip Johnson. Regular exhibitions explore the history of American design and its European influences. The academy is quartered in a 19th-century dollhouse mansion, remodeled by Ogden Codman in 1913. Inside you will find all the ingredients of a classic townhouse: checkered floors, ornate ceilings, columns, and, of course, a winding Cinderella staircase. Open Wed.-Thurs. and Sat.-Sun. noon-5pm, Fri. noon-8pm. Admission $3.50; seniors, students, and children under 16 $2. Free Fri. 5-8pm.

New Museum of Contemporary Art, 583 Broadway (219-1355), between Prince and Houston St. Subway: N or R to Prince; or B, D, F, or Q to Broadway-Lafayette. Dedicated to the destruction of the canon and of conventional ideas of "art," the New Museum supports the hottest, the newest, and the most controversial. Interactive exhibits and video tricks aplenty. Many works deal with politics of identity—sexual, racial, and ethnic. Most major exhibitions are complemented by "Gallery Talks" in which the artist holds court at the museum to discuss the work and answer questions. Open Wed.-Fri. and Sun. noon-6pm, Sat. noon-8pm. Admission $3.50, artists, seniors, and students $2.50, children under 12 free. Sat. 6-8pm free.

Old Merchants House, 29 E. 4th St. (777-1089), between Lafayette St. and the Bowery. Subway: #4, 5, or 6 to Bleecker St. Walk 3 blocks north up Lafayette St. and a block east. New York City's only family home preserved intact from the 19th century. Built in 1832, the house was owned by Seabury Tredwell, a prosperous merchant, and preserves his family's furniture, clothing, and family memorabilia. Open Sun.-Thurs. 1-4pm. Admission $3, seniors and students $2.

Parsons Exhibition Center, at Parsons School of Design, 2 W. 13th St. (229-8987), at Fifth Ave. Subway: #4, 5, 6 or L, N, R to 14th St. A variety of exhibitions, many of student work, including photography, computer art, painting, and sculpture. Open Mon.-Sat. 9am-6pm. Free.

Police Academy Museum, 235 E. 20th St. (477-9753), near Second Ave. Subway: #6 to 23rd St. On the second floor of the city's police academy. An esoteric and somewhat perplexing collection of crime-related artifacts. Intriguing displays of counterfeit money and firearms, including Al Capone's personal machine gun. Interspersed throughout are intimidatingly posed mannequins in uniform, as well as old trophies that the police squad's various sports leagues have won. Call one day or more in advance to get a reservation. Open Mon.-Fri. 9am-2pm. Free.

Nicholas Roerich Museum, 319 W. 107th St. (864-7752), between Broadway and Riverside Dr. Subway: #1 or 9 to 110th St. A friend and close collaborator of

Stravinsky on Diaghilev's *Ballets Russes,* Nicholas Roerich painted, philoso-phized, archaeologized, studied things Slavic, and founded an educational institu-tion to promote world peace through the arts. Located in a stately old townhouse, the museum brims with Roerich's landscape paintings, books, and pamphlets on art, culture and philosophy. Open Tues.-Sun. 2-5pm. Free.

Schomburg Center for Research in Black Culture, 515 Lenox/Malcolm X Ave. (491-2200), at 135th St. Subway: #2 or 3 to 135th St. This branch of the New York Public Library has one of the world's largest collections of documentation on black history and culture, including taped oral history, photographs, and personal papers. Shows by African and African-American artists, and regular exhibitions concerning African-American issues. Open Mon.-Wed. and Fri.-Sat. 11am-6pm. Free.

Abigail Adams Smith Museum, 421 E. 61st St. (838-6878), between York and First Ave. Subway: #4, 5, 6, N, or R to 59th St.-Lexington Ave. Although the house bears her name, Abigail never actually lived (or even slept) here; in fact, this building was once her stable. Now refurbished with nine rooms of 18th-century articles, including a letter from George Washington. Open Sept.-May Mon.-Fri. noon-4pm, Sun. 1-5pm. Admission $3, students and seniors $2.

Studio Museum in Harlem, 144 W. 125th St. (864-4500), between Adam Clayton Powell Jr. Blvd. and Lenox/Malcolm X Ave. Subway: #2 or 3 to 125th St. Founded in 1967 at the height of the Civil Rights movement and dedicated to the collection and exhibition of works by black artists. Photographs, paintings, and sculptures in three broad categories: African-American art, Afro-Caribbean paintings, and African art and sculpture. Open Wed.-Fri. 10am-5pm, Sat.-Sun. 1-6pm. Admission $5, seniors and students $3, children $1; seniors free on Wed.

Ukrainian Museum, 203 Second Ave. (228-0110), between 12th and 13th St. Sub-way: L to Third Ave. This tiny upstairs museum exhibits late 19th- and early 20th-century Ukrainian folk art, including pottery, hand-carved candelabra, and tradi-tional embroidered ceremonial clothing. Also hosts special shows, such as the recent exhibition of art by New Yorkers of Ukrainian descent. Interesting for Ukraine buffs and those in the neighborhood. Seasonal exhibits on Christmas and Easter crafts as well as numerous courses in Ukrainian embroidery, baking, and Christmas ornament-making. Open Wed.-Sun. 1-5pm. Admission $1, seniors and students 50¢, children under 12 free.

The Whitney Museum of American Art at Philip Morris, 120 Park Ave. (878-2453 or 878-2550), at 42nd St. Subway: #4, 5, 6, 7 or S to 42nd. A small, one-gal-lery extension of the uptown mothership, featuring contemporary American installations in both its gallery and its larger indoor sculpture garden. Gallery talks on Wed. and Fri. at 1pm. Gallery hours Fri.-Wed. 11am-6pm, Thurs. 11am-7:30pm; sculpture garden Mon.-Sat. 7:30am-9:30pm, Sun. 11am-7pm. Free.

Yeshiva University Museum (718-960-5390) on 185th St. in the Bronx. Subway: #1 or 9 to 181st or 190th St. Features exhibitions concerning the Jewish commu-nity. Open Tues.-Thurs. 10:30am-5pm, Sun. noon-6pm, or call for appointment. Admission $3, senior and children under 17 $1.50.

Galleries

The city overflows with small galleries that exhibit (and, of course, vend) a wild diversity of art. Spend a few hours gallery-hopping and you're likely to be presented with every genre and medium of art you've ever imagined—paintings, sculptures, drawings, photographs, painted drawings, sculpted paintings—everything. Most gallery exhibits are interesting in some way (things always seem to be more interesting when they're free), and some are truly amazing. Last summer's show by Bill Burns at the 303 Gallery, titled "Safety Gear for Small Animals," featured a number of antique stuffed animals wearing items to protect them from present-day living conditions: an otter was outfitted with a respirator, a rat wore a fluorescent orange safety vest, and a rabbit wore hearing protectors. At the opposite end of the artistic spectrum, last year's inaugural exhibition at the Ace Gallery by Michael Heizer was huge and stunning. A tall, gray, metal door led into the middle of a long hall; variously sized rooms lit by skylight opened off the hall, and within each, large concrete and stone sculptures pierced the floors, graced the walls, and hung from the ceiling.

To get started, pick up a free copy of the *Gallery Guide* at any major museum or gallery; it lists the addresses, phone numbers, and hours of virtually every showplace in the city and comes equipped with several handy maps to orient you on your art odyssey. Extensive gallery information can also be found in the "Art" section of *New York* magazine as well as in the omniscient "Goings On About Town" in *The New Yorker.*

SoHo is a wonderland of galleries, with a particularly dense concentration lining Broadway between Houston and Spring St. More than 40 different establishments in this two-block stretch can keep you busy for a while. Madison Ave. between 70th and 84th has a generous sampling of ritzy showplaces, and another gaggle of galleries festoons 57th St. between Fifth and Sixth Ave. Most of these places are open from Tuesday to Saturday, from 10am or 11am to 5pm or 6pm. In the summer, galleries often close on Saturdays and many are open by appointment only (and, for the most part, only to those serious about buying) from late July through early September. One of the nicest things about gallery-hopping is that during the week, especially in the summer, galleries are air-conditioned and relatively empty. Try to go during off-hours to enjoy some of the widest open spaces in Manhattan for free.

Nearly all galleries throw "openings" for their exhibitions; these are often open to the public, offering the chance to drink wine, eat cheese, and pose, pose, pose (check the *Village Voice,* the *New Yorker,* and the *New York Press*). Stumbling upon an installation-in-progress can also be interesting, as walls are painted, bulky structures are erected, and artsy types actually sweat with the physical exertion.

While gallery-hopping can be great fun, remember that many of the commercial galleries have an elite image to maintain and aren't the most accommodating places for tourists not planning to shell out five grand for a 200-lb. granite porcupine. Always ask before invading the premises, especially if you travel in a pack of two or more.

■■■ SOHO

Hard economic times have sent the galleries in SoHo into a state of flux. Not only do they open and close with amazing rapidity, but many of them have had to cut their losses and sell what they call "bread and butter" art—a landscape that goes well with a yuppie sofa or a soothing sunset to remind the investment banker of his upcoming Club Med holiday. The avant-garde is having trouble getting its foot into the door of the ground level, more commercial galleries that line West Broadway.

With so many galleries packed into this tiny neighborhood, it's easy to get lost; look over your copy of *Gallery Guide* carefully so you don't miss a show that leaves tomorrow.

Some galleries can always be relied on for good shows. You might want to start at the **Alternative Museum,** 594 Broadway, fourth floor (966-4444)—which, unlike most SoHo galleries that bill themselves as alternative, actually *is* alternative, focusing on socially conscious art. (Open Tues.-Sun. 11am-6pm. See Museums.) On the second floor of the building is **American Primitive** (966-1530), which shows works by folk and self-taught American artists of the 19th and 20th centuries, most of whom are contemporary. The sculptures and paintings are generally very colorful and depict urban people and scenes; the style of folksy art presented here has become pervasive in the SoHo restaurant and bar scene. (Open Mon.-Sat. 11am-6pm; closed Sat. during July and Aug.) Also on the second floor of this building is the **Helander Gallery** (966-9797), a small exhibition space for such big names as Jennifer Bartlett, David Hockney, Francisco Clemente, and Larry Rivers. (Open Tues.-Sat. 11am-6pm; closed Sat. in July; closed entirely in Aug.) Just down the hall (and *still* on the second floor) is **Heineman Galleries** (334-0821), which specializes in cartoon art of graphic illustration such as that found in the *New Yorker* or newspaper op-ed pages. It's the largest commercial gallery of its kind in NYC. (Open Tues.-Sat. 10:30am-6pm.) On the third floor of the same building is the **Richard Meyer Gallery of African Art** (941-5968), which holds a fascinating collection of Western and Central African art, including masks, tapestries, and sculpture. (Open Sept.-May Fri.-Sat. 11am-5pm or by appointment.)

A mere skip away from this art-packed building lies the **Stuart Levy Gallery,** 588 Broadway, third floor, (941-0009). It features five to six one-person shows and several groups shows a year of all media incorporating photography. A major exhibition for 1995 will feature a selection of newly released photos from the Russian State Archives. (Open Sept.-July Tues.-Sat. 10am-6pm.) A branch of the famed **Leo Castelli Gallery** (431-6279) makes its home on the fourth floor of the Prince Building at 578 Broadway. Here you can see the smaller works of some big names in peace and quiet. Rauschenberg, Oldenburg, Artschweiger, and Johns are just a few standouts. (Open Sept.-June Tues.-Sat. 10am-6pm, July Tues.-Fri. 11am-5pm, closed Aug.) Adjacent to the Prince Building is 568 Broadway, at Prince St., which is home to a whopping 12 galleries. Among these is the **John Gibson** (925-1192), on the first floor above the lobby, which generally presents thematic installations such as last year's "Universe," in which the walls were painted a chlorophyll green, a small greenhouse was erected in one corner of the room using post-consumer, reprocessed plastic, and strawberry plants were grown using a strange hydroponic structure. (Open Sept.-June Tues.-Sat. 10am-6pm, July-Aug. Tues.-Fri. noon-6pm.) Around the corner, at 63 Crosby near Spring St., is the **A.I.R. Gallery** (966-0799), for women artists. (Open Tues.-Sat. 11am-6pm, closed late June-early Sept.)

Cross Broadway and walk west one block to Mercer St.; hang a right and head up two blocks to the corner of Houston St., where former uptown giant **Holly Solomon** now makes her home at 174 Mercer St. (941-5777). Among the gallery's featured artists is William Wegman, whose famous photographs of his Weimareiners in all sorts of guises have achieved mass-market appeal and have even made it onto T-shirts. (Open Sept.-June Tues.-Sat. 10am-6pm, July-Aug. Tues.-Fri. 10am-5pm.)

A block west on Houston St. and a few doors down on Greene St., **Metro Pictures,** 150 Greene St. (925-8335), is a flashy haven for photographers as well as select sculptors and painters, and is well-stocked with mainstays like Cindy Sherman, Robert Longo, and Louise Lawler. (Open July Tues.-Fri. 10am-6pm; Sept.-June Tues.-Sat. 10am-6pm.) A few steps farther south on Greene St. is the famed **Pace Gallery,** 142 Greene St. (431-9224), a huge open space where you can see the works of biggies like Julian Schnabel and Claes Oldenburg. (Open Mon.-Thurs. 10am-6pm, Fri. 10am-4pm; mid-Sept.-early June Tues.-Sat. 10am-6pm.) Continuing down Greene St. will bring you to the entertaining **303 Gallery,** 89 Greene St.

(966-5605), which hosted last year's show by Bill Burns titled "Safety Gear for Small Animals." (Open Tues.-Sat. 10am-6pm; closed Sat. in July-Aug.) Farther down on Greene St., near Spring, is the **Blum Helman Warehouse,** 80 Greene St. (226-8770). Lesser-known but key artists show here right alongside the brand names. Spend time with works by Chuch Agro, Karin Davie, and Richard Serra. (Open Sept.-June Tues.-Sat. 10am-6pm; July-Aug. by appointment only.)

Artists Space, a fixture of the New York art scene, recently moved to 38 Greene St., third floor (226-3970), at Grand St. A non-profit gallery that brings new talents to light, the Space lets you see them while they're hatching—especially in September. Every year 10 to 15 artists are chosen from the organization's slide file of unknowns for a group exhibition. (Open late Sept.-mid-July Tues.-Sat. 10am-6pm; closed Tues. mid-July to late Sept.)

If you're not so sick of art that you're going to yench if you see another canvas, walk west one block on Grand St. and go right on Wooster St. to the **Drawing Center,** 35 Wooster St. (219-2166). The Center presents work by established artists such as Richard Serra but focuses more on exhibitions intended to bring attention to the work of emerging and underrepresented artists. (Open Tues. and Thurs.-Fri. 10am-6pm, Wed. 10am-8pm, Sat. 11am-6pm.) The **Brooke Alexander Gallery,** 59 Wooster St., second floor (925-4338), between Spring and Broome St., often hosts some interesting thematic exhibits, such as last summer's "Drawn in the '70s," which featured work by a large group of artists, including Richard Artschweiger and Bruce Nauman. (Open Tues.-Sat. 10am-6pm; early July to mid-Aug. Tues.-Fri. 11am-5pm.) Head farther up Wooster St. and stop in at the hard-to-find **Gagosian Gallery,** 136 Wooster St. (228-2828), which features Henry Moore, David Salle, and Peter Halley. (Open Mon.-Sat. 10am-6pm.) The excellent **Paula Cooper Gallery,** 149-155 Wooster St. (674-0766), holds court near the corner of Houston St. and shows Jackie Winsor, Elizabeth Murray, Jennifer Bartlett, Julian Lethbridge, and Dara Birnbaum. (Open mid-Sept. to mid-June Tues.-Sun. 10am-6pm; mid-June to mid-Sept. Mon.-Fri. 9:30am-5pm.)

Walk back down Wooster St. and hang a right to get to 130 Prince St. Six galleries populate this building; the **James Danzinger** (226-0056) shows many well-known photographers, including Mapplethorpe, Leibowitz, and Weber, as well as artists working in other mediums. (Open Tues.-Sat. 11am-6pm; closed in Aug.)

Continue on Prince St. to W. Broadway and go right, up toward Houston St. **Martin Lawrence Galleries,** 457 W. Broadway (995-8865, open Sun.-Thurs. 10am-7pm, Fri.-Sat. 10am-8pm), and **Martin Lawrence Modern,** 426-428 W. Broadway (941-5665, open Mon.-Thurs. 10am-7pm, Sat. 10am-8pm, Sun. 11am-7pm), both near Houston St., are much more crowded and commercial than most, with price tags placed prominently on the walls next to the paintings. Both specialize in Pop Art: Warhol, Lichtenstein, Haring, Kostabi, and others.

Down the block, **Leo Castelli** (431-5160) has its main branch on the second floor of 420 Broadway, mixing new works in all media by young and old artists. See the Starn twins with re-run stars Ellsworth Kelly, Frank Stella, Rauschenberg, and Warhol. (Open mid-Sept. to mid-June Tues.-Sat. 10am-6pm; mid-June to mid-Sept. Tues.-Fri. 11am-5pm.) In the same building is **Sonnabend** (966-6160), which features contemporary paintings by American and European artists. Jeff Koons, John Baldessari, and Robert Rauschenberg top the bill. (Open Tues.-Sat. 10am-6pm; July-Aug. by appointment only.) Now walk across the street to **Mary Boone,** 417 W. Broadway (431-1818), where the likes of Sean Scully and Yoko Ono are featured, as well as Barbara "You where you are shown" Kruger and Eric Fischl. (Open Tues.-Sat. 10am-6pm; no public exhibitions from late June through early Sept.)

Also check out the **O.K. Harris Gallery,** 383 W. Broadway (431-3600), which has a range of artists and mediums from installation pieces to photographs to reliefs, as well as four one-person shows each year. (Open Tues.-Sat. 10am-6pm, first 2 weeks of July Tues.-Fri. noon-5pm; closed mid-July through Labor Day.) **Nahan Galleries,** 381 W. Broadway (966-9313), is one of the best-established and most commercial galleries in the area, recently having celebrated its 35th anniversary; the gallery mainly represents contemporary artists, including Papart, Tobiasse, and Coignard. (Open Mon.-Fri. 10am-6pm, Sat. 11am- 6pm, Sun. noon-6pm.)

A bit distant from the main SoHo scene but well worth the trip is **Ace Gallery,** 275 Hudson St. (255-5599), just south of Spring St. This huge gallery, with its lofty ceilings and skylights, is as somber and daunting as a temple (but without an altar). Within the gallery is also a bookstore with works focusing on 20th-century art, architecture, and poetry. (Open Tues.-Sat. 1-6pm.)

■■■ UPPER EAST SIDE

M. Knoedler & Co., Inc., 19 E. 70th St. (794-0550). One of the oldest and most respected galleries in the city, it shows Abstract Expressionists like Olitski and Motherwell. Recently, contemporary trends infiltrated the time-honored institution, which now mounts shows like "Robert Rauschenberg: Bicyclords, Urban Bourbons & Eco-Echo." Open Mon.-Fri. 9:30am-5pm.

Hirschl and Adler Galleries, 21 E. 70th St. (535-8810). A wide variety of 18th- to 20th-century European and American art. Good contemporary work. Open Mon.-Fri. 9:30am-4:45pm. Also **Hirschl and Adler Modern** upstairs.

■■■ 57TH STREET

Fuller Building, 41 E. 57th St., between Madison and Park Ave. Stylish Art Deco building hosts 12 floors of galleries. Contemporary notables such as Robert Miller, André Emmerich, and Susan Sheehan, collectors of ancient works like Frederick Schultz, and several galleries handling modern works. The **André Emmerich Gallery** (752-0124) features important contemporary work by Hockney et al. Most galleries in the building keep hours of Mon.-Sat. 10am-6pm, but there is extreme variation, and from Oct.-May most will be closed Mon.

Marlborough Gallery, 40 W. 57th St. (541-4900), between Fifth and Sixth Ave. A great diversity of forms, including painting, mixed media, and sculpture, featuring artists from throughout the world. Artists of note include Red Grooms, John Davies, and Marisol. Open Mon.-Sat. 10am-5:30pm.

Pace Gallery, 32 E. 57th St. (421-3292). Four floors dedicated to the promotion of widely disparate forms of art. **Pace Gallery** specializes in painting, sculpture, and drawing, **Pace Editions** in prints both old and new, **Pace MacGill** in photography, and the unfortunately named **Pace Primitive** in African works. Open Tues.-Fri. 9:30am-5:30pm, Sat. 10am-6pm.

Sidney Janis Gallery, 110 W. 57th St. (586-0110), between Sixth and Seventh Ave. Spanning artistic epochs from Cubism to Minimalism, this gallery has hosted one-man shows by de Kooning, Gorky, Gottlieb, Pollock, and Rothko. It has also examined the links between its favored artists in large-scale conceptual shows, like the recent "An American Homage to Matisse," which included works by Avery, Kelly, Lichtenstein, and others. Open Mon.-Sat. 10am-5pm.

Entertainment & Nightlife

Being in New York at night is like being in a huge room full of beautiful people, all of whom look at you with longing eyes. From the blindingly bright lights of Times Square to the dark, impenetrably smoky atmosphere of a Greenwich Village or SoHo bar, New York pulls you in a million directions at once. Find some performance art; hear some jazz; go to an all-night diner—heck, even get a tattoo. A cab ride home at 3am through empty streets with the windows down is always sure to make your spirits soar. Incomparable during the day, the city is unbelievable at night. We guarantee your head will swivel.

Choosing a show or club from among the city's dizzyingly broad array of entertainment and cultural activity is a common problem. The theaters, halls, and clubs, and hundreds of other independent venues that are together responsible for New York's cultural hegemony over the rest of the country all compete fiercely for popular attention and critical credibility. *Let's Go* lists New York's more essential venues and hot spots, but you should plan to check local sources to find out about other places and to get the scoop on present offerings. A number of publications print daily, weekly, and monthly entertainment and nightlife calendars; try *New York* magazine, the *Village Voice,* and *The New York Times* (particularly the Sunday edition). The most comprehensive survey of the theater scene can be found in *The New Yorker*. The monthly *Free Time* calendar ($1.25) lists free cultural events throughout Manhattan. Try the NYC Parks Department's **entertainment hotline** (360-3456; 24 hrs.) for the lowdown on special events in parks throughout the city. Call the **NYC/ON STAGE hotline** (768-1818) for a comprehensive listing of all the theater, dance, and music events taking place each week. Also try **765-ARTS,** which lists music, theater, art, and other events at more than 500 venues.

■■■ THEATER

Broadway is currently undergoing a revival—ticket sales are booming, and mainstream musicals are receiving more than their fair share of attention. Dorky, old-fashioned productions such as *Crazy For You* and *Guys and Dolls* are very popular, and tickets can be hard to get. The many Off-Broadway and Off-Off-Broadway shows throughout the city offer a cheaper and less mainstream alternative for theatergoers.

Consult *The New Yorker* for superior short descriptions of current shows, or try *The New York Times*. For listings of Broadway, Off-Broadway, and Off-Off-Broadway shows, see *Listings,* a weekly guide to entertainment in Manhattan ($1). **The Broadway Line** (563-2929) is an interactive phone service which gives show descriptions, performance schedules, and ticket prices for all types of shows, and it even forwards your call to a ticket agent if you are ready to make a purchase. For information on shows and ticket availability, you can also call the **NYC/ON STAGE hotline** at 768-1818. The NYC Department of Cultural Affairs **Arts Hotline** (956-2787) offers an actual person to advise you (open Mon.-Fri. 9am-5pm).

Though Broadway tickets usually run upwards of $50, there are many ways to save money. Some theaters have recently introduced $15 seats on the farthest reaches of the balcony, though these seats are predictably hard to come by. **TKTS** (768-1818 for recorded info) sells half-price tickets to many Broadway and some of the larger Off-Broadway shows on the same day of the performance, from a booth in the middle of Duffy Square (the northern part of Times Square, at 47th and Broadway). The board near the front of the line posts the names of the shows with available tickets. There is a $2.50 service charge per ticket, and only cash or traveler's checks are accepted. (Tickets sold Mon.-Sat. 3-8pm for evening performances; Wed. and Sat. 10am-2pm for matinees; and Sun. noon-8pm for matinees and evening performances.) The lines can be long, snaking around the traffic island a few times, but they move fairly quickly. To beat the lines, arrive before selling time. The lines are often shorter downtown, where TKTS has an indoor branch in the mezzanine of 2 World Trade Center. (Booth operates Mon.-Fri. 11am-5:30pm, Sat. 11am-3:30pm; Sunday matinee tickets sold on Sat.)

You can get a similar discount with **"twofers"** (i.e., two fer the price of one), ticket coupons that float around the city at bookstores, libraries, and the New York Visitors and Convention Bureau. They are usually for old Broadway warhorses— shows that have been running strong for a very long time.

Full-price tickets may be reserved over the phone and paid for by credit card through **Tele-Charge** (239-6200, 24 hrs) for Broadway shows, **Ticket Central** (279-4200, open 1-8pm daily) for Off-Broadway shows, and **Ticketmaster** (307-7171, 24 hrs.) for all types of shows. All three services assess a per-ticket service charge; make sure you ask before purchasing. These fees can be evaded by purchasing tickets directly from the box offices.

The renowned **Shakespeare in the Park** series, founded by the same Joseph Papp who founded the Joseph Papp Public Theater (see below), is a New York summer tradition that practically everyone in the city has attended (or attempted to attend). From late June through August, two Shakespeare plays are presented at the Delacorte Theater in Central Park, near the 81st St. entrance on the Upper West Side, just north of the 79th St. Transverse (861-7277 or 598-7100). The glorious outdoor amphitheater overlooks Turtle Pond and its mini-Dunsinane. Top-notch productions—plus the opportunity to perform Shakespeare in the great outdoors— attract the most important actors around. Recent performances have included *The Taming of the Shrew* with Morgan Freeman and Tracey Ullman, *Richard III* with Denzel Washington, and *Othello* with Raoul Julia and Christopher Walken. Kevin Kline serves as the festival's artistic director. For free tickets, wait in line at the Delacorte Theater (Tickets available from 1pm; try to get there by 11:30am. Also available from 1-3pm at the Public Theater at 425 Lafayette St. downtown. Limit of two tickets per person. Doors open Tues.-Sun. at 7:30pm, shows start at 8pm).

For years, the **Joseph Papp Public Theater,** 425 Lafayette St. (598-7150), was inextricably linked with its namesake founder, one of the city's leading producers and favorite sons (he died in 1991). The six theaters here present a wide variety of shows; recently, an exhaustive and exhausting Shakespeare Marathon included every single one of the Bard's plays down to *Timon of Athens.* Ticket prices $15-35. The Public Theater saves about one quarter of the seats for every production, to be sold for about $10 on the day of performance (starting at 6pm for evening performances and 1pm for matinees).

The city also boasts the widest variety of ethnic theater in the country. The **Repertorio Español,** currently housed in the Gramercy Arts Theater at 138 E. 27th St. (889-2850), presents many productions in Spanish (tickets $15-20). The **Negro Ensemble Company** (575-5860) rents out spaces to perform works by and about African-Americans, such as Charles Fuller's *A Soldier's Play,* which won the Pulitzer Prize in 1983 (tickets $15-20). The **Pan Asian Repertory Theater** (245-2660) is the largest Asian-American repertory theater in the U.S., located in the Church of St. Clements at Playhouse 46, 423 W. 46th St. The **Irish Arts Center,** at 553 W. 51st St. (757-3318), presents contemporary and classic Irish and Irish-American plays (tickets $20-25).

New York is the birthplace of the elusive amalgam called **"performance art,"** a combination of stand-up comedy, political commentary, theatrical monologue, and video art. The Brooklyn Academy of Music's famous **Next Wave festival** specializes in performance art, as do these Manhattan places: **The Kitchen,** at 512 W. 19th St. (255-5793), **Franklin Furnace,** at 112 Franklin St. (925-4671), **Performance Space 122 (P.S. 122),** at 150 First Ave. (477-5288), and the **Theater for the New City,** at

155 First Ave. (254-1109). **La Mama,** at 74a E. 4th St. (254-6468), the most venerable of the lot, helped Sam Shepard get started.

BROADWAY

Most Broadway theaters are located north of Times Square, between Eighth Ave. and Broadway and the streets that connect them. Broadway theaters are open only when a play is in production, and most have no phones. Call **Telecharge** (239-6200) or one of the other information lines listed above for information, or check the papers.

Ambassador Theater, 219 W. 49th St., between Broadway and Eighth Ave. Built on a slant. Spencer Tracy played here in *The Last Mile* in 1930. In *The Straw Hat Revue* (1939), Danny Kaye, Jerome Robbins, and Imogene Coca parodied the rest of the shows playing on Broadway, anticipating *Forbidden Broadways* to come.

Belasco Theater, 111 W. 44th St., between Sixth and Seventh Ave. Built in 1907 by David Belasco, a producer extraordinaire who acted, designed, directed, and believed fervently in spectacle. He equipped the place with an elevated stage that could be lowered for set changes as well as a backstage elevator that would ascend to his private apartments. In 1935, the legendary Group Theater brought Clifford Odets's *Awake and Sing* to the Belasco. The Group Theater proved the most politically explicit act on Broadway, and 4 decades later the very nude revue *Oh! Calcutta!* exploded here as the most sexually explicit.

Booth Theater, 222 W. 45th St., between Broadway and Eighth Ave. Designer Herts dressed it up in early Italian Renaissance in 1913 and Melanie Kahane modernized it in 1979. Kaufman and Hart's *You Can't Take It With You* opened here, as did Noel Coward's *Blithe Spirit*. Ntozake Shange's poetic *For Colored Girls Who Have Considered Suicide When the Rainbow is Enuf* lasted 742 performances. Recent productions have included Arthur Miller's *Broken Glass,* which may still be running.

Broadhurst Theater, 235 W. 44th St., between Broadway and Eighth Ave. Designed in 1917 by Herbert J. Krapp, the man who churned out these theaters at the top of the century. Helen Hayes crowned the place with her legendary performance in *Victoria Regina* back in 1935. *Grease* first rocked here, as did *Godspell*. And *Dancin'* hoofed here for 3 years. Ian McKellan played Salieri to Tim Curry's Mozart and Jane Seymour's Constanze in the American premier of *Amadeus*. Patrick Stewart has taken off his Star Trek uniform the past 2 holiday seasons for an energetic 1-man performance of Dickens's classic *A Christmas Carol.* The theater's most successful recent production has been *Kiss of the Spider Woman,* starring Vanessa Williams, which won 7 Tony Awards in 1993, including Best Musical.

Broadway Theater, 1681 Broadway, between 52nd and 53rd St. Built as a movie house in 1924 with a whopping capacity of 1765. Its first theatrical venture, *The New Yorkers* by Cole Porter and Herbert Fields, closed in 20 weeks—it was hard to sell tickets for $5.50 during the Depression. Benefits, including Irving Berlin's *This Is the Army* with a cameo by Irv himself, raised money for the Emergency Relief fund during World War II. Soon Oscar Hammerstein did a jazzed-up all-black *Carmen*. A few operas and dance troupes later, the stage saw another musical: *Mr. Wonderful,* starring Sammy Davis Jr. and Sr. Soon *The Most Happy Fella* dropped in, *The Body Beautiful* dropped out, and Les Ballets de Paris, the Beryozka Russian Dance Company, and the Old Vic flew in to do Shakespeare. Then Ethel Merman brought musical comedy belting back with *Gypsy*. In 1972, *Fiddler on the Roof* ended its run here, breaking previous records with its tally of 3242 performances. Harold Prince revived Leonard Bernstein's *Candide* with labyrinthine staging and multi-level seating; he then went on to stage *Evita* here. Here Anthony Quinn starred in the revival of *Zorba,* and most recently, the theater has hosted *Miss Saigon,* which in 1994 was in its fourth year and will most likely run throughout 1995 (tickets $15-65).

Brooks Atkinson Theatre, 256 W. 47th St. (719-4099), between Broadway and Eighth Ave. Designed in 1926 as the Mansfield by very busy architect Herbert J. Krapp. In 1930 *The Green Pastures* opened here, setting Southern blacks amidst

THEATER

Old Testament events; it enjoyed a run of 640 performances and won the Pulitzer Prize. Marc Blitzstein's revolutionary *The Cradle Will Rock* opened here during the memorable snowstorm of December 26, 1947. In the 50s, the struggling theater served as a TV playhouse. Then, in 1960, it was named for the much-loved *New York Times* theater critic and Harvard grad who had retired from reviewing plays that spring. John Steinbeck's *Of Mice and Men* was revived here with James Earl Jones as Lenny. Ellen Burstyn and Charles Grodin conducted their annual fling here in *Same Time, Next Year* for 1453 performances. *She Loves Me* closed in June 1994.

Circle in the Square Theatre, on W. 50th St. between Broadway and Eighth Ave. Delightfully in the round, a charming hotbed of things Shavian and Shepardian. Modeled after the downtown theater by the same name but half the size, it opened with *Mourning Becomes Elektra* in 1972. The circular stage has brimmed with sand for Tina Howe's *Coastal Disturbances* and was once strung up with laundry for a production of *Sweeney Todd*. Much Molière here, too.

Cort Theater, 138 W. 148 St., between Sixth and Seventh Ave. Built in the style of Louis XVI, with a lobby of Pavanozza marble and 999 seats. Katherine Hepburn made her debut here in 1928 in *These Days*; it closed in a week, but she returned in the 50s to star in a blockbuster run of *As You Like It*. Grace Kelly made her first Broadway appearance here. In 1994, the current production was *Twilight: Los Angeles, 1992,* a celebrated play about that year's riots in L.A.

Ethel Barrymore Theater, 243 W. 47th St., between Broadway and Eighth Ave. In 1927 the celebrated Ethel was blithely appearing in a Maugham play at another theater when playwright Zoe Atkins approached her and promised that the Shuberts would build her a theater if she would agree to do a play called *The Kingdom of God*. Ethel Barrymore read and liked it and soon found herself starring in this play and a series of others. Alfred Lunt, Lynn Fontanne, and Noel Coward appeared here in Coward's *Design for Living*. Described as "a kettle of venom" by Brooks Atkinson, Claire Booth Luce's scathing play *The Women*, with a cast of 40 females, ran for 657 performances. *A Streetcar Named Desire* opened here in 1947, starring Jessica Tandy and Marlon Brando, as did Lorraine Hansbery's acclaimed *Raisin in the Sun*, starring Sidney Poitier. *The Sisters Rosenweig* was running in 1994.

Eugene O'Neill Theater, 230 W. 49th St., between Broadway and Eighth Ave. Using the Georgian style, Krapp designed this one too, born as the Forrest Theater back in 1925. In 1959, it was renamed in honor of playwright Eugene O'Neill, who had died in 1953. Arthur Miller's *All My Sons* opened here, as did his *A View From the Bridge*. A slew of musicals have come and gone here, followed by a host of Neil Simon plays and some sterner stuff. Recently, controversial Trumpette Marla Maples starred here in *The Will Rogers Follies*. In 1994 the O'Neill began a revival of *Grease,* which may still be running; to promote the musical, the outisde of the theater was painted bright, fluorescent pink and covered with graffiti in black paint.

Gershwin Theater, on W. 50th St. between Broadway and Eighth Ave. Neo-Art Nouveau. It started up in 1972 as the Uris, hosting *Porgy and Bess*, *Sweeney Todd*, and *The Pirates of Penzance*, who spent the summer in Central Park. Both *The King and I* and *Mame* were reviewed here.

Golden Theater, 252 W. 45th St., between Broadway and Eighth Ave. Built by Krapp, commissioned by the Chanin brothers, the production whiz-kids who wanted the 800-seat space to accommodate intimate artistic work. When *Angel Street*, a strange piece of Victoriana, opened here, skeptical producers ordered only 3 days' worth of playbills—but the show ran for 1293 (3 x 431) performances. Some revues swept through—starring Mike Nichols and Elaine May, Yves Montand, and finally the likes of Peter Cook and Dudley Moore in *Beyond the Fringe*. A recent long-running production at the Golden, *Jackie Mason—Politically Incorrect,* may still be running (tickets $42-47.50).

Helen Hayes Theater, 240 W. 44th St., between Broadway and Eighth. It opened in 1912 with only 299 seats and was soon appropriately christened the Little Theatre. Originally designed to stage intimate and non-commercial works, it didn't do too well commercially and closed. It served as New York Times Hall from 1942-

1959 and as the ABC TV Studio from 1959-1963, but then went on to host the long-running comedy *Gemini* and Tony Award-winning *Torch Song Trilogy*. In 1994, *Sally Marr and Her Escorts*, about Lenny Bruce's mother and starring Joan Rivers, went into production.

Imperial Theater, 249 W. 45th St., between Broadway and Eighth Ave. Built in 1923, it entered the big leagues with *Oh, Kay!* by the Gershwins (story by P.G. Wodehouse and Guy Bolton). Rodgers and Hart, with George Abbot, conflated American musicals and Russian ballet in their 1935 hit *On Your Toes*. Cole Porter's *Leave It To Me* introduced to the Broadway stage Mary Martin and a chorus blue-boy named Gene Kelly. Martin returned in *One Touch of Venus*, a show by unlikely collaborators Kurt Weill, S.J. Perelman, and Ogden Nash. Ethel Merman proved there's no business like show business in *Annie Get Your Gun*. *Fiddler on the Roof* opened here on September 22, 1964. *Cabaret* had a brief stint, followed by *Zorba* and *Minnie's Boys*, a musical about the Marx Brothers. *Les Misérables* has jerked tears here since October, 1990, and almost certainly will continue through 1995 (tickets $15-65).

Lunt-Fontanne Theater, 205 W. 46th St. (575-9200), between Broadway and Eighth Ave. Built in 1910 as the Globe. Carrière and Hastings planned the seating and equipped the place with an oval ceiling-panel that could be removed in fair weather. Fanny Brice dazzled here in the *Ziegfeld Follies of 1921. No, No Nanette*, featuring the song "Tea for Two," was a hit here in the 20s. The Globe went dark during the Depression, and then became a movie house. In 1957, the City Investing Company fixed it up and named it after dashing drama couple Alfred Lunt and Lynn Fontanne. The restored house hosted new musicals *The Sound of Music* and *The Rothschilds* as well as revivals *A Funny Thing Happened on the Way to the Forum* and *Hello, Dolly!* Sandy Duncan flew here as *Peter Pan.*

Lyceum Theater, 149 W. 45th St., between Sixth and Seventh Ave. The oldest of the lot, designed by Herts and Tallant back in 1903, topped by a 10-story tower with scene shops, carpentry studios, and extra dressing rooms galore. It faced demolition in 1939; playwrights George S. Kaufman and Moss Hart chipped in with some friends, bought it in 1940, and sold it to the Shubert Organization in 1945. *Born Yesterday*, with Judy Holliday, opened here in 1946. *Look Back in Anger* stormed over from England in 1957. In 1980, the 1939 flop *Morning's at Seven* was revived here—and won a Tony Award.

Majestic Theater, 247 W. 44th St., between Broadway and Eighth Ave. The largest legit theater in the district and the last of the former Chanin chain. Rodgers and Hammerstein's *Carousel* opened here, as did their short-lived *Allegro* and their hot ticket *South Pacific*, which ran for 1925 performances. *Camelot*, with Julie Andrews and Richard Burton, charmed Broadway for 873 performances. Nowadays, Andrew Lloyd Webber's *Phantom of the Opera* skulks on after seven lucrative years.

Mark Hellinger Theater, 237 W. 51st St., between Broadway and Eighth Ave. On April 22, 1930, it opened as the Hollywood Theater Moviehouse. It became the 51st Street Theater in 1936. In 1940, Laurence Olivier and Vivian Leigh were Romeo and Juliet here, but soon the movies started playing again. Then, in 1949, Anthony Farrell bought the place and named it for Broadway columnist Mark Hellinger. The 50s saw revues and Gilbert and Sullivan. Musical comedy reared its feathered head in 1955 with *Plain and Fancy*, a stylish musical about the Amish. In 1956, *My Fair Lady* won innumerable awards and ran for 2717 performances. *Jesus Christ Superstar* premiered at this theater; the hall has since been bought by the Times Square Church, ironically.

Martin Beck Theatre, 302 W. 45th St., between Eighth and Ninth Ave. When built in 1924, it was the only Byzantine-style American theater. The Abbey Irish Theater Players performed here in 1932 in classics like *Juno and the Paycock* and *Playboy of the Western World*. Katharine Cornell played Juliet here to Basil "Sherlock" Rathbone's Romeo and Orson Welles's Tybalt. Tennessee Williams found his way here with *The Rose Tattoo*, starring Maureen Stapleton and Eli Wallach, and *Sweet Bird of Youth*, starring Geraldine Page and Paul Newman. Liz Taylor

THEATER

made her Broadway debut here in *The Little Foxes*. The classic musical *Guys and Dolls* should remain in production here through 1995 (tickets $40-50).

Minskoff Theatre, 200 W. 45th St. at Broadway. Less streamlined than its neighbor, the Gershwin, but equally high-tech. Its 1621 seats are 35 ft. in the air. It opened on March 13, 1973, with Debbie Reynolds in a revival of *Irene*. Rudolf Nureyev pirouetted through here with the Murray Lewis Dance Company in 1978, followed by a series of short-lived musicals: *The King of Hearts,* a *West Side Story* revival, and *Can-Can,* a fast-stomping extravaganza that closed after 5 days. *Sunset Boulevard* was scheduled to premier here in November 1994 and could enjoy a long run through 1995.

Music Box Theater, 239 W. 45th St., between Broadway and Eighth Ave. Cute, charming, built in 1921 by Sam Harris and Irving Berlin to house Berlin's *Music Box Revues.* This stage braved the Depression with French comedy *Topaze* by Marcel Pagnol and Noel Coward's "Mad Dogs and Englishmen" ditty (not to be confused with Joe Cocker's flailing album of the same name) sung by Beatrice Lillie in *The Third Little Show.* The Music Box production *Of Thee I Sing* became the first musical comedy to win the Pulitzer Prize. When romantic comedies upstaged revues, the Music Box churned out the tuneless *I Remember Mama,* introducing a young Marlon Brando to the stage; Tennessee Williams's *Summer and Smoke;* and William Inge's *Bus Stop. Sleuth* mysteriously endured for 1222 performances, *Deathtrap* for a prime 1609. Irving Berlin maintained a lively financial and emotional interest in the theater until his death. *Blood Brothers,* a musical, could continue here through 1995 (tickets $45-65).

Nederlander Theater, 208 W. 41st St., between Seventh and Eighth Ave. It opened as the National Theater in 1921. Noel Coward and Gertrude Lawrence trod the stage in a group of plays called *Tonight at 8:30.* Orson Welles and John Houseman transported their Shakespearean productions from the smaller Mercury Theater. Here Sir John Gielgud and Lillian Gish starred in a failed production of *Crime and Punishment,* and Edward Albee premiered his successful *Who's Afraid of Virginia Woolf*—starring Uta Hagen and directed by Alan Schneider— and his more obscure *Tiny Alice.* The Royal Shakespeare Company's *A Midsummer Night's Dream* directed by Peter Brook, came to visit, as did Tom Stoppard's *Jumpers* and Harold Pinter's *Betrayal.* In 1980 the National-turned-Billy Rose-turned-Trafalgar was dubbed *The Nederlander* in honor of late theater owner David Tobias Nederlander.

Neil Simon Theater, 250 W. 52nd St., between Broadway and Eighth Ave. Tireless designer Herbert J. Krapp built this in 1927 as the Alvin Theater with a capacity of 1400. The Lunts' *The Taming of the Shrew,* staged for the Finnish Relief Fund, was followed by Robert E. Sherwood's Pulitzer Prize-winning *There Shall Be No Night,* about Russia's invasion of Finland. The Alvin found lighter fare with long-running *A Funny Thing Happened on the Way to The Forum* and Tom Stoppard's landmark farce *Rosencrantz and Guildenstern Are Dead.*

Palace Theatre, 1564 Broadway at 47th St. Sarah Bernhardt, Ethel Barrymore— you name them, they played the Palace. Once a vaudeville haunt for Houdini, W.C. Fields, and the Marx Brothers, the Palace became a movie house with few spells of musical theater from the 30s to the 50s. Then in 1965, James Nederlander restored it. Lauren Bacall stopped by to be *The Woman of the Year,* later followed by the more outrageous men of the year in *La Cage aux Folles.* The Palace debuted Disney's blockbuster musical adaptation *Beauty and the Beast* in 1994; it should continue through 1995 (tickets $20-65).

Plymouth Theater, 236 W. 45th St., between Broadway and Eighth Ave. Built in 1917, Krapp designed it to seat 1000. Thornton Wilder's *Skin of Our Teeth* played here in 1942. A British invasion began with *Equus, Piaf,* and *The Real Thing;* English visitors completely reconstructed the house for the Royal Shakespeare Company's 8-hr., Dickensian marathon *Nicholas Nickleby,* which won Tonys for actor Roger Rees and directors Trevor Nunn and John Caird. 1994's main production was *Passion,* which won the 1994 Tony Award for Best Musical and which should continue through 1995 (tickets $40-65).

Richard Rodgers Theatre, 226 W. 46th St., between Broadway and Eighth Ave. Krapp sloped the seats L-Z upward for short people in the back. Here *Finian's*

THEATER

Rainbow charmed Broadway with an Irish lilt—725 performances worth. *Guys and Dolls* opened here in 1950, won 8 Tony Awards, and lasted 1194 performances. Audrey Hepburn was transmogrified into Jean Giraudoux's lyrical sprite in *Ondine* in 1954. In 1975, Sir John Gielgud directed Maggie Smith in a revival of *Private Lives*, and Bob Fosse staged the hit *Chicago*. The 80s brought the sizzling musical *Nine*, based on Fellini's *8½*. Neil Simon's *Laughter on the 23rd Floor* played here in 1994.

Roundabout Theatre, 1530 Broadway (719-9393). This tiny, 500-seat theater is just large enough to be considered Broadway. It produces classics and revivals of plays and musicals. One of 1994's main productions was Ibsen's *Hedda Gabler*, which starred Kelly McGillis (of *Top Gun* fame). Tickets average $45-60.

St. James Theater, 246 W. 44th St., between Broadway and Eighth Ave. Built in 1927. Seats 1600 in Georgian splendor. Here "April in Paris" was first sung, and this was the first American stage on which Hamlet soliloquized. John Houseman and Orson Welles collaborated on Richard Wright's chilling *Native Son*. *Oklahoma!* whirled in 1943, dazzling New York, running for 2248 performances, and launching Rodgers and Hammerstein. Yul Brynner first took the Broadway stage here in *The King and I* in 1951. Laurence Olivier and Anthony Quinn even traded roles at whim in their remarkable production of Anouilh's *Becket*. Joseph Papp brought his musical version of *Two Gentleman of Verona*. Straight out of 60s vinyl, The Who's legendary rock opera *Tommy* now tilts and flashes here.

Shubert Theatre, 225 W. 44th St., between Broadway and Eighth Ave. Built in 1913 by Lee and J.J. Shubert in memory of their deceased brother Sam. The Shubert exemplifies the Venetian Renaissance. 1932 brought *Americana*, with its Depression song "Brother, Can You Spare a Dime?" In 1943, Paul Robeson played Othello, co-starring with Uta Hagen and José Ferrer. Katherine Hepburn thrilled audiences with *The Philadelphia Story* for 417 sold-out performances. *A Chorus Line* opened and closed here after its record-breaking run. The musical *Crazy for You* will be into its fifth year as of February 1995.

Theater Royale, 242 W. 45th St., between Broadway and Eighth Ave. Designed by Krapp, this house seats over 1000 and caters mostly to musicals. Tennessee Williams's first Broadway play, *The Glass Menagerie*, starring Laurette Taylor, moved here from the Off-Broadway Playhouse. Julie Andrews made her debut in *The Boy Friend*, a 1954 takeoff on 1920s musicals. Thornton Wilder's *The Matchmaker* previously flopped as *The Merchant of Yonkers* and later got musicalized as *Hello, Dolly!* here in 1955. Mary Tyler Moore took the man's role in *Whose Life Is It Anyway?*, continuing the tradition of profuse gender confusion initiated by Jagger, Bowie, and the rest of the "glam" movement of the 70s. J.B. Priestley's *An Inspector Calls* is likely to continue here in 1995.

Virginia Theater, 245 W. 52nd St., between Broadway and Eighth Ave. On April 13, 1925, President Coolidge pushed a button in Washington, D.C., that set the floodlights flowing over Shaw's *Caesar and Cleopatra*, starring Helen Hayes and Lionel Atwill. Next, Lunt and Fontanne came here with Shaw's *Arms and the Man*. Edward G. Robinson graced the stage in 1927 in Pirandello's *Right You Are If You Think You Are*. A series of flops forced the Theater Guild to lease out the place as a radio playhouse from 1943-50. The American National Theater and Academy (ANTA) then took over and started sponsoring experimental productions and straight plays such as *J.B.*, *A Man For All Seasons*, and a revival of *Our Town* with Henry Fonda.

Walter Kerr Theater, 225 W. 48th St. Built in a record 66 days in 1921 as The Ritz and only recently christened the Walter Kerr in honor of the gentle critic. When it was the WPA Theater, the Federal Theater Project staged *Pinocchio* and T.S. Eliot's *Murder in the Cathedral* here. Renovated in 20s-style by Karen Rosen, the Kerr reopened in 1983 with the juggling, entertaining *Flying Karamazov Brothers*. Tony Kushner's extraordinary *Angels in America*, a two-part epic on gay life comprised of *Millennium Approaches* and *Perestroika*, play here today.

Winter Garden Theater, 1634 Broadway, between 50th and 51st St. It opened in 1911 as a hall "devoted to novel, international, spectacular and musical entertainment." Al Jolson first appeared in blackface here. The Winter Garden has always been graced by new musical successes, from *Wonderful Town* to *West Side Story*

THEATER

to *Funny Girl.* Here Zero Mostel revived *Fiddler on the Roof,* Angela Lansbury revived *Gypsy,* and the multi-media blitz *Beatlemania* revived Beatles worship. Most recently, designer John Napier clawed the place apart to create his fantasy set for *Cats,* which will likely continue to play through 1995 (tickets $37.50-65).

OFF-BROADWAY AND OFF-OFF BROADWAY

Off-Broadway theaters are a group of smaller theaters, mostly located downtown. Officially, these theaters have between 100 and 499 seats; only Broadway houses have over 500. Off-Broadway houses frequently offer more offbeat or quirky shows, with shorter runs, but occasionally these shows have long runs or jump to Broadway houses. Many of the best of the Off-Broadway houses huddle in the Sheridan Square area of the West Village. Eugene O'Neill got his break at the **Provincetown Playhouse,** and Elisa Loti made her American debut at the **Actors Playhouse.** Tickets cost $15-35; TKTS sells tickets to the larger Off-Broadway houses. It is often possible to see shows for free by arranging to usher; this usually entails dressing neatly and showing up at the theater around 45 min. ahead of curtain, helping to seat ticket-holders, and then staying for about 10 min. after the performance to help clean up. Call the theater about a week in advance to set this up.

Off-Off-Broadway is not a joke but an actual category of cheaper, younger, and smaller theaters. In the '90s, many of these theaters are among the most activist, with frequent productions related to gay and lesbian issues. Some Off- and Off-Off Broadway theaters have easily definable missions and aesthetics. **Playwrights Horizons** and **Manhattan Theater Club,** for instance, are among the nation's most prestigious launching pads for new American plays.

Many of the theaters listed below have varied and eclectic offerings, and many of them host several different companies. Your best bet is to check the listings and reviews in the *Village Voice.*

Actors Playhouse, 100 Seventh Ave. S. (691-6226).

Alice's Fourth Floor, 432 W. 42nd St. (967-0400).

American Place Theater, 111 W. 46th St. (840-2960 for a schedule, 840-3074 for the box office). Contemporary drama such as Barnaby Spring's *The Mayor of Boys Town,* which ran in 1994.

Astor Place Theater, 434 Lafayette St. (254-4370).

Cherry Lane, 38 Commerce St. (989-2020), at Grove St. Started in the 1920s by theater mavens unhappy with what they perceived as the commercial drift of the Provincetown Playhouse, Cherry Lane has hosted such avant-garde productions as Beckett's *Waiting for Godot* and plays by Ionesco and Albee.

Circle in the Square Downtown, 159 Bleecker St. (254-6330), at Thompson St. The original Circle in the Square company of the 1950s got their name from their round theater within Sheridan Square. At their new, non-round space on Bleecker, *The Iceman Cometh* by Eugene O'Neill was put on, and Jason Robards and Geraldine Page got their starts here.

Douglas Fairbanks Theatre, 432 W. 42nd St. (239-4321). The musical comedy *Nunsense* has been playing here for the past nine years; its sequel is scheduled to join it in late 1994 or early 1995 (tickets $35-37.50).

Ensemble Studio, 549 W. 52nd St. (247-4982), at Eleventh Ave. Produces non-musicals and compilations of short-plays by both established and lesser-known playwrights. Tickets free to $25.

Harold Clurman Theater, 412 W. 42nd St. (279-4200).

Here, 142 Ave. of the Americas (647-0202).

Hudson Guild, 441 W. 26th St. (760-9800).

John Houseman Theater, 450 W. 42nd St. (967-9077).

Joseph Papp Public Theater, 425 Lafayette St. (598-7150).

Lamb's, 130 W. 44th St. (997-1780). Two spaces (one with 349 seats, the other with 29) host family-oriented plays and musicals such as *Johnny Pie* and *Smoke on the Mountain.* Tickets $25-35.

Lucille Lortel, 121 Christopher St. (924-8782). Primarily known for its 1950s production of the *Threepenny Opera* by Brecht, with a cast that included Bea Arthur, Ed Asner, and John Astin.

Manhattan Theater Club, 453 W. 16th St. (645-5590).

New York Theater Workshop, 79 E. 4th St. (505-1892).

Orpheum, 126 Second Ave. (307-4100).

Pan Asian Repertory, 423 W. 46th St. (245-2660).

Playhouse 91, 316 E. 91st St. (831-2000). Currently houses the Jewish Repertory Theater, affiliated with the 92nd St. YMHA/YWHA. Under the artistic direction of Ran Avni, the JRT puts on plays geared towards the Jewish experience.

Playwrights Horizons, 416 W. 42nd St. (279-4200). Dedicated to the support and development of new American playwrights, lyricists, and composers and to productions of their work. Has developed and produced more than 300 new plays and musicals, including 3 Pulitzer Prize winners. Tickets $10-30.

Promenade Theatre, 2162 Broadway (580-1313).

Provincetown Playhouse, 133 MacDougal St. (477-5048). Some of the most noteworthy Villagers are associated with this playhouse, including Eugene O'Neill and Edna St. Vincent Millay. Starting out in 1915 as plays produced on a porch in Cape Cod, the Provincetown put on many controversial, avant-garde acts in the 1920s, such as Dada drama and the puzzling works of e.e. cummings. A huge figure in Village history, it no longer holds such a luminary place in the confrontational theater of the '90s.

Ridiculous Theatrical Company, 1 Sheridan Sq. (691-2271). Challenges assumptions about what theater really is. Starts their 29th year of productions in 1995.

Samuel Beckett Theater, 410 W. 42nd. St. (594-2826), between Ninth and Tenth Ave. Artsy productions of contemporary drama, sometimes including post-performance discussions with members of the casts. Tickets $8-12.

SoHo Repertory Theatre, 46 Walker St. (977-5955). This 100-seat theater stages contemporary avant-garde works by American playwrights. Tickets $10-15.

Sullivan Street Playhouse, 181 Sullivan St. (674-3838). Home to *The Fantasticks* since May 1960, making it the longest running show in U.S. history. Grab a twofer pass. All seats $35; shows Tues.-Fri. 8pm, Sat. 3 and 7pm, Sun. 3 and 7:30pm.

Theater at Saint Peter's Church, 619 Lexington Ave. (935-2200).

Vineyard Theater, 309 E. 26th St. (683-9772).

Westside Theater, 407 W. 43rd St. (315-2244). Rental theater hosting a variety of plays, comedies, and musicals, including the likes of Penn and Teller. Recently featured Sherry Glaser's one-woman comedy *Family Secrets.* Tickets $30-40.

■■■ MOVIES

If Hollywood is *the* place to make films, New York City is *the* place to see them. Most movies open in New York weeks before they're distributed across the country, and the response of Manhattan audiences and critics can shape a film's success or failure nationwide. Dozens of revival houses show motion picture classics year round. And independent filmmakers from around the reel world come to New York to flaunt their work.

First-run movies show all over the city. Big-screen fanatics should check out the cavernous **Ziegfeld,** 141 W. 54th St. (765-7600), between Sixth and Seventh Ave, one of the largest screens left in America, showing first-run films. Consult local newspapers for complete listings. Tickets run $8 for adults and $4.25 for children under 12. **MoviePhone** (777-FILM) allows you to reserve tickets for most major movie-houses and pick them up at showtime from the theater's automated ticket dispenser; you charge the ticket price plus a small fee over the phone.

MUSEUMS AND OTHER VENUES

Adam Clayton Powell, Jr., State Office Building, 163 W. 125th St. (873-5040), at Adam Clayton Powell Blvd. Second floor gallery highlights contemporary and classic cinema created by and about African-Americans, as well as work done by black filmmakers from South America, Africa, and the Caribbean. Admission $5, seniors and students with ID $3. Lectures by contemporary filmmakers $3, but prices vary.

American Museum of the Moving Image, 35th Ave. at 36th St., Astoria, Queens (718-784-0077). Has three full theaters showing everything from silent classics to retrospectives of great directors. Recent programs have ranged from 1950's *Father of the Bride* to *Fast Cars and Women.* (Free with admission to museum: $5, seniors $4, students and children under 12 $2.50.)

The Asia Society, 725 Park Ave. (288-6400), at 70th St. Subway: #6 to 68th St. Films from or about Asia. Ticket prices vary. Call 517-ASIA for tickets.

Cineplex Odeon Worldwide, 340 W. 50th St. (246-1583), between Eighth and Ninth Ave. Offers second-run, big Hollywood movies on 7 screens for $2.

French Institute/Alliance Française, in Florence Gould Hall, 55 E. 59th St. (355-6100). Francophiles can satisfy their craving for Godard by inquiring about current film offerings. Films are screened Wed. at Tinker Auditorium, 22 E. 60th St. Tickets $6, students $4.50.

Goethe Institute, 1014 Fifth Ave. (439-8706), between 82nd and 83rd St. Shows German films (usually with English subtitles) each week at locations around the city. Ticket prices vary.

Japan Society, 333 E. 47th St. (752-3015). Mounts yearly retrospectives of the greatest Japanese achievements in film. Schedule can be obtained by visiting the society or by calling. Tickets $7; students, seniors, and members $5.

Metropolitan Museum of Art, Fifth Ave. at 82nd St. (570-3930). The Met shows art-related movies throughout the week, as well as standard classic and foreign films on Saturdays, at 4pm and 6:30pm. They are free with museum admission. (Box office at the Uris Center Information Desk opens at 5pm on the day of the performance; limit 4 tickets per person).

Museum of Modern Art: Roy and Nivta Titus Theaters, 11 W. 53rd St. (708-9490). The MoMA serves up an unbeatable diet of great films daily in its two lower-level theaters. The film department holds what it claims to be "the strongest international collection of film in the United States," and it's hard to doubt them. Film tickets are included in the price of admission and are available upon request. Also ask about screenings in the video gallery on the third floor.

New York Public Libraries. For a real deal, check out the library. All show free films: documentaries, classics, and last year's blockbusters. Screening times may be a bit erratic, but you can't beat the price. (For complete information on New York libraries, see Practical Information: Libraries).

Symphony Space, 2537 Broadway (864-5400), at 95th St. Subway: #1, 2, 3, or 9 to 96th St. Throughout every July the Foreign Film Festival showcases the expanding canon of quality foreign films. Tickets $6.

Walter Reade Theater, at Lincoln Center (875-5600). Subway: #1 or 9 to 66th St. New York's performing arts octopus flexes yet another cultural tentacle with this two-year-old theater in the Rose Building next to the Juilliard School. Foreign, famous, and critically-acclaimed American independent films dominate. Schedule and ticket prices vary.

REVIVAL AND INDEPENDENT FILM HOUSES

Angelika Film Center, 18 W. Houston St. (995-2000), at Mercer St. Subway: #6 to Bleecker St. or B, D, F, Q to Broadway-Lafayette. Eight screens of alternative (not quite underground) cinema. Come here to see the movies that hipper-than-thou people at cocktail parties mention—the films that everyone has seen reviews of but never got around to seeing. Come early on weekends. Cafe upstairs has excellent espresso. Tickets $7.50; seniors and children under 12 $3.50 Mon.-Fri. before 5pm.

Anthology Film Archives, 32 Second Ave. (505-5181) at E. 2nd St. Subway: F to Second Ave. A forum for independent filmmaking, focusing on the contemporary, off-beat, and avant-garde chosen from U.S. and foreign production. The resident cinema guru has created the Archives' most enduring series—"The American Narrative"—featuring 300 great American films. Tickets $6, students with ID $5.

Cinema Village, 22 E. 12th St. (924-3363), at University Pl. Subway: N, R, L, 4, 5, or 6 to Union Sq. Features independent documentaries, both domestic and foreign. Great seats that lean back. Tickets $7.50, seniors $4.50 before 5pm.

Film Forum, 209 W. Houston St. (727-8110), near Sixth Ave. and Varick St. Subway: C or E to Spring St., or 1 or 9 to Houston St. Three theaters showing the best in independent filmmaking, movie classics, and foreign films. Tickets $7.50, seniors $4.50.

Joseph Papp Public Theater, 425 Lafayette St. (598-7150). Subway: #6 to Astor Pl. Quirky selection of old movies, particularly "art" classics and film history milestones. There is also a theater auditorium featuring live "experimental" performance pieces. No screenings on Mon. For info call 598-7107. Tickets $5-8.

The Kitchen, 512 W. 19th St. (255-5793), between Tenth and Eleventh Ave. Subway: C or E to 23rd St. World-renowned showcase for off-beat happenings. Features experimental and avant-garde film and video, as well as concerts, dance performances, and poetry readings. Most shows are from New York-based struggling artists. Season runs Oct.-June. Call for information or check advertisements in *The Village Voice.* Ticket prices vary by event.

Millennium Film Workshop, 66 E. 4th St. (673-0090). Subway: F to Second Ave. More than just a theater, this group presents an extensive program of experimental films and offers classes and workshops. Tickets $6.

For more extensive listings of revival houses and independent films check *The Village Voice* or *The New Yorker.*

■■■ TELEVISION: LIVE IN THE STUDIO

If you didn't get enough TV before you got here, New York is the place to dose up. Here in the city you can do the impossible—pass right through the TV screen itself—and plop down directly in front of your favorite actors and most beloved talk show hosts. For free. Plan ahead, though. It's best to order your tickets two to three months in advance, although standby tickets are often available. Here's a little sampler of what the Big Four (count 'em—four) are offering and how to get on the ticket.

CBS (975-3247) scored big by bringing David Letterman into its fold. Order tickets for his *Late Show* well in advance by writing: Dave Letterman Tickets, 1697 Broadway, New York, NY 10019. Call CBS for information on obtaining day-of-show standby tickets. Daytime talker Geraldo Rivera also tapes through CBS. Call 265-1283 for more information.

NBC currently opens three shows to guests: *Saturday Night Live, The Phil Donahue Show,* and the new *Late Night with Conan O'Brien.* Call 664-3055 for general information. Only *Late Night* is active during the summer; tapings are scheduled Mon.-Fri. 5:30-6:30pm, and tickets are given out on the day of the show only, beginning at 9am, from the page desk in the main lobby of NBC at Rockefeller Center. *SNL* and *Donahue* go on hiatus June-Aug.; order tickets for these shows well in advance by sending one postcard per show to NBC Tickets, 30 Rockefeller Plaza, New York, NY 10012. Be warned, though: not only are you not given the option to choose specific dates, but because requests are lotteried you might not find out you've been rejected until four months after you send off your request. *SNL* accepts ticket orders during the month of August only. You just might want to get in line on the mezzanine level of Rockefeller Center (50th St. side) at 8am the morning of the show for a chance at standby tickets.

For general information on **ABC's** offerings, call 456-7777. When this book went to press, *Regis and Kathie Lee* was the only show to which ABC admitted guests (456-3537). Send a postcard with name, address, phone number, and your request for up to four tickets to Live Tickets, Ansonia Station, P.O. Box 777, 10023. Expect an eight-month wait. For standby tix, line up at the corner of 67th St. and Columbus Ave. at 8am. Or before. No one under 18 admitted to this one.

Fox (452-3600) currently opens two shows to audiences: *Rush Limbaugh* (397-7367) and *Montel Williams* (840-1700). Call these numbers for further information.

■■■ OPERA

Lincoln Center (875-5000) is New York's one-stop shopping mall for high-culture consumers; there's usually opera or dance at one of its many venues. Write Lincoln Center Plaza, New York, NY 10023, or drop by its Performing Arts Library (870-1930) for a full schedule and a press kit as long as the *Ring* cycle. The **Metropolitan Opera Company** (362-6000), opera's premier outfit, plays on a Lincoln Center stage as big as a football field. Regular tickets run as high as $160—go for the upper balcony (around $22; the cheapest seats have an obstructed view) unless you're prone to vertigo. You can stand in the orchestra ($14) along with the opera freaka-zoids who've brought along the score, or all the way back in the Family Circle ($15). (Regular season runs Sept.-April Mon.-Sat.; box office open Mon.-Sat. 10am-8pm, Sun. noon-6pm.) In June, watch for free concerts in city parks (call the Met ticket line at 362-6000). The 1994-95 Met season features works by Mozart, Verdi, and Puccini.

At right angles to the Met, the **New York City Opera** (870-5570) has a new sound under the direction of Christopher Keene, who became general director in 1989. Beverly Sills, its previous head, was renowned for beating old masterworks into the ground. Keene's first season got rave reviews, although the opera's financial problems may soon force it out of Lincoln Center. The company now performs pop classics and contemporary U.S. operas in addition to the old faithfuls. "City" now has a split season (Sept.-Nov. and March-April) and keeps its ticket prices low year-round ($15-73). Call on the night before the performance you want to attend to check the availability of $10 rush tickets; then wait in line the next morning.

In July, look for free performances by the **New York Grand Opera** at Central Park Summerstage (360-2777) every Wednesday night. Check the papers for perfor-mances of the old warhorses by the **Amato Opera Company,** 319 Bowery (228-8200; Sept.-May). Music schools often stage opera as well; see Classical Music for further details. The **World Trade Center,** Church St. at Dey St. (435-4170), hosts free opera concerts on Mondays in July and August presented by America Opera Projects, the Bronx Opera Company, and the PALA Opera Association. Perfor-mances are at 12:15pm, repeated at 1:15pm.

■■■ DANCE

The New York State Theater (870-5570), another Lincoln Center fixture, is home to the late, great George Balanchine's **New York City Ballet.** This is the country's old-est and, arguably, most famous dance company. Though Balanchine is best-known for modern, abstract masterpieces such as *Apollo* and *Jewels,* his versions of the clas-sics are still the repertoire's biggest sellers. Decent tickets for the *Nutcracker* in December sell out almost immediately. (Performances Nov.-Feb. and April-June. Tickets $12-57, standing room $8.) The **American Ballet Theater** (477-3030) dances at the Metropolitan Opera House at Lincoln Center from late April to mid-June. Under Mikhail Baryshnikov's guidance, A.B.T.'s eclectic repertoire has ranged from grand Kirov-style Russian, for which it is best known, to experimental Ameri-can (tickets $16-95).

The **Alvin Ailey American Dance Theater** (767-0940) bases its repertoire of modern dance on jazz, spirituals, and contemporary music. It often takes its moves on the road, but always performs at the **City Center** in December. Tickets ($15-40) can be difficult to obtain. Write or call the City Center, 131 W. 55th St. (581-7907), weeks in advance, if possible. Look for half-price tickets at the Bryant Park ticket booth (see below).

The **Martha Graham Dance Co.,** 316 E. 63rd St. (832-9166), performs original Graham pieces during its October New York season. The founder of modern dance and of perhaps the most famous experimental company, Graham revolutionized 20th-century movement with her psychological, rather than narrative, approach to choreography (tickets $15-40).

Keep an eye out for performances of the **Merce Cunningham Dance Company** (255-8240), of John Cage fame, and the **Paul Taylor Dance Company** (431-5562). Both companies stage a one- to two-week season of performances at the City Center (581-1212) each year, along with other performances throughout New York and the rest of the country. The **Dance Theater Workshop** (691-6500) also stages works in Manhattan throughout the year, and the Joyce Theater, 175 Eighth Ave. (242-0800), between 18th and 19th St., offers a year-round schedule of experimental dance troupes (tickets $15-40).

In Queens, the **Ballet Folklorica de Dominican Republic,** 104-11 37th Ave. (718-651-8427), in Corona, specializes in traditional ethnic folk dance. **Central Park Summerstage** (320-2777) hosts dance companies from around the world. 1994 featured the Parsons Dance Company, Israeli dance troupes, and the Blind Boys of Alabama. Ballet connoisseurs should call the Brooklyn Center for Performing Arts at Brooklyn College (see Classical Music), which introduces a major foreign ballet company to New York every year.

Half-price tickets for many music and dance events can be purchased on the day of performance at the **Bryant Park** ticket booth, on W. 42nd St. (382-2323) between Fifth and Sixth Ave. (Open Tues.-Sun. noon-2pm and 3-7pm; tickets for Monday shows available Sunday; cash and traveler's checks only.) Call for daily listings. Full-price tickets are also available here for all Ticketmaster events.

■■■ CLASSICAL MUSIC

Musicians advertise themselves vigorously; you should have no trouble finding the notes. Begin with the ample listings in *The New York Times, The New Yorker,* or *New York* magazine. The *Free Time* calendar ($1.25) can clue you in on free classical events throughout the city. Remember that many events, such as outdoor music, are seasonal.

LINCOLN CENTER

The Lincoln Center Halls have a wide, year-round selection of concerts. The **Great Performers Series** (875-5020), featuring famous and foreign musicians, packs the Avery Fisher and Alice Tully Halls and the Walter Reade Theater, from October until May (call 721-6500; tickets from $11).

Avery Fisher Hall (875-5030) paints the town ecstatic with its annual Mostly Mozart Festival, featuring performers like Itzhak Perlman, Alicia de Larrocha, Jean-Pierre Rampal, and Emanuel Ax. Show up early; major artists and rising stars usually give half-hour pre-concert recitals, beginning one hour before the main concert and free to ticketholders. The festival runs from July to August, with tickets to individual events running from $12 to $30. The **New York Philharmonic** (875-5656) begins its regular season at Fisher Hall in mid-September. The 1994-95 season includes performances by Andre Watts and Yo-Yo Ma as well as premieres of works by John Williams and many others. Tickets range from $10 to $60. (Call CenterCharge for tickets at 721-6500; Mon.-Sat. 10am-8pm, Sun. noon-8pm.) During the Philharmonic's regular season, students and seniors can sometimes get **$5 tickets;** call ahead to check availability, then show up 30 minutes before the concert (Tues.-Thurs. only). $10 tickets are sometimes sold for the odd morning rehearsal; again, call ahead (anyone is eligible for these). In August for a couple of weeks, the Philharmonic heads for the hills and lawns of New York's parks. Kurt Masur and friends lead the posse at **free concerts** on the Great Lawn in Central Park, in Prospect Park in Brooklyn, in Van Cortland Park in the Bronx, and around the city. Select nights are enlivened by fireworks after the program. For information on these outdoor events call the summer hotline at 875-5709. Avery Fisher Hall is wheelchair-accessible.

Alice Tully Hall, in the Juilliard School at Lincoln Center, features an eclectic mix of music, dance, theater, video, and performance art. Composer Philip Glass is a regular here. Founded six years ago, the Serious Fun! Series brings big-name avant-garde, mixed-media, and performance artists into the realm of corporate sponsorship. The series lasts three weeks in July; tickets go from $22 to $30 per event. (875-5050; box office open Mon.-Sat. 11am-6pm, Sun. noon-6pm, or call CenterCharge at 721- 6500.) The **Chamber Music Society** offers students and seniors heavily discounted seats for its performances in Alice Tully Hall (call 875-5788; students from $9, seniors from $14, others from $20). Wheelchair-accessible.

The **Juilliard School of Music** itself is one of the world's leading factories of classical musicians. Juilliard's **Paul Recital Hall** hosts free student recitals almost daily during the school year from September until May; Alice Tully Hall holds larger student recitals, also free, most Wednesdays from September to May at 1pm. Orchestral recitals, faculty performances, chamber music, and dance and theater events take place regularly at Juilliard and never cost more than $10—you can see the next generation's Yo-Yo Ma for a third of the cost of seeing this one's. Call 769-7406 for a complete Juilliard schedule. Wheelchair-accessible.

Free **outdoor** events at Lincoln Center boggle the mind every summer, with everything from modern dance premieres to country-music festivals; call 875-5400 for the daily boggle.

OTHER HALLS AND VENUES

Carnegie Hall (247-7800), Seventh Ave. at 57th St. Subway: N or R to 57th St., or B, D, or E to Seventh Ave. The New York Philharmonic's original home was saved from demolition in the 1960s by Isaac Stern and is still the favorite coming-out locale of musical debutantes. Top soloists and chamber groups are still booked regularly. Box office open Mon.-Sat. 11am-6pm, Sun. noon-6pm; tickets $10-60.

92nd Street Y, 1395 Lexington Ave. (996-1100). Subway: #6 to 96th St. Cultural life on the Upper East Side revolves around the 92nd Street Y. The Y's Kaufmann Concert Hall seats only 916 people and offers an intimate setting unmatched by New York's larger halls, with flawless acoustics and the oaken ambience of a Viennese salon. The Y is the home of the **New York Chamber Symphony** under the fiery direction of Gerard Schwartz. The Chamber Symphony's repertoire covers everything from Telemann and Rameau to the works of contemporary masters like Pijton, Diamond, and Stravinsky. In addition, the Y plays host to a panoply of world-class visiting musicians. The Distinguished Artists Series, dating back to the late 30s, has featured all the big names from Segovia and Schnabel to Yo-Yo Ma, Alfred Brendel, and Schlomo Mintz. In the 1994-1995 season, Nadia Salerno-Sonnenberg, Dawn Upshaw, Young Uck Kim, and Isaac Stern will be performing. Other notable series include Chamber Music at the Y, Lyrics and Lyricists, Keyboard Conversation, and Young Concert Artists. Non-musical events include an ongoing series of literary readings at the Poetry Center and some of most engaging lectures in New York. Readings $8-12, lectures $15, concerts $15-40.

Town Hall, 123 W. 43rd St. (840-2824), between Sixth Ave. and Broadway. Subway: #1, 2, 3, 9, N, or R to 42nd St. This landmark is an elegant pavilion with excellent acoustics. Tenacious trio McKim, Mead & White designed the place in 1921; it has since hosted a wide variety of cultural events, including lectures by such luminaries as Sandra Bernhard, jazz festivals, and concerts of all kinds. Joan Sutherland made her debut here. The building has a seating capacity of 1495. Box office open daily noon-6pm.

Merkin Concert Hall, 129 W. 67th St. (362-8719), between Broadway and Amsterdam Ave. Subway: #1 or 9 to 66th St. Quartered in Abraham Goodman House, the Merkin Concert Hall offers eclectic, ethnic, and contemporary music alongside more conventional selections. A typical week at the Merkin might include love songs and dirges spanning 400 years, classical and modern Chinese music, and the choral, folk-inspired works of Bartok and Shostakovich. Traditional Jewish and 20th-century classical music seems to be Merkin's specialty. One of New York's best spaces for chamber music, the intimate theater seats 457. Season Sept.-June; tickets $10-15.

Symphony Space (864-5400), at Broadway and 95th. Subway: #1 or 9 to 96th St. The misleadingly named Symphony Space is a former skating rink and cinema that now hosts all kinds of cultural events. The performance season (Sept.-June) corrals classical and traditional ethnic musical performances along with plays, dance companies, and the "Selected Shorts" program of fiction readings by famous actors. An annual Gilbert and Sullivan operetta packs the space, and during the summer it sponsors an ambitious program of old and new foreign films. Pick up a Symphony Space program guide at the Space itself. Box office open Tues.-Sun. noon-7pm. Most movies $6, other events free or up to $35.

Metropolitan Museum of Art (535-7710: see Museums). The Met posts a schedule of performances covering the sound spectrum from traditional Japanese music and Russian balalaika to all-star classical music recitals. Chamber music in the bar and piano music in the cafeteria on Fri. and Sat. evenings, free with museum admission; some of the other concerts charge $10 and up for tickets. For ticket information or brochure, call Concerts and Lectures at 535-7710.

Museum of Modern Art (708-9480; see Museums). On most weekends in July and August, the Museum of Modern Art's "Summergarden" program presents free concerts of "avant-garde" contemporary classical music by Juilliard students in the museum's Sculpture Garden; concerts are on Fri. and Sat. at 7:30pm. Enter the Sculpture Garden through the (normally locked) back gate at 14 W. 54th St. between 6pm and 10pm.

Frick Collection (288-0700; see Museums). From Oct. through May, the Frick Collection hosts free classical music concerts Sundays at 5pm (occasional summer concerts Tues. at 5:45pm). Tickets are limited to 2 per applicant; written requests must be received by the third Mon. before the concert. If you're not in the mood to fill out forms, show up 5 minutes before the show and try to steal the seats of no-shows.

Cooper-Hewitt Museum (860-6868; see Museums). Free concerts—ranging from classical to soul to hip hop—come to the garden of the Cooper-Hewitt Museum from late June through August.

Cathedral of St. John the Divine, 1047 Amsterdam Ave. (662-2133), at 112th St. Subway: #1 or 9 to 110th St. Presents an impressive array of classical concerts, art exhibitions, lectures, plays, movies, and dance events. Ticket prices vary, so call.

Theater at Riverside Church (864-2929), on Riverside Dr. between 120th and 122nd St. Subway: #1 or 9 to 125th St. Hosts theater, music, dance, and video performances for up to 275 people. Prices vary.

St. Paul's Chapel (602-0747, 602-0873), on Broadway between Church and Fulton St. Subway: A or C to Broadway-Nassau St. Built in 1766, St. Paul's is Manhattan's only surviving pre-Revolutionary War church. George Washington came here to pray after his inauguration. The exquisite interior, lit by Waterford crystal chandeliers, provides the perfect setting for concerts of well-loved classical standards by Mozart, Haydn, Shostakovich, Bach, et al, as well as occasional lesser-knowns. Noonday concerts (Sept.-June) Mon. and Thurs. at noon. Suggested donation $2.

Trinity Church, 74 Trinity Pl. (602-0873), at Wall St. Subway: #4 or 5 to Wall St. With St. Paul's Chapel, Trinity Church presents the **Sundays at Four** classical-concert series Sept.-June. Tickets $15-20; students and seniors can reserve standard seating for $10.

World Financial Center (945-0505), Battery Park City. Subway: C or E to World Trade Ctr. Free concerts at the Winter Garden, the Center's main atrium, occasionally include classical artists, but more often feature modern serious composers such as John Cage.

Brooklyn Academy of Music, 30 Lafayette St. (718-636-4100), between Felix and Ashland Pl. Subway: #2, 3, 4, 5, D, or Q to Atlantic Ave. Founded in 1859, the Brooklyn Academy of Music (B.A.M.) has compiled a colorful history of magnificent performances: here Pavlova danced, Caruso sang, and Sarah Bernhardt played Camille. The oldest performing arts center in the country, it focuses on new, non-traditional, multicultural programs (though it sometimes features classical music as well). Jazz, blues, performance art, opera, and dance can be enjoyed here. Every May brings Dance Africa, which features West African dancing as well as crafts. Call for the constantly changing schedule. B.A.M.'s annual Next Wave Festival, Oct.-Dec., features contemporary music, dance, theater, and performance art; it broke artists like Mark Morris and Laurie Anderson. B.A.M. is home to the **Brooklyn Philharmonic Orchestra,** which performs from Sept.-March and hosts a brief opera season March-June. Orchestra and opera tickets $10-40. Manhattan Express Bus makes the round trip to B.A.M. from 51st St. and Lexington Ave. for each performance ($4); subway: #2, 3, 4, 5, D, Q to Atlantic Ave. or B, M, N, R to Pacific St.

Brooklyn Center for Performing Arts (718-951-4500 or 951-4522), 1 block west of the junction of Flatbush and Nostrand Ave. on the campus of Brooklyn College. Subway: #2 or 5 to Flatbush Ave. The Brooklyn Center for Performing Arts At Brooklyn College (B.C.B.C.) prides itself on presenting many exclusive events each year. In 1993-94 it brought Leontyne Price, André Watts, the Garth Fagan Dance Company with Wynton Marsalis, Joan Rivers, and Jerry Lewis. Season Oct.-May; tickets $20-40.

Colden Center for the Performing Arts (718-793-8080), at Queens College in Flushing, Queens. Subway: The Colden Center has a beautiful, 2143-seat theater, which houses the **Queens Symphony Orchestra** and hosts an excellent program of jazz and dance concerts. Special effort is made to present work by emerging artists whose works reflect the borough's cultural diversity. Season Sept.-May; tickets $12-25. Subway: #7 to Main St., Flushing, then Q17 or Q25-34 bus to the corner of Kissena Blvd. and the Long Island Expressway.

Ukrainian Bandura Ensemble of New York, 84-82 164th St. (718-658-7449) in Jamaica, Queens. This ensemble keeps the 56-stringed bandura alive, playing at parades, festivals, and various other events around the city as the occasion arises.

MUSIC SCHOOLS

One of the best ways for the budget traveler to absorb New York musical culture is to visit a music school. Except for opera and ballet productions ($5-12), concerts at the following schools are free and frequent (especially September to May): The **Juilliard School of Music,** Lincoln Center (see above); the **Mannes School of Music,** 150 W. 85th (580-0210), between Columbus and Amsterdam Ave.; the **Manhattan School of Music,** 122 Broadway (749-2802); the **Bloomingdale House of Music,** 323 W. 108th St. (663-6021), near Broadway.

■■■ JAZZ

Jazz in New York comes in two versions: smoky or smoke-free. You can check out one of the many hazy dens that bred lingo like "cat" and "hip." (A "hippie" was originally someone on the fringes of jazz culture who talked the talk but was never really in the know.) Summer spawns cleaner but humid sets in parks and plazas.

Central Park Concerts/Summerstage, at 72nd St. (360-2777) in Central Park, divides its attention between many performing arts, including jazz, opera, rock, and folk. Call or pick up Central Park's calendar of events, which is available at the Dairy in Central Park (see Sights: Central Park). The season runs from mid-June to early Aug. and concerts are free.

Head to the **Lincoln Center Plazas** and Damrosch Park's **Guggenheim Bandshell** to hear free jazz, salsa, and big-band delights. The Lincoln Center's new **Midsummer Night Swing Dancextravaganza,** held from late June until late July every night from Wednesday to Saturday, invites couples and singles to tango, swing, shimmy, or foxtrot. The center provides a dance floor, a café, and bands fronted by such musicians as Illinois Jacquet. (Dancing Wed.-Sat. 8:15pm, lessons Wed.-Thurs. 6:30pm.) **Alice Tully Hall,** also at Lincoln Center, presents a summer jazz series (875-5299). Guest soloist Wynton Marsalis trumpeted the inaugural season.

The **JVC Jazz Festival** blows into the city in June. All-star performances in the 1994 series included Julius Hemphill, Ray Charles, Billy Taylor, and Mel Torme. Tickets go on sale in early May, but many of the best events take place outdoors in the parks and are free. **Bryant Park** hosts a large number of these concerts, as does **Damrosch Park** at Lincoln Center. Call 787-2020 in the spring for information, or write to: JVC Jazz Festival New York, P.O. Box 1169, Ansonia Station, New York, NY 10023.

The **Guggenheim Museum** (423-5000; see Museums) has live jazz and worldbeat music in its rotunda on Fridays and Saturdays from 5 to 8pm. Museum admission is required, but Fridays 5 to 8pm is pay-what-you-wish. The **Museum of Modern Art** (708-9480; see Museums) also has jazz in its Garden Cafe on Fridays from 6 to 8pm. Museum admission is required, but Fri. 5:30-8:30pm is pay-what-you-wish. The **World Financial Center Plaza** (945-0505) hosts free concerts from June to September. The range of jazz styles is wide, ranging from Little Jimmy Scott to the Kit McClure Big Band, an all-female jazz orchestra, though jazz concerts are infrequent. The **World Trade Center,** on Church St. at Dey St. (435-4170), hosts free lunchtime jazz concerts in its plaza each Wednesday during July and August. Two performers are featured each week, one performing at noon and the other at 1pm. The **South Street Museum** (732-7678) sponsors a series of outdoor concerts from July to early September at Pier 17, Ambrose Stage, and the Atrium.

In the heart of Rockefeller Center, entertainment palace **Radio City Music Hall** (247-4777) boasts a bill of great performers that reads like the invitation list to the Forbes Anniversary bash; Ella Fitzgerald, Frank Sinatra, Ringo Starr, Linda Ronstadt, and Sting, among others, have all performed at the legendary venue. The Rockettes still kick out the lights here every year at Christmas and Easter. (Box office at 50th St. and Sixth Ave. Open Mon.-Sat. 10am-8pm, Sun. 11am-8pm.) Tickets range from $20 to $1000 for the "Night of 100 Stars."

New York's churches wed the pristine to the upbeat in their capacity as music halls. Though the true godfathers of gospel keep the faith farther uptown, the midtown sacred-jazz scene belongs to **Saint Peter's,** 619 Lexington Ave. (935-2200) at 52nd St. On the first Sunday of every month, St. Peter's hosts a gala jazz mass. On other Sundays, jazz vespers are intoned at 5pm, followed at 7pm or 8pm by a full-fledged jazz concert ($5-10 donation for the concert). Informal jazz concerts are also held Wednesdays at 12:30pm ($4 donation), and classical concerts are given on Sunday afternoons (except in summer). In addition, the hippest ministry in town brings you art openings and exhibits, theater, lectures, and more (see Theater and Sights: Midtown). John Garcia Geyel, Pastor to the Jazz Community, oversees all tuneful good deeds.

Most of the music schools and halls listed under Classical Music have jazz offerings. And the **Coca Cola Concert Series,** though primarily a rock festival, also brings jazz and reggae concerts to **Jones Beach** (516-221-1000; June-early Sept.; tickets $20-27.50).

JAZZ CLUBS

Expect high covers and drink minimums at the legendary jazz venues. Most of them crowd tables together and charge $5 a drink. While hearing the jazz gods costs an arm and a leg, there are a few bars, like Augie's, which supply a reliable selection of no-names free of charge.

Apollo Theatre, 253 W. 125th St. (749-5838, box office 864-0372), between Frederick Douglass Blvd. and Adam Clayton Powell Blvd. Subway: #1, 2, 3, or 9 to 125th St. Historic Harlem landmark has heard Duke Ellington, Count Basie, Ella Fitzgerald, Lionel Hampton, Billie Holliday, and Sarah Vaughan. A young Malcolm X shined shoes here. Now undergoing a resurgence in popularity. Ticket prices vary, but the legendary Amateur Night (where the audience is reputed to boo inferior acts off the stage, à la *Gong Show*) is still only $5.

Augie's, 2751 Broadway (864-9834), between 105th and 106th St. Subway: #1 or 9 to 103rd St. Small and woody. Jazz all week until 3am. The saxophonist sits on your lap and the bass rests on your table. Quality musicians and an unpretentious crowd. No cover; $3 drink min., $5 Fri.-Sat. Sets start around 10pm. Open daily 6pm-4am.

Birdland, 2745 Broadway (749-2228), at 105th St. Subway: #1 or 9 to 103rd St. A supper club serving reasonably good food and top jazz. The place feels Upper West-nouveau but the music is smoked-out-and-splendid 52nd St. Blue Note Records makes recordings here. Appetizers $7, entrees $12-18, sandwiches $8-11. Sun. jazz brunch. Fri.-Sat $5 cover plus $5 min. per set at bar; $10 cover and $15 min. per set at tables. Sun.-Thurs. $5 cover plus $5 min. per set at tables; no cover at bar. No cover for brunch Sun. noon-4pm. Open Mon.-Sat. 4pm-4am, Sun. noon-4pm and 5pm-4am. First set nightly at 9pm.

Blue Note, 131 W. 3rd St. (475-8592), near MacDougal St. Subway: A, B, C, D, E, F, or Q to Washington Sq. The Carnegie Hall of jazz clubs. Now a commercialized concert space with crowded tables and a sedate audience. Often books top performers. Cover $25 and up. More reasonable Sun. jazz brunch ($14.50 for drinks and jazz, noon-6pm, shows at 1 and 3:30pm). Other sets Sun.-Thurs. 9 and 11:30pm, Fri.-Sat. 9pm, 11:30pm, and 1:30am.

Bradley's, 70 University Pl. (473-9700), at 11th St. Subway: #4, 5, 6, L, N, or R to Union Sq. Nightly piano and bass duos (and other small ensembles) cut through the smoke. Usually crowded. Cover $12, $8 drink min. Sets at 10pm, midnight, 2am. Music daily 9:45pm-4am.

Cotton Club, 666 W. 125th St. (663-7980), between Broadway and Riverside Dr. More tourists than regulars at this way-famous jazz hall of the greats. Most shows pretty expensive, but some affordable ones. Cover $8 and up. Shows at 8 and 10pm.

Dan Lynch, 221 Second Ave. (677-0911), at 14th St. Subway: #4, 5, 6, L, N, or R to Union Sq. Dark smoky room with Casablanca fan, long bar, and "all blues, all the time." Swinging, beautifully friendly deadhead crowd envelops the dance floor. Pool table in back. Blues and jazz start at 10pm. Jam session Sat.-Sun. 4-9pm. Cover Fri.-Sat. $5. Open Mon.-Thurs. 8am-2am, Fri.-Sat. 8am-4am, Sun. noon-2am.

Fat Tuesday's, 190 Third Ave. (533-7900), between E. 17th and 18th St. Subway: L to Third Ave. A small club with big names. Dependable mainstream jazz artists have included Betty Carter, Astrud Gilberto, and the Les Paul Trio. Cover $20, plus $10 drink min. Sets Tues.-Thurs. 8pm and 10pm, Fri.-Sat. 8pm, 10pm, and midnight.

Honeysuckle West, 170 Amsterdam Ave. (873-4100), at 68th St. Subway:#1 or 9 to 66th St. Cool jazz (and occasional R&B) blended with uptown chic. Open daily 11am-1am. Cover usually $10, with $10 food and drink minimum.

Indigo Blues, 221 W. 46th St. (221-0033), between Broadway and Eighth Ave. Subway: #1, 2, 3, 9, N, or R to 42nd St.; or C or E to 50th St. Located in the basement of the Hotel Edison. Jazz and blues served up nightly in a high-modernist glass and brick den. Heavyweight guests have included Milt Jackson, Freddie Hubbard, Frank Bruno, Betty Carter, and Stanley Jordan. Music starts after 9pm. Cover $10-20 depending on the attraction, plus a variable min. if you sit at a table (no ingestive min. at the bar). Occasional nights of comedy; call ahead if you're headed for the music.

Metropolis Cafe, 31 Union Square (675-2300). Subway #4, 5, 6, L, N, R to 14th St. Live jazz downstairs Mon.-Tues. and Thurs. (shows at 8pm and 10:30pm); upstairs jazz other nights. Entrees $5-15. Open all day but come between 1 and 2am.

Michael's Pub, 211 E. 55th St. (758-2272), at Third Ave. Subway: #4, 5, or 6 to 59th St. New Orleans traditional jazz. Woody Allen occasionally plays clarinet here on Mon. nights, more frequently since the brouhaha over his domestic troubles. ("He needs the adulation," says one commentator.) Mel Torme and other jazz stars also come in sometimes; try your luck. Sets Mon. 8:40pm and 11pm, Tues.-Sat. 9:15pm and 11:15pm and at 1:30am "if people are still here." Cover $15-20 plus 2-drink min.; Mon. no cover but $35 min. on food or drink. Open 24 hrs.

Red Blazer Too, 349 W. 46th St. (262-3112), between Eighth and Ninth Ave. Subway: C or E to 50th St. Dance cheek to cheek in the stardust of fab golden oldies.

Tuesdays are a musical romp through the '20s and '30s, Thurs. big bands take the stage for '40s swing, Fri.-Sat. is blistery Dixieland, and Sun. night is ragtime. Jazz Age crowd. Sun. jazz brunch 1-5pm. Fri. cocktail hour 6-8pm with big band music and free hors d'oeuvres. Music nightly Sun. 7pm-midnight, Mon. 8pm-midnight, Tues.-Thurs. 8:30pm-12:30am, Fri.-Sat. 9pm-1:30am. Cover $5 and 2-drink min. except Mon.

Sweet Basil, 88 Seventh Ave. (242-1785), between Bleecker and Grove St. Subway: #1 or 9 to Christopher St./Sheridan Sq. Serves mostly traditional jazz with dinner. Lots of tourists, some regulars. Check the *Village Voice* for occasional star sets. Cover $15, plus $10 min. No cover at jazz brunch (Sat.-Sun. 2-6pm). Shows Mon.-Fri. 9pm and 11pm, Sat.-Sun. 10pm, midnight, and 1:30am.

Village Vanguard, 178 Seventh Ave. (255-4037), south of 11th St. Subway: #1, 2, 3, or 9 to 14th St. A windowless cavern shaped like a wedge, as old and hip as jazz itself. The walls are thick with memories of Lenny Bruce, Leadbelly, Miles Davis, and Sonny Rollins. Every Mon. the Vanguard Orchestra unleashes its torrential big-band sound on the sentimental journeymen at 10pm and midnight. Cover Sun.-Thurs. $12 plus $8 min., Fri.-Sat. $15 plus $8 min. Sets Sun.-Thurs. 9:30pm and 11:30pm, Fri.-Sat. 9:30pm, 11:30pm, and 1am.

■■■ ROCK, POP, PUNK, AND FOLK

New York City has a long history of producing bands on the vanguard of popular music and performance, from the New York Dolls to DNA to Dee-Lite to Pavement. If New York City's home-grown bands fail to satisfy the craving for live music, keep in mind that virtually every band that tours the U.S. comes to New York City. Call the **Concert Hotline** (249-8870), or check out the exhaustive and indispensable club listings in the *Village Voice* to find out who's in town.

The annual **New Music Seminar** (473-4343) is a trade convention of the alternative-rock industry. Over 600 bands and thousands of hangers-on, journalists, and radio people invade 30-plus clubs for a week of rock, pop, rap, and networking, usually during the last week in July. Nirvana and Jane's Addiction played here way back when; last year, biggies like Violent Femmes and ignored geniuses like Helium, Magnetic Fields, and Butterglory came here to get (more) noticed. Passes include admission to all shows, lectures, seminars, and parties, but they cost $380 to $440; almost every one of the NMS nighttime shows is open to the public for $5 to $15.

At 12th St. in Coney Island, Brooklyn, is the **Coney Island Circus Sideshow,** which features great indie rock shows as part of its "Sideshows by the Seashore" program on most Friday nights in the summer (admission $6; first band at 10pm). The adjacent snack bar is a great place to sip your Rolling Rock ($2) and chat with NYC underground rock luminaries. Call 718-372-5159 for information on all Sideshow happenings.

If arena rock is more your style, check out **Madison Square Garden,** Seventh Ave. and W. 33rd St. (465-6000), perhaps America's premier entertainment facility, hosting over 600 events and nearly six million spectators every year. Apart from rock concerts, regular offerings include exhibitions; trade shows; boxing matches; rodeos; monster trucks; dog, cat, and horse shows; circuses; tennis games; and the odd presidential convention (tickets $20-50). **Radio City Music Hall** (247-4777) and New Jersey's **Meadowlands** (201-935-3900) also occasionally stage equally high-priced performances.

ABC No Rio, 156 Rivington St. (254-3697), near Clinton St. Subway: B, D, or Q to Essex St. Walk a block north and then 3 blocks east. A non-profit, community-run space featuring lots of hardcore and other punk-related genres, as well as occasional poetry readings, art exhibits, etc. No alcohol served. All ages. Cover $2-5.

Academy, 234 W. 43rd St. (307-7171), at Seventh Ave. Subway: #1, 2, 3, 7, or 9 to 42nd St. Broadway theater turned concert club. Wide variety of rock styles, from Luscious Jackson to the Beastie Boys. Call for showtimes. Tickets $15-25.

A.K.A., 77 W. Houston St. (673-7325), between W. Broadway and Wooster St. Subway: #1 or 9 to Houston St.; or N or R to Prince St./Broadway. Dark and gothic and hard to find (look for the small green awning and head upstairs), A.K.A. draws all sorts of bands, from heavy metal to acid jazz, into its excellent room. Mainly a chic crowd of in-the-know locals. Live acts Wed.-Sat. Cover $5-10.

Beacon Theatre, 2124 Broadway (496-7070), between 74th and 75th St. Subway: #1, 2, 3, or 9 to 79th St. Mid-sized concert hall featuring mid-sized alternative rock names, as well as special events such as world beat concerts and multi-media performance events. Call or check the *Village Voice* for schedule; there's usually something every weekend. Tickets $15-40.

The Bitter End, 147 Bleecker St. (673-7030), at Thompson St. Subway: A, B, C, D, E, F, Q to W. 4th St., or #6 to Bleecker St. Small space hosts sweet-sounding folk and country music; they claim artists like Billy Joel and Rita Rudner got their start here. Recently in some kind of rent dispute, they have succeeded in re-securing their lease, though it still may close soon. Call for show times. Cover $5-15.

Bottom Line, 15 W. 4th St. (228-7880 or 228-6300), at Mercer St. Subway: #1, 9 to Christopher St., or A, B, C, D, E, F, Q to W. 4th St. A somber, loft-like space where rainbows weave on the walls, set against black. If you can't find a seat, you can sit at the comfy bar (even without ordering a drink) surrounded by old show photos. A mixed bag of music and entertainment—from jazz to kitsch to country to theater to good old-time rock and roll by over-the-hill singer/songwriters. Double proof of age (21 and over) required, but some all-ages performances. Shows nightly 7:30pm and 10:30pm. Cover $15.

CBGB/OMFUG (CBGB's), 313 Bowery (982-4052) at Bleecker St. Subway: #6 to Bleecker St. The initials stand for "country, bluegrass, blues, and other music for uplifting gourmandizers," but everyone knows that since 1976 this club has been all about punk rock. Blondie and the Talking Heads got their starts here, and the club continues to be *the* place to see great alternative rock. CB's has adjusted to the post-punk '90s with more diverse offerings, but the punk spirit lives on in the grotty, famously narrow interior, the multi-colored layers of graffiti on the bathroom walls, and the wistful eyes of some of the clientele. Shows nightly at around 8pm, Sun. (often hardcore) matinee at 3pm. Cover $5-10. **CB's Gallery** next door also offers live music. Both venues 16+.

Continental Divide, 25 Third Ave. (529-6924), at St. Mark's Pl. Subway: #6 to Astor Pl. An East Village fixture booking lots and lots of local bands—some good, some bad, most ugly. No cover Sun.-Thurs.; Fri.-Sat. $3-5.

Irving Plaza, 17 Irving Pl. (777-6800), at 15th St., between Third Ave. and Union Sq. Subway: L, N, R, 4, 5, or 6 to 14th St.-Union Sq. A mid-sized venue decorated in a puzzling *chinoiserie* style. Features rock, comedy, feminist performance art, and other entertainment in its barn-like perfomance space. Sat. night becomes **Grey Gardens** dance club. Cover varies. Doors open Mon.-Fri. at 8pm, Sat. at 7:30pm. Box office open Mon.-Fri. 11am-6pm.

Knitting Factory, 47 E. Houston St. (219-3055), between Mott and Mulberry St. Subway: #6 to Spring St. or B, D, F, Q to Broadway-Lafayette St. Free-thinking musicians anticipate the Apocalypse with a wide range of edge-piercing performances complemented by great acoustics. Several shows nightly. Sonic Youth played here every Thurs. night for years (alas, no more). Big names like Laibach share space with Joe Coleman and Brinssly Slopchop. The last Sun. of each month features "Cobra," a musical genre invented by avant-garde jazz composer John Zorn. Cover (usually $10) for entrance to the back room/performance space only; entry to the cozy bar up front is always free. $3 pints of Brooklyn Brown Ale and Brooklyn Lager are yummy.

Lovesexy, 104 Hudson St. (201-656-1136), just off 1st St. in Hoboken, NJ. Subway: B, D, F, N, Q, or R to 34th St., then PATH train ($1) to the 1st stop in Hoboken. (PATH train also leaves from the 23rd and 14th St. stations of the F train, as well as from its own stations at 9th St./Sixth Ave. and Christopher St./Greenwich St.) From the PATH station, walk along Hudson Pl. to Hudson St. and up two blocks. This bar features local bands, usually on weekends, but occasionally during the week. The club is in the back of a remarkably seedy bar. Cover $5, drinks $3-3.50. Shows at 9:30pm.

Maxwell's, 1039 Washington St. (201-798-4064), at 11th St. in Hoboken, NJ. Subway: B, D, F, N, Q, or R to 34th St., then PATH train ($1) to the 1st stop in Hoboken. (PATH train also leaves from the 23rd and 14th St. stations of the F train, as well as from its own stations at 9th St./Sixth Ave. and Christopher St./Greenwich St.) Once there, walk along Hudson Pl. to Hudson St., up one block to Newark St., left two blocks to Washington St., right 10 blocks to 11th St. Strong underground rock, punk, and pop acts from America and abroad have plied their trade in the back room of this Hoboken restaurant for about 15 years. New Order played its first U.S. show here, the Feelies were once regulars, and Ira Kaplan of Yo La Tengo manned the soundboard for a while. Now it's graced by the likes of angry girls Bikini Kill, hardcore band Surgery, and dream-poppers Stereolab. Cover $5-10; shows occasionally sell out, so get tix in advance from Maxwell's, Pier Platters in Hoboken (see Shopping: Record Stores), See Hear in the East Village, or Ticketmaster.

McGovern's, 305 Spring St. (627-5037), between Greenwich and Hudson St. Subway: 1 or 9 to Canal St.; or A, L, or E to Canal St. Tiny, worn, and a little bit seedy; a world away from the glitzy SoHo scene. Out of the way, with a mostly young, local crowd; live rock Wed.-Sun. Cover Fri.-Sat. after 10pm $5.

Mercury Lounge, 217 E. Houston St. (260-4700), at Ave. A. Subway: F to 2nd Ave.-E. Houston St. The Mercury has attracted an amazing number of big-name acts to its fairly small-time room, running the gamut from folk to noise to pop. Past standouts have included Lenny Kravitz, Morphine, They Might Be Giants, and Bikini Kill. Music nightly; cover usually $5-15.

New Music Café, 380 Canal St. (941-1019), at W. Broadway. Subway: #1 or 9 to Canal St.; or J, N, R, or 6 to Canal St. Tends to be more up-scale and mainstream than avant-garde; music ranges from acid jazz to noise pop. Music nightly; cover about $10.

Rock-n-Roll Café, 149 Bleecker St. (677-7630), two blocks west of Broadway. Subway: B, D, or F to Broadway/Lafayette, or #6 to Bleecker St. All covers, all the time. This club books tribute bands only. See your favorite Bruce Springsteen or Jim Morrison lookalike sing his doppleganger's greatest hits. Shows Sun.-Thurs. 8 and 9:30pm, Fri.-Sat. 8:30 and 10:30pm. Cover varies.

Roseland, 239 W. 52nd St. (247-0200), at Eighth Ave. and Broadway. Subway: C or E to 50th St. Decently priced concert club featuring mostly They-Might-Be-Giants-style, major-label college rock, with the occasional descent into Mötley Crüe-type territory. Also the occasional night of ballroom dancing. Tickets $15-25.

Tramps, 45 W. 21st St. (727-7788), between Fifth and Sixth Ave. Subway: F, N, or R to 23rd St. Screaming violins and clattering washboards pack the sweaty dance floor. Louisiana zydeco rocks nightly with help from blues, reggae, and rock bands. Surprisingly agile crowd. Sets usually around 8:30 and 11pm. Doors open at 7pm. Cover $5-15.

Wetlands Preserve, 161 Hudson St. (966-4225), near Laight St. in TriBeCa. Subway: #1, 9, A, C, or E to Canal St. A giant Summer of Love mural in the back room sets the tone, a Volkswagen bus curio shop swims in tie dyes, and mood memorabilia harken to the Woodstock years in this 2-story whole-earth spectacular. The back-to-nature theme is backed up by regular Tues. night "Ecosaloon" lectures on environmental concerns (7pm, free). Nightly live music includes Grateful Dead tributes each Tues., "Psychedelic Psaturdays," and rock-underground-alternative-whatever Wed.-Fri. Sun. caters to the 16-and-over crowd. Cover usually $7-10; usually free Mon.-Tues.; shows usually kick off at either 9 or 10pm.

OTHER MUSIC CLUBS

Ballroom, 253 W. 28th St. (244-3005), at Eighth Ave. Subway: C or E to 23rd St. A slinky cabaret on the edge of Chelsea. Borderline Art Deco decor with a funky, vegetable-heavy *tapas* bar. Eclectic offerings range from Long Island Retro to Village avant-garde. Often dance, comedy, or performance art enriches the music. Open Tues.-Sat. 4:30pm-1am, Sun. noon-1am. Showtime Tues.-Sun. 9pm. Cover $15-20, plus 2-drink min.

Louisiana Community Bar & Grill, 622 Broadway (460-9633), between Bleecker and Houston St. Subway: B, D, F, or Q to Broadway-Lafayette St.; or N or R to

Prince St. Large and youthful NYU crowd. Interior is an attempt to create a pure Cajun atmosphere, with open beams across the ceiling, "unfinished walls," and massive alligators made of papier-mâché. Soul, blues, folk, and zydeco nightly; never a cover. They really stick you with the beer prices (up to $4 a bottle), so it's best to get lubricated—if you're into getting lubricated—before you come. Music starts Sun. at 8pm, Mon.-Thurs. at 9pm, Fri.-Sat. at 11pm

Sounds of Brazil (SOB's), 204 Varick St. (243-4940), at the corner of Seventh and Houston in the Village. Subway: #1 or 9 to Houston. This luncheonette-turned-dance-club presents bopping musicians playing the sounds of Brazil, Africa, Latin America, and the Caribbean in a setting overrun with tropicana. Open for dining Tues.-Thurs. 7pm-2:30am, Fri.-Sat. 7pm-4am. Most shows Sun.-Thurs. 8 and 10pm; Fri.-Sat. 10:30pm and 1am, or 10pm, midnight, and 2am. Cover $10-16, depending on the act.

■■■ DANCE CLUBS

> *A wilderness of human flesh / Crazed with avarice, lust and rum / New York, thy name's Delirium.*
> —Byron R. Newton, Ode to New York, 1906

The New York dance club is an unrivaled institution. The crowd is uninhibited, the music unparalleled, and the fun unlimited—as long as you uncover the right place. Honing in on the hippest club in New York isn't easy as a tourist. Clubs rise, war, and fall, and even those "in the know" don't always know where to find the hot spot. The best parties are often "raves" or "outlaws," advertised only by word of mouth, which convene late at night in abandoned warehouses, closed bars, or unknown clubs. Many clubs move from space to space each week, although true clubbers still manage to find them. Make friends with someone on the inside. *Let's Go* could only dream of being cool enough to be totally on top of the club scene.

The rules are simple. You have to have "the look" to be let in. Doormen are the clubs' fashion police, and nothing drab or conventional will squeeze by. Wear black clothes and drape your most attractive friends on your arms. Don't look worried or fearful; act like you belong. Most clubs open their doors around 9pm, but come after 11pm unless you crave solitude; things don't really get going until 1 or 2am. Most clubs stay open until 4am; a few non-alcoholic after-hours clubs keep getting busy until 5 or 6am, or later.

Most good clubs are good on only one or two nights a week. The right club on the wrong night can be a big mistake, particularly if you've already paid the $5-15 cover charge. The cover can rise to $20 on weekend nights when the *too-cool* B&T crowd (who reach Manhattan from New Jersey and Long Island by bridge and tunnel) attempt to get past the bouncers *en masse.*

Alternative and downtown nightlife often blend; the hippest clubs have one or two "gay nights" a week, and same-sex couples can go "clubbing" in most places without any hassle. The distinction between "dance clubs" and other types of clubs or bars is also somewhat fuzzy; as it is possible and sometimes overwhelmingly tempting to dance anywhere with music, you may find people shakin' their thangs at some of the bars (See Eating and Drinking: Bars) and music clubs listed earlier in this book. Doing the "headless chicken" to muzak in a skyscraper lobby may be somewhat out of line, though.

Let's Go has ranked the following dance clubs according to fun and value. The suggestions could well have changed by the summer of '95, as hipness factors tend to fluctuate wildly. Call ahead to make sure that you know what (and whom) you'll find when you arrive.

Bar Room, 432 W. 14th St. (366-5680), at Washington St. Subway: A, C, or E to 14th St. When it's not the Clit Club or Jackie 60 (see Gay and Lesbian Clubs below), the Bar Room still is a hip place to be. Wed. night is **Sin Sister** (no theme

4 West 31st Street
New York, New York 10001

Let's Go Travel

Harvard Student Agencies
53A Church Street
Cambridge, MA 02138

but cool people, $5), and Thurs. night is **Aqua Booty** (229-7777), where Willie Ninja from Dee-lite spins the deep house tunes ($5). Doors open at 10:30pm.

Tunnel, 220 Twelfth Ave. (695-7292), near 28th St. Subway: C or E to 23rd St. Immense club; 3 floors and a mezzanine packed with 2 dance floors, lounges, glass-walled live shows, and a skateboarding cage. Enough room for a multitude of diverse parties in this labyrinthine club. The unisex toilet/bar is especially convenient. Open Fri.-Sat.; Sat. nights are queer. Cover $20.

Webster Hall, 125 E. 11th St. (353-1600), between Third and Fourth Ave. Subway: #4, 5, 6, N, or R to Union Sq.-14th St. Walk 3 blocks south and a block east. New and very popular club offers a rock/reggae room and a coffeeshop in addition to the main, house-dominated dance floor. "Psychedelic Thursdays" often feature live bands and $2.50 beers. Open Wed.-Sun. Cover $5-15.

Limelight, 47 W. 20th St. (807-7850), at Sixth Ave. Subway: F or R to 23rd St. Once a church and some nights are about as much fun as Sunday school. The real attraction is Wed. night's Disco 2000 party, where funky things happen. Queer on Fri. and Sat. nights. Sun. night is live heavy metal. Cover usually $15.

Nell's, 246 W. 14th St. (675-1567), between Seventh and Eighth Ave. Subway: #1, 2, 3, or 9 to 14th St. A legendary hotspot; some faithful admirers hang on even through its decline. Dingy neighborhood belies the opulence of the huge Victorian-style sitting room inside. Overstuffed chairs, chandeliers, and bejeweled Beautiful People upstairs. Angular dance floor downstairs. Every other Mon. is **Funky Buddha**—funk and hip-hop with guest bands. Cover Mon.-Wed. $7, Thurs.-Sun. $15. Open daily 10pm-4am.

Palladium, 126 E. 14th St. (473-7171), at Third Ave. Subway: #4, 5, 6, L, N, or R to 14th St. Started by megaclub moguls Steve Rubell and Ian Schrager. Once Madonna and her friends set the pace, now big hair has replaced big crowds. But the music is still good and the space is still cool. Look in stores in the Village for invites offering free or discounted admission. Club MTV used to be filmed here. Funky, funky, funky. The alternative Michael Todd Room hosts somewhat mainstream alternative-rock shows. Open Fri.-Sat. 10pm-4am. Cover $20.

The Pyramid, 101 Ave. A (420-1590), at 6th St. Subway: #6 to Astor Pl. No sign over the door, just a pink triangle. Transvestite punk and '60s lighting in this small bar and dance space. Psychedelic lounge downstairs. Those seeking the unusual will fit right in. Avant-garde performances nightly with great and frequent lip-synch shows. Mostly a gay club, though Fri. nights are straight. Transvestite go-go dancers on the bar (yes, on the bar). Gay cabaret Sun. night. Cover $5-10.

Love Sexy, 31 Union Square (675-2300), in the Metropolis Café Wed. nights. Subway #4, 5, 6, L, N, R to 14th St. Glam model-types boogie-ing the night away to top 40 dance. See or be seen. Cover $8-15.

The Bank, 225 E. Houston St. (505-5033) at Essex St. on the Lower East Side. Subway: F to Delancey St. A stately bank converted into a slick club. Clear sight-lines make it great for live music. Reliable, if journeyman, music. Underground vault a great spot for the wee hours. Call for information on the erratic schedule. Cover usually around $8.

China Club, 2130 Broadway (877-1166), at 75th St. Subway: #1, 2, 3, or 9 to 72nd St. Rock-and-roll hot spot where Bowie and Jagger come on their off nights. Models and long-haired men make it a great people-watching spot. Pudgy, rich men trying to get by the doorman make it a great people-mocking spot. Mon. night is one of New York's hottest club nights for the "beautiful people" crowd. Be well-dressed or you probably won't get in. Go elsewhere for great dancing. Cover around $10. Opens daily at 9pm.

Au Bar, 41 E. 58th St. (308-1546), between Park and Madison Ave. Subway: #4, 5, 6 to 59th St., or N, R to Lexington Ave. Au dear. Très Euro. Gypsy Kings music on the dance floor. Lots of thirtysomething men in Armani suits, cigars in hand, put the moves on women. Mon. nights is **Milk,** where Asian-Americans rub elbows with East Villagers braving the trek uptown. Serves "supper" to the refined and "breakfast" to the diehards. Open Tues.-Sun. 9pm-4am. Cover Sun. and Tues.-Wed. $10, Thurs.-Sat. $15. No cover before midnight Sun. and Tues.-Wed.

■■■ GAY AND LESBIAN CLUBS

The New York gay scene extends visibly throughout the city. The West Village, especially around Christopher St., has long been the hub of the city's alternative life. Chelsea, just north of Village, has emerged as the new hangout of gay men disgusted with the Guppie lifestyle. A hard-core gay crowd also occupies the East Village on First and Second Ave. south of E. 12th St. Wealthier types cruise the Upper West Side in the upper 70s; Columbus Ave. on Sundays is a great place to drive. Gay communities are not restricted to Manhattan; Park Slope in Brooklyn has long been home to a large and important lesbian community.

Each week the *Village Voice* and *New York Native* publish full listings of gay events. The free *NY Press* is also a good resource. The Gay and Lesbian Student Organization of Columbia University sponsors a huge dance on the first Friday and the third Saturday of each month in Earl Hall at 116th St. and Broadway (Subway: #1 to 116th St.; Cover $7, students with ID $5). The *Pink Pages* is a phone book for the queer community with all sorts of listings, including bars and clubs. You can pick one up in some of the gay/lesbian bars, or call 1-800-982-4717 to get information on where to pick one up.

Following is a list of clubs (some of them dance-oriented, others geared more towards conversation and drinking) at the center of gay and lesbian nightlife. Remember to bring two forms of ID to prove you're over 18 or 21, as needed. *Let's Go* has ranked the clubs, taking fun and value into account.

Clit Club, 432 W. 14th St. (529-3300), at Washington St. Fri. nights in the Bar Room. This is *the* place to be for young, beautiful, queer grrls. Host Julie throws the hottest party around every Fri. night, with go-go girls, house music, and babes galore. Hit on the femme of your dreams at the pool table, or just chill out in the video room. Cover $3 before 11pm, $5 after 11pm. Doors open at 9:30pm.

Jackie 60, 432 W. 14th St. (366-5680), at Washington St. Tues. nights at the Bar Room. Drag queens work it while the (sometimes) celebrity crowd eggs them on to even more fabulous feats of glamor. You go, girl! Cover $10. Doors open at 10pm.

Uncle Charlie's, 56 Greenwich Ave. (255-8787), at Perry St. Subway: #1 or 9 to Christopher St. Biggest and best-known gay club in the city. Mainstream and preppy, with guppies galore. It's still fun, if a bit crowded on the weekends. Women are welcome, but few come. Open daily 4pm-4am. No cover.

Duplex, 61 Christopher St. (255-5438), at Seventh Ave. Bright lights, drag queens, cabarets...check out this, the oldest continuing cabaret in the city, if you're doing the queer NYC tour. Lady Bunny struts her stuff here periodically and must be seen. Cover varies: $3-12, with a 2-drink min. Concerts start around 7 or 8pm.

Limelight, 47 W. 20th St. (807-7850), at Sixth Ave. Subway: F or R to 23rd St. Hosts a club within a club, **Lick It!,** on weekend nights plus a gay back room always. Check out the Plexiglas "feel-me" booth. Cover usually $15.

DT's Fat Cat, at W. 4th St. and W. 12th St. (243-9041). Subway: A, C, E, or L to 14th St. Yes, these two streets do intersect in the non-Euclidean West Village, near Eighth Ave. Piano bar which provides a relaxed scene for lesbians. Very low-key, but pretty definitely queer. No cover. Open daily until 4am.

The Spike, 120 11th Ave. (243-9688), at W. 20th St. Subway: C or E to 23rd St. Caters to an adventurous crowd of leather-clad men (and some women) who know how to create a spectacle. Open daily 9pm-4am.

The Monster, 80 Grove St. (924-3558), at 4th St. and Sheridan Sq. Subway: #1 or 9 to Christopher St. Look for the horrifying light display outside. Cabaret-style piano bar with downstairs disco; heats up on Fri. and Sat. nights. Guys galore trying to get phone numbers amidst decadently lush vegetation. Really hoppin'. Cover Fri.-Sat. $5. Open daily 4pm-4am.

The Pyramid, 101 Ave. A (420-1590), at 6th St. Subway: #6 to Astor Pl. Also known by its street address, this dance club mixes gay, lesbian, and straight folks. Vibrant drag scene. Continues to push the limits of exotic with the freshest mixes. Fri. is straight night. Cover $5-10. Open daily 9pm-4am.

Crazy Nanny's, 21 Seventh Ave. South (366-6312, 929-8356), near LeRoy St. Subway: #1 or 9 to Houston St. Glamour dykes and the women who love them come here to shoot some pool and just hang out. Dancing nightly. Open daily 4pm-4am.

Henrietta Hudson, 438 Hudson St. (924-3347), between Morton and Barrow St. Young, clean-cut lesbian crowd. Mellow in the afternoon, packed at night and on the weekends. No cover. Open daily 3pm-4am.

The Roxy, 515 W. 18th St. (645-5156), near Tenth Ave. A mixed club in a good space with a heavily gay crowd on Sat. and Sun. (and sometimes Tues.). Often features roller-skating. Crowd makes up for sometimes tired mixes with serious moves on the dance floor. Security can be tight. Cover $7-15. Open 10am-4am.

The Works, 428 Columbus Ave. (799-7365), at 81st. Cheerfully dim, long, narrow, and popular spot for gay men. Behind a one-way window; it always looks closed from the outside. Amusing mural. Faint tropical theme. Good age range. $1 margaritas on Thurs. On Sun. guzzle all the beer you can for $5. Open daily 2pm-4am.

■■■ MISC. HIPSTER HANGOUTS

Collective Unconscious, 28 Ave. B (505-8991), between 2nd and 3rd St. Subway: F to Second Ave. Walk 3 blocks east and 2 blocks north. This performance space/ commune offers performances of various sorts, including an open mike night Sun. at 9pm ($3), plays, rock shows, and other performances (cover usually $5-7), as well as an ongoing serial play on Sat. at 8pm ($5). Lots of men sporting the bald/pot belly/goatee look. Friendly people, and usually something interesting to see. No frills—you might have to sit on the floor. No alcohol or other refreshments served either, but you're welcome to bring your own.

Nuyorican Poets Café, 236 E. 3rd St. (505-8183), between Ave. B and Ave. C. Subway: F to Second Ave. Walk 3 blocks north and 3 blocks east. New York's leading venue for the currently in-vogue "poetry slams" and spoken word performances. A mixed bag of unintentioned doggerel with occasional gems. Other types of performances too. Cover $5-10.

■■■ COMEDY CLUBS

The Next Big Thing only a few years ago, comedy clubs are now on the wane. While venues vary tremendously in size and atmosphere, nearly all impose a hefty cover and a drink minimum that's more like a maximum on Fridays and Saturdays. Invariably, there'll be an annoying emcee who'll jab at the Kansans in the front row between acts; if you dare to sit up close, be prepared.

Boston Comedy Club, 82 W. 3rd St. (477-1000), between Thompson and Sullivan. Subway: A, B, C, D, E, F, or Q to W. 4th St. Boston memorabilia everywhere, including photos of Michael Dukakis and the Cheers bar. But no more Boston than anything else—just coarse humor and lots of yuks. Cover Sun.-Thurs. $5-7, Fri.-Sat. $10. 2-drink min. Shows Sun.-Thurs. 9:30pm, Fri. 9:30pm and 11:45pm, Sat. 10pm and 12:15am.

Comedy Cellar, 117 MacDougal St. (254-3630), between W. 3rd and Bleecker St. Subway: A, B, C, D, E, F, or Q to W. 4th St. Subterranean annex of the artsy Olive Tree Café. Dark, intimate, atmospheric, packing the people in late on early Sat. morning. Features rising comics like John Manfrellott and drop-ins by superstars like Robin Williams. Cover $10 plus 2-drink min. per person. Shows Sun.-Thurs. 9pm-2am, Fri. 9pm and 11pm, Sat. 9pm, 10:45pm, and 12:30am. Make reservations on weekends.

Chicago City Limits, 351 E. 74th St. (772-8707), between First and Second Ave. Subway: #6 to 77th St. If you're looking for something a little different from the usual stand-up, check out New York's longest running theater-style improvisational comedy group. Shows are careful syntheses of cabaret, scripted comedy sketches, and improvisation, often with a political bent. Extemporaneous skits are heavily dependent on audience suggestions for plot direction, allowing the crowd to get into the act. 4500 improvised performances already. No alcohol served. Call to find out about frequent children's shows. Shows Mon. and Wed.-Thurs. 8:30pm, Fri.-Sat. 8pm and 10:30pm. Cover Mon. $10, Wed.-Thurs. $15, Fri.-Sat. $20. New Year's Eve and Labor Day are big "laff-a-thon" nights.

The Comic Strip Inc., 1568 Second Ave. (861-9386), between 81st and 82nd St. Subway: #6 to 77th St. Sunday comics characters Dagwood and Dick Tracy line the walls of this well-established pub-style club. Jim Morris honed his Reagan impressions here. Mon. is audition night, when lucky wanna-bes who signed up the previous Fri. are chosen by lottery for their brief moments in the spotlight. Shows Sun.-Thurs. 9pm, Fri. 8:30pm and 10:45pm, Sat. 8pm, 10:30pm and 12:30am. No cover charge Mon. On Sun. and Tues.-Thurs. $7 cover and 2-drink min., Fri.-Sat. $12 cover and 2-drink min. Make reservations.

Dangerfield's, 1118 First Ave. (593-1650), between 61st and 62nd St. Subway: #4, 5, or 6 to 59th St., or N or R to Lexington Ave. Rodney's respectable comic launching pad. Rising stars from throughout the country perform here, and HBO specials featuring the likes of Roseanne Barr, Sam Kinison, and Jerry Seinfeld have been taped at the club, and be prepared for a surprise (the line-up is only available the day of the show and unannounced guest comedians occasionally appear). Shows Sun.-Thurs. 8:45pm; Fri. 9pm and 11:15pm; Sat. 8pm, 10:30pm, and 12:30am. Cover Sun.-Thurs. $12.50, Fri.-Sat. $15.

The Original Improvisation, 433 W. 34th St. (279-3446), between Ninth and Tenth Ave. Subway: A, C, or E to 34th St. A quarter-century of comedy—acts from Saturday Night Live, Johnny Carson, and David Letterman. Richard Pryor and Robin Williams got started here. Shows Wed.-Sat. 9pm, Fri.-Sat. also 11:30pm. Cover $10, $9 drink min.

■■■ RADIO

Some of the most interesting programming is on the **college stations** clustering around the lower end of the dial, where you'll find jazz, country, Latin, Caribbean, blues, classical, heavy metal, and underappreciated rock. WFMU 91.1 from Upsala College in New Jersey (usually receivable only on the west side of Manhattan, south of Midtown, and in New Jersey) has amazing **underground rock** shows scattered generously through their free-form programming, and WNYU 89.1 collects the best indie rock for its New Afternoon show (weekdays 4-7:30pm). WSOU 89.5 from Seton Hall specializes in **heavy metal,** and WXCR 89.9 from Columbia University fills the airwaves with an eclectic mix of non-rock. **Rap** shows tend to show up at night on stations like WRKS 98.7 or WBLS 107.5. Morning **talk shows** are a great way to get into the day; the emperor of the talk show scene is Howard Stern, whose show airs each morning on WXRK 92.3 (so popular is Howard that his fans got him on the ballot for the 1994 gubernatorial election).

Classic Rock: WXRK 92.3, WNEW 102.7
Top 40: WPSC 88.7, WPLJ 95.5, WRCN 103.9
Urban Contemporary: WRKS 98.7, WBLS 107.5
Oldies: WRTN 93.5, WCBS 101.1
Country: WYNY 103.5
Classical: WNYC 93.9, WQXR 96.3
Jazz: WBGO 88.3
College/Indie/Alternative: WNYU 89.1, WSOU 89.5, WFMU 91.1, WDRE 92.7, WHTZ 100.3, WAXQ 104.3
Foreign-language Programming: WADO 1280AM, WWRV 1330AM, WKDM 1380AM, WZRC 1480AM, WNWK 105.9
News: WABC 770AM, WCBS 880AM, WINS 1010AM, WBBR 1130AM
Public Radio: WNYC 93.9, WBAI 99.5
Sports: WFAN 660AM

Sports

While most cities would be content to field a major-league team in each big-time sport, New York opts for the Noah's Ark approach: there are two baseball teams, two NHL hockey teams, and two NFL football teams (although the Giants and Jets are now quartered across the river in New Jersey), as well as an NBA basketball team. In addition to local teams' regularly scheduled season games, New York hosts a number of celebrated world-class events such as the New York Marathon and the United States Tennis Association Open (a.k.a. the U.S. Open). The city papers overflow with information on upcoming events.

■■■ SPECTATOR SPORTS

BASEBALL

The national pastime thrives in New York from late March to early October, when two high-exposure teams make their exploits off the field almost as melodramatic as those on it. The legendary **New York Yankees** play ball at **Yankee Stadium** in the Bronx (718-293-6000), though short-tempered boss George Steinbrenner is threatening to move the Yanks elsewhere. Relations with the Bronx turned particularly sour in 1994, when a member of the Yankees front management allegedly likened the neighborhood youths to "monkeys." On the playing field, recent acquisitions Paul O'Neill, Wade Boggs, and Jimmy Key have joined long time Yank Don Mattingly in propelling the club to the upper-tier of the division, after some dismal seasons in the late '80s. Plenty of tickets are usually available, from $6.50 for bleacher seats to $17 for lower box seats. On Family Day every Monday, the deserving brood can get half-price seating.

Over the past few years, the **New York Mets** have lost virtually all their superstars, including Howard Johnson and slugging rightfielder Darryl Strawberry, retaining only Bobby Bonilla and a faltering Dwight Gooden. The Mets suffered nightmare seasons in 1992 and 1993 and were sporting a losing record as of press time in 1994. Hope springs eternal for '95. Watch them go to bat at **Shea Stadium** in Queens (718-507-8499). Tickets range from $6.50 for bleacher seats to $15 for lower box seats, the best of which are often difficult to obtain. On promotion dates, sponsors give away baseball cards, action figures, wallets, helmets, banners, and other memorabilia. Avoid family days unless you really love screaming kids.

FOOTBALL

Though both New York teams once battled in the trenches at Shea Stadium, nowadays they play across the river at **Giants Stadium** (201-935-3900) in East Rutherford, New Jersey. The mighty **New York Giants** are looking for their third Super Bowl ring. Meanwhile, the **Jets,** long seeking to return to the glory of the Namath years, have played well recently and went 8-8 in 1993. Jets tickets are hard to come by; Giants tickets nigh impossible—season ticket holders have booked them all for the next **40 years.** See *Let's Go: New York City 2035* for details. Tickets for the Jets start at $25 (cash only at the Meadowlands box office).

BASKETBALL

After years of mediocrity, the **New York Knickerbockers** (usually referred to as the Knicks) are finally a force in the NBA, winning the Eastern Conference in 1994 under the towering leadership of center Patrick Ewing but losing in the NBA Finals to Houston in seven games. The Knicks do their dribbling at **Madison Square Garden** (465-6741) from late fall to late spring; tickets, which start at $13, are fairly hard to come by and nearly impossible during the playoffs. On the college level, the second-tier N.I.T. and Big East collegiate tournaments take place at Madison Square Garden in March.

HOCKEY

In a town known for its speed and turbulence, it's not hard to understand why New Yorkers attend hockey games with such fervor. The **New York Rangers** play at **Madison Square Garden** (465-6741 or 308-6977) from late fall to late spring. Long-suffering fans, after enduring 54 dry years, were finally rewarded with a huge, gleaming piece of silverware when their Rangers captured the Stanley Cup in June 1994. Indoor fireworks exploded as the final buzzer sounded, and one ecstatic fan spoke for many when he held up a sign saying, "Now I can die in peace!" Tickets start at $12; reserve well in advance. Meanwhile, the lowly **New York Islanders** are now mired near the bottom of the league, after winning four consecutive Stanley Cups in the early '80s. They hang their skates at the **Nassau Coliseum** (516-794-9300) in Uniondale, Long Island. Tickets start at $14.

TENNIS

Tennis enthusiasts who get their tickets three months in advance can attend the prestigious **United States Open,** held in late August and early September at the United States Tennis Association's (USTA) Tennis Center in Flushing Meadows Park, Queens (718-271-5100). Tickets start at $25 for day matches and $18 for evening matches. The **Virginia Slims Championship,** featuring the world's top women players, comes to Madison Square Garden (465-6741) in mid-November. Tickets for the opening rounds start at $15.

HORSERACING

Forsake the rat race for some equine excitement. Thoroughbred fans can watch the stallions go at **Belmont Park** (718-641-4700) every day except Monday from May through July and from September to mid-October, and may even catch a grand slam event. The **Belmont Stakes,** run in early summer, is one leg in the Triple Crown. The "Belmont Special" train leaves from Penn Station every 20 minutes from 9:45am to noon ($7 round-trip, including $1 off admission). Meanwhile, **Aqueduct Race-track** (718-641-4700), next to JFK Airport, has races from late October to early May, every day except Tuesday. (Subway: A or C to Aqueduct.) Grandstand seating at both tracks costs $2. Racing in New York is suspended during the month of August, when the action goes upstate to Saratoga.

PEOPLERACING

On the third Sunday in October, two million spectators line rooftops, sidewalks, and promenades to cheer 22,000 runners in the **New York City Marathon** (16,000 of whom actually finish). The race begins on Verrazano Bridge and ends at Central Park's Tavern on the Green.

■■■ PARTICIPATORY SPORTS

Amateur and recreational athletes also twist and flex in New York, and you can too. Although space in much of the city is at a premium, the City of New York Parks and Recreation Department (360-8111; 360-3456 for a recording of park events) manages to maintain numerous playgrounds and parks in all boroughs, for everything from baseball and basketball to croquet and shuffleboard.

SWIMMING

Beaches

Coney Island Beach and Boardwalk (2½ mi.), on the Atlantic Ocean, from W. 37th St. to Corbin Pl., in Brooklyn (718-946-1350). Subway: B, D, F, or N to Coney Island.

Manhattan Beach (¼ mi.), on the Atlantic Ocean, from Ocean Ave. to Mackenzie St. in Brooklyn (718-946-1373).

Orchard Beach and Promenade (1¼ mi.), on Long Island Sound in Pelham Bay Park, Bronx (885-2275). Subway: #6 to Pelham Bay Park.

Rockaway Beach and Boardwalk (7½ mi.), on the Atlantic Ocean. From Beach 1st St., Far Rockaway, to Beach 149th St., Neponsit, Queens (718-318-4000). Lifeguards on duty daily 10am-6pm through the summer. Subway: A, C, or H to any Beach St. stop.

Staten Island: South Beach, Midland Beach, and **Franklin D. Roosevelt Boardwalk** (2½ mi.), on Lower New York Bay. From Fort Wadsworth to Miller Field, New Dorp. Take bus #51 from the ferry terminal.

Pools

Public pools are scattered throughout all the boroughs of New York, but they can be dangerous, as several incidents of sexual assault have occurred in the past couple years. Often this takes the form of girls or women being surrounded by a circle of boys or men, who close in and molest the victim in what is called "whirlpooling." The NYC Parks Department has added security and is considering segregating some pools by sex. If you can find the few pools that aren't in troubled neighborhoods, though, public pools can be a cheap way to escape from the sweltering summer heat. All outdoor pools are open from early July through Labor Day from 11am to 7 or 8pm, depending on the weather. All are free. Call 718-699-4219 to reach the Parks Aquatic Information Line.

Indoor pools can be somewhat safer than outdoor pools and tend to be open year-round, but most require some sort of annual membership fee of $10 and up.

BICYCLING

From spring to fall, daily at dawn and dusk and throughout the weekend, packs of dedicated (and fashion-conscious) cyclists dressed in biking shorts navigate the trails and wide roads of **Central Park.** (The circular drive is car-free Mon.-Thurs. 10am-3pm and 7-10pm, and Fri. 10am-3pm and 7pm until Mon. 6am.) (See Jogging below for tips on where to ride in Central Park.) On the West Side, along the Hudson bank, **Riverside Park** between 72nd and 110th draws more laid-back riders. Other excellent places to go on weekends include the deserted **Wall Street** area or the unadorned roads of Brooklyn's **Prospect Park.** For quick same-day excursions, plenty of bike shops around Central Park rent out two-wheelers by the hour. See Essentials: Getting Around for more information on biking in New York City.

JOGGING

In New York, joggers and cyclists go hand in hand—not exactly a harmonious combination. When running in **Central Park** during no-traffic hours (see Bicycling above), stay in the right-hand runners' lane to avoid being mowed down by some reckless pedal-pusher. Stay in populated areas and stay out of the park after dark. Avoid venturing up beyond 96th St. unless you have a companion or are familiar with the route. Recommended courses include the 1.58-mi. jaunt around the Reservoir and a picturesque 1.72-mi. route starting at Tavern on the Green along the West Drive, heading south to East Drive, and then circling back west up 72nd St. to where you started. Another beautiful place to run is **Riverside Park,** which stretches along the Hudson bank from 72nd to 116th; don't stray too far north. See Essentials: Getting Around for more information on jogging in New York.

BOWLING

There are only a few places left for strikes and spares in Manhattan. Try the 44-lane **Bowlmor,** 110 University Pl. (255-8188), near 13th St., on the third and fourth floors. With such limited alley space, call ahead to check lane availability. ($3.25 per game each person, $1 shoe rental. Open Sun.-Wed. 10am-1am, Thurs. 10am-2am,

Fri.-Sat. 10am-4am.) **Tennis** courts are on the higher floors; call 989-2300 to reserve space and check prices.

GOLF

Although New York golf courses don't measure up to those at Pebble Beach, New Yorkers nonetheless remain avid golfers, jamming all of the 13 well-manicured city courses during the weekends. Most are found in the Bronx or Queens, including **Pelham Bay Park** (885-1258), **Van Cortlandt Park** (543-4595), and **Forest Park** (718-296-0999). Greens fees are $19 during the week and $21 Saturdays and Sundays for non-NYC residents. Reservations for summer weekends suggested 7-10 days in advance.

ICE SKATING

The first gust of cold winter air brings out droves of aspiring Brian Boitanos and Katarina Witts. While each of the rinks in the city has its own character, nearly all have lockers, skate rentals, and a snack bar. The most popular and expensive is the tiny sunken plaza in **Rockefeller Center,** Fifth Ave. and 50th St. (757-5730), which doubles as the chic American Festival Café during the spring and summer months. You can do your Bolero thing at the Donald Trump-owned **Wollman Memorial Rink** (517-4800), located in a particularly scenic section of Central Park near 64th St. **Sky Rink** (695-6555), at W. 21st St. and the Hudson River, boasts two full-sized Olympic rinks. Call for hours, prices, and skate rental fees for recreational skating.

HORSEBACK RIDING

Horseback riding in Central Park for those experienced in English saddle operates out of **Claremont Stables,** at 175 W. 89th St. (724-5100; open Mon.-Fri. 6:30am-1 hr. before dusk, Sat.-Sun. 6:30am-4pm; $33 per hour; make reservations). In Queens, **Lynne's Riding School** (718-261-7679) and **Dixie Do Stables** (718-263-3500) give guided trail rides through Forest Park (open 8am-7pm; $20 per hour).

CRICKET AND CROQUET

The two bastions of British civilization, cricket and croquet, are both played in this most un-English of cities. You won't see Ian Botham swinging his chunk of willow, but you can turn your arm over for a few overs of off-spin at **cricket fields** throughout the boroughs. Fields include **Flushing Meadows-Corona Park** in Queens (call 718-520-5932 for the $10 permit); **Canarsie Beach Park** in Brooklyn (718-965-8919); and **Van Cortlandt Park** in the Bronx (718-430-1890 for the $25 permit). During the summer months, weekend permits at any of the three parks are nearly impossible to come by. All welcome spectators, though, and Flushing Meadows-Corona Park has just added three new fields.

For a quick dose of mallet and wicket, head to the croquet lawn in Central Park, north of Sheep Meadow (call 929-9440 for permits; open May-Nov.).

■ Shopping

At the Whitney Museum, you can buy a $60 canvas sack imprinted with a bold, constructivist message that reads "I Shop Therefore I Am." As Descartes would recognize, image is what sells in this City of Images, whether that image is an "I Love Brooklyn" sweatshirt or a Polo-emblazoned pair of socks from Ralph Lauren's believe-me-or-not *palazzo* on Madison.

■■■ DEPARTMENT STORES AND SHOPPING MALLS

New York has more ritzy department stores than Beverly Hills. Start with **Macy's,** the world's "finest" department store; it used to bill itself as the world's "largest" until recently, when a store in Germany was built one square foot larger. You can eat breakfast, lunch, and dinner at Macy's, get a facial and a haircut, mail a letter, have your jewelry appraised, exchange currency, purchase theater tickets, and get lost. Of course, you can also shop. The colossus sits at 151 W. 34th St. (695-4400), between Broadway and Seventh Ave.

Grab a store directory at the entrance to help you navigate Macy's mazes. Macy's has its own Visitors Center, located on the first-floor balcony, where the concierge service (560-3827) will assist anyone looking for anything. They will also arrange free tours, make dining or entertainment reservations, provide information on upcoming entertainment events, and arrange for interpreters to accompany non-English speakers through the store. Those too busy making money to spend any of it themselves can hire others to spend it for them, using the "Macy's by Appointment" service on the third floor. A staff of fashion consultants, home-accessories experts, and corporate specialists act as consumer therapists, walking clients through the store if necessary to help them discover what they really want (for an appointment, call 560-4181). All these services are free. (Open Mon. and Thurs.-Fri. 10am-8:30pm, Tues.-Wed. and Sat. 10am-7pm, Sun. 11am-6pm. Subway: #1, 2, 3, or 9 to Penn Station, or B, D, F, N, Q, or R to 34th St.

Courtly **Lord and Taylor,** 424 Fifth Ave. (391-3344), between 38th and 39th St., has made a specialty of stocking clothes by American designers, but its furniture transcends the trendy with such couture classics as Henredon sofas, Chinese porcelain lamps, and reproductions of Louis XV tables. Scores of New Yorkers come to be shod at the legendary shoe department and treated in Lord's manner: caring service, free coffee in the early morning, and unsurpassed Christmas displays. The first in history to use the picture window as a stage for anything other than merchandise, the store began this custom in 1905 during an unusually balmy December that failed to summon the appropriate meteorological garnish; Lord and Taylor filled its windows with mock storms and blizzards, reviving the Christmas spirit for gloomy city-dwellers. (Open Mon.-Tues. 10am-7pm, Wed.-Fri. 10am-8:30pm, Sat. 9am-7pm, Sun. 11am-6pm. Subway: B, D, or F to 42nd St.; or N or R to 34th St.)

Also renowned for its window displays is **Barney's New York** (945-1600). The mother store, a 10,000-sq.-ft. coliseum, overlooks the Hudson River at 2 World Financial Center. Barney's features collections of sportswear, formal wear, shoes, and oh-so-fine shirts from Truzzi. (Open Mon.-Fri. 10am-7pm, Sat. 10am-6pm, Sun. noon-5pm.) Another outlet (929-9000) does business at Seventh Ave. and 17th St. (Open Mon.-Thurs. 10am-9pm, Fri. 10am-8pm, Sat. 10am-7pm; Sept.-June also on Sun. noon-6pm.)

Saks Fifth Avenue, 611 Fifth Ave. (753-4000), between 49th and 50th St., is subdued and chic. This institution has aged well and continues to combine good taste with smooth courtesy. The perfume-sprayers are more restrained, although no less adept, than those at Bloomingdale's. (Open Mon.-Wed. and Fri.-Sat. 10am-6:30pm, Thurs. 10am-8pm, Sun. noon-6pm.)

Bloomingdale's, 1000 Third Ave. (705-2000), at E. 59th St., affectionately known as Bloomie's, is "an extraordinary shopping experience." More to the point, Bloomie's is nine floors dedicated to yuppie decadence—the totally consuming need to shop. Watch the eternal tango between casual shoppers and perfume spritzers on the first floor, and dodge the throngs of foreign tourists buying up the Clinique counter. There's something for everyone here, but most of it is far too hopelessly chic for the average budget peasant. Just remember, though: bathrooms are on floors 2, 7, and 8, the chairs are soft and cushy for when your friend takes longer in the fur salon than you'd anticipated, and there's 8.25% sales tax on all purchases in NYC. (Open Mon., Fri., and Sat. 10am-7pm, Tues.-Wed. 10am-10pm, Thurs. 10am-9pm, Sun. 11am-7pm.)

Sit in luxury's lap at the legendary, extortionate **Bergdorf-Goodman** clothing mansion, on both sides of the street at 745 and 754 Fifth Ave. (753-7300), between 57th and 58th St., where expensive people buy pricey jewelry and swank outfits by the crystal light of chandeliers. (Open Mon.-Wed. and Fri.-Sat. 10am-6pm, Thurs. 10am-8pm.)

If the name doesn't set you rolling, the smorgasbord of bizarre merchandise will; **Hammacher Schlemmer,** 157 E. 57th St. (421-9000), between Third and Lexington Ave., is a gadget-fancier's fantasyland. Marvel at such essential items as a self-stirring French saucepan, an air-conditioned doghouse, a computerized fortune teller, and the Whiz Bang Popcorn Wagon. More redeemingly, Hammacher's zeal for automated convenience has also provided the world with the steam iron, electric razor, and pressure cooker. Masquerade as a serious consumer while test-driving the floor models of various massage machines. (Open Mon.-Sat. 10am-6pm.)

Abraham & Strauss (A&S) (594-8500), the inventor of the vertical shopping mall, ascends to commodity heaven in the **A&S Plaza** (465-0500) at Sixth Ave. and 33rd St., with eight levels of fashion, toys, electronics, and hard-to-find items. The Plaza's colored lights and fantasy-land exterior appear to herald an amusement park, and all is movement inside, with the silver escalators and the constant parade of humanity. Four glass elevators haloed in lightbulbs slide up and down the walls, eliciting the same sinking feeling as an advanced-technology ferris wheel. The building is twisted into a doughnut shape, intended to focus shoppers' attention inward and away from the real life on the streets outside. The top level, called "Taste of the Town," is an international food court, an entire floor of noshing and funk. (Plaza open Mon. and Thurs.-Fri. 9:45am-8:30pm, Tues.-Wed. and Sat. 9:45am-6:45pm, Sun. 11am-6pm.)

The **Trump Tower** (832-2000), at 57th St. and Fifth Ave., gleams with marble and gold. Inside, a fountain of plenty climbs the walls of a six-story atrium of upmarket boutiques and restaurants. The 1980s are alive and well here, if slightly worse for wear. (Boutiques open Mon.-Sat. 10am-6pm. Atrium open daily 8am-6pm.)

At the **SoHo Emporium,** 375 W. Broadway (966-6091), between Broome and Spring St., some 25 independent boutiques vie with each other tooth and claw for your patronage. Everything goes on sale here, from furs and jewelry to crafts and crystal. A fortune teller, on hand, can help you define your most urgent shopping needs. (Open daily noon-8pm.) Mall-shopping on a global scale transpires at the 60 shops and restaurants in the concourse of the **World Trade Center** (435-4170) at West and Liberty St. (shops open Mon.-Fri. 7:30am-6:30pm, Sat. 10am-5pm).

Anyone from the American hinterland who's feeling a little homesick won't want to miss the **Staten Island Mall,** off Richmond Rd. near the center of the island. With a huge, sprawling, one-floor selection, it's so similar to those all over the country that it's easy to imagine yourself anywhere but Staten Island, New York. Roam from Sears to Macy's to the Gap to B. Dalton—all the big names of Mall-dom are here. (Mall open Mon.-Sat. 10am-9:30pm, Sun. noon-6pm.) To get here, take the S44 bus from the ferry terminal and ride for about 45 minutes.

■ SECAUCUS AND PARAMUS, NJ

No sales tax on clothes! Though these two cities are sort of a schlep from Manhattan, the intrepid shopper should definitely make the 20-30 minute trek to these two towns. If Manhattan is defined by 42nd St., the East Village by St. Mark's Place, and Brooklyn by bagels, then northern New Jersey is summarized by these two shopping-mall meccas. Prostrate yourself to the glories of suburbia.

Secaucus is Outlet Store Central for the mid-Atlantic region. Hold onto your big consumer-maven hat, honey; the whole town is a conglomerate of small factory outlet stores. There are four outlet centers, each with many outlets grouped together near the same parking lot, and there are also some 50-odd individual outlets dotted on the streets like fleas on a dog. Some of the more noteworthy outlets include Anne Klein, 9 West, Calvin Klein, Liz Claiborne, and a plethora of stores specializing in discount designer labels. Most stores are closed Sundays.

Paramus, on the other hand, is mall-o-mania. No fewer than seven malls sit in climate-controlled splendor here. These are not really megalopolis malls like the Mall of America—they are smaller, discrete units with about 30 stores per mall, rather than having hundreds of stores all under one roof. Look for **The Paramus Mall, Garden State Plaza** on Rte. 17, and **Riverside Square** on Rte. 4.

The best way to get to these two scenic sights of beautiful New Jersey is, fittingly, by the suburbanite car via the Lincoln Tunnel or the George Washington Bridge, but NJ Transit also runs buses from New York City for the urban denizen homesick for childhood. From Port Authority, take the NJ Transit #129 to the Secaucus outlets ($1.90). Take the NJ Transit #168 to Paramus ($3.25 to Paramus Park Mall, $2.55 to Bergen Mall). In Paramus, the Mall-Link B16 bus links Garden State Plaza to Paramus Park Mall to Bergen Mall ($1).

■■■ CLOTHES

In SoHo, enormous **Canal Jean Co.,** 504 Broadway (226-1130), the original home of the surplus clinic, brims with neon ties, baggy pants, and silk smoking jackets. Fashion-conscious (public) high school students buy their black here. Poke around in the bargain bins out front. (Open Sun.-Thurs. 11am-7pm, Fri.-Sat. 10am-8pm.) On weekends, check out the **flea market** at the western end of Canal St. for honest-to-goodness antiques along with the usual funk junk.

In the NYU area, the **Antique Boutique,** 712 Broadway (460-8830) near Astor Pl., sells both stunning vintage clothing and interesting (but expensive) new designs. (10% discount for students with ID. Open Mon.-Sat. 10am-10pm, Sun. 10am-8pm.) **Reminiscence,** 74 Fifth Ave. (243-2292), near 14th St., may spark high school memories. But now it's even cheaper—a few items cost under $10. (Another store at 109 Ave. B (353-0626), near 14th St. Both stores open Mon.-Sat. 11:30am-8pm, Sun. 1-6pm.) At 16 W. 8th St. between Fifth and Sixth Ave., the clothes at **Andy's Cheepee's** (460-8488) aren't really all that chee-pee, but are definitely worth a peek (if only for that distinctive vintage clothing aroma; open Mon.-Sat. 9am-8pm, Sun. noon-7pm). Another location at 691 W. Broadway near W. 4th St. (420-5980; open Mon.-Sat. 9am-11pm, Sun. noon-8pm).

Known for its large selection of cashmere, **Fishkin Knitwear Co.,** 314-318 Grand St. (226-6538), carries Adrienne Vittadini and others at 30-50% off (open Mon.-Thurs. 10am-5pm, Fri.-Sat. 10am-4pm, Sun. 9:30am-4:30pm). Uptown, those with the stamina to burrow through mountains of clothes can find amazing bargains at **Gabay's,** 225 First Ave. (254-3180) between 13th and 14th, which sells seconds from department stores (open Mon.-Sat. 9am-5pm, Sun. 10am-4pm). Go early: the best buys are gone by 11am. You can also find clothes and shoes of all descriptions, generally in fine condition, at the mammoth **Salvation Army,** 208 Eighth Ave. between 20th and 21st (open Mon.-Fri. 10am-7:15pm, Sat. 10am-5:30pm).

The shopping experience on the Upper West Side along Columbus Ave. is designed primarily for those with Roman numerals after their names. Hit the boutiques during the January and July sales. A few havens for the not-so-rich-or-famous do exist. Still a favorite of the young and hip is **Alice Underground,** 380 Columbus Ave. (724-6682) at 78th St. (also at 481 Broadway; 431-9067). Alice Underground offers wonderful cummerbunds, bow ties, and silk dinner jackets to give men that Bond, James Bond sheen. Women have choices galore, from chic to funk to Victorian. (Open on Columbus Sun.-Fri. 11am-7pm, Sat. 11am-8pm; on Broadway daily 11am-7:30pm.) Daryl Hannah, Diane Keaton, and Annie Lennox stop at **Allan and Suzi,** 416 Amsterdam Ave. (724-7445) at 80th St. From new Gault-ier Madonna-wear at 70% off to $40 original Pucci dresses, this store is cheap, chic chaos. A large assortment of platform shoes surrounds the melee. No men's clothes. (Open daily noon-8pm.)

Across town, buy highfalutin' designer clothes second-hand at **Encore,** 1132 Madison Ave., second floor (879-2850), at 84th St. (open Mon.-Wed. and Fri. 10:30am-6:30pm, Thurs. 10:30am-7:30pm, Sat. 10:30am-6pm, Sun. noon-6pm; closed Sun. July-mid-Aug.), or at **Michael's,** 1041 Madison Ave., second floor (737-7273), between 79th and 80th (open Mon.-Wed. and Fri.-Sat. 9:30am-6pm, Thurs. 9:30am-8pm). For new, mid-range designer clothes, go to the two-story **Daffy's,** 335 Madison Ave. (557-4422) at 44th St., or 111 Fifth Ave. (529-4477) at 18th St. Be prepared to go through piles of unsorted items to find those 70%-off gems you thought you'd never have. (Madison branch open Mon.-Fri. 8am-8pm, Sat. 10am-6pm, Sun. noon-6pm; Fifth Ave. branch open Mon.-Sat. 10am-9pm, Sun. 11am-6pm.) Great bargains on normally expensive designer clothes can be had at **Dollar Bills,** 99 E. 42nd St. (867-0212), at Vanderbilt Ave., right outside Grand Central Station. It's hit or miss, but when you hit, you hit far. Armani, Fendi, and other chic European designers can all be found here with careful sifting and little luck. (Open Mon.-Fri. 8am-7pm, Sat. 10am-6pm.)

Stripey oxfords, tasteful ties, Father's Day every day—why, it's **Brooks Brothers!** At 346 Madison Ave. (682-8800) at E. 44th St., stock up on male-related accoutre-ments and finger the ties admiringly. (Open Mon., Thurs. 8:30am-7pm; Tues.-Wed. 8:30am-6pm, Fri. 8:30am-6pm, Sat. 9am-6pm.)

■■■ ELECTRONICS

Amps, CD players, cameras, tape decks, VCRs—you name it, New York sells it for less. Every other block has a combo camera/electronics/luggage store. With few exceptions, avoid these tourist traps; the salesmen will likely sell you something you'll regret buying. When dealing with equipment costing several hundred dollars or more, try to stick to new goods with original manufacturer's American warranties.

To eliminate most hassles, shop at the bigger and more reputable electronics stores in New York. Recently, **The Wiz** has been publicizing their long-held but for-merly obscure policy of matching advertised competitors' prices. They proudly pro-claim that "Nobody Beats The Wiz" and then dare you to find a lower-priced ad for anything sold in their stores. If you find a valid ad, they'll beat it and return 10% of the price difference. Take them up on their little challenge; get hold of the Sunday *New York Times* or the latest copy of the *Village Voice*, in which you'll find ads from **6th Ave. Electronics** and **Uncle Steve,** two stores that consistently beat The Wiz's prices. In Manhattan, The Wiz's locations include 337 Fifth Ave. (684-7600), at 33rd St. opposite the Empire State Building; 871 Sixth Ave. (594-2300), at 31st St.; 12 W. 45th St. (302-2000), between Fifth and Sixth Ave.; and 17 Union Sq. West (741-9500), at 15th St. (Open Mon.-Sat. 10am-7pm, Sun. 1-7pm.) **J & R Music World,** at 23 Park Row (732-8600) near City Hall, will also meet most of your electronics needs with competitive prices. (Open Mon.-Sat. 9am-6:30pm, Sun. 11am-6pm. Sub-way: #4, 5, or 6 to City Hall.) Mega-store **47th Street Photo,** 67 W. 47th St. (921-1287), deals in cameras, dark room equipment, computers, and electronics at excel-lent prices. Get your *Gone with the Wind* mouse pad here. (Open Mon.-Wed. 9:30am-7pm, Thurs. 9:30am-8pm, Fri. 9:30am-3pm, Sun. 10am-5pm.)

■■■ RECORD STORES

They're not just for records anymore, as CDs, cassettes, and even music videos tend to dominate many so-called "record stores." But whatever the format (unless you're looking for the new Tori Amos 8-track), in New York you can get your eardrums buzzing with music from almost every era and genre.

If you're not the scrounge-and-search type, go straight to **Tower Records,** 692 Broadway (505-1500) at E. 4th St. This one-stop music emporium, nearly a block long with four full floors of merchandise, is one of the largest on the East Coast. Gadgets like the music-video computer let you preview select songs before purchasing them, while a touch-screen store directory makes tracking down that elusive album by your favorite mainstream artist a cinch. (Open daily 9am-midnight. Subway: #6 to Bleecker St.) There's a branch uptown at 1961 Broadway at 66th St. (same hrs.).

HMV at 86th St. and Lexington Ave. is another "music superstore," looking like dad's study filled with CDs and large posters of the Breeders and the Beastie Boys. His Master's Voice provides a wide range of classical, jazz, new age, show tunes, and rock pop schlock for you and your little disc-spinnin' dog. (Open Sun.-Thurs. 10am-10pm, Fri.-Sat. 10am-11pm.)

For those music enthusiasts on the lookout for more obscure titles or labels, at least a dozen smaller stores can be found east of Tower Records in the East Village and round about Bleecker St. in the West Village. Though they may lack the stock and organization of larger stores, many of these places specialize in hard-to-find alternative rock imports, dance remixes, rare oldies, and the insurgent 7-inch single. Several of these smaller stores also sell used records, cassettes, and CDs at bargain prices. Perseverance pays off in this city; if you can't find what you want here, you're probably not looking hard enough.

Bleecker St. Golden Disc, 239 Bleecker St. (255-7899). Subway: A, B, C, D, E, F, or Q to W. 4th St. Basement full of jazz LPs; street level full of rock, reggae, country, and "oldies." Not an especially discriminating selection, but there are so many LPs that there's probably something here you've been seeking. Some bootlegs. Open Mon.-Fri. 11:30am-6:15pm, Sat. 11:30am-7:30pm, Sun. 1-5:30pm.

Colony Records, 1619 Broadway (265-2050), at 49th St. Subway: #1 or 9 to 50th St., or N or R to 49th St. Extensive selection of all forms of new and used music on CD, tape, and vinyl—from rock to Cajun to folk. Check out the vintage sheet music and the selection of autographs, memorabilia, and movie scripts. Open Mon.-Sat. 9:30am-1am, Sun. 10am-midnight.

Dance Tracks, 91 E. 3rd St. (260-8729), near Ave. A. Subway: #4, 5, or 6 to Bleecker St. The latest in all kinds of dance music—house, hip-hop, and various permutations thereof. Lots of expensive imports. Open Mon.-Thurs. noon-9pm, Fri. noon-10pm, Sat. noon-8pm, Sun. 1-6:30pm

Disc-O-Rama, 186 W. 4th St. (206-8417), between Sixth and Seventh Ave. Subway: #1 or 9 to Christopher St.; or A, B, C, D, E, F, or Q to W. 4th St. Cheap popular albums. All CDs (all!!) $10 or below; grab a coupon from the *Voice* and knock off a buck more. Strong alternative section in addition to the more standard Mariah Carey-type Top 40. Downstairs, Vinyl City stacks house and R&B singles for $5 and all kinds of used LPs for $2-5. Open Mon.-Fri. 11am-11:30pm, Sat. 10:30am-12:30am, Sun. 11:30am-8pm.

Generation Records, 210 Thompson St. (254-1100). All kinds of alternative and underground rock on CD and vinyl—the hardcore selection is especially strong. Fairly low prices (CDs $11-13) and many hard-to-find imports. Open Sun.-Thurs. 11am-10pm, Fri.-Sat. 11am-1am

Gryphon Record Shop, 251 W. 72nd St., #2F (874-1588), near West End Ave. Subway: #1, 2, 3, or 9 to 72nd St. A 2nd-floor apartment with walls, tables, and crates of classical LPs, many rare or out of print. Real collector atmosphere; proprietor seems to have the knowledge to match. Open Mon.-Sat. 11am-7pm, Sun. noon-6pm.

Kim's Underground, 144 Bleecker St. (260-1010), two blocks west of Broadway. Subway: B, D, or F to Broadway-Lafayette, or #6 to Bleecker St. Mostly a tremendous video showcase specializing in independent and foreign films, but the rear of the store contains a small, startlingly strong selection of independent and import CDs for (almost) reasonable prices. Also carries contemporary 7-in. releases. Occasionally hosts small concerts in-store. Open daily 9am–midnight.

Midnight Records, 263 W. 23rd St. (675-2768), between Seventh and Eighth Ave. Subway: #1, 9, C, or E to 23rd St. A mail-order and retail store specializing in hard-to-find rock records. Posters plaster the walls; every last mildewy nook is crammed with records—over 10,000 in stock. Prices aren't cheap, but if you're looking for the Prats' album *Disco Pope,* this may be the only place to find it. Lots of '60s and '70s LPs. Most LPs $9-20. Open Tues.-Sat. noon-7pm.

Pier Platters, 56 Newark St. (201-795-4785 and -9015), in Hoboken. Subway: B, D, F, N, Q, or R to 34th St., then PATH train ($1) to the first stop in Hoboken. Walk along Hudson Pl. to Hudson St., up one block to Newark St., then left. In 1982, a homesick Irishman longing for something other than the new-wave pap on the radio started this phenomenal record store, which now features the best alternative-rock selection in the Greater New York area, if not the Western Hemisphere. Celebrated members of the musical underground shop here regularly, perusing the incredibly extensive, high-quality collection of rare singles and full-length records, with an emphasis on independent releases from the U.S. and New Zealand. CDs downstairs, vinyl upstairs. Check out the *Sassy*-fied magazine rack too. Open Mon.-Sat. 11am-9pm, Sun. noon-8pm.

Rebel Rebel, 319 Bleecker St. (989-0770), between Grove and Christopher St. Subway: #1 or 9 to Christopher St. A small store specializing in British top 40, underground, and dance imports. LPs, CDs, and 7-in. singles. Rare stuff. Open Mon.-Wed. 12:30-8pm, Thurs.-Sat. 12:30-9pm, Sun. 12:30-7pm.

Revolver Records, 45 W. 8th St. on the 2nd floor (982-6760), between Fifth and Sixth Ave., near MacDougal St. Subway: A, B, C, D, E, F, or Q to W. 4th St. From Deep Purple to Guns-n-Roses, this place specializes in guitar rock through the decades, whether classic, metal, or thrash. New releases are mostly American metal. Bargains on the odd non-metal items. They buy back used stuff and have an extensive collection of out-of-print records, including a vast collection of all things Beatle (including bootlegs). Open Sun.-Thurs. 11am-10pm, Fri.-Sat. 11am-midnight.

Rocks in Your Head, 157 Prince St. (475-6729), between Thompson and West Broadway. Subway: #6, C or E to Spring St. Yet another one of the many alternative rock/import record stores in the area. Used CDs around $8; some LPs $2-5. Open Mon.-Thurs. noon-9pm, Fri.-Sat. noon-10pm., Sun. 1-9pm.

Second Coming Records, 235 Sullivan St. (228-1313), near W. 3rd St. Subway: A, B, C, D, E, F, or Q to W. 4th St. Vinyl, and lots of it. An especially strong selection of underground 7"s. While records proliferate, CD covers languish in plastic wrappers, and tapes huddle in locked cabinets. Very into the local music scene—come here to see who's playing where. Open Mon.-Thurs. 11am-10pm, Fri.-Sat. 11am-midnight, Sun. noon-8pm

Smash Compact Discs, 33 St. Mark's Pl. (473-2200), between Second and Third Ave. Subway: #6 to Astor Pl. Come here if you can't find a '60s or classic-rock album at Sounds. Used CDs $8-10. Open Mon.-Wed. 11am- 9:30pm, Thurs. 11am-10:30pm, Fri.-Sat. 11am-11:30pm, Sun. noon-9:30pm.

Sounds, 20 St. Mark's Pl. (677-3444), between Second and Third Ave. Subway: #6 to Astor Pl. Good fair-priced selection of alternative and dance music. Used CD folders offer the best values, but be prepared to search. Racks of used LPs. New CDs $9-13, used ones $5-9. For used CDs, they'll pay (in cash) up to 50% of their resale value. **CD & Cassette Annex** at 16 St. Mark's Pl. (677-2727). Open Mon.-Thurs. noon-10:20pm, Fri.-Sat. noon-11:20pm, Sun. noon-9pm.

Vinylmania, 60 Carmine St. (924-7223), at Bedford St. Subway: A, B, C, D, E, F, or Q to W. 4th St. The dance center—they carry house, hip-hop, rap, R&B, and some jazz as well. Vinyl in the front (better for the scratch mix) and CDs in the back. Pick up flyers here for *the* latest happenings and hippest clubs. Open Mon.-Fri. 11am-9pm, Sat.-Sun. 11am-7pm.

■■■ SPECIALTY STORES

All of New York is a specialty store. From the highbrow chic boutiques to the funky avant-garde, if it's been made, you'll find it in this city. Here's a partial list of interesting places to browse:

The Ballet Shop, 1887 Broadway (581-7990), at 62nd St. Subway: #1 or 9 to 66th St. LPs, CDs, photographs, books, posters, and memorabilia related to ballet. Open Mon.-Sat. 11am-7pm, Sun. noon-5pm; Sept.-March Mon.-Sat. 11am-7pm.

Bird Jungle, 401 Bleecker St. (242-1757), at 11th St. Subway: #1 or 9 to Christopher St. Colorful, gregarious parrots fly around the shop window schmoozing with passersby. (They're not dead.) Take home domestically bred rainforest birds, from ordinary canaries to the $10,000 hyacinth macaw. Open Mon.-Fri. 12:30-6:30pm, Sat. 11am-6:30pm, Sun. 11am-5:30pm.

Books and Binding, 33 W. 17th St. (229-0004), between Fifth and Sixth Ave. Subway: L or F to Sixth Ave.-14th St. A budget bookstore with a bookbinding department on the 2nd floor ($30-125). Open Mon.-Thurs. 9am-9pm, Fri.-Sat. 9am-8pm, Sun. 11am-5pm.

Condomania, 351 Bleecker St. (691-9442), near W. 10th St. Subway: #1 or 9 to Christopher St. "America's first condom store," this latex-heavy boutique is refreshingly free of the snickery gag gifts that pervade other condom stores—it's just condoms, dental dams, and lube. Friendly staff answers all questions and gives safer-sex tips. Open daily 11am-11pm.

Dollhouse Antics, 1343 Madison Ave. (876-2288), at 94th St. Subway: #6 to 96th St. Furniture that'll fit your tiny NYC hovel of a room! First-class doll real estate plus most miniaturized mundanities: coffee sets, Scrabble boards, toilets, napkins, and tables covered by artfully stitched baby-tablecloths. Immortalize your own family pet in a hand-painted 2- by 3-in. portrait to hang above a Lilliputian mantle ($75, clear photo required). Open Mon.-Fri. 11am-5:30pm, Sat. 11am-5pm; hours may vary in the summer, so call ahead.

East Village Cheese, 34 Third Ave. (477-2601). Subway: #6 to Astor Pl. The name says it all. Actually, it doesn't, because this store also sells many varieties of crackers and snack foods in addition to the many different varieties of *fromage*. Check out the bargain bin. Open Mon.-Fri. 9am-6:30pm, Sat.-Sun. 9am-5:30pm.

Economy Candy, 108 Rivington St. (254-1531), on the Lower East Side. Subway: F, J, M, or Z to Delancey St.-Essex St. Imaginatively named store purveys sugar in all its most attractive forms. Imported chocolates, jams, oils, and spices, plus countless bins of confections, all at rock-bottom prices. Treat yourself to a huge bag of gummibears ($1) or a pound of chocolate-covered espresso beans ($5). Open Sun.-Fri. 8:30am-5:30pm, Sat. 10am-5pm.

Enchanted Forest, 85 Mercer St. (925-6677), between Broome and Spring St. Subway: N or R to Prince St. Lots of craft and folk items like jewelry and trinkets and marionette puppets and books on spirituality and handmade toys. Out of the way, with a fun, nature-loving atmosphere. You may think you've been to places like this before, but prices here are more reasonable than most. Open Mon.-Sat. 11am-7pm, Sun. noon-6pm.

The Erotic Baker, 582 Amsterdam Ave. (721-3217), between 88th and 89th St. Subway: #1 or 9 to 86th St. Decadent baked goods, shaped to approximate nature's designs. Some PG-13 baking, too. Place custom orders (usually around $20) 24 hrs. in advance (phone orders only). Open Tues.-Sat. 10am-6pm.

Game Show, 1240 Lexington Ave. (472-8011), at 83rd St. Subway: #4, 5, or 6 to 86th St. Sick of painting the town red? Why not stay inside and play board games? Everything from *Monopoly* and *Pictionary* to the ever-loved *Kosherland,* the original *Hüsker Dü,* and a discreet section of "adult" games like *Talk Dirty to Me.* Lots of puzzles too. Open Fri.-Wed. 11am-6pm, Thurs. 11am-7pm; closed Sun. from Memorial Day to Labor Day.

Godiva Chocolatier, 560 Lexington Ave. (980-9810), between 50th and 51st St. in the G.E. Building. Subway: #6 to 51st St. or E, F to Lexington-Third Ave. You'd think they were selling jewelry with all the mini-chandeliers and gold; in fact it's much more precious—some of the finest chocolates on earth sit here, teasing you from behind the glass. Even if you don't buy it, come take a calorie-free look at the best-pressed chocolate in the world, or try to take advantage of the occasional free samplings. Open Mon.-Fri. 9am-7pm, Sat. 11am-5pm.

The How-To Video Source, 953 Third Ave. (486-8155), at 57th St. Subway: #4, 5, or 6 to 59th St., or N or R to Lexington Ave. A store that specializes in how-to videos. Learn to rhumba while speaking Spanish, cooking Chinese food, and improving your sex life and golf game. Only in New York. Open Mon.-Fri. 10am-8pm, Sat.-Sun. 11am-7pm.

The Leather Man, 111 Christopher St. (243-5339), between Bleecker and Hudson St. Subway: #1 or 9 to Christopher St. Check out that window display! Not for the timid—chains, leather, and, in the basement, sex toys for the adventurous, including a mold kit for your favorite one-eyed snake (on the tamer side). Staff is friendly and helpful toward all genders and orientations. Open daily noon-midnight.

Little Rickie, 49½ First Ave. (505-6467), at 3rd St. Subway: F to Second Ave. Collectible offbeat cultural icons, like topical Pee Wee Herman decals, Madonna tapestries, and Elvis lamps, as well as marionettes of the Pope and Indonesian penis dolls. Open Mon.-Sat. 11am-8pm, Sun. noon-7pm.

Maxilla & Mandible, 451-5 Columbus Ave. (724-6173), between 81st and 82nd St. Subway: #1 or 9 to 79th St. Shelves and boxes of well-displayed shells, fossils, eggs, preserved insects, and—most of all—bones from every imaginable vertebrate (including *Homo sapiens*). A giant walking-stick insect under glass and an 11-ft. alligator skeleton stand out prominently among the merchandise. Malachite-colored jewel beetles "for the kids" $9. Caters to international collectors. Macabre but neato. Open Mon.-Sat. 11am-7pm, Sun. 1-5pm.

Rita Ford Music Boxes, 19 E. 65th St. (535-6717), between Madison and Fifth Ave. Subway: #6 to 68th St. Tinkle, tinkle, tinkle. Not just a plastic pop-up ballerina in a box here; all kinds of music boxes, from 19th-century antiques to Disney-endorsed *Beauty and the Beast* models. Expensive, yes (no budget buys here), but well worth a peek. Open Mon.-Sat. 9am-5pm.

Schoepfer Studios, 138 W. 31st St. (736-3939), between Sixth and Seventh Ave. Subway: N or R to 34th St. A gallery-store of great breadth in the realm of stuffed and mounted dead animals. Buy a genuine rattlesnake (from $100), or get just the rattles in the form of a pair of earrings ($18). Steer skulls start at $75, and the mounted barnyard chicken goes for $175. Snake head keychains also available. Open Mon.-Fri. 9:30am-5pm

Tender Buttons, 143 E. 62nd St. (758-7004), between Third and Lexington Ave. Subway: #4, 5, or 6 to 59th St., or N, R to Lexington Ave. A treasure-trove of billions of buttons. If you carelessly lost the button on your favorite Renaissance doublet, you will find a replacement here. Also has cuff links and buckles to match buttons, or vice versa. Fork out $1000 for a button off one of George Washington's coats. Open Mon.-Fri. 11am-6pm, Sat. 11am-5pm.

Warner Bros. Studio Store, 1 E. 57th St. (754-0300), at Fifth Ave. Subway: B or Q to 57th St.-Sixth Ave., or N or R to 57th St.-Seventh Ave. A three-story shrine to the characters of Looney Tunes, with a few DC Comics superheroes thrown in for good measure. Find Bugs Bunny, the Tasmanian Devil, Pepe le Peu, and Yosemite Sam emblazoned and embroidered on every conceivable type of item, from hats to housewares. No, you can't get any of those Acme products that Wile E. Coyote relied upon, but you can get Acme-label clothing. That's all, folks. Open Mon.-Sat. 10am-8pm, Sun. noon-6pm.

■■■ BOOKSTORES

Whether your taste runs to European fine art or Third World revolution, whether you seek a Lithuanian dictionary or a first-edition copy of Freud's *On the Interpretation of Dreams,* Manhattan is the island for you. Chains like **Barnes and Noble** (807-0099), **B. Dalton** (674-8780), **Doubleday** (397-0550), and **Waldenbooks** (269-1139) discount current best-sellers. If the books you want are harder to find, you can try either one of the larger shops like the Strand (nearly 2 million volumes) or a specialized shop like Murder Ink.

GENERAL INTEREST

Barnes and Noble, 107 Fifth Ave. (897-0099), at W. 18th St. Subway: L or F to Sixth Ave.-14th St. Although part of a chain, this store began it all. The "biggest bookstore in the world" with tons of titles, many at heavy discounts. Buys college textbooks for up to ½-price. Open Mon.-Fri. 9:30am-7:45pm, Sat. 9:30am-6:15pm, Sun. 11am-5:45pm. Check out the **Barnes and Noble Bargain Annex,** 128 Fifth Ave. (633-3500) too. The B&N information line is 675-5500.

Barnes and Noble, 2289 Broadway (362-8835), at 82nd St. Subway: #1 or 9 to 79th St. Bigger than the Chelsea branch, this vast store offers comfortable chairs and couches to read in, a café, a well-stocked magazine section, and just about any book you want. Reportedly, this is one of the hot new pick-up scenes for literary-minded New Yorkers. Open Sun.-Thurs. 9am-11pm, Fri.-Sat. 9am-midnight.

Books and Company, 939 Madison Ave. (737-1450), between 74th and 75th St. Subway: #6 to 77th St. Isabelle Allende, Gary Snyder, and Jamaica Kincaid have all read in this small store. Excellent section of literature, criticism, and literary periodicals. Call for information on free (but often extremely crowded) readings. Open Mon.-Fri. 10am-7pm, Sat. 10am-6pm, Sun. noon-6pm.

Burlington Book Shop, 1082 Madison Ave. (288-7420), at 81st St. Subway: #6 to 77th St. Books, books, and more books (both new and out-of-print) are crammed into this tiny but charming neighborhood shop. Great staff knows what's worth reading, so don't be shy about asking for advice. Open Mon.-Fri. 9:30am-6pm, Sat. 10am-6pm, Sun. noon-5pm. Used books bought and sold upstairs at the **Compulsive Collection** (open Wed.-Sat. 1-6pm).

Coliseum Books, 1771 Broadway (757-8381), at 57th St. Subway: #1, 9, A, B, C, or D to 59th St. Mainly stocks new releases, but also has a fine selection of drama and music (the store is just a stone's throw from Lincoln Center and Carnegie Hall), as well as poetry. Open Mon. 8am-10pm, Tues.-Thurs. 8am-11pm, Fri. 8am-11:30pm, Sat. 10am-11:30pm, Sun. noon-8pm.

Gotham Book Mart, 41 W. 47th St. (719-4448). Subway: B, D, F, or Q to 47-50th St. Legendary and venerable bookstore selling new and used volumes. Largest selection of contemporary poetry in the city plus a huge stock of drama, art, and literary journals. Join the James Joyce society for $7.50 per year and chat with other literary types, or just browse through one of the changing exhibits in the upstairs art gallery. Open Mon.-Fri. 9:30am-6:30pm, Sat. 9:30am-6pm.

Gryphon, 2246 Broadway (362-0706), between 80th and 81st St. Subway: #1 or 9 to 79th St. Small and homey, with used books. Varied selection. Open daily 10am-midnight.

St. Mark's Bookshop, 31 Third Ave. (260-7853), at 9th St. Subway: #6 to Astor Pl. The ultimate East Village bookstore. Excellent selection, with an emphasis on current literary theory, fiction, and poetry. Helpful staff. Open daily 11am-11:30pm.

Strand, 828 Broadway (473-1452), at 12th St. Subway: #4, 5, 6, L, N, or R to 14th St. New York's biggest and most-loved used-book store. A must-see. 8 mi. of shelf space holding nearly 2 million books. Staffers will search out obscure titles at your bidding. Ask to see a catalog, or better yet, get lost in the shelves on your own. The best of the best. Open daily 9:30am- 9:30pm.

SPECIALTY BOOKS

Applause Theater and Cinema Books, 211 W. 71st St. (496-7511), at Broadway. Subway: #1, 2, 3, or 9 to 72nd St. Great selection of scripts, screenplays, and books on everything from John Wayne to tap dancing. Over 4000 titles. Knowledgable staff. Open Mon.-Sat. 10am-8pm, Sun. noon-5pm.

Argosy Bookstore, 116 E. 59th St. (753-4455). Subway: #4, 5, or 6 to 59th St.; or N or R to Lexington Ave. Buys and sells rare and used books, as wells as autographed editions, Americana, and some truly swell maps. Extremely helpful staff and a quite friendly clientele to boot. Open Mon.-Fri. 9am-6pm; Oct.-May also Sat. 10am-6pm.

Asahiya Bookstore, 52 Vanderbilt Ave. (883-0011), at E. 45th St. Subway: #4,5,6,7, or S to 42nd St. Japanese-language books and periodicals. Origami, some stationery, and a few English-language books on Japan for the *kanji/hiragana*-illiterate. Open daily 10am-8pm.

Biography Bookstore, 400 Bleecker St. (807-8655), at W. 11th St. Subway: #1 or 9 to Christopher St. Rediscover your previous incarnations. Biography-browsing at its best. Very strong gay/lesbian section as well as bestsellers. Open Mon.-Fri. noon-8pm, Sat. noon-10pm, Sun. noon-6pm.

Books of Wonder, 132 Seventh Ave. (989-3270), at 18th St. Subway: #1 or 9 to 14th St. Small bookstore stocked with children's literature. The selective used-book section is worth exploring. Open Mon.-Sat. 11am-7pm, Sun. noon-6pm.

The Complete Traveller Bookstore, 199 Madison Ave. (685-9007), at 35th St. Subway: #6 to 32nd St. Possibly the widest selection of guidebooks on the Eastern Seaboard. New addition of antiquarian travel guides. Open Mon.-Fri. 9am-7pm, Sat. 10am-6pm, Sun. 11am-5pm.

Forbidden Planet, 821 Broadway (473-1576), at 12th St. Subway: N, R, L, 4, 5, or 6 to Union Sq.-14th St. New and used comic books, D&D figurines, a whole section of V.C. Andrews books, piercing books, and a shelf of serial killers at this large sci-fi/fantasy warehouse. Unhealthily thin boys and the death-goth girls who love them congregate here. Open Mon.-Tues. and Sat. 10am-7:30pm, Wed.-Fri. 10am-8:30pm, Sun. noon-7pm.

Hacker Art Books, 45 W. 57th St. (688-7600), between Fifth and Sixth Ave. Subway: B or Q to 57th St. Texts on fine and applied art. Catch up on Michelangelo or learn how to build a birdhouse for your fire escape. A *New York Times* article once raved, "You won't get lost in Hacker's, you won't get fleeced, and no one is too busy to talk to you." It's still true. Open Mon.-Fri. 9am-6pm.

Judith's Room, 681 Washington St. (727-7330), at Charles St. Subway: #1 or 9 to Christopher St. A bookstore by, for, and about women (gay and straight). Excellent selection, all kinds of feminist periodicals, and an assortment of community-oriented flyers. Open Tues.-Thurs. noon-8pm, Fri.-Sat. noon-9pm, Sun. noon-7pm.

Kitchen Arts and Letters, 1435 Lexington Ave. (876-5550), at 93rd St. Subway: #6 to 96th St. Sick of *Let's Go* restaurant reviews, but don't know what you can do about it? The wide range of cookbooks here will help you break away from the monotony of bland Chinese and cheap burger joints. Also books on wine and culinary history and scholarship, as well as antique culinary tomes. Open Mon. 1-6pm, Tues.-Fri. 10am-6:30pm, Sat. 11am-6pm.

Liberation Bookstore, 421 Lenox Ave. (281-4615), at 131st St. Subway: #2 or 3 to 135th St. Great selection of African and African-American history, art, poetry, and fiction. Open Mon.-Fri. 11am-7pm, Sat. 11:30am-6:30pm.

Murder Ink, 2486 Broadway (362-8905), between 92nd and 93rd St. Subway: #1, 2, 3, or 9 to 96th St. New and used, happily cluttered. Mystery everywhere. Open Mon.-Wed. and Fri.-Sat. 10am-7:30pm, Thurs. 10am-9pm, Sun. 11am-7pm.

Oscar Wilde Memorial Bookstore, 15 Christopher St. (255-8097), at Gay St. Subway: #1 or 9 to Christopher St. Stocks a wide selection of books by, for, and about gay men. Lesbians get their own side of the bookstore, just as complete. Videos, pins, flags, rings, and witty T-shirts too. Open daily 11:30am-7:30pm.

Pathfinder Books, 191 Seventh Ave. (727-8421), between 21st and 22nd St. Subway: C or E to 23rd St. Small Trotskyite bookstore with an esoteric and sometimes provocative selection of political tracts. Open Mon.Tues. and Thurs. noon-3pm and 5:30-8:30pm, Wed. and Fri. 5:30-8:30pm, Sat. 10:30am-6pm.

A Photographer's Place, 133 Mercer St. (431-9358), between Prince and Spring St. Subway: R to Prince St. Photography books, photo this and photo that. Open Mon.-Sat. noon-8pm, Sun. noon-6pm.

Revolution Books, 13 E. 16th St. (691-3345), between Union Sq. and Fifth Ave. Subway: #4, 5, 6, L, N, or R to 14th St. Ironically one of the most successful chains of independent booksellers, a real entrepreneur in books on Marx, Mao, and Martin Luther King, Jr. Open Mon.-Sat. 10am-7pm, Sun. noon-5pm.

See Hear, 59 E. 7th St. (505-9781), between First and Second Ave. Subway: #6 to Astor Pl. A small store exclusively (well, almost exclusively) dedicated to books, 'zines, and magazines about rock music, mostly of the underground variety. Excellent selection of Chick religious tracts as well. Open daily noon-8pm

Daytripping from NYC

This city drives me crazy, or, if you prefer, crazier; and I have no peace of mind or rest of body till I get out of it.
— Lafcadio Hearn, 1889 (he later fled to Tokyo)

■■■ ATLANTIC CITY

The riches-to-rags-to-riches tale of Atlantic City began half a century ago when the beachside hotspot was tops among resort towns. Vanderbilts and Girards graced the boardwalk that inspired *Monopoly*, the Depression-era board game for coffee-table high rollers; fans of the game will enjoy seeing the real Boardwalk and Park Place they've squabbled over for years. But the opulence has faded. With the rise of competition from Florida resorts, the community chest closed. Atlantic City suffered decades of decline, unemployment, and virtual abandonment.

In 1976, state voters gave Atlantic City a reprieve by letting it legalize gambling. Casinos soon rose out of the rubble of Boardwalk. Those who enter soon forget the dirt and dank outside, especially since the managers see to it that you need never leave. Each velvet-lined temple of tackiness has a dozen restaurants, big-name entertainment, even skyways connecting it to other casinos. The chance to win big draws everyone to Atlantic City, from international jet-setters to seniors clutching plastic coin cups. One-third of the U.S. population lives within 300 miles of Atlantic City, and fortune-seeking foreigners flock to its shore to toss the dice. Budgeteers can even take a casino-sponsored bus from Manhattan—pay $15 for the trip and get it all back in quarters upon arrival. How can you lose?

PRACTICAL INFORMATION

Emergency: 911.

Visitor Information: Atlantic City Convention Center and Visitors Bureau, 2314 Pacific Ave. (348-7130, 800-262-7395; they play "Under the Boardwalk" while you're on hold). Home of the Miss America Pageant. Main entrance on the Boardwalk between Mississippi and Florida Ave. There is also a booth on the Boardwalk at Mississippi Ave. Personal assistance daily 10am-6pm; leaflets available 24 hrs. **Atlantic City Special Improvement District Visitor Information Center,** 1716 Pacific Ave. (344-8338), and booths along the Boardwalk. Open Mon.-Fri. 9am-5pm, Sat.-Sun. 1-9pm.

Atlantic City International Airport: (645-7895, 800-728-4322). Located just west of Atlantic City in Pamona with service to Washington, Philadelphia, and New York (around $50 one way).

Amtrak: (800-872-7245) at Kirkman Blvd. near Michigan Ave. Follow Kirkman to its end, bear right, and follow the signs. To New York (1 per day, 2½ hr., $28). Open Sun.-Fri. 9:30am-7:40pm, Sat. 9:30am-10pm.

Buses: Greyhound (345-6617). Buses every hr. to New York (2½ hr., $19). **New Jersey Transit** (800-582-5946). Runs 6am-10pm. Hourly service to New York City ($21). Also runs along Atlantic Ave. (base fare $1). Both lines operate from **Atlantic City Municipal Bus Terminal,** Arkansas and Arctic Ave. Both offer casino-sponsored round-trip discounts, including cash back on arrival in Atlantic City. Bally's has a particularly good deal—you get your full fare ($15) back in quarters upon arrival. Terminal open 24 hrs.

Pharmacy: Parkway, 2838 Atlantic Ave. (345-5105), one block from TropWorld. Delivers locally and to the casinos. Open Mon.-Fri. 9am-7pm, Sat. 9am-6pm.

Hospital: Atlantic City Medical Center (344-4081), at the intersection of Michigan and Pacific Ave.

Bookstore: Atlantic City News and Book Store (344-9444), at the intersection of Pacific and Illinois Ave. Most comprehensive collection of gambling-strategy literature east of Las Vegas. Buy with your head, not over it. Open 24 hrs.

Help Line: Rape and Abuse Hotline (646-6767). 24-hr. counseling, referrals, and accompaniment. **Gambling Abuse** (800-GAMBLER/800-426-2537). 24-hr. help for gambling problems.

Post Office: (345-4212), at Martin Luther King and Pacific Ave. Open Mon.-Fri. 8:30am-5pm, Sat. 10am-noon. **ZIP code:** 08401.

Area Code: 609.

Atlantic City lies about half-way down New Jersey's coast, accessible via the **Garden State Parkway** and the **Atlantic City Expressway,** and easily reached by train from Philadelphia and New York. *Let's Go* can never recommend hitchhiking as a safe method of transport; especially in these parts, it's exceptionally stupid.

Gamblers' specials make bus travel a cheap, efficient way to get to Atlantic City. Many casinos will give the bearer of a bus ticket receipt $10-15 in quarters and sometimes a free meal. **Gray Line Tours** in New York, 900 Eighth Ave. (397-2600), between 53rd and 54th St., offers several round-trip excursions daily to Atlantic City ($21, $23 on weekends). Your ticket receipt is redeemable for up to $15 in cash, chips, or food from a casino when you arrive. When this book went to press, Caesar's, the Taj Mahal, and TropWorld had the best offers ($15 in cold, flexible cash). You can buy Gray Line tickets at many NYC convenience stores (look for the sign in the window) or at the bus station itself. The bus drops you off at the designated casino and picks you up three hours later.

Atlantic City's attractions cluster on and around the Boardwalk, which runs east-west along the Atlantic Ocean. All but two of the casinos (the Trump Castle and Harrah's) overlook this paradise of soft-serve ice cream and fast food. Running parallel to the Boardwalk, Pacific and Atlantic Ave. offer cheap restaurants, hotels, and convenience stores with "We Buy Gold and Jewelry for Cash" signs. Getting around Atlantic City is easy on foot. When your winnings become too heavy to carry, you can hail a **Rolling Chair,** quite common along the Boardwalk. It's a bit of an investment ($1 per block for 2 people, 5-block min.), but sometimes-entertaining Atlantic City locals or erudite foreign students might chat with you while they push. The less exotic and less expensive **yellow tram** runs continuously for $2 one-way or $5 for an all-day pass. On the streets, catch a **jitney** ($1.25), which runs 24 hrs. up and down Pacific Ave., or a NJ Transit Bus ($1) covering Atlantic Ave.

ACCOMMODATIONS AND CAMPING

Large, red-carpeted beachfront hotels have bumped smaller operators out of the game. Smaller hotels along **Pacific Avenue,** a block from the Boardwalk, have rooms for less than $60, and rooms in the city's guest houses are reasonably priced, though facilities there can be dismal. Reserve ahead, especially on weekends. Many hotels lower their rates mid-week. Winter is also slow in Atlantic City, as water temperature, gambling fervor, and hotel rates all drop significantly. Campsites closest to the action cost the most; the majority close September through April. Reserve a site if you plan to visit in July or August.

Irish Pub and Inn, 164 St. James Pl. (344-9063), near the Boardwalk, directly north of Sands Casino. Clean, cheap rooms fully decorated with antiques. Victorian sitting rooms open onto sprawling porch lined with large rocking chairs. Laundry in basement. Singles $29. Doubles $40, with private shower $60. Quads $60. Cot in room $10. Key deposit $5. Breakfast and dinner $10, children $8. Open Feb.-Nov.

Hotel Cassino, 28 Georgia Ave. (344-0747), at Pacific Ave. Named after a *cassino* in the Italian hometown of kindly proprietors Felix and Mina. Multi-cultural atmosphere. A little run-down, but no sleaze. Strictly a family business. Rates negotiable depending on specific room, day, time of year, and number of people. Singles $30-45. Doubles $35-50. Key deposit $10. Open May-early Nov.

Birch Grove Park Campground (641-3778), Mill Rd. in Northfield. About 6 mi. from Atlantic City, off Rte. 9. 50 sites. Attractive and secluded. Sites $15 for 2 people, with hookup $18.

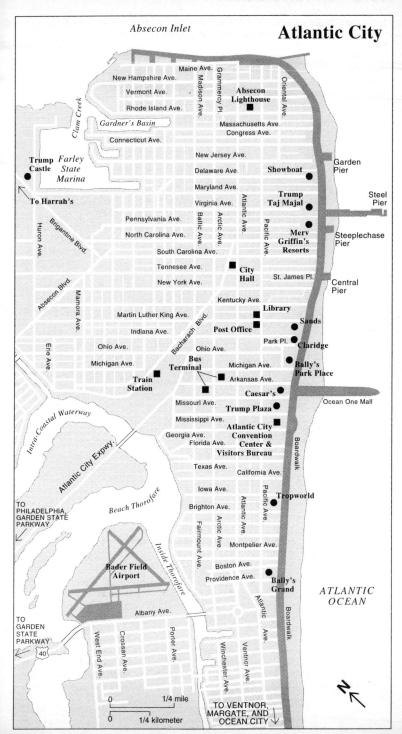

Pleasantville Campground, 408 N. Mill Rd. (641-3176). About 7 mi. from the casinos. 70 sites. Sites $24 for vans with full hookup, $27 for RVs and motor homes.

FOOD

After cashing in your chips, you can visit a **casino buffet** (about $10 for dinner; $6-7 for lunch). The town provides higher-quality meals in a less noxious atmosphere. For a complete rundown of local dining, pick up a copy of *TV Atlantic Magazine, At the Shore,* or *Whoot* (all free) from a hotel lobby, a restaurant, or a local store.

Your best bet for cheap dining in Atlantic City is the **Inn of the Irish Pub,** at 164 St. James Pl. (345-9613), which serves hearty, modestly priced dishes like deep-fried crab cakes ($4.25), honey-dipped chicken ($4.25), and Dublin beef stew ($5). The lunch special (Mon.-Fri. 11am-2pm) gets you a pre-selected sandwich and cup of soup for $2. This oaky, inviting pub has a century's worth of Joycean élan and Irish memorabilia draped on the walls. (Open 24 hrs.)

Pacific Avenue is cramped with steak, sub, and pizza shops. Celebrity supporters of the **White House Sub Shop,** Mississippi and Arctic Ave. (345-1564, 345-8599), include Bill Cosby, Johnny Mathis, and Frank Sinatra, who is rumored to have these immense subs flown to him while he's on tour ($6-8, half-subs $3-4; open Mon.-Sat. 10am-midnight, Sun. 11am-midnight). For renowned Italian food, including the best pizza in town, hit **Tony's Baltimore Grille,** 2800 Atlantic Ave. at Iowa Ave. (345-5766). Feel like Donald Trump as you sit in a booth and twiddle the knobs on your own personal jukebox. (Pasta around $5, pizza $5-8. Open daily 11am-3am; bar open 24 hrs.) Though the crowds may put you off, you can get great slices of pizza ($1.75) from one of the many **Three Brothers from Italy** joints on the Boardwalk. For a traditional and toothsome oceanside dessert, try custard ice cream or saltwater taffy, both available at vendors along the Boardwalk.

CASINOS

You don't have to spend a penny to enjoy yourself in Atlantic City's casinos; their vast, plush interiors and spotless, marble bathrooms can entertain a resourceful and voyeuristic budget traveller for hours. Watch the blue-haired old ladies shove quarter after quarter in the slot machines with vacant, zombie-like stares. Gaze in admiration at the fat, seventy-something men dressed in polyester, trying to act like James Bond at the blackjack tables.

Thousands of square feet of flashing lights and plush carpet stupefy the gaping crowds; everyone pretends not to notice the one-way ceiling mirrors concealing big-brother gambling monitors. The luring rattle of chips, clicking of slot machines, and clacking of coins never stops. Outside the gambling matrix, coffee shops teem with con-men, bargain-blazing seniors, and dealers. Glittery crooners crow away.

The casinos on the Boardwalk all fall within a dice toss of one another. Your best bet for sheer gaudiness and bombast is the **Taj Mahal** (449-1000) at Pennsylvania Ave.—Donald Trump's meditation on sacred Indian art and architecture. Here you can eat at the "Gobi Dessert" or "The Delhi Deli." It was missed payments on this tasteless tallboy that cast the financier into his billion-dollar tailspin. Trump has two other casinos, each screaming out his name in humungous, lighted letters—the **Trump Castle** (441-2000) and **Trump Plaza** (441-6000).

Don't miss **Caesar's Boardwalk Resorts** (348-4411) at Arkansas Ave. (look for the giant statue of Julius beckoning you to come, see, and conquer), which features "Pompeii's Pasta Pavilion" and "Circus Maximus," an auditorium graced by the likes of Natalie Cole and Chicago. (Unfortunately, in a surprising deviation from the ancient Roman original, the performers are not fed to the lions.) The newly expanded **Sands** (441-4000) at Indiana Ave. is a close third in the big-and-ostentatious sweepstakes with its pink and green seashell motif.

The other casinos are also worth exploring: **Bally's Park Place** (340-2000), **Harrah's Marina Hotel** (441-5000), the **Claridge** (340-3400) at Indiana Ave., **Showboat** (343-4000) at States Ave., and **TropWorld Casino** (340-4000) at Iowa Ave. Be sure to check out the celebrity handprints at the main entrance of Merv Griffin's **Resorts International** (344-6000).

Open nearly all the time, casinos lack windows and clocks, denying you the time cues that signal the hours slipping away. Free drinks (coffee and juice) and bathrooms at every turn keep you peppy and satisfied. To curb inevitable losses, stick to the cheaper games: blackjack, slot machines, and the low bets in roulette and craps. Minimum bets go up in the evenings and on weekends. Stay away from the cash machines. A book like John Scarne's *New Complete Guide to Gambling* will help you plan an intelligent strategy, but keep your eyes on your watch or you'll have spent five hours and five digits before you know what hit you.

The minimum gambling age of 21 is strictly enforced. Even if you sneak by the bouncers posted at the doors, you cannot collect winnings if you are underage. When an underage gambler hit a $200,000 jackpot, claiming his father had won, the casino reviewed videos to discover the kid had pulled the lever. It was the casino's lucky day, not his.

High-priced casino entertainment, featuring magicians, comedians, songstresses, and musicals, can sometimes be endured at a discount. Call casinos to find out or consult *Whoot,* the weekly free "entertainment and casino newspaper." Atlantic City and adjacent shore towns maintain an active nighttime schedule, and many clubs host solid rock and jazz outfits: consult *Whoot* or *Atlantic.* Blow your winnings at the **Shops On Ocean One** (347-8086), a shopping complex on the Boardwalk opposite Caesars featuring 120 stores. (Open daily 10am-10pm; restaurants open earlier and stay open later.)

BEACHES AND BOARDWALK

Atlantic City squats on the northern end of long, narrow **Absecon Island,** which has seven miles of beaches—some pure white, some lumpy gray. The **Atlantic City Beach** is free and often crowded. Walk, jog, or bike west to adjacent **Ventnor City's** sands, which are quieter. The legendary **Boardwalk** of Atlantic City has given itself over to junk-food stands, souvenir shops, and carnival amusements.

■■■ NEW HAVEN

Today New Haven is simultaneously university town and depressed city. Academic types and a working-class population live somewhat uneasily side by side—bumper stickers proclaiming "Tax Yale, Not Us" embellish a number of street signs downtown. But there is more than mere political tension here. New Haven has a reputation as something of a battleground, and Yalies tend to stick to areas on or near campus, further widening the rift between town and gown. Despite efforts by Yale to revitalize New Haven, including financial incentives for faculty members to buy houses near the university, the difference between the controlled, wealthy academic environment and the rest of the town is apparent in every facet of the city, from architecture to safety.

Yet the hype of "Yale is dead" is vastly overstated. New Haven is currently undergoing somewhat of an economic revival and offers a vibrant and strikingly diverse community. Yale itself is recovering from the ravages of ex-President Benno Schmidt's fiscal irresponsibility and is briskly renovating its beautiful neo-Gothic campus. Indeed, Yale lives on.

PRACTICAL INFORMATION AND ORIENTATION

Two hours from New York City, New Haven lies at the intersection of I-95 (110 mi. from Providence) and I-91 (40 mi. from Hartford). At night, don't wander too freely out of the immediate downtown and campus areas, as surrounding sections are notably less safe. The Yale area is well patrolled by campus police. The downtown area is also patrolled by police mostly on the lookout for illegally parked cars. On weekdays tow trucks are out in full force, so read parking signs carefully.

New Haven is laid out in nine square units. The central one is **The Green,** which, despite the fact that it lies between Yale University and the downtown area, is a pleasant escape from the hassles of city life. A small but thriving business district borders the Green on Chapel St., consisting mostly of bookstores, boutiques, cheap sandwich places, and other establishments catering to students and professors.

Visitor Information: Greater New Haven Convention and Visitors Bureau, 1 Long Wharf Dr. (203-777-8550 or 800-332-7829). From Union Station take city bus J or U to the Green and transfer to bus Z; the bureau is located in the back of a huge office complex. Take the G bus back to downtown New Haven. Free street maps and information on current events in town. For recorded events information, updated weekly, call 498-5050, ext. 1310. Open Mon.-Fri. 8:30am-5pm. **Yale Information Center,** inside the Phelps Gateway, 344 College St. (203-432-2302, recording 432-2300), facing the Green. Free campus maps. Pick up a $1 walking guide and *The Yale*, a guide to undergraduate life ($3). Open daily 10am-3:30pm. Free 1-hr. tours Mon.-Fri. at 10:30am and 2pm, Sat.-Sun. at 1:30pm.

Trains: Amtrak (800-872-7245), Union Station, Union Ave. Newly renovated station but area is unsafe at night. Trains to New York $22; take the *Metroliner*. **Metro-North Commuter Railroad** (800-638-7646 or 212-532-4900), Union Station. Runs trains to New York's Grand Central Station for half of Amtrak's fare ($10.15; $13.50 rush hour). Trains run once an hour (more frequently during peak times); the ride takes 90 min. Ticket counter in NYC open daily 6am-10:30pm; in New Haven, Mon.-Fri. 5:55am-10:15pm, Sat.-Sun. 6:40am-10:15pm.

Buses: Greyhound (in NYC 547-1500; in New Haven 203-772-2470 or 800-231-2222), Union Station. Area is unsafe at night. Frequent bus service to: New York ($13, 2½ hrs.), Boston ($22), and Providence ($19). Ticket office open daily 8:30am-7:30pm. **Peter Pan Bus Lines,** Connecticut Limousine Terminal, 10 Brewery St. (203-878-6054), offers buses to New York ($12). Terminal accessible to and from Yale only by taxicab. **Connecticut Transit,** 470 James St. (203-624-0151), provides city transit within New Haven and the surrounding area. Most buses depart from the Green. Fare 95¢; free transfers available. Information booth, at 200 Orange St., open Mon.-Fri. 9am-5pm.

Taxis: Metro Cab (777-7777). Yale campus to Union Station $4-5.

Zip Code: 06511

Area Code: 203

ACCOMMODATIONS

If you have any friends at Yale (or acquaintances whom you could pretend to be friends with, stay with them. Inexpensive accommodations are scarce in New Haven. The hunt is especially difficult around Yale Parents Weekend (mid-Oct.) and commencement (early June). The nearest park for camping is **Hammonasset Beach** (245-2785 or 245-1817, sites $12), 20 minutes away.

Hotel Duncan, 1151 Chapel St. (787-1273). Decent singles ($40) and doubles ($55), both with bath. Boasts the oldest elevator in CT. The safest elevator is elsewhere. Reservations recommended on weekends.

Nutmeg Bed & Breakfast, 222 Girard Ave. (236-6698), Hartford. Reserves doubles in New Haven B&B's at $35-45. Open Mon.-Fri. 9am-5pm.

Bed & Breakfast Ltd. (469-3260). Mon.-Fri. 4-9pm, Sat.-Sun. anytime.

FOOD

Food in New Haven is reasonably cheap, catering to the student population, especially along Chapel St. and Broadway. The Little Italy district on Wooster St., east of downtown, features superb pizza, understandably the pride of New Haven.

Frank Pepe Pizzeria Napoletana, 157 Wooster St. (865-5762), 1 block east of Olive St. From the Green, walk east on Chapel St., turn right at Olive St., and then turn left at Wooster St. Also accessible by city bus Z Mon.-Sat. This showy restaurant with green cushions and lots of white tile opens into a huge kitchen where you can watch your pizza being prepared and then baked in a massive oven. Pizzas with various combinations of traditional toppings range from a straightforward small tomato pie ($4) to a large clam tomato pie ($16.70). Open Mon. and Wed.-Thurs. 4-10:30pm, Fri.-Sat. 11:30am-midnight, Sun. 2:30-10:30pm.

Sally's Pizza Restaurant, 237 Wooster St. (624-5271), near Olive St. From the Green, walk east on Chapel St., turn right at Olive St., and then turn left at Wooster St. Also accessible by city bus Z Mon.-Sat. A tiny, slightly drab pizzeria that makes thin-crust pizza very, very well. Small pizzas $3-4.45, large $9-13.45. Open Tues.-Thurs. 5-11pm, Fri.-Sat. 5pm-midnight, Sun. 5-10pm.

Daily Caffè, 316 Elm St. (776-5063). Started by a Yale graduate; quickly becoming the haunt of the university's coffee-and-cigarette set. The swirly, psychedelic windows and the colorful chalkboard menu should tip you off that this is where the lit. majors go to caffeinate. No smoking, but the heavy-duty discussions probably cause lung cancer by themselves. Open Mon.-Sat. 8am-1am, Sun. 8am-midnight.

Claire's, 1000 Chapel St. (562-3888). A homey restaurant that touts its gourmet vegetarian menu, which has Mexican and Middle Eastern selections. Brunch until 11am; extensive selection for under $6. Quiche $5.75 and many glossy, rich cakes for around $2.65 per slice. Open daily 8am-10pm.

Willoughby's Coffee and Tea, 1006 Chapel Street (789-8400), near College St. Coffee factory for those who want good coffee without the trappings of pretense. The whining, bean-churning machines add that touch of industrial intrigue to the cup of joe. Large coffee $1.05, espresso $1. Another Willoughby's at 258 Church St. (777-7400). Open Sun.-Thurs. 8am-6pm, Fri.-Sat. 8am-9pm.

Bangkok Gardens, 172 York St. (789-8718 and 789-8684), off Chapel St. Nice, generic Thai food for those who don't want any more pizza or coffee in New Haven. Lunch prices $4.50-5.50; dinner $7-9. Open Mon.-Fri. 11:30am-10pm, Sat. noon-11pm, Sun. noon-10pm

Atticus Café, 1082 Chapel St. (776-4040), at High St. A charming bookstore/café with friendly (if harried) service. Try their soups served with delicious half-loaves of bread ($4); lunch specials $5. Open 8am-midnight.

Louis Lunch, 263 Crown St. (562-5507). The wife-and-husband team serves the best flame-broiled burger on the East Coast for $2.50. They say the menu hasn't changed in 40 years. They also claim to have invented the hamburger. Whatever. Open Mon.-Fri. 8:30am-4pm, Sat. 11am-3pm.

SIGHTS

The main reason to come to New Haven is, of course, **Yale University.** With such diverse alums as George H.W. Bush, Jodie Foster, Cornelius Vanderbilt, and Sara Gilbert from *Roseanne,* the Yale campus is justifiably proud.

From **Phelps Gate,** the piece of architecture at 344 College St. that looks like a rook on a chessboard, enter the **Old Campus,** where first-year students now live. Statues of former University presidents (and Nathan Hale) litter the verdant lawn. Check out the shiny foot of one of the presidential statues—Yale seniors rub it for good luck at Commencement.

Walk straight through Old Campus and look at the huge Gothic tower on High St.; **Harkness Tower** can be seen from almost every place at Yale (except, of course, when you're right under it), and during the school year it features daily carillon bell performances. Harkness is part of Branford College, one of the 12 residential dorms for upperclassmen. This system was lifted from Oxford, as were many things at Yale. Evincing great anxiety of influence about this, Yale took great pains to artificially age the campus architecture (built mostly in the early 20th century). Bricks were buried in different soils to give them that Industrial Revolution look, windows were shattered, and cobblestones were imported. As a result, Yale's neo-gothic look always appears to be on the verge of a nervous breakdown. All the colleges stand in close proximity to each other—check to see where your favorite alum lived.

Down High St. towards Chapel St., stop by and examine a small, dark, unlabeled building right next to the overpass. This is **Skull and Bones,** Yale's elite secret society—so hush-hush that members are supposed to walk out of a room if the name is even mentioned. Test this out at your next Yale alum party, or next time you want member George Bush to skedaddle. ("Skull and Bones! Skull and Bones!"). The obnoxious people will leave.

Walking the other way down High St., take note of the round sculpture with the water pouring off it. Maya Lin, the Yale grad who designed the Vietnam memorial, was commissioned to design a sculpture to commemorate women at Yale. The result was **The Women's Table.** The numbers spiraling out from the vertex represent the numbers of women enrolled. Yale went co-ed in 1969; the numbers for previous years represent graduate schools.

Across the way from the Women's Table is the **Sterling Memorial Library,** 120 High St. (432-1775), designed by James Gambel Rodgers, a firm believer in the sanctity of printed material. The building looks like a cathedral; even the telephone booths are shaped like confessionals. Rodgers spared no expense in making Yale's library look "authentic," even decapitating the figurines on the library's exterior to replicate those at Oxford, which, because of decay, often fall to the ground and shatter. Inside, check out the "altarpiece" over the check-out counter. This slightly sacrilegious work features Mother Yale in Mary's place, with the Yale seal in her hand instead of the Bible. (Open in summer Mon.-Wed. and Fri. 8:30am-5pm, Thurs. 8:30am-10pm, Sat. 10am-5pm; during academic year Mon.-Thurs. 8:30am-midnight, Fri. 8:30am-5pm, Sat. 10am-5am, Sun. 1pm-midnight.)

Walk through the library and you'll end up on Yale's own Wall Street. Across from the library is the **Law School,** where Bill and Hillary Clinton first met (and where Hillary kicked Bill's butt in class). The Neo-Gothic gargoyles perched on the building are in fact cops and robbers. Walking east on Wall St., notice the massive, windowless **Beinecke Rare Book and Manuscript Library,** 121 Wall St. (432-2977). Instead of windows, this intriguing modern structure is panelled with Vermont marble cut thin enough to be translucent. A persistent but untrue rumor is that its volumes, including one Gutenberg Bible and an extensive collection of William Carlos Williams's writings, can survive a nuclear war (joy!). (Open Mon.-Fri. 8:30am-5pm, Sat. 10am-5pm.)

Turn right onto College St. from Wall St. and look down **Cross Campus** for a beautiful view of the Sterling Library. The dorms here were deliberately separated to preserve the view. If you're hungry, walk to **Naples Pizza,** 90 Wall St. (776-9021 or 776-6214). Yale students hang out obsessively here. (Open June-Aug. Mon.-Wed. 7-10pm, Thurs.-Fri. 7-11pm; Sept.-May Sun.-Thurs. 7pm-1am, Fri.-Sat. 7pm-2am.)

Yale also has quite a few museums. The **Yale University Art Gallery,** 1111 Chapel St. at High St. (432-0600), open since 1832, claims to be the oldest university art museum in the Western Hemisphere. Its collections of Asian art and Italian Renaissance works are especially notable. (Open Tues.-Sat. 10am-5pm, Sun. 2-5pm. Closed Aug. Suggested donation $3.)

The **Yale Center for British Art,** 1080 Chapel St. (432-2800), features the most extensive collection of British art outside England. A must for Anglophiles. (Open Tues.-Sat. 10am-5pm, Sun. noon-5pm. Free.)

The **Peabody Museum of Natural History,** 170 Whitney Ave. (recorded message 432-5050), is on Science Hill, the ghetto of the non-humanities at Yale and a 15-minute walk from the Old Campus. It houses Rudolph F. Zallinger's Pulitzer Prize-winning mural, which portrays the North American continent as it appeared 70 to 350 million years ago. Filled with regional pride, it features exhibits on rocks of Connecticut, birds of Connecticut, Native Americans of Connecticut, meteors which have struck Connecticut, and dinosaurs who presumably didn't live in Connecticut, as well as Central American artifacts. Take the J bus if your legs are pooped. (Open Mon.-Sat. 10am-5pm, Sun. noon-5pm. Admission $4, seniors $3, children 3-15 $2.50. Free Mon.-Fri. 3-5pm.)

ENTERTAINMENT

New Haven offers plenty of late-night entertainment. The *New Haven Advocate* has good current listings. Check **Toad's Place,** 300 York St. (562-5694, recorded information 624-TOAD), to see if one of your favorite bands is in town. This huge bar has hosted impromptu gigs by Dylan and the Stones and now features folks like Juliana Hatfield and Joan Jett. While you get tickets, grab a draft beer ($1) at the bar. (Box office open daily 11am-6pm; tix available at the bar after 8pm. Bar open Sun.-Thurs. 8pm-1am, Fri.-Sat. 8pm-2am.) The **Anchor Bar,** 272 College St. (865-1512), is the kind of place that serves Corona and St. Pauli Girl; a local paper rated its jukebox the best in the region, though the judges clearly like easy-listening more than students do. (Open Mon.-Thurs. 11am-1am, Fri.-Sat. 10am-2am.)

Less mainstream types flock to the **Tune Inn,** 29 Center St. (772-4310 or 865-9371), right off Church St. Call for current bookings—this place sponsors such anomalies as the "Connecticut Hardcore Fest!!!!"

Once a famous testing ground for Broadway-bound plays, New Haven's thespian community carries on today on a lesser scale. The **Shubert Theater,** 247 College St. (526-5666, 800-228-6622), a significant part of the town's on-stage tradition, still mounts shows. (Box office open Mon.-Fri. 10am-5pm, Sat. 11am-3pm.) Across the street, the **Palace,** 246 College St. (784-2120, box office 624-6497), hosts big-name concerts and revues.

Yale itself accounts for an impressive portion of the theater activity in the city. The **Yale Repertory Theater,** 222 York St. (432-1234) at Chapel St., has turned out such illustrious alums as Meryl Streep, Glenn Close, and James Earl Jones, and it continues to produce excellent shows. (Open Oct.-May; tickets usually under $8.) In summer, the Green is the site of free **New Haven Symphony** concerts (865-0831), the **New Haven Jazz Festival** (787-8228), and other free musical series. The **Department of Cultural Affairs** (787-8956), 770 Chapel St., can answer questions about concerts on the Green.

■■■ PRINCETON

Princeton slumbers peacefully 50 miles southwest of New York City off Rte. 1 in New Jersey. This disarmingly quiet and preppy town's only attraction, some students say, is Ivy League **Princeton University,** which has turned out presidents (James Madison and Woodrow Wilson), tycoons (J.P. Morgan), writers (F. Scott Fitzgerald), movie stars (Jimmy Stewart), and jeans models (Brooke Shields). A stroll through the leafy and lovely campus will give you a healthy dose of centuries-old Gothic buildings, cloistered lawns, and intellectual history. The streets of the surrounding, upscale town provide bookstores, abundant cheap and ritzy eateries, and an amount of black and orange that exceeds all established standards of good taste.

PRACTICAL INFORMATION AND ORIENTATION

Located in the green heart of the Garden State, Princeton is within commuting distance of both New York and Philadelphia. Driving from New York City, take the Holland Tunnel to the New Jersey Turnpike and exit at Hightstown, thereby avoiding the slow, ugly U.S. 1. The Dinky train (see below) lets you off at the end of University Place; merely stroll onto the green areas surrounded by stone buildings to get to the heart of the campus. **Nassau Street** is Princeton's main strip, with shops clustered on the north side and the university set back on the south side. **Palmer Square,** the center of Princeton's business district, lies right off Nassau between Witherspoon and Chambers St.

Visitor Information: Princeton University Communication/Publication Office, Stanhope Hall (258-3600). Campus maps and current information, including the *Princeton Weekly Bulletin,* with a calendar of events. Open Mon.-Fri. 8:30am-4:30pm. **Orange Key Guide Service,** 73 Nassau St. (258-3603), in the back entrance of MacLean House. Free campus tours, pamphlets, and maps. Hour-long tours leave from MacLean Mon.-Sat. at 10 and 11am, 1:30 and 3:30pm, Sun. at 1:30 and 3:30pm. Office open Mon.-Sat. 9am-5pm, Sun. 1-5pm. **Princeton University Telephone Information,** 258-3000. Open daily 8am-11pm.

Trains: New Jersey Transit, in-state 800-772-2222, out-of-state 201-762-5100, hearing-impaired 800-772-2287. Leaves NYC for Princeton about every hr., leaves Princeton for NYC less frequently. 1-hr. trips start at 6am ($9.85 one-way, $14 round-trip). Prices include a 5-min. ride on the "Dinky," probably the shortest commuter train in the world, which runs directly to the Princeton campus, stopping across from the McCarter Theater. **Amtrak** (800-872-7245) connects Princeton Junction, 3 mi. south of Princeton on Rte. 571, to NYC. 7 trains run daily from New York to Princeton (between 6am and 4pm), 9 from Princeton to New York (between 6am and 9pm). 1-hr. trip costs $23 one-way, $38 round-trip.
Buses: New Jersey Transit, 800-772-2222. Runs 6am-midnight within Princeton. Buses stop at Princeton University and Palmer Sq. **Suburban Transit** (908-249-1100, 800-222-0492) has 2 locations, in Palmer Sq. and Princeton Shopping Center, about 5 blocks from the center of town. Departures every ½hr.; call for times. To NYC $7.50 one-way, $14.65 round-trip.
Taxi: Associated Taxi Stand, 924-1222. Open Mon. 5:30am-midnight, Tues.-Fri. 6am-midnight, Sat.-Sun. 7am-midnight.
Post Office: (921-9563), in Palmer Sq. behind Tiger Park . Open Mon.-Fri. 8am-4:30pm, Sat. 8:30am-12:30pm. **ZIP code:** 08542 (08540 for main branch)
Area code: 609.

ACCOMMODATIONS

The only cheap beds in Princeton proper are found by befriending a hospitable student. Otherwise cruise Rte. 1 south of town for any number of fairly inexpensive chain motels. **Camping** is available about 20 mi. away at Delaware and Raritan Canal State Park, 2185 Daniel-Bray Hwy. (397-2949), 3 mi. north of Stockton on Rte. 29. They have 75 sites for tents and trailers with toilets and showers (no hookups) for $10 per night.

McIntosh Inn (896-3700), U.S. 1 and Quaker Bridge Mall. Ideal for more than 1 person. Rooms come clean and large. Not too many frills here, but cable TV and free morning coffee make up the difference. Next to fast food and a mall. Singles w/ queen-sized bed $44. Doubles with 2 beds $56.
Howard Johnson's (896-1100), 2995 U.S. 1, 5 mi. south of Princeton. You know what to expect: large, well-kept, and generic rooms. Extremely reasonable, especially for groups of 2 or more. Outdoor pool, cable TV, free continental breakfast at the in-house restaurant. Up to 4 people pay $74.50 for a room with 2 double beds.

FOOD

Princeton's two main feeding areas are in the Palmer Square area and down Nassau St. It's hard to find cheap places that let you sit down—perhaps you might picnic amid the squirrels on the University campus.

Teresa's Pizzetta Caffé, 21 Palmer Sq. East (921-1974). Personalized gourmet pizzas with poetic toppings in a clean, well-lit, modern café. Since recent renovations, Teresa's size has doubled and its prices have risen, but the spinach, eggplant, and fresh garlic pizza is still a good deal at $6.50. Lines are super long here. Entrees $7-9. Open Mon.-Thurs. 10am-11pm, Fri.-Sat. 10am-midnight, Sun. 10am-10pm. For those impatient with what can easily be a 1½-hr. wait, there is also a take-out and delivery branch, **Café Colóre,** at 124 Nassau St. (924-0777; slices around $2; open Sun.-Thurs. 11am-midnight, Fri.-Sat. 11am-1am).
Small World Coffee, 14 Witherspoon St. (924-4377). Seattle comes to Princeton in this terminally hip, graduate-student-encrusted coffee bar. Periodically features bad folk singers, but the coffee is good. Medium coffee of the day $1.25, double espresso $1.75. Open Mon.-Fri. 6:30am-midnight, Sat.-Sun. 7:30am-midnight.
Thomas Sweet's Ice Cream (683-1655), Palmer Sq. across from the Nassau Inn. Massive selection of ice cream and frozen yogurt changes daily. The Snickers and cookie-dough flaves are faves, as are rum raisin and the delicious bittersweet chocolate yogurt. Ice cream $1.60 per scoop, yogurt $1.75. Make sure to grab

some free chocolate samples in the connected candy store while you're there. Open Sun.-Thurs. 11am-10:30pm, Fri.-Sat. 11am-11pm.

P.J.'s Pancake House, 154 Nassau St. (924-1353). A Princeton tradition. Old wooden tables etched with student graffiti. Typical college hangout—loud, crowded, inexpensive. Fresh, tasty food; breakfast served all day. Try the pancakes with fresh fruit ($4.75) or the hamburger platter ($5.25; order it well-done). Open Sun.-Thurs. 7:30am-10pm, Fri.-Sat. 7:30am-midnight.

Chuck's Spring Street Café, 16 Spring St. (921-0027). Specializes in buffalo wings but also serves a variety of sandwiches in a local and student hangout. Open Sun.-Thurs. 11am-9pm, Fri.-Sat. 11am-10pm.

Hoagie Haven, 242 Nassau St. (921-7223). Several blocks from the action (and high real estate prices) of Palmer Sq., this is but one of the many cheap joints in this area, but perhaps the best bargain. Hoagie $3-4; half-hoagie $2-2.50. Open daily 9am-1am.

The Athenian, 25 Witherspoon St. (921-3425). Bizarro hybrid: coffee shop collides with Greek pastry shop and Italian pizzeria. Good pizza by the slice ($1.50) and by the pie ($4.75-$7.75). Gaze at the Parthenon while you gnaw on a wedge of pepperoni. Top it all off with *baklava.* Sandwiches and entrees under $7. At $6 the Greek special *is* special. Open Mon.-Wed. and Sun. 11am-10pm; Thurs. 11am-11pm; Fri. and Sat. 11am-midnight.

SIGHTS

The landscaped, Gothic campus of Princeton University will wow you with its 2500 acres (although 1900 acres house the supercollider down on Rte. 1). James Madison acquired his debating skills here, Woodrow Wilson served as president, and both F. Scott Fitzgerald and Eugene O'Neill dropped out. Albert Einstein also worked here at the high-powered Institute for Advanced Study, and his house still sits relatively close to campus at 112 Mercer St. The **Orange Key** (see Practical Information above) provides free tours geared toward prospective students intent on hearing the myths and legends of the nation's fourth-oldest school (founded in 1746).

Start a tour of Princeton by the **Nathaniel Fitzrandolph Gate** on Nassau St. (right across from Burger King). Or maybe don't—the legend says that Princeton undergraduates who walk through the gate won't graduate with their class. Straight down the path from this cursed gate is **Nassau Hall.** Upon completion in 1756 it stood as the colonies' largest stone edifice and Princeton's original university building; it also served as the capitol building of the original U.S. colonies for several months in the summer of 1783. The two magnificent bronze tigers represent the school's mascot. Each class plants ivy on the walls of this building; if the ivy grows to the top, good luck is supposedly in store for that class. Try not to snicker at the dead sprigs of ivy for the Class of 1904.

To the left of Nassau Hall is the oddly shaped **Chancellor Green Center,** the student center of Princeton. Inside, free copies of the *Village Voice* lie in a disheveled heap during the school year, and students grab coffee and watch sitcoms on the gigantic TV in the café (258-2825; coffee and pastries under $1; open daily 9am-1am during the school year, 9am-10pm in summer). Past the Green Center to the east is Princeton's intellectual kingpin, **Firestone Library** (258-3180), which houses original manuscripts by Woodrow Wilson, Adlai Stevenson, and F. Scott Fitzgerald, as well as an extensive graphic arts collection and countless other books. (Open Mon.-Fri. 8:30am-4:30pm.) Next to the library is the **University Chapel** (258-3047), an ornate Gothic structure designed by a Yale architect, with a wonderful stained glass window, a 16th-century French pulpit, and a 17th-century lectern. (Open Sept.-June 9am-9pm; July-Aug. 9am-4:30pm.)

Straight down the path between Nassau Hall and the Green Center are **Whig Hall** and **Clio Hall,** home to the oldest college literary and debating club in the U.S. Go down the stairs, take a left, and match stares with Picasso's *Head of a Woman,* which sits outside the impressive **University Art Museum** (258-3787). The museum holds everything from Northwest Coast Indian art and Pre-Columbian objects to Renaissance masterpieces to Jean-Michel Basquiat's postmodern experiments.

P R I N C E T O N

There is also a fine contemporary collection, in which women artists such as Louise Nevelson and Nancy Graves are well-represented. Also of interest is Cézanne's *La Montaigne Sainte Victoire*. (Open Tues.-Sat. 10am-5pm, Sun. 1-5pm. Free.) The Princeton campus is likewise a gallery for a number of beautiful sculptures such as Picasso's. While there are occasional revolving exhibits such as Brooke Shields '87, the more permanent pieces are part of the Putnam Collection, which has works of Alexander Calder, Henry Moore, and David Smith scattered throughout campus. The museum gives tours of these works on Saturdays at 2pm.

From the museum, walk to the left and through the ornate iron gates to the **Prospect Gardens,** a huge bed of flowers in the shape of Princeton's shield, which is particularly beautiful in the summertime. Watch out for inebriated couples during the school year. Exiting Prospect Gardens, walk down the path until you reach Washington Rd. (Take note of the black squirrels here—they were specially imported to give the campus a more Oxford-esque feel.) Across the street is the **Woodrow Wilson School of Public and International Relations.** The school's building features an oddly lumpy sculpture with water jetting out all over, and a reflecting pool, often used as a wading hole.

Heading east from Washington Rd. is **Prospect Street,** the social center of Princeton. The **eating clubs,** the social groups of upperclassmen, are all located here, each with various reputations but all quite notorious in their own ways. Some have a complicated rush system (called "bicker"); some are "open invite." F. Scott Fitzgerald's haunt, the **Cottage Club,** is the fifth club down the street from campus on the right. Edging Prospect and Olden St. is the **E-Quad,** the engineering campus. Note especially the large, erectile sculpture on Olden St., often the site of feminist safer-sex demonstrations. Back on Washington Rd., heading south past Ivy Lane takes you to the frumpy **Fine Hall,** the tallest building on campus (the University Chapel is the most altitudinous). Get one of the scruffy math-heads to let you in, and go up to the 12th floor. From here there's a great view of Princeton's entire verdant expanse.

The most notable sight off-campus is probably **Einstein's House,** 112 Mercer St., at the western end of Nassau St. This is where Albert Einstein lived his last 22 years; it is currently the home of the unfortunate individual in the physics department chosen to fill his shoes. A Hollywood team recently increased the pressure by filming *IQ* here, starring Walter Matthau as Albert and Meg Ryan as his zany niece. This prompted a sign reading, "IQ Crew: Please Do Not Park On The Azalias!"

The town of Princeton is home to a few other historical landmarks. The **Bainbridge House,** 158 Nassau St. (921-6748), is a Georgian building that was the home and birthplace of Commodore William Bainbridge, commander of "Old Ironsides," the *U.S.S. Constitution.* (Open March-Dec. Tues.-Sun. noon-4pm. Free.) Bainbridge House also houses the **Historical Society of Princeton** (921-6748), which can give you historical information and a map for a self-guided walking tour of town. The tour takes in **Morven** (683-1514), a Georgian-style governor's mansion, and the former home of black artist-athlete-performer Paul Robeson.

Near town is the **Princeton Battlefield State Park,** Rte. 158 (921-0074), which commemorates George Washington's defeat of the British on January 3, 1777. (Open Wed.-Sat. 10am-noon and 1-4pm, Sun.1-4pm.) Near the park, on Rosedale Rd. off Rte. 206, lurks the bane of every student in America, the **Education Testing Service (E.T.S.)** (921-9000). The tests they administer—the SAT, GRE, LSAT, MCAT, GMAT—have inspired a loathing equalled by few institutions in America.

New Jersey's **Washington Crossing State Park** (737-0623) marks the point where General George gained fame for standing up in a crowded rowboat while crossing the Delaware River. The park is on the banks of the river, 12 miles southwest of Princeton on Rte. 29, off U.S. 206. (Open June-Aug. daily 8am-8pm; Sept.-May daily 8am-4:30pm. $3 per car on summer weekends.)

ENTERTAINMENT

On May 17, 1955, Princeton students held one of the first pro-rock 'n roll demonstrations in the U.S., blaring Bill Haley and the Comets' "Rock Around the Clock" until 1am, when the Dean woke up and told them to knock it off. This tradition continues at the **Terrace Club,** 62 Washington Rd. (683-4426), the "alternative" eating club. This small, intimate setting hosts smoke-laden, underground pop concerts during the school year, letting weary road-tripping bands crash for the night between their gig in Philly and their gig at Maxwell's. Bands that have played here include Tiger Trap, Tsunami, and the Village People. They book irregularly, and the weekend concerts are by Princeton ID only—try to go with your Tiger-buddy, or beg at the door. For less nicotined but more boozey fun, traipse down Prospect Ave. to the Princeton **eating clubs,** where alcohol and sex are reputed to swim together. Once again, Princeton U. ID is needed, so go with your Princeton friends (or make some quickly).

The school itself provides amusement as well. **Crazy students** attempt life-threatening pranks, like smashing safety lights with their heads, jumping onto the electrified Dinky train (and subsequently suing the university), and falling from great heights while attempting to steal objects off towers. If you are fortunate enough to be in Princeton on the occasion of the first snowfall of the academic year, get off the grass quickly, or the bare-butt sophomores running amok in the **Nude Olympics** will mow you down. Take photos like the upperclassmen do.

For more sedate Princeton goings-on, like lectures or classical music, see the *Princeton Weekly Bulletin.* Students and professional actors perform at **McCarter Theater** (683-8000). The **Princeton Record Exchange,** at 20 Tulane St., sells new and used records, cassettes, and CDs. Prices start at 99¢. Good stuff, cheaply (921-0881; open Mon.-Sat. 10am-8pm, Sun noon-6pm).

■■■ LONG ISLAND

While in theory "Long Island" includes the entire 120-mi.-long fish-shaped landmass, in practice the term excludes the westernmost sections, Brooklyn and Queens. The residents of these two boroughs will readily remind you that they are officially part of the City. This leaves Nassau and Suffolk Counties to constitute the real Long Island. East of the Queens-Nassau line, people read *Newsday,* not the *Times* or the *Daily News;* they back the Islanders, not the Rangers, and they enjoy their role as neighbor to, rather than part of, the great metropolis.

Until the 20th century, Long Island was a sparsely populated, typically Northeastern jumble of farms and villages on land considered especially good for potato farming; its docks and ports sustained a strong maritime industry. Parts of Suffolk County still preserve the small-town tradition (although for the most part they preserve it in order to capitalize on its value as a tourist draw).

In the early part of the 20th century, Long Island became the playground for Manhattan's rich and famous. New York millionaires built their country houses on the rocky north shore, creating the exclusive "Gold Coast" captured in its 1920s heyday in F. Scott Fitzgerald's *The Great Gatsby.* Later emigres pushed further east to Montauk and the Hamptons. The 1950s were a turning point for the Island: New York City expanded, cars became more affordable, and young couples enjoying postwar prosperity sought dream houses for their baby-boom families. Most important, new Long Island neighborhoods such as Levittown provided an escape from the city and a safe, wholesome environment in which to raise children.

The 1950s also saw the expansion of Long Island's highway system, the essential link to New York City for hordes of commuters. For years, the Long Island Railroad (LIRR) provided the only major connection from Long Island across the Nassau-Queens border and into the city. During the 50s the Island's main artery, the Long Island Expressway (LIE, officially called State Highway 495), grew to include 73 exits on the 85-mi. stretch from Manhattan to Riverhead. Today the Island's population has outgrown all its forms of transportation, and traffic jams are seemingly incessant on the expressway during rush hour (which basically extends from 7am to midnight). Because of this traffic, many Islanders still commute to the city by train, but the sights of Long Island are most easily accessible by car.

Although the Island gives the impression of uninterrupted suburbia, parts of the eastern end are quite rural, while other towns, like Hicksville in eastern Nassau County, are relatively urban (despite the name). Dozens of mega-malls dot Long Island; it is no mistake that they appear on road maps, highlighted as points of interest. The cluster of communities along the South Fork, known collectively as the Hamptons, is home to wealthy, Upper East Side, summering Manhattanites and modern-day Gatsbys. The area jams in July, as traffic backs up miles on Highway 27. Each Hampton has its own sands, style, and stereotype. Look in Southampton for old money, Westhampton for new money, and East Hampton for artists. Bridgehampton, appropriately enough, lies between Southampton and East Hampton.

PRACTICAL INFORMATION

Visitor Information: Long Island Convention and Visitors Bureau (794-4222). This number offers an interactive recorded schedule of events with operators available. The Bureau also operates two visitor centers. The first is located on the LIE, eastbound between exits 51 and 52 (open daily May-Sept. 9:30am-4:30pm). The second is on the Southern State Pkwy., eastbound between exits 13 and 14, opposite the State Police Barracks (open May-Sept. Wed.-Sun. 9:30am-4:30pm).

Trains: Long Island Railroad (LIRR) (train information 822-5477, tour information 718-990-7498, lost articles 718-990-8384). The Island's main public-transportation facility has 5 central lines, all but one of which meet at the main station in Jamaica, Queens. In Manhattan, you can connect from the subway to the LIRR at Penn Station (34th St. at 7th Ave.), which is served by the #1, 2, 3, 9, A, C, and E subway lines. In Brooklyn, you can transfer from the subway to the LIRR at the Flatbush Ave. station, which is served by the B, D, M, N, Q, R, 2, 3, 4, and 5 subway lines. In Queens, the #7 subway line connects with the LIRR at stations in Long Island City, Hunters Point Ave., Woodside, and Main St., Flushing. The E, J, and Z subway lines connect with the LIRR at Jamaica Station. Fares vary according to destination and time of day ("peak" or "off-peak"). Peak fares (charged on trains scheduled to arrive at western terminals between 6 and 10am, and on trains departing those terminals between 4 and 7pm) range from $4.25-14. Off-peak fares (usually about 30% less) range from $3-9.50. Tickets may be purchased aboard trains, but tickets purchased on trains when the station ticket office is open cost more, so buy before you board. The LIRR offers educational and recreational tours, as well as escorted sightseeing tours from May-Nov.

Buses:

Metropolitan Suburban Bus Authority (MSBA): Daytime bus service in Queens, Nassau, and western Suffolk (766-6722). Service runs along most major highways, but the routes are complex and irregular—make sure you confirm your destination with the driver. Some buses run every 15 min., others every hr. In Nassau, the fare is $1.50, but crossing over into Queens from Nassau Cty. costs an additional 50¢; transfers are 25¢. Disabled travelers and senior citizens pay half-fare. Children under 44 in. tall ride free. The MSBA has daily service to and from Jones Beach during the summer months, connecting with the LIRR in Freeport, Nassau ($2.25 each way). Buses also run in summer from the LIRR station in Babylon, Nassau to Robert Moses State Park on Fire Island ($1.75 each way). Call for current schedule.

Suffolk Transit: (852-5200, open Mon.-Fri. 8am-4:30pm). Fare policy same as Nassau. The S-92 bus loops-the-loop back and forth between the tips of the North and South Forks, with 9 runs daily, most of them between East Hampton and Orient Point. Call to confirm stops and schedules. The route also connects with the LIRR at Riverhead, where the forks meet. No service Sun. Fare $1.50, senior and the disabled 50¢. Transfers 25¢. Children under 5 ride free.

Greyhound: 24-hr. reservation number 800-231-2222. Terminal locations in Hempstead (483-3230), Melville (427-6897), and Islip (234-2445). Manhattan to Islip $10 one-way, $20 round-trip. More expensive and less comfortable than the LIRR; taking Greyhound makes little sense unless you're coming in to New York on it from outside the area, in which case continuing connection on to Long Island may be much cheaper.

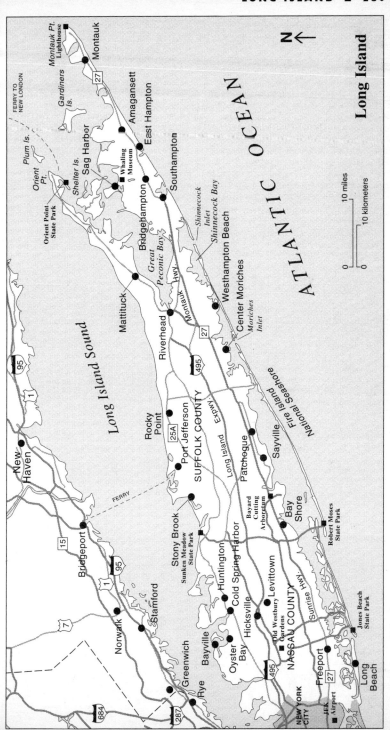

LONG ISLAND

Long Island

Hampton Express: (212-861-6800, on Long Island 874-2400). Buses depart 10-11 times on Fri., 6-7 times per day Sat.-Thurs. Buses to destinations on the South Fork depart Manhattan from 86th and Columbus, 81st and Third, 42nd and Third, 72nd and Madison, and 72nd and Lexington. Fare $15 to all destinations, children 4-11 $10. Reservations recommended, but tickets may be purchased aboard bus. Call for schedule information and exact locations of stops.

Sunrise Express: (800-527-7709, in Suffolk 477-1200). Their "NY Express" runs 4 times per day Fri.-Sat. and 3 times per day Sun.-Thurs. from Manhattan to the North Fork ($15, $29 round-trip). Catch buses on the southwest corner of 44th St. and Third Ave., or in Queens (LIE exit 24 to Kissena Blvd., in front of Queens College's Colden Ctr. at the Q88 bus stop). They go directly to Riverhead, then stop at almost all villages on the north fork to Greenport. The Greenport stop is right near the Shelter Island Ferry terminal. Disabled travelers pay $22 round-trip and lapkids ride free. Reservations recommended. Bicycles ($10) and pets ($5) allowed. Call for schedule information.

Taxis and Car Services: See the phone book for local cab companies; the following are useful for longer distances.

Ollie's Airport Service (829-8647), in Nassau. Vans, limousines, and cars. Runs its vans on set lines from the major airports in Queens out to Nassau and will be cheaper than a taxi, but public transport will be cheaper still. Open 24 hrs.

Long Island Airports Limousine Service (234-8400; Queens 718-656-7000). Similar to Ollie's; focuses on van lines from the Queens airports out onto the island at less-than-taxi rates. Farthest this "line-service" extends is Riverhead in Suffolk Cty. Also standard taxi service. Buses, cabs, and vans available 24 hrs.

Car Rental:

Avis Rent-a-Car (nationwide reservations 800-331-1212). In Nassau, 357 Old Country Rd. (222-3255), in Westbury (open Mon. and Fri. 7am-8pm, Tues.-Thurs. 7am-7pm, Sat.-Sun. 9am-5pm). In Suffolk, 20 West Jericho Turnpike (271-9300), Huntington Station (open Mon.-Fri. 7am-8pm, Sat.-Sun. 9am-5pm). Any rental will run upwards of $50 per day, even on multi-day packages (but free unlimited miles!). Renting from smaller outfit in Manhattan definitely advised (see NYC listings). Must be at least 25 with a major credit card.

Hertz Rent-a-Car (worldwide reservations 800-654-3131). In Islip, Suffolk Cty., at the MacArthur Airport (737-9200; open Mon.-Fri. 6am-11pm, Sat.-Sun. 7am-7pm). Also at the East Hampton Airport in Suffolk Cty. (537-5365; open Sun.-Thurs. 9am-5pm, Fri.-Sat. 9am-7pm). Upwards of $50 per day during the week, reaching $100 per day on weekends. Rent in Manhattan and save a lot of dough (see NYC listings). Must be at least 25 with a major credit card.

Bicycle Rental:

Country Time Cycles, 11500 Main Rd. (298-8700), in Mattituck. All bikes $15 per day, or $50 for five days. Open Mon.-Sat. 9am-6pm, Sun. 10am-5pm. Credit card required ("and they don't take American Express...").

Piccozzi's Service Station, Rte. 114 (749-0045), at the Mobil in Shelter Island Heights. A 10-min. walk from the north ferry up Rte. 114 (Bridge St.). 3-speeds $12 for 4 hrs., $17 for 8 hrs.; 12-speeds $14 for 4 hrs., $19 for 8 hrs.; 21-speeds and mountain bikes $17 for 4 hrs., $21 for 8 hrs. Open daily 7:30am-7:30pm. Cash deposit or credit card required.

Ferries: Many of the smaller islands off the shore of Long Island are popular with vacationers. Listed below are several of the ferry services from Long Island to the various islands. Call for schedules, which vary with day and destination.

To Fire Island: From **Bay Shore** (665-3600), ferries sail to Fair Harbor, Ocean Beach, Ocean Bay Park, Saltaire, and Kismet. (Round-trip fare $10.50, children under 12 $5.) From **Sayville** (589-8980), ferries leave for Sailor's Haven (round-trip fare $8, children under 12 $4.50) and Cherry Grove and Fire Island Pines (round-trip fare for either $10, children under 12 $5). From **Patchogue** (475-1665), ferries go to Davis Park and Watch Hill (round-trip to either $10, children under 12 $5.50). LIRR stations lie within a short distance of the 3 ferry terminals, making access from New York City relatively simple. (All ferries May-Nov.)

To Shelter Island: from the North and South Forks. **North Fork: Greenport Ferry** (749-0139), North Ferry Rd., on the dock. Passenger and driver $6.50, round-trip $7, each additional passenger $1, walk-on (without a car) $1. Ferries run daily every 15 min., with the first ferry leaving Greenport at 6am and the last ferry departing the island at 11:45pm. **South Fork: North Haven Ferry** (749-1200), 3 mi. north of Sag Harbor on Rte. 114, on the dock. Car and driver $6 one-way, $6.50 round-trip, additional passengers $1 each, walk-ons $1 round-trip. Ferries run daily at approximately 10 min. intervals 6am-1:45am.

To Block Island: Viking Lines, P.O. Box 730 (668-5709), in Montauk. Take LIE to exit 70 and follow signs to Rte. 27 E.; follow this through Montauk and one mile farther east; turn left on West Lake Dr. and follow it 3 mi. to the dock. Fare $15 one-way, $30 same day round-trip (children 5-12 $10 and $15); bicycles $3 one-way and $5 same day round-trip. Ferry leaves daily at 9am, returns from Block Island at 4:30pm, with additional sailings mid-July through Sept. Crossing time 1½ hrs. No reservations necessary. No cars.

To Connecticut: Steamboat Co., 102 West Broadway (473-0286), in Port Jefferson. Peak rates effective from noon Fri. through Sun. To Bridgeport (1¼ hr.): car and driver $31, off-peak $26; each additional passenger $8, off-peak $7; unlimited passengers (off-peak only) $35; walk-ons $11, off-peak $9; children 6-12 $5, off-peak $4. Tues. is Gentlemen's Day—walk-ons of the appropriate gender pay $10 round-trip; Thurs. is Ladies' day and same fares apply for women. Ferries leave every 1½ hrs. or so from 6am-7pm. Call for exact times and reservations. **Fisher's Island Ferry,** (203-443-6851 or 203-442-0165), State St., New London, CT. Fisher's Island to New London: automobile (not including driver) $10, each adult (with or without car) $4, each child 5-12 $2. Any trip leaving New London after 3:45pm costs $1 extra. Ferries run daily 5am-9:30pm with varying frequency; call for schedule. Crossing time 45 min. **Viking Lines,** P.O. Box 730 (668-5709), in Montauk. Montauk to New London: ferries run late May-early Sept. From July to Sept., 2 trips per day every Fri., Sun., and Wed., leaving Montauk at 6am and 7pm, and leaving New London at 8am and 9pm. Ferries Fri. and Sun. only during May and June. Fare $15 each way; children 5-12 $10 one-way, $15 round-trip; bicycles $5 round-trip. Passengers only. Crossing time 1½ hrs. each way.

Help Line: Rape Hotline 222-2293.
Area Code: 516.

ACCOMMODATIONS

Finding a place to stay on The Island can be a daunting prospect for the budget traveler. Daytrippers in Nassau would probably be better off heading back to the city to crash for the night. Most of the decent larger hotels in Nassau exact indecent rates ($100-150 per night) and cater to a McDonald's-eating, mini-van driving, family-of-four-or-more set, while the few smaller hotels which rent for less are often seedy enough to make you want to keep driving (some advertise special rates for "short stays"). Suffolk County provides a wider variety of accommodations and, with its open spaces, more opportunities for camping (Be Young. Have Fun. Go Camping.). In general, however, places close during the off-season and fill up quickly during the summer.

Nassau County

Freeport Motor Inn and Boatel, 445 South Main St. (623-9100), in Freeport, LIE Exit 38. Head south on the Meadowbrook State Pkwy. to exit M9. Turn right off the exit and bear left onto Mill Rd. Turn left onto South Main, and it's a few minutes ahead on the left. Only 5 min. from Jones Beach, next to a marina and a nice strip of water. Clean and comfortable, with TVs, private baths, and phones in all rooms. Sun.-Thurs. singles $60, doubles $65. Fri.-Sat. singles and doubles $67. Continental breakfast. Reservations urged for summer weekends.

Days Inn, 828 S. Oyster Bay Rd. (433-1900, fax 433-0218) in Hicksville. LIE exit 435, then right (south) on S. Oyster Bay Rd. The Inn is about 2¼ mi. ahead on your right (a little ways south of Old Country Rd.). Your standard "budget" motel room—clean, spacious, and comfortable. What's to say? Singles $80, doubles $82, but specials as low as $59 run throughout the year. Reservations recommended for summer weekends.

Suffolk County

Montauket, Tuthill Rd. (668-5992), in Montauk. Follow the Montauk Hwy. to Montauk. At the traffic circle take Edgemere, which becomes Flamingo, and make a left onto Fleming and then another left. The Island's best bargain, though difficult to find. Perched on a hill with a great ocean view—bring your golf clubs and practice driving from one of the astroturf "greens" atop the hill, toward the target which floats off shore. From March-May and Oct.-Nov. 15, only 4 rooms are open; the whole hotel opens for the summer season. Make reservations for summer weekends starting March 1st—it fills up quickly. Almost always full on weekends. Doubles $35, with private bath $40.

Pines Motor Lodge, corner of Rte. 109 and 3rd St. (957-3330), in North Lindenhurst. LIE to Southern State Pkwy. E., Exit 33. Go southeast on Babylon Farmingdale Rd. (which is Rte. 109); it's just beyond the intersection of Straight Path. Affordable roadside motel. Rooms clean, with all the standard amenities (TV, private bath, phone). Singles or doubles Fri.-Sat. $65, Sun.-Thurs. $55. Off-season rates lower; call ahead.

132 North Main Guest House (324-2246 or 324-9771), in East Hampton, 1 mi. from the beach. LIE Exit 70 to Sunrise Hwy., which becomes Montauk Hwy., which in turn becomes Main St.; veer left onto N. Main at the fork in front of the windmill green. A main house, a newly renovated guest house, cottages, and cabana on 2 acres of grounds. Weekdays: singles $65-90, doubles $70-110. Weekends: doubles $120-160. Call ahead, as further renovations in 1995 could raise rates.

Easterner Resort, 639 Montauk Hwy. (283-9292), in Southampton. Sunrise Hwy. Exit 66 to the Montauk Hwy. east. It's 3 mi. west of the Southampton Village Center. Fully renovated in spring of 1994. Very nice 1- and 2-bedroom cottages with kitchenettes, TV, and A/C. Swimming pool. Sun.-Thurs. $65, summer weekend packages from $135 per night (and generally a 2-night min. stay required). Open June-Sept. Call ahead for weekend reservations.

Shelter Island

The Belle Crest House, 163 North Ferry Rd. (749-2041), in Shelter Island Heights. Just up the hill from the north ferry. Beautiful old country home with lovely garden. Large rooms furnished with an eye toward antique detail—most beds have canopies. Great spot for a romantic getaway. From May 1 to Oct. 31: Mon.-Thurs. doubles $65-70 with shared bath, $95 with private bath; Fri.-Sun. $80 and $165. Two night min. for weekends in summer. Off-season rates dip as low as $45 for a shared bath; call for details. Includes a full country breakfast.

Referral Services

Twin Forks Reservation, P.O. Box 657, Hampton Bays, NY 11946 (728-5285). B&B in private homes on both forks of the East End. Doubles $80-105, with the higher rates charged for weekend stays and for south fork homes.

A Reasonable Alternative, Inc., 117 Spring St., Port Jefferson, NY 11777 (928-4034). Rooms in private homes all along the shores of Nassau and Suffolk. Prices increase the farther east you go. Singles or doubles $50-100.

Camping

Camping makes by far the most financial sense if you plan to spend any amount of time on the Island without spending too much money. On the down side, there are only a few months when the weather blows fair enough for comfort, and even then the humidity can be oppressive. You will also find the Island's campsites tangled in a mystifying web of local, state, and federal regulations. Most Island camping facilities are restricted to local residents; you can camp on most of the Island only if you already live there. State parks are generally the most welcoming to visitors, and a few private campgrounds open their arms as well. Those planning an extended stay should contact **Hither Hills State Park** (668-2254 or 800-956-2267), on the Old Montauk Hwy. near Montauk. Reservations are required, and you must stay for at least one week (fee $84 per week). Reservations are taken up to 90 days in advance and, seriously, should be made as close to that far ahead as possible. **Wilderness camping** is available near Smith Point West on Fire Island. Camping is free but requires a hike of about 1½ mi. to get into the camping area. You must pick up a permit from Smith Point Visitors Center (281-3010; open daily 9am-5pm) on the day you go down. To get to Smith Point, take exit 68, head south, and follow the signs.

Battle Row (572-8690), in Old Bethpage, Nassau. Take LIE exit 48 and go south on Old Swamp Rd. At the fourth traffic light, turn left onto Bethpage-Sweethollow Rd., and then make the first right onto Claremont St. Adjacent to the Village Restoration. 8 tent sites and 50 trailer sites available on a first-come, first-served basis. Electricity, restrooms, showers, grills, and a playground. Tent sites $6.75 for Nassau residents, $8.50 for visitors. Trailer sites $10 for residents, $15 for visitors. 21 and over—unless you're a family. Reservations strongly recommended.

Heckscher Park (800-456-2267 or 581-4433), in East Islip, Suffolk. Take LIE exit 53 and go south on the Sagtikos State Pkwy. Follow signs onto the Southern State Pkwy. east, and follow this as it turns south and becomes the Heckscher Spur Pkwy. The Park is at the end of the Pkwy. A state-run facility. Make reservations by calling the toll-free state number. 69 tent and trailer sites. Restrooms, showers, food, grills, a pool, and a beach. $12.50 for the first night and $11 per additional night. Limit of two tents and six people per site. Reservations recommended and must be made at least 7 days in advance. Open May-Sept.

Wildwood Park (800-456-2267 or 929-4314), at Wading River. LIE exit 68 and go north onto Rte. 46 (Wm. Floyd Pkwy.): follow it to its end and go right (east) on Rte. 25A. Follow the signs from there. Near the location of Mackay Radio Station, source of Voice of America and one of the largest stations in the country (not open to the public). Former estate of Charles and John Arbuckle, multi-millionaire coffee dealers who, brilliantly, packaged coffee instead of selling it in bulk. 300 tent sites and 80 trailer sites with full hook-ups, restrooms, showers, food, and a beach. Tent sites $11.50 first night and $10 each additional night; sites with a concrete platform $12.50 first night and $11 thereafter. Reservations urged for summer weekends and must be made at least a week in advance (by calling the toll-free number).

FOOD

Nobody has ever confused Long Island with a hungry budget traveler's paradise. Tourist food, found mostly in the fashionable resorts out east, is wonderful if you have already made your first million but otherwise not worth discussing. Restaurants catering to Islanders, on the other hand, do very well for themselves without the droves of rich Manhattan patrons. Many of these Island favorites specialize in such ethnic fare as Chinese, Italian, and Greek. You might have to overcome your hangups about style and locale, though; if you refuse to eat in a strip mall you're seriously limiting your options. For some of the best food on the Island, scope out the bountiful farm stands of the East End and the mostly infallible seafood restaurants of Suffolk.

Nassau County

An amazing variety of reasonably priced restaurants, from Turkish to Viennese, helps to diversify Nassau, pleasing those whose wallets have been depleted in New York. Mega-malls offer some of the most affordable food options on the Island. You are practically always assured of a good meal at one of the Island's Chinese eateries, which are found at virtually every shopping center in Nassau. Some good moo-shi vegetables or beef and broccoli should send you on your way with a full stomach for less than $10.

No trip to Long Island is complete without a stop at one of its regionally unique diners. Originally, these were decommissioned dining cars parked on street-sides to provide short-order cooking; the diner on Long Island has since become a field-stone-modernist extravaganza, with potted palms, hosts, mints at the exit, and two-foot glossy menus.

Stango's, 19 Grove St. (671-2389) in Glen Cove. LIE Exit 39N onto Glen Cove Rd. heading north. Bear right at the fork onto Cedar Swamp Rd. (and away from Rte. 107). At the fourth traffic light make a left onto Grove St. Since 1914, this neighborhood southern Italian restaurant has been serving up delicious bargain food. Green checked tablecloths and garlic bread. Ravioli $6.50, side of meatballs $3. Sausage and pepper sandwich $5.25. Open Tues.-Sun. 4-11:30pm.

Christiano's, 19 Ira Rd. (921-9892), in Syosset. LIE to Exit 41N (S. Oyster Bay Rd.), go north, cross the Jericho Tpke., continue on Jackson Ave. for 1 mi., and hang a right onto Ira Rd. Legend has it that this unassuming eatery inspired local youth Billy Joel to write his chestnut "Scenes from an Italian Restaurant." (The original 45 is still on the jukebox, replete with a dedication; on a very lucky day you might have the good fortune to glimpse the Piano Man himself nursing a tallboy at the bar.) Order a bottle of blush chablis to enjoy with the excellent food (entrees $6.50-11). Try the baked ziti parmagiana ($6.50). Half-price drinks with lunch (Mon.-Fri. 11am-3pm). Open Mon.-Thurs. 11am-1am, Fri.-Sat. 11am-2am, Sun. noon-1am.

To Fu, 8025 Jericho Tpke. (921-7981 or 921-7983), in Woodbury. Take LIE exit 43N and turn left (north) at the light onto S. Oyster Bay Rd. Hang a right (go east) on Jericho Tpke., and it's on the left after the third light. Chinese and Japanese food to rave about on a huge menu. Fine selection of sushi and sashimi—try the "Woodbury Roll" ($7.50). Entrees $7.50-10. Lunch specials, including soup, fried rice, green salad, and egg roll ($7). Open Mon.-Thurs. 11:30am-10pm, Fri. 11:30am-11pm, Sat. noon-11pm, Sun. 1-10pm.

Suffolk County

On the North and South Forks, upscale seafood eateries abound. Trust decor as an indicator of price, but not necessarily of the quality of the food; many expensive dives lurk about.

For a truly wholesome food experience, stop at any roadside produce stand that looks appealing; or, if you're feeling especially participatory, visit one of **Lewin Farms'** two separate pickin' patches. At the one on Sound Ave. in Wading River (929-4327), you can pick your own apples, nectarines, and peaches. (Open May-Dec. Mon.-Tues. 9am-4pm, Wed.-Sun. 8am-5:30pm. LIE to Exit 68, go north to Rte. 25A and east to Sound Ave.—it's the first farm on Sound Ave.) At the other, 123 Sound Ave. in Calverton (727-3346), you can pick strawberries, raspberries, plums, pears, peaches, nectarines, beans, onions, peas, squash, and tomatoes. Pumpkins too. (Open late May-late Nov. daily 9am-4pm. LIE to Exit 71N, drive on Edwards Ave. to Sound Ave.; the farm is ¼ mi. down on the left.) Crops are (obviously) seasonal, so always call ahead to confirm that some crop is ripe for the picking.

Driver's Seat, 62 Jobs Lane (283-6606), in Southampton; Jobs Ln. begins just across from Hill St. (Rte. 27E) in the town center. A well-known meeting place in the posh Hamptons. Eat indoors, outdoors, or at the bar. Entrees like jumbo burgers, quiche, and local seafood run $6-18. On Wed. entrees are 2-for-1. Open daily 11:30am-11pm; on weekends burgers and bar food served until midnight.

Shelter Island Pizza and Eatery, Rte. 114 at Jaspa Rd., Shelter Island (749-0400), near the Shelter Island Center. Excellent, inexpensive food—great thin-crust pizza (slice $1.25, whole large pie $9) and BBQ'd or herb rotisserie chicken (whole $7, half $4). Lunch specials offer hero sandwiches for $3.69—a great deal (served Mon.-Fri. 11:30am-2:30pm). Open daily 11am-9pm.

56th Fighter Group, Republic Airport, Rte. 110 (694-8280), in Farmingdale. LIE to Exit 49 onto Rte. 110 south; follow signs to the airport. It's on the left just past the Polytech University building. English farmhouse in the midst of a World War II encampment, complete with bunkers, sandbags, abandoned medical trucks, and Glenn Miller's trombone-tugging dance tunes. Lunches $5-10, dinners $15-20.

Entrees range from pastas to pork chops. Open Mon.-Thurs. 11am-11pm, Fri.-Sat. 11am-midnight, Sun. 11am-10pm.

Peter's Pasta Specialties, 132 W. Main St. (422-9233), in Babylon. Take the Southern State Parkway East to Exit 33. Go south on Rte. 109 all the way to Rte. 27A (Main St.) in Babylon Village and go left. A cozy Italian restaurant of soothing pastels where, if nothing on the menu makes your mouth water, you can dream up your own meal and then watch the chef prepare it. The specials are always so special, and the service is amazing. Entrees $8-12. Lunch specials—choose from 6 pasta and 14 sauces—are a great deal at $5. On weekends, the lines sometimes stretch out the door. Open Mon. 5-9pm, Tues.-Thurs. noon-9:30pm, Fri.-Sat. noon-10pm, Sun. 3-9pm.

Spinnaker's, Main St. (725-9353), in Sag Harbor. LIE Exit 70 to Rte. 27, left at the monument on Bridgehampton Tpke. Stay to the right, follow it all the way into Sag Harbor—the restaurant's in the middle of the block of shops on the right. This inviting American/Italian eatery is quite a draw—there's usually a wait on weekends for the primavera (the most popular dish by far), and the warm, delicious, homemade bread at every table. Creative pasta entrees (e.g. "stir-fry roast garlic bell peppers, cremini mushrooms, scallions, lemongrass fettucini, and a roasted beef broth") $15-20. Steak and seafood entrees $16-21. Open Sun.-Thurs. 11:30am-10pm, Fri.-Sat. 11:30am-11pm. On "theater nights" (weeknights when the nearby Sag Harbor Theater has a show) the place stays open until 10:30pm.

Fish Net, 122 Montauk Hwy., Hampton Bays (728-0115), a ¼-mi. west of the Shinnecock Canal Bridge. Some of the best local fish on the South Fork, served in a worn, homey atmosphere, eaten with sleeves rolled up. Shoes required, but all else is optional. Still, though, the prices are strictly South Fork: dinners $11-15. Open Sun.-Thurs. 11:30am-10pm, Fri.-Sat. 11:30am-11pm.

SIGHTS

Nassau County

Nassau's distinctive regional museums, sprawling garden estates, and historical preserves offer a relaxed alternative to the hectic Manhattan scene, although the negotiations of traffic involved in reaching these places can often leave you feeling anything but relaxed. Many of the following sights can be reached by public transport from Manhattan via the Long Island Railroad and the public bus lines. Directions are almost always complicated, though, especially when trying to get from one sight to another. The best idea is to call ahead and speak to a staff member directly.

The **United States Merchant Marine Museum,** on Steamboat Rd. in King's Point (773-5000 for recording, 773-5515 for a staff member), is housed on the grounds of the U.S. Merchant Marine Academy. Disciplined midshipmen keep watch over the museum's exhibits on the history and past glories of the Merchant Marine (Open Tues.-Wed. 11am-3pm, Sat.-Sun. 1-4:30pm. Free. Take LIE to Exit 33 and go north on Community Dr. Continue to the road's end and then go right on W. Shore Rd. Take a right on King's Point Rd., and then a left on Steamboat Rd.)

Among the finest of Nassau's famous Gold Coast estates is **Old Westbury Gardens,** on Old Westbury Rd. (333-0048), in Westbury. The huge and elegant manor house here roosts comfortably at the center of acres of formal, flower-filled gardens; it is the gardens which should claim most of your attention. If the day is beautiful, your time and money would be better spent on the grounds admission only, rather than the grounds-and-house combined admission. The two lakes are ornamented by sculptures, gazebos, and water lilies. A vast rose garden adjoins a number of theme gardens (such as the Grey Garden, which contains only plants in shades of silver and deep purple). Sunday afternoon classical concerts performed by Juilliard students once a month in May, June, September, and October (free with regular admission). (Open Wed.-Mon. 10am-5pm. Garden admission $6, seniors $4, children 6-12 $3. House and garden admission $10, seniors $7, children 6-12 $6. To reach the gardens, take LIE to Exit 39S. Follow the service road parallel to the expressway eastbound for 1.2 mi. and turn right onto Old Westbury Rd.)

Another sprawling Gold Coast property now open to the public, larger but less formally lavish than Old Westbury Gardens, is the **Planting Fields Arboretum,** the site of insurance magnate William Robertson Coe's Oyster Bay home, **Coe Hall** (922-0479 or -9206). Constructed in 1921 in the Tudor Revival style, the residence has rows upon rows of mind-boggling windows. But only eight decorated rooms are open to the public; unless you are an interiors enthusiast, you may be better off saving the entrance fee and admiring the building from the outside. (House open Sun.-Fri. 12:30-3:30pm. Admission $3.) The massive arboretum consists of 409 acres of some of the most valuable real estate in the New York area. Two huge greenhouses, covering 1½ acres, contain the largest camellia collection in the Northeast. The flowers burst into bloom during the unlikely months of January, February, and March, when most city-dwellers have begun to forget what flora looks like. Other quirky highlights include a "synoptic garden" of plants obsessively arranged according to their Latin names, from A to Z; every letter is represented except J and W. The **Fall Flower Show,** held for two weeks in early October, attracts huge crowds every year. The arboretum hosts a summer concert series; past seasons have seen the likes of Joan Baez, the Indigo Girls, and Spyro Gyra. (Grounds open daily 9am-5pm; admission $3 per vehicle. To reach the arboretum, take LIE to 41N, go north on U.S. 106 to Rte. 25A, take a left, and follow the signs.)

Those tired of manicured gardens and delicately pruned trees can find nature in a less tame condition at one of the preserves scattered throughout the county. The **Garvies Point Museum and Preserve,** Barry Dr. (571-8010), in Glen Cove, includes a small museum devoted to regional geology and Native American archaeology, and 62 acres of woods, thickets, fields, and ponds. The preserve is right on the shore and offers access to some secluded beaches and spectacular overlooks—pick up a trail map at the museum. The museum hosts a popular annual **Indian Feast** the weekend before Thanksgiving. (Museum open Wed.-Sat. 10am-4pm, Sun. 1-4pm. Admission $1, children 5-12 50¢. Take LIE to Exit 39N and follow Glen Cove Rd. north. Continue on the Glen Cove bypass (Rte. 107)—keep left at the fork—to its end, and follow the signs.)

A National Historical Site and perhaps the most important residence in Nassau County, **Sagamore Hill,** off Sagamore Hill Rd. northeast of Oyster Bay, was the summer residence of Theodore Roosevelt during his presidential term. In the summer of 1905, Roosevelt met here with envoys from Japan and Russia to set in motion negotiations that would lead to the Treaty of Portsmouth, which ended the Russo-Japanese War. The house is jam-packed with "Teddy" memorabilia, and its Victorian clutter convincingly evokes Roosevelt's era; the collection of antlers, for instance, reflects his sporting interests. (Open Wed.-Sun. 9:30am-5pm. Tours leave every ½-hr.; you must have a tour ticket to enter. To get here, take LIE Exit 41N to Rte. 106 north, turn right (east) at the junction with Rte. 25A and follow the signs.)

Since the days of Herman Melville, American culture has given a suitably prominent place to that longest of mammals, the whale. To indulge a cetacean obsession or merely to catch up on what you've been missing, nothing compares to the **Cold Spring Harbor Whaling Museum** (367-3418), on Main St. in Cold Spring Harbor. Built in honor of the small whaling fleet that sailed from Cold Spring Harbor in the mid-19th century, the museum features a 30-ft.-long, fully rigged vessel, one of only six remaining whaleboats of its kind in the world. The collection of scrimshaw—detailed whalebone carvings done to pass the long hours at sea—testifies to the joys of the seafaring tradition. (Open daily 11am-5pm; closed Mon. in fall and winter. Admission $2, seniors and children 6-12 $1.50. To get here, take LIE Exit 41 N to Rte. 106 north, and turn right (east) at the junction with Rte. 25A. Follow this all the way into Cold Spring Harbor, where it becomes Main St. The museum is past the commercial center a short distance on the left.)

The **Old Bethpage Village Restoration** (572-8401), on Round Swamp Rd. in Old Bethpage, is a "history preserve" in which fragments of Long Island's 19th-century heritage have been gathered and reassembled in the form of a typical pre-Civil War village. As you enter the general store or the blacksmith's shop, employees clad in period costume will explain their occupations. The hatter is especially informative. Special events take place every weekend afternoon; stick around for sheep shearing. Of course, the charm of Americana can wear off, especially in the summer when this place is packed solid with tourists. Winter visitors, on the other hand, may have to dodge school groups. Columbus Day weekend brings the **Long Island Fair,** a popular old-fashioned festival. (Village open Wed.-Sun. 10am-5pm. Admission $5, seniors and children 5-12 $3. Take LIE to Exit 48, then hang a right onto Round Swamp Rd. and a left onto the winding driveway.)

Jones Beach State Park (785-1600) is convenient and crowded, overflowing with daytrippers from the city. There are nearly 2500 acres of beachfront here, and the parking area accommodates 23,000 cars. Only 40 minutes from the City, Jones Beach packs in the crowds during the summer months; the beach becomes a sea of umbrellas and blankets with barely a patch of sand showing. Along the 1½-mi. boardwalk you can find deck games, roller-skating, miniature golf, basketball, and nightly dancing. The **Marine Theater** inside the park hosts rock concerts (see Entertainment: Nassau). There are eight different public beaches on the rough Atlantic Ocean and the calmer Zachs Bay, plus a number of beaches restricted to residents of certain towns in Nassau County. In the summer you can take the LIRR to Freeport or Wantaugh, where you can get a bus to the beach. **Recreation Lines** (718-788-8000) provides bus service straight from mid-Manhattan from Memorial Day to Labor Day on Sat. and Sun. Buses leave Manhattan from 56th St. at Second Ave. at 8:30 and 9am, and return from the beach at 4 and 4:30pm; the round-trip fare is $18. By car, take the LIE east to the Northern State Pkwy., go east to the Meadowbrook (or Wantaugh) Pkwy., and then south to Jones Beach.

Suffolk County

The peaceful villages of Suffolk County, only a few hours' drive from Manhattan, are New York's version of the tradition-steeped towns of New England. Many of Suffolk's colonial roots have been successfully preserved, and the county offers some fine colonial house-museums. Salty old towns full of shady streets—refreshing retreats from the din of New York—line the lazy coast.

On the other hand, Suffolk is transformed during the summer, when the water warms, the sun shines, the hotels double their rates, and it seems as if half of New York is tagging along as you stroll along the streets. The traffic nightmare can be avoided by traveling during off-peak hours. If you are going for the weekend, leave before 3pm or after 10pm on Friday. Or visit mid-week, when lodging is cheaper and beaches are all but empty.

Break up your trip by stopping at one of numerous roadside farm stands, where you can sometimes pick your own produce. Better yet, pull over and take a tour of one of Long Island's vineyards and wineries, many of which offer free tours and tastings (see Wine Country below).

After shopping at the Walt Whitman Mall, the nearby **Walt Whitman's Birthplace** (427-5240) will seem a more appropriate memorial to the great American poet whose 1855 *Leaves of Grass* introduced a democratic free-verse style that revolutionized poetry. The small, weathered farmhouse at 246 Old Walt Whitman Rd., Huntington Station, was built in 1816 by Walt Whitman, Sr., a carpenter and the father of the Bard of Long Island. The family moved to Brooklyn when the poet was only four years old, but the house is still able to offer an interesting commentary on his life. Especially worthwhile is the short still-frame movie consisting of pictures of the poet's life and loves accompanied by passages from *Leaves of Grass*. A visitors center is scheduled to open in June 1995. (Open Wed.-Fri. 1-4pm, Sat.-Sun. 10am-4pm. Free. Take LIE to Exit 49N, drive 1¾ mi. on Rte. 110, and turn left onto Old Walt Whitman Rd.; signs will guide you.)

Sagtikos Manor (665-0093), on Rte. 27A in Bay Shore on the South Bay, completed on an estate of 150 acres in 1697, remains the finest example of Colonial architecture on the Island. The hub of Long Island's pre-Revolutionary aristocracy, the 42-room mansion housed the commander of the British forces during the

Revolution and then perfidiously hosted George Washington during his presidency. Built by the Van Cortlandt family, it soon passed into the hands of the Thompsons, who lived here until the 20th century. Its current owner, Robert Gardiner, descends from another family of early Suffolk settlers. All of the original colonial structure (as opposed to the several later additions) is open to the public. Highlights include the fine period rooms—one containing an ancient desk with a set of cubby-holes into which the mail of James Madison and Thomas Jefferson was received when they were on the island—and the parlor which still displays the house's original paint made of lime, buttermilk, and blueberries. (Open July-Aug. Wed.-Thurs. and Sun. 1-4pm; June and Sept. Sun. 1-4pm. Admission $3, children under 12 $1. Take the Southern State Pkwy. to Exit 40 and go south on the Robert Moses Causeway. Turn left (east) on the Montauk Hwy. (Rte. 27A) and go 1½ mi. The Manor is on the left just past Manor Ln.)

Historians and sadists alike should check out the **Southampton Historical Museum** (283-1612), located near the center of town at the corner of Meeting House Lane and Main St. Start with the pillory, where thieves and those *accused* of adultery were publicly flayed. Or try your neck in the stocks, the clever device used to humiliate (and hurt) the drunkards and disrespectful children of old Southampton. Sniff original try-pots, the huge urns where whale blubber was once boiled to produce oil for pre-Edisonian lamps. Inside the house, walk upstairs to see an excellent collection of old children's toys, which includes a merry-go-round and several rocking horses, as well as some fascinating dolls and dollhouses. Downstairs don't miss seeing the whaling logs which 18th-century captains kept while at sea. (Open in summer Tues.-Sun. 11am-5pm. Admission $2, children 6-11 50¢. Take Rte. 27E to Southampton Center.)

The **Guild Hall Museum** 158 Main St. (324-0806), in East Hampton, ensures that sophisticated New Yorkers escaping to the Hamptons won't have to suffer from total art withdrawal. The collection specializes in well-known artists of the eastern Island region, from the late-19th century to the present. Guild Hall hosts changing exhibitions, films, lectures, concerts, plays, art classes, and special events (see Suffolk: Entertainment & Nightlife). A recent major exhibition displayed a number of important works by Willem de Kooning. (Open June-Aug. daily 11am-5pm, Sept.-May Wed.-Sun. 11am-5pm. Admission $5, seniors $2.)

For those who have had their fill of museums, art exhibits, and historical sites (or those who just like animals, the **Long Island Game Farm and Zoo** (878-6644) in Manorville (2 mi. south of LIE, exit 70) is the perfect place to go for a hands-on good time. Check out the petting zoo, where many of the zoo's countless farm animals make their home. The **Oceanarium Sea School Theater** here presents sea-lion shows several times a day. (Open week after Easter to Columbus Day 10am-6pm. Admission to park, shows, and all rides but the Sky Slide $12, seniors $6, children 2-11 $9.)

Wine Country

Long Island does not readily conjure up images of plump wine-grapes just waiting to be plucked by epicurean Islanders, but a visit to one of the East End's more than 40 vineyards can be a pleasant and interesting surprise. The wineries and vineyards here produce the best Chardonnay, Cabernet Sauvignon, Merlot, Pinot Noir, and Riesling in New York State. Local climate and soil conditions rival those of Napa Valley. Many of the Island wineries offer free tours and tastings; call ahead to make an appointment (all tasting for those 21 and over).

To get to the wine district, take the LIE to its end (Exit 73), then Rte. 58, which becomes Rte. 25 (Main Rd.). North of and parallel to Rte. 25 is Rte. 48 (North Rd. or Middle Rd.), which claims a number of wineries. Many wineries ferment on the South Fork as well.

Palmer Vineyards, 108 Sound Ave. (722-9463), in Riverhead. Embark on a guided or self-guided tour of the most advanced equipment on the Island and enjoy a tasting room with an interior assembled from two 18th-century English pubs. On Oct. weekends you can take a hayride to the vineyards. (Open daily 11am-6pm. Guided tours hourly Sat.-Sun. 1-5pm. Always 3 free tastings; other tastings available for a fee. Hours and tours shorter in off-season; call ahead.)

Bridgehampton Winery (537-3155), Sag Harbor Tpke., Bridgehampton. Holds special summer events, including the effervescent Chardonnay Festival in mid-Aug. Guided tours June-Sept. daily 11am-5pm. Free tastings always available.

Mattituck Hills Winery (298-9150), Bergen and Sound Ave., Mattituck. Hosts both a Strawberry Festival (in which you can sample chocolate-covered strawberries with house wines) and a Pre-Harvest Festival (which includes a grape stomp), as well as free daily tastings and tours on summer weekends. (Open Mon.-Fri. 11am-5:15pm, Sat.-Sun. 11am-6pm.)

Sag Harbor

Out on the South Fork's north shore droops Sag Harbor, one of the best-kept secrets of Long Island. Founded in 1707, this port used to be more important than New York Harbor since its deep shore made for easy navigation. In 1789 Washington signed the document creating ports of entry to the United States and, of the two named, "Sagg Harbour" appeared before New York City. At its peak, this winsome village was the fourth-largest of the world's whaling ports. James Fenimore Cooper began his first novel, *Precaution,* in a Sag Harbor hotel in 1824. During the Prohibition years, the harbor served as a major meeting-place for smugglers and rum-runners from the Caribbean.

In the past few years an increasing number of tourists has returned bustling activity to the quiet, tree-lined streets of salt-box cottages and Greek Revival mansions. This is a different bustle than that of the past, but the legacy of Sag Harbor's former grandeur survives in the second-largest collection of Colonial buildings in the U.S., and in the cemeteries lined with the gravestones of Revolutionary soldiers and sailors. In town, check out the **Sag Harbor Whaling Museum** (725-0770), in the former home of Benjamin Hunting, a 19th-century whale-ship owner. A huge whale rib towers in an arch over the front door. Note the antique washing-machine, made locally in 1864, and the excellent scrimshaw collection. (Open May-Sept. Mon.-Sat. 10am-5pm, Sun. 1-5pm. Admission $3, children 6-13 $1. Tours by appointment.)

Montauk

At the easternmost tip of the south fork, Montauk is one of the most popular destinations on Long Island. With good reason, considering the thrill of looking out at the Atlantic Ocean and realizing that you've reached the end—nothing but water between you and Limerick. Though the trip from Manhattan takes three hours by car, the peaceful, salty air of Montauk Point makes the drive well worth it. Take the LIE to Exit 70 (Manorville), then go south to Sunrise Hwy. (Rte. 27), which becomes Montauk Hwy., and drive east. It's impossible to go too far—at least without turning the inside of your car into an aquarium.

At the island's edge stands the **Montauk Point Lighthouse and Museum** (668-2544). The 86-ft. structure went up in 1796 by special order of President George Washington, but back then it was 297 ft. off the shoreline. Thanks to the wonders of geology, it's now fully attached, surrounded by the Montauk Pt. State Park. If your lungs are willing, you should definitely climb the 138 spiralling steps to the top, where you can look out over the seascape, across the Long Island Sound to Connecticut and Rhode Island. Try to spot the *Will o' the Wisp,* a ghostly clipper ship sometimes sighted on hazy days under full sail with a lantern hanging from its mast. Experts claim that the ship is a mirage resulting from the presence of phosphorus in the atmosphere, but what do they know? (Open Sun.-Fri. 10:30am-6pm, Sat. 10:30am-8pm. Admission $2.50, children 6-11 $1. Parking $3 until 4pm, free after 4pm.)

Try **Viking** (668-5700) or **Lazybones'** (668-5671) for half-day fishing cruises ($24; equipment and bait included). During the summer, most trips go after fluke, but these two companies also offer seasonal outings for bluefish, cod, and tuna.

Okeanos Whale Watch Cruise (728-4522) offers excellent six-hour trips for spotting fin, minke, and humpback whales ($30, children under 13 $15).

The Island's Islands: Fire And Shelter

Fire Island, one of the more extraordinary natural sites off Long Island's shores, is a 32-mi.-long barrier-island buffering the South Shore from the roaring waters of the Atlantic. The state has designated most of Fire Island either a state park or a federal "wilderness area"—both of which are legally protected from development—but 17 summer communities have designated the rest of it their resort area and forged their own niche here. Fire Island's unique landscape will make you forget there ever was such a city as New York. Cars are allowed only on the easternmost and westernmost tips of the island; there are no streets, only "walks." Fire Island was a hip countercultural spot during the 60s and still maintains a laid-back atmosphere. Two of Fire Island's many resorts, Cherry Grove and The Pines, are home to predominantly gay communities. (For ferry information see Practical Information above.)

The **Fire Island National Seashore** (289-4810 for the headquarters in Patchogue) is the main draw here, and in summer it offers fishing, clamming, and guided nature walks. The facilities at **Sailor's Haven** (just west of the Cherry Grove community) include a marina, a nature trail, and a famous beach. Similar facilities at **Watch Hill** (597-6455) include a 20-unit campground, where reservations are required. **Smith Point West,** on the eastern tip of the island, has a small visitor-information center and a nature trail with disabled access (281-3010; center open daily 9am-5pm). Here you can spot horseshoe crabs, whitetail deer, and monarch butterflies, which flit across the country every year to winter in Baja California.

The **Sunken Forest,** so called because of its location down behind the dunes, is another of the Island's natural wonders. Located directly west of Sailor's Haven, its soils support an unusual and attractive combination of gnarled holly, sassafras, and poison ivy. From the summit of the dunes, you can see the forest's trees laced together in a hulky, uninterrupted mesh.

Shelter Island bobs in the protected body of water between the north and south forks. Accessible by ferry (see Practical Information above) or by private boat, this island of about 12 sq. mi. offers wonderful beaches (locals tend to favor Wades Beach and Hay Beach) and a serene sense of removal from the intrusions of the city. But that doesn't mean you'll have to rough it here, since the island has virtually everything that you could possibly need, including a coalyard, four insurance agencies, and a real-estate attorney. A detailed map of the island is available from most inns and other places of business. If you don't have or choose not to bring a car, you should definitely consider renting a bike (see Practical Information above), since the island offers no public transport.

ENTERTAINMENT AND NIGHTLIFE

The best nightlife for most Long Islanders exists in Manhattan. The selection is severely limited out on the Island, but there's still no reason to sit at home reading a book after the sun sets over the Long Island Sound. Huge multi-screen theaters pepper the island and tickets are cheaper than in the city. See *Newsday* for full listings.

Nassau County

Nassau has never been known as a late-night paradise; post-movie options are limited. You can relax to some live jazz at **Sonny's Place,** 3603 Merrick Rd. (826-0973), in Seaford. Sonny extracts an $8 cover charge here on Friday and Saturday nights and enforces a two-drink minimum. During the week the music plays on without the cover or minimum if you sit or stand at the bar, but for those sitting at tables a $2 cover and 2-drink minimum is enforced. Music plays Sunday through Thursday 9pm-1am, Friday-Saturday 9:30pm-2am. From the LIE, take Exit 44S to the Seaford-Oyster Bay Expressway and head south; take Exit 1W onto Merrick Rd. and go west one block.

For dancing, try **Gatsby's,** a fashionable spot on a stretch past the green light at 1067 Old Country Rd. in Westbury (997-3685). The DJ starts spinning at 9pm from Tuesday to Saturday, and there are occasional live shows on Thursday, Friday, and Saturday nights. Cover for live shows is usually about $5; ladies sometimes drink free—call for details.

Nassau also bows to the more refined. The **Long Island Philharmonic** (293-2222), a highly respected orchestra, performs at the Tilles Center for the Performing Arts and offers free evening concerts at area parks during the summer (call for info.). Located on the C.W. Post Campus of Long Island University, on Northern Blvd. in Greenvale, the **Tilles Center** (299-2752, box office 299-2356) sponsors a wide variety of performances throughout the academic year. Enjoy a concert under its slopy white ceiling. The **Arena Players Repertory Theater,** 296 Rte. 109 in East Farmingdale (731-1100), and the **Broadhollow Theater** at 229 Rte. 110, Farmingdale (752-1400), have full calendars of productions. Performances can be uneven, especially by New York standards, and shows are often overly commercial. Still, the theaters have matured, and are worth a look when a favorite goes up. Local universities also have active theaters—notably the **John Cranford Adams Playhouse** at Hofstra University, on Fulton Ave. in Hempstead (463-6644).

National rock concert-tours stop during the summer at the **Jones Beach Marine Theater,** Jones Beach State Park, Wantaugh (221-1000, recorded concert hotline 422-9222). Joining the bandmembers for some slam-dancing is impossible here unless you have a rowboat; the stage is separated from the bleachers by a wide stretch of water. In a production of *Showboat,* the actors made their entrances and exits by motorboat. Now the theater hosts concerts exclusively. The **Westbury Music Fair,** on Brush Hollow Rd. in Westbury (334-0800), has a theater in the round and hosts big names on tour.

Suffolk County

The most exciting nighttime entertainment in Suffolk (besides breathing the night air and listening to the crickets) can be found on the grounds of the parks and museums, which host harpsichord and piano recitals. This outdoor musical life, as with most things in Suffolk, becomes much more active in the summer. Performance dates and times vary; ask at community museums or pick up a copy of one of the free papers or magazines such as *Dan's Papers* (see below), which are ubiquitous around the entrances of most establishments. Some of these parks restrict admission to local residents or charge exorbitant fees to exclude tourists like yourself—get the dope before setting out. The **Guild Hall Museum** in East Hampton hosts a number of impressive films, lectures, concerts, plays, and special events. The Guild Hall's John Drew Theater hosts most of these performances, including a series of author's readings by such prominent writers as Robert Bly and Robert Lipsyte. The Hall's Jazz Festival takes place in the latter half of each July (call 324-0806 for information). *Dan's Papers,* published in Bridgehampton, provides information on concerts and other nighttime happenings.

CPI (the Canoe Place Inn), located on the East Montauk Hwy. east of Hampton Bays (728-4121), is by far the South Fork's biggest draw for the college and twenty-something crowd. It's not uncommon for CPI to feature three DJs and two live bands in a single night (for a cover of about $10). Live shows can sometimes be great bargains—the Violent Femmes played a recent show here which was free before 11pm and after that only $5. (Open Fri.-Sat. 10pm-4am, with occasional special shows on Wed. nights.)

Another big draw for the post-college crowd is **Co-Co's Water Café,** at 117 New York Ave., Huntington (271-5700), but beware: the minimum age for men is always 23 and rises to 28 on singles night (Tues.). Women need only be 21. (Open nightly until 2am.)

On the South Fork, **East Hampton Bowl,** 71 Montauk Hwy. (324-1950) just west of East Hampton, offers a great escape from the area's big-money scene. And yes—it is a spot for nightlife: the bowling alley and attached bar stay open until at least midnight every night, and Sat. nights feature "Rock-'n'-Bowl," a big draw in which the lights are put out and a disco ball descends, a live DJ starts to play, and, of course, people keep on bowling. (Bowling $3.40 per game; shoe rental $2.)

For stand-up comedy in Suffolk, look to either **Thomas McGuire's Comedy,** 1627 Smithtown Ave. (467-5413), Bohemia, with a $10 cover and shows Friday and Saturday nights or the **East Side Comedy Club,** at 1815 Rte. 110 (249-6061), Farmingdale, with shows Wed.-Sun. (2 on Fri.-Sun.) and a $7.50-12.50 charge.

The **New Community Cinema,** 423 Park Ave., Huntington (423-7653), just over the Nassau border, is a local secret and one of the only places on Long Island where you can safely call your movie a "film." The cinema screens offbeat documentaries and foreign art-flicks. Shows are often preceded by introductions or concluded with question-and-answer sessions with the filmmakers themselves or simply those in the know. Eat brownies and siphon herbal tea while you wait for the lights to go down (they won't start the film until everyone is seated). Tickets cost $6, students with ID $4, children under 13 $3. Shows on Sat. after 6pm are 50¢ more. (To get here take LIE Exit 49N to Rte. 110 and continue north into the village of Huntington; from the town center take a right onto Park Ave.

Appendices

■■■ FREE NEW YORK

New York may cost an arm and a leg to live in, but you can visit it without having the Midas touch. Free entertainment abounds; you just need to know where to look. Both the *Times* (especially good on Fridays) and *Village Voice* (each Wednesday) print extensive lists of free events throughout the city, as does the *Free Time* monthly ($1.25).

Some museums—such as the **Cooper-Hewitt** on Tuesdays—have weekly free times. Others have voluntary-donation policies; if you're on a budget, you can choose to pay less at the **Alternative Museum**, the **American Museum of Natural History**, the **Black Fashion Museum**, the **Brooklyn Museum**, the **China House Gallery**, the **Cloisters**, the **Metropolitan Museum**, the **Museum of American Folk Art**, and the **Museum of Television and Radio**. On Friday from 6 to 8pm, the **Guggenheim** invites visitors to "pay what you wish." The Museum of Modern Art offers the same policy Thurs. and Fri. 5:30-8:30pm, as does the New Museum of Contemporary Art Sat. 6-8pm. Smaller galleries and some museums never charge admission; without spending a penny, you can visit the **American Numismatic Society**, the **Forbes Magazine Galleries**, the **Garibaldi-Meucci Museum** on Staten Island, the **Hall of Fame for Great Americans**, the **Hispanic Society of America**, the **Museum of American Illustration**, the **Nicholas Roerich Museum**, the **Police Academy Museum**, the **Schomburg Center for Research in Black Culture**, and countless art galleries clustered throughout SoHo and the rest of the city. For those who prefer more animate entertainment, the **Bronx Zoo** is free Wednesday.

For free, you can tour **Grand Central Station**, the **Lincoln Center Library**, the **New York Stock Exchange**, and the **Commodities Exchange Center** at the World Trade Center. Paying your respects at **Grant's Tomb** and the **U.N. General Assembly** (Sept.-Dec.) costs nothing. And colonial dwellings like the **Dyckman House** and **Hamilton Grange** welcome their modern-day visitors free of charge.

Shakespeare shows for free in Central Park, but to obtain a ticket, you have to wake up early. Central Park's **Summerstage** brings amazing music and writers for free performances from late June through early August; check the *Village Voice* or call 360-CPSS. Past performers include Buddy Guy, Los Lobos, Alceu Valença, Patti Smith, Joan Baez, and more. Music schools don't charge for their concerts: try **Juilliard**, the **Greenwich Music School**, and the **Bloomingdale House of Music**. You can listen to a prestigious free lecture series at the **Cooper Union** or to free poetry at the **92nd Street Y**.

Come summertime, troopers willing to brave the heat enjoy concerts, dances, comedy, theater, and film at absolutely no charge. The *Summer in New York* brochure, available free at the Visitors Bureau and other information booths (see Essentials: Getting Acquainted), presents a full catalog of gratis summertime events.

The **JVC Jazz Festival** (787-2020) and the **Serious Fun!** comedy series offer several free events throughout the city's parks when they come to town in June and July. Try the 24-hour information line of the **City of New York Parks and Recreation Department** (360-3456) for a schedule of concerts and events. **Bryant Park**, at Sixth Ave. between 40th and 42nd St., offers many lunchtime jazz recitals during the summer, as well as free screenings of classic movies on Monday nights June-Aug.

Assorted corporate magnates mount their own musical agendas. From June through August, **Rockefeller Center** (632-3975) holds concerts on Tuesday and Thursday at 12:30pm at the Garden at 1251 Sixth Ave. On Wednesdays in July and August, the Rockefeller series moves to the McGraw Hill Minipark at 48th St. and Sixth Ave. (also at 12:30pm). The **World Financial Center** (945-0505) hosts its own summer bash from June to September, mostly free: a fittingly global parade of art, chamber music, contemporary dance, and jazz by greats like Dave Brubeck. The Duke Ellington Orchestra, the Artie Shaw Orchestra, and Buster Poindexter have all played here in the past. Serious classical music wafts alongside strains of classic rock and roll; the Shostakovich String Quartet shared the bill with Flash Cadillac, the beat boys from *American Graffiti*.

The **World Trade Center** (435-4170) also maintains a full summer entertainment schedule in July and August at its Austin J. Tobin Plaza. Each day has a different theme, such as oldies, opera, or jazz. Most concerts here start at 12:15pm and are then repeated at 1:15pm. In August, **Lincoln Center** (875-5400) holds a series of music and dance concerts six days a week, day and evening, on the plazas. Offerings include folk, blues, and classical music. **Damrosch Park,** at Lincoln Center, sponsors shows several nights a week in the summer.

The **South Street Seaport Museum** (732-7678) presents a wide variety of free outdoor entertainment, ranging from rock concerts to classical recitals to celebrations of street hockey. The Museum of Modern Art (708-9480) holds its free **Summer Garden Series** of classical music in its delightful sculpture garden at 14 W. 54th St. (July-Aug. Fri.-Sat. 7:30pm).

The Central Park **Dairy** (794-6564) provides information on free New York parks activities, like the Central Park Dairy's calcium-enriched Sunday afternoon recitals. The **Lower Manhattan Cultural Council** (432-0900) stages music and dance performances and public readings at various downtown sites; it also organizes and provides information on the free concerts held at the World Trade and Financial Centers. **American Landmark Festivals** (866-2086) include a series of free concerts year-round at various locales.

The **Brooklyn Summer Series** fills the bill with concerts in Brooklyn parks, playgrounds, and even shopping malls. **Celebrate Brooklyn** (718-788-0055), a multimedia extravaganza, swarms Brooklyn's Prospect Park Bandshell with jazz, rock, world beat, blues, and big brass, as well as dance, ballet, and theater. The **Brooklyn Botanical Garden** (718-622-4433) hosts summer Shakespeare and outdoor chamber music.

The **Queens Council on the Arts** (718-647-3377) organizes its own **Arts in the Park Festival** at the Forest Park Seufert Bandshell, at Forest Park Dr. and Woodhaven Blvd. Concerts take place July through August in the late afternoon and evenings and feature a variety of musical styles, ranging from gospel to classical to country; concerts for children are held on Thursday mornings. Check the council's bimonthly calendar of events, the *Queens Leisure Guide,* or call the above number.

■■■ MAJOR ANNUAL EVENTS

January	Black History Month	*events citywide*
	Winter Festival	*Central Park*
	National Boat Show, Jan. 6-15	*New York Coliseum*
February	Jazz Festival	*Snug Harbor Cultural Center, Staten Island*
	Chinese New Year	*Chinatown*
March	Ringling Bros. and Barnum & Bailey Circus	*Madison Square Garden*
	St. Patrick's Day Parade	*Fifth Avenue*
April	Easter Show	*Radio City Music Hall*
	International Auto Show	*Jacob Javits Convention Center*
	Spring Flower Show	*Brooklyn Botanic Garden*
	Cherry Blossom Festival	*Brooklyn Botanic Garden*
	Earth Day Parade	*TBA*
May	Fleet Week '95	*Intrepid Museum*

	Ninth Ave. International Food Festival	*Ninth Ave. between 37th and 57th St.*
	Memorial Day Celebration	*South Street Seaport*
	Seafest '95	*South Street Seaport*
June	Tony Awards	*TBA*
	Summer Stage	*Central Park*
	Bronx Week	*events throughout the borough*
	Buskers Fare Festival	*street performances in lower Manhattan*
	Puerto Rican Day Parade, Jun. 11	*Fifth Ave.*
	Museum Mile Festival	*Fifth Ave. museums open free, 6pm-9pm*
	Midsummer Night Swing Dances	*outdoors under the stars at Lincoln Center*
	Mermaid Parade	*Coney Island*
July	Macy's Firework Display (July 4)	*lower Hudson River*
	Mostly Mozart Music Festival	*Lincoln Center*
	Serious Fun Festival	*avant garde performing arts at Lincoln Center*
	Salute to New York City	*New York Philharmonic in Central Park, with fireworks*
	free Shakespeare performances	*Delacorte Theater, Central Park*
	Macy's "Tap A Mania"	*34th St. and Broadway*
August	U.S. Open	*National Tennis Stadium, Flushing, Queens*
	Harlem Week	*Harlem*
	Summer Stage	*Central Park*
September	New York Film Festival	*Lincoln Center*
	Chile Pepper Fiesta	*Brooklyn Botanic Gardens*
	ice skating begins	*Rockefeller Center and Wollman Rink, Central Park*
October	United Nations 50th Anniversary Celebration	*events TBA*
	Halloween Parade	*Sixth Ave. from Spring St. to 23rd St.*
November	New York City Marathon	*Fifth Avenue*
	Macy's Thanksgiving Day Parade	*Broadway (Huge balloon floats assembled the previous evening at 79th and Central Park West)*
December	Christmas Tree lighting, Dec. 2	*Rockefeller Center*
	Lighting of Giant Chanuka Menorah	*Fifth Ave. and 59th St.*
	New Year's Eve	*Times Square—at midnight, a big apple drops from Times Tower, ushering in the new year.*
	New Year's Eve Fireworks	*South Street Seaport and Prospect Park, Brooklyn*

■ Index

★ FREE T-SHIRT ★

JUST ANSWER THE QUESTIONS ON THE FOLLOWING PAGES AND MAIL TO:

Let's Go Survey
Macmillan Ltd.
18-21 Cavaye Place
London SW10 9PG

WE'LL SEND THE FIRST 1,500 RESPONDENTS A LET'S GO T-SHIRT!

(Make sure we can read your address.)

■ LET'S GO 1995 READER ■ QUESTIONNAIRE

1) Name _____

2) Address _____

3) Are you: female   male

4) How old are you?   under 17   17-23   24-30   31-40   41-55   over 55

5) Are you (circle all that apply):   at school   at college or university
                                        employed   unemployed   retired

6) What is your annual income?
   £10,000- £15,000   £15,000 - £25,000   £25,000 - £40,000   Over £40,000

7) Have you used *Let's Go* before?

   Yes   No

8) How did you hear about *Let's Go* guides?

   Friend or fellow traveller
   Recommended by bookshop
   Display in bookstore
   Advertising in newspaper/magazine
   Review or article in newspaper/
     magazine

9) Why did you choose *Let's Go*?

   Updated every year
   Reputation
   Prominent in-store display
   Price
   Content and approach of books
   Reliability

10) Is *Let's Go* the best guidebook?

   Yes
   No (which is?) _____
   Haven't used other guides

11) When did you buy this book?

   Jan   Feb   Mar   Apr   May   Jun
   Jul   Aug   Sep   Oct   Nov   Dec

12) When did you travel with this book? (Circle all that apply)

   Jan   Feb   Mar   Apr   May   Jun
   Jul   Aug   Sep   Oct   Nov   Dec

13) Roughly how much did you spend per day on the road?

   Under £10   £45- £75
   £10- £25   £75- £100
   £25- £40   Over £100

14) What were the main attractions of your trip?
    (Circle top three)

   Sightseeing
   New culture
   Learning language
   Sports/Recreation
   Nightlife/Entertainment
   Local cuisine
   Shopping
   Meeting other travellers
   Adventure/Getting off the beaten
     path

15) How reliable/useful are the following features of *Let's Go*?

   v = very, u = usually, s = sometimes
   n = never, ? = didn't use

   Accommodations   v u s n ?
   Camping   v u s n ?
   Food   v u s n ?
   Entertainment   v u s n ?
   Sights   v u s n ?
   Maps   v u s n ?
   Practical Info   v u s n ?
   Directions   v u s n ?
   "Essentials"   v u s n ?
   Cultural Intros   v u s n ?

16) Would you use *Let's Go* again?

Yes
No (why not?) _____

_____

_____

17) Which of the following destinations are you planning to visit as a tourist in the next five years?
(Circle all that apply)

Australasia
Australia
New Zealand
Indonesia
Japan
China
Hong Kong
Vietnam
Malaysia
Singapore
India
Nepal

Europe And Middle East
Middle East
Israel
Egypt
Africa
Turkey
Greece
Scandinavia
Portugal
Spain
Switzerland
Austria
Berlin
Russia
Poland
Czech/Slovak Republic
Hungary
Baltic States

The Americas
Caribbean
Central America
Costa Rica
South America
Ecuador
Brazil
Venezuela
Colombia
Canada
British Columbia
Montreal/Quebec
MaritimeProvinces

18) What **major** destinations (countries, regions, etc.) covered in this book did you visit on your trip?

_____

_____

_____

_____

_____

_____

_____

_____

_____

_____

_____

_____

19) What other countries did you visit on your trip?

_____

_____

_____

_____

_____

20) How did you get around on your trip?

Car   Train   Plane
Bus   Ferry   Hitching
Bicycle   Motorcycle

Mail this to:

Let's Go Survey

Macmillan Ltd.
18-21 Cavaye Place
London SW10 9PG

Many Thanks For Your Help!

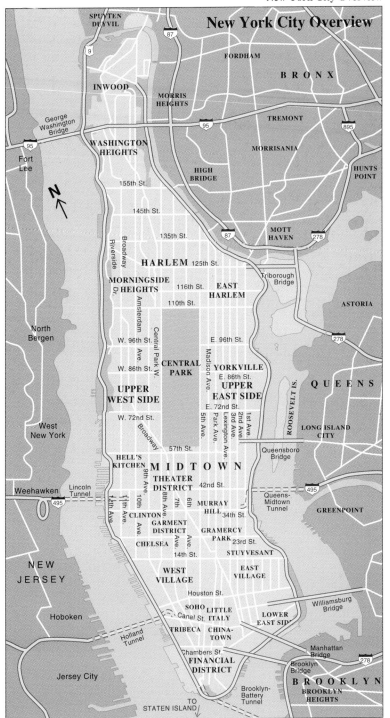

New York City Overview

New York City Subways

Subways

Stops are not served by all trains at all times.
Refer to Transit Authority map for descriptions
of express, local, and limited service.

LEGEND

K,B   Line
168 St   Terminal

Downtown Manhattan

Downtown Manhattan

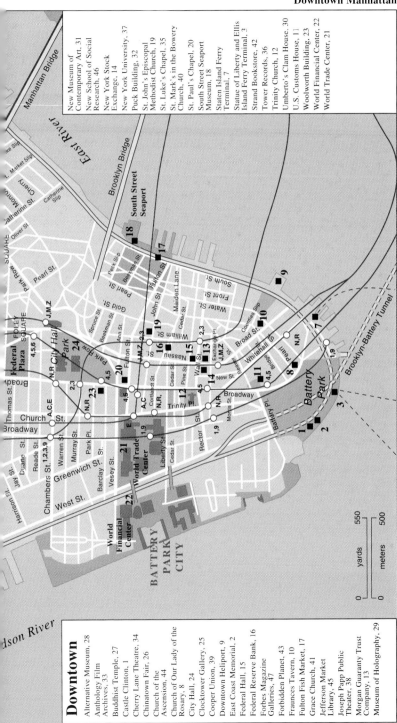

Midtown Manhattan

East River

Queensboro Bridge

Queens-Midtown Tunnel

FDR Dr.

TURTLE BAY

United Nations

First Ave.

Second Ave.

Third Ave.

Lexington Ave.

Park Ave.

Madison Ave.

Fifth Ave.

E. 60th St.
E. 59th St.
E. 58th St.
E. 57th St.
E. 56th St.
E. 55th St.
E. 54th St.
E. 53rd St.
E. 52nd St.
E. 51st St.
E. 50th St.
E. 49th St.
E. 48th St.
E. 47th St.
E. 46th St.
E. 45th St.
E. 44th St.
E. 43rd St.
E. 42nd St.
E. 41st St.
E. 40th St.
E. 39th St.
E. 38th St.
E. 37th St.
E. 36th St.
E. 35th St.
E. 34th St.
E. 33rd St.

Citicorp Center

Grand Central Terminal

New York Public Library

Bryant Park
W. 40th St.

MURRAY HILL

Empire State Building

Museum of Modern Art

Rockefeller Center

Grand Army Plaza

Park Avenue South

Central Park South

Carnegie Hall

GARMENT DISTRICT

HERALD SQUARE

Broadway

Seventh Ave.

TIMES SQUARE

Eighth Ave.

Port Authority Bus Terminal

General Post Office

Ninth Ave.

W. 34th St.

Dyer Ave.

Tenth Ave.

HELL'S KITCHEN

Eleventh Ave.

Twelfth Ave.

Lincoln Tunnel

New York Convention & Visitors Bureau

COLUMBUS CIRCLE

W. 60th St.
W. 59th St.
W. 58th St.
W. 57th St.
W. 56th St.
W. 55th St.
W. 54th St.
W. 53rd St.
W. 52nd St.
W. 51st St.
W. 50th St.
W. 49th St.
W. 48th St.
W. 47th St.
W. 46th St.
W. 45th St.
W. 44th St.
W. 43rd St.
W. 42nd St.
W. 41st St.
W. 39th St.
W. 38th St.
W. 37th St.
W. 36th St.
W. 35th St.
W. 33rd St.

A,B,C,D, 1,2,3,9
N,R
B,Q
4,5,6
B,D,F,Q
E,F
6
4,5, 6,S
7
N,R
B,D,E
C,E
A,C,E
1,2,3, N,R,9
B,D,F,Q,7
1,2,3,9
1,2,3,9

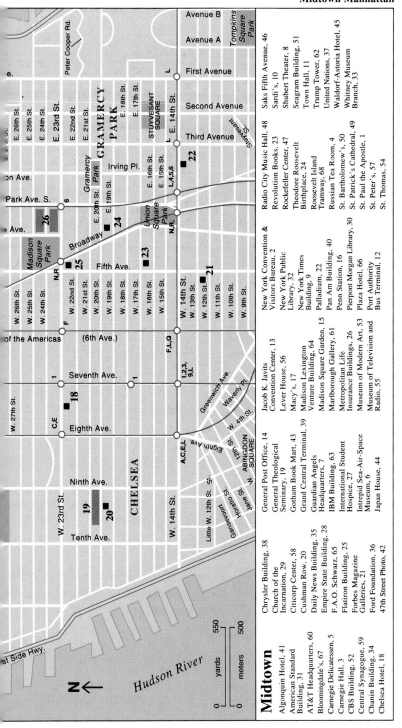

Avenue B

Avenue A

First Avenue

Second Avenue

Third Avenue

GRAMERCY PARK

STUYVESANT SQUARE

Tompkins Square Park

Peter Cooper Rd.

Gramercy Park

Irving Pl.

Madison Square Park

Union Square Park

Broadway

Fifth Avenue

Park Ave. S.

of the Americas   (6th Ave.)

Seventh Ave.

Eighth Ave.

CHELSEA

Ninth Ave.

Tenth Ave.

ABINGDON SQUARE

Greenwich Ave.

Waverly Pl.

West Side Hwy.

Hudson River

N ←

yards 0 … 550 … 500

meters 0 … 500

Uptown

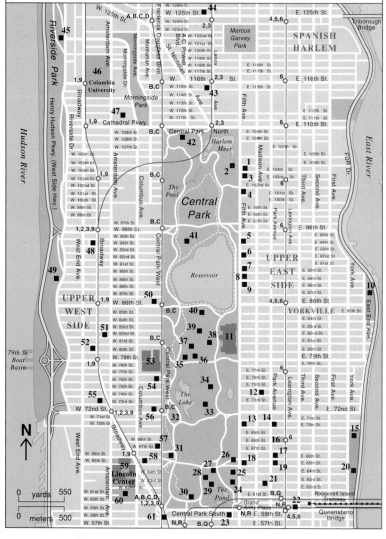